FOOD
FUNDAMENTALS

FOOD
Fourth Edition
FUNDAMENTALS

Margaret McWilliams, Ph.D., R.D.
California State University, Los Angeles

JOHN WILEY & SONS
New York • Chichester • Brisbane • Toronto • Singapore

Other books by Margaret McWilliams

Fundamentals of Meal Management
Illustrated Guide to Food Preparation
Experimental Foods Laboratory Manual
Nutrition for the Growing Years
Living Nutrition (with F. J. Stare)
Nutrition for Good Health (with F. J. Stare)
Understanding Food (with L. Kotschevar)
Modern Food Preservation (with H. Paine)
Food for You (with L. Davis)
World of Nutrition (with H. Heller)

Cover Painting: ''The Table'' by Pierre Bonnard
The Tate Gallery, London

Library of Congress Cataloging in Publication Data:

McWilliams, Margaret.
  Food fundamentals.

  Includes bibliographies and index.
  1. Food   I. Title.
TX354.M28 1985   641   84-27071
ISBN 0-471-81369-9

Printed in the United States of America

10 9 8 7 6 5 4 3 2 1

PREFACE

As an area of study, food is a fascinating subject, for it affords opportunities for creativity and scientific understanding of the very substances needed for pleasure, as well as for survival. Internationally, affairs of state are conducted using food—such as President Reagan's turkey dinner for Chinese officials in Peking—to promote understanding and goodwill. Domestically, public officials have made their mark by focusing attention on food and food problems. Availability and quality of food are concerns of everyone. How well these concerns are met is determined partially by the knowledge of the person doing the shopping and preparation. By studying the selection, storage, functions, preparation, and service of food, you can add to your own pleasure and health as well as to the welfare of those around you.

If you are planning a career in food science, nutrition, or dietetics, a thorough understanding of the various foods and their behaviors alone and in combination during preparation is the starting point for building your career. Whether you are responsible for counseling others about food choices, for supervising others who are preparing food, or for developing and/or producing food products, you will be using this knowledge constantly.

All of us are consumers, and food is something that we all consume each day. We have the choice of preparing foods from basic ingredients at home, of buying convenience foods for use in the home, or of dining out. Added pleasure and often better nutrition can be gained by knowing how to make wise food choices and to prepare appealing foods.

This book has been completely rewritten to help you learn the fundamentals of food and its preparation, with attention directed to providing study aids. Each chapter begins with a detailed listing of the topics included in the chapter. Key words are defined in the margins, and a special feature—''Science Notes''—has been added to highlight important scientific concepts underlying preparation procedures. The influence of preparation techniques on nutrient content and various aspects of nutrition are included throughout the book.

With the knowledge gained from studying the various chapters, you will be prepared to move ahead with your plans for entering a food-related professional career and/or to expand your culinary horizons as a gourmet. No longer will you be limited to eating only what you can buy in the store or what somebody else prepares for you. You will be able to prepare products of high quality and to recognize why they turned out the way they did. In other words, you will be ready to take charge of food preparation and even to explain the fundamentals to others!

Because the sequence of topics covered in university and college food classes varies from institution to institution, the chapters in this book have been written to be independent entities. Thus, it is possible to study the chapters in the order preferred by the professor. No prerequisites are presumed for this course, but the scientific discussions in the ''Science Notes'' will be of considerable interest to those students who have had organic chemistry and/or physics. However, the ''Notes'' have been written so that students who have not had previous science courses also will be able to gain greater understanding of food principles. This understanding will be strengthened through work in the laboratory or at home. Appropriate material for laboratory study coordinated with this book is contained in the laboratory manual, ''Illustrated Guide to Food Preparation'' (Plycon Press).

It is a real pleasure to thank my many students who over the years have given me their thoughtful and helpful suggestions regarding the development of *Food Fundamentals* through its various editions and particularly this edition. Special recognition and thanks are due Dr. Zoe Ann Holmes, Associate Professor of Food and Nutrition at Oregon State University for her very careful reading and thoughtful suggestions for this edition. Thanks also to Barbara Chasse for her interest and diligent efforts in exploring the literature to help make this revision a thorough presentation. And to Mary Kramer, my colleague in teaching food courses at Cal State, I wish to express continuing gratitude for her very helpful and stimulating suggestions for this and previous editions.

In this edition, I would also like to acknowledge the following reviewers: Patricia T. Berglund, North Dakota State University and Mary Sonander, Miami University–Ohio. To Earl Shepherd, my first editor at John Wiley & Sons, goes a big thank you for providing guidance and encouragement in the writing of this and other books over the past two decades. I am very grateful to Debbie Wiley, Ray O'Connell, and now Katie Vignery for their editorial support and guidance in the various editions of *Food Fundamentals* and to the many interested people in the Production Unit who have combined their talents to make this edition a beautiful reality.

May 1985   **Margaret McWilliams**
Redondo Beach, California

CONTENTS

PART ONE

PREPARATION

Cornelius Jacobsen (Delft) "Kitchen Still Life with Peasant Woman"/Bettmann Archive.

CHAPTER 1

FACTORS IN FOOD PREPARATION

Food preparation affords a wonderful opportunity to combine the aesthetic qualities of foods with the scientific elements that influence the overall palatability of meals and their ingredients. All of the senses participate in savoring food that is being eaten: pleasing shapes and colors attract the eyes; aroma encourages acceptance and then combines with taste to define flavors; texture and other characteristics such as crunchiness, tenderness, and temperature round out the eating experience. The total appeal is a combination of how well a single food meets all these sensory measures. When food is prepared well, all these conditions will be fulfilled. The chapters of Part One provide the background needed to ensure quality food preparation. The principles underlying the selection and preparation of various foods and different ways in which cooking can be accomplished lay the foundation for your becoming a professional in the realm of food.

MEASURING

Replication is an important characteristic of quality food preparation, and it can only be achieved through clear recipes and controlled amounts of all the ingredients to be used. To achieve these accurate and reproducible measurements, home cooks in the United States usually use volumetric measures, but in Europe and also in food research laboratories, ingredients commonly are weighed. Weighing is ordinarily done using the metric system. In this discussion of measuring, first volume measuring techniques are reviewed; then the metric system is considered.

Dry Ingredients

Depending upon the amount to be measured, dry ingredients are measured either in graduated measuring cups (ordinarily a set consisting of ¼ cup, ⅓ cup, ½ cup, and 1 cup) or graduated measuring spoons (usually ¼ teaspoon, ½ teaspoon, 1 teaspoon, and 1 tablespoon). Measurement is done by stirring or sifting and then spooning the dry ingredient into the appropriate measuring cup(s) until the cup is overflowing. Then the straight edge of a spatula is used to level the measure. Only full measures should be used. For example, measuring ¾ cup of sugar would require filling the ½ cup and the ¼ cup measures; similarly, ½ tablespoon would mean using the 1 teaspoon and the ½ teaspoon measures. To know what measures to use in the various cases, it is necessary to know certain equivalent measures. Those commonly needed in home food preparation are provided in Table 1.1.

Dry ingredients often pack down in the package or form lumps. To avoid discrepancies resulting from close packing, these ingredients should be stirred to eliminate lumps and consequent excesses in measurements. This is particularly important when measuring cornstarch, which tends to pack considerably during shipping and storage.

Flour is another dry ingredient that has a tendency to pack, which can lead to significant variations in the amounts measured. To eliminate this

Table 1.1 Equivalents of Common Household Measures

Measure		Equivalent	Measure	Equivalent
1 tablespoon (T)	3	teaspoons (tsp)	1 fluid ounce (oz)	2 tablespoons
¼ cup (c)	4	tablespoons	1 cup	8 fluid ounces
⅓ cup	5⅓	tablespoons	1 pint (pt)	2 cups
½ cup	8	tablespoons	1 quart (qt)	4 cups
1 cup	16	tablespoons	1 gallon (gal)	4 quarts

problem, recipes are developed based on the practice of sifting flour one time and then lightly spooning it into the measuring cup, being careful not to tap the cup or otherwise cause the flour to pack. This technique results in a measured cup of all-purpose flour weighing between 92 and 120 grams, while measuring without sifting may result in a cup weighing as much as 150 grams. Obviously, such variation would cause wide variation in a recipe from one time to the next.

Different types of sugar require somewhat different measuring techniques. Powdered sugar, like flour, tends to pack; sifting prior to measuring is recommended. Brown sugar needs to be stirred to eliminate any lumps before being pressed gently, but firmly, into the appropriate graduated measuring cup(s). The packing should be just firm enough so that the sugar will hold the shape of the cup if the cup is inverted to remove the sugar. Granulated sugar only needs to be stirred to eliminate any lumps before being measured like any other dry ingredient.

Fats and Oils

Solid fats ordinarily are measured by pressing them firmly into the appropriate graduated measuring cup and then leveling with a spatula. Care must be

Success in food preparation requires careful measuring of ingredients, using a glass measuring cup for liquids, graduated measuring cups for fats and dry ingredients, and measuring spoons for smaller quantities.

taken to be sure that there are no air pockets remaining when the fat has been packed in.

Some people use the water displacement method for measuring solid fats, but this method is inaccurate because the measurement includes the water clinging to the fat. The water acquired by this method is a particular problem when making pastry. To use this method, however, water is placed in a glass measuring cup to equal the difference between the desired amount of fat and one measuring cup. Then the fat is pressed into the cup until the water level rises to the one-cup mark. It is essential that the fat be pressed below the surface of the water when measuring by this method to achieve any degree of accuracy. To use this technique to measure ⅓ cup of fat, first ⅔ cup of water is put in a glass measuring cup and then the fat is pressed until the water level reaches 1 cup. The water is drained from the fat in the cup before the fat is removed and added to the other ingredients.

Oils are measured by pouring into a glass measuring cup until the level of the oil reaches the desired marker on the cup. The cup should be placed on the counter and the measure taken by bending over to look across rather than down on the surface.

Liquids

Liquids are measured easily in a standard glass measuring cup placed on a level surface. Accurate readings require bending over until the eye is at the same height as the cup and then pouring in liquid until the meniscus reaches the desired level. The glass measuring cup works well with liquids because there is no need to do any mechanical leveling. The glass cup itself also has the advantage of extending a bit above the 1 cup mark, which makes it possible to carry the measured liquid without spilling it.

SCIENCE NOTE: USING METRICS

Although the United States has decided not to convert to metric measures as a national policy now, the metric system is the system used in the research aspects of food and other sciences. Therefore, professionals will need to be familiar with metrics and to be able to convert between our traditional units and metric measures.

The metric system is based on units of 10, with prefixes providing the necessary information about size and the suffixes indicating the type of unit, that is, volume, weight, or distance. Specifically, the suffixes are liter (l) for volume, gram (g) for weight, and meter (m) for length (distance).

The prefixes attached to these root words define each unit of 10, making it possible to describe metric measures in comparatively simple numbers. Table 1.2 presents the common prefixes for metrics.

Table 1.2 Common Prefixes in the Metric System

Prefix	Symbol	Definition
Tera	T	$1,000,000,000,000 = 10^{12}$
Giga	G	$1,000,000,000 = 10^{9}$
Mega	M	$1,000,000 = 10^{6}$
Kilo[1]	k	$1,000 = 10^{3}$
Hecto	h	$100 = 10^{2}$
Deka	da	$10 = 10^{1}$
Deci[1]	d	$0.1 = 10^{-1}$
Centi[1]	c	$0.01 = 10^{-2}$
Milli[1]	m	$0.001 = 10^{-3}$
Micro[1]	μ	$0.000,001 = 10^{-6}$
Nano	n	$0.000,000,001 = 10^{-9}$
Pico	p	$0.000,000,000,001 = 10^{-12}$

[1]Prefixes used commonly in food and nutrition.

Measures in metric are expressed by combining the appropriate prefix with the type of measurement being made. For example, if volume were being measured, the expression for the volume might be in milliliters. In this sytem, half a liter would be expressed as 0.5 liter, or 500 milliliters (note that 1 liter equals 1000 milliliters or 10^3 milliliters). Similarly, 1 kilogram is the same as 1000 grams (10^3 grams).

Not only do food scientists need to be able to work within the metric system, but they also need to be able to convert between these laboratory units and household measures. This is a matter of simple arithmetic if certain equivalent measures are known. It is helpful to know that there are about 236 milliliters in a common measuring cup and that there are approximately 454 grams in a pound. With these equivalencies and others provided in Table 1.3, calculations can be done quickly.

Table 1.3 Common Equivalent Measures and Conversion Factors

Equivalents	Conversion Factors
Weights	
1 kilogram = 2.2 pounds	Ounces (avdp) × 28.35 = grams
454 grams = 1 pound	Pounds (avdp) × 0.454 = kilograms
28.35 grams = 1 ounce	Grams × 0.035 = ounces (avdp)
1 gram = 0.035 ounce	Kilograms × 2.2 = pounds (avdp)
Measures	
1 liter = 1.06 quarts	Quarts × 0.946 = liters
1 gallon = 3.79 liters	Gallons × 0.0037 = cubic meters
1 quart = 946.4 milliliters	Liters × 1.056 = quarts
1 cup = 236.6 milliliters	Cubic meters × 264.172 = gallons
1 fluid ounce = 29.6 milliliters	
1 tablespoon = 14.8 milliliters	

Yet another type of measurement done in the laboratory is that of determining temperatures used in food preparation. Consumers ordinarily use the Fahrenheit scale in the United States, while scientists use Celsius. Conversions may need to be made between the two scales. Comparisons are shown in Figure 1.1. Familiar reference points are the

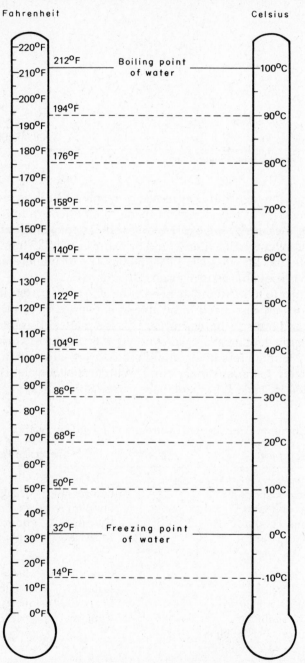

Figure 1.1 Comparison of the Fahrenheit and Celsius scales.

boiling point of water (212° Fahrenheit or 100° Celsius at sea level) and the freezing point (32°F or 0°C).

To convert from the Fahrenheit (F) scale to the Celsius (C) temperature, the following equation is used:

$$\text{\small 5/9} \, (\underline{\quad}°F - 32) = \underline{\quad}°C$$

For example, to convert 140°F to the Celsius scale:

$$\text{\small 5/9} \, (140°F - 32) = \underline{\quad}°C$$
$$\text{\small 5/9} \, (108) = 60°C$$

Conversion from Celsius to Fahrenheit is done by using this equation:

$$(\text{\small 9/5} \times \underline{\quad}°C) + 32 = \underline{\quad}°F$$

Thus, 60°C is converted to the Fahrenheit scale as follows:

$$(\text{\small 9/5} \times 60°C) + 32 = \underline{\quad}°F$$
$$108 + 32 = 140°F$$

TEMPERATURES IN FOOD PREPARATION

Expressions such as "freezing cold" and "boiling hot" are used frequently in conversation to describe temperature extremes, but in food preparation, the range of temperatures actually is considerably greater than the implied range of 32°F to 212°F. When dealing only with pure water, these two temperatures represent the range of extremes. However, food preparation involves using an array of foods and food mixtures and also different means of heating. As a result, temperatures in food and cooking equipment may range from about 0°F to 450°F. For example, deep-fat frying often is done in oil heated to 375°F, and an oven temperature of 425°F or even 450°F sometimes may be used in baking.

Freezing Temperatures

Water is a key component of many foods—not only sauces and soups but also for such foods as gelatins and ice creams that do not flow. Because of this abundance of water in foods, the temperature at which foods freeze often is quite close to the freezing temperature of water. The transition of water from its liquid state into ice is essential in the making of ice cream and certainly is an important textural determinant in frozen fruits, vegetables, meats, and other frozen foods.

Heat of Solidification Heat given off when water is transformed into ice; 80 kilocalories per gram of water.

Freezing is the transition of a liquid into a solid, and the freezing point is the temperature at which this happens. This process of solidification results in a heat loss of 80 kilocalories per gram of water converted to ice, referred to as the *heat of solidification*. The converse occurs, that is an absorption of 80 kilocalories per gram occurs when ice is changed back into liquid. This is the reason why the mouth feels so cold when letting an ice cube melt.

The temperature at which freezing occurs influences the preparation and the quality of frozen foods. While such a statement may sound simplistic—for everyone has learned since childhood that water freezes at 32°F—the fact is that substances dissolved in water will alter the temperature at which the solution freezes. In practical terms, this means that sugars and soluble salts, such as table salt, dissolve in water and modify the freezing point.

Sugar in solution depresses the temperature at which the freezing of the solution occurs; the freezing point drops 1.86°C for each gram molecular weight of sugar per liter. Consequently, an ice cream made with a large quantity of sugar will take a long time to freeze and will require a lower temperature for freezing to occur than would a less sweet ice cream. The high sugar content also means that the ice cream will melt more rapidly than will a product with less sugar. Thus, this sweet ice cream will be somewhat difficult to serve.

The fact that salt ionizes results in an even greater drop in the freezing point of salt solutions than of comparable sugar solutions. Although salt solutions are unpalatable at concentrations sufficient to have significant effect on freezing points, this property of salt is utilized advantageously in making ice cream in an ice cream freezer. The container holding the ice cream mixture is chilled and the ice cream is frozen by placing the container in a mixture of salt and ice. Because the ice cream is freezing much faster than when only melting ice is used, not only is energy saved, but more important smaller ice crystals form, which results in an ice cream with a smooth texture.

Intermediate Temperatures

Many foods are stored and/or prepared at temperatures that lie between the freezing and boiling points of water. Protein-containing foods have the potential for causing food poisoning if they are held at temperatures promoting the growth of microorganisms. Storage just above freezing (between 33° and a maximum of 40°F) in the refrigerator is important to slow the reproduction of microorganisms and to also control spoilage in other foods. Protein-containing foods being held for delayed service need to be maintained at temperatures outside the danger zone (preferably at 140°F) to avoid food poisoning. Careful control of the temperature of foods is critical to maintaining both food safety and food quality.

Some foods (a notable example being a stirred custard) are particularly sensitive to temperatures during cooking. A controlled, fairly low heat is important to achieving the desired thickening without overheating and damaging the protein in custards and several other protein-containing foods. A double boiler, which is a two-part pan, has been designed specifically to avoid letting such heat-sensitive items heat too quickly and boil. Water placed in the lower container is heated to produce steam all around the upper container where the food is being heated. This arrangement makes it impossible to bring the mixture in the upper container to a boil and helps to ensure gentle enough heating for heat-sensitive foods. Many ranges are equipped with a simmer setting to permit comparable rates of heating without the inconvenience of using a double boiler.

Lukewarm Approximately body temperature; about 100°F.

Scalding Temperature used to loosen fruit skins and perform other similar functions; about 150°F.

Simmering Range of temperatures between 180° and 211°F; bubbles form and rise, but rarely break the surface; more gentle heat treatment than boiling.

Boiling Active agitation of liquid and transition of some liquid to the vapor state; occurs when vapor pressure just exceeds atmospheric pressure.

Vapor Pressure Pressure within a liquid for individual molecules to escape from the liquid; varies with the temperature of the liquid and with dissolved substances.

Atmospheric Pressure The pressure of the atmosphere pressing downward on the surface of a liquid; varies with changes in elevation.

Heat of Vaporization Energy required to convert boiling water into steam; 540 kilocalories per gram of water.

Descriptive words are used to indicate the desired temperature in working with such foods as yeast or milk, which require careful temperature control for success. The coolest of these temperatures is *lukewarm*, or a temperature of about 100°F, a little above body temperature. Scalding temperatures are used to prepare milk for use in bread making, for loosening skins on tomatoes, and for a few other procedures. *Scalding* water (about 150°F) can be characterized as having large bubbles collecting on the sides and bottom of the pan, but with little movement. Between 180°F and 211°F is the range designated as *simmering*. Water held in this temperature range will have large bubbles forming and rising almost to, but not breaking the surface of the water.

Boiling Temperatures

Boiling is extremely active agitation of a liquid, at which time some of the liquid changes to the vapor state. This occurs when the *vapor pressure* (pressure in a liquid to escape) of a liquid just exceeds *atmospheric pressure* (downward pressure on the liquid). The temperature at which boiling occurs is the boiling point, which is 212°F for water at sea level. Interestingly, pure water at sea level will remain at 212°F regardless of how fast the water is boiling. The heat can be turned higher, and the water will boil more rapidly than before, but the temperature will remain constant.

To change water from the liquid state into the gaseous state, or steam, requires an input of a considerable amount of energy, called the *heat of vaporization*. In fact, to convert a gram of boiling water into steam requires 540 kilocalories! This is almost seven times as much energy as is involved in the heat of solidification. When water is being heated, the temperature will rise quickly until the boiling point is reached, but there will be a lag before boiling actually begins because of the tremendous heat input needed to supply the energy needed for vaporization (steam) to occur. The situation is reversed when steam condenses into water, as occurs when steam comes in contact with skin. The serious burns resulting from contact with steam reflect the fact that 540 kilocalories are given off onto the skin when steam is converted back into water. This is one of the reasons to be careful to avoid contact with steam.

Atmospheric pressure The pressure being exerted downward upon a pan of water must be overcome before boiling can occur. Therefore, this pressure has an instrumental role to play in determining the temperature at which boiling will happen. Atmospheric pressure is influenced by the altitude; in the mountains there is less atmosphere above the surface of the ground than there is at sea level. Consequently, atmospheric pressure is lower at high elevations than at low ones. This means that boiling will take place more easily at a high elevation than at sea level; in other words, the temperature at boiling is lower on a high mountain than it is at the ocean. In fact, the boiling temperature of water drops 1°F for each 500 feet of gain in elevation (1°C for each 960 feet of gain).

People who live at an elevation of 8000 feet boil vegetables at a temperature of 196°F in contrast to a temperature of 212°F at the ocean. This is why vegetables or other foods cooked in boiling water in the mountains require a longer time to become tender than they do at lower elevations. A remarkable illustration of this drop in the temperature of boiling is noted in people's accounts of expeditions on Mt. Everest, where the extremely high elevations and the consequently low atmospheric pressure cause such a decrease in the boiling temperature of water that it is possible to reach directly into a pot of boiling water and not be burned!

Atmospheric pressure can be modified intentionally by special devices. Sometimes in food processing, the temperature of boiling is reduced so that water can be evaporated without causing a cooked flavor to develop. This is desirable when making orange juice concentrate. In processing the concentrate, the industry utilizes a partial vacuum, which reduces the atmospheric pressure above the orange juice, to cause the original orange juice to boil at a cool temperature. This technique promotes the evaporation of water yet avoids actually "cooking" the orange juice.

The reverse of a partial vacuum often is needed in cooking to shorten cooking times. Pressurized systems enable the atmospheric pressure to be increased significantly, resulting in a high temperature for boiling. In the home, pressure saucepans and pressure canners are available for this purpose. Commonly, 15 pounds of pressure will be generated within this very tight system, which raises the cooking temperature to about 240°F. This high temperature significantly shortens the cooking time needed to tenderize a food. Commercially, pressurized equipment accomplishes this same increase in temperature of the cooking medium.

Vapor Pressure The energy of water molecules trying to escape the liquid system (vapor pressure) is influenced by the temperature of the water. At room temperature, vapor pressure is quite low, but it increases rather rapidly as water temperature rises toward the boiling point. With adequate heat, vapor pressure will just exceed atmospheric pressure, and some of the water molecules will begin to escape into the air above the pan.

Substances that form a true solution in water reduce the vapor pressure of the solution. For boiling to take place, additional heat must be supplied to raise the vapor pressure to the point at which vapor pressure just exceeds atmospheric pressure. The net result of the addition of a solute to water is to raise the boiling point. The greater the concentration of solute, the higher the temperature of the boiling solution. This effect is utilized in the preparation of candies, which are boiled to specified final temperatures. For example, fudge usually is cooked to 234°F, a temperature well above the 212°F temperature of boiling water. Several minutes of active boiling are required before the thermometer will finally reach the desired temperature because it is necessary to evaporate much of the liquid to concentrate the sugar sufficiently. It is this high concentration of sugar that successfully reduces the vapor pressure of the solution sufficiently to cause boiling to occur at 234°F (or even higher in some other candies with still greater concentrations of sugar). Thus, the temperature is a reliable indicator that the concentration of sugar has reached the desired point. This subject is discussed in some detail in Chapter 6.

The molecules of sugar, as pointed out, are small enough to go into solution. Molecules smaller than 1 millimicron are able to form true solutions and will reduce vapor pressure. Salt (sodium chloride) ionizes when it is placed in water, resulting in the formation of two ions (sodium and chloride) from a single molecule of salt. As a consequence, salt has twice as great an effect on vapor pressure as sugar. However, the unpalatable quality of a salty solution makes this effect of little practical use in cookery.

Many substances in foods are much larger than a millimicron. Proteins, for example, are large molecules that are unable to go into solution but form a *colloidal dispersion*. Therefore, they have no appreciable effect on the boiling point. Gelatin, starch, gums, cornmeal, and countless other food items can be added to boiling water in high concentrations or low, but they will not cause a measurable change in the boiling point because they form *coarse suspensions*, not true solutions.

Colloidal Dispersion
System containing protein or other molecules or particles between 1 and 100 millimicrons in size dispersed in a continuous phase, in this case in water.

Coarse Suspension
Dispersion of particles larger than colloidal size mixed in water or other liquid.

Frying Temperatures

With the exception of sugar solutions, cookery in boiling water is done at 212°F or less unless a pressurized system is used. However, much higher temperatures can be utilized when fat is the cooking medium, because fat does not boil even when the temperature rises as high as 475°F. Fat can be maintained at desirable temperatures for frying (usually around 375°F). Such hot fat means that foods will reach their desired degree of doneness quite quickly in comparison with the length of time that would be needed if they were to be boiled in water at 212°F. After all, boiling water is more than 150°F cooler than the fat used in frying.

The temperatures utilized in the preparation and storage of food generally range over a temperature span of almost 500°F! To be successful in food preparation and management, knowledge of the appropriate temperatures and ways of controlling them will be a vital part of this field. An overview of the various temperatures and their applications is provided in Figure 1.2.

Such high temperatures highlight the need for being safety conscious in preparing foods. Burns occur all too easily when people fail to appreciate the extremely high temperatures of boiling candies or of the fat being used in deep-fat frying. In fact, kitchen counters with vinyl or formica tops can be damaged simply by placing a pan with a boiling candy solution or deep fat on them.

A related danger exists when water is added to a caramelizing sugar or to hot fat. The extreme temperature difference between a caramelizing sugar or hot fat and cold water causes excessive splattering, which may result in burns on the hands, arms, or face—wherever the spatters reach the skin. For this reason, water should be boiling when it is added to caramelizing sugar and potato slices for french frying should be blotted as dry as possible with paper towels before being added to the fat.

A meat thermometer is a convenient and accurate means of determining the degree of doneness of large cuts of meat and poultry. Other special thermometers to check temperatures in deep-fat frying, candy making, and in refrigerators, freezers, and ovens help to assure safe food of high quality.

Thermometers

To help ensure good temperature control in food preparation and handling, appropriate thermometers are used, generally, a candy thermometer, a deep-

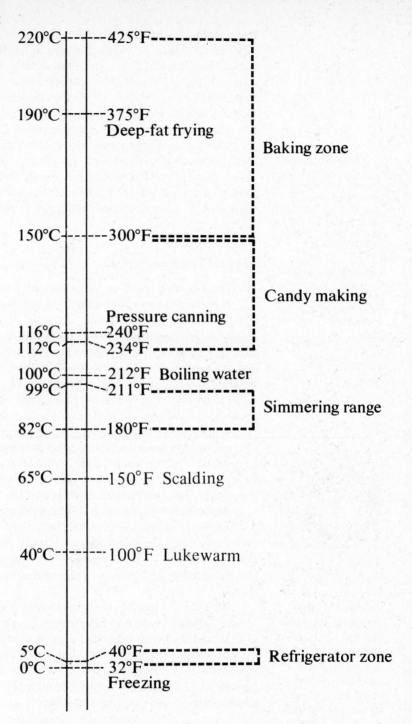

Figure 1.2 Temperatures of importance in food preparation.

fat frying thermometer, and a meat thermometer. The thermometer for candy making will need to have an upper limit of approximately 325°F to allow a margin of safety above the probable high of 300°F needed for some candies. The deep-fat frying thermometer will have an upper limit of at least 500°F. A meat thermometer will register up to about 185°F and should have a short sensing rod to accommodate to roasting in the oven.

Appliances occasionally may fail to maintain their thermostatic control. A refrigerator thermometer and an oven thermometer are useful checks on appliances to be sure that food is being held at safe temperatures. Food service professionals in industry may find a small pocket-sized thermometer invaluable in ensuring that foods on the steam table are being held at a high enough temperature and that refrigerated items are being stored at safe temperatures.

PRINCIPLES OF HEATING FOODS

Conduction

Conduction Transfer of heat from one molecule to the next.

Heat can be transferred by the process of *conduction*, that is, heat is transferred directly from one molecule to another. In cooking, heat is transferred by conduction from the metal of an electrical coil on a range directly to the metal of the pan in which a food is being heated. This method of heat transfer works slowly, but it is fairly successful when good conductors are used. Aluminum pans, for example, provide quite uniform heating if they are thick. In contrast, stainless steel conducts heat unevenly, causing some pans made with this metal to develop some spots that are too hot, while others may be too cool.

Convection

Convection Transfer of heat throughout a system by movement of currents of heated air, water, or other liquid.

When water, oil or other fat, or air is heated, currents begin to develop within the system and aid in moving the heat throughout the food. This circulation of heated liquids or air is a process called *convection*. It is on this principle that the convection oven is based. By forcing the circulation of heated air currents in this type of oven, foods will be heated and baked significantly more quickly than they will be when circulation of heated air is limited.

All ovens contain some circulation of heated air during operation, but the amount of convection in a normal oven is quite low. When conventional ovens are loaded so that baking pans extend to the sides, front, or back of the oven, the normal flow pattern of the hot air currents will be obstructed, and uneven baking results. It is important to avoid placing one pan directly beneath another or to prevent loading an oven with pans being jammed right against each other and against the oven walls if even baking and browning are to be achieved. Convection currents are the key to successful baking in both convection and conventional ovens.

Convection is also a significant part of the heating process when foods are being heated on the range, too. The pan holding the food will be heated by conduction, but the heat begins to move through the food itself with the aid of warming currents of water or other liquid. Stirring is an added aid in helping to distribute the heat uniformly through the food.

Radiation

Radiation Transfer of energy directly from the source to the food being heated.

Radiation is the direct transfer of energy from the energy source to the food. Broiling is a familiar example of this type of heating. The energy involved in radiation from broiling is in the infrared range, being somewhat longer waves than are in the range of visible light.

Microwave Oven Special type of oven that is able to heat food by sending waves of 915 or 240 mHz from a magnetron directly into foods, where water and/or fat molecules vibrate and heat foods.

Microwave ovens also utilize the infrared frequency range for a unique way of heating foods. In microwave ovens, a *magnetron tube* is used to generate waves of a frequency above the length of visible light, specifically either 915 or 2450 megahertz (MHz). These waves penetrate as much as an inch into a food, causing rapid vibrations of individual molecules of water or fat. It is these vibrations that cause the food to begin to heat rapidly.

Magnetron Tube Tube generating the microwaves in a microwave oven.

Although these are distinctly different types of heating, most foods are heated by a combination of at least two of these cooking techniques. For instance, a broiled steak will be heated by conduction as well as by radiation. A soup being heated in a pan will be heated by conduction and convection.

Microwaves Form of electromagnetic energy; 915 and 2450 MHz are the assigned frequencies for microwave ovens.

Dipole Molecule having both a positive and a negative charge.

SCIENCE NOTE: HEATING BY MICROWAVES

Food is heated in a microwave oven by penetrating into the product with microwave energy, thus heating by radiation. *Microwaves* are a form of electromagnetic radiation, the waves being generated by a magnetron vacuum tube that converts electrical energy received by an amplifier into microwave radiation. The Federal Communications Commission has assigned two frequencies, 915 and 2450 MHz, for radiation in microwave ovens. Both these frequencies are above the visible light range. The 2450-MHz frequency has a shorter wavelength than the signal at 915 MHz; hence, it does not penetrate as deeply into the food mass as does the longer wavelength at 915 MHz.

These waves generate heat in food because of the electrical nature of water molecules, water actually being a *dipole*, that is, one portion of a water molecule carries a positive electrical charge, while another part of the molecule will carry a negative charge. The microwave energy penetrating the food is characterized by its very, very rapid alternating of electrical charge. This constant change causes the water molecules to vibrate very actively, and that vibration generates heat. Unlike other forms of cookery, this energy is generated within the food rather than traveling only from the surface toward the interior. Once the food begins to heat because of the dipolar nature of the food in relation to the microwave energy, conduction also occurs, helping to equalize the temperature throughout the meat or other food. The standing time recommended in many microwave oven recipes acknowledges the importance of allowing conduction to contribute to the overall cookery mode.

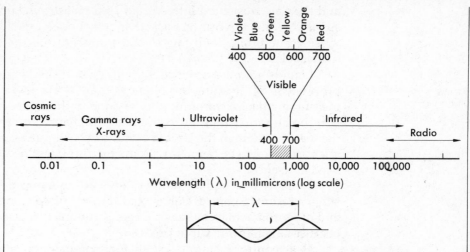

The frequencies assigned to microwave ovens (915 and 2450 MHz are above visible light. (From *Life of the Green Plant* by Arthur Galston, 2nd edition, © 1964 by Prentice-Hall, Inc., Englewood Cliffs, N.J. p. 4. Reprinted by permission of Felix Cooper.

For food to be heated by microwave energy, there must be some water or fat present, although a large quantity is not essential to success. Fat becomes very hot even more quickly than water does in a food being heated by microwaves. Thus, butter or other fats can be melted very quickly in a microwave oven. Similarly, meats tend to be overheated quickly by microwave cookery unless the slices are relatively thin, and the progress of the microwaves into the meat is monitored with extreme care.

Microwave ovens must be operated only when water or food has been placed in them for the microwaves introduced into the cavity must have a substance to absorb them. Otherwise, the waves will be bounced right back toward the magnetron tube, causing irreparable damage to the tube. An empty pan or dish will not absorb the microwaves any better than the empty cavity. Even if food is present, microwaves will arc back toward the magnetron if metal is placed within the unit. Consequently:

1. Do not operate a microwave oven without food or water.
2. Never use metal in a microwave oven.

SUMMARY

Measuring is important to quality control when preparing foods. Dry ingredients can be measured accurately by use of graduated measuring cups. Flour is sifted before being spooned lightly into the appropriate cup and leveled with a metal spatula. Other dry ingredients are generally stirred to lighten them and then are measured into a graduated measuring cup and leveled. Brown sugar is gently, but firmly, packed tightly enough to hold the shape of the cup when turned out. Solid fats also are pressed into the appropriate cup and then leveled.

Liquids are measured carefully in glass measuring cups filled to the appropriate level. Reading of volume is done at eye level. These and the other measurements are continuing to be done in the units used commonly in the U.S. home rather than in metric measurements. The proposal to convert to the metric system in the United States has been put aside. Nevertheless, food scientists need to be familiar with the metric system because this is the system used in science.

Freezing and boiling temperatures are influenced by the percentage of sugar present. Sugar dissolves and lowers the freezing point of ice creams and other foods high in sugar. Sugar solutions boil at elevated temperatures because sugar lowers vapor pressure.

Heat control is important in food preparation and storage. Moderate heats include lukewarm, scalding, and simmering. These can be achieved by use of a double boiler or a very low heat setting on a range.

High elevations and/or partial vacuums will cause water to boil at a lower temperature than normal. The converse is provided by pressure saucepans or pressure cookers, which reach elevated temperatures, thus reducing cooking times. Deep-fat frying is another technique that provides fast cooking because temperatures in fat can be about 375°F or even a bit higher.

Food may be heated by conduction, convection, radiation, or a combination of these methods. Radiation is quite fast, resulting in a saving in cooking time compared with either convection or conduction ovens; microwaves cause water and fat molecules within a food to vibrate rapidly, resulting in heat generation.

Selected References

Arlin, M. L. et al. Effect of different methods of flour measurements on the quality of plain two-egg cakes. *J. Home Econ. 56*: 339. 1964.

American Home Economics Association. *Handbook of Food Preparation*. AHEA. Washington, D.C. 8th ed. 1980.

Holmes, Z. A. and M. Woodburn. Heat transfer and temperature of foods during preparation. *CRC Critical Reviews in Food Sci. Nutr. 14*: 231. 1981.

Lovingood, R. P. and R. C. Goss. Electric energy used by major cooking appliances. *Home Econ. Res. J. 8*: 234. 1980.

Mathews, R. H. and O. M. Batcher. Sifted versus unsifted flour. *J. Home Econ. 55*: 123. 1963.

McWilliams, M. *Illustrated Guide to Food Preparation*. Plycon Press. Redondo Beach, Calif. 4th ed. 1982.

Peet, L. J. et al. *Household Equipment*. John Wiley. New York. 8th ed. 1979.

Rosen, C. Effect of microwaves on food and related materials. *Food Tech. 26(7):* 39. 1972.

Voris, H. H. and F. O. VanDuyne. Low wattage microwave cooking of top round roasts: energy consumption, thiamin content, and palatability. *J. Food Sci. 44*: 1447. 1979.

Study Questions

1. Describe the way to measure flour and explain the rationale for the technique.
2. What is the best way to measure ¾ cup of rice using a recipe in the home?
3. What is the most accurate way of measuring 3 teaspoons of baking powder? Of measuring 5⅓ tablespoons of sugar?
4. What is the recommended method for measuring ½ cup of shortening? Describe a second method sometimes used to measure solid fats in the home. Why is this method less desirable than the first?
5. What are the suffixes used in the metric system for designating units of length, weight, and volume, respectively?
6. What is the meaning of milli, kilo, centi? What is the symbol for each of these prefixes?
7. Convert 50°C to degrees Fahrenheit. Convert 150°F to degrees Celsius.
8. Why does the temperature rise when a sugar solution is boiled actively for several minutes?
9. How can atmospheric pressure be modified? What influence does atmospheric pressure have on the boiling point of water?
10. Describe the ways in which heat is transferred into foods.

Sir Luke Fides, detail from "Dolly." Warrington Art Museum, The Bridgeman Art Library/Art Resource.

CHAPTER 2

VEGETABLES

Vegetables! This word is likely to elicit reactions that range from applause to moans and groans. In recent years, however, the high interest in good nutrition and the popularity of vegetarian diets have drawn favorable attention to vegetables (and also other plant foods). People who are eating for good health and are selecting diets adequate in vitamins and minerals without being high in calories have been staunch supporters of vegetables. This increasing popularity of vegetables is even evidenced by the fact that many restaurants are not only offering a comparatively wide variety of vegetables, but they are also doing excellent jobs of preparing and serving them.

High-quality preparation of vegetables is a challenge, for vegetables can be truly beautiful to look at and appealing to eat, but they also can be ruined by poor cooking techniques. Mastery of vegetable cookery is an essential aspect of the study of foods. When vegetables are selected and prepared with imagination and skill, they can add exciting color, flavor, and textural contrast to a meal.

Imagine how drab the main course of a meal would be if the bright red of a tomato, the striking orange of carrots, the intense green of broccoli, the pearly white of cauliflower, or some other color accent were absent. Slightly crisp cooked green beans, fluffy mashed potatoes, or the crunch of a celery strip add essential textural interest to a meal. And what would many meals be without the flavor lift of an onion, a summer squash, or broccoli?

Vegetable Herbaceous plant containing an edible portion suitably served with the main course of a meal.

Today, people do agree that vegetables are nutritious and should be a regular part of the diet, but there is still a lack of agreement on the definition of a *vegetable*. The argument involves foods such as tomatoes and pumpkins that are viewed by some people as fruits and by others as vegetables. The confusion can, however, be resolved in good order by using the following definition of a vegetable: a plant, usually herbaceous (with little or no woody tissue), containing an edible portion that is suitably served with the main course of a meal. Corn, beans, and most other vegetables are from plants that wither after the growing season, a characteristic common to herbaceous plants. The limited sweetness of most vegetables suits these foods to the main course rather than to dessert. Thus, this definition helps to classify tomatoes as vegetables, even though they are the fruit of the plant on which they grow.

CLASSIFICATION

Almost all parts of plants can be used as vegetables, but specific portions of the various plants are selected for use in meals. It is on the basis of the part of the plant that is eaten that vegetables are classified. For example, although the tender green tops of onions may be used, the bulb is the main portion eaten, so onions are classified as bulbs. The roots of carrots are the portion ordinarily consumed, while tubers, leaves and stems, fruits, and seeds of various other plants are viewed as the vegetable. Table 2.1 illustrates the classification for many of the common vegetables.

Table 2.1 Classification of Vegetables

Bulb	Root	Tubers[1]	Leaves, Stems	Fruits	Seeds
Garlic	Beets	White potatoes	Broccoli	Tomatoes	Legumes[2]
Leeks	Carrots	Sweet potatoes	Brussels	Eggplant	(lima beans
Onions	Radishes	Jerusalem artichoke	sprouts	Peppers	kidney beans
Shallots	Parsnips	Jicama	Celery	Okra	red beans
	Rutabagas		Cabbage	Sweet corn	navy beans
	Turnips		Chinese	Squash,	pinto beans
	Daikon		cabbage	summer and	chick peas
	Celeriac		Endive	winter	black-eyed
	(celery		Parsley	Cucumbers	peas
	root)		Cilantro	Chinese snow	split peas
			Leaf lettuce	peas	black beans)
			Head lettuce	Artichokes	
			Kale	Green beans	
			Kohlrabi	Wax beans	

[1]Enlarged, edible fleshy stems growing under the ground.
[2]Seeds from the *Leguminosae* family, a family of plants unique for the ability to fix nitrogen into the soil, thus enriching the soil.

STRUCTURE

Parenchyma Cell Type of cell comprising most of the pulp of a vegetable or fruit.

Cellulose Complex carbohydrate made up of glucose and not digested by people.

Pectic Substances Complex carbohydrates acting as cementing substances between cells; sequence of change during ripening is protopectin to pectin to pectic acid.

Hemicelluloses Complex carbohydrates made up of several different sugars and sugar derivatives.

Vegetables vary somewhat in their structure from one type of vegetable to another type, but generally they have an outer covering (dermal tissue), a transport system (vascular system), and the pulp, which is composed primarily of *parenchyma cells*. These parenchyma cells have permeable walls to permit some substances to pass back and forth. Some rigidity is provided by the presence of *cellulose*, with additional strength being the result of *pectic substances* and *hemicelluloses* serving as connecting links between cells. These various substances are types of carbohydrates.

SCIENCE NOTE: STRUCTURE OF PLANT FOODS

The strong, thick nature of the dermal layer is evident when peeling fruits or vegetables. This is a protective layer with a high concentration of cellulose in the cell walls. Cellulose, like other structural carbohydrates, is not digested and absorbed for energy by people. This seems surprising when its content of only glucose units is known, for that is the same building material found in starch. However, the glucose units in cellulose are linked together differently from the linkage found in starch. The cellulose linkage is termed a 1,4-β-glucosidic linkage, whereas that in starch is a 1,4-α-glucosidic linkage. These two types of linkages are shown below. Note that the only difference is found on the carbon labeled *1*. The union on the fourth carbon of the next glucose unit is the same in both cellulose and starch.

$$1,4 = \beta - \text{Glucosidic linkage}$$
Cellulose fragment

$$1,4 = \alpha - \text{Glucosidic linkage}$$
Starch fragment

Hemicelluloses also are important components of cell walls in fruits and vegetables. These compounds are more difficult to define than cellulose because hemicelluloses contain a variety of different sugar-related products. These include derivatives of some sugars with five carbons (arabinose and xylose) as well as galactose and mannose, each of which contains six carbons. The pectic substances, discussed in detail in Chapter 16, are made up of galacturonic acid units. These units are derivatives of galactose and undergo chemical changes during ripening of fruits. Unlike hemicelluloses, pectic substances are found between cells, where they act as substances to cement cells together rather than as parts of the cell wall.

The parenchyma cells constitute the bulk of the edible portion of fruits and vegetables. Their structure, therefore, is of special interest. Within the parenchyma cell, as can be seen in Figure 2.1, there are special structures, the *plastids*, within the *cytoplasm*. The various types of plastids perform specific, unique functions and provide diverse characteristics to specific vegetables. For instance, in green vegetables chlorophyll is formed in a special plastid called a chloroplast. *Chloroplasts* are in

Plastids Special structures within the cytoplasm of parenchyma cells.

Cytoplasm Viscous layer just inside the cell wall of the parenchyma cell; contains plastids.

Chloroplasts Plastids containing chlorophyll in parenchyma cells.

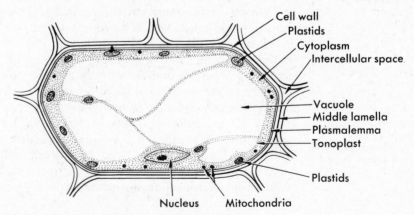

Figure 2.1 Key parts of a parenchyma cell.

Chromoplasts Plastids containing carotenoids (orange pigments) in parenchyma cells.

Leucoplasts Plastids serving as the site for formation and storage of starch in parenchyma cells.

Vacuole Largest region of the parenchyma cell; the portion encircled by the cytoplasm.

the cytoplasm layer just inside the cell. The orange pigments in vegetables are found in other plastids called *chromoplasts*, which also are in the cytoplasm just next to the cell wall. Starch is found in still other plastids called *leucoplasts*.

A large portion of each of the parenchyma cells is occupied by the *vacuole*. The vacuole is of particular interest because this is the region where the fluid of the cell is concentrated and where such important flavor constituents as sugars, acids, and salts are found. This is also the location of the flavonoid (white or bluish to reddish-purple) pigments. When a vegetable is cut or peeled, many parenchyma cells are opened, allowing considerable loss of pigments and other compounds found in the vacuole.

NUTRIENT CONTENT

Vegetables often are recommended in abundance in reducing diets because of their very small energy contribution and their large amount of water. In fact, green beans, cabbage, broccoli, asparagus, and many other vegetables are more than 90 percent water. Few vegetables other than legumes have less than 80 percent water.

Carbohydrate content varies, both in form and amount. Immature vegetables will have a gradual transition of some of the sugar in them to starch as they mature. Starch levels in potatoes are around 15 percent for white potatoes and 25 percent for sweet potatoes, while cooked legumes average around 20 percent starch. In contrast, the carbohydrate level in cabbage is only about 5 percent (Table 2.2), and that is largely sugar rather than starch. The carbohydrate levels of most vegetables range between these figures, but tend toward 10 percent or less.

In addition to starch and sugars, which are digestible carbohydrates, much of the physical structure of vegetables is provided by the generally indigestible pectic substances, hemicelluloses, and cellulose, all of which have been described briefly. The most durable of the structural components actually is not a carbohydrate; it is a woodlike substance called lignin and is used in the body only as roughage.

Protein and fat levels generally are very low in vegetables, thus partly accounting for the low energy value of most vegetables. The exceptions to this statement are the legumes, which are very useful sources of incomplete protein at a comparatively low cost. The protein content of cooked legumes averages approximately 8 percent, which is well below the protein content of meats, but much higher than the content of other vegetables and fruits. This amount of protein influences the cookery techniques needed for optimal quality.

Minerals and vitamins are found in widely varying amounts (Table 2.3) in the different vegetables, with some vegetables being notable in their content of specific nutrients. For example, the provitamin A content of dark green,

Table 2.2 Approximate Composition of Selected Vegetables (1 Cup)

Vegetable	Water (%)	Protein (g)	Fat (g)	Total Carbohydrate (g)
Asparagus, cooked	92	3	Trace	5
Beans (green), cooked	92	2	Trace	6
Beets, cooked	88	2	Trace	16
Broccoli, cooked	90	5	Trace	8
Brussels sprouts, cooked	85	6	1	12
Cabbage, raw	92	1	Trace	5
Carrots, cooked	92	1	1	9
Cauliflower, cooked	92	3	Trace	6
Corn, sweet, cooked	78	2	1	16
Lettuce, raw	95	5	1	13
Lima beans, cooked	64	16	1	48
Onions, cooked	90	2	Trace	18
Peas, cooked	82	8	1	19
Potatoes, baked	75	3	Trace	21
Spinach, cooked	91	6	1	6
Split peas, cooked	70	20	1	52
Squash, summer, cooked	96	2	Trace	7
Sweet potatoes, baked	64	2	1	36
Tomatoes, raw	94	2	Trace	6

Source: Compiled from Nutritive values of the edible part of foods. *Home and Garden Bulletin* No. 72. U.S. Dept. Agriculture. Washington, D.C. 1981.

leafy vegetables and orange vegetables is noteworthy, accounting for the recommendation of one of these vegetables at least every other day to ensure sufficient vitamin A is in the diet. Thiamin is relatively high in legumes, while folacin is found in excellent amounts in the leafy vegetables, and vitamin C plus other B vitamins are in other vegetables. Calcium and magnesium are found in useful amounts, too.

Flavoring substances also are vital to the appeal of vegetables. The organic acids in vegetables certainly heighten the interest of the various flavors; some sulfur-containing compounds contribute the unique flavor overtones found in onions and members of the cabbage family.

SURVEY OF VEGETABLES

One of the pleasures of vegetables is their great variety. With the excellent transportation and storage facilities now available for marketing vegetables, it no longer is necessary to restrict menus to corn, peas, beans, and carrots. The array in some markets may be almost puzzling; the paragraphs that follow will help to identify many different vegetables and highlight their storage and preparation.

Table 2.3 Vitamin and Mineral Content of Selected Vegetables (1 Cup)

Vegetable	Calcium (mg)	Iron (mg)	Vitamin A (I.U.)	Thiamin (mg)	Riboflavin (mg)	Niacin (mg)	Ascorbic Acid (mg)
Asparagus,							
cooked	30	0.9	1,310	0.23	0.26	2.0	38
canned	44	4.1	1,240	0.15	0.22	2.0	37
Beans, lima,							
cooked	80	4.3	480	0.31	0.17	2.2	29
Beans, green,							
cooked	63	0.8	680	0.09	0.11	0.6	15
Beans, wax,							
cooked	63	0.8	290	0.09	0.11	0.6	16
canned	81	2.9	140	0.07	0.10	0.7	12
Beets, cooked	14	0.5	20	0.03	0.04	0.3	6
Beet greens,							
cooked	144	2.8	7,400	0.10	0.22	0.4	22
Broccoli,							
cooked	158	1.4	4,500	0.16	0.36	1.4	162
Brussels sprouts,							
cooked	50	1.7	810	0.12	0.22	1.2	135
Cabbage, raw,	34	0.3	90	0.04	0.04	0.2	33
cooked	64	0.4	190	0.06	0.06	0.4	43
Carrots, cooked	48	0.9	15,220	0.08	0.07	0.7	9
Cauliflower,							
cooked	25	0.8	70	0.11	0.10	0.7	66
Corn, sweet,							
cooked	2	0.5	310	0.09	0.08	1.0	7
Lettuce, raw							
(1 head)	91	2.3	1,500	0.29	0.27	1.3	29
Peas, cooked	37	2.9	860	0.44	0.17	3.7	33
Potato, baked	9	0.7	Trace	0.10	0.04	1.7	20
Spinach,							
cooked	167	4.0	14,579	0.13	0.25	1.0	50
Squash, cooked,							
summer	52	0.8	820	0.10	0.16	1.6	21
winter	57	1.6	8,610	0.10	0.27	1.4	27
Tomatoes (1 raw)	24	0.9	1,640	0.11	0.07	1.3	42

Source: Compiled from Nutritive values of the edible part of foods. *Home and Garden Bulletin* No. 72. U.S. Dept. Agriculture. Washington, D.C. 1981.

Anise

Also called sweet fennel, anise is unique among vegetables because of its flavor; in fact, it can be described as licorice-flavored celery. The bulb can be eaten raw or may be cut up and cooked by boiling, steaming, or braising. Storage following purchase should be in the hydrator drawer of the refrigerator.

Artichokes

Globe (or French) artichokes, the artichoke type found commonly in U.S. markets, are actually the flower of a thistlelike plant. The Globe artichoke has an edible portion at the base of each leaf and under the choke (fuzzy portion), called the heart. These beautiful vegetables are deceptive in terms of quantity because of their limited amount of edible pulp in relation to fibrous petals and choke. However, the ceremony of dipping the base of each petal into a sauce of some type and then delicately scraping the pulp from the petal with the front teeth gives any meal a festive appeal. Globe artichokes can be stored in the refrigerator for a few days in a plastic container or in the hydrator drawer. After being boiled, steamed, or baked, Globe artichokes may be served hot or cold.

Jerusalem artichokes, sometimes called sunchokes, are quite different and for this reason are classified as a tuber. Despite their name, Jerusalem artichokes are thought to be natives of North America. Their use ranges from raw slices in salads and garnishes to serving as a boiled or broiled alternative to potatoes.

Asparagus

Whether the beautiful green or highly prized white asparagus, this vegetable is available fresh for only a very brief period in the spring, and even then, its price is often high. For best results, storage time should be kept short, in the hydrator drawer in the refrigerator. Boiling, steaming, and stir-frying are all excellent techniques for preparing asparagus. Sometimes cooked asparagus is chilled before serving and used in salads.

Beans

Fresh beans generally available in the market include green or snap beans, wax beans, lima beans, and fava beans (a bean similar to lima beans). Refrigerator storage should be limited to about three days, in a closed plastic bag or the hydrator drawer. Boiling, stir-frying, and steaming are suitable cookery methods.

Dried beans include an array of varieties: red, kidney, navy, pinto, black, pink, white, garbanzo, and lima. Unlike the other vegetables discussed here, dried beans can be stored at room temperature for several months as long as they are in their dried state. A tightly closed bag is recommended for storage in a damp climate. An extended soaking and/or cooking period rehydrates and tenderizes dried beans.

Beets

The deep red color of beets has made them prized (or cursed when spilled) as a vegetable dye. When harvested quite young, the greens are excellent either steamed or boiled. Preparation usually involves boiling, followed by peeling and slicing. Sweet-sour sauces, such as the sauce used in Harvard beets, are used sometimes to heighten the flavor interest. Beet pickles are another popular means of preparing this vegetable.

Broccoli

Meal planners seeking ways to raise nutrient content choose broccoli often. Not only is it nourishing, but it also is attractive on the plate, with its combination of little flowers and the stem of the plant. Optimal quality is obtained when the flowers are deep bluish-green; yellowing is an indication of "age." Boiling or steaming are the most frequent preparation methods, but sometimes broccoli is deep-fat fried or stir-fried. Prior to cooking, storage needs to be in a hydrator drawer or tightly covered container to avoid moisture loss.

Brussels Sprouts

These "little cabbages" can add considerable appeal of line, color, and flavor in a meal when properly prepared. Each sprout should be a tight, small head with no trace of yellowing on the green leaves. A comparatively short storage period in the hydrator drawer of the refrigerator will be possible without losing quality significantly.

Cabbage

Cabbage, a rather short word, covers an intriguing range of vegetables. The common green cabbage is known to most markets and is particularly valuable as a source of vitamin C when eaten in quantity. Heads should be firm, with a good green color and smooth leaves. A similar description can be made for red cabbage, with the exception of the color, which should be a deep purplish-red in red cabbage. Savory cabbage is a close relative of green cabbage, but the leaves are characterized as being deeply crinkled. Chinese cabbage is quite different in appearance, having a wide and prominent central rib in each leaf and an overall shape of an elongated head. Since all of these are susceptible to loss of moisture from their leaves and consequent loss of crispness, careful hydrator storage is necessary. These various forms of cabbage are served either raw in salads or cooked, usually by boiling.

Carrots

The lacy tops on carrots suggest the fact they they belong to the parsley family; other relatives of this varied group include celery and parsnips. The bright orange color and delicate flavor of high-quality carrots have made them a favorite vegetable, either raw or cooked. One of their virtues is their comparatively low cost and availability throughout the year. When stored without their tops, carrots can be kept in a hydrator drawer or plastic bag for many days. Carrots are remarkably versatile, being used raw as carrot curls or sticks, or shredded in a salad with raisins; boiled or steamed and served plain or with sauces; and even grated and used in carrot cake.

Cauliflower

A white, compact head, free of dark blemishes or spots, is the cauliflower to select in the grocery store. Its cabbagelike flavor indicates its descendancy from cabbage. Some people use small flowerets raw for dipping or in vegetable salads. In addition, the head may be cooked whole by boiling, or individual flowerets may be broken off and boiled or steamed.

Celery

Celery is one of the stem vegetables particularly popular in its raw form. Pascal is the variety generally preferred because of its reduced stringiness and mild flavor.

Celeriac is a relative of celery. However, it is the bulblike root that is used for the vegetable. Its large cross section requires thorough cooking to tenderize it, a problem that can be minimized by cutting the root into cubes before cooking. The gnarled skin of celeriac should be removed.

Corn

Sweet corn, quite a different product from the field corn used to feed cattle, is a highlight of summer when served boiled or steamed on the cob. Occasionally, it is roasted in a tight foil wrap. Enthusiasts often have a pot of water boiling before rushing corn from its place on the corn stalk to the pot for a brief boiling before eating. This ceremony reflects the rapid reduction in sugar content that happens after picking. The shortest possible elapsed time between picking and cooking results in the highest content of sugar.

Daikon

The influx of immigrants from the Far East has led to an increased availability of vegetables unique to that area of the world. Daikon, also called the Japanese radish, is a striking example of these vegetables. Its white length may extend as much as 18 inches. Use of daikon can be similar to the use of white radishes when washed and peeled. It provides a flavor highlight and crispness of texture that is particularly appealing in raw vegetable salads.

Eggplant

Originally found in India and China, eggplant now is a particularly popular vegetable for Middle Eastern meals. The deep purple, glossy skin of the eggplant is unique among vegetables. Size varies, but often eggplants will be as big as 6 inches in diameter. For best results, eggplant should be held only briefly in the refrigerator before cooking. Sauteed slices or baked eggplant are particularly popular ways of preparing this vegetable.

Greens

Greens may be either salad greens served raw or cooked greens. Although spinach is used both ways, most greens are used only as the raw or as the cooked version. Those used for cooking include kale, turnip greens, beet greens, mustard greens, and collard. During cooking, these greens will wilt drastically as water departs from the leaves, and the fragile cell walls collapse. For optimal quality, greens should be stored in the hydrator drawer of the refrigerator for only a day or two and then should be cooked just until they are wilted.

Green salads are extremely popular, but their quality and interest are influenced by the careful selection and proper storage of the greens. Considerable interest can be added to salads by selecting different-types of lettuce to add variety of color and texture. For instance, the butterhead (Boston and bibb) lettuces, with their moderate, slightly yellow-green color and almost oily, undulating leaves, are excellent for liners under other salads as well as for use in green salads. Bibb lettuce sometimes is known as "limestone" lettuce. Endive, a green with long, thin, curly leaves, has a scratchy texture, while escarole is somewhat less abrasive in the mouth and throat. Leaf lettuces afford yet another choice when looking for good salad greens. Some leaf lettuce is bronze or red in color.

Jicama

Jicama is a vegetable introduced to the United Sates from Mexico. Its skin must be pared before it is used—raw or boiled. Its most popular uses currently are in the raw state, as sticks for dips and as cubes in raw vegetable salads.

Mushrooms

Mushrooms are highly prized as a complement to steaks, in sauces and gravies, and as a vegetable ingredient. Commercial production of this delicacy requires careful control of humidity, temperature, and ventilation, as well as a rich mulch and dark growing conditions, but the excellent financial returns have caused a healthy industry in mushroom growing. Refrigerator storage is the recommended way of storing mushrooms, but even this method should be limited to only a few days.

Some people like to go mushroom gathering in the woods, an idyllic pastime. Unfortunately, many varieties are highly toxic, a fact that has caused fatalities.

Okra

Creole cookery, gumbo, and okra are inseparable. The comparatively small pods of okra contain a slippery exudate that can be minimized by drying the

Okra is a vegetable associated with southern cookery and is one of the key ingredients in making the popular gumbos.

pods thoroughly before cutting them. Most often, okra is used as a sliced vegetable in soups and gumbos, but it also can be batter-dipped and fried.

Onions

Onions and their relatives are valued for their unique flavor contributions to foods, both from the bulbs themselves and also, frequently, from the green tops. The choices range from large, dry Spanish onions to tiny scallions and chives. The globe-shaped or flat-topped dry onions are useful in heightening flavors of many different foods. Red onions, because of their attractive appearance and pleasing flavor, are a useful ingredient in salads. Shallots (onionlike bulbs) are yet another possibility for flavoring. Boiling onions, small dry onions about an inch in diameter, are popular for skewering on kabobs and for the primary ingredient in creamed onions. All types of dry onions should be stored in a cool, dry place to delay root growth and possible decay.

Green onions are onions that are harvested before the bulb develops fully. Scallions, another member of this cluster of edible and flavorful group from the lily family, ordinarily are harvested when the shoots are well developed but the bulb has not formed. Chives have become a familiar sight in gourmets' kitchens where they provide an attractive touch of green and a continuing supply of flavorful shoots for garnishes. Leeks are the hardiest of the green onionlike foods. They have a somewhat flat, thick edible stalk noted for its onion flavor. For optimum quality, these various types of green onions, with the exception of chives planted in pots, need to be refrigerated in the hydrator drawer and used within a matter of days.

Peas

Peas, like sweet corn, are sweetest when they can go directly from the vine to the pot. Delays result in a change from sugar to an increasing starch content. The maturity of the pea also influences the development of starch, with mature peas being less sweet and more starchy in flavor than new peas. Storage of peas should be in the pod and in the hydrator drawer of the refrigerator.

The Chinese or snow pea is a strain of pea that has been gaining rapidly in popularity recently in this country. This delicate pea is cooked and consumed pod and all, with only the tips of the pods being broken off before cooking. The bright color and crispness of the pod add both textural interest and eye appeal to many Oriental and other dishes.

Although not used in large quantities in the typical American diet, dried peas should be noted. Split peas are one type of legume that can be stored for comparatively long period in a dry storage area. Their most popular use is in making split pea soup, usually flavored with a ham bone.

Peppers

The word "pepper" seems to spell "hot" to people, and yet the sweet peppers are anything but hot. Both red and green sweet bell peppers are the source of pleasing color accents and intriguing flavors. Sometimes the top is cut off, the seeds are removed, and then the remaining whole pepper shell is parboiled in preparation for stuffing and baking. Often, green and red peppers are diced or sliced and are used raw in salads or as ingredients in casseroles.

Other types of peppers also find their way to the table in different ways. For instance, paprika, one of the most common of the spices, is prepared for market by drying and grinding paprikas (sweet red peppers). Various hot peppers (chiles) are the hallmark of Mexican cuisine, as well as others, notably Thai and neighboring cultures. Flavors range from spicy to hot, depending on the variety of chile. Some of the varieties available in the United States include jalapeño, serano, Anaheim (California), and pasilla. Removal of all of the seeds in these chiles is important unless searing characteristics are desired. Sensitive people even wear rubber gloves when handling chiles to avoid skin irritations.

Potatoes

Potatoes form the backbone of diets in some areas of the world. In fact, the spread of this native South American food to Europe created such shifts in diet patterns that the Irish suffered an extremely serious famine in the mid-nineteenth century when the potato crop failed.

Potatoes occupy a unique place among vegetables because of their excellent keeping qualities when stored properly and their remarkable versatility in preparation. There even are whole cookbooks devoted to ways to prepare potatoes. Although potatoes are found in markets throughout the year all across the country, the specific varieties available in different regions vary according to the types that will grow best in the local climate. The basic types of potatoes are

1. Round white.
2. Russet.
3. Round red.
4. Long white

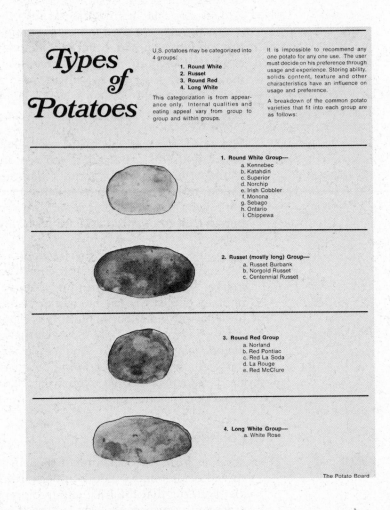

Examples of the varieties in each of the four categories of potatoes.

The storage temperature will influence the starch and sugar content of potatoes. The recommended temperature is about 60°F, or somewhat cooler than the average room. At this temperature, the sugar/starch levels in potatoes remain approximately the same as they were when the potatoes entered storage. However, when temperatures dip to around 45°F, sugar begins to accumulate, and starch levels drop; these changes are detrimental to optimal quality when cooked.

Sweet potatoes are available in markets throughout the year, with the choice generally being between those with a light-colored skin and a somewhat dry interior and the deeper-colored moist variety. This latter variety often is called yams, even though they are not actually yams. True yams are not available in the markets in this country. Whether selecting the broad, bulky sweet potatoes with their tapered ends or ''yams,'' the ends need to be dry and free from any hint of rot. Otherwise, they will not keep well in cool, dry storage.

Radishes

The red, globular-shaped radish is popular as a garnish or sliced in salads. The ability of the radish to fan out or to unfold when thin cuts are made in the vegetable is extremely useful when preparing garnishes to beautify a dinner plate or salad. White radishes, although lacking the bright color of the red radish, are extremely pleasing flavor accents when sliced into salads or simply eaten raw.

Rutabagas

Some vegetables have been used extensively for many years because they can be held in cool storage over the winter months. The rutabaga is an excellent, relatively inexpensive example. When coated with wax, this vegetable can be held for an extended period, but the wax needs to be peeled from rutabagas before they are boiled. After boiling, this yellow-fleshed vegetable often is mashed.

Squash

Summer squash are noted for their intriguing shapes, subtle flavors, and high water content. These squash are able to be kept in refrigerated storage only a few days without losing quality. Zucchini is perhaps the best known of the summer squashes, being used widely raw in sticks for dips or in salads and also being cooked in a variety of ways. Other summer squashes include yellow crookneck, yellow straightneck, pattypan or scallop, and cocozelle.

The hard-shell winter squashes, in sharp contrast to the softer-skinned summer varieties, can be held in cool, dry storage (but not in the refrigerator) for several months. The hard shell and relatively low moisture content of winter squashes necessitate thorough cooking, often by baking, to make them highly palatable. Familiar winter squashes include Hubbard, table queen (acorn), buttercup, butternut, Turk's turban, and banana.

Spaghetti squash is an unique squash that separates into spaghettilike strands and is an important vegetable in a meal.

Tomatoes

Although actually the fruit of the tomato plant, their common use in the main part of a meal causes tomatoes to be classified as a vegetable. The versatility of the tomato as a raw vegetable simply sliced as a component of vegetable salads or cooked in many ways, including extensive use in sauces and casseroles, makes this one of the most popular and widely accepted vegetables. Considerable research effort has been expended to develop tomato varieties suited for specific purposes and with the desired growing characteristics. For example, the elongated tomato was developed to fulfill the needs of commercial canners. The cherry tomato has found its niche in the hearts of salad lovers.

Turnips

With the institution of salad bars in U.S. restaurants and fast-food franchises, the turnip has gained in stature. Its white, crisp character adds interest to salads, either in grated form or in julienne strips. This vegetable is also sufficiently strong for use with dips. Of course, the vegetable can also be cooked. When fresh, the tops of turnips are excellent for boiling or steaming and serving as greens.

Other Vegetables

This is far from an exhaustive list of vegetables that might be available fresh, frozen, or canned in the market. However, it does highlight some of the ones that are likely to be available. The broadening interest in other cuisines doubtless will increase the availability of cilantro, bok choy, gobo, and other vegetables popular with the various ethnic groups in this country.

HARVESTING AND MARKETING

The high quality of vegetables in the food supply today is something that is taken almost for granted. Farmers utilize modern farming techniques, including use of fertilizers and pesticides, to produce a crop that is high both in quantity and quality. However, the need for care and attention continues into the harvesting and marketing operations to help retain maximum nutrient content and palatability. From the moment the vegetables are harvested, proper temperature and moisture controls are necessary, for metabolic processes continue in the harvested food. Control of these chemical changes is essential to the retention of vitamins and to the overall palatability of produce.

When fresh vegetables are crated, the temperature in the crates slowly begins to rise, even though the crates generally have an open design. This is the consequence of the respiration that is continuing in the harvested food. For instance, the temperature in a crate of spinach has been measured to rise to as high as 100°F, causing a soft rot to develop rapidly. Although leafy greens have a faster respiration rate than do other types of vegetables, the increase in temperature in crates of all types of vegetables still causes reduced quality. This problem can be alleviated by packing vegetables loosely in crates, preferably along with some crushed ice.

The next step is to transport the freshly harvested produce rapidly to the processing plant if it is to be canned or frozen. The shorter the time and the better the temperature is controlled between harvest and processing, the higher will be the nutrient value and the palatability of the processed vegetables. If the vegetables are to enter the retail market as fresh produce, proper temperature control must be maintained from harvest until they are cooked and consumed in the home. Ordinarily, vegetables are loaded efficiently into refrigerated trucks or refrigerated railroad cars for transport to wholesale and, ultimately, the retail markets. These special trucks or railroad cars work in opposite fashion at different seasons of the year, chilling the vegetables in the summer and keeping them from freezing with the assistance of heaters in the winter.

By paying careful attention to the circulation of air, maintenance of a desirable level of humidity, and control of temperature during transport in refrigerated cars, vegetables can be shipped clear across the country and arrive on the opposite coast in excellent condition. In fact, when vegetables shipped in refrigerated storage across the continent are compared with those grown locally and marketed without chilling, the refrigerated and transported produce may be of higher quality than that from local fields.

Local marketing arrangements are important if the consumer is to be able to purchase high-quality produce. Refrigerated transport from wholesale

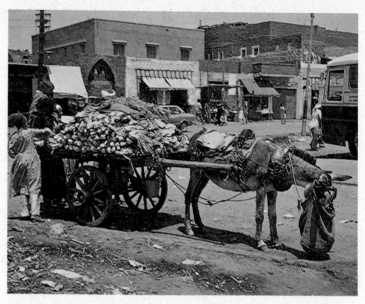

Produce being marketed locally can be brought to market even in such simple fashion as this animal-drawn cart in Egypt. In countries where supply lines are long, as in urban areas in the United States, refrigerated trucks or railroad cars are essential if quality is to be maintained.

markets or warehouses to the retail outlet is essential. Within the market, the retailer must have adequate refrigerated storage to maintain quality of produce awaiting display for purchase. Retail markets doing a high volume of business have the advantage of rapid turnover of produce, which is important in maintaining quality and nutritive value. Some small retail stores suggest that their produce is particularly high in nutrients by labeling items as being ''organically grown.'' In fact, the nutrient level of such produce may even be lower than that of the produce available in the supermarket. The key to nutrient content of produce is freshness and controlled storage during marketing; the application of chemical or organic fertilizers does not influence nutrient value.

Market Order Regulations for the marketing of specific food products under the guidance of a board, which is authorized by the U.S. Department of Agriculture.

One important part of the marketing procedure is the *market orders* established as a result of the Agricultural Marketing Agreement Act of 1937. This legislation enables the U.S. Department of Agriculture to draw up and enforce marketing agreements and orders to regulate quality, quantity, standardization of packs, research and development projects, specification of unfair trade practices, required filing of selling prices, and collection of marketing information for the producers of the commodity specific to the marketing order. Such marketing boards have had considerable impact over the years in influencing the development of markets for their products and promoting improvements intended to benefit producers and consumers alike.

SELECTION

Selection of specific vegetables for a meal begins with the decision to buy them fresh, frozen, canned, or, in some cases, dried. Individual preference may influence this decision, but price and availability often play key roles in the choice. When a vegetable is in season so that the quality is high, the price usually will be competitively low, making purchase of the fresh form often the best choice. However, the convenience of preparing frozen or canned vegetables may motivate people to select one of these forms even when the fresh food is comparatively inexpensive and of high quality.

Fresh Vegetables

The eye often is the best guide to selecting fresh produce, although wholesalers may use grading as an aid at that point in the marketing process. The quality of fresh vegetables is influenced by the season of the year and the handling during the marketing process, with the peak harvest period ordinarily providing a particular vegetable of the highest quality. Table 2.4 is a guide to the normal schedule of availability of various fresh vegetables, thus serving as an aid in anticipating what vegetables might reasonably be available fresh at sensible prices.

Grade standards have been established for many vegetables by the Agricultural Marketing Service of the U.S. Department of Agriculture by the authority of the Agricultural Marketing Act of 1946. This optional service is useful in the wholesale phase of marketing, but it is not ordinarily visible to consumers directly. Typically two grade designations are used for a particular type of vegetable, although four grade designations can theoretically be used.

Consumers usually rely on their own knowledge and experience in selecting fresh vegetables to meet their personal standards. Such characteristics as crispness, color, and freedom from blemishes are characteristics that frequently can be used by consumers in making wise selections in the produce department. Some suggested guides for selecting fresh vegetables are presented in Table 2.5.

Wise selection depends not only on quality of the item selected, but also sometimes on the variety chosen. For instance, a choice might need to be made between buying large beefsteak tomatoes or cherry tomatoes for making a salad. Onions are yet another type of vegetable requiring some decision between varieties. When a recipe calls for pea pods, the variety to choose is the Chinese or snow pea, with its tender, flat pods. Regular garden peas have a pod that is too tough to provide the delicate crispness desired.

Potatoes are the cornerstone of a meal for many people, but the pleasure afforded by this vegetable is related to the type of potato selected for making specific recipes. Some potatoes, termed *waxy potatoes*, are relatively high in sugar and low in starch. The opposite type, *nonwaxy* (sometimes termed mealy) *potatoes*, have a high starch content and are low in sugar. Waxy potatoes have a low specific gravity and, consequently, float in water. Conversely,

Waxy Potatoes Potatoes with a high content of sugar and low amount of starch; best suited for boiling and other preparations where shape is important.

Nonwaxy Potatoes Potatoes with a low sugar content and high starch level; best suited for baking, mashing, and frying.

Table 2.4 A Guide to Average Monthly Availability of Fresh Vegetables

Vegetable	Jan	Feb	Mar	Apr	May	Jun	Jul	Aug	Sep	Oct	Nov	Dec
Artichokes	M	M	P	P	P	M	M	M	M	M	M	M
Asparagus	N	M	A	A	P	M	N	N	N	N	N	N
Beans, snap	M	M	M	M	P	P	P	P	M	M	M	M
Beets	M	M	M	M	M	P	P	P	P	P	M	M
Broccoli	P	P	P	P	M	M	M	M	M	P	P	P
Brussels sprouts	P	P	M	M	M	N	N	N	M	P	P	P
Cabbage	P	P	P	P	P	P	P	P	P	P	P	P
Carrots	P	P	P	P	P	P	P	P	P	P	P	P
Cauliflower	M	M	M	M	M	M	M	M	P	M	M	M
Celery	P	P	P	P	P	P	P	P	P	P	P	P
Chinese cabbage	M	M	M	M	M	M	M	M	M	M	M	M
Corn, sweet	N	N	M	M	P	P	P	P	P	M	M	N
Cucumbers	P	P	P	P	P	P	P	P	P	P	P	P
Eggplant	M	M	M	M	M	M	M	P	P	P	M	M
Escarole, endive	P	P	P	P	P	P	P	P	P	P	P	P
Endive, Belgian	M	M	M	M	M	N	N	N	N	M	M	M
Greens	P	P	P	P	P	P	P	P	P	P	P	P
Lettuce	P	P	P	P	P	P	P	P	P	P	P	P
Mushrooms	M	M	M	M	M	M	M	M	M	M	M	M
Okra	N	N	M	M	M	M	M	M	M	M	N	N
Onions, dry	P	P	P	P	P	P	P	P	P	P	P	P
Onions, green	M	M	P	P	P	P	P	P	M	M	M	M
Parsley	M	M	M	M	M	M	M	M	M	M	P	P
Parsnips	M	M	M	M	M	N	N	N	M	M	M	M
Peppers, sweet	P	P	P	P	P	P	P	P	P	P	P	P
Potatoes	P	P	P	P	P	P	P	P	P	P	P	P
Radishes	P	P	P	P	P	P	P	P	P	P	P	P
Spinach	P	P	P	P	P	M	M	M	M	M	M	M
Squash	P	P	P	P	P	P	P	P	P	P	P	P
Sweet potatoes	P	P	P	P	M	M	M	M	P	P	A	P
Tomatoes	P	P	P	P	P	P	P	P	P	P	P	P
Turnips	M	M	M	M	M	M	M	M	M	M	M	M
Rutabagas	M	M	M	M	M	M	M	M	M	M	M	M

Source: Adapted from information provided by the United Fresh Fruit and Vegetable Association. Washington, D.C.
N = Nonexistent or scarce; M = moderate supply; P = plentiful; A = abundant.

nonwaxy potatoes have a high specific gravity and will sink to the bottom of a solution containing 11 parts of water to 1 part salt (Mackey and Joiner, 1960).

Nonwaxy potatoes will tend to slough off and to lose their shape during boiling, while waxy potatoes hold their shape well during boiling. This is not surprising, for the high starch content of the nonwaxy potatoes means that

Table 2.5 Guide to Selection of Fresh Vegetables

Vegetable	*Criteria*
Artichoke	Plump, firm, heavy in comparison with size; green petals with absence of brown discoloration
Asparagus	Good green color extending down much of stalk; closed and compact tips; crisp and tender stalk
Beans (green and wax)	Bright color for variety; pods firm and crisp rather than flabby
Beets	Fresh-looking tops if still attached; surface that is smooth and deep red, firm and round with slim tap root
Broccoli	Dark green to bluish bud clusters with no trace of yellow; smooth stalks of moderate size with no traces of spoilage
Brussels sprouts	Fresh green color void of yellow leaves; tight outer leaves free of injury; tight heads
Cabbage	Firm head; fresh color in outer leaves, crisp leaves
Carrots	Crisp rather than flabby; good orange color free from sunburned green at top
Cauliflower	Uniform creamy white color with no trace of dark discoloration; solid and compact head; fresh leaves, if attached
Celery	Crisp stalks with a solid feel; glossy surface on stalk; crisp leaves; no discoloration on inside surface of large outer stalks
Corn	Ear well covered with plump young kernels; fresh husks that are green and unwilted; silks free of decay
Cucumbers	Firm, moderate size; green color all over
Eggplant	Smooth and firm with deep purple skin free of blemishes
Greens	Crisp appearance with good green color typical of the type of green; free from rust and other blemishes; no wilted or decaying areas
Lettuce	Crisp quality to leaves, with butter lettuces being somewhat less crisp, but still succulent; free of decay; good color for the variety
Mushrooms	Caps closed around the stem; surface of cap light-colored and gills (if showing under cap) should be light rather than dark; smooth and firm cap with no suggestion of drying out
Okra	Pods tender enough to bend under some pressure; less than 4½ inches long; fresh green color; no blemishes
Onions, dry	Firm and dry with small necks; no decay
Onions, green	Crisp, bright green tops; free from decay
Parsnips	Smooth and firm; small to medium size; free from blemishes
Peas	Crisp pods with fresh green color; pods full but not bulging

Table 2.5 (*Continued*)

Vegetable	Criteria
Peppers	Firm, deep color; no trace of flabbiness or decay
Potatoes	Firm; free from sunburned green areas; no decay; skin intact and free from blemishes
Radishes	Medium size; firm and plump; fresh red color
Squash	Well developed with no soft areas, firm; summer squash has glossy and tender skin; winter squash has tough, hard skin
Sweet potatoes	Firm, no signs of decay at ends; good color
Tomatoes	Smooth; good color for stage of ripeness; firm if not fully ripe; free from blemishes
Turnip and rutabagas	Firm and smooth; free of blemishes

Examples of the various greens commonly boiled in the United States. All are rich sources of provitamin A

there will be considerable swelling of the cells during the cooking of the non-waxy ones because of the gelatinization or swelling of the starch in these potatoes. These characteristics make nonwaxy potatoes excellent for mashing and baking. In contrast, the waxy potatoes, with their low starch and comparatively high sugar content, retain their shape during preparation, making them well suited to preparations such as potato salad where shape of the pieces is important.

Fried potatoes, particularly french fries, are popular ways of preparing potatoes. Here again, the type of potato selected will influence the quality of the finished product. As predicted, waxy potatoes (such as the Red Pontiac) will not perform well when fried, because the high sugar content causes them to brown quite quickly or even to burn before the interior of the piece is cooked. Nonwaxy potatoes, however, with their low sugar content, brown rather slowly, thus allowing time for the heat to cook the interior of the piece before the exterior becomes too dark. The familiar example of nonwaxy potatoes is the Russet Burbank. Its long, flat shape is excellent for making the long slices desired in french fries.

It is desirable to buy the right variety of potato for the intended use, but people who use potatoes infrequently may find that the purchase of a single type of potato is appropriate. In such instances, an all-purpose potato, such as the White Rose, may be selected. The products prepared may not be quite as good as they would be if the correct type of potato had been used, yet the

Potatoes that float when placed in a salt water brine (ratio 1:11) have a low specific gravity and tend to retain their shape when boiled, a characteristic typical of waxy potatoes. Those that sink have a high specific gravity and exhibit the characteristics of a nonwaxy potato.

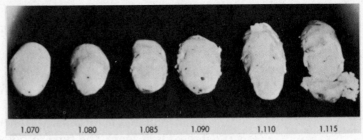

| 1.070 | 1.080 | 1.085 | 1.090 | 1.110 | 1.115 |

Boiled potatoes arranged according to specific gravity. Waxy potatoes have a low specific gravity, whereas the nonwaxy potato reveals a high specific gravity and a distinct tendency to slough off.

quality is satisfactory for any type of preparation (boiling, mashing, or even frying). Although the White Rose often will not make mashed potatoes as light and fluffy as those from Russet Burbanks, the White Rose is comparatively excellent when contrasted with the rather dark, somewhat gummy character of mashed potatoes made with Red Pontiac potatoes. The suggested uses of several common varieties are presented in Table 2.6.

Frozen and Canned Vegetables

Canned vegetables are a mainstay in the menu plans of some people. They have the advantages of being convenient to store and quick and easy to serve because they are cooked fully during canning. Since canned vegetables can be

Table 2.6 Preferred Preparation Methods for Selected Varieties of Potatoes[1]

Variety	Suitable Types of Preparation
Cherokee	Boiling, baking
Chippewa	Boiling
Cobbler	Boiling, medium acceptability baked
Green Mountain	Boiling, baking
Hunter	Boiling, baking
Katahdin	Boiling, french frying
Kennebec	Boiling, baking, french frying
Keswick	Boiling, baking
Norgold Russet	Boiling, french frying
Norland	Boiling
Pungo	Boiling, baking
Red LaSoda	Boiling
Red Pontiac	Boiling
Russet Burbank	Baking, french frying
Sebago	Boiling, baking
White Rose	Boiling

Source: Adapted from *Buying Guide for Fresh Fruits, Vegetables, and Nuts.* Blue Goose, Inc. Fullerton, Calif. 1971. P. 84.

stored for many months at room temperature, they can be bought when on sale and held for later use without a significant loss in quality. No special equipment is needed to prepare commercially canned vegetables. In fact, salads often include canned vegetables that have simply been drained before being incorporated into the salad. Of course, canned vegetables can be used in many different recipes, even ones involving complex preparation steps.

The textures of canned vegetables basically will be soft because of the rigorous heat treatment involved in safe processing of canned vegetables. The other limitation in canned vegetables is the color of green vegetables. Again, the intense and extended heat treatment required to prevent the possibility of botulism in canned vegetables always changes the bright green color of fresh green vegetables into the familiar olive drab green observed in such vegetables as green beans and spinach.

Frozen vegetables have gained an important segment of the vegetable market as a result of some creative marketing as well as inherently pleasing quality. The bright green color of frozen peas and beans is a real plus for these and other frozen green vegetables. Although frozen vegetables do require a bit of cooking to make them ready to eat, the time actually is very short, particularly when the vegetables are being heated in a microwave oven. This gives them a real advantage over fresh vegetables, which require some time to prepare them for cooking and then a cooking period usually at least 10 minutes long. To enhance sales, manufacturers have created some exciting vegetable combinations, several with sauces to add a gourmet touch to the frozen food section. Although comparatively expensive, these frozen vegetable products have been well accepted.

A disadvantage of frozen vegetables is the requirement for frozen storage space. The freezer compartment in most refrigerators is adequate to accommodate the amount of frozen vegetables many families might wish to store for a week or longer. For people having a freezer, frozen vegetables can be purchased when special sales occur and then stored for use perhaps as long as six months later.

Grading standards for quality have been established by the U.S. Department of Agriculture, the same agency that is responsible for monitoring enforcement of these regulations. The three grades for canned and frozen vegetables are U.S. Grade A or Fancy, U.S. Grade B or Extra Standard, and U.S. Grade C or Standard. To use these federal grades, packers must have a federal inspector from the U.S. Department of Agriculture present constantly. These inspectors monitor to be sure that the grade specifications are being satisfied. For U.S. Grade A, vegetables must be of top quality and have the appropriate color for the vegetable, have a high degree of tenderness, and be free of blemishes. U.S. Grade B is characterized as being slightly more mature than U.S. Grade A and less carefully selected for color and tenderness. Vegetables in U.S. Grade C are lacking in uniformity and have poorer color and flavor. This lowest grade is perfectly adequate for use in casseroles and soups and can save consumers money.

Packers are not required to use the federal grades. They can use their own grade designations or even designate their grades as Grade A or Fancy if they choose. Unless the grade designation is *U.S.* Grade A, B, or C, it is not

Table 2.7 Estimated Servings of Fresh, Frozen, and Canned Vegetables

Vegetable	Estimated Servings from:		
	Fresh (1 lb)	*Frozen (10 oz)*	*Canned (1 lb)*
Asparagus	4	2½	2–3
Beans, green or wax	5	3–4	3–4
Beans, lima	2 (in pods)	3–4	3–4
Beets	4	—	3–4
Broccoli	3–4	3	—
Brussels sprouts	5	3–4	—
Cabbage	4	—	—
Carrots	4	3–4	3–4
Cauliflower	3	3	—
Corn	1 per ear	3–4	3–4
Peas	2 (in pods)	3–4	3–4
Potatoes	3–4	3–4	3–4
Spinach	4	2–3	2–3
Tomatoes	4	—	4

Source: Adapted from *Handbook of food preparation.* American Home Economics Association. Washington, D.C. 8th ed. 1980; Peterkin, B. and C. Cromwell, Money's worth in foods, *Home and Garden Bulletin* No. 183, Ag. Res. Serv., USDA, Washington, D.C. 1977; Thompson, E. R. How to buy canned and frozen vegetables, *Consumer Marketing Service Bulletin.* No. 167. Washington, D.C. 1969.

mandatory to have a federal inspector supervising the grading process. Consumers often use the brand name as the guide to quality rather than reading the grade designation. By noting quality and uniformity available in different brands, it is possible to make purchasing decisions that integrate quality and price to meet specific needs.

The suggested serving size for cooked vegetables is half a cup. To ensure that enough vegetable is being purchased to provide the appropriate number of servings, it is helpful to have a guide to estimated yields of fresh, frozen, and canned vegetables. The number of servings for common market units of vegetables is provided in Table 2.7.

STORAGE

Fresh vegetables, with a few exceptions, should be stored in the refrigerator. Since refrigerator space often is limited, trimming of the tops of radishes and carrots, as well as the removal of leaves around a head of cauliflower and other inedible portions may be done before storing produce. The cool air of the refrigerator will slow respiration and help to delay deteriorative changes, but the dryness of the air causes serious loss of moisture unless storage is in the closed hydrator drawers or in sealed plastic bags.

Although all vegetables rely on their moisture content for part of their crisp texture, moisture is particularly important for succulents, such as the various greens. The combination of the cool air (which will be saturated with only limited loss of moisture from the leaves) and the small amount of air surrounding greens in the hydrator drawer or plastic bag is the best possible combination to help keep the cells in the leaves of the greens filled with their normal amount of water. Many other fresh vegetables, such as sweet corn, broccoli, and peas, also will maintain quality best by storage in the refrigerator in the hydrator drawers.

The chief exceptions to the rule of storing fresh vegetables in the refrigerator hydrator drawers are potatoes, winter squash, Spanish and other dry onions, dry legumes, and other dried foods. All of these types of vegetables should be stored in a dark, dry, and somewhat cool place with some air circulation. As mentioned earlier, the temperature control for potatoes is of particular importance because of the potential for shifts in the type of carbohydrate in the stored potatoes. About 60°F is considered optimal. Low temperatures cause an accumulation of sugar, and warmer temperatures raise the level of starch.

VEGETABLES IN MENU PLANNING

Vegetables have the potential for being the highlight of the meal when they are chosen carefully and prepared with skill. The attractive colors, distinctive shapes, and assorted flavors can be utilized to add just the right touch to a menu that might otherwise be a bit dull. Selection of the vegetable and the way it will be prepared should be based on color, texture, shape, and flavor of the vegetable in relation to the other foods being served. For instance, confetti corn (sweet corn with diced green pepper and pimiento) adds excitement to a meal of white fish and rice pilaf. The bright flavor of a broiled tomato accents a dinner featuring baked halibut. Mashed potatoes provide a pleasing textural contrast when served with slightly crisp, buttered, boiled carrots as the vegetables in a meal. Some vegetables can be cut into different shapes to give the desired line to a plate. For instance, carrots can be cut into slices or into matchstick pieces or even left whole, depending upon the other foods being included in the meal. These are but a few examples of the types of choices that can be made when considering the vegetables for a meal.

FACTORS IN VEGETABLE COOKERY

Nutritional Factors

Vegetables have a well-deserved reputation as being good sources of nutrients, but the truth is that the way in which vegetables are prepared can have a definite influence on the actual nutritive value of the vegetable. Even more important than the nutrient content in a vegetable is its palatability and general appeal. A vegetable can be a good source of nutrients, but it will not provide these nutrients to the body until the vegetable is eaten. Preparation for maximum palatability is clearly an important factor in the nutrient contribution of vegetables.

Efficient transport of vegetables through the marketing process to the table is essential to maintaining maximum nutrient content. It is the vitamins that are at risk during the marketing period. Vitamins A and C (ascorbic acid) are the vitamins that undergo oxidative losses most easily. Keeping cut surfaces to a minimum during preparation reduces oxidation and maximizes the levels of vitamins A and C. By avoiding peeling and/or cutting into small pieces, oxidation also is minimized.

The length of time vegetables are cooked will influence nutrient retention, and so will the method used in cooking. By placing vegetables into water that is boiling, rather than starting with cool tap water, the cooking time is reduced and loss of the water-soluble vitamins will be minimized. The sudden, intense heat expels some oxygen and halts enzyme action. The B vitamins and vitamin C are lost to an extent into the cooking water because they are water soluble; losses are accelerated if the water is alkaline. Soda should not be added to the cooking water because this is particularly destructive to thiamin (a B vitamin) content, as shown in Table 2.8.

Microwave cookery is one technique for helping to keep vitamin losses to a minimum. The extremely small amount of water used is helpful in retaining the water-soluble vitamins. Additionally, the cooking time is relatively short in microwave cookery. Another technique involving almost no water is stir-frying. This is a very quick way of cooking vegetables, and it conserves vitamins, for the numerous cut surfaces that promote vitamin losses are offset by the very short cooking time required to tenderize the thin slices. Steaming is another cooking method effective in conserving nutrients. A pressure saucepan provides yet another alternative for cooking vegetables. This causes some increase in vitamin loss despite the short cooking time because the cooking temperature is higher than that of boiling water.

TEXTURE

Denaturation of protein, gelatinization of starch, and softening of the cellulose and other structural elements are changes taking place when vegetables are cooked. These physical changes result in distinct changes in texture, with

Table 2.8 Properties of Vitamins Important in Food Preparation

		Sensitivity to:		Heat in Presence of	
Vitamin	Solubility in Water	Oxygen	Light	Acid	Alkali
Vitamin A	No	Sensitive	Sensitive	Stable	Stable
Thiamin	Yes	Stable	Stable	Sensitive	Sensitive
Riboflavin	Yes	Stable	Sensitive	Stable	Sensitive
Niacin	Yes	Stable	Stable	Stable	Stable
Ascorbic acid	Yes	Sensitive	Sensitive	Sensitive	Sensitive
Vitamin D	No	Stable	Stable	Stable	Stable

the final effect being determined by how long the vegetable is cooked. The softening in texture that occurs during cooking is due primarily to softening of cellulose and conversion of some of the cementing pectic substances into more soluble pectic compounds. When these changes have proceeded to suit individual taste, the palatability of some vegetables is enhanced.

The acidity or alkalinity (pH) of the cooking water will have a definite influence on the softening occurring during boiling of a vegetable. The texture quickly becomes mushy and the shape blurs if there is a bit of soda added to make the water alkaline. This change is detrimental to palatability (as well as being harmful to thiamin retention). Ordinarily, soda is not used with vegetables because of the detrimental effects. However, the softening of dried beans can be speeded significantly by adding a maximum of ⅛ teaspoon of soda per cup of beans, an amount that does not cause undue loss of thiamin. Even this small amount of baking soda does cause the beans to be slightly lower in thiamin than they would be if no alkali were added to the soaking and/or cooking water.

If lemon juice or other acid is added to the water used for boiling a vegetable, the effect on texture will be just the opposite of the effect of alkali. In fact, the vegetable will be extremely resistant to softening over an extended boiling period if water is acidified. This effect is particularly important to remember, for some vegetable recipes involve the use of acid. For example, in the preparation of Harvard beets, first the beets are softened by boiling them in water. When tender, the sliced beets are combined with a vinegar (acidic) sauce and heated to serving temperature. Unless the beets are tender before they are combined with the sauce, the slices will be too crisp to enjoy. Similarly when lemon butter sauce is to be combined with boiled carrots or other boiled vegetable, the vegetable must be cooked until the desired degree of tenderness is achieved before the acidic lemon juice is added.

Calcium ions are often found in hard water, and these ions can combine with pectic substances to form insoluble salts in the vegetables. The apparent result is a hard vegetable that is extremely resistant to softening during cooking. This is a particular problem when dried beans are being cooked. However, food processors use this ion to advantage when processing tomatoes. By the addition of a calcium salt (usually calcium chloride), tomatoes can be kept in their original round form, instead of becoming mushy and indistinct.

Molasses is an acidic food ingredient that has a fair amount of calcium ions. When baked beans are being prepared with molasses in the sauce, it is imperative that the beans be softened to the desired degree of tenderness before the flavorful, molasses-containing sauce is added and baked with the beans. If added too soon, the beans will not be tender enough.

pH Hydrogen ion potential; values less than 7 are acidic, while those above, are alkaline.

Color

The eye has a tremendous influence over the acceptance of vegetables. Color is a key aspect of the visual appeal of vegetables. The problem in vegetable preparation is to optimize color by proper cooking techniques, being sure that the cooking medium and the cooking time are controlled to give the desired results. The specific techniques that are appropriate differ with the pigments predominating in the various vegetables.

There are three principal pigment categories (Table 2.9), with each of these categories having subgroups within them. The green vegetables have *chlorophylls* as their predominant pigment type. The orange and yellow vegetables, as well as some of the red vegetables, are colored by various *carotenoids*. Xanthophyll and lycopene are carotenoid pigments found in tomatoes. Different amounts of these pigments will be formed, depending on the light conditions under which they are ripened. Tomatoes protected from intense light will develop a high lycopene content (reddish color), whereas a more yellow color will dominate under conditions with more intense light. When tomatoes are ripened at temperatures consistently higher than 104°F, carotenoids are not developed, and the chlorophyll of the green tomato does not decompose.

The orange-colored vegetables, such as sweet potatoes, carrots, and rutabagas, contain carotenes. This pigment group not only provides the attractive color of these vegetables, but several of the carotenoid pigments also are nutritionally important as precursors of vitamin A. Beta-carotene is a particularly important form from the perspective of nutrition.

The vegetables that are white, blue, purple, and purplish-red contain the third group of pigments, the *flavonoids*. Some flavonoids provide the white pigment, as seen in cauliflower. This flavonoid belongs to a group called the *anthoxanthins*. The rather deep reds, purples, and blues are the result of the pigment group known as the *anthocyanins*.

This discussion is something of an oversimplification, for a blend of pigments commonly occurs in vegetables, with one of the pigments predominating over the others. This blending accounts for the range of colors observed.

Chlorophyll Green, magnesium-containing pigment in fruits and vegetables.

Carotenoids Carotenes and related compounds producing the orange pigments in fruits and vegetables.

Flavonoids Class of pigments contributing white and red to blue colors in fruits and vegetables; two main divisions are anthoxanthins and anthocyanins.

Anthoxanthins Group of flavonoids providing the white or creamy colors in fruits and vegetables.

Anthocyanins Group of flavonoids providing the reddish to bluish hues of fruits and vegetables.

Table 2.9 Common Vegetable Pigments

Pigment	Color	Vegetable
Chlorophylls		
Chlorophyll a	Intense blue-green	Lettuce, spinach, peas, green
Chlorophyll b	Yellow-green	beans, broccoli
Pheophytin a	Pale green-gray	Green vegetables cooked more
Pheophytin b	Olive-green	than 7 minutes
Carotenoids		
Carotenes		
Alpha-carotene	Yellow-orange	Winter squash, carrots, sweet
Beta-carotene	Red-orange	potatoes, rutabagas
Lycopene	Red	Tomatoes, watermelon
Xanthophylls		
Cryptoxanthin	Yellow	Sweet corn
Lutein	Orange	Spinach
Flavonoids		
Anthocyanins	Red, purple, blue	Red cabbage
Anthoxanthins	White	Cauliflower, white onions, turnips

SCIENCE NOTE: PIGMENTS

Chlorophyll pigments (chlorophyll a and chlorophyll b) are susceptible to changes in their chemical structure during cooking. In the raw vegetable, these two structures differ only in the functional group attached to one of the rings in the structure. Actually, the structure of chlorophyll resembles that of heme (in hemoglobin), except that the metal complexed in chlorophyll is magnesium rather than the iron atom found in heme. In chlorophyll a, a methyl group ($-CH_3$) is the functional group, resulting in a fairly intense blue-green pigment color. This is seen in the blue-green buds on broccoli. The aldehyde ($-C\overset{\displaystyle /\!\!/O}{\underset{\displaystyle \backslash H}{}}$) group in chlorophyll b imparts a rather yellow-green hue to green vegetables.

When chlorophyll-containing vegetables are cooked for at least 5 minutes, magnesium ions are released from some of the molecules of chlorophyll and are replaced by hydrogen. This reaction results in the formation of pheophytin a from chlorophyll a or pheophytin b from chlorophyll b. Pheophytin a causes the color to be a greenish-gray; pheophytin b is a distinctive olive drab. The combination of these two types of pheophytin yields the familiar, and rather dull, olive-green color characteristic of canned green vegetables.

*Pheophytin forms when magnesium (Mg) is replaced by hydrogen (H)

Chlorophyll

Note: R is Ch$_3$ in chlorophyll a and $C\overset{\displaystyle /\!\!/O}{\underset{\displaystyle \backslash H}{}}$ in chlorophyll b.

The carotenoid pigments are highly unsaturated, as can be seen in the accompanying structure. These conjugated (alternating double and single bonds) double bonds account for the bright pigments of the carotenoid compounds.

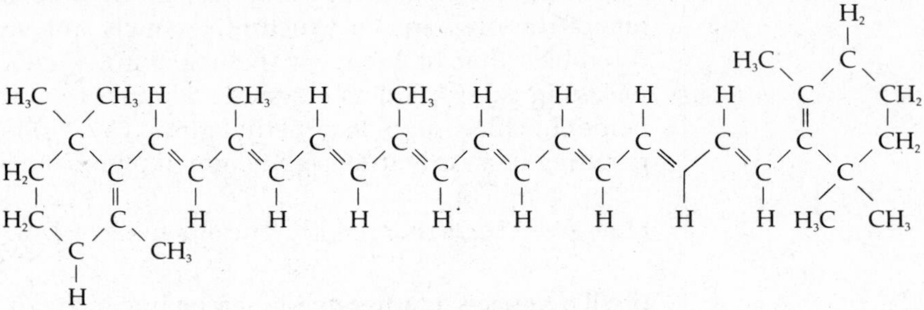

β–Carotene

Beta-carotene is but one example of the carotenes, all of which contribute color to vegetables. When this particular carotenoid (β-carotene) is split in the body, it yields vitamin A. The structures of the various carotenes are quite similar, varying only slightly in one of the rings at the end of the carbon chain. Lycopene (the red pigment in tomatoes) has no rings. The carotenes are quite stable pigments.

Xanthophylls are carotenoid pigments that are very similar to the carotenes, the exception being that xanthophylls have some oxygen (in the form of —OH or hydroxyl groups), while the carotenes lack this element. Examples of the xanthophylls are the cryptoxanthin in corn and lutein, an orange compound in spinach (but masked by chlorophyll).

Unlike the chlorophylls and carotenoids, which are contained in plastids, the flavonoids are in the vacuole of parenchyma cells, which causes these pigments to be released into the cooking water when vegetables containing them are cut or peeled. The various flavonoids are derivatives of the parent compound, flavone. Anthoxanthins are the white or colorless pigments in vegetables, such as cauliflower. The three-carbon unit in the middle of the structure of anthoxanthins includes a carbonyl (C=O); the reddish, purple, or blue colors of anthocyanins are the result of a somewhat different structure, for they lack this carbonyl, as shown in the structure.

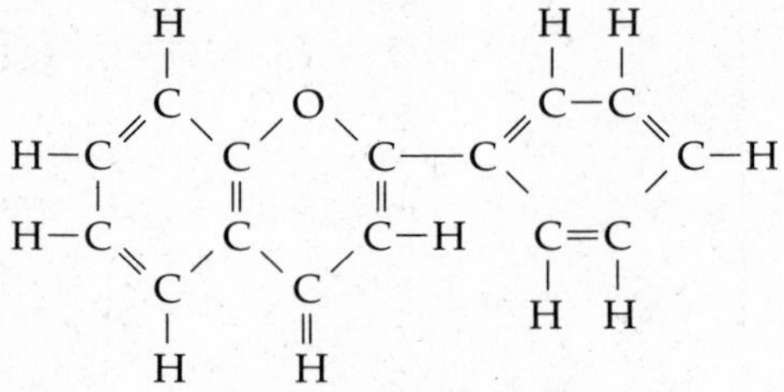

Flavone

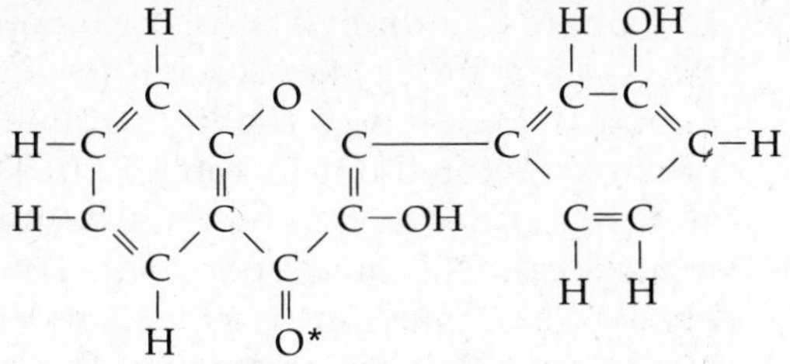

Flavonol (an *anthoxanthin*)

*Carbonyl of anthoxanthins is replaced with hydrogen in anthocyanins.

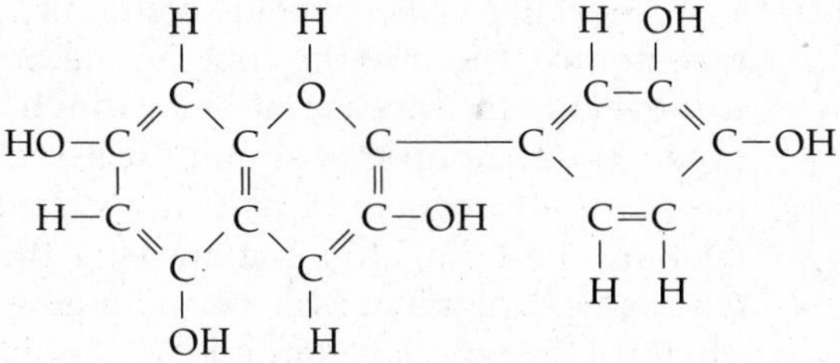

Cyanidin (an *anthocyanin*)

Shifts in the pigment color of the anthocyanins occur as a result of the number of hydroxyl (—OH) groups on the molecule. An increase in hydroxyl groups shifts the pigment from a reddish color toward a more bluish hue. The color shifts toward red in acid and toward blue in alkaline media, paralleling the change of color observed with litmus paper.

Metal ions (notably iron, tin, and aluminum) complex with flavonoids if they come in contact. These complexes result in unattractive hues of blue, ranging from slate blue to a greenish-blue. Such colors are not appealing in foods and should be avoided by removing metal sources of contamination.

Pigments sometimes change color or hue when a vegetable is cooked, with the results ranging from pleasing to distinctly unpalatable. Because of this potential for detrimental changes, pigments require special consideration when planning cooking methods. The initial change that can take place is an intensification of the original color when vegetables are plunged into boiling water. This drastic change in temperature apparently causes expulsion of the small amount of air between the cells, making pigments (particularly chlorophyll) appear even brighter than before heating. This abrupt start to heating vegetables has the added advantage of keeping cooking times as short as possible, which helps to avoid converting chlorophyll to pheophytin and also aids in retaining nutrients.

The acidity or alkalinity of the water in which vegetables are being boiled will modify the colors of all pigments except the carotenoids. The vegetables containing chlorophyll will take on an olive-drab color gradually while they are cooking if the water is acidic (or if the cooking period exceeds about 5 to 7 minutes). However, a slightly alkaline medium promotes retention of chlorophyll, as pointed out in Table 2.10. The flavonoids, both the anthoxanthins and the anthocyanins, retain a desirable color in a slightly acidic medium, while alkali will cause poor color. For instance, the white of cauliflower in a barely acidic medium is considered desirable, but yellow cauliflower, the result of alkali, is not acceptable. The color change from the rather pinkish-red seen in red cabbage cooked in a mild acid to the bluish color of a barely alkaline medium can cause complete rejection of that vegetable simply because of the change in the anthocyanin pigment with increasing alkalinity.

Vegetable cells naturally contain some mild organic acids, but these acids may be released into the cooking medium, causing pigment changes to begin to develop. In the case of chlorophyll, the change will be toward an olivegreen, a transition that should be avoided if possible. If green vegetables are boiled in an uncovered pan, the volatile organic acids will escape from the cooking medium, thus maintaining the water close to neutral. The desired chlorophyll pigment will be maintained and conversion to the undesirable pheophytin will be retarded by removing the lid once the water returns to boiling after the vegetable has been added.

The technique for boiling the flavonoid-containing vegetables is the reverse of that for chlorophyll. Both the anthocyanin and anthoxanthin pigments are considered to be more desirable in an acidic than in an alkaline medium. Thus, using a lid on the pan retains the volatile organic acids and protects the pigments.

Carotenoids can be viewed as pigments that are comparable in boiling water, regardless of the acidity or alkalinity. There is no compelling reason either for using or for not using a lid on carotenoid-pigmented vegetables from the perspective of color.

Table 2.10 Color Reactions of Vegetable Pigments

Pigment	Example	Color in Acid	Color in Alkali	Color Reaction to Metals
Chlorophyll	Broccoli	Olive-green[1]	Bright green[2]	Copper, iron: bright green
Carotenoids	Carrots	Orange	Orange	
Flavonoids:				
Anthoxanthins	Cauliflower	Colorless, white	Yellow	Aluminum: yellow Iron: brown
Anthocyanins	Red cabbage	Red	Blue to green	Iron: blue Tin: purple

[1]Pheophytin.
[2]Chlorophyllin.

Flavor

Although color will have a very strong influence on the acceptance of vegetables, other sensory qualities of vegetables also play a role. Flavor and the related characteristic, aroma, are key aspects of palatability. The aroma of onions cooking may be tempting to many, but the strong odor of cabbage boiling may completely repel others. Aromas are important because they contribute to the perceived flavor of a food, too. Vegetables with a strong aroma will also have a strong flavor and may be rejected on that basis.

To help promote a desirable flavor in vegetables, it is advisable to cover a pan when a mild-flavored vegetable is being prepared. Conversely, do not use a cover when a strong-flavored vegetable is being boiled so that the volatile flavoring compounds can escape from the product. Remember, any odor escaping into the air is simply that much less odorant remaining to strengthen the flavor of the finished product.

Anyone who has ever sampled the cooking water from boiled cabbage is well aware of the solubility of some of the flavoring components. By using enough water to cover strong-flavored vegetables with an excess of about ¼ inch of water, the flavoring components will be diluted by the leaching action of the cooking medium. This small excess will help to weaken the sometimes overpowering flavor of the various members of the cabbage family, thus promoting palatability. When mild-flavored vegetables are being prepared, however, using just enough water to barely boil over the vegetable will assure uniform boiling of the vegetable with a minimum influence on losing flavoring compounds into the cooking water.

The length of cooking time has a distinct influence on the flavors of certain key vegetables. The onion family, with its intense sulfur-containing flavoring components, will grow increasingly mild with continued heating. This is because some of the key flavoring compounds (including propionaldehyde, hydrogen sulfide, and sulfur dioxide) are volatile and lost from the vegetable. While a certain reduction in quantity of these intense substances is helpful, excessive loss leads to uninteresting flavors. The desired compromise can be achieved by cooking onions for a moderate length of time without a cover.

Sinigrin Compound in the cabbage family that ultimately is converted to hydrogen sulfide, causing an unpleasant flavor.

In contrast to onions, the cabbagelike vegetables develop increasingly intense flavors with extended cooking. Raw cabbage contains *sinigrin*, a glycoside found in the various members of this family. In the presence of water and heat, sinigrin is converted to allyl isothiocyanate and ultimately to hydrogen sulfide, a strong and unpleasant-smelling compound. The longer the cooking time, the greater the production of hydrogen sulfide. By keeping cooking time short for members of the cabbage family, palatability will be increased significantly.

For optimum flavor of cooked vegetables, the preparer must determine (1) whether to use a lid or not, (2) how much water is needed, and (3) how long the cooking period should be. Appropriate decisions with regard to these three variables will yield significant dividends in the preparation of highly pleasing cooked vegetables.

PREPARATION PROCEDURES
FOR FRESH VEGETABLES

Preliminary Steps

For all fresh vegetables, careful washing is essential. Many vegetables are cleansed well by washing them directly under a stream of cold, running water, using a vegetable brush or plastic scouring pad for scrubbing potatoes or other vegetables with stubborn dirt clinging to them. The quickest and most efficient way of cleaning mud from the veins and convolutions of greens is to fill the sink with cold water and then slosh the leaves up and down vigorously in the water to remove the dirt. Drain the water from the sink, being sure to rinse the dirty sediment on down the drain. Then refill the sink with fresh, cold water. Repeat the vigorous sloshing action and draining until the water remains clean and sediment no longer collects in the bottom of the sink as the rinse water is drained.

Following washing, careful inspection of fresh produce to remove all blemishes provides an important quality control check. At this point, any trimming, paring, and cutting needed should be done judiciously. For example, corn-on-the-cob is prepared by removing the husks and also the fine corn silks caught in the rows between kernels of corn. Similarly, green beans are trimmed at both ends to eliminate the very tough cellulosic areas sealing off the ends of the pods. Practically all fresh vegetables will need some judicious trimming to eliminate woody stalks, heavy, tough leaves, or other features that are not appropriate for human consumption.

Not all vegetables require extensive trimming prior to cooking. For instance, cabbage wedges should be cut so that enough of the core remains with each piece to ensure that the wedge will remain intact during boiling. Beets are left whole, with the root still attached and at least an inch of the stem remaining. These precautions help to avoid damaging any of the cells holding the anthocyanin pigments.

Paring is done to remove the skins of potatoes, carrots, and a few other vegetables. Use of a vegetable peeler helps to keep trimming losses to a minimum, although a paring knife also is a convenient way of removing skins. To reduce oxidative losses of vitamins and also to avoid possible discoloration, paring should be done right before cooking the vegetable. Discoloration in some potatoes is caused by enzyme action causing formation of a pigment called melanin from the amino acid tyrosine. This color change progresses through a brownish pink finally to a gray color. If potatoes have to stand after paring, discoloration can be minimized by placing the potatoes in a bowl of cold water to cover the entire surface and prevent oxygen from reaching the potatoes.

Many vegetables are cut into various shapes and pieces prior to being cooked. This permits vegetables to enhance the line and design of the menu.

Boiling

Probably the most common way of preparing cooked vegetables is by boiling them. Most fresh vegetables can be tenderized by boiling in water, with or without a lid, depending on color and flavor considerations. In preparation for boiling vegetables, enough water should be brought to boil in a covered pan to barely cover the vegetable (or to exceed this depth by about ¼ inch for strong-flavored vegetables). The cleaned and cut or whole fresh vegetables then are added to the boiling water, with the lid being replaced or removed, depending upon the specific vegetable. Boiling is continued just until the vegetables can be cut conveniently with a fork, but are not "mushy." Guidelines for boiling selected vegetables appear in Table 2.11.

Table 2.11 Suggested Techniques for Boiling Selected Fresh Vegetables

Vegetable	Use of Cover	Reason to Cover or Uncover	Amount of Water	Size of Piece	Boiling Time, (min)[1]
Artichoke, Globe	Covered[2]	Steam needed	¾ in.	Whole	35–45
Asparagus	Uncovered	Green color	Small[3]	Tips,	5–10
				stalks	10–20
Beans, green	Uncovered	Green color	Small	Whole	20–30
Beets	Covered	Mild flavor	Small	Whole	30–90
Broccoli	Uncovered	Green color, strong flavor	—[4]	Split stalk	10–20
Cabbage, green	Uncovered	Green color, strong flavor	Large[5]	Whole	10–20
				Wedge	7–15
Cabbage, red	Uncovered	Strong flavor	Large	Wedge	10–15
Carrots	Covered	Mild flavor	Small	Small, whole	15–30
Cauliflower	Uncovered	Strong flavor	Large	Whole, flower	15–25 / 8–15
Corn	Covered	Mild flavor	Small	Kernels	5–7
Corn-on-cob	Covered	Mild flavor	To cover	Whole	5–10
Onions	Uncovered	Strong flavor	Large	Whole	15–40
Parsnips	Uncovered	Strong flavor	Large	Whole	20–40
Peas	Uncovered	Green color	Small	Whole	10–20
Potatoes	Covered	Mild flavor	Small	Whole	20–40
Spinach	Covered to wilt, then uncovered	Green color	Clings to leaves	Leaves	5–10
Sweet potatoes	Covered	Mild flavor	Small	Whole	20–40
Tomatoes	Covered	Mild flavor	None	Whole	7–15

[1]Variation in cooking time depends on size and maturity of vegetables, as well as personal preference.
[2]Chlorophyll turns olive green with or without a cover because of the long cooking time needed for artichokes, so cover is used to trap steam in the pan to aid in retaining the flavor.
[3]Just enough water is used to bubble to the top of the vegetable when the water is boiling gently.
[4]Water to within ¼ in. of flowers when broccoli is standing upright in water.
[5]Enough water is used to provide an extra ¼ in. of water over the vegetable.

Mixtures of vegetables can be combined very successfully, particularly in making delicious homemade soups.

Steaming

Steaming requires a rack to hold vegetables in the steam above the water boiling in a pan. Many variations of these steamers and steamer baskets are on the market today. Steamed vegetables generally retain the water-soluble nutrients that leach out into the cooking water when vegetables are boiled. The time required for steaming is longer than the time for boiling if home-style steamers are used. Commercially, pressurized steamers are fairly common. The elevated temperature of the steam under pressure makes it possible to steam vegetables to the desired stage of doneness more quickly than they could be boiled.

Some green vegetables may be less palatable when steamed than when boiled because steaming requires that a cover be on the steamer throughout the cooking period, resulting in at least an overtone of olive-green unless steaming time is less than 5 minutes. Strong flavors may seem to be intensified by steaming because the lid traps volatile flavoring components; in addition, there is limited loss of soluble substances into the steam, as contrasted with the probable escape of these flavors into the boiling water when vegetables are boiled.

Mild-flavored, sweet vegetables are particularly adaptable to steaming, acquiring a tender, yet slightly crisp texture while retaining desirable flavor characteristics. Table 2.12 outlines some appropriate preparation techniques for many vegetables.

Simmering

The high protein content and low moisture level in dried legumes necessitate special preparation techniques for these nutritious vegetables. Rehydration is necessary, and this is a fairly slow process compared with the preparation of fresh vegetables. To promote the rehydration and softening of legumes, a

Table 2.12 Suggested Methods for Preparing Various Vegetables

Vegetable	Raw	Boiled or Steamed	Broiled	Baked	Fried	Stir-fried
Artichoke, Globe		X				X
Asparagus		X				X
Beans, string		X				X
Beans, dried lima		Simmered		X		
Beans, fresh lima		X				
Beets		X		X		X
Broccoli		X			X	X
Brussels sprouts		X				X
Cabbage, green	X	X				X
Cabbage, red	X	X				
Carrots	X	X		X		
Cauliflower	X	X			X	X
Celery	X	X				X
Corn		X		X		
Eggplant				X	X	
Mushrooms	X		X		X	X
Okra		X			X	
Onions	X	X	X	X	X	
Parsnips		X		X	X	
Peas		X				
Potatoes		X		X	X	
Spinach	X	X				X
Squash, acorn				X		
Squash, summer		X				
Sweet potatoes		X				
Tomatoes	X	X	X	X	X	
Zucchini		X		X	X	

soaking period (use of ⅛ tsp soda being optional) is the first preparation step. Either an overnight soaking period or a 2-minute boiling period followed by an hour of soaking in the same water can be used equally well to shorten the simmering time needed to tenderize the beans. The exceptions to this soaking period are lentils and split peas, for they will become tender when simply simmered for about an hour or less.

Ordinarily legumes are simmered in the water used to soak them so that the water-soluble B vitamins leaching into the soaking water will be retained with the cooked beans. The recommended amount of water for soaking is a maximum of 3 cups per cup of dried beans. The anticipated final yield of cooked beans from a cup of the original beans is about 2 to 3 cups after the simmering period of 90 minutes or more. At this point, the starch in the legumes will have gelatinized and caused the beans to swell significantly. The comparatively mild heat treatment will denature the protein, tenderize the cellulose and pectic substances, and eliminate possible toxic substances as well as inactive a trypsin inhibitor. The net result of these changes is that simmered legumes are palatable and comparatively inexpensive sources of protein that can be utilized fairly well by the body, particularly when cereals (rice, for example) or nuts are served with them.

If pectic substances in legumes are precipitated by calcium, tenderizing is difficult. Usually, the phytic acid found in legumes is able to bind calcium ions to prevent combination with pectic substances and formation of insoluble pectinates. The difficulty in softening legumes is compounded if molasses is added before adequate softness has been achieved by simmering. This problem is the result of the calcium ions and acid in the molasses. Hard water causes a similar problem due to calcium salts. Baked beans need to be tender before the molasses-containing sauce is added to make the popular, flavorful main dish. Acids, such as tomatoes, also should not be added before the legumes are softened by simmering because of the retarding effect that all acids will have on the softening of the pectic substances and cellulose.

Broiling

Broiling is a direct heat method of preparing tender vegetables quickly. Tomatoes (cut in half) and stuffed mushroom caps are two vegetables that can be broiled successfully. A few other vegetables, such as boiling onions, are excellent broiled if they have been parboiled first. The parboiling almost to the point of tenderness prior to broiling ensures that the center of the vegetable will be appropriately tender by the time the exterior of the broiling vegetable becomes a pleasing, golden brown color.

Baking

Baked potatoes are practically a national institution, but other vegetables, for instance winter squash and eggplant, also are suitable for baking because their skins protect them from drying excessively while baking. Onions and roasting ears of corn are other vegetables particularly well suited to baking.

Many other vegetables, with the exception of green vegetables, can be baked satisfactorily if they are placed in a covered casserole to help keep moisture in while baking.

Temperatures for baking vegetables may range anywhere from 300°–425°F, depending upon the other items that may be in the oven at the same time. Energy conservation suggests that baking vegetables when some other menu item also is being baked is good use of resources. Toaster ovens are useful for baking vegetables when they are the only item to be baked.

Frying

French-fried potatoes and onion rings are popular menu items despite the advice that the amount of fat should be reduced in the typical American diet. The techniques used in frying vegetables can be geared toward keeping the fat level of such items as low as possible when they are being prepared. The fat for deep-fat frying should be at about 375°F before the vegetables are placed in the fat. This temperature is hot enough for rather fast cooking of the vegetable, but not so hot that the vegetable burns on the exterior before it is soft in the center. With cooler temperatures than 375°F, the vegetable will absorb increasing amounts of oil as the cooking time is extended. By placing small amounts of the raw vegetable into the frying oil, the temperature of the fat will drop only slightly from the desired frying heat. Careful draining of the fried food, complete with blotting thoroughly on paper towels before serving, is another important measure to help keep the fat content of deep-fat fried foods comparatively low.

Vegetables to be fried sometimes are dipped in a batter prior to frying, and sometimes they are blotted rather dry with paper towels and then dropped carefully into the hot fat. French-fried potatoes are always fried without batter, while onion rings and such familiar Japanese tempura morsels as sliced sweet potatoes, carrots, and green beans are enhanced by being immersed in a batter first.

Shallow-fat frying of vegetables is done to a limited extent. Potatoes often are prepared in this way, with cottage fries and hash browns being two of the very popular recipes. Since the fat level is too shallow to check with a thermometer, the rule is to keep the fat from getting so hot that it smokes.

Stir-Frying or Panning

Wok Metallic, bowl-shaped pan developed in the Orient for stir-frying.

Stir-frying or panning, utilizing either a *wok* or a frying pan, is a method of vegetable cookery borrowed from Oriental cuisines. A wok is a metal vessel with a curved bottom that is placed on a stabilizing metal ring over a heat source; an electrical version of a wok has the heat source built into the base of the appliance. Both styles of woks rely on intense heat at the bottom of the bowl to cook thin slices of the vegetable very quickly in a small amount of oil. As soon as the vegetable slice browns slightly, it is pushed up the side, where heat conduction will keep finished portions warm while other slices are being fried in the bottom.

By slicing vegetables into thin strips and stir-frying them briefly in a wok, the nutritive value, color, and flavor are all retained well.

One of the delights of stir-frying is that vegetables, despite their thin slices, maintain just a suggestion of crispness. Another plus for this method of vegetable cookery is its speed. This not only saves preparation time, but also helps to retain nutrients. The combination of the very short preparation time and the limited contact with water results in good retention of vitamin C and other water-soluble nutrients, in spite of the large surface area exposed by the thin slices. Other advantages of stir-frying are the fresh and vibrant green color maintained in chlorophyll-containing vegetables and the fresh flavors.

Although many vegetables will become sufficiently tender just with the heating that occurs while the slices are being browned slightly, some require additional time to achieve the desired texture. With extended frying in the intense heat of the wok, too dark a brown color or even burning can occur before the slices are done and the texture is sufficiently tender. In preparing vegetables that tenderize slowly, stir-frying is initiated as usual (i.e., with a small amount of margarine or salad oil in the bottom of the wok). However, the wok is covered with a lid whenever stirring is not being done and just a little water is added to form to help tenderize the slices.

Other Techniques

Microwaving Microwave ovens, familiar pieces of equipment in many kitchens today, offer yet another means of preparing vegetables comparatively quickly. One of the advantages of a microwave oven is the rapid cooking that can happen if only small quantities are being prepared. Although cookery methods in the microwave oven frequently include adding a small amount of liquid and covering the vegetable with a paper towel or other suitable protection to trap moisture, the retention of the water-soluble vitamins (even the elusive vitamin C and the B vitamins) is good.

The texture of fresh vegetables that have been prepared in a microwave oven is often more tenacious and chewy than is true of similar vegetables that have been boiled. This is considered undesirable by some people, but quite acceptable by many others who find the excellent color and flavor sufficient compensation. Microwaving of vegetables results in uneven cooking of various parts of the vegetable. This can be offset to a degree by stirring once or twice during the cooking period if the vegetables are in slices or pieces. Even then, the loss of water from parenchyma cells will be greater in microwaved vegetables than in boiled counterparts; this loss explains, in part, the difference in texture resulting from these two cookery methods.

Pressure Cooking Some time can be saved in cooking vegetables by using a pressure saucepan, but the greatest savings are gained with vegetables requiring 20 minutes or more to become appropriately tender. The use of a pressure saucepan is particularly helpful at high altitudes where the reduced temperature of boiling water at atmospheric pressure causes considerable delay in tenderizing vegetables.

Petcock Small opening in the cover of a pressure saucepan to let steam escape and on which the pressure gauge is placed.

A small amount of water is placed in a pressure saucepan along with the washed and trimmed vegetables. The cover is secured, and the pan is heated, keeping the *petcock* open. When steam begins to come continuously through the open petcock, the pressure gauge (15 pounds) is put in position and full heat is continued until the gauge begins to jiggle. At this time, the desired pressure has been reached, and the timing of the cooking begins. Since the pressure is creating a very hot temperature, timing must be done carefully, for an error of 30 seconds can cause a significant variation from the desired result in tenderizing the vegetable. As soon as the desired time has elapsed, the pressure saucepan is removed from the heat and is held under cool running water briefly to reduce the pressure inside before the pressure gauge is removed and the lid opened. Strong-flavored and green vegetables are suited less well to pressure saucepan cookery than are other vegetables, but many vegetables can be cooked successfully this way.

PREPARING CANNED
AND FROZEN VEGETABLES

Canned Vegetables

Basically, the preparation of vegetables canned commercially is as simple as opening the can and either heating them to serving temperature in their own juice or draining them and using them cold in salads. The canning process has cooked the vegetables completely. Reheating can be done by microwaving the vegetables in a glass dish, with only enough of the liquid added to provide the juice desired in serving the vegetable—often only the liquid clinging to the vegetable as it is spooned from the can. No cover is required for this brief period of microwaving unless a sauce, such as that on creamed corn, is being heated with the vegetable.

Home-canned vegetables present the potential hazard of being a source of the toxin produced by *Clostridium botulinum*. Since this toxin can be fatal in even extremely small amounts, home-canned vegetables should be boiled actively for at least 15 minutes before they are even tasted. To use home-canned vegetables without following this precaution is to take a risk that could result in death (see Chapter 17). The sole exception to the rule of boiling for 15 minutes is tomatoes, for they are an acidic vegetable that does not favor growth of *Cl. botulinum* spores.

Frozen Vegetables

Blanching Boiling or steaming for a brief period to inactivate enzymes prior to freezing.

Frozen vegetables have been *blanched* before freezing to inactivate enzymes that might cause oxidative changes during frozen storage. This brief cooking period is enough to begin to soften the cell walls and shorten the subsequent cooking period required when the frozen vegetable ultimately is cooked. Usually, the block of frozen vegetable is placed in a small amount of boiling water (ordinarily about half a cup of water for a 10-ounce portion of vegetable) and is boiled just until the vegetable is tender. A lid can be used to help trap the steam for melting the upper portion of the frozen block. Even green vegetables can be cooked from their frozen state to their serving time with the pan covered because the oxidative enzymes that promote pheophytin formation have been inactivated by the prior blanching period. In addition, the very short boiling period is unlikely to result in pheophytin being formed from chlorophyll.

Microwaving works particularly well for preparing frozen vegetables. As the frozen block softens during the heating process, the vegetables should be stirred to promote even heating. The texture of microwaved frozen vegetables is close to those that are boiled, because the changes in the cell walls resulting from the blanching period and the formation of ice crystals during freezing usually result in adequate tenderizing of the vegetables, even with a fairly brief cooking period in the microwave oven.

ADDING INTEREST

Even when vegetables have been prepared perfectly, they may seem monotonous if only a narrow range of vegetables is prepared, particularly if only one or two preparation techniques are being used. The use of sauces, seasonings, and spices can add considerable appeal to the vegetables in meals. Sauces that are appropriate for vegetables include lemon butter, Hollandaise, bechamel, and mornay, as well as sweet-sour sauces. Imaginative use of herbs is another way of accenting vegetables. Basil, dill, marjoram, mint, oregano, chopped parsley, chopped chives, rosemary, sage, savory, tarragon (very sparingly), and thyme are some of the popular herbs for vegetables.

Attractive and appetizing service of vegetables is important to acceptance. Careful draining before serving is essential if a sauce is going to be added or if the vegetable will be served directly on the main dinner plate. Herbs may be stirred into the drained vegetable, along with the margarine or butter, before serving the vegetable. A squeeze of lemon juice stirred into the vegetable is another way of adding a subtle flavor accent.

SUMMARY

Vegetables often are classified according to the part of the plant that is used as food, the resulting classifications being bulbs, roots, tubers, leaves and stems, fruits, and seeds. Vegetables have an outer covering, a vascular transport system, and pulp (composed mostly of parenchyma cells). The structural components of vegetables are primarily cellulose, hemicelluloses, and the pectic substances. Within the parenchyma cells, starch is formed and stored in the plastids called leucoplasts, carotenoid pigments in the chromoplasts, chlorophylls in the chloroplasts, and flavonoid pigments, plus sugars, acids, and salts, in the large portion of the cell, called the vacuole.

Vegetables are valuable sources of nutrients when they are prepared and served in tempting ways. Among the nutrients contained in vegetables are many of the vitamins (particularly provitamin A in the dark green, leafy, and yellow vegetables) and minerals. A few are also excellent sources of starch. An important contribution of vegetables in the diet is the fiber in them, which is useful in promoting intestinal motility.

Throughout the year, a wide range of fresh vegetables can be obtained in large supermarkets. Many of these need to be stored in the refrigerator, carefully wrapped to protect against moisture loss in the home. A few, potatoes being a notable example, should be stored about 10°F below room temperature to promote optimum quality retention. At 60°F, starch content of nonwaxy potatoes remains high, thus promoting their excellent performance for mashing, baking, and frying. Waxy potatoes held at this temperature will retain adequate amounts of sugar, yet starch content will be controlled to enable them to be used for their best preparation modes, for boiling and in salads and casseroles.

Considerable nutrients and palatability can be lost if care is not exercised in the handling of vegetables from the farm to the market and ultimately the family table. Temperature control is vital to nutrient retention and the avoidance of spoilage. Control of the moisture level in the surrounding environment during storage also is important. The eye can be a good guide to the selection of vegetables of high quality and nutrient value.

Cookery techniques should be designed to optimize color, flavor, total palatability, and nutrient content. This is a large order, but appropriate decisions regarding the amount of water to use in boiling, the use of a lid, and length of cooking can be made. Green vegetables will retain their chlorophyll rather than form pheophytin if the cooking time is kept short and a lid is not used. A tiny bit of acid helps to retain the desired color in the flavonoids (anthoxanthins and anthocyanins), but adding much acid will cause vegetables to remain hard. Using a lid on a boiling vegetable helps to hold in the natural organic acids. A minimum amount of water to just boil over a fresh vegetable and the use of a lid will promote optimum flavor in a mild-flavored vegetable, whereas uncovering a strong-flavored vegetable like cabbage helps to increase palatability by weakening the flavor. If either color or flavor is improved without the lid, the cover should be left off for maximum palatability.

In addition to boiling, vegetables can be prepared by steaming. Legumes are simmered because they take a long time to soften. Broiling, baking, frying, and stir-frying are other techniques suited to preparing some vegetables. Microwave cookery of vegetables, particularly of canned and frozen vegetables, is yet another quick technique. A pressure saucepan is a time-saver in cooking vegetables that require at least 20 minutes to soften appropriately; it is of particular merit when cooking vegetables in the mountains.

Selected References

Adams, J. B. Blanching of vegetables. *Nutr. and Food Sci. (73)*: 11. 1981.

Agricultural Marketing Service. *Marketing Agreements and Orders for Fruits and Vegetables*. Program Aid No. 1095. U.S. Dept. Agriculture. Washington, D.C. 1975.

Agricultural Marketing Service. *Grade Names for Fresh Fruits and Vegetables*. U.S. Dept. Agriculture. Washington, D.C. 1976.

American Home Economics Association. *Handbook of Food Preparation*. AHEA. Washington, D.C. 8th ed. 1980.

Bailey, S. D. et al. Volatile sulfur components of cabbage. *J. Food Sci. 26*: 163. 1961.

Ballentine, C. L. and M. L. Herndon. Who, why, when, and where of food poisons. *FDA Consumer 16(6)*: 25. 1982.

Bisogni, C. A. and G. Armbruster, Quality comparisons of room ripened and field ripened tomato fruits. *J. Food Sci. 41*: 333. 1976.

Boelens, M. et al. Volatile flavor compounds from onions. *J. Agr. Food Chem. 19*: 984. 1971.

Borchgrevink, N. C. and H. Charley. Color of cooked carrots related to carotene content. *J. Am. Dietet. Assoc. 49*: 116. 1966.

Bowman, F. et al. Microwave vs. conventional cooking of vegetables at high altitude. *J. Am. Dietet. Assoc. 58*: 427. 1971.

Bressani, R. et al. Reduction of digestibility of legume proteins by tannins. *J. Plant Foods 4(1)*: 438. 1982.

Charley, H. Fruits and vegetables. In *Food Theory and Applications*. Eds. P. Paul and H. H. Palmer, John Wiley. New York. 1972. P. 251.

Consumer and Food Economics Institute. Conserving Nutritive Values in Foods. *Home and Garden Bulletin* No. 90. U.S. Dept. Agriculture. Washington, D.C. 1971.

Consumer and Food Economics Institute. Vegetables in Family Meals. *Home and Garden Bulletin* No. 105. U.S. Dept. Agriculture. Washington, D.C. 1975.

Cromwell, C. Organic foods—an update. *Family Economics Review (Summer)*: 8. U.S. Dept. Agriculture. Washington, D.C. 1976.

Davis, E. A. et al. Scanning electron microscope studies on carrots: effects of cooking on the phloem and xylem. *Home Ec. Research J. 4*: 214. 1976.

Deshpande, F. S. and M. Cheryas. Changes in phytic acid, tannins, and trypsin inhibitory activity on soaking of dry beans. *Nutr. Reports International 27(2)*: 371. 1983.

Eheart, M. S. and C. Gott. Chlorophyll, ascorbic acid, and pH changes in green vegetables cooked by stir-fry, microwave, and conventional methods. *Food Tech. 19*: 867. 1965.

Emodi, A. Carotenoids—properties and applications. *Food Tech. 32(5)*: 38. 1978.

Fennema, O. Loss of vitamins in fresh and frozen foods. *Food Tech. 31(12)*: 32. 1977.

Haard, N. J. Postharvest physiology and biochemistry of fruits and vegetables. *J. Chem. Ed. 61*: 277. 1984.

Hopkins, H. Coming out of soybeans and whey. *FDA Consumer 17(9)*: 8. 1983.

Ide, L. E. How to Buy Potatoes. *Home and Garden Bulletin*. No. 198. U.S. Dept. Agriculture. Washington, D.C. 1972.

Johnston, D. E. and W. T. Oliver. Influence of cooking techniques on dietary fiber of whole boiled potatoes. *J. Food Tech. 17(1)*: 99. 1982.

Ku, S. et al. Extraction of oligosaccharides during cooking of whole soybeans. *J. Food Sci. 41*: 361. 1976.

Lipton, W. J. and C. M. Harris. Controlled atmosphere effects on the market quality of stored broccoli (Brassica oleracae L. Italica group). *J. Am. Soc. Hort. Sci. 99*: 200. 1974.

Little, A. C. Colorimetry of anthocyanin pigmented products: Changes in pigment composition with time. *J. Food Sci. 42*: 1570. 1970.

Longe, O. G. Effect of boiling on carbohydrate constituents of some non-leafy vegetables. *Food Chem. 7(1)*: 1. 1981.

Mackey, A. and S. Joiner. *Science in Cooking—Potatoes*. Circular of Information No. 600. Ag. Expt. Sta. Oregon State University. Corvallis, Ore. 1960.

MacLeod, A. J. and G. M. MacLeod. Effects of variations in cooking methods on the flavor volatiles of cabbage. *J. Food Sci. 35*: 744. 1970.

Maga, J. A. and J. A. Twomey. Sensory comparison of four potato varieties baked conventionally and by microwaves. *J. Food Sci. 42*: 541. 1977.

Maruyama, F. T. Identification of trimethyl sulfide as a major aroma component of cooked brassicaceous vegetables. *J. Food Sci. 35*: 541. 1970.

Moyer, W. C. *Buying Guide*. Blue Goose, Fullerton, Calif. 1981.

Muneta, P. Enzymatic blackening of potatoes: influence of pH on dopachrome oxidation. *Am. Potato J. 54*: 387. 1977.

Odland, L. D. and M. S. Eheart. Ascorbic acid retention and organoleptic properties of green vegetables cooked by several techniques using ammonium carbonate. *Home Ec. Research J. 2*: 241. 1974.

Patil, C. B. et al. Metabolism of solanine and chlorophyll in potato tubers as affected by light and specific chemicals. *J. Food Sci. 36*: 474. 1971.

Peterkin, B. and C. Cromwell. Your Money's Worth in Foods. *Home and Garden Bulletin.* No. 183. U.S. Dept. Agriculture. Washington, D.C. 1977.

Powers, J. R. and S. R. Drake. Effect of cut and field-holding conditions on activity of phenylalanine ammonia-lypase and texture in fresh asparagus spears. *J. Food Sci.* 45: 509. 1980.

Preston, R. D. Cellulose, *Sci. Amer. 197 (3):* 157. 1957.

Quast, D. C. and S. D. daSilva. Temperature dependence of the cooking rate of dry legumes. *J. Food Sci. 42:* 371. 1977.

Rick, C. M. The tomato. *Sci. Amer. 239 (2):* 76. 1978.

Shannon, S. et al. Firmness of canned carrots and red beets during storage. *J. Food Sci.* 42: 1674. 1977.

Somers, G. F. and K. C. Beeson. Influence of climate and fertilizer practices upon vitamin and mineral content of vegetables. *Adv. Food Res. 1:* 291. 1948.

Study Questions

1. Compare the cost and palatability of the following vegetables in their fresh, frozen, and canned forms: corn, peas, string beans, carrots, and potatoes. Which products represent the most economical choices? The greatest palatability?

2. Make a list of the various gourmet vegetables in the frozen food section. What types of sauces or special ingredients are incorporated in these items? How does the cost compare with the cost of the plain frozen vegetables?

3. What are some vegetables that are examples of each of the pigment categories? What color changes may be anticipated in each in the presence of acids and alkalis? How can cookery technique influence the color of cooked vegetables?

4. Describe the techniques involved in cooking vegetables by each of the following methods: boiling, steaming, broiling, baking, frying, stir-frying, microwaving, and pressure cooking. Name at least one vegetable suitable for each method.

5. Explain the use of a lid and the amount of water to be used in boiling each of the following fresh vegetables: corn, broccoli, onions, red cabbage, Brussels sprouts, spinach, cauliflower, beets, carrots. Explain why you chose each of your answers.

Peter de Hooch, "Interior with People." Wallace Collection/Art Resource.

CHAPTER 3

FRUITS

Fruits—fresh, frozen, canned, or dried—are favorite foods for many people. They are popular at all meals of the day and as snack foods, too, for their high palatability when eaten raw makes them among the easiest of foods to prepare. In contrast to vegetables, which require some skill and imagination to bring them to the table as a meal highlight, fruits have flavors tinted with sweetness and textures ranging from crisp to very soft to brighten any meal or snack. The challenge with fruits is to select fruits of high quality and to store them appropriately until they are prepared for simple and elegant service.

The array of fruits available to today's consumers throughout the year would have amazed even royalty 50 years ago, for wealth alone could not have bought items considered standard fare today. The secret of this difference is a combination of significant changes in shipping and marketing practices, plus agricultural innovations.

Summer is still the height of the fruit season, but even in winter, the choices extend far beyond the traditional oranges, grapefruit, and apples of yesteryear. Not only are many fruits available, but also choices must be made between the fresh, frozen, canned, and dried fruits in the market. This chapter considers the fascinating array of fruits, their selection, nutritive value, care, and preparation.

CLASSIFICATION

Fruits are defined as being the edible, more or less succulent products of a tree or plant and consist of ripened seeds and adjacent tissues. Although a few of these fruits actually will end up classified as vegetables because of their use in the main course of a meal (tomatoes, for example), the majority will be used for salads and desserts because of their naturally sweet flavor. Some order can be made out of the many fruits by classifying them into groups or families on the basis of shape, cell structure, type of seed, or natural habitat. Commonly, fruits are categorized according to the following groups: berries, citrus, drupes, grapes, melons, pomes, and tropical and subtropical fruits.

Berries

Berries typically are small fruits with a fragile, easily damaged cell structure. These fruits rely heavily on a high content of water within the cells to give the juicy plumpness associated with berries. This high water content accompanied by thin cell walls causes berries to lose their notably juicy and slightly firm character (as a result of the formation of sharp ice crystals and the consequent rupturing of cells walls) during freezing and thawing. Familiar members of the berry group include blackberries, blueberries, boysenberries, red and black raspberries, youngberries, cranberries, gooseberries, huckleberries, and strawberries. Less familiar berries that can be found occasionally are lingonberries, cloud berries (natives of the Arctic Circle), and dew berries.

As a group, berries often are used fresh as desserts, either served simply in a bowl or made into baked products, such as a fresh berry pie or other types of bakery goods. They also can be made into gourmet pies by preparing a glaze into which the fresh berries are stirred in preparation for filling a baked pie crust.

Raspberries, blueberries, and strawberries have a wide sale in the frozen food market. Blueberries are even marketed in blueberry muffin mixes. Pancakes and waffles become festive when they are topped with berries in the form of the fresh fruit, syrups, or even jams and jellies. Cranberries earn their special place by being available in the fall when many other fruits have faded. They are unique among the berries in their diverse forms in cranberry sauce, jelly, and juice.

Citrus Fruits

Nutritionists recommend serving a citrus fruit or other rich source of vitamin C daily. The inability of the body to store vitamin C efficiently has been a boon to the citrus industry, for oranges and other citrus fruits are year-round crops and a comparatively inexpensive source of this essential, but somewhat elusive, vitamin. The menu need not be limited to oranges, however; grapefruit, lemons, tangerines, limes, and temple oranges are other citrus sources of vitamin C. Kumquats and citron are eaten only rarely, yet they also can provide this vitamin.

Strawberries are just one of the several types of berries available fresh during the spring and summer.

Citrus fruits include grapefruit, tangerines, oranges, and lemons; these fruits are available fresh most of the year.

The two common types of oranges in U.S. markets are Valencias and navels. Valencia oranges, preferred for juice, can be distinguished from navel oranges by examining the bottom of the orange. The bottom of the Valencia is smooth, whereas the bottom of the navel has a formation that is the beginning of an orange within an orange. Navels peel more easily than do the Valencias, are seedless, and slice readily; these attributes make navel oranges particularly popular for eating.

The popularity of oranges extends far beyond their role as a provider of vitamin C. The delightful flavor of oranges lends a pleasing accent to other foods; the bright color is yet another asset of oranges. Commercially, the production of orange juice to be marketed fresh, canned, or as frozen concentrate is a big business, for this is a convenience food that is a welcomed time-saver in many U.S. homes. Of interest, too, is the fact that the orange is a major source of pectin in the manufacture of jams and jellies; a major source of commercial pectin is the white (albedo) portion of the skins of citrus fruits.

The tangerine, another type of citrus, has the shape of a slightly flattened orange. Its particular virtue is the loosely fitting skin, which can be peeled off with almost no effort; on the other hand, the sections of flesh contain a number of seeds that have to be removed. Mandarin oranges, actually a type of tangerine, are utilized in the canned form frequently as a salad and dessert ingredient. A close relative is the tangelo, which is a hybrid between a grapefruit and a tangerine. Temple oranges are another result of breeding experiments by botanists. This very pleasing citrus fruit has the juiciness of oranges and the easy peeling of tangerines.

Grapefruit, the largest of the citrus fruits, is enjoyed not only in the United States, but also from South Africa to Israel. The flesh may be either white or pink. Although grapefruit frequently are eaten simply cut in half, they are excellent also when broiled, perhaps topped with a bit of brown sugar and served hot.

Lemons are a particular boon to people who are trying to follow weight-reduction diets because a squeeze of lemon juice or a bit of grated lemon rind can add an exciting flavor accent to many different foods without adding enough calories to mention. For instance, a touch of lemon on a green salad can replace a high-calories salad dressing, yet give a pleasing flavor. However, lemons can also be used in high-calorie preparations such as lemonade and lemon meringue pies as well as in other desserts that rely on large quantities of sugar to compensate for the tartness of the lemon juice.

Two other, less familiar citrus fruits are kumquats and citron. Kumquats are only about an inch long and, because of their size, make an attractive garnish when used raw, preserved, or candied. Citron resembles a large avocado with a very thick peel. Citron is valued for its edible peel, which ordinarily is candied and used in fruit cakes and some holiday cookies.

Drupes

Drupes Fruit with a single seed surrounded by edible pulp.

Fruits with a single large seed surrounded by edible pulp are classified as *drupes*. Apricots, cherries, peaches, plums, and prunes are drupes. These fruits are very popular in many forms—fresh, frozen, canned, in jams and jellies, and sometimes even dried. A showy example of a drupe is the maraschino cherry, which is made by bleaching sweet cherries with sulfur dioxide and then adding food coloring. Prunes, apricots, and peaches are popular dried; apricots and peaches usually are sulfured to retain their familiar orange color.

Grapes

Cherries are an example of a drupe, a type of fruit recognized by its single seed.

Grapes are an important fruit crop in many parts of the world, valued both for the fruit itself and for the wine that can be made from certain varieties. Table grapes are available in such varieties as Thompson seedless, Flame Tokay, Emperor, Muscat, Malaga, and Concord. These stem from two basic types—the American grape with its round shape and the European grape, typified by an oval outline. The familiar blue Concord grape is an example of an American grape, and the Thompson Seedless is classified as European.

Concord grapes are eaten fresh in season, but they also are the basis of many commercial products, including grape jelly, jam, conserves, juice, and frozen grape juice concentrate. Other grapes also are used to make commercial products. Thompson seedless grapes are canned in fruit cocktail and are made into raisins by sun drying. Muscat grapes and currants also are popular products when dried.

Melons

Unlike most other fruits, melons generally are restricted to use as the fresh fruit. Preservation methods cause undesirable textural changes, with the exception of watermelon pickles. Even freezing presents problems, for the delicate cell structure of melons is damaged by freezing, resulting in a slippery, slightly unpleasant texture when thawed.

Fortunately, melons can be grown over a rather wide geographic area from north to south so the growing season for melons is fairly long. For instance, melons grown in the Imperial Valley of southern California are shipped to markets from the middle of May until early July, at which time northern California takes over the market, only to relinquish it again to the Imperial Valley for a fall crop.

Muskmelon One of two general subdivisions of melons; includes cantaloupe, honeydew, and other melons characterized by having a thick pulp surrounding a large central cavity full of small seeds.

The two general categories in the melon group are watermelons and muskmelons. *Muskmelons*, with their central cavity filled with seeds and thick, colorful pulp under a thin outer skin, are subdivided into several familiar varieties: cantaloupe, honeydew, Persian, casaba, honey ball, and Cranshaw.

Persian melons, noted for their thick, orange-colored flesh, are a close relative of the cantaloupe, while the casaba has a soft flesh and a creamy color. The Persian and casaba melons were crossed to produce the Cranshaw variety, a melon with a rich flavor and a lovely salmon color. Casaba and Cranshaw melons have an excellent marketing characteristic, for they are best picked green and ripened off the vine, which makes shipping comparatively easy. Cantaloupe and Persian melons present problems in shipping because they are best when they are allowed to ripen on the vine before being harvested. The lovely, delicate green color and very sweet flavor of the honey-

Melons are categorized as watermelons or muskmelons, the latter including cantaloupe, honeydew, cranshaw, and Persian melons.

dew are a distinct contrast to the other muskmelons. Occasionally, the honey ball melon is seen in the markets. It has an exterior closely resembling a honeydew melon, while the interior is similar to a mild-flavored cantaloupe.

Pomes

Fruits from the botanical family *Malaceae* all have a central core containing five encapuslated seeds surrounded by a thick and fleshy edible layer. This core

Pome Fruit with a core containing five seeds and surrounded by thick, edible pulp; apples, pears, and quince are examples.

Pears are classified as pomes because of their central core and five encapsulated seeds; varieties include (left, top to bottom—Bartlett, Red Bartlett, Anjou, Bosc; above, top to bottom—comice, Nelis, Forelle, Seckel.)

structure is characteristic of all of the fruits classified as *pomes* (see Figure 3.1). Familiar pomes are apples, pears, and quince. Apples are particularly common in the American diet, due to their great versatility and their excellent keeping qualities. Commercially, apples are processed into juice, vinegar, jelly, apple butter, applesauce, and pie fillings. They may also be dried in slices or used in frozen pie fillings. In the home, numerous recipes for apples are used. Baked apples, apple pie, fruit salads, and apple fritters are just some of the ways in which apples are incorporated into the diet.

Pears can be used in many recipes interchangeably with apples. For instance, pears can be used in fruit salads and in making a pear pie. The greater juiciness of pears makes it necessary to make some adjustments in some products, such as quick breads where liquid levels are particularly important. Bartlett pears are a rich yellow color when ripe; d'Anjou pears are still green

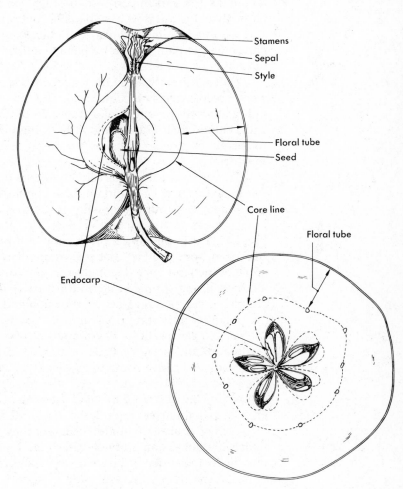

Figure 3.1 An apple is classified as a pome because it contains 5 encapsulated seeds within the core line.

in color but yield slightly to pressure when ripe; Bosc pears have a brown network on the skin, called russeting, which makes them look brown when ready to use.

Tropical and Subtropical Fruits

With today's excellent transportation facilities, the range of fruits in the market has expanded tremendously. Tropical and subtropical fruits, despite the fact that they have to be shipped from distant ports, usually are available throughout the year. This has been particularly important in providing alternative sources of vitamin C in the diet, as well as adding interest to diets.

Among the popular tropical and subtropical fruits are avocados, pineapples, papayas, mangoes, bananas, figs, dates, and pomegranates. The avocado is unique among fruits because of its comparatively high fat content (about 13 percent) in contrast to other fruits having negligible levels of fat. Gros Michel is the variety of banana commonly used for eating and in salads and various baked products. Caribbean recipes call for another type of banana, the plantain, a starchy banana suitable for frying and baking, but not ordinarily consumed raw.

Dates, formerly an exotic fruit from distant oases overseas, now are being grown commercially in California. The three stages of ripening (*khalal*, developing of a yellow or red color; *rutab*, softening; and *tamar*, time for curing the fruit) culminate in the curing of dates high in sugar content. Their sweetness makes them popular in baked products, salads, and confections as well as in milk drinks.

Figs are best known as canned kadota figs or as the filling in fig newtons. But fresh figs may be found for a brief period of time in some markets.

Pineapple, found originally in Central America, now is available on a large scale from Hawaii, with Puerto Rico and Florida also adding to the supply. In Hawaii, pineapple production and processing still represent a key industry, despite the fact that real estate ventures are beginning to crowd out some of the land once devoted to raising this key tropical fruit. Nevertheless, a large volume of pineapple, in the form of juice, spears, rings, crushed, and chunks, is shipped regularly to the mainland.

Another important tropical fruit exported from Hawaii to the mainland is the papaya. The delicate flavor and lovely orange color make this fruit a welcome addition to fruit salads or poultry salads; papayas also are excellent when served alone, sometimes heightened by a squeeze of lime or lemon juice. Surprisingly, even the seeds of papayas can be used as food, for they can be ground and used in salad dressing. The papaya also is a source of the enzyme papain, used in tenderizing less tender cuts of meat.

Pomegranates are unique fruits for they are valued for their edible seeds, which contain a comparatively large amount of a flavorful, red juice. The juice may be extracted from the seeds to make grenadine and fruit juice combinations. In the home, the seeds are prized as an attractive red color accent in fruit salads.

Papayas are tropical fruits with a bland flavor that is heightened by adding lime or lemon juice after the seeds are removed. (left)

Papaya tree with its valuable crop of golden fruit. (right)

The mango is a tropical fruit with a very large seed in the center of its pulp.

Kiwi fruit is a relative newcomer to produce markets. Its delicate flavor and beautiful green interior are beautiful to serve after the fuzzy brownish peeling has been removed.

COMPOSITION OF FRUITS

Most fruits have a high water content, ranging between 80 and 90 percent, with watermelons and muskmelons at the upper end (about 92 percent moisture level). Even dried fruits are about 25 percent water. The carbohydrate levels in fresh fruits range generally from about 3 to 14 percent. Protein and fat are notably low in fruits (except the avocado). Table 3.1 provides information on the composition of some familiar fruits.

The type of carbohydrate found in individual fruits varies with the maturity of the fruit, but the total amount of carbohydrate remains relatively constant as the fruit develops from the green to mature state. Starch content, high in immature fruits, usually declines as ripening occurs, whereas the sugar level rises. This relationship in these two forms of carbohydrate reflects the gradual transition of starch into sugar with maturation, a change that can be detected in the sweet flavor of ripened fruits. Actually, there is a remark-

Table 3.1 Average Values Obtained in the Analysis of Selected Fruits[1]

Fruit[2]	Water (%)	Calories	Carbohydrate (g)	Vitamin A Value (I.U.)	Ascorbic Acid (mg)
Apples					
1 medium	85	70	18	50	3
Apricots					
3	85	55	14	2890	10
Avocado,					
½ of 10 oz	74	185	6	310	15
Banana,					
1 medium	76	85	23	170	10
Cantaloupe,					
½ of 5″	94	40	9	6590	63
Grapefruit,					
½ medium	89	50	14	10	50
Navel orange,					
1 large	86	70	17	270	83
Peach,					
1 medium	89	35	10	1320	7
Pear,					
3″ × 2½″	83	100	25	30	7
Pineapple,					
1 c, diced	85	75	19	180	33
Strawberries,					
1 c	90	55	12	90	89
Watermelon,					
4″ × 8″ slice	92	120	29	2530	26

Source: Adapted from Nutritive values of the edible part of foods, *Home and Garden Bulletin* No. 72. U.S. Dept. Agriculture. Washington, D.C. Rev. 1981.
[1]All values are for the raw fruits.

able range in the sugar levels found in ripe fruits, from only about 1 percent for avocados to about 61 percent in dates. The types of sugars include fructose, invert sugar (an equal combination of glucose and fructose), sucrose, and glucose, all of which add a sweet taste to the fruits in which they are found.

Much of the structural material of fruits is other types of indigestible carbohydrates, commonly referred to as fiber or roughage. These structural components, so important to the texture of different fruits, occur in differing proportions in the various fruits. Cellulose is one of the key constituents (see Chapter 2), particularly in the dermal cells forming the protective skin in fruits. The vascular cells (those carrying food and water to the parenchyma cells) also contain cellulose in their cell walls. The parenchyma cells are the type of cell comprising most of the edible pulp in fruits, and these also have some cellulose in their walls. In addition to cellulose, hemicelluloses add to the strength of cell walls, particularly in the parenchyma cells. The pectic substances are complex carbohydrates that help to cement the individual cells together in fruits. Changes in pectic substances are responsible in large measure for the change observed in the hard texture of green fruit to the mushiness of very ripe fruit.

Other important constituents in fruits are enzymes and organic acids. The enzymes are of interest because they are responsible for effecting changes in fruits during the ripening process, including softening of the fruit and development of sugar, as well as other flavor components of the ripened fruit. Unfortunately, sometimes enzyme action causes browning on the cut surfaces of fruits. Organic acids are of importance both because of contributions to flavor and to the role they play in preservation techniques, specifically in canning and in making jams and jellies (see Chapter 16).

PIGMENTS

The pigments found in fruits are classified in the same categories discussed in Chapter 2. As is true in vegetables, fruits contain a blending of pigments, and oranges afford an excellent illustration of this. The rind (flavedo) of most oranges shows just a bit of chlorophyll in addition to the characteristic carotenoid pigments that gave this fruit its name. Oranges are susceptible to a process called regreening, in which the chlorophyll may begin to dominate the carotenoids, often causing consumers to think (erroneously) that the regreened oranges are not yet ripe. Other pigments also are found in oranges. The white area (albedo) just under the flavedo contains anthoxanthin pigments, while blood oranges contain anthocyanins in the pulp of the fruit.

Very few vegetables provide examples of anthocyanins, but fruits illustrate the range of anthocyanins clearly. Delphinidin is a blue anthocyanin found in Concord grapes; other fruits run the gamut of potential colors in the anthocyanin group, from the blue of the Concord grape through purples to a bright red. Examples of these pigments are found in Table 3.2.

Table 3.2 Anthocyanin Pigments in Fruits

Anthocyanin Compound	Color	Examples in Fruit
Delphinidin	Blue	Concord grape
Cyanidins	Purple to deep red	Bing cherries, sour cherries, blueberries, black raspberries, boysenberries
Pelargonidin	Red	Strawberries, red raspberries

Although color changes during cooking are not generally a problem in fruit cookery, there is considerable potential for problems when fruits containing anthocyanins are combined. The addition of an acidic juice such as lemon juice to an anthocyanin-containing fruit juice will heighten the red, which is usually acceptable. However, the juices containing anthocyanins may become blue when they come in contact with hard water or are otherwise brought to an alkaline reaction. The pigments in strawberries and cranberries are quite stable, which makes them useful as ingredients when a red color needs to be maintained in a fruit juice mixture.

Flavonoids (both anthocyanins and anthoxanthins) are capable of complexing readily with metal ions, causing undesirable color changes. Thus, fruits containing these pigments should be kept away from aluminum, iron, or tin.

NUTRITIVE VALUE

People have long been aware that fruits are important sources of nutrients, even though the specific nutrients in individual fruits may have remained a mystery to them. As can be seen in Table 3.1, some of the yellow fruits (apricots, peaches, and cantaloupe, for example) are excellent potential sources of vitamin A because they contain carotenes, which can be converted to vitamin A in the body. Several other fruits are outstanding sources of ascorbic acid or vitamin C, and most fruits contain at least some of this vitamin. Citrus fruits are abundant year-round and are rich sources of vitamin C, while many of the tropical and subtropical fruits and also berries afford other outstanding sources of this vitamin.

Fruits also contribute toward the day's total intake of minerals. Dried fruits are relatively good sources of iron. Calcium is provided by oranges in particular, with other fruits contributing minor amounts of calcium. Even oranges, however, are useful only in supplementing the calcium from milk, for their calcium levels are inadequate as the primary source of this key mineral.

The need for fiber to help promote motility of the digestive tract is extremely important from the standpoint of good health, even though the fiber is not actually absorbed into the body and used in the ways that nutrients are. Therefore, fruits are important foods in the diet, for they provide excellent amounts of hemicelluloses, pectic substances, and cellulose, all of which are components of fiber.

Fruits also are a good source of energy because of the sugar they provide in the diet. The actual contributions of the various fruits include a range of nutrients, but fruits, as a group, are important nutritionally primarily for their contributions of vitamins A and C, supplemental contributions of calcium and other minerals and vitamins, as well as their excellent fiber content.

MARKETING ASPECTS

Since fruits often are produced far from the markets where they will be purchased by consumers, shipping must be done quickly and economically to bring products to stores while they are still of excellent quality and high in nutrients. To do this, refrigerated trucks and railroad cars are utilized. Control of humidity within vehicles and storage areas is vital, for too much moisture favors mold formation and too little causes dehydration and shriveling.

Deterioration during storage and shipping of fruits also can be retarded by controlling the carbon dioxide level in the storage area, for carbon dioxide gas inhibits yeast and mold growth as well as retards the ripening process. Unfortunately, too much carbon dioxide promotes the formation of alcohol in apples and pears. Use of carbon dioxide in storing fruits is not limited to commercial operations. Plastic containers especially designed with a tight cover and small openings to permit some entry of oxygen and to regulate moisture level are available for home use to aid consumers in controlling the ripening of immature fruits. In these containers, the carbon dioxide is produced by the fruits themselves and is trapped in the closed container, a system that functions rather efficiently.

Apples are a particularly good fruit for long-term storage, due in part to their excellent dermal layer. Most other fruits have to move through the marketing chain comparatively rapidly after harvest, which results in close to a glut, with low prices at some times and only ''greenhouse'' products at astronomical prices during the remainder of the year.

Grapes are an especially perishable commodity because of their tendency to promote mold growth during shipping and storage. The use of sulfur dioxide gas in the storage environment is an aid in reducing problems due to mold.

Bananas and avocados are fruits that will continue to ripen after they have been harvested. This allows them to be picked green and shipped while they are still quite firm, thus reducing the damage incurred during shipping. On the other hand, pineapple, citrus fruits, and some melons (cantaloupe and Persian melons) fail to develop their full flavor potential when picked before becoming ripe.

Ethylene gas is a valuable adjunct to the marketing of some fruits because of its ability to promote ripening and the resultant color changes in fruits. Chlorophyll can be decomposed to reveal the desired carotenoid pigments in

Bananas can be ripened on the tree in Thailand because they are so close to the market, but bananas in the markets in the United States have been picked green and then ripened artificially because they have to be transported from Central and South America.

oranges when ethylene gas is present in the storage atmosphere. Although the flavor is not changed in these oranges, the enhanced color makes these oranges very marketable. Oranges, bananas, and a few other fruits are ripened in storage by the use of ethylene gas.

Selection of fruit is based to a large extent on the visual message provided by the color and appearance. Since 1922, citrus fruits have been waxed to enhance their appearance. Carnauba wax (from palm fronds) is applied in an extremely thin film to apples, peaches, cantaloupe, and some other fresh produce in such a small amount that a gallon of the wax will coat 5 tons of apples! In the case of oranges about six drops are applied to each orange, then buffed with brushes to add to the eye appeal. This wax also serves as a protective coating to reduce moisture loss and resultant shriveling and as a shield against decay. Thus, a wax coating helps to extend the period when quality of the fruit will be high.

SELECTION

Fresh Fruits

When buying fresh fruits, select those that are fresh and plump, free from bruises and blemishes, at the desired degree of ripeness, and an appropriate size for the intended use of the fruit. Freshness can be seen visually by looking for plump, rather than limp fruits. If at all possible, avoid blemishes and bruises, for these are the areas in which spoilage begins during storage.

When fruits are available in more than one size, the larger size almost invariably will be appreciably higher in price than the smaller one. If the fruit is to be displayed in an arrangement or to be served whole or as a garnish, the large size may be worth the price, but the small size often can be used very satisfactorily in recipes at a significant saving.

Fruits often are graded according to federal grading standards, although consumers usually do not see the designation. The Agricultural Marketing Service of the U.S. Department of Agriculture is the agency charged with grading standards for fruits. At the wholesale level, grade is an important determinant of price, which ultimately is passed on to consumers. The federal grades established by the Agricultural Marketing Service are

U.S. Fancy   Premium produce.

U.S. No. 1   Chief trading grade.

U.S. No. 2   Intermediate quality range.

U.S. No. 3   Lowest commercially useful grade.

Often only two of these grades may be used when a specific fruit is being graded. Any fruit undergoing federal grading will have its container marked with an official USDA grade shield or a label stating "Packed Under Continuous Inspection of the U.S. Department of Agriculture" or else "Packed by _____ Under Continuous Federal-State Inspection."

Since customers are unable to see the grade designations when they are shopping, they need to be able to make wise decisions unaided by grading. Table 3.3 provides some information regarding factors to note when making selections in the market. By making mental notes regarding the quality of fruits selected, shoppers can gradually build up an ability to select excellent fruits.

Table 3.3   A Guide to the Selection of Fresh Fruits

Fruit	Desirable Qualities	Characteristics to Avoid
Apples	Firm; crisp; good color for the variety of apple	Overripe; soft and mealy; bruises
Apricots	Uniform, golden color; plump; juicy; barely soft	Soft or mushy; hard; pale yellow or green color
Avocados	Firm if to be used later, slightly soft for immediate use	Dark patches; cracked surfaces
Bananas	Firm; bright color; free from bruises	Bruises; discolored skin
Blueberries	Dark blue with silver bloom; plump; firm; uniform size	Soft, spoiled berries; stems and leaves
Cherries	Dark color in sweet cherries; bright red in pie cherries; glossy; plump	Shriveling; dull appearance; soft, leaking fruit; mold
Cranberries	Plump and firm; lustrous; red color	Soft and spongy; leaking
Grapefruit	Firm; well-shaped; heavy for size; thin skin indicates juiciness	Soft and discolored areas; mold

Table 3.3 (*Continued*)

Fruit	Desirable Qualities	Characteristics to Avoid
Grapes	Plump; yellowish cast for white or green grapes; red color predominating for red grapes; stems green and pliable	Soft, wrinkled; bleached area around stem; leaking
Lemons	Rich yellow color (pale or greenish yellow for higher acid content); firm; heavy	Hard or shriveling; soft spots; mold; dark yellow
Limes	Glossy skin; heavy	Dry skin; decay
Melons:		
Cantaloupes	Smooth area where stem grew; bold netting; yellowish cast to skin	Soft rind; bruises
Casaba	Yellow rind; slight softening at blossom end	Decayed spots
Cranshaw	Deep golden rind; very slight softening of rind; good aroma	Decayed spots
Honeydew	Faint odor; yellow to creamy rind; slight softening at blossom end	Greenish-white rind; hard and smooth skin
Persian	Same as cantaloupe	Same as cantaloupe
Watermelon	Slightly dull rind; creamy color on the underside	Cracks; dull rind
Nectarines	Slight softening; rich color; plump	Hard or shriveled; soft
Oranges	Firm and heavy; bright, fresh skin either orange or green tint	Light weight; dull skin; mold
Peaches	Slightly soft; yellow color between the red areas	Very firm, hard; green ground color; very soft; decay
Pears	Firm, but beginning to soften; good color for variety (Bartlett, yellow; Anjou or Comice, light green to yellow green; Bosc, greenish-yellow with skin russeting; Winter Nellis, medium to light green)	Weakening around the stem; shriveled; spots
Pineapples	Good pineapple odor; green to yellow color; spike leaves easily removed; heavy for size	Bruises; poor odor; sunken or slightly pointed pips
Plums	Good color for variety; fairly firm	Hard or shriveled; poor color; leaking
Raspberries	Good color for kind; plump; clean; no caps	Mold; leaking
Strawberries	Good red color; lustrous; clean; cap stem attached	Mold; leaking; large seeds
Tangerines	Bright lustrous skin	Mold; soft spots

Sometimes choices must be made between varieties as well as within varieties of a fruit. Choice of the right variety depends upon the intended end use for the fruit. For example, Bing cherries and sour (pie) cherries may be available at the same time. The Bing cherries will give particularly good results in salads or simply for eating, while the sour cherries are excellent for making cherry pie.

Several varieties of tangerines may also be on the market at the same time. If the fruit is being chosen for a child's school lunch, the few seeds and

Table 3.4 Suggested Uses for Selected Varieties of Apples

Variety	Fresh and Salads	Pie	Sauce and Coddling	Baking
Delicious				
Red	Excellent			
Golden	Excellent	Excellent	Good	Good
Gravenstein	Good	Good	Good	Good
Grimes golden		Good		
Jonathan	Good	Good	Excellent	Good
McIntosh	Excellent	Excellent	Good	
Newtown pippin	Good	Excellent	Good	Good
Northern spy				Good
Rhode Island greening		Excellent	Excellent	Good
Rome beauty	Good	Good	Excellent	Excellent
Wealthy	Good	Good	Good	
Winesap	Excellent	Good	Excellent	Good
Yellow transparent		Excellent	Good	

easy peeling typical of the Satsuma Mandarin would make this a good choice, while the difficulty of peeling the Orlando Tangelo and removing its many seeds would make this a poor choice. Of the tangerines, the Dancy is the variety found most commonly; its easy peeling and tart flavor help to compensate for the annoyance of removing so many seeds.

Apples found in the market vary in varieties greatly from one part of the country to another, and new varieties continue to be developed by researchers. Some varieties are particularly well suited to eating raw and in salads, while others may be used to good advantage in such cooked preparations as sauce, coddling or poaching, baking, and in pies or other baked products. Table 3.4 provides a partial guide to the use of various apples in food preparation.

The seasonal nature of many fruits limits their use in the fresh form to a rather short time period. Knowledge of the usual times when each of the fruits may be expected to be available (Table 3.5) is an aid in menu planning. Generally, the quality of fruits will be the best and the price will be lowest when the fresh fruit is at the height of its season. At such times, generous use of fresh fruits can add considerable interest as well as nutrients to the diet. Of course, many fruits can be obtained as the frozen, canned, or dried products at any time of the year.

Canned and Frozen Fruit

The Agricultural Marketing Service of the U.S. Department of Agriculture is responsible for the federal standards used for grading frozen and canned fruits. The top grade, U.S. Grade A or Fancy, is characterized by fruit of excel-

Table 3.5 A Guide to Average Monthly Availability of Fresh Fruits

Fruit	Jan (%)	Feb (%)	Mar (%)	Apr (%)	May (%)	Jun (%)	Jul (%)	Aug (%)	Sep (%)	Oct (%)	Nov (%)	Dec (%)
Apples	10	9	10	9	8	5	3	4	9	12	10	11
Apricots	—	—	—	—	11	60	27	2	—	—	—	—
Avocados	9	7	8	8	8	7	7	8	7	9	11	11
Bananas	8	8	10	9	8	8	7	7	7	8	9	9
Berries	—	—	—	—	2	30	39	14	8	5	2	—
Blueberries[1]	—	—	—	—	1	26	43	28	2	—	—	—
Cantaloupes	—	—	3	4	10	20	25	22	11	4	1	—
Cherries	—	—	—	—	11	41	43	5	—	—	—	—
Cranberries	—	—	—	—	—	—	—	—	8	26	48	18
Grapefruit	12	12	12	11	10	6	4	3	3	8	10	9
Grapes	4	3	3	3	2	6	11	17	18	15	10	8
Honeydews	1	1	3	5	7	12	10	20	22	15	3	1
Lemons	8	6	8	8	9	11	11	9	7	8	7	8
Limes	6	4	5	5	9	12	13	12	10	8	7	9
Mangos	—	1	3	6	17	23	28	17	4	1	—	—
Nectarines	—	—	—	—	1	19	36	30	12	—	—	—
Oranges	11	12	13	11	10	7	5	4	4	5	8	10
Papayas	6	6	6	7	10	10	9	8	8	10	11	9
Peaches	—	—	—	—	6	17	31	29	15	1	—	—
Pears	7	7	7	6	4	2	4	13	16	17	10	7
Pineapples	7	7	11	10	12	12	9	7	6	5	7	7
Plums–prunes	—	—	—	—	1	15	33	32	15	2	—	—
Strawberries	3	5	8	18	29	16	7	5	4	2	1	2
Tangelos	23	4	—	—	—	—	—	—	—	—	33	39
Tangerines	21	8	7	4	2	—	—	—	—	5	20	32
Watermelons	—	—	1	3	10	28	31	20	5	1	—	—

Source: From *Supply guide—Average monthly availability of fresh fruits and vegetables.* 9th ed. United Fresh Fruit and Vegetable Assoc., Washington, D.C. 1975. Percentages are estimates only because production varies slightly with the seasons.
[1]Mostly raspberries, blackberries, and dewberries.

lent color, uniform size, optimum ripeness, and few or no blemishes. When canned or frozen fruits are being used in fruit plates, as a baked or broiled accompaniment to an entree, or served alone as a simple dessert, U.S. Grade A or Fancy is the best choice. In other words, this top grade will provide optimum eye appeal. U.S. Grade B or Choice is used to designate fruit that is somewhat less perfect than fruits in the top category. Fruits in this grade are perfectly fine for use in molded gelatin products and in fruit mixtures where perfect, large pieces are not needed. The lowest grade available to consumers is U.S. Grade C or Standard; such fruits are perfectly wholesome and nourishing, but they will have uneven pieces and occasional blemishes. These are well suited to making sauces, jams, cobblers, or other products where individual pieces are not of great importance.

Consumers are aided in picking frozen and canned fruits because of labeling requirements. This is fortunate, for the packages usually obstruct the view of the fruit inside, which makes grading or other labeling information essential. Required information includes

1. Common or usual name of the fruit.
2. Form (whole, slices, halves, pitted) if not visible in the container.
3. Some fruits must list variety or color.
4. Syrups, sugar, or liquid used in packing. Canned fruits may be packed in syrups of varying viscosities (extra heavy, heavy, light, extra light) or simply in a water pack. Frozen fruits usually are packed in sugar.
5. Net weight of contents in ounces (also in pounds and ounces or pounds and fractions of pounds for containers between 1 and 4 pounds.
6. Ingredients, including spices, flavoring, coloring, and any other additives.
7. Any special type of treatment.
8. Packer's or distributor's name and place of business.

Nutrition labeling is an optional feature unless nutritional claims are made for the product. When nutrition labeling is done, it must conform to federal requirements for such labels. If the fruit has been canned or frozen under continuous inspection by the U.S. Department of Agriculture, the USDA grade shield can be printed on the label.

Gradually, definitions are being established for fruit-containing processed fruit products. For instance, various orange juice products have been defined by the U.S. Department of Agriculture as follows:

Orange juice drink blend   Product containing 70–95 percent orange juice.

Orange juice drink   Product containing 35–70 percent orange juice.

Orange drink   Beverage containing 10–35 percent orange juice.

Orange-flavored drink   Beverage containing more than 0 percent but less than 10 percent orange juice.

Since the various definitions provide a wide range of orange juice, the label must indicate to the nearest 5 percent the percentage of juice actually included in the beverage.

Dried Fruits

Since federal grading standards rarely are applied to dried fruits, selection must usually be based on prior experience and color, if the fruit can be seen through the packaging material. Fruits should be firm, yet pliable. Dried apples usually have a creamy color, which has been retained through the use of a dip in acidic fruit juice or ascorbic acid prior to drying. Similarly, dried pears are treated to help retain the desired, somewhat yellow color. Apricots, peaches, and golden seedless raisins ordinarily are exposed to sulfur dioxide

Raisins being made by drying grapes in the sun.

fumes while drying so that the desired orange color will not give way to a drab brown. Raisins, prunes, and currants become a deep brown when they are being dried. Regardless of the type of dried fruit, prices in the market parallel the size of the fruit, with prices increasing as the fruits progress from small to medium, to large, and extra large.

Sun drying has been the method for preserving certain fruits for many, many years, but newer methods have evolved and now include freeze-drying, dehydration, and vacuum drying. The moisture levels, regardless of the technique used, are brought to below 25 percent. The exception to this practice is in the case of prunes, some of which are marketed in special packages that inhibit mold development even though the moisture level is above 25 percent. This comparatively high moisture level results in prunes that are soft and pliable, having the advantage of being easily rehydrated by stewing.

STORAGE IN THE HOME

The length of time fruits can be stored successfully in the home depends on the type of fruit and the condition when purchased. When fruits are ripe at the time they are purchased, they need to be consumed as soon as possible and stored at the appropriate temperature, usually in the refrigerator until served. Berries of all types are particularly susceptible to spoilage, necessitating a short storage period. Because of their fragile nature and their problems with mold formation, berries should be sorted before they are stored to be sure that any spoiling berries are removed. If this is not done, the spoiled areas will promote spoilage throughout the container in a fairly efficient and wasteful manner. Since high moisture promotes molding, berries are not washed when being prepared for storage; instead, they are washed when being prepared and served. Other fruits only need to be inspected before being stored if they were not checked when being selected at the market.

Some tropical and subtropical fruits retain their quality better if they are stored at a cool room temperature rather than refrigerated. Bananas, pineapples, and melons are best held at room temperature unless they are fully ripe. Then they need to be refrigerated to retard the ripening process. However, banana skins will develop a startling brown color at refrigerator temperatures. Citrus fruits ideally are stored just above the temperature in the refrigerator, a difficult condition to provide in most homes. Consequently, refrigerator storage often may be necessary.

Peaches, plums, pears, and similar fruits frequently are rather green when purchased at the store. Such fruits should be kept at room temperature until they achieve the desired degree of ripening. Then, they should be held in the refrigerator and used rather soon.

When fruits are likely to be eaten without being washed after they are taken from the refrigerator, the fruit should be washed and wiped dry before being placed in the refrigerator. Exceptions to this recommendation are berries, cherries, and grapes, for these are fruits that tend to mold even during refrigerator storage if their moisture content is high. Fresh fruits in the refrigerator should be in the hydrator drawers where the small volume of cold air limits the moisture lost from the fruits and helps to retain high quality in the fruit. Dried fruits, because they should have a low moisture content, can be stored in the main compartment of the refrigerator. Unopened canned fruits retain their nutrient levels best if stored in a dark, cool cabinet for less than a year.

PREPARATION

Raw Fruits

Preparation of fresh fruits often is as simple as washing the fruit and serving it raw (whole or sliced) or in salads or as a dessert. Both appearance and nutritive value need to be kept in mind when preparing raw fruits. In particular, attention should be directed to maximizing vitamin C levels in fruits. Fortunately, the acidic nature of most fruits is helpful in retaining vitamin C. The key problems to remember in trying to keep vitamin C levels high are the possibility of oxidation by exposing cut surfaces to air and loss by placing in water for soaking. Fruits that are good sources of vitamin C should be prepared as close to serving time as possible and by coating cut surfaces with a solution of ascorbic acid or an acidic fruit juice (lemon, orange, or pineapple work well). These same practices will help to retain vitamin A levels, too.

Fruits have tremendous potential for beautifying a meal when served and arranged artistically. Attractive slices of fruit arranged in a pleasing style may be slightly less nourishing than uncut fruit, but the appealing appearance may tempt people to eat more of it than they would otherwise, with the result

With the aid of a melon baller, interest can be added to fruit combinations.

that more nutrients actually are consumed. For example, an orange that has been sliced and arranged carefully on a plate is more approachable than is an unpeeled orange. Melon balls, pineapple chunks, ellipses of bananas, and peach slices are some of the variety of shapes available when fruits are cut creatively. The design element of line can be very important when arranging fruits. The bit of extra time required for arranging fruits is more than compensated for by the beauty created.

Browning of cut surfaces can be a problem in certain raw fruits, such as apples, peaches, and bananas. This color change is caused by action of oxidative enzymes, especially phenol oxidase, on catechin, leucoanthocyanins, and some other flavonoid compounds. Since this change requires oxygen, the enzyme cannot cause this oxidative change unless the fruit has been cut to expose the cut surfaces to air. The key to avoiding this problem is to block air from the surface. This can be done by dipping the cut fruit into an acidic fruit juice or by sprinkling some granulated sugar on the surface and stirring to spread the sugar uniformly. The sugar draws some water from the cut cells to make a sugar solution on the surface, thus effectively blocking air from the fruit itself. A solution of ascorbic acid is yet another means of preventing browning, in this case by providing ascorbic acid to interact with oxygen and protect the pigments. Browning problems also are reduced by keeping fruit chilled in the refrigerator between the time that it is cut and service actually occurs.

Simmered Fruits

Poaching Simmering a food in water or other liquid just below boiling until the food is tender.

Fruits can be heated gently in water to tenderize them. When fruits are heated in water just below boiling, they are said to be poached, simmered, or stewed. *Poaching* softens the cellulose and other fibrous tissue, modifies the flavor, and halts enzymatic browning. Usually, a limited amount of water is heated to just below boiling in a covered pan containing the fruit. By controlling the heat at simmering, the agitation associated with active boiling is avoided, and the shape of the fruit is retained rather well. Retention of the delicate flavors of fruits is aided by keeping the cover on throughout the simmering period, thus reducing loss of volatile flavoring components.

Apples, pears, and peaches are well suited to simmering without losing their shape. Cranberries and rhubarb also are simmered to make sauces, but their structures are broken, and their shapes become quite blurred during cooking. Dried fruits frequently are simmered to tenderize and rehydrate them before being served or used in other recipes. Prunes are done when the pit may be removed easily; other dried fruits are ready when they can be cut with ease. The actual simmering time required depends on the amount of soaking done prior to simmering, the size of the pieces of fruit, and the amount of cut surface exposed. By soaking dried fruit in warm water for an hour before simmering is begun, the simmering time is shortened. Dried fruits with cut surfaces rehydrate more quickly than do whole fruits because the cut cells provide easy entry into the fruit.

Other Preparation Procedures

A few fruits, notably apples and pears, are well suited to baking, their skins serving as an adequate protection against drying while baking. A considerable amount of pressure can build up in these fruits because of the conversion of some of the juice to steam during baking. To avoid a possible explosion of the fruit, a narrow strip of skin should be peeled around the equator of the fruit. Considerable time can be saved by microwaving rather than baking these fruits. Since browning is not necessary, the lack of browning typical of microwave oven cookery does not present a problem. However, the rapid heating of the fruit is very effective in retaining a good skin color and excellent fresh fruit flavor.

Broiling is a quick way of adding interest to fruits. Grapefruit halves can be broiled, sometimes with a light sprinkling of brown sugar for color and fla-

Osmotic Pressure The pressure exerted to move water in or out of cells to equalize the concentration of solute in the cell and in the surrounding medium.

Coddling Simmering of fruit in a sugar syrup.

SCIENCE NOTE: OSMOTIC PRESSURE

Fruits have cells with walls that are semipermeable membranes, that is, water can pass in and out of the cells, but other substances are blocked by the wall. Equilibrium exists when the concentration of solute is the same on both sides of the cell membrane. However, a change in the concentration of the solute in the solvent outside the cells can cause water to move in or out of the cell, depending on the external concentration. The pressure that builds up to attempt to equalize the concentrations is termed *osmotic pressure*.

Fruits naturally contain sugars dissolved in the water inside the cells. If apples or other fruits are placed in water and simmered, water will begin to move into the cells in an attempt to dilute the sugar present in the cells. The osmotic pressure created in this circumstance can cause so much water to go into the cells that some of the walls will rupture, creating a mushy texture. This is desirable in making a pureed product, such as applesauce. And this is the reason that sugar is added to taste only after the desired mushy texture has been achieved when making applesauce. The rehydration of dried fruits is also promoted by simmering them in water without adding sugar.

The reverse may also occur with *coddling* fruits, or simmering of fruits in a sugar syrup. The aim is to have just enough sugar in the cooking syrup to approximate the level in the cells. Then water will pass into and out of the cells in equilibrium, but will not build up excess water in the cells. A very slightly lower level of sugar in the cooking syrup will cause a small amount of water to be drawn into the cells of the coddled fruit, giving just a suggestion of plumpness. With prolonged use of the sugar syrup, the loss of water will begin to raise the relative concentration of sugar, and water may start to move from the fruit into the sugar syrup to attempt to equalize the two solutions. When this happens, the fruit being coddled will start to look wizened due to loss of water from the cells. By simply adding a bit of water to the sugar syrup, water can once again be moved back into the fruit cells.

The coating of berries or other fruit with some dry sugar can have a dehydrating effect on the fruit. Again, osmotic pressure develops because of the high concentration of sugar outside the cells, which draws water out of cells. Evidence of this is seen when strawberries are allowed to sit for a while after sugar has been added. Juice from the berries will begin to collect in the bottom of the bowl, and the berries will begin to droop. Thus, berries should be sweetened just before they are served.

---

vor, to make a special breakfast treat or a light dessert after a heavy meal. Canned or fresh peach halves also broil quickly to provide eye-catching garnishes for a meat platter.

Frying is yet another means of preparing fruits. Apple rings can be fried in shallow fat to provide a tasty complement to pork chops. Fruit slices can be dipped in a medium batter and then fried in deep fat at 375°F until a golden brown and served hot with powdered sugar or syrup.

Fruits are featured in many different recipes for baked products. Some quick breads gain their distinctive flavors from fruits incorporated in their batters. Cranberry, blueberry, orange, date, prune, apple, fig, and lemon muffins are some of the variations possible with a basic muffin recipe. Special breads may be made using various mashed, stewed, canned, frozen, fresh, grated, or candied fruits. Pies may have a sweetened filling made from fresh, canned, or frozen fruits thickened with starch. Grated citrus rinds are excellent flavoring substances for meringue and chiffon pies when care is taken to grate only the flavorful and colorful flavedo of the rind. Cream pies often are made with a layer of various fruits, such as bananas, peaches, or strawberries.

Fruits combine well with other foods to make special desserts. For instance, sliced fruits may be served with a cream pudding, in combination with yogurt, with ice cream in sundaes or parfaits, or even in a cheese cake. Cherries jubilee, peach melba, fruit tortes, fruit-filled angel food cakes, and fruit souffles are other examples of the excitement that fruits can bring to a dessert. Of course, fruit-flavored ice creams and sherbets also have become very popular uses of fruits.

Preparation Using Canned and Frozen Fruits

Canned fruits are used frequently in food preparation because of their convenience and availability throughout the year. Many recipes are based on the use of canned fruits, particularly for the preparation of pies and other desserts. For success in preparing these recipes, it is important to drain the fruit well, using only the amount of juice specified in the recipe to avoid too thin a product. Extra juice can be reserved for some other use or discarded.

When pineapple is an ingredient in gelatin products, it is important to use only canned pineapple, never the fresh or frozen fruit. The heat treatment in the canning of pineapple is sufficient to destroy the proteolytic enzyme in pineapple. However, the enzyme is active in fresh or frozen pineapple; the result is a gelatin mixture that simply will not set.

Frozen fruits retain the bright color and bright flavors of their fresh counterparts, but their texture is altered significantly by freezing because the ice crystals break cell walls. If frozen fruits can be served while they still have a few ice crystals, the texture will be more appealing than when the fruit has thawed to the point where the pieces are flabby. If only the pieces of fruit are to be used in a recipe, the thawed juice needs to be drained before the fruit is used. Otherwise, there will be too much liquid in the recipe.

SUMMARY

The various classifications of fruits include berries, citrus fruits, drupes, grapes, melons, pomes, and tropical and subtropical fruits. Characteristically, fruits are very high in water and contain a moderate amount of carbohydrate, usually in the form of sugars and fiber. In addition to fiber, fruits are rich sources of vitamins A and C and of modest amounts of other vitamins and minerals, particularly of calcium and iron.

The cell walls in fruits are abundant sources of cellulose, hemicelluloses, and pectic substances (which often occur in the intercellular spaces). Fruits have a dermal layer surrounding their vascular cells and parenchyma cells. The parenchyma cells have chloroplasts, chromoplasts, and leucoplasts containing pigments and starch in the cytoplasm. Their large vacuole is the site of the flavonoid pigments, sugars, acids, and many other flavoring substances, as well as water.

Careful control of temperature and atmosphere is necessary during the marketing of fruit because fruits are very susceptible to spoilage. When selecting fresh fruits, blemishes and spoiled areas are to be avoided. Each type of fruit has certain desirable qualities to guide consumers in selection, and knowledge of these qualities is important since grade designations are not ordinarily available to consumers. The best variety for the type of preparation being planned should be selected when making choices among apples and other fruits with more than one variety on the market at the same time. Canned and frozen products can be selected by reading labels carefully and also remembering previous experience with particular brands.

In the home, temperature control is required to maintain the fruit at its optimum until it is served. Usually, refrigerator storage is recommended, although a few fruits, such as bananas, should be stored in a cool room.

Preparation of raw fruit requires attention to washing and then cutting and arranging close to serving time to avoid loss of vitamin C and the possible problem of enzymatic browning. Always simmer fruits; boiling should be avoided because of its destructive effect on the shape of the fruits. The level of sugar in the cooking liquid should be appropriate to the type of preparation being done so that osmotic pressure will help to achieve the desired texture. Baking, broiling, and frying are other cookery techniques appropriate to the preparation of some fruits. Many fruits also can be used in baked products of many types, as well as in elegant dessert combinations. Canned and frozen fruits can be used in some recipes satisfactorily if they are drained to avoid getting extra juice in them. The texture in frozen fruits usually is quite soft and mushy unless they are served while some ice crystals are still present. Canned pineapple can be used satisfactorily in gelatin products, but fresh and frozen pineapple should be avoided because gelatin will not set when these forms are used.

Selected References

Abers, J. E. and R. E. Wrolstad. Causative factors of color deterioration in strawberry preserves during processing and storage. *J. Food Sci.* 44: 75. 1979.

Agricultural Marketing Service. *Grade Names for Fresh Fruits and Vegetables*. U.S. Dept. Agriculture. Washington, D.C. 1976.

American Home Economics Association. *Handbook of Food Preparation*. AHEA. Washington, D.C. 8th ed. 1980.

Bartley, I. M. and M. Knee. Chemistry of textural changes in fruit during storage. *Food Chem.* 9: 47. 1982.

Baruah, P. and T. Swain. Action of potato phenolase on flavonoid compounds. *J. Sci Food Agr. 10*: 125. 1959.

Bate-Smith, E. C. Flavonoid compounds in foods. *Adv. Food Res. 5*: 261. 1954.

Consumer and Food Economics Institute. Fruits in Family meals. *Home and Garden Bulletin* No. 125. U.S. Dept. Agriculture. Washington, D.C. 1975.

Charley, H. Fruits and vegetables. In *Food Theory and Application*, Eds. P. Paul and H. Palmer. John Wiley. New York. 1972. P. 306.

Fennema, O. Loss of vitamins in fresh and frozen foods. *Food Tech. 31(12)*: 32. 1977.

Haard, N. F. Postharvest physiology and biochemistry of fruits and vegetables. *J. Chem. Ed. 61(4)*: 277. 1984.

Labuza, T. P. Drying food: technology improves on the sun. *Food Tech. 30(6)*: 37. 1976.

Luh, B. S. et al. Textural changes in canned apricots in the presence of mold polygalacturonase. *J. Food Sci. 43*: 713. 1978.

McWilliams, M. and H. Paine. *Modern Food Preservation*. Plycon. Redondo Beach, Calif. 1977.

Moyer, W. C. *Buying Guide*. Blue Goose, Fullerton, Calif. 4th ed. 1971.

Palmer, J. K. Enzyme reactions and acceptability of plant foods. *J. Chem. Ed. 61(4)*: 284. 1984.

Peterkin, B. and C. Cromwell. Your Money's Worth in foods. *Home and Garden Bulletin* No. 183. U.S. Dept. Agriculture. Washington, D.C. 1977.

Vettel, R. and C. H. Davis. Storing Perishable Foods in the Home. *Home and Garden Bulletin* No. 78. U.S. Dept. Agriculture. Washington, D.C. 1973.

Williams, M. and G. Hrazdina. Anthocyanins as food colorants: effects of pH on the formation of anthocyanin-rutin complexes. *J. Food Sci. 44*: 66. 1979.

Study Questions

1. Visit a grocery store to see what fresh fruits are available. How does the cost of the fresh fruits compare with their canned and frozen counterparts?

2. How does the cost of reconstituted frozen orange juice concentrate compare with fresh orange juice and with a powdered imitation orange drink?

3. How are the following fruits classified: oranges, avocados, strawberries, kumquats, apricots, plums, apples, nectarines, tangerines, Thompson seedless grapes, cranberries, pears, cantaloupe, quince, pomegranates, currants, Tokay grapes, bananas, and pineapple. When is each of these usually available?

4. How can osmotic pressure be controlled to aid in making applesauce and coddled apples?

5. Why is ascorbic acid added to some fruits?

P. Antsen, detail from "Market Scene, Rotterdam." Museum Boymans van Beuningen/Kavaler/Art Resource.

CHAPTER 4

SALADS AND SALAD DRESSINGS

THE NUTRITIONAL PERSPECTIVE

The abundance of salad bars in restaurants of many different types throughout the country is ample evidence of the interest in salads to U.S. consumers of all ages. Salads seem to have become as important to Americans as pastas are to the Italian cuisine. Versatility is the keystone of salad-making, for a salad can be created out of practically any ingredients to fit any occasion. Recipes are legion, but creativity is the most vital ingredient.

Salad variations can be created to suit any occasion and any temperature or weather condition; only imagination sets limits on what a salad can and will be. Cookbooks can be used to provide suggestions, but salad time well may be adventure time to experienced or inexperienced cooks alike. Salads may be the means of adding variety to the temperatures and textures in a meal. A hot potato salad provides a warm and hearty touch to a meal; a frozen fruit or gelatin salad will bring a cooling touch to the palate when a spicy meal is served. Textures often are crisp in salads, but combinations of ingredients afford a variety of textures even within the salad itself. For example, the use of crisp celery slices in a shrimp salad provides a sharp textural contrast. Gelatin salads feel smooth, cold, and slippery in the mouth, presenting quite a contrast to the other textures in a meal.

The spectrum of foods used in salads keeps expanding. A few years ago, alfalfa sprouts and fresh slices of zucchini would rarely have been found in salads, yet they are frequent salad ingredients today. In fact, many vegetables that formerly would always be cooked before serving now are being added to salads in raw, crisp pieces. Similarly, the range of dressings used on salads has increased remarkably.

Specifics regarding the nutritional value of salads cannot be listed because salads are so variable in their ingredients. Frequently, salads are excellent sources of vitamins and minerals. Some salads—potato and pasta salads, for example—are good sources of carbohydrate, while others containing fish, meat, eggs, or cheese are good sources of protein. If a large amount of dressing is served on a salad, the salad probably will be high in fat, whereas salads with little or no dressing generally provide almost no fat. Fiber is often abundant in salads.

The Basic Four, discussed in Chapter 18, is also a useful way of looking at the range of ingredients that may be found in various salads. In fact, ingredients from each of the four groups often are major components of salads:

Milk and dairy products Cheeses of many types and sometimes yogurt.

Meats and meat alternatives Beef, pork, ham, chicken, turkey, fish, eggs, legumes, and nuts.

Fruits and vegetables Practically any fruits and vegetables.

Breads and cereals Macaroni and other pastas, croutons.

Because of this representative use of foods from all of the food groups in making salads, it is perfectly possible to plan a large salad to serve as the main course of a meal, providing about a third of the day's recommended nutrient intake, as well as a desirable amount of fiber.

Fruits and vegetables are frequently the main ingredients in salads, but tuna fish or other food high in protein from the category of meats and meat alternatives, cheese from the milk and dairy products, and pastas or croutons also are popular salad components to help round out the Basic Four at a meal.

PLANNING SALADS

Role in the Meal

The plan for a salad begins with deciding on its role in the meal. Is it to be a bit of interest on the main plate of the meal or an accompaniment salad on a separate plate? Will it be served as an independent course or even as the main course for a luncheon? Is it to serve as the dessert for a meal? All of these are possibilities, depending on the total menu plan.

Once the role in the menu has been identified, certain aspects of planning the salad will be clarified. For example, an appetizer salad ideally will be a conservative size to whet rather than sate appetites; however, a salad for a main course must be much larger and give more satiety value (a satisfied feeling). Accompaniment salads can vary in size, depending on the remainder of the menu plan. A large dinner will be complemented by a small salad, whereas a light entree requires a somewhat hearty salad. After the role of the salad, its size, and its satiety value have been defined, the specific plans for ingredients and their combination can be made.

Arrangement and Shape

All food has the potential for beauty, but salads offer the greatest opportunity to create artistic and tempting arrangements. Care given to making attractive salads can pay real dividends; a salad with asparagus spears loses its appeal when the stalks are jumbled like fallen logs in a storm-swept forest. On the other hand, these same spears become a tempting unit when they are aligned neatly as a center of interest for a vegetable salad. This same attention should be given whether arranging individual salads or a buffet salad platter. Balance between various parts of the arrangement is necessary, along with a definite center of interest. A frame of salad greens often adds a unifying component to provide the diner with a truly beautiful and tempting salad.

When arranging salads, be sure to use a plate or bowl large enough to hold the salad comfortably. Greens hanging over the edge of the plate make a salad look poorly prepared and disheveled. If the salad is arranged so precariously that removal of a single piece appears to be tempting gravity, diners will have trouble approaching the salad with enthusiasm for fear that the whole arrangement may slide right off the plate.

Designs in salad arrangements can be orderly, but abstract. Some people approach salad making with the air of a serious painter. When a pear half and some added decoration are merged to create a rabbit or peach halves end up making a "snowman" salad, children may be delighted, but many adults will not applaud. The anticipated design preferences of the people who will be eating the salad should serve as the guide to the design approach to use.

Color

Salads have the potential of providing a wonderful, bright touch of color in a meal. By developing an awareness of color and the potential of various ingredients for heightening color interest and harmony, truly beautiful salads can be created. Sometimes the use of color may be understated, as is the case when a mixed green salad is made by drawing upon the full spectrum of greens, from perhaps the deep green of spinach or romaine, the medium to almost yellow green of butter lettuce, to the rather light green of iceberg lettuce. A sharp contrast is a colorful tossed salad made with not only a variety of greens, but also cherry tomatoes, slivers of red cabbage, chopped green onions, radish slices, and bits of celery. A Waldorf salad can lack color if the apples are pared, but the use of yellow-skinned Golden Delicious and bright red of Red Delicious apples cut into cubes sporting their colorful skins and accented by Flame Tokay grapes will brighten any meal.

Flavor

The flavors provided by a salad need to combine well and enhance the total flavor impression of a meal. An accompaniment salad with some julienne strips of a cheese containing a touch of hot peppers can provide some zip to a bland meal; the saltiness of a ham dinner may be offset by serving a fruit-filled gelatin salad.

The ingredients should combine to provide a pleasing impression of the flavor of the salad. A touch of green pepper cut into a cole slaw does wonders in heightening the flavor of the cabbage, whereas the addition of cauliflower pieces is of little value in enhancing the flavor of the salad. Skillful addition of herbs and spices are other ways of adding flavor highlights. Celery seed, dill weed, and mustard are but a few of the possibilities in the spice rack. For instance, celery seed and mustard, when augmented with diced fresh onion, add flavor excitement to a potato salad.

Texture

A variety of textures within a salad can be very helpful in creating an appealing salad. Crisp and soft textures combine well. The comparatively soft texture of tuna fish contrasts with textural accents of crispness provided by diced fresh celery and green pepper. The softness of a tomato wedge complements the crispness of the greens in a tossed salad.

Excitement in texture, flavor, and color is the result of creating an artistic salad featuring fresh spinach accented with red onion rings, rounds of fresh zucchini, thin slices of mushrooms, and sections of canned mandarin oranges.

The texture of other foods in the meal also needs to be considered when planning a salad. A meal of mashed potatoes, baked fish, and sliced avocado certainly provides a monotonous texture. This menu could be improved by substituting a crisp vegetable salad for the avocado. On the other hand, crisp fried chicken would be a pleasing contrast to the avocado salad. Many different approaches are available; the important point is to consider the texture of both the salad alone and the salad with the rest of the meal.

TYPES OF SALADS

Fruit Salads

The sweetness of fruits makes fruit salads excellent choices when the salad is to serve as a dessert, though fruit salads can be used as the main course of a luncheon or as an accompaniment to the main course. A large, dramatic platter of fruit can be the salad for a buffet meal. Even for small family dinners, a modest array of fruits can be combined to make a very pleasing salad. By cutting fruits into shapes that can be arranged artistically, individual fruit salads can gain considerable appeal. Any cutting should be done to enhance the appearance of the fruit and accent the natural beauty of its line. When fruit is cut into quite small, nondescript cubes, much of the visual appeal of the salad is lost. Larger, recognizable pieces of fruit can be made attractive and tempting.

The fruits themselves may be the source of interesting ideas for serving a fruit salad. A dessert salad of pineapple, fresh strawberries, and banana gains real distinction when a boat of a quarter of the pineapple, resplendent with some of the green pineapple leaves, is used to present the mixture of pineapple cubes, strawberry halves, and banana slices. Grapefruit can be scooped out to serve as baskets for salads. A watermelon half makes an admirable salad bowl for a fruit salad at a buffet when the interior has been scooped out to make melon balls and the shell has been scalloped or cut into ''Vs'' all around the top edge.

Hot summer days can be made pleasant when fresh fruit plates are the main menu item for the day. A scoop of cottage cheese, some fruit sherbet, a dollop of yogurt, or some cheese can be added to provide even more nutrients, particularly some calcium and (with the exception of the sherbet) protein.

Another approach to using fruits in summer meals is afforded by a frozen fruit salad. These salads usually are made with a base of whipped cream, mayonnaise, sugar, and sometimes cream cheese. Fresh or canned fruits cut into pieces are folded into this mixture and then frozen. Although some added sugar will help to blend the flavor of the whipped cream with the fruit, this is not absolutely necessary. In fact, excessive use of sugar can make a frozen fruit salad difficult to serve on a hot day, because the sugar lowers the freezing point of the mixture, causing the salad to soften and even flow quickly at room temperature.

Vegetable Salads

Practically any vegetable can be an ingredient in a salad. Some are used raw; others may be cooked and chilled. Canned vegetables are a convenience for use in salads, for they merely require chilling and draining.

Artistry can be brought to vegetable salads when color, line, and design are combined to advantage. An important part of creating beauty in vegetable salads is the skillful cutting of vegetables to create julienne strips, thin slicing of fresh mushrooms in silhouettes, or creating other pleasing shapes. Tomatoes, carrots, and onions are but some of the types of vegetables that can be cut in many ways to add interest to the design of vegetable salads. The range of colors available in vegetables is broad: the yellow of corn, the stark white of fresh cauliflower, the bright red of tomatoes, the deep purplish-red of red cabbage, and the great variety of shades of green seen in different salad greens illustrate the tremendous impact that color can have in vegetable salads.

Some vegetable salads are good sources of nutrients and fiber but quite low in calories, for example, various types of green salads if they have only a modest amount of dressing. Mixed green salads made with two or three types of greens—spinach, bibb or leaf lettuce, and iceberg lettuce—can be beautiful studies in shades of green, yet they are high in fiber and provide a useful amount of provitamin A, folacin, and some minerals. Despite these assets, green are primarily a source of water and provide minimal amounts of energy—properties that make them high on the list for people seeking to lose weight. In addition to the familiar greens—raw spinach, bibb lettuce, and iceberg lettuce—others—such as romaine, Chinese cabbage, leaf lettuce, red lettuce, watercress, escarole, and endive—can also be used in making interesting salads. Many of these are useful as liners under other salads, too.

Flavor accents often are important in adding interest to vegetable salads. The bright flavor of a green onion, including pieces of its fresh green top, is one means of bring a salad alive. Other times, a marinated vegetable, perhaps artichoke hearts or button mushrooms, can be the highlight. The sparkle afforded by the tartness of a beet pickle or other type of pickle is another suggestion for enhancing flavor.

Vegetables also provide the opportunity for varying texture. Even mixed green salads can get a lift by combining the sturdiness of romaine with the soft, buttery bibb or other butterhead lettuces. And a kidney bean salad gains excitement by adding diced celery for crispness.

Actually, the variety of vegetable salads that can be made is almost limitless. Among the favorites are potato salads. These often are prepared as the cold potato salad, but hot potato salad, with its piquancy and overtone of bacon and onion, is appropriate during the cold weather months. Cabbage salads, usually called simply cole slaw, are inexpensive and popular types of salads. By combining other ingredients, such as grated carrots, pineapple tidbits, diced green peppers, or other accents, cole slaw can be individualized to complement other menu items. At the other end of the price range for vegeta-

Head lettuce is a very popular salad green, but interest in salads can be heightened by using other greens, such as escarole, romaine, curly endive, and Belgian endive.

ble salads are those featuring such ingredients as hearts of palm or asparagus spears and pimiento garnish.

Gelatin Salads

Gelatin salads are popular because they can be (in fact, should be) prepared a day in advance of a meal and still be of excellent quality. This makes them ideal for holiday meals or other occasions when preparation time is limited. Commonly, flavored gelatins are the base for these salads, for they provide not only the desired flavor, but also the color needed to convey the desired image of the salad. Some gelatin salads are made with the unflavored gelatin, as is done when preparing tomato aspic. The unflavored gelatin also is void of color. In the case of tomato aspic, the red of the tomato is sufficient to provide the desired color.

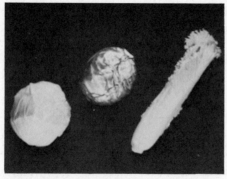

Green, red, or Chinese cabbage can be used to provide a firm, yet crisp texture and distinctive flavor in salads. (top left)

Spinach, parsley, watercress, and chives (in the pot) are a deep green color, and each one has a unique flavor characteristic that can add zip to salads. (top right)

Bibb and Boston are butterhead lettuces, so named because of their somewhat oily feel when rubbed between the fingers. They provide a range of green—from a moderately dark green in the outer leaves to a yellow green in the interior. (bottom)

The usual practice is to add some other ingredients to a gelatin salad. Fruits and vegetables of many different types can be selected to complement particular flavored gelatins. Grated carrots, finely diced celery, and grated cabbage are common ingredients. Sometimes mayonnaise or cottage cheese is blended with the gelatin before the gel sets, giving an opaque appearance and a modified flavor to the salad.

High-Protein Salads

When salads are to be the primary portion of a meal, they need to include adequate protein. For instance, a shrimp salad nestled on a bed of half an avocado is a significant, but expensive source of protein. Other protein-rich foods well suited to use in salads include tuna fish, kidney and other beans (except green and wax), hard-cooked or deviled eggs, cheeses of many types, ground ham or other ground meats, or poultry. Almost always, these protein-rich foods have been cooked or processed prior to use in salads. The most notable exception to this is the use of a raw egg in a Caesar salad.

Garnishes

Garnishes are intended to accent color and flavor in a meal, not to be a main feature. To meet this goal, garnishes usually are quite small. They might be a brilliantly orange carrot curl, perhaps a radish rose spreading to reveal its bright white interior and outer red petals, or even a small spoonful of a corn relish with diced pimiento and green pepper. A few crisp cucumber slices, celery curls, rings of green pepper, disks of onion, or hollowed-out dill pickle rings holding thin carrot sticks are just some of the possible garnishes that can be eaten and serve as a very small salad.

PRINCIPLES OF PREPARATION

Freshness of salad ingredients is vital to preparing a pleasing salad. In addition, cleanliness of those ingredients must be assured. Quality of ingredients and quality of preparation are the cornerstones of salad preparation.

Washing

Greens are likely to have sand or dirt trapped in their convoluted leaves, and this soil must be removed. To begin, run a large amount of water in the sink and slosh the greens in the water to help loosen the sand and soil. The greens may need to be subjected to several washings before the water no longer is loaded with sediment from the leaves. Particularly dirty produce may need to be washed under running water, leaf by leaf in addition to the treatment in the sinkful of water. Be sure to keep changing the washing water until no more sediment is found. Thorough draining following washing is important; otherwise, dressing will be diluted and salad plates will be unattractive because of the water draining from the greens.

Fresh mushrooms can add an unplanned texture to salads if they are not washed adequately. An individual, gentle scrub is the key to eliminating the soil that sometimes clings so tenaciously. Zucchini is another vegetable with a particularly tight hold on dirt. However, all fresh produce needs to be rubbed while being held under running water to be sure all dirt is dislodged and removed.

Handling of Greens

The key to quality in many salads is the presentation of the greens. The ideal is an attractive leaf or pieces of leaf. Proper storage is essential to achieving this goal, for greens rely on a high concentration of water in their cells to give the desirable crispness. Even carrots and celery, as well as most other vegetables used in salads, rely on proper refrigerator storage to maintain the normal level of water in their cells. Clean lettuce and other fresh produce should be stored in the hydrator drawer or a tightly covered container to keep evaporative losses to a minimum, thereby maintaining a crisp texture.

Lettuce cups often are used as liners for individual salads. To obtain leaves free of disfiguring tears, the core of the head needs to be removed, a job done easily with a paring knife. When cold water is run forcefully into the

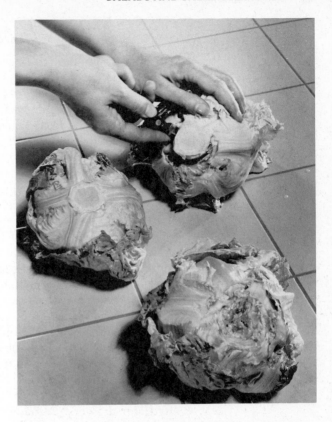

Lettuce cups for salad liners are prepared in advance by cutting out the core and then running cold water into the conical hole to help separate the leaves without tearing them. The leaves can be wrapped loosely in paper toweling and held in the hydrator drawer of the refrigerator until needed later in the day.

resulting cavity, the leaves will begin to separate gradually, making it easy to ease individual leaves from the head.

Although all salad ingredients need to be well drained, greens require particular attention. Otherwise, their curled and twisting surfaces will hold little pockets of water that subsequently drain and collect at the bottom of the salad, diluting dressings and creating a careless appearance. A short period of standing in a colander, a quick spin in a spinner, sharp shakes of the leaves, and a very gentle blotting with absorbent toweling are useful techniques to eliminate excess moisture on lettuce and other greens. After this has been done, the leaves can be used whole or broken into pieces the desired size. Tearing, rather than cutting with a knife, is recommended because the jagged edge that results adds eye appeal to the salad.

Turgor The tension in cells caused by water pressing against cell walls; a desirable characteristic in salad ingredients.

SCIENCE NOTE: TURGOR

Any plant with limited fiber in cell walls relies on water within the cells to hold the cell walls in an extended position, and greens are excellent examples of plants needing a large amount of water inside their cells. The presence of water within the cell exerts pressure against the cell walls, helping to hold them in an extended position. The greater the amount of water in the cell, the greater is the push against the cell walls. This pressure creates *turgor*, a state of tension in the walls. Loss of water from cells reduces this tension, the cells begin to collapse, and greens lose their crispness and begin to droop.

Since crispness in greens is so important, storage and preparation techniques must consider ways of keeping the water level in cells high enough to maintain the desired turgor. One problem is keeping evaporative losses to a minimum. Storage in an environment where the air is saturated with moisture reduces evaporative losses. Lettuce or other greens will contribute moisture to their surrounding environment in an attempt to saturate the air.

Two factors can be controlled to reduce the amount of water required to achieve saturation: the volume of air to be saturated and the temperature of that air. Obviously, a very small volume of air will require less moisture for saturation than will a large volume. By storing greens in a tightly closed, small space, the air will be saturated easily. Evidence of this is seen in the condensation occurring on the ceiling of hydrator drawers. Perhaps less obvious, but of no lesser importance, is the fact that cold air cannot hold as much moisture as warm air. Consequently, cold air will become saturated with only a small amount of moisture, while warm air will cause a considerable loss of water from greens before becoming saturated.

The desirable circumstance is to store greens in very small areas that are chilled so that the cells will retain moisture and maintain their turgor. However, it is possible to return some moisture to drooping greens by placing the leaves in a damp towel and refrigerating the wrapped leaves until cells become plump once again with water.

Turgor also can be lost after dressings are added to greens. The loss of water from cells is the result of unfavorable osmotic pressure that develops when the greens are in contact with the dressing and its salts for a period of time. Water will be drawn from the cells into the dressing in a vain attempt to equalize the concentration on both sides of the semipermeable cell walls. To minimize this problem, dressing should be applied to tossed, mixed green, or similar salads just before serving.

Gelatin Salads

The smooth coolness of a gelatin salad contrasts pleasingly with the various ingredients that commonly are a part of a gelatin salad. However, the desired final effect relies on good preparation techniques. A critical part of preparing a gelatin salad is the complete dispersion of the gelatin. Unflavored gelatin needs to be hydrated by soaking in cold water (¼ cup water per tablespoon gelatin) as a preliminary step because its coarse particles take up water less readily than do the finer particles used in the flavored gelatins. A measured amount of boiling liquid, usually water or a fruit juice, is poured over either flavored or hydrated unflavored gelatin to begin the process of dispersion. Slow stirring is needed to facilitate the solution of the gelatin particles, and this should be continued until absolutely no particles of gelatin can be seen. In particular, stirring needs to be directed toward scraping all gelatin particles from the bottom of the container where they tend to settle. Unless this is done, an undesirable rubbery layer may form.

When the gelatin has been dissolved completely, the remainder of the liquid specified in the recipe is stirred into the gelatin dispersion. This portion of the liquid may be cold liquid or even ice cubes. The use of ice speeds the cooling of the dispersion and initiates the formation of the gelatin gel structure quickly. It is necessary to stir while the ice cubes are melting so that the concentration of gelatin is uniform throughout the mixture and the entire dispersion is cooled at the same rate. If stirring is not done, the gelatin will begin

To unmold gelatin salads, dip them briefly in warm water, shake the mold sideways sharply once or twice to loosen, and then invert a plate over the molded salad. A quick flip of the plate and mold (held tightly together) will release the salad onto the serving plate. At least a brief chilling again in the refrigerator helps to firm the surface of the salad before serving.

to set in regions adjacent to the melting ice and will contribute to a lumpy texture in the finished product. With steady stirring throughout the cooling gelatin, gelation will begin to occur rather slowly. The first sign of gelation is the development of a syruplike consistency. Any unmelted ice should be removed at this point and fruit or other ingredients stirred in until dispersed appropriately. This mixture then is refrigerated in a bowl or mold until gelled.

Sol Colloidal system in which the discontinuous phase is a solid and the continuous phase is a liquid.

Gel Colloidal system in which a solid forms the continuous phase and a liquid is the discontinuous phase.

SCIENCE NOTE: GELATIN GELS

A gelatin dispersion represents a colloidal dispersion, either a *sol* or a *gel*. The gelatin molecules are proteins of a moderate size and are categorized as the solid phase when considering colloidal dispersions. A sol is a colloidal system in which the solid is dispersed in a liquid; that is, the solid is termed the discontinuous phase and the liquid is the continuous phase. In other words, it is possible to get from one gelatin molecule to another only by passing through the liquid in which it is dispersed when the system is a sol. This is the colloidal system being formed when gelatin is being dispersed in boiling liquid in preparing a gelatin salad.

When the gelatin sol begins to cool, the gelatin molecules gradually move slower and slower through the liquid. These fibrous molecules begin to bump against each other and occasionally form hydrogen bonds between molecules. The cooler the system gets, the more slowly the protein molecules move, and the greater is the likelihood of hydrogen bonds beginning to hold one gelatin molecule close to another one. Gradually, many molecules are cross-linked by hydrogen bonding into a jumbled network in which water becomes trapped. Finally, the gelatin molecules form a continuous network, and the water is trapped in discontinuous pockets within this network. In short, the colloidal system has undergone a transition from the original sol to a different colloidal system, that of a gel. A gel no longer exhibits the flow properties characteristic of a sol. This makes it possible to mold gelatin and serve it in a defined shape.

The ease with which gelatin molecules can cross-link to each other to establish the gel structure is influenced by the pH of the dispersion. The addition of some acid to help bring the system to a pH of 5 makes it easy for the gel to form because this is the isoelectric point of gelatin, and at this pH there will be a minimum electrical charge on each molecule. This lack of electrical charge on the surface helps to keep similarly charged molecules from repelling each other. When molecules can get close together, hydrogen bonds are able to form comparatively easily. If the system is acidified to a pH lower than 5 or is more alkaline than 5, it still is possible for hydrogen bonds to form between gelatin molecules and establish a gel. However, this occurs more slowly and gives a gel with somewhat less strength than one at a pH of 5.

The amount of gelatin in a gelatin product clearly influences the strength of the gelatin gel, for there will be fewer molecules to hydrogen bond and form the continuous network when the gelatin concentration is low than when it is great. A low concentration of gelatin forms a weak gel or may even not gel at all. On the other hand, too high a concentration of gelatin gives such a dense network that the gelatin gel is too tough to be enjoyed. A ratio of a tablespoon of gelatin per cup of liquid produces a good gel.

If sugar is increased in a gelatin recipe, the gel will be more tender than the original product. In fact, a very large increase can even prevent gelation. The effect is attributed to the reduction in the concentration of protein when sugar is increased.

Gels look like solids, but actually they are undergoing continual change during storage. Evidence of this is the difficulty of trying to serve a gelatin product that has been firm for only an hour versus one that has been chilled for six hours or more. The gelatin will be more resistant to melting and easier to serve after an extended period of chilling. The difference is due to the gradual formation of more and more hydrogen bonds between gelatin molecules, which serves to draw the structure ever more tightly together and toughen the gel. This, plus the accompanying squeezing out of water, explains the gradual development of a tough, almost rubbery texture during extended storage.

Bromelin Proteolytic enzyme occurring in fresh and frozen pineapple.

The ability of gelatin molecules to establish a network is dependent on their long molecules being hydrogen bonded together. If a proteolytic (protein-digesting) enzyme is added to the system, as occurs when fresh pineapple is added, the gelatin molecules will be altered to shorter molecules and will lose the ability to form a gel. *Bromelin*, the enzyme contained in pineapple, splits the gelatin molecules into shorter units rather quickly, whereas the heat treatment utilized in canning this fruit alters the bromelin molecules, making them incapable of catalyzing the digestive breakdown of gelatin. Papain from papayas and actinidin from kiwi have a similar proteolytic effect.

Recipes for gelatin salads are based on proportions known to produce the desired consistency, so that the salad can be served easily without softening and flowing. Careless measurements of the liquid can affect results. But the most common point of error is in the addition of fruits. To avoid getting extra liquid in the recipe, fruits should be drained thoroughly. The drained juice can be used in making the gelatin if this juice is treated as part of the liquid in the recipe. The problem occurs when poorly drained fruit is added to a gelatin mixture already containing the correct level of liquid.

SERVING SALADS

Salads are particularly appealing when they are served with careful attention to detail. For example, cold salads assume great importance at a meal when served as a separate course, with the chilled salad being arranged attractively on a chilled plate, accompanied by a chilled fork. Dressing to be tossed with a salad is added right before serving. Individual salads should fit the salad plate used, with a bit of a border of the plate itself. Leaves of lettuce extending over the edge or an arrangement that looks like pieces are about to fall off are uninviting. Plates should also be free of splatters or smears.

Gelatin salads often need to be unmolded before serving. This task should be done at least half an hour before serving so that the unmolded gelatin can be chilled again in the refrigerator to firm the outer portion. Unmolding is done by dipping the thoroughly gelled gelatin mold very briefly into warm water, being careful not to get any water into the mold. This can be done easily by filling a sink with warm water to about the level of the mold. A gentle shake of the mold should be enough to loosen the gelatin. If not, the mold may need to be returned again briefly to the warm water. When the gelatin shakes loose from the edges of the mold, the service plate is inverted on the mold, and then the assembly is turned over quickly to unmold the gelatin directly on the plate. The unmolded gelatin is then placed in the refrigerator to reverse the softening and firm the structural design of the molded salad.

SALAD DRESSINGS

Emulsion Colloidal dispersion of two immiscible liquids, with one type of liquid being dispersed as droplets in the other type of liquid.

Discontinuous (disperse) phase Droplets in an emulsion.

Continuous phase Liquid surrounding the suspended droplets in an emulsion.

Salad dressings are of many different types, but the majority contain an oil, an acidic liquid, and seasonings. The combination of oil with an aqueous liquid is often an unstable arrangement because oil and water do not blend together naturally. However, under certain conditions, these two types of liquids can be combined to form a colloidal system called an *emulsion*. Salad dressings usually have droplets of oil (the *discontinuous phase*) suspended in water (the *continuous phase*). Since these salad dressings are droplets of oil in water, the type of emulsion is classified as oil-in-water (written simply as o/w). Emulsions also are classified on the basis of their stability or tendency to separate into two distinct layers, with the oil layer floating on the water layer.

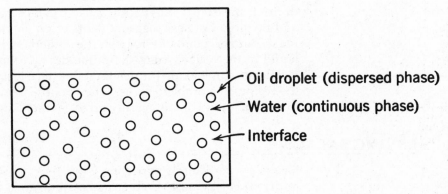

Diagram of an oil-in-water (o/w) emulsion.

Temporary Emulsion

Temporary Emulsion
Emulsion that separates very quickly into two layers.

Salad dressings that have to be shaken each time they are used to distribute the ingredients uniformly are classified as *temporary emulsions*. French and Italian dressings are familiar examples of temporary emulsions. The physical act of shaking breaks the oil up into small droplets, but they coalesce with each other and quickly form an oily layer when allowed to stand even briefly. The only interference keeping one droplet from merging with another is the dry ingredients, such as dry mustard and paprika, which often are part of the seasonings.

The ingredients in temporary emulsions include a flavorful vinegar or another acid ingredient, such as lemon juice, to add flavor interest. The oil used might be olive oil, but often people select corn, soybean, peanut, safflower, or other oil because of the extended shelf life of these types of oils and their mild flavors. Usually about two to three times as much oil as vinegar is used in making ''vinegar-and-oil'' dressings (temporary emulsions), which results in fairly fluid dressings.

Semipermanent Emulsion

Semipermanent Emulsion
Emulsion that is quite viscous and separates into two layers very slowly.

Semipermanent emulsions tend to remain intact for a few days. The viscosity of these emulsions, about like heavy cream, reduces the ease of oil droplets bumping into each other and coalescing to break the emulsion. Sometimes this increased viscosity is the result of a viscous liquid in the recipe, possibly honey, a cooked sugar syrup, an undiluted canned soup base, or a starch-thickened sauce. Commercial dressings of this type often contain such stabilizers as gum tragacanth, gum arabic, pectin, or gelatin to increase viscosity and promote stability.

Sweet dressings for fruit salads, herb dressings, and other readily pourable dressings are semipermanent emulsions. When these dressings do separate, the emulsion can be reformed rather easily by some stirring.

Permanent Emulsion

Permanent Emulsion
Viscous emulsion containing an emulsifying agent that rarely separates into two layers.

Emulsifying Agent
Substance forming a protective coating on the surface of droplets (the interface) in an emulsion.

Lecithin Compound in egg yolk that is attracted to both oil and water, making it a very effective emulsifying agent.

Mayonnaise is the classic example of a *permanent* oil-in-water *emulsion*. The definitely thick character of the dressing restricts the movement of oil droplets throughout the dressing and hinders separation of the oil from the vinegar. In addition to this stabilizing effect, permanent emulsions contain an adequate amount of a very effective *emulsifying agent*, usually egg yolk. An emulsifying agent is capable of forming a protective coating around the spherical surface of each oil droplet, thus preventing oil in one droplet from directly touching the oil in another droplet, which blocks coalescence of the droplets. Egg yolk is effective as an emulsifying agent because it contains *lecithin*, a compound attracted to both oil and water. Lecithin aids emulsion formation by forming a thin protective coating around the oil droplets. Lecithin is much more effective as an emulsifying agent than are the various powdered spices because lecithin has chemical functional groups that allow it to cover a large surface area between the two diverse liquids in the emulsion.

Mayonnaise can be made easily by mixing together the seasonings, egg yolk, and part of the vinegar. Then oil is added dropwise to start forming the emulsion. This is done with beating to help split the oil into small droplets. As the amount of oil is increased and the total volume of mayonnaise begins to be sufficient to be picked up by the beater blades well, the addition of oil can be increased a bit, but still needs to be very deliberate. If too much oil is introduced at any time, the emulsion will break, and the mayonnaise will have a dreadfully curdled appearance. This problem can be remedied by starting with a fresh egg yolk in a clean bowl and gradually beating in the broken emulsion, treating it as oil. The amount of oil that potentially can be incorporated in mayonnaise is somewhere between 70 and 80 percent of the total weight of the ingredients. At these high levels of oil, the mayonnaise will become so firm that it can be sliced. Eventually, it is possible to add so much oil that the emulsion will break, and fluid oil will separate.

Permanent emulsions can be broken not only by adding too much oil, but also by freezing or by storage in a very warm place, which will cause oil droplets to coalesce. Although excessive shaking during shipping or handling can be another cause of a broken mayonnaise, this is rarely seen because of the stability of the mayonnaise itself and the excellent present-day control in storing and shipping food products.

Cooked Salad Dressings

Other salad dressings are made with formulations quite different from those just described. In fact, there is a commercial product group marketed as "salad dressing" and used in many applications in place of the more costly mayonnaise. The Food and Drug Administration's definition of mayonnaise lists specific required ingredients, including a high percentage of oil, whereas salad dressings can have a thickening agent to help give the viscosity normally acquired through the use of a fairly costly salad oil. These salad dressings require only 30 percent oil or more, which reduces their cost and also their calories. Although several different thickening agents can be used, starch is one effective and inexpensive way of producing a cooked salad dressing of the desired viscosity.

Homemade cooked salad dressings usually are thickened by starch and egg protein. Starch mixtures are brought to a boil to ensure maximum thickening and a cooked flavor before the egg is added and then heated again slightly to thicken the proteins in the egg. The dressing is not boiled or cooked very long after the egg is added because the egg proteins might give a curdled appearance to the dressing treated in this way. Homemade dressings in which fruit juices or other acidic liquids are used should be made by adding the acidic liquid after the starch has been thickened. Otherwise, the starch will break down and result in a thin product. Starch cookery and egg cookery principles are discussed in Chapters 7 and 10, respectively.

Varying Salad Dressings

Basic salad dressings can be modified to special dressings by adding appropriate ingredients. For instance, a creamy-type dressing can be made using sour

Flavorful additions to basic salad dressings may include (bottom, left to right) oregano, parsley flakes, chili powder, freeze-dried shallots, nutmeg, cloves, freeze-dried chives, paprika; (center, left to right) black pepper, bay leaves, dill weed, curry powder, onion flakes; (top, left to right) dill seed, mustard seed, caraway seed, dried red pepper, and rosemary.

cream, cream, milk, yogurt, or cream cheese. Exciting flavors can be introduced through the addition of chopped pickles, diced cheeses of many types (including Roquefort-type), pickle relish, and grated onions, as well as many other types of spices and condiments. Many commercial salad dressing packets are available in the market to provide a skillfully blended assortment of spices for the "do-it-yourself" touch.

Evaluating Salad Dressings

The popularity of salads has caused many consumers to turn into "salad dressing gourmets," the people who whip up their own dressings, often using commercial products as aids. Dressings should have a pleasing flavor that blends with the flavors that will be contained in the salad ingredients themselves. Such dressings should be thin enough to blend easily with the salad ingredients, yet not so fluid that they drain rapidly to the bottom of the salad. Droplets of oil should not be evident on the surface of permanent emulsions, such as mayonnaise; cooked salad dressings should be free of lumps.

SUMMARY

Salads have the potential for adding virtually all of the nutrients to the diet in many different ways. They can be used in any part of the meal, from appetizer to dessert, with each salad being an artful combination of arrangement and shape, color, flavor, and contrasting textures. Fruits, vegetables, gelatin, meats, fish, poultry, eggs, and cheese are all possible ingredients in various salads.

Preparation of salads requires careful washing of fresh produce and proper storage and service to assure that greens exhibit the optimal amount of turgor. Gelatin gels can be made from unflavored or flavored gelatin. With careful preparation and unmolding, these salads add beauty and pleasure to dining. Unmolded gelatins hold their shape well if they are refrigerated briefly following the removal of the mold.

Salad dressings are usually oil-in-water emulsions, with their stability ranging from temporary, to semipermanent, and permanent. French and Italian dressings are fluid, have little in the way of emulsifying ingredients, and separate readily, which is why they are termed temporary emulsions. Semipermanent emulsions are considerably more viscous and stable than the temporary emulsions. Permanent emulsions rarely break, although freezing, high temperatures, and considerable shaking can cause even mayonnaise to break. Egg yolk contains lecithin, a particularly effective emulsifying agent, which aids greatly in making mayonnaise a thick, stable permanent emulsion. Some dressings contain less oil than the permanent emulsions, yet are similar in function to permanent emulsions. These dressings often are thickened using starch or eggs.

Salad dressings should have a fresh flavor characteristic of the type of dressing. They should coat the salad ingredients, yet not be so thick that they will not flow.

Selected References

Ferry, J. D. Protein gels. *Adv. Prot. Chem. 4*: 8. 1948.

Grass, J. Collagen. *Sci. Amer. 204(5)*: 121. 1961.

Hansen, H. and L. R. Fletcher. Salad dressings stable to frozen storage. *Food Tech. 15*: 256. 1961.

Harrington, W. F. Structure of collagen and gelatin. *Adv. Prot. Chem. 16*: 1. 1961.

Hecht, A. and J. Willis. Sulfites: preservatives that can go wrong. *FDA Consumer 17(7)*: 11. 1983.

Idson, B. and E. Braswell. Gelatin. *Adv. Food Res. 7*: 236. 1957.

Vincent, R. et al. Surface activity of yolk, plasma, and dispersions of yolk fractions. *J. Food Sci. 31*: 643. 1966.

Worrell, L. Flavors, spices, condiments, and essential oils. In *Chemistry and Technology of Food and Food Products*. M. B. Jacobs, Ed. Interscience. New York. 1951. Ch. 32, Vol. 2.

Study Questions

1. Compare the cost of commercial and homemade salad dressings. Be sure to include an estimate of the amount of time and the value of the time required to prepare the product at home. Under what conditions would you make your own dressing? Buy your dressing already prepared?

2. Describe a salad to be served as (a) the main course of a luncheon, (b) an appetizer, (c) an accompaniment to the main course, and (d) a dessert. Why do you think these salads are appropriate for each application? What characteristics distinguish each type of salad?
3. Why does the viscosity of a salad dressing influence the stability of an emulsion?
4. Identify each of the basic categories of salad dressings and name an example. Identify the ingredients in the individual recipes that contribute to the stability of the emulsion.
5. Explain the preparation of a gelatin salad. How is a gelatin gel formed and what happens as it ages?
6. What is the effect of adding fresh pineapple to a gelatin salad? How can this effect be avoided?

Black figured amphora, c. 520 B.C. The Granger Collection.

CHAPTER 5

FATS AND OILS

CONTROVERSIAL INGREDIENTS

Lipids Comprehensive term including fats, oils, and some other organic compounds containing carbon and hydrogen, and only a very small amount of oxygen.

Among nutritionists and weight-conscious people, fats and oils (particularly saturated fats) are an important diet and health concern because of their relationship to nutritional status and health and the U.S. consumer's fondness for *lipids*. Fats and oils are calorie-dense food items, providing more than twice as many calories, gram per gram, as do either carbohydrates or proteins. Even alcohol, with its 7 calories per gram is lower in calories than fats and oils, with 9. Not only are fats and oils high in calories, they often are found in foods containing only a limited amount of water. As a result, many foods rich in fats and oils are concentrated sources of calories.

Nutritionally, people want to avoid consuming too much fat (because of the association with overweight and heart disease) and keep down the level of saturated fats in particular. In preparing foods, any reduction in fat usage will reduce the calorie content. A clear indication of this point is exemplified in the "nouvelle cuisine" from France, in which the rich sauces so typical of "haute cuisine" have been modified by significantly reducing the quantities of butter and cream.

Ideally, fats and oils are selected for use in specific recipes to fulfill the roles of the fat in the dish being prepared. Knowledge of the properties of the many different types of products available today will make it possible to make optimal choices, resulting in high-quality products without a high level of fats.

TYPES OF FATS AND OILS

Lard

Leaf Lard Fat obtained from the abdominal cavity of hogs; the premium type of lard.

Lard, a fat rendered from hogs, has been used in cooking for centuries wherever hogs were raised for food. *Leaf lard*, considered to be the prime lard, is obtained by rendering the fat from the abdominal cavity around the kidneys. All lard has a modestly distinctive flavor that can be a pleasing addition to the delicate flavor quality of pastry and other baked products. Sometimes lard will begin to develop a grainy texture. To alleviate this problem, lard can be processed and marketed as "rearranged" lard. The tendency to become rancid, hence strongly flavored, can be retarded significantly simply by storing lard in the refrigerator.

Butter

The other type of fat from animals is butter. Like lard, butter has been used for centuries as a fat in cooking. However, its popularity today is significantly higher than that of lard, for its attractive yellow color and pleasing flavor make it useful as a table spread as well as a fat for cooking. Butter is made by churning milk until the original oil-in-water emulsion in milk breaks and a water-in-oil emulsion forms. Although a considerable amount of water is removed from butter, the end product still contains about 16 percent water, a distinct contrast to the absence of water in lard.

Butter is graded, with AA being the top grade designated by the U.S. Department of Agriculture standards. Usually butter has a small amount of salt added to it for flavor and to enhance keeping quality; unsalted butter (also called sweet butter) is available in most markets, too. Carotene may be added for color.

Some recipes specify using clarified butter, which can be prepared by melting butter and then carefully pouring the melted fat from the milk solids settling in the bottom of the pan. Removal of the milk solids reduces the likelihood of scorching sauces containing butter.

Margarine

Margarines (occasionally called oleomargarine) represent some remarkable achievements in food technology. The goal of the extensive research in margarines originally was to develop a product from vegetable oils with the characteristics of butter. To do this, oils from any of several plants (corn, soybean, cottonseed, safflower, sunflower) are hydrogenated to change them into spreadable solid fats. Coloring, flavorings, vitamins A and D, emulsifying agents, and water are added to approximate the desirable characteristics of butter.

Stick margarines are marketed as a spread that can be substituted for butter in any of the preparations for which butter is designated. Their labels will indicate the ingredients used in making the specific margarines. As is true with all labels, the ingredients must be listed in descending order of weight in the product, beginning with the most abundant item. A comparison of margarine labels allows consumers to make choices between margarines made of only one specific type of oil or a mixture of oils. It also indicates whether an oil or a hydrogenated fat is the most abundant ingredient, a matter of interest to people seeking a high intake of polyunsaturated fats in relation to saturated fats. When an oil is listed as the first ingredient, the margarine will be higher in polyunsaturated fatty acids than if a partially hydrogenated or hydrogen-

Microphotograph of margarine (500×) showing the various size droplets of the disperse phase (oil) of the emulsion under ordinary light. The liquid and crystalline fat are not shown in detail. (left)

Microphotograph of margarine (500×) under polarized light shows the crystalline portions as light areas. The liquid portions do not show. (right)

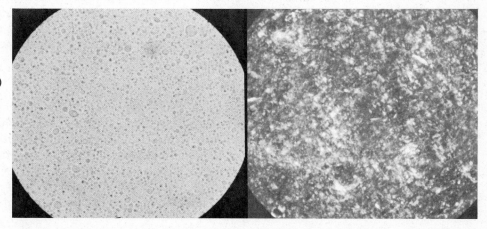

ated fat is the first item. All margarines, however, are higher in polyunsaturates than butter is.

Soft margarines are marketed in tubs because they contain such a high proportion of polyunsaturates that they will not hold the molded stick form at room temperature. The oil sources for making soft margarines are the same as those used in manufacturing the stick margarines. The lower melting point of tub margarines makes them easier to spread on bread than stick margarines, but even the stick margarines are much easier to spread than butter when they are first removed from the refrigerator.

Diet margarines offer yet another choice to consumers. These are products formulated with a percentage of water far exceeding the usual 16 percent in other margarines. By replacing much of the fat with water, the caloric contribution of diet margarines is reduced appreciably. The high water content limits the use of diet margarines to serving as a spread. They have no cooking applications.

Whipped Spreads

Both butter and margarine are also marketed in whipped form. Whipping adds air and increases the volume of these spreads, which tends to limit the amount normally spread on bread or a roll. On a volume basis, whipped butter or margarine contains approximately half as many calories as the unwhipped form.

Shortenings

In a sense, shortenings are the first cousins of margarines, for they are products manufactured from the same types of oils used in making margarines. Hydrogenation is done to modify the oils into the desired solid form. Key differences between shortenings and margarines are the absence of water, flavorings, and (usually) color in shortenings. Shortenings have little flavor and can be stored at room temperature for a relatively long period without becoming rancid. Color is sometimes added during the manufacturing of a shortening to satisfy consumers who want to use a yellow fat in their baking.

Shortenings have been designed primarily for use in baked products. The inclusion of monoglycerides and diglycerides aids in emulsifying the ingredients in cake batters to promote a fine texture and retards staling.

Salad Oils

Salad oils commonly are the oils expressed from one or more of the following: corn, safflower, cottonseed, soybean, peanut, sunflower seed, or olives. These oils from plant sources are generally high in polyunsaturates, although olive oil and palm oils are rather low. The distinctive flavor of olive oil is prized by some as an ingredient in vinegar and oil dressings and in a number of recipes for pasta and vegetable dishes of Italian, Greek, or Middle Eastern origins. The other salad oils also are utilized as ingredients in salad dressing.

They are of great importance as the frying medium for shallow or deep-fat frying because of their high smoke point. Most salad oils can be used several times for deep-fat frying before their smoke point drops below frying temperatures (about 375°F). The good stability of oils at high temperatures stems from the absence of water in them. Unlike butter and margarine, salad oils consist entirely of fatty compounds and have neither water nor milk solids to promote breakdown of the oil during frying.

FUNCTIONS IN FOOD PREPARATION

Palatability

Color, flavor, and aroma are all aspects of palatability that can be influenced by the type of fat selected. The golden color of butter, margarines, or yellow-colored shortenings is considered to be a positive contribution of these fats toward palatability of the foods in which they are used. Regardless of the color of fat selected, baked products do achieve a pleasing golden brown color when fats are included in the recipe.

The flavor and aroma of butter, olive oil, lard, and most margarines are of importance in determining palatability of foods containing them. Usually, butter and margarines are considered to be important for their flavors in foods. Lard is enjoyed for its flavor by some people, while others may avoid the use of lard because of its flavor, which can be distinguished fairly easily. Olive oil, like lard, has its devotees and its detractors.

Textural Influences

Two textural qualities, tenderness and flakiness, are influenced by fats. Tenderness is one aspect of texture that is of great importance in baked products. Cakes and pastries usually are assessed for their tenderness, and the amount and type of fat selected can have a significant effect on this characteristic. Fats promote tenderness by impeding the contact of water with the protein (gluten) in flour, which toughens the product. The fat also adds a lubricating quality, another factor in preventing toughness. The consequence of these actions of fats during the mixing of batters and doughs is increasing tenderness with increases in the proportion of fat.

Fats can be cut into pieces, as is done in making pastry and biscuits. These pieces melt during baking and become incorporated in the cell walls, leaving holes where the pieces had been in the initial mixture. This contributes significantly to the textural characteristic called flakiness. In products in which flakiness is desired, the use of a hard fat is important.

Cooking Medium

Fats and oils can be heated to 375°F and higher, temperatures way above the temperature of boiling water, thus adding considerable opportunity for variety in food preparation. When foods are fried, they develop a crisp character on the outside and remain pleasingly moist in the interior. The flavors of fried foods are a combination of the richness afforded by the absorbed fat, possible unique flavors of the specific fat used, and the cooked food itself.

SELECTING FATS

Selection of the best fat for a particular task in cookery will be an important part of preparing a top-quality product, yet simply buying the most expensive fat is not a guarantee of the best choice. The role that fat is to play in making the product will determine the type to choose.

Spreads

The choice of a spread is largely an individual matter. Butter is more difficult to spread immediately after being removed from the refrigerator than are the various margarines. If many sandwiches are to be made quickly, margarine may be a time-saver. Preference for a specific brand of margarine or of butter often is based on flavor and level of polyunsaturates rather than on plasticity or spreadability.

Tub margarines are particularly easy to spread because of their softness, the result of a high ratio of polyunsaturated fats in their formulation. This softness makes attractive service of these margarines at the table very difficult, a disadvantage that causes some people to avoid them.

If margarine is to be used as an ingredient in a batter or dough product or for frying, choice of a diet margarine will prove unsatisfactory. The low fat content and high water level will create tough baked products, and considerable splattering will be a problem in frying. The smoke point of diet margarines is very low, another reason for not frying with them.

Butter or regular margarines generally can be used interchangeably because of their similar composition and characteristics. Some people maintain that they can distinguish between butter and any margarine and are willing to pay the higher cost of butter. Others do not detect any important difference and opt for margarines, either on the basis of economy or the desire for fewer saturated fats and a higher level of polyunsaturates. Clearly, this is a matter of individual preference.

Frying

Some people like to use butter or margarine for shallow-fat frying because of the flavor and color contributed by these fats. However, both butter and margarine can be used only a very short period of time before they begin to smoke and break down. This is due to their fat composition and the presence of water as well as to the presence of milk solids. Burning of these fats (actually, the milk solids in them) also can be a problem affecting both appearance and flavor. Clarified butter burns less readily than butter.

Lard and shortenings are other fats sometimes used for frying. Unfortunately, these have comparatively low smoke points, which usually make both lard and shortening poor choices. The addition of mono- and diglycerides to shortenings during manufacturing reduces shortenings' suitability for frying, for they break down and start smoking soon after frying is begun.

Salad oils, with the exception of olive oil, are the clear choice for frying. Peanut oil has a slightly distinctive flavor enjoyed by some, but avoided by others. The other salad oils have high smoke points and are essentially taste-less, characteristics that make them particularly well suited to use in deep-fat frying. Their content of antioxidants is an aid in extending shelf life.

Salad Dressings

Salad oils are often selected for use in making salad dressings; their viscosity and clarity make them key components of dressings. Although the flavor of many dressings is derived from the seasonings and vinegar used in them, olive oil sometimes is the oil chosen for its distinctive contribution to flavor. A disadvantage of using olive oil is that it will solidify in the refrigerator, making it necessary to warm the oil enough to be poured. Other salad oils have had their components with a high melting point removed during processing, which prevents crystals from forming and immobilizing the oil during refrigerator storage.

Baked Products

Breads Fat is a minor ingredient in most breads and sometimes is not even included, as is the case in French bread. In yeast breads, butter or margarine often is chosen because of the flavor and color contributions despite the fact that only a small amount is used. It is possible to use shortening or an oil, although the color and flavor contributed by the butter or margarine will be lacking.

Quick breads are so varied that it is necessary to comment on the type of fat best suited for several different products. For instance, muffin preparation requires the fat to be in liquid form. That liquid may be a salad oil or melted shortening. Butter and margarine are not used because they would provide less fat than desired and more liquid than is appropriate.

Biscuits are prepared by cutting the fat into the dry ingredients. To do this, the fat must be capable of being split apart easily and remaining separated. Lard and hydrogenated shortenings have this capability and, hence, are the preferred fats for this purpose. Butter and margarine are difficult to cut into small pieces when cold and will tend to cream together during mixing when warm.

Some quick loaf breads, such as banana nut bread, are made by creaming the fat with the sugar to establish a fine grain in the bread. Hydrogenated shortenings are excellent choices because they are very plastic and readily creamed without becoming too soft. Butter has the disadvantage of sometimes becoming too soft during creaming, so that the emulsion in the batter ultimately breaks, resulting in a slightly coarse texture.

Cakes   Shortened cakes require thorough creaming of the fat and sugar as the initial step in mixing the ingredients. Although butter and margarine can be creamed, they may become too soft. They also do not have the emulsifying agents (mono- and diglycerides) that are added to shortenings to enhance their performance in making fine-textured cakes. There is a trade-off between the flavor and color contributions of butter and margarine and the fine texture resulting from the use of hydrogenated shortening. Sometimes lard is used in cakes. The fairly compact nature and lack of emulsifying agents in lard cause lard cakes to be a bit heavy, with a slightly greasy crumb.

Chiffon cakes are unique among the foam cakes because they use fat in the recipe. Foam cakes, which rely on light egg white foams for their airy quality, cannot be made with solid fats. Salad oil, however, can be blended with the other ingredients to give added tenderness to chiffon cakes without making them heavy.

Pastry   The ratio of fat to liquid in pastries is particularly crucial. With too much water or too little fat, a pastry can quickly become very tough. Excellent results can be obtained using either lard or hydrogenated shortening, for both of these fats are entirely fat and do not contain water. If butter or margarine is substituted into a pastry, the amount of fat actually being added to the other ingredients will be about 16 percent less than is needed, and the amount of water actually is being increased, both changes being clearly counter to producing a high-quality pastry. On the other hand, use of an oil would provide the correct level of fat without adding liquid. However, the fluidity of oils allows them to flow and be distributed uniformly throughout the dough. The dough will be extremely tender, but very oily, and will lack the desired flakiness because oil cannot be cut into particles.

Puff pastries are specialty items prepared by placing butter between thin layers of dough. The butter aids in keeping the dough layers separated and also adds important color and flavor. The water in the butter helps by generating steam between the layers during baking, which promotes the puffing of the numerous layers to make a high pastry. Shortening and lard are not used in puff pastry because they lack flavor and water needed for steam development.

Cookies   The melting characteristics of butter, margarines, and shortenings are different, and these differences are quite evident in making cookies. Most cooky recipes require a fairly rich dough. During mixing, the doughs may seem quite similar in their handling characteristics, regardless of which of these three types of fats is used. However, drop cookies will spread quite differently during baking, depending upon the type of fat used. Cookies made with shortening will hold their shape and flow less readily than will those containing butter or margarine. With careful development, a cooky recipe can be formulated for a particular type of fat. Butter and margarine can be used interchangeably, but they cannot be substituted for shortening unless the recipe is adjusted.

STORING FATS

Cold temperatures are helpful in extending the shelf life of any fat or oil because the enzyme action leading to the development of rancidity is retarded. However, limitations on refrigerator space and the inconvenience of needing to allow fats to reach room temperature for ease in using may favor room temperature storage, at least at times. If fats are to be used within a matter of only a few days, refrigerator storage may not be necessary. This is particularly true for salad oils. Salad oils, with the exception of olive oil, can be stored in a cool, dark cabinet for several weeks without becoming rancid. Generally, this is the preferred way to store these products because of convenience, but refrigerator storage extends shelf life. Hydrogenated shortenings also can be stored in a cool, dark place. The covers should be fastened securely on oils and shortenings to help prevent easy entry of air, which would promote the development of oxidative rancidity.

Butter, margarines, and lard should be stored in the refrigerator to help them achieve a reasonable storage life. They need to be covered securely to prevent contact with air and to avoid absorbing volatile flavors from other foods in the refrigerator. Fats are avaricious in their ability to acquire flavors from onions, cheeses, or other items that might be exuding volatiles not considered desirable in butter or other fats. Uncovered or loosely wrapped butter or margarine can add surprising flavors to cookies or other items in which they might be used. A tight cover for refrigerated fats is the only protection against this problem.

Occasionally, fats of various types may be on sale. If appropriate, butter or margarines can be bought in quantity and frozen until needed. However, even frozen fats should be used within about six months because freezing does not completely halt the development of rancidity.

Storage of olive oil presents a real dilemma. It becomes rancid frustratingly quickly at room temperature, but olive oil develops so many fat crystals in the refrigerator that it must be warmed before any can be poured from the container. With proper planning, olive oil can be stored in the refrigerator and removed well in advance of the time it will need to be poured. However, if stored at room temperature, purchase only what will be used within a matter of a week or two. Rancidity develops much more rapidly in olive oil than in many other familiar fats.

Glycerol Alcohol containing three carbon atoms and three hydroxyl groups; common to the fats used in food preparation.

SCIENCE NOTE: CHEMISTRY OF FATS

All fats of concern in food preparation contain one component in common—*glycerol*. Although it is a small alcohol containing only three carbon atoms, glycerol is unique in that it has three hydroxyl ($-OH$) groups (in contrast to the sole functional group usually found in alcohols). Each of these hydroxyl groups can combine with a fatty acid to form an ester linkage by eliminating a molecule of water:

H
|
H—C—OH
|
H—C—OH +
|
H—C—OH
|
H

$$O \diagdown C—(CH_2)_x—CH_3 \diagup HO$$

$$\xrightarrow{-HOH}$$

H
|
H—C—OH
|
H—C—OH
|
H—C—O—C—(CH_2)_xCH_3
|
H

| Glycerol | Fatty acid | Monoglyceride showing ester linkage (dashed lines) |

Fatty Acid Organic acid containing between 4 and 24 carbon atoms; combines with glycerol to form a fat.

Fatty acids in fats are responsible for the varying physical characteristics of different fats. The fewer the carbon atoms present in a fatty acid, the lower the melting point in comparison with a fatty acid with a longer chain length. Fats containing fatty acids with 16 or more carbon atoms will be firmer at room temperature than will those with short chains because of the difference in the melting point of the fatty acids.

Another variation in fatty acids that helps to determine whether a fat will be a fluid or a solid is the amount of saturation with hydrogen. Each carbon atom within the fatty acid chain is capable of holding two hydrogen atoms. When this situation exists, the fatty acid is said to be saturated; that is, it cannot hold any more hydrogen. Sometimes adjacent carbon atoms will have only one hydrogen atom apiece, rather than two, thus creating a double bond or an unsaturated fatty acid. Many plant oils contain molecules of fat that have two or three double bonds in their fatty acids. These fatty acids are designated as being polyunsaturated. An increase in the amount of unsaturation lowers the melting point temperature. Thus, vegetable oils, with their comparatively high amount of polyunsaturation, will remain fluid at room temperature, in contrast to the firm saturated fats in butter and other solid fats.

The carbon chain in a fatty acid ordinarily proceeds in a linear fashion, but at double bonds, there is the possibility of altering the direction of the next portion of the chain. The configuration at a double bond that causes the chain to continue in its linear fashion is a *trans* form; the *cis* form is the arrangement causing a change in the direction of the molecule at the double bond. The *cis* form at a double bond causes the melting point of that fatty acid to be significantly lower than is the comparable fatty acid containing the *trans* form. The importance of the form (*cis* or *trans*), the length of chain, and the degree of unsaturation in determining melting points is illustrated in Table 5.1.

Trans Configuration at the double bond of an unsaturated fatty acid resulting in a continuation of the linear chain.

Cis Configuration at the double bond of an unsaturated fatty acid resulting in a change in the direction of the chain of a fatty acid.

Mono-, Di-, Triglycerides Fat molecules containing, respectively, one, two, or three fatty acids esterified with glycerol.

Fats not only differ in the length and degree of saturation of the fatty acids they contain, but they also differ in the number of fatty acids in a molecule. When a fat contains a single fatty acid, it is called a *monoglyceride*. This fatty acid can be esterified at the terminal carbon or the central carbon position. *Diglycerides* will have two fatty acids, esterified to glycerol at either the two terminal carbon atoms or at two adjacent carbon atoms. The ultimate configuration of most fats used in food preparation is that of a *triglyceride,* in which all three carbon positions have been esterified with fatty acids. These various possibilities are depicted in Table 5.2.

Table 5.1 Characteristics of Selected Fatty Acids and Fats Occurring in Foods

Type	Structure and Configuration	Chain Length	No. of Double Bonds	Melting Point, °F	Appearance	Source
Fatty Acid						
Butyric	$CH_3CH_2CH_2COOH$	4	0	18 to 24	Colorless liquid	Milk fat
Stearic	$CH_3(CH_2)_{16}COOH$	18	0	157	Colorless waxy solid	Animals, plants
Oleic	$CH_3(CH_2)_7CH=CH(CH_2)_7COOH$ *(cis)*	18	1	61	Yellow liquid	Animals, plants
Elaidic	$CH_3(CH_2)_7CH=CH(CH_2)_7COOH$ *(trans)*	18	1	111	Solid	
Linolenic	$CH_3(CH_2CH=CH)_3(CH_2)_7COOH$	18	3	12	Colorless liquid	Soy
Fats						
Tripalmitin		16	0	150	White crystalline solid	
Tristearin		18	0	161	White crystalline solid	
Triolein		18	1	25	Yellow liquid	

Source: Selected from *Biochemists' handbook.* Ed. C. D. Long. Van Nostrand. Princeton, N.J. 1961.

Table 5.2 General Structures of Fats in Foods

Type of Fat	Possible Structures

Monoglyceride

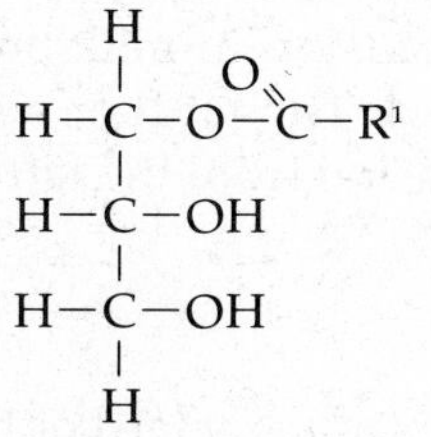

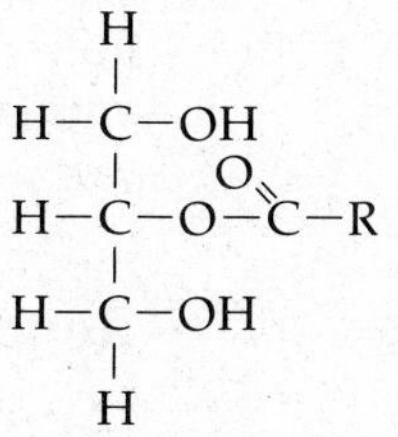

Diglyceride

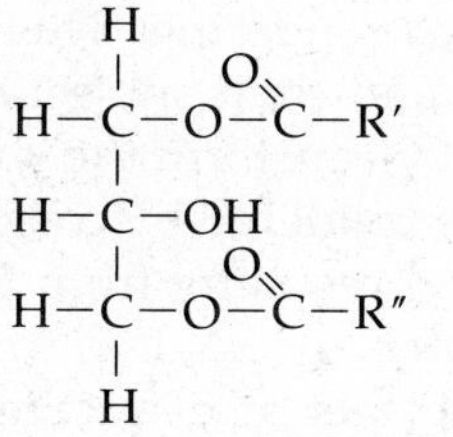

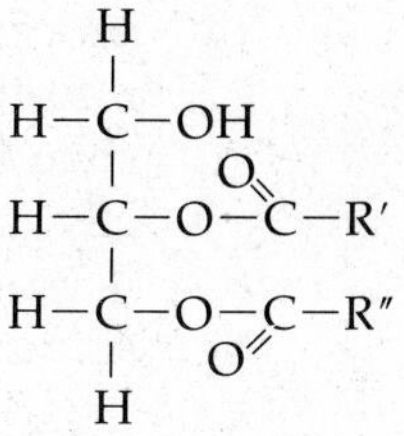

Triglyceride

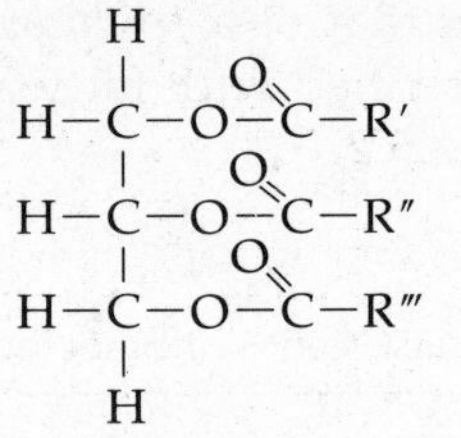

$$
\begin{array}{c}
\text{H} \\
|\\
\text{H}-\text{C}-\text{O}-\overset{\displaystyle\overset{\text{O}}{\diagup}}{\text{C}}-\text{R}' \\
|\\
\text{H}-\text{C}-\text{O}-\overset{\displaystyle\overset{\text{O}}{\diagup}}{\text{C}}-\text{R}'' \\
|\\
\text{H}-\text{C}-\text{O}-\overset{\displaystyle\overset{\text{O}}{\diagup}}{\text{C}}-\text{R}''' \\
|\\
\text{H}
\end{array}
$$

[1]R, R′, R″, and R‴ represent the remainder of the carbon–hydrogen chain; $R = (-CH_2)_x CH_3$, in which x represents between 2 and 22 CH_2 groups.

TECHNOLOGY OF FATS

Origin of the Fat

Fats vary in their natural characteristics depending upon their origin. For example, in milk fat, fatty acids range in chain length from 4 to 26 carbon atoms, with nine different saturated and seven unsaturated fatty acids being prominent. In contrast, many other fats will have only three saturated and two unsaturated fatty acids in abundance in their structures. Cattle fat is higher in saturated fatty acids than is the fat from chickens and other poultry, pigs, or lambs. Even the location of the fat within the animal influences the composition of the fat; fats near the surface are softer and higher in polyunsaturated fatty acids than are those in the leaf fat surrounding the internal organs.

Some modification in the fatty acid composition of nonruminants can be accomplished by modifying the diet. The fat of pigs can be changed somewhat in this way. However, cows will continue to deposit their typical fatty acid pattern in their fats regardless of the diet because bacteria in their rumen modify fats prior to passage into the intestinal region where they are absorbed.

The fats of commercial interest from animals are milk fat, lard, and tallow. Milk fat is the forerunner of butter and is made available by churning milk until the emulsion in milk breaks and reverses to form the water-in-oil emulsion of butter. The fat that will be marketed ultimately as lard or as tallow must be extracted from the fatty tissues of pigs and cows, respectively.

Rendering

The first step in producing lard or tallow is the extraction of fat from tissues, a process known as rendering. This is accomplished by chopping fatty tissues into fine pieces and then subjecting them to between 40 and 60 pounds of steam pressure to transform the solid fats into liquids for removal. Occasionally, lard may be rendered by cooking the fatty tissues in an open kettle. The dry rendered lard resulting from this processing has a cooked flavor, which some people prefer.

In rendering fats or extracting them from plant sources, however, the portion of the plant containing the oil, ordinarily the seed, may be pressed to express the oils or may be treated with a solvent to extract the fat-soluble materials. Following extraction, the oils are heated briefly in steam to coagulate any protein that might be present and render the protein insoluble.

Refining

The fats and oils resulting from rendering or extraction are contaminated with such undesirable materials as free fatty acids and other substances. To improve the quality of fats and oils, it is necessary to refine the raw material, by adding alkali to the fat to form an emulsion, which then is heated, broken, and separated. By additional washings and centrifugation, fats pass through a continuous process until the free fatty acid content is decreased to between 0.01 and 0.05 percent, a degree of purity essential to the production of a fat with a reasonable shelf life. Once the fats have been purified to this extent, they are bleached and deodorized.

Hydrogenating

Hydrogenation Process of adding hydrogen to polyunsaturated fatty acids to change oils into solid fats.

Hydrogenation, the addition of hydrogen to unsaturated fatty acids, is a key process in the preparation of margarines and shortenings. Through the action of a nickel catalyst in an environment held between 100° and 200°C and at 15 atmospheres of pressure, hydrogen is added (2 atoms of hydrogen at each double bond) to transform oils into solids. By increasing the saturation of polyunsaturated fatty acids, their melting points rise as unsaturation decreases. Hydrogenation can be controlled to achieve the degree of saturation desired. To maintain as high a content of polyunsaturated fatty acids as feasible, margarines may be manufactured by mixing unhydrogenated oil with some fat that has undergone a fairly thorough process of hydrogenation. This permits the manufacture of a spreadable product, yet one with the desired high content of polyunsaturates.

Blending and Tempering

Fats can be tailored to provide the physical characteristics desired for a particular application. Oils can be blended with solid fats to produce a fat with excellent spreading and creaming characteristics over a wide temperature range. To obtain the fine crystalline structure desired in solid fats, the solid fats are warmed and mixed thoroughly with the oils being added. Then this mixture is supercooled rapidly with agitation to achieve a matrix of very tiny fat crystals in which the oil droplets are trapped. This supercooling and rapid crystallization is accomplished by placing the fluid fat into a closed system containing nitrogen to cool the fat to 65°F in 30 seconds. Then the fat is worked for up to 4 minutes to help achieve the desired fine crystals. A holding period at a controlled cool temperature for a couple of days to temper the fat completes the manufacturing process. This tempering period aids in achieving stable, fine crystals that are of considerable benefit in any solid fat.

SCIENCE NOTE: FAT CRYSTALS

Solid fats are composed of many, many crystals of fat with some oil trapped between the crystals. The ease with which these crystals form is influenced by the fatty acids in the fat molecules. Not surprisingly, polyunsaturated fatty acids with the *trans* configuration at the double bonds will precipitate and form crystals more readily than will the *cis* form (see the melting point comparison in Table 5.1). The configuration of the *trans* form permits molecules to approach each other readily and form hydrogen bonds to help bind one molecule close to another. The angular form of *cis* double bonds makes it difficult for molecules to congregate and form crystals, although they can do so when cooled sufficiently.

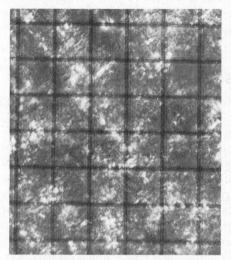

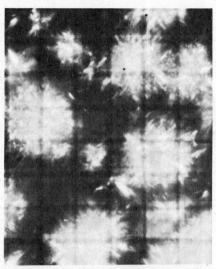

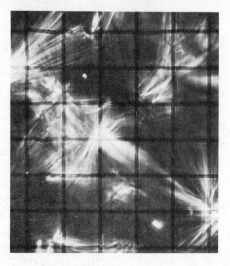

Photomicrograph of beta prime fat crystals in polarized light (200×). Grid lines represent 18 microns. (top left)

Photomicrograph of intermediate fat crystals in polarized light (200×). Grid lines represent 18 microns. Comparison with the beta prime crystals shows the significant difference in size between the two forms of crystals. (top right)

Photomicrograph of beta fat crystals in polarized light (200×) reveals the large size and the sharp angularity of the largest of the four types of fat crystals. Grid lines represent 18 microns. (bottom)

The crystal forms in solid fats may be any of four different types: alpha (α), beta prime (β'), intermediate, or beta (β). The α form is a transitory crystal that very quickly melts and recrystallizes in the fairly stable β' form. The β' crystals are actually very small and give the appearance of an extremely smooth surface, as seen when a can of shortening is opened. If shortenings and other solid fats are held at cool storage temperatures, they will retain the desirable β' crystals for months. However, if they are warmed a bit, the crystals will begin to melt, and when they recrystallize, they will be in the larger intermediate crystal form. The intermediate crystals give a somewhat coarse appearance to the surface of a fat.

Anyone who has ever melted butter or margarine and then allowed it to cool undisturbed has seen the very large crystals known as β crystals. Fats with β crystals are not recommended for use in shortened cakes, for example, where the fat is creamed with sugar. The very coarse β crystals result in the formation of a coarse-textured cake.

Actually, any melted fat will cool in the form of β crystals unless quick cooling and thorough agitation are used to crystallize the fat. The procedure used in the solidification or crystallization of fats in making margarines and shortenings is designed to precipitate β' crystals rather than intermediate or β crystals. These desirable β' crystals will remain during storage and marketing as long as temperatures are fairly cool. It is particularly important in warm weather to avoid letting margarine get warm, for the β' crystals will melt, and the transition to the intermediate and even to the very stable β crystals may take place with prolonged warm storage. Shortenings and lard need cool storage (60°F for shortening and 40°F for lard) to keep β' crystals.

Lard crystals are particularly unstable, which tends to give lard a grainy appearance. The fatty acids on the molecules of lard can be stripped off during manufacturing and rearranged to modify the form of the lard crystals. Lard that has undergone this special treatment is called *rearranged lard*. Another technique to help maintain lard in the desired β' crystals is to add flakes of a fat in the β' form to the cooling lard to help seed the crystallizing lard in the desired form.

Rearranged Lard Lard that has been processed to remove the fatty acids from the glycerol and then to reunite them in a somewhat different configuration to achieve a product that tends to form β' crystals.

Winterizing Process of chilling an oil to 45°F and then filtering it to remove any fat crystals.

Winterizing

Salad oils are designed so that they can be kept chilled without having crystals of fat forming in them. To accomplish this, the oils are chilled to 45°F and then filtered to remove any crystals that have formed. This chilling and filtering process is called *winterizing*. By this process, it is possible to store salad oils and salad dressings containing these oils in the refrigerator and to pour them from their bottles without heating them to melt crystals.

Shortening Value

Shortening Value
Ability of a fat to interfere with gluten development and tenderize a baked product.

The ability of a fat to aid in tenderizing baked products is called its *shortening value*. This terminology is derived from the ability of fats to shorten gluten (protein) strands, the structural protein network in wheat-containing batters and doughs. In other words, fats contribute to structural weakness, helping to keep baked products tender. This is accomplished by spreading the fat into thinner and thinner layers along the developing gluten strands as mixing is done. This slippery coating of fat helps to keep water from reaching the gluten and inhibits the hydration of the gluten. The type of fat used will influence the effectiveness in tenderizing the product. The plasticity of a fat and its ability to cover surface area are two important qualities determining the shortening value of fats.

Plasticity Ability of a fat to be spread easily into quite thin films.

Plasticity An ideal fat for tenderizing will be soft enough to be spread easily, but not so fluid that it runs out of the mixture. Hard fats are limited in their effectiveness as shortening agents because they resist efforts to spread them into thin layers during mixing, thus limiting the protective action of the fat.

Fats that are soft enough to be spread into rather thin films during mixing are said to possess *plasticity*. Shortenings are good examples of fats that are plastic over a rather wide temperature range, making them excellent choices in many baked products. In contrast, butter has a narrow temperature range over which it exhibits plasticity. When first removed from the refrigerator, it is too hard to spread, yet in a warm room, butter becomes quite fluid. This limited plasticity makes butter less effective as a shortening agent than shortening.

Surface Area The composition of a fat will determine how effectively the fat blocks water from reaching gluten. Fats with added mono- and diglycerides are useful shortenings because the hydroxyl (—OH) group(s) will be attracted to the interface between water and fat. Similarly, polyunsaturated fatty acids in salad oils are able to cover a large surface area along the gluten strands because the double bonds also are drawn to both water and fat. When molecules have structural features attracted to the interface between water and oil, fats

Oil / Water — Saturated fatty acid

Oil / Water — One double bond

Oil / Water — Two double bonds

Oil / Water — Three double bonds

are very good shortening agents. The accompanying diagrams illustrate the particularly effective configuration of a fatty acid with three double bonds, a situation common in salad oils. Note that fatty acids with either one or two double bonds are equally effective in covering surface area because it is physically impossible for the second double bond to be drawn back to the interface. However, any polyunsaturated fatty acid is more effective at covering the surface at the interface than is a saturated fatty acid.

Frying

Fat is the cooking medium utilized in both shallow-fat and deep-fat frying. Many different fruits, vegetables, meats, eggs, poultry, fish, and even some doughs and batter-dipped products may be fried. In fact, frying is a quick and popular way of preparing many foods, in large part because of the crisp texture that develops on the surface of well-prepared fried foods.

Shallow-Fat Frying   Good heat control is the key to successful shallow-fat frying. The food should be frying briskly, but with little spattering and no smoking of the fat. If the heat is too high, the fat will start to smoke, which is irritating to the eyes and also causes a greasy buildup on kitchen walls over a period of time. Moreover, the food will become tough and dry or may even be burned on the exterior if the fat is too hot. Too low a heat creates greasy food due to the absorption of extra fat during the extended frying period.

Deep-Fat Frying   A thermometer is an important adjunct to successful deep-fat frying, for temperature control must be maintained if the food is to be cooked through without burning or becoming greasy. Most deep-fat frying is done at 375°F, and the fat should be heated to this temperature before any food is added. If the fat is not hot enough, grease will be absorbed readily by the food. The addition of food to hot fat will cause the temperature of the fat to drop below the desired frying temperature of 375°F, but a fast rate of heating will quickly restore the desired temperature unless large quantities of food are added to the fat at one time. Even as little as 2 ounces of potatoes being french fried will cause 4 pounds of oil to drop almost 18 F°. A thermostatically controlled fryer will quickly regain the desired temperature because the drop immediately triggers the heating unit to heat. Despite this action, it still is important to avoid overloading a deep-fat fryer so that food will be fried at the correct temperature rather than being heated at a lower temperature and becoming greasy.

The appearance of deep-fat fried foods can be a deceptive indication of doneness, particularly if the frying oil is too hot. Even at 375°F, foods brown very readily on the exterior, considerably ahead of the rate of heat penetration into the interior of thick pieces, such as chicken. As a result, foods can be beautifully browned and look wonderful, yet be almost raw in the center. This is a greater problem when thick pieces (such as chicken) are being fried than when something thin (like onion rings) is being prepared. Fortunately, the browning process proceeds far more slowly after the initial browning, which makes it possible to fry foods until they are done in the center without burning them if the temperature is controlled properly.

When the correct amount of time has elapsed for deep-fat frying, a final check of doneness can be made by cutting a very small slit in the product to the center and checking for doneness. If the food is done, it should be drained on a paper towel to remove excess fat clinging to the surface. For optimum quality, the fried food should be served just as soon as possible. If it must be

---

SCIENCE NOTE: CHEMICAL CHANGES IN FATS

Heat Reactions

The high temperatures of frying cause fats to undergo hydrolysis and polymerization of the fatty acids. The first stage in the breakdown of fats in frying is *hydrolysis*, in which a molecule of water is utilized to split a free fatty acid from the fat molecule, ultimately releasing glycerol. The glycerol molecule then loses two molecules of water, forming a very irritating aldehyde called *acrolein*. This reaction is shown here.

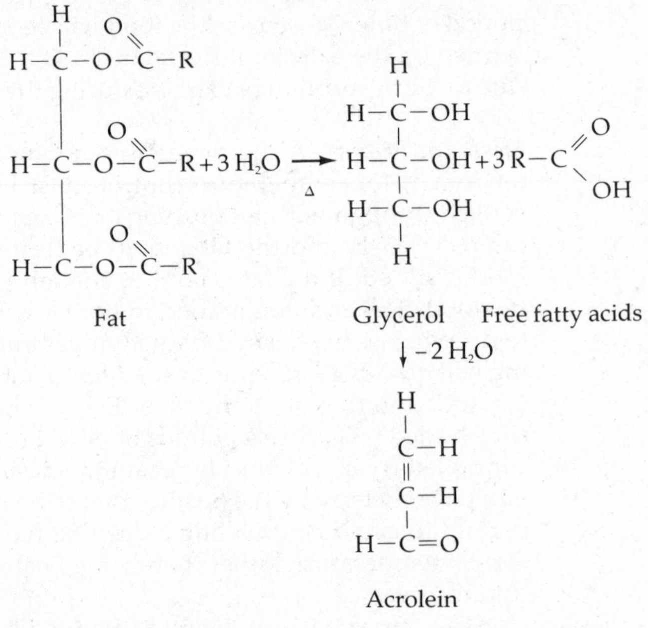

Hydrolysis Chemical reaction in which a molecule of water is used to split a compound into two molecules.

Acrolein Aldehyde formed when glycerol loses two molecules of water.

Fat   Glycerol   Free fatty acids

Acrolein

The free fatty acids released during extended use of oils polymerize into long chains. The increase in viscosity noted in oils that have been used for a period of time for deep fat frying is the visual evidence of this *polymerization* process. The long carbon chains resulting from this chemical change present much more resistance to movement than does a single fatty acid.

Polymerization The joining together of free fatty acids to make long chains; occurs in heated oils.

The release of free fatty acids and formation of acrolein are accompanied by smoking of the fat. The temperature at which this can be seen is the *smoke point*. The smoke point is not a constant value but, instead, drops gradually as the fat begins to break down. Oils will have a smoke point well above the temperature needed for frying when they first are used, but they will begin to smoke during frying after a period of time. Hydrogenated shortenings are not suitable for deep-fat frying because their monoglycerides will quickly lose the single fatty acid, and the free glycerol will promptly form acrolein, causing smoking to occur at the temperature used in frying.

Rancidity

Fats slowly undergo deteriorative chemical changes that create undesirable odors and flavors due to oxidation or hydrolysis. The first detectable change, *reversion*, is noted in polyunsaturated fats when they develop a slightly fishy flavor and aroma. This precedes actual rancidity.

Oxidative Rancidity Unsaturated fatty acids in fats become rancid when they take up oxygen at the double bonds following removal of a hydrogen atom from the carbon atom adjacent to the point of unsaturation. Heat and light promote the initial oxidation process, but the reaction will continue even in the dark once rancidity is started. The result is the formation of peroxides due to the uptake of oxygen. Consequently, *oxidative rancidity* is measured by determining the *peroxide value* of a fat; the higher the peroxide value, the lower the quality of the fat.

Oxidative rancidity is retarded by antioxidants, such as the tocopherols, that may be present naturally in oils or added during processing (see Chapter 18). Antioxidants are effective because they take up the oxygen more readily than the fatty acids do. Metals (particularly copper, iron, and nickel) catalyze oxidative rancidity by lowering the energy needed for peroxide formation. Traces of these minerals need to be kept from contact with fats. Hematin (an iron-containing compound in meat) can catalyze oxidative reactions in the fats of meat even during frozen storage. Lipoxidases are enzymes in vegetables capable of catalyzing oxidative rancidity. However, freezing or heat will inactivate lipoxidases.

Hydrolytic Rancidity *Hydrolytic rancidity* occurs when free fatty acids are split from fat molecules as a result of the action of *lipases* (enzymes catalyzing the breakdown of fats) during storage. The measurement of hydrolytic rancidity is done by determining the level of free fatty acids in the fat.

Cold temperatures retard the development of hydrolytic rancidity, but even frozen storage does not halt this gradual deterioration of quality. Flavor changes are particularly objectionable when hydrolytic rancidity results in free fatty acids with 12 or fewer carbon atoms. Fortunately, heat is effective in inactivating lipases.

Smoke Point Temperature at which a fat smokes due to chemical breakdown to free fatty acids and acrolein.

Reversion Development of a fishy quality in polyunsaturated fats.

Oxidative Rancidity Uptake of oxygen (with loss of hydrogen at points of unsaturation in a fatty acid), causing undesirable flavor and aroma changes.

Peroxide Value Content of peroxides in a fat; a measure of oxidative rancidity.

Hydrolytic Rancidity Release of free fatty acids due to lipase action during storage of fats.

Lipase Enzyme catalyzing the release of fatty acids from fats.

held, place the fried food between two layers of paper towels and hold at 140°F in the oven until served.

The oil used for deep-fat frying can be used more than once. However, even when care is taken to store the oil properly, the smoke point of the fat will drop gradually, causing the foods fried in it to be less appealing than they would be if fresh oil were used. The useful life of oils for frying can be extended by heating the oil just long enough prior to frying to preheat it and then cooling it promptly as soon as the food has been fried. Deterioration occurs rather rapidly at the high temperatures used in frying so the time of heating should be kept as short as possible.

Keeping the water in foods to be fried to an absolute minimum will also help to extend the useful life of the oil. For example, when water comes in contact with hot oil, there is considerable splattering, which introduces oxygen into the oil and also adds water. Both of these additives accelerate the breakdown of oil, which causes a lowering of the smoke point. Using paper towels to blot potatoes for french fries and other foods that may contain water before frying will reduce this problem.

Foreign particles in oil for deep-fat frying also hasten the chemical breakdown and lowering of the smoke point. After frying, the cooled oil can be strained to help filter out small particles of food that may have fallen into the oil during frying.

SUMMARY

Wise selection and use of fats and oils is important from the standpoint of nutrition and weight control as well as food quality. There are numerous fats and oils from which to choose. Lard and butter are familiar animal fats, while margarines, shortenings, and salad oils are produced commercially from several plant sources, including corn, soybeans, safflower, cottonseed, sunflower, palm, and olives.

In many areas of food preparation, fats are used to enhance palatability by modifying texture, color, and flavor and by promoting tenderness. Oils and fats are used for frying foods, too. Butter and margarine are used for spreads and sometimes in cakes and cookies. Frying is most satisfactory when salad oils are used, but butter or margarine can be used if frying is to be brief. Salad oils are well suited to making salad dressings, with olive oil being a favorite choice for some. For most baked products, shortenings are particularly suitable, although lard may be preferred by some in making pastry. Specific baked products may be made using oil; chiffon cakes require oil as the lipid, and muffins can be made with oil rather than melted fat, if desired.

Refrigerator storage extends the shelf life of fats and oils, although shortening and salad oils usually can be stored at room temperature for weeks without becoming rancid. Butter, margarine, and lard should be stored in the refrigerator to retard the development of rancidity unless they are to be used promptly.

Fats are composed of glycerol and fatty acids (usually three fatty acids) in each molecule. The melting point of fats is determined by the number of carbon atoms and the amount of unsaturation in the fatty acids. To prepare fats and oils for the commercial market, the fats are rendered or extracted from their animal or plant sources, after which they are refined and sometimes hydrogenated to convert some oils into solid fats. Blending and tempering are done to achieve the desired mix of fats and oils to achieve a fat that will be quite stable in the beta prime (β^1) crystal form. Oils are winterized to remove crystals of fat that form at refrigerator temperatures.

When fats are used to tenderize baked products, their shortening value is of importance, for this determines how much protection a particular fat will afford gluten during mixing. Fats with short chain fatty acids and polyunsaturated fatty acids will spread readily to give good coverage. Monoglycerides and fatty acids with at least one double bond will help to block water from gluten by collecting at the interface between the fat and water.

Frying, either shallow- or deep-fat frying, causes some breakdown of fats. Careful temperature control aids in producing a high-quality fried product with a minimum of fat clinging to it. During extended heating of fat used in frying, fatty acids split from glycerol, and the glycerol then breaks down to acrolein. The fatty acids polymerize as heating continues, causing increased viscosity of the oil. The smoke point drops as these changes take place.

Rancidity develops as a result of oxidation or of hydrolysis during extended storage of fats. Oxidative rancidity can be catalyzed by lipoxidases and is evidenced by an increase in the peroxide number due to the loss of hydrogen at double bonds and the uptake of oxygen. Metals and oxygen in the presence of stored fats promote oxidative rancidity, while antioxidants retard this change by reacting readily with oxygen that may be present. Hydrolytic rancidity, the splitting off of fatty acids, results in an increasing level of free fatty acids as rancidity develops. The presence of water promotes this reaction, but lipases can catalyze hydrolytic rancidity even in dehydrated foods. Heat inactivates lipases.

Selected References

Bauer, F. J. Acetin fat. I. Products made from mixed acetin fats. *J. Am. Oil Chem. Soc.* *31*: 147. 1954.

Bennion, M. et al. Changes in frying fats with batters containing egg. *J. Am. Diet. Assoc. 68*: 234. 1976.

Boothby, L. New technology of oils and fats. *Food Manufacture 57(2)*: 27. 1982.

Brignoli, C. A. et al. Comprehensive evaluation of fatty acids in food. V. Unhydrogenated fats and oils. *J. Am. Diet. Assoc. 68*: 224. 1976.

Coenen, J. W. Hydrogenation of edible oils. *J. Amer. Oil Chem. Soc. 53*: 382. 1976.

Deuel, H. J. *The Lipids. Vol. 1. Chemistry.* Interscience. New York. 1951.

Frankel, E. N. Lipid oxidation, *Prog. in Lipid Research 19(1)*: 1. 1980.

Glass, R. L. Food rancidity: Its nature and prevention. *Baker's Digest 40*: 34. 1966.

Hoerr, C. W. and D. F. Waugh. Some physical characteristics of rearranged lard. *J. Am. Oil Chem. Soc. 32*: 37. 1955.

Hoerr, C. W. Morphology of fats, oils, and shortenings. *J. Am. Oil Chem. Soc.* 37: 539. 1960.

Hoerr, C. W. X-ray diffraction of fats. *J. Am. Oil Chem. Soc. 41(7)*: 4. 1964.

Husted, H. H. Interesterification of edible oils. *J. Amer. Oil Chem. Soc.* 53: 390. 1976.

Hutchinson, P. E. et al. Effect of emulsifiers on the texture of cookies. *J. Food Science* 42: 399. 1977.

Kreulen, H. P. Fractionation and winterization of edible fats and oils. *J. Amer. Oil Chem. Soc.* 53: 393. 1976.

Landers, R. E. and D. M. Rathman. Vegetable oils: effects of processing, storage, and use on nutritional values. *J. Am. Oil Chem. Soc. 58(3)*: 255. 1981.

Mai, J. et al. Effects of microwave cooking on food fatty acids: no evidence of chemical alteration or isomerization. *J. Food Sci. 45(6)*: 1753. 1980.

McComber, D. and E. M. Miller. Differences in total lipid and fatty acid composition as influenced by lecithin, leavening agent, and use of frying fat. *Cereal Chem.* 53: 101. 1976.

Nawar, W. W. Chemical changes in lipids produced by thermal processing. *J. Chem. Ed. 61*: 299. 1984.

Ottenstein, D. M. et al. Trans fatty acid content of commercial margarine samples determined by gas-liquid chromatography on OV-275. *J. Amer. Oil Chem. Soc.* 54: 207. 1977.

Perkins, E. G. Nutritional and chemical changes occurring in heated fats. *Food Tech.* 14: 508. 1960.

Puri, P. S. Winterization of oils and fats. *J. Am. Oil Chem. Soc. 57(11)*: 848. 1980. (a)

Puri, P. S. Hydrogenation of oils and fats. *J. Am. Oil Chem. Soc. 57(11)*: 850. 1980. (b)

Robertson, J. A. Sunflower: America's neglected crop. *J. Amer. Oil Chem. Soc.* 49: 239. 1972.

Roth, H. and S. P. Rock. Chemistry and technology of frying fats. I. Chemistry. *Baker's Digest 46(4)*: 1972.(a)

Roth, H. and S. P. Rock. Chemistry and technology of frying fats. II. Technology. *Baker's Digest 46(5)*: 38. 1972. (b)

Sherwin, E. R. Antioxidants for vegetable oils. *J. Amer. Oil Chem. Soc.* 53: 430. 1976.

Sherwin, E. R. Oxidation and antioxidants in fat and oil processing. *J. Am. Oil Chem. Soc. 55(11)*: 809. 1978.

Sreenivasan, B. Interesterification of fats. *J. Am. Oil Chem. Soc. 55(11)*: 796. 1978.

Weihrauch, J. L. et al. Fatty acid composition of margarines, processed fats, and oils: new compilation of data for tables of food composition. *Food Tech. 31(2)*: 80. 1977.

Young, V. Processing of oils and fats. *Chem. and Ind.* 18: 692. 1978.

Study Questions

1. Make an inventory of the various types of fats and oils available in a supermarket. How do the ingredients compare among (a) brands and (b) types of products. Compare the price per pound of each item.
2. Using the same recipe for each product, prepare pastry using each of the following fats: shortening, butter, stick margarine, lard, and salad oil. Compare the ease of preparation and the palatability characteristics of each pastry.
3. What factors influence the fluidity of a fat?
4. Why is it important that fat crystals be in the β' form when fats are used for

making cakes? Does the type of fat crystal in fats have significance if fats are to be used for frying?

5. What changes occur in a fat during prolonged heating?
6. In what ways do fats become rancid? How can use and storage practices help to delay the onset of rancidity?
7. What fats are the most effective tenderizing agents? Why?

Grandma Moses, "Sugaring Off." © Grandma Moses Properties/Galerie St. Etienne.

CHAPTER 6

CARBOHYDRATES: SUGAR COOKERY

INTRODUCING THE CARBOHYDRATES

Carbohydrate Organic compounds containing carbon, hydrogen, and oxygen, with the hydrogen and oxygen being in the ratio of water (H_2O); category includes sugars, starches, pectic substances, cellulose, gums, and other complex substances.

Carbohydrates are recognized in nutrition as an important source of energy, a function viewed negatively by some weight-conscious people. It is true that some foods are rather concentrated sources of carbohydrate, but still pure carbohydrates provide less than half as many calories per gram as are derived from a comparable amount of pure fat.

In food preparation, the various carbohydrates serve some key roles meriting special discussion. The simplest of the carbohydrates are the sugars. Many foods, particularly fruits, contain sugars, which are responsible for pleasingly sweet flavors. Other foods contain appreciably less sugar than the levels in fruits. However, sugars in various forms are used in making candies, various desserts, and even sauces for meats and vegetables.

Foods naturally contain many other carbohydrates that are more complex than sugars. Starch is the best known of these complex carbohydrates, but the fiber in fruits and vegetables also contains carbohydrates in such forms as cellulose, hemicelluloses, pectic substances, and gums. These different forms of complex carbohydrates are valued in food preparation for their contributions to the texture of foods and to structure.

At first glance, it would seem that sugar and its sweet flavor would have almost nothing in common with the complex structural and texturizing carbohydrates. Why are these simple and complex substances clumped collectively into the category of organic compounds called carbohydrates? The answer lies in the fact that they are all made up of the same elements—carbon, hydrogen, and oxygen—and in approximately the same proportions. The term *carbohydrate* is a combination of carbon and hydrate (H and OH, or water). This relationship of hydrate to carbon holds regardless of the size and complexity of a particular carbohydrate.

SUGARS IN THE MARKETPLACE

The sugars marketed today are quite different in quality, quantity, and price from the first sugar known in the Near East. Although sugar was once a rare item available only to royalty, today it is a household item in most kitchens around the world. The history of sugar began sometime between 300 and 600 A.D. when various techniques were developed in the Near East to refine and crystallize sugar. News of this remarkable food was carried to Europe by the returning Crusaders and eventually reached the New World when Columbus introduced sugar to Santo Domingo in 1493.

Of course, changes in sugar production have taken place over the centuries, but perhaps the single most important discovery was the realization by a nineteenth-century German chemist that the sugar beet is an outstanding source of sugar. By the beginning of this century, the sugar beet was approaching sugarcane as a source of sugar for commercial production. Levels of consumption of cane versus beet sugar vary in different sections of the country.

Sugarcane is a very tall crop; the stalk is squeezed to remove the sugar-rich sap, which then is processed ultimately into various sugar products.

The sugar beet, a very large, white variety of beet, serves as the source of a significant amount of sugar for the consumer market. The sugar products resulting from the processing of sugarcane or sugar beets are the same regardless of the original source of the sugar.

Cane sugar is produced by squeezing the sugar-containing juice from the washed cane stalks, heating the juice in the presence of lime to aid in removing impurities, and then evaporating the mixture to a highly viscous syrup and to raw sugar crystals. It is these raw sugar crystals that are the starting material for the refining process. The coarse, yellow raw sugar is transformed from its sticky state into white, fine sugar crystals by the use of charcoal and careful recrystallization of the sugar.

Beet sugar, the product of sugar beets, is extracted from this special type of beet and processed to the refined sugar product in much the same manner as the process used for making cane sugar. The end product of both of these manufacturing processes is the same sugar, sucrose, and is marketed simply as granulated sugar or in related sugar products. Since there is no difference in cane sugar and beet sugar, either type can be chosen. The sugar market for both types of sugar is regulated by the federal government, in that it establishes the levels of sugar imports authorized each year.

An interesting by-product of sugar manufacturing is monosodium glutamate, often referred to simply as MSG. This is a sodium derivative of sugar, yet is not itself sweet tasting. Its merit is as a flavor enhancer to help heighten the existing flavors in foods. It is used particularly frequently in various Oriental cuisines.

Granulated Sugar

Between 50 and 85 percent of factory sugar production is devoted to granulated sugar because of its important roles in many food products. The source of granulated sugar, whether cane or beet, will be found on the package label although both products are the same.

White or refined granulated sugar may be purchased in different granule sizes, ranging from superfine to regular granulated sugar. The name dessert sugar, a synonym for superfine, indicates that this type of sugar is preferred for making hard and soft meringues and other desserts where the ease of solubility of these very tiny crystals is important. Regular granulated sugar is perfectly suitable for most uses and has the advantage of being less expensive than dessert sugar.

Cube sugar is simply granulated sugar that has been moistened with a white syrup, molded into cubes, and then dried in that shape. These cubes are used for sweetening individual cups of tea and coffee.

Frosting Sugar

When making uncooked icings, the easy solubility of the bubbles of frosting sugar is convenient. These bubbles are basically made of sucrose; no filler is added.

Powdered (Confectioners) Sugar

One problem with any sugar is its tendency to cake when stored in a moist environment. To counteract the tendency to lump when sugar pulverized to a fine powder is stored, cornstarch can be added, and this is just what is done in the manufacturing of powdered sugar. Cornstarch, at a level of 3 percent, is sufficient to absorb the moisture that would otherwsie cause caking in this very-fine-particle sugar. Powdered sugar customarily is used for making icings and for sweetening certain fruits, such as strawberries.

Raw Sugar

Raw sugar, a semirefined sugar that is a light tan color, has gained a place on the market shelf because of consumers' demand for natural products. However, there is no nutritional merit in using raw sugar in place of granulated sugar. (Raw sugar is not the unrefined product, for the unrefined product is not safe to eat.) The raw sugar at the market behaves very much like brown sugar in food preparation and is sometimes used to sweeten fruits or to make cookies and other baked products. The tan color will show when this sugar is used in light-colored baked products. The cost of raw sugar is surprisingly high in view of the fact that the processing is slightly easier than that for white granulated sugar.

Brown Sugar

Because of its pleasing and distinctive flavor, brown sugar frequently is used in baked products. The color and flavor of brown sugar are correlated with the state of refinement; a dark, strong-flavored brown sugar has undergone less filtration and purification than has a light, mild-flavored product. Either can be used very satisfactorily. The comparatively high moisture content of brown sugar tends to promote the development of hard lumps during storage. The use of such special packages as plastic bags with tight closure helps to minimize this problem. A pourable, pelletlike brown sugar is also available, although this is more costly than regular brown sugar.

Maple Sugar and Syrup

The tapping of sugar maple trees and the boiling of the collected sap to make maple syrup and sugar date back to Colonial days in America. It still is possible to buy maple syrup and sugar, but limitations in the production process have hampered output and caused prices to be relatively high for these products.

Maple syrup and sugar have a sweet taste and a pleasing, distinctive flavor, which contribute to its popularity. The demand for maple flavoring has stimulated considerable effort to develop a synthetic counterpart, and the result is a reasonably comparable flavoring at a significantly reduced price. Synthetically flavored maple syrup is a familiar and widely used topping for pancakes and waffles and may even be used occasionally in baked products for sweetening.

Molasses

Molasses is a sugarcane derivative that may be marketed as unsulphured molasses, sulphured molasses, or blackstrap molasses. Sulphured molasses ranges in color from rather light to a medium dark brown, depending on whether it is prepared by centrifuging the first (the lighter color) or second boiling of the sugarcane juice. Sulphured molasses is a by-product remaining after cane sugar has been crystallized and removed from the cane juice. Sulfur fumes are in contact with the liquid when sugar is the principal product being prepared and molasses is merely a by-product. Unsulphured molasses is a full-flavored, reddish-brown liquid that has not been exposed to sulphur fumes. Aging enhances the flavor of unsulphured molasses. Blackstrap molasses, often used as animal food, is the material remaining after the sugar has been extracted from the boiled cane juice.

Corn Syrup

All of the sweeteners discussed so far are acquired by refining or otherwise processing parts of plants that are high in their sugar content. Corn syrup is unique in that it is produced from starch, a complex carbohydrate, by a series of chemical changes called hydrolysis. This hydrolytic breakdown is accomplished by treating starch from corn with hydrochloric or sulfuric acids in the presence of heat and pressure to produce a mixture of breakdown products. Although cornstarch itself does not have a sweet taste, the small units splitting from the starch (glucose, maltose, and some dextrins) are sweet. Corn syrup, which is a very viscous liquid, gains much of its sweetness from its high glucose content.

The abundance and comparatively low cost of cornstarch are valued qualities that have helped to make corn syrup a popular sweetener. However, there still is a need to find ways of using or marketing the surplus of cornstarch available, and this has prompted efforts to derive new products from it. One creative approach has involved the development of a new corn syrup called *high-fructose corn syrup*. Chemically, this is an interesting product, for the enzyme *isomerase* is used to convert some of the glucose in the corn syrup into another sugar, fructose. Theoretically, this high-fructose corn syrup (actually only about 30 percent fructose) has an advantage over the original corn syrup because fructose is about twice as sweet as glucose. This means that less fructose-containing corn syrup can be used to sweeten a product than would be needed if ordinary corn syrup were used. This difference is an advantage in beverages or other fluid applications but not in baked products. Nevertheless, there are many applications of high-fructose corn syrup by food manufacturers. High-fructose corn syrup is not yet available directly to consumers at the marketplace level.

High-Fructose Corn Syrup Corn syrup in which isomerase has converted some of the sugar to fructose.

Isomerase Enzyme utilized to convert glucose to fructose in making high-fructose corn syrup.

Honey

Honey is the only sweetener derived from animal sources. Bees, using nectar from different flowering plants, produce this distinctive sweetening liquid. Frequently, the sources of nectar for the bees are clover and alfalfa, but there are many types of honey, such as orange blossom, available with varying flavor qualities. Honey is an excellent sweetener because it contains an abundance of fructose and adds a distinctive flavor to products containing it. The disadvantages of honey are the comparatively high price and the excessively fast browning when batters and doughs containing honey are baked.

Other Sweeteners

Saccharin is a noncarbohydrate, nonnutritive sweetener that has been used as a sweetener by diabetics for years. The consumption of saccharin no longer is limited to diabetics, for many weight-conscious people are now selecting foods made with saccharin rather than with sugar in order to reduce their caloric intake. Saccharin is marketed in many commercial food products and in the granular and fluid forms for sweetening foods at home. Saccharin can be used in products, such as beverages, where sugar serves only a sweetening function, although some people find the aftertaste objectionable. Saccharin is not a suitable substitute for sugar in traditional candy recipes or batter and dough products where sugar performs other roles in addition to sweetening.

Other nonnutritive sweeteners may be anticipated in the future, although considerable time is required to gain the approval of the Food and Drug Administration for any new product. Extensive tests on the safety of any proposed new additive, including sweeteners, must be completed before such items can be used in any food. Cyclamates were previously on the market, but subsequently banned when some evidence of carcinogenicity was found in experimental animals fed impossibly high doses of the sweetener.

Aspartame is a low-calorie sweetener recently approved for use in many different food products. This substance is a dipeptide, that is, it behaves like a protein. A gram of aspartame will provide 4 kilocalories of energy, but the sweetness contribution is sometimes as great as 200 times that of sucrose. Since only small amounts of aspartame are needed, its use as a sweetener can reduce the calorie content of beverages or some other food items in which sucrose traditionally would be used. The two amino acids making up aspartame are aspartic acid and phenylalanine, the latter being a concern for people needing to keep their intake of this amino acid low (those with phenylketonuria).

Applications in which aspartame may be used are still being explored, but problems have been observed in loss of sweetness in baked products. This loss appears to be due to the change in the structure of this dipeptide when heated. The primary use of aspartame in the home market is as a sweetener for tea and coffee.

Aspartame

SWEETENING POWER

The sweetening power of pure sugars and of products containing sugars is of importance in formulating recipes, for the sweet taste of any food must please the diner's palate. People vary in their taste sensitivity, with some people being able to detect sweetness at a far lower concentration than others can. One way of considering sugars as ingredients is to determine how sweet one sugar is in comparison with another. The sweetest sugars will be able to be detected as being sweet at much lower concentrations than will those that are only slightly sweet. Such tests ordinarily are conducted using dilute sugar solutions tested at room temperature. Results of such comparisons are presented in Table 6.1, with sucrose being set arbitrarily at 100.

Table 6.1 Comparative Sweetness of Sugars and Related Products

Product	Sweetness	Product	Sweetness
Saccharin	30,600	Maple syrup	64
Aspartame	20,000[1]	Glucose	64
Fructose	115	Galactose	59
Sucrose	100	Maltose	46
Honey	97	Lactose	30
Molasses	74	Corn syrup	30

Source: Adapted from *Food Research* 22:206. 1957.
[1]Manufacturer's information.

SCIENCE NOTE: Mono- and Disaccharides

The sugars found naturally in foods are classified on the basis of the number of carbon atoms in their basic units and on the complexity of the total molecule. Some five-carbon sugars, called pentoses, are found in foods, but they have limited application in home food preparation. Ribose and arabinose are pentoses. Of more importance in food preparation are the hexoses, which are named because of their content of six carbon atoms. Glucose, fructose, and galactose are the three hexoses of particular interest. Their structures are shown below.

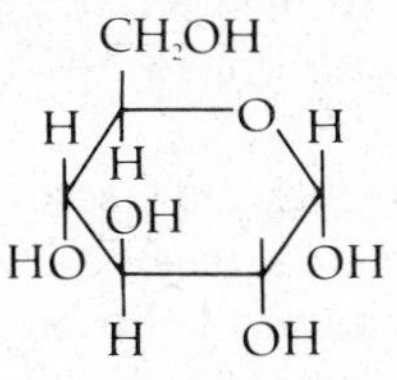

Glucose 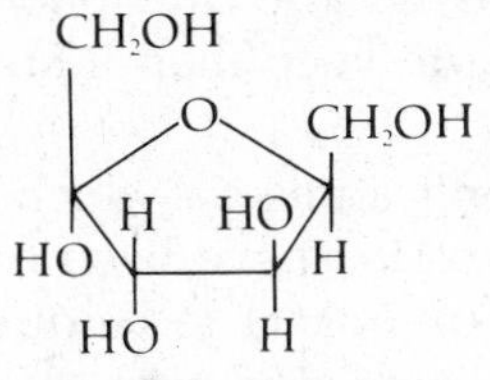   Fructose 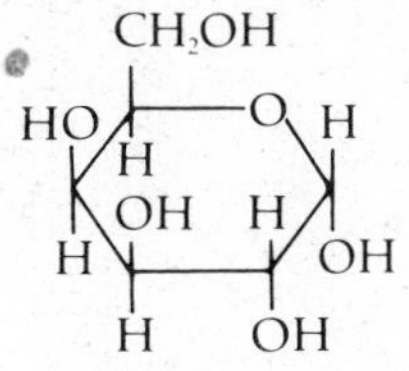   Galactose

Monosaccharide Sugar composed of five or six carbon atoms.

Disaccharide Sugar composed of two monosaccharide units joined by eliminating a molecule of water.

These three *monosaccharides* are used in the formation of three common disaccharides. Each molecule of a disaccharide is composed of two monosaccharides that have been united with the expulsion of a molecule of water. All three of the disaccharides of greatest importance in food contain one unit of glucose. In fact, maltose contains two units of glucose. Lactose contains galactose in addition to glucose, and fructose is the second monosaccharide in sucrose. Their structures are presented below.

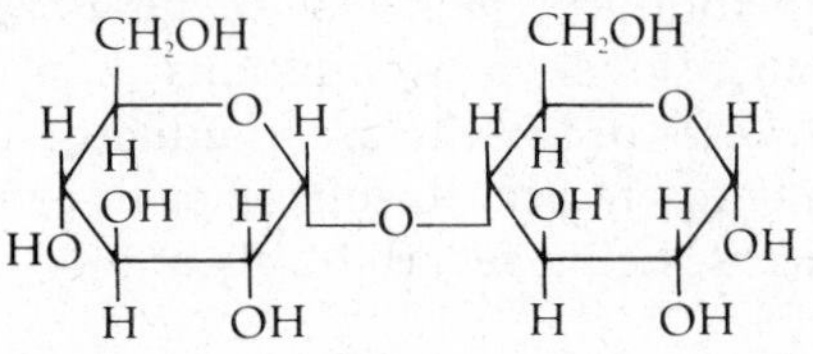

Maltose 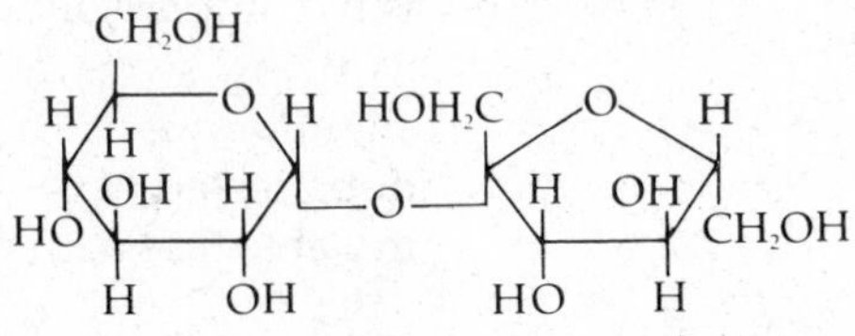   Sucrose

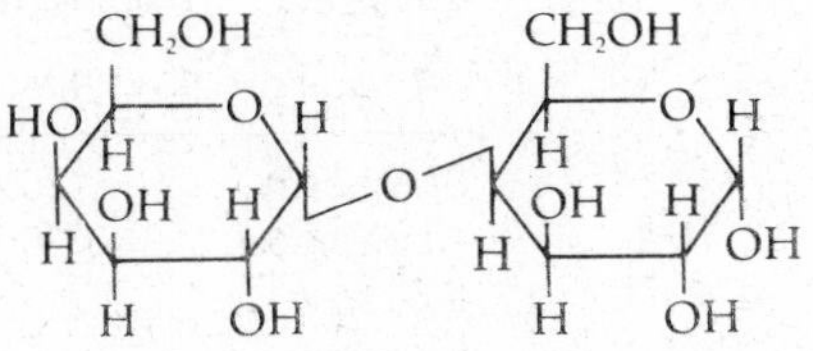

Lactose

Sucrose is the most common of the disaccharides and is used widely in food preparation. Lactose is the sugar in milk and sometimes is referred to as "milk sugar."

Caramelization

Sucrose can be heated by itself until it becomes so hot that it melts and fairly rapidly goes from a colorless liquid to a golden brown and then to a deep brown, followed by black if heating is continued. At the same time that the color is changing, the aroma becomes caramel-like and eventually will smell like burning sugar unless cooled promptly. The temperature of caramelizing sugar is very high, and the chemical breakdown of the sugar proceeds so rapidly that boiling water usually is poured into the molten sugar at the desired stage of caramelization to cool the mixture and halt the caramelization. Even when the added water is boiling, there is a large temperature differential between the molten sugar and the boiling water, which results in some spattering briefly. This added water not only halts caramelization, but also dilutes the sugar to make a caramelized sugar syrup for use in recipes. Otherwise, the undiluted sugar will solidify into a hard, brittle mass that cannot be incorporated with other ingredients.

Hydrolysis

Invert Sugar A mixture of equal amounts of glucose and fructose resulting from the hydrolysis of sucrose.

Inversion Specific term for the hydrolysis of sucrose to glucose and fructose.

Sucrose can undergo the severe chemical breakdown involved in caramelization, or it can be subjected to a milder change—that of hydrolysis. Hydrolysis of sucrose results in the formation of *invert sugar* (equal amounts of two simple sugars, glucose and fructose). This change, specifically called *inversion*, affects the sugar-containing products in which hydrolysis occurs because the usual end result is a mixture of sucrose and invert sugar, which together will crystallize less easily than will sucrose alone.

SCIENCE NOTE: Caramelization Reactions

When heated without water, sucrose crystals melt, and then chemical breakdown begins. First, the linkage between the fructose and glucose units of sucrose break. Continued heating then creates many different chemical compounds as a result of the breaking of the ring structure of both monosaccharides. Prominent among the compounds created by caramelization are organic acids. Evidence of the formation of these acids is seen when baking soda is added to caramelizing sugar; the alkaline ingredient combines with the acids to form carbon dioxide, causing the caramelized liquid to bubble and become porous. An application of this reaction to produce CO_2 is the making of peanut brittle, for this type of candy is heated to the point where caramelization is occurring, and then baking soda is added before the very viscous mixture has an opportunity to cool enough to become solid. The reaction of the soda with the organic acids in the candy causes the brittle to become opaque and porous as a result of the large amount of carbon dioxide generated.

Inversion is promoted when sugar is cooked in a solution to which an acid has been added. In making crystalline candies, cream of tartar frequently is added as the acid ingredient to ensure that a moderate amount of invert sugar will be formed to help in achieving a smooth texture. A moderate to slow rate of cooking will result in an appreciable amount of inversion, while a fast rate of boiling a crystalline candy will permit less time for inversion to occur.

Some inversion is desirable when making crystalline candies because the presence of more than one sugar helps to inhibit crystal formation during the cooling period, thus aiding in creating a smooth-textured candy. However, excessive inversion presents a problem; too much inversion of sucrose to glucose and fructose can interfere with crystal formation so much that the resulting candy will be too soft. The addition of a small amount of cream of tartar, combined with a moderate rate of heating, will provide the combination needed to produce an appropriately firm, smooth-textured crystalline candy.

Invertase Enzyme catalyzing the inversion of sucrose to glucose and fructose.

Another means of causing hydrolysis is with the use of the enzyme *invertase*. Invertase, which is available commercially but not in the home market, is able to catalyze the inversion of sucrose when allowed to interact with a finished candy for a few days. As is true with any enzyme, invertase must not be heated if it is to retain its catalytic ability. Consequently, commercially produced chocolate creams are made by creating a fairly firm center filling that is mixed with the invertase prior to dipping in chocolate. After a period of several days of storage, invertase will have inverted so much of the sucrose that the filling will have softened to the desired consistency.

TYPES OF CANDIES

Candy is called *khandi* in Arabic and *sweets* in England, but there is universal appeal regardless of the name. From the perspective of nutrition, candy certainly is not essential, but its popularity in various forms around the world indicates that candy likely is here to stay as a pleasure in life. The various candies are classified as crystalline or amorphous, depending upon their internal organization. *Crystalline candies* are the candies that can be bitten easily and can be cut with a knife. When viewed under a microscope, there are many areas in crystalline candies where organized crystal structure can be seen, along with some liquid. Fondant, fudge, panocha, divinity, and creams are examples of crystalline candies.

Crystalline Candies Candies with an organized crystal structure; easily bitten into or cut with a knife.

Amorphous Candies Candies with such a high sugar content that they are too viscous to permit an organized crystal structure to develop; very hard to extremely chewy candies.

The *amorphous candies*, as the name implies, lack an organized structure. These candies generally have a higher concentration of sugar than the crystalline candies. Their cooked syrups are so viscous that sugar crystals cannot form any type of organization. The amorphous candies, with their lack of organized crystal structure, are not chewed easily or cut with a knife. They range in texture from extremely chewy caramels to very hard or even brittle products, such as toffee.

Although crystalline and amorphous candies are both examples of sugar cookery, their preparation problems are quite different. They both require

The coating on caramel or taffy apples, nut brittles, taffy, popcorn balls, and caramels are all examples of amorphous candies. Fudge is one of the various candies that are classified as crystalline candies.

careful cooking to the correct final temperature, but the problems associated with making crystalline candies are quite different from those involved in making high-quality amorphous candies.

Amorphous Candies

During the cooking of amorphous candies, water is evaporated until the correct concentration of sugar has been achieved. This is determined by the temperature of the boiling candy, which ranges from about 260° to 300°F, depending upon the type of amorphous candy being prepared. As water is being evaporated, the sugar concentration is effectively increasing, with the result that the boiling point of the solution keeps rising (see Chapter 1 for the discussion of the effect of sugar on vapor pressure and the temperature of boiling). These candies become extremely viscous in the later stage of cooking, making it difficult to keep the candy in total contact with the thermometer. If air is trapped around the bulb, the reading will be inaccurately low, and overcooking to the point of scorching may occur. Scorching may also be a problem if amorphous candies are boiled in pans that heat unevenly; a heavy aluminum pan with a perfectly flat bottom provides uniform heat distribution to avoid possible burning of any portion of the candy. Careful stirring during the entire boiling period is an additional aid in making high-quality amorphous candies.

Amorphous candies are evaluated on the basis of their texture and flavor. There is no single criterion for texture of amorphous candies, for they vary with the type of candy. Caramels should be wonderfully chewy, while taffy ordinarily is a bit too hard to bite, and toffees and brittles break easily when hit with a knife handle. A particular amorphous candy is judged on whether or not it fits the expected chewiness or hardness for the specific candy being made. The flavor should not have any trace of scorching or burning and should be pleasingly rich and characteristic of the ingredients and flavorings used.

Crystalline Candies

The problems in making high-quality crystalline candies are quite different from those involved in making amorphous candies. The concentration of sugar in crystalline candies is appreciably lower than in the amorphous candies, which means that they are not boiled as long or to as high a temperature (see Table 6.2). As a result, the likelihood of scorching and of obtaining an inaccurate temperature reading is reduced significantly. As with amorphous candies, however, a pan with even heating characteristics must be used. Since the temperature of boiling candies reflects the sugar concentration, very accurate temperature control is vital to obtaining the correct firmness of crystalline candies. A small error on the low side will cause the candy to be too soft, and a degree or two above the correct temperature will create a crumbly, hard product.

Two other factors, in addition to the final temperature reached, will influence the firmness of a crystalline candy. One is the rate of heating. If a candy is heated unusually slowly, the amount of inversion that occurs will be excessive. The large proportion of the resulting glucose and fructose will interfere more than normally in the crystallization process, and the candy will be a little

Table 6.2   Ingredients and Final Temperatures for Some Typical Candies

Candy	Basic Ingredients	Final Temperature, °F
Crystalline		
Fondant	Granulated sugar, corn syrup or cream of tartar, water	238
Fudge	Granulated sugar, cocoa or chocolate, milk, corn syrup, butter	234
Panocha	Brown sugar, granulated sugar, milk, corn syrup, butter	234
Amorphous		
Caramels	Granulated sugar, corn syrup, butter, cream	245
Taffy	Granulated sugar, corn syrup, water	260
Toffee	Granulated sugar, butter, water, corn syrup	300

softer than the final temperature would suggest. This problem can be avoided simply by being sure to use a pan large enough to allow the boiling candy to boil vigorously without spilling over the top.

The second factor that might cause a crystalline candy to be too soft relates to making candy on a rainy day. This is not an old wives' tale; there is scientific evidence to support the result. Sugar is very *hygroscopic* material—it attracts or absorbs water readily; this is particularly true when it is in a hot solution. Thus, while crystalline candies are cooling in an extremely humid environment, moisture will be removed from the air and held in the cooling candy. The result is that the candy will have a higher moisture content after standing than it did when it was first removed from the heat. In crystalline candies, the moisture level is so critical to the firmness of the candy that this small amount of absorbed moisture will make the candy just a bit too soft. To compensate for this, on a rainy day crystalline candies should be cooked about a degree Fahrenheit higher than the recipe states. This adjustment is unnecessary for amorphous candies because their moisture level is slightly less critical.

In addition to the firmness, crystalline candies are evaluated on their smoothness. Ideally, a crystalline candy will feel perfectly smooth when rubbed with the tongue against the roof of the mouth. There should be no suggestion of grittiness or rough crystals even though these candies are defined as having an organized crystalline structure. For success, the crystals must be very small, rather than in large aggregates, for it is these large clumps of crystals that feel rough on the tongue.

There are three areas of concern in preparing crystalline candies with a very smooth, velvety texture: (1) interfering agents, (2) adequate beating, and (3) rapid crystallization.

Interfering agents are ingredients or components of a candy that make it difficult for sugar crystals to form and clump together in large aggregates. Butter and the fat in chocolate are examples of interfering agents in fudge. The use of corn syrup is another; its viscous quality and the presence of a mixture of sugars (maltose and glucose) are useful in blocking crystals from aggregating. Cream of tartar or other acidic ingredients interfere indirectly by promoting the inversion of sucrose to give a mixture of sugars.

By beating crystalline candies when crystallization is starting and continuing throughout the crystallization until the candy converts to a solid, the sugar crystals are kept in motion and are not able to congregate together into coarse aggregates. This constant interference with crystals to prevent their bonding together is important in maintaining the desired, very smooth crystalline candy texture. Beating does not cause the candy to get hard; it simply influences how readily the crystals grow together. It also modifies the color of crystalline candies by trapping air throughout the solidifying, crystallizing candy. The combination of the air and the numerous sugar crystals produces an opaque, white or lighter-colored candy than would result if beating were omitted.

Beating is an important part of preparing high-quality crystalline candies. It is necessary to continue beating from the time crystallization begins until

Hygroscopic Water attracting.

Interfering Agent Butter, corn syrup, or other ingredient inhibiting crystal formation in candies.

Crystals from fondant cooked to 235°F, cooled to 105°F, and then beaten until the mass was stiff and kneadable (200×). The sugar solution was very supersaturated when beating was initiated in this candy. (Left)

Crystals from fondant cooked to 235°F and then beaten immediately and continuously until the mass was stiff and kneadable (200×). Note the large crystal size resulting from this treatment compared with the crystals in the photo on the left. (Right)

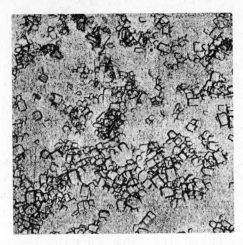

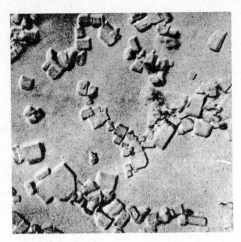

Heat of Crystallization Heat energy released when a viscous sugar solution crystallizes and forms a solid mass.

the candy softens slightly just before becoming firm. However, even diligent and vigorous beating cannot prevent a slight amount of graininess if crystallization begins too early in the cooling process.

The last factor influencing the smoothness of crystalline candies is the point when crystallization begins. If crystals are formed very rapidly, the candy will become locked into a fine crystalline structure that will change very little over time. The fine crystals remain separated; they do not rearrange into large aggregates if the total crystallization process can occur within an extremely brief period of time. This circumstance occurs when all of the sugar in a crystalline candy is dissolved during the boiling period and the candy is allowed to cool to about 110°F without any disturbance. If beating is initiated at this point, there will be extremely rapid formation of many sugar crystals and little opportunity for crystals to clump and create a grainy texture.

When beating crystalline candies, it may be difficult at first to spot the exact point when beating should be stopped, and the candy should be spread in preparation for cutting into pieces. The clue to the stopping point is the very slight softening of the candy due to the *heat of crystallization*. The heat of crystallization is the heat energy released when the very viscous sugar solution changes into the solid state (crystals). With experience, this softening can be detected, but it is difficult to see in small batches of candy because the heat is dissipated so rapidly. If the candy is not spread in time, it still is possible to produce a candy with a good appearance. This is accomplished by kneading the crumbly candy mass gently with the fingers until it works into a cohesive candy that can be modeled into the desired thickness.

Sometimes crystalline candies do not meet expectations. Perhaps they are too hard or too soft, or maybe they have a gritty texture. Unlike a number of food products, such candies can be salvaged. Water needs to be added to the candy in a pan and then the dissolved candy should be reheated until the correct final temperature is reached. The cooling and beating are done the same as they would be done for any crystalline candy.

Crystalline candies will soften slightly due to heat of crystallization just before they become solids, and they should be spread quickly at this point. Kneading is necessary if the candy is not spread at this point.

SCIENCE NOTE: Saturated and Supersaturated Solutions

In sugar cookery, sugar is a solute that is dissolved in a solvent (water or milk usually) to make a true solution. This is a true solution because it is homogeneous; that is, the content of samples taken from different portions of the mixture will all be the same. The ability of water to dissolve sugar varies with the temperature of the solution. This is quite apparent when making candy. At first, the solution is gritty no matter how much it is stirred because much of the sugar cannot be dissolved until the temperature rises. Gradually, the sugar all goes into solution, and the temperature of the boiling mixture starts to rise. This solution now is a *saturated solution*, which means that no more sugar can be dissolved in that amount of water at that temperature. However, the percentage of sugar in solution continues to rise in the boiling candy as the temperature rises and water evaporates. Throughout this boiling and evaporation period, the candy is a saturated solution, although the percentage of sugar in solution continues to increase until the final temperature is reached and the candy is removed from the heat.

Once the candy has been removed from the heat, the solution will begin to cool. This may seem to be perfectly natural, but in candy cookery, the cooling needs to be considered in relation to the sugar in the solution. Remember that less sugar should be in solution at a cooler temperature than could be dissolved in a saturated solution at the higher

Saturated Solution
Homogeneous mixture that has as much solute in solution as is possible at that temperature.

temperature reached during cooking. In other words, more sugar has been placed in solution by going to the higher final temperature than theoretically can be in solution as the candy cools. And yet, it is possible to keep this extra sugar in solution for quite a long time during the cooling period. By this careful cooling, a *supersaturated solution* is created, which means that more sugar is in solution than theoretically can be in solution at that temperature. The cooler the candy gets, the more unstable the supersaturated solution becomes because less and less sugar can be dissolved as the temperature drops. Ideally, a highly supersaturated state will be created.

If some nucleus is introduced into a supersaturated solution, the excess sugar in solution begins to crystallize and precipitate. The presence of a crystal of sugar, a piece of lint, or any other object can serve as the starting point for crystals of sugar to form. If this occurs when the candy has cooled only a little, there will be rapid crystallization of the small amount of dissolved sugar that should not have been in solution. Gradually, as the candy continues to cool, the extra sugar will continue to crystallize, adhering to the existing crystalline nucleus and creating a gritty texture even if beating is done continuously from the time the crystals start to form until the candy becomes solid.

In the ideal circumstance, a crystalline candy will cool to 110°F before any crystals form, a condition creating an extremely unstable situation. If beating is started at this point, the large excess of dissolved sugar will start to crystallize almost simultaneously, and the candy will become a solid mass within a matter of a very few minutes. Crystal aggregates simply cannot grow large under this circumstance if beating is vigorous until the candy solidifies. This is the reason that careful cooling to create a highly supersaturated solution is so important to success in making smooth crystalline candies.

Supersaturated Solution Solution in which more solute is dissolved than theoretically can be dissolved; created by boiling a true solution to a high temperature and then cooling very carefully.

When a high-quality crystalline candy has been prepared, it will improve even more by undergoing a 24-hour ripening period in a tightly covered container. During this ripening period, there will be a slight softening and an increase in smoothness. However, longer storage will allow small crystals to dissolve in the mother liquor and recrystallize on larger crystal aggregates. The *mother liquor* is the saturated sugar solution that is found between the sugar crystals throughout the candy. This is the liquid that helps to soften a crumbly, overbeaten candy into a workable mass during kneading. Since the smallest sugar crystals in a candy are the ones most susceptible to being dissolved in the saturated mother liquor, crystalline candies gradually become grainy during prolonged storage.

Mother Liquor Saturated sugar solution between the crystals in crystalline candies.

Commercially, candies are divided into three categories, according to the ingredients they contain:

1. Candies made entirely of sugar with or without flavor and color (hard candies, creams, stick candies).

2. Candies containing at least 95 percent sugar and a maximum of 5 percent nonsugar ingredients (pectin jellies, marshmallows, nougats).

3. Candies with a minimum of 75 percent sugar and between 5 and 25 percent nonsugar ingredients (fudge, caramels, starch jellies, chocolates).

The problems encountered in commercial confectionery are a composite of the problems encountered in making homemade candies, plus storage and shipping hazards. Some of these problems can be alleviated by the use of appropriate additives. For instance, glycerol and large quantities of corn syrup are helpful in maintaining moisture in candy and in retarding the development of a gritty texture in creams and mints. Various emulsifiers, including monoglycerides, are helpful in retarding staling and toughening of candies having a starch-jelly base.

Inversion to promote a mixture of sugars and a smooth crystalline candy is aided by adding cream of tartar in commercial candies. Invertase is a vital additive in softening cream centers after chocolates have been dipped.

For candies that are gels (orange slices, for example), gums are essential to form the gel. Most gums used in candy production are carbohydrates derived from seaweed, plant seeds, or tree exudates. The seaweed extracts, such as agar and Irish moss, have been used commercially for a long time, but often now are replaced in commercial candy-making by starch and pectin. Carrageenan (Irish moss) is used to prevent the "oiling off" that occurs in high-fat candies such as caramels, toffees, and nougats in hot weather. Two tree exudates, gum arabic and gum tragacanth, have the dual functions of preventing crystal growth and emulsifying fat to avoid fat separation in candies.

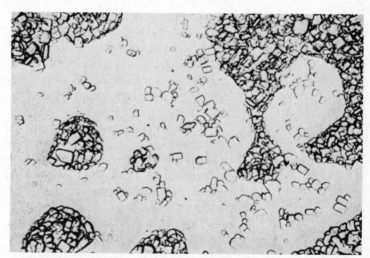

After 40 days of storage, the fondant (shown in the photo on page 158), cooked to 235°F and beaten when cooled to 105°F, shows coarse crystal aggregates resulting from solution in the mother liquor and recrystallization (200×).

SUMMARY

Carbohydrates are important sources of energy in the diet, whether in the form of various sugars or starch; other complex carbohydrates are valued as roughage. In food preparation, the simple carbohydrates, the sugars, are used as sweeteners to add to the pleasure of eating. The word *carbohydrate* is derived from the fact that, chemically, all compounds in this class are hydrates of carbon.

Among the many sweeteners available to consumers today, the various types of cane and beet sugars are used in by far the greatest quantity, with granulated sugar being the most common form selected. Frosting sugar and powdered or confectioner's sugar are other refined sweeteners, the latter having cornstarch added to it to keep the fine powder from lumping. Raw sugar, a partially refined sugar, is nutritionally comparable to refined sugar, and is more expensive. Light and dark brown sugar contain impurities that alter their color and flavor. Maple syrup and sugar have unique flavors attributable to the impurities in the maple sap from which they are made. Molasses is another distinctive sweetener and is the by-product, either sulphured or unsulphured, resulting from the processing of cane sugar.

Corn syrup is made by hydrolyzing cornstarch. A variation produced from corn syrup is high-fructose corn syrup, the result of the action of isomerase (an enzyme) on the sugars in corn syrup. Honey also is a fluid sweetener, this one being naturally high in fructose. The distinctive flavor of honey varies with the source of the nectar the bees collect, but all types result in very rapid browning in baked products.

Saccharin is a nonnutritive sweetener used by many to avoid calories from sugar and by diabetics as a means of limiting sugar intake. The bitter aftertaste is objectionable to some people. Aspartame, a dipeptide, is a low-calorie sweetener. Its intense sweetness means only small amounts of aspartame are needed to sweeten a beverage or other food item.

The sugars are classified as monosaccharides and disaccharides, with the disaccharides being made up of two units of the monosaccharides. Glucose, fructose, and galactose (all hexoses) are the common monosaccharides, and these are combined in various ways to form sucrose (table sugar), maltose, and lactose (milk sugar).

Sucrose, the sugar commonly used in cookery for sweetening, tenderizing, browning of baked products, and other purposes, undergoes a severe chemical breakdown when it is heated to very high temperatures. This process, called caramelization, results in the formation of many different compounds, including organic acids. Hydrolysis is a less severe reaction and results in the formation of an equal mixture of two sugars (glucose and fructose); the mixture is called invert sugar.

The two types of candies are crystalline and amorphous, the difference being that the crystalline candies have organized crystals of sugar throughout, while the amorphous candies are completely disorganized and range from chewy to very hard. The type of candy, whether crystalline or amorphous, is determined in large measure by the final cooking temperature; crystalline candies are cooked to lower temperatures than are the amorphous candies. The lower temperature of crystalline candies means that the concentration of sugar is somewhat lower than in the amorphous candies, a difference that enables the sugar crystals to form an organized network in the cooling, fairly viscous crystalline candies.

Amorphous candies should be the correct texture for the type of candy (ranging from chewy caramels to brittle toffees) and should not have any trace of scorching, the most common problem in preparing amorphous candies. In contrast, crystalline candies are evaluated on the basis of being firm yet soft enough to bite easily and having a velvety smooth texture. This texture is the result of achieving a highly supersaturated solution and then beating adequately until the structure sets. Commercial candies are categorized according to the percentage of sugar they contain. Many of these have various additives to enhance the quality of the candy when it reaches consumers.

Selected References

Baldwin, R. E. and B. M. Korschgen. Intensification of fruit-flavors by aspartame. *J. Food Sci. 44*: 938. 1979.

Cloninger, M. R. and R. E. Baldwin. L-aspartyl-1-phenylalanine methyl ester (aspartame) as sweetener. *J. Food Sci. 39*: 347. 1974.

Doner, L. W. Sugars of honey—a review. *J. Sci. Food Ag. 28*: 443. 1977.

Fenner, L. That lite stuff. *FDA Consumer 16(5)*: 10. 1982.

Fruin, J. C. and B. L. Scallet. Isomerized corn syrups in food products. *Food Tech. 29(11)*: 40. 1975.

Guy, E. J. Lactose. *Baker's Digest 45 (Apr.)*: 34. 1971.

Heaton, K. C. F. et al. Sorbitol. *IFST Proc. 13(3)*: 157. 1980.

Hoseney, R. C. Chemical changes in carbohydrates produced by thermal processing. *J. Chem. Ed. 61*: 308. 1984.

Inglett, G. E., ed. *Symposium: Sweeteners.* Avi Publishing Co. Westport, Conn. 1974.

Johnson, R. E. et al. Formation of sucrose pyrolysis products. *J. Agr. Food Chem. 17*: 22. 1969.

Keal, E. J. Sweeteners for baked foods. *Baker's Digest 47 (Oct.)*: 80. 1973.

Lee, C. K. and M. G. Lindley. *Developments in Food Carbohydrates.* Applied Science. New York. 1982.

Life Sciences Research office. Evaluation of health aspects of sucrose as a food ingredient. FDA. Bethesda, Md. 1976.

Meade, G. P. Sugar and sirups. In *Chemistry and Technology of Food Products.* Ed. M. B. Jacobs. Interscience. New York. Ch. 41, Vol. 3. 2nd ed. 1951.

Mermelstein, N. H. Immobilized enzymes produce high-fructose corn syrup. *Food Tech. 29(6)*: 20. 1975.

Newton, J. M. and E. K. Wardrip. High fructose corn syrup. In *Symposium: Sweeteners.* Ed. G. E. Inglett. Avi Publishing Co. Westport, Conn. 1974. P. 87.

Pintauro, N. D. *Sweeteners and Enhancers.* Noyes Data Corp. Park Ridge, N.J. 1977.

Salant, A. Nonnutritive sweeteners. *Handbook of Food Additives.* Ed. T. E. Furia. CRC Press. Columbus, Ohio. 2nd ed. 1972.

Schiffman, S. S. et al. Qualitative differences among sweeteners. *Physiol. Behav. 23*: 1. 1979.

Schiffman, S. S. et al. Multiple receptor sites mediate sweetness: evidence from cross adaption. *Pharmacol. Biochem. Behav. 15*: 377. 1981.

Schoen, M. Confectionery and cacao products. In *Chemistry and Technology of Food Products*. Ed. M. B. Jacobs. Interscience. New York. Ch. 42. Vol. 3. 2nd ed. 1951.

Schultz, H. W. et al., ed. *Carbohydrates and their Rules*. Avi Publishing Co. Westport, Conn. 1969.

Study Questions

1. What is the result of a very slow rate of heating on a crystalline candy? Explain the reaction that occurs.
2. What influence does the amount of beating have on a crystalline candy?
3. Does the time of initiation of beating influence the quality of a crystalline candy? Explain.
4. What is the purpose of adding the following ingredients to a basic fondant recipe: cream of tartar, corn syrup, chocolate, butter? Explain the action of each.
5. Why does the temperature of boiling candy rise gradually?

Pieter Bruegel, The Elder, "The Harvesters." The Metropolitan Museum of Art, Rogers Fund.

CHAPTER 7

CARBOHYDRATES: STARCHES AND CEREAL COOKERY

Starch, a Key Polysaccharide

Sources
Starch in food preparation
Dextrinization
Gelatinization

Science Note—A Chemical and Physical Portrait

Factors influencing properties

Science Note—Chemical Degradation

Starch gels
Starch products

Starch Cookery

White sauces
Gravies
Cream soups
Cornstarch puddings

Cereals

Cereals in the diet
Grain structure
Nutritional contribution
Commercial processing
Corn and barley
Rice

Science Note—Characteristics of Rice Grains

Wheat
Storage
Preparation of cereals

Summary

Selected References

Study Questions

STARCH, A KEY POLYSACCHARIDE

Sources

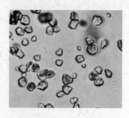

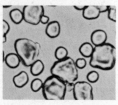

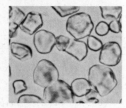

Root starches (tapioca and potato) and cereal starches (rice, corn, waxy corn, and wheat) on pages 168 and 169. Magnification 500×.

Rheology Study of flow properties of matter.

Dextrinization Chemical breakdown of starch to a more soluble carbohydrate as a result of intense, dry heat.

Starch, the form in which plants store energy, is an important complex carbohydrate, both in cookery and in nutrition. The energy value to the body is the same (4 kilocalories per gram) as that from sugar, but the behavior of starch in food products allows it to be used in cookery in ways quite different from the uses for sugar. A particularly valuable quality of starch is its ability to thicken food products.

Several plants are good sources of starch, including some from roots, others from cereals, and even one from a tree. The tree starch, called sago, is fairly common commercially, but is not familiar as a thickener for use in the home. The root starches tend to be comparatively expensive, although they are prized by some people for special applications. Root starches include arrowroot, tapioca (the root of the cassava, which sometimes is called manioc), and potato. The cereal starches are perhaps the most familiar and are generally the least expensive of the starches. Included among the cereal starches are cornstarch, rice, and wheat, this last cereal being used most commonly simply as flour.

Each of the types of starch has its own characteristic appearance when seen under a microscope. As can be seen in the figures, the shapes range from spherical to angular, with some being large and others small. For example, potato starch is found in large, fairly round granules, quite a contrast to the typically small and angular rice starch granules, which are the smallest of the cereal starches. Wheat starch granules are the largest of the cereals.

Starch in Food Preparation

Food owes part of its palatability to its *rheology* (flow properties), and starch is a very useful ingredient to achieve the desired viscosity. This thickening ability is a primary reason for using starch in such food products as gravies, sauces, soups, casseroles, puddings, pie fillings, and other desserts. In various baked products, and particularly in cakes, starch helps to give structure to the framework.

Sometimes starch is mixed with liquids and heated to effect a physical change. Occasionally, it is heated by itself to a high temperature to cause a chemical change. These types of changes merit further study and a close examination to clarify the importance and use of starch in food products.

Dextrinization

Sometimes starch (usually in the form of wheat flour) is heated alone in a heavy skillet until the color begins to change to a golden brown, after which this browned flour is used to make a sauce. A similar situation exists when bread is toasted. Such rigorous heat treatment causes a chemical change in the starch, a change called *dextrinization*. Actually, some of the starch is changed into a somewhat more soluble carbohydrate with reduced thickening

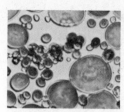

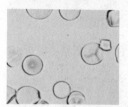

ability. The new carbohydrate is called dextrin. When starch or flour is dextrinized to make a brown sauce, it is necessary to use more starch than usual to provide adequate thickening, thus compensating for the reduced thickening ability.

Gelatinization

At various temperatures, starch dispersed in water will exhibit different characteristics. In cold water, a limited amount of swelling will occur, but for the most part, starch in cold water can only be maintained in suspension by stirring. The root starches are somewhat more soluble in cold water and will swell a bit more than the cereal starches without applying heat.

For starch to serve as an effective thickening agent, adequate heat and water must be present. If either the heat or the water is missing, thickening will not occur. This thickening action of starch is the result of a process called gelatinization. *Gelatinization* is the process of absorbing water into the starch granules in the presence of adequate heat. Although this sounds quite simple, the process may give an unsatisfactory result unless the starch is dispersed thoroughly and gelatinization is done with careful control of heating and stirring.

The first step is the smooth dispersion of the starch granules in water. Three different procedures can be used for ensuring a smooth dispersion:

1. Mixing the starch with cold water to make a smooth *slurry* (thin paste).
2. Mixing the starch with oil or melted fat to make a smooth paste.
3. Combining the starch with a fairly large quantity of another dry ingredient before adding liquid.

Notice that in each of these techniques, the requirements of both water and heat are not satisfied. Consequently, the gelatinization process does not begin during this mixing period, and mixing can be accomplished without lumps forming.

Once the ingredients have been combined smoothly, heating of the mixture is done to gelatinize the starch and thicken the product. Stirring is essential when gelatinizing starch to thicken any kind of sauce, soup, or other liquid product. Without stirring, the gelatinizing starch mixture will vary in its temperature from one part of the mixture to another, and the hottest areas will have gelatinized starch granules, which will be considerably more viscous than the other areas and will form lumps in the product.

During gelatinization, some of the water in the product will be absorbed into the individual starch granules and held there tightly, actually becoming *bound water*. Bound water no longer is able to flow; the water that is bound in the granules causes the granules themselves to swell significantly. It is the combination of less free water actually available in the system and the physically swollen starch granules that is responsible for the very obvious thickening that occurs during gelatinization of starches.

Accompanying the obvious thickening of gelatinizing starch mixtures is an increase in the translucency of the system, a clear change from the milky,

Gelatinization Physical change in starch when heated sufficiently in the presence of water; swelling of starch granules because of the entry of water.

Slurry Starch paste.

Bound Water Water held so tightly by other substances that it cannot flow.

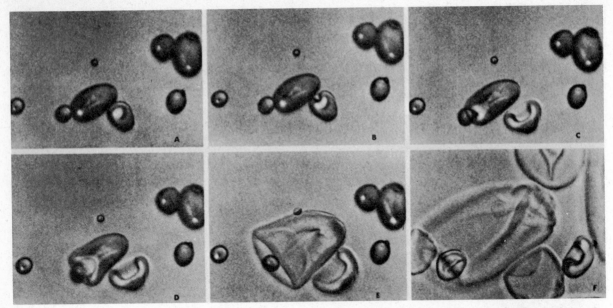

Potato starch gelatinization during the 10 seconds between initial swelling (a) to complete swelling (f). Note the change in translucency and size.

opaque quality of ungelatinized starch suspensions. This increased translucency is caused by the solution of some of the portions of crystalline structure within the granule and the loss of some of the starch from the granule into the surrounding water. In fact, one way of telling when gelatinization is completed is the translucent quality. However, there is a considerable variation in this characteristic, depending on the type of starch being gelatinized. The root starches are more translucent than the cereal starches. Flour, which is often gelatinized in cookery, remains opaque even when gelatinization is completed; the protein in the flour continues to block the transmission of light through the starch paste even when the starch itself is altered enough to let light pass through.

Amylose Linear starch fraction (1,4-α–glucosidic linkages) that is soluble and capable of forming gels.

Amylopectin The rather insoluble, non-gel-forming fraction of starch; contains both 1,4- and 1,6-α-glucosidic linkages, resulting in a bulky, branching molecule.

SCIENCE NOTE: A Chemical and Physical Portrait

Starch is a very short word representing the complex polysaccharide in plants that can cause thickening when heated in water. However, this is not a very specific term. Chemists have differentiated between two components of starch—*amylose* and *amylopectin*. These two carbohydrates are both made up of glucose as the single building unit, but amylose is basically a linear molecule in which the glucose units are linked by an alpha-glucosidic linkage between the first carbon of one glucose and the fourth of the next unit. This linearity is important, for it permits amylose molecules to escape from the starch granule by dissolving to an extent in the water. It also makes it possible for amylose molecules to cross-link to each other in fairly low-energy systems to form gels. The structure for amylose is shown, in part, below. Actually, there are probably more than 600 glucose units in a single molecule of amylose.

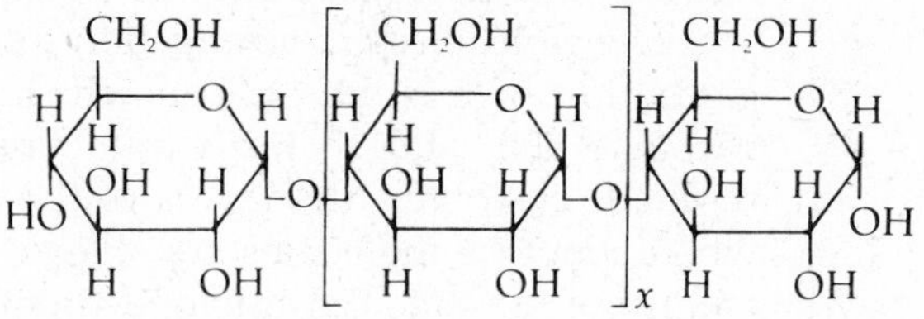

Amylose

The other starch fraction, amylopectin, has many portions in which the glucose units are linked by the same 1,4-α-glucosidic linkage seen in amylose. However, after each 20 to 25 units with the linear arrangement, a 1,6-α-glucosidic linkage occurs. It is this linkage to the carbon outside the ring structure that causes a branching in the amylopectin molecules, giving them a bulky structure. As a consequence, amylopectin molecules are rather insoluble and do not link together readily to form gels. The smallest of the amylopectin molecules probably contains at least 1000 glucose units, and complex ones are as large as 1500 glucose units. The structure has many branch points, a portion of the molecule being shown below.

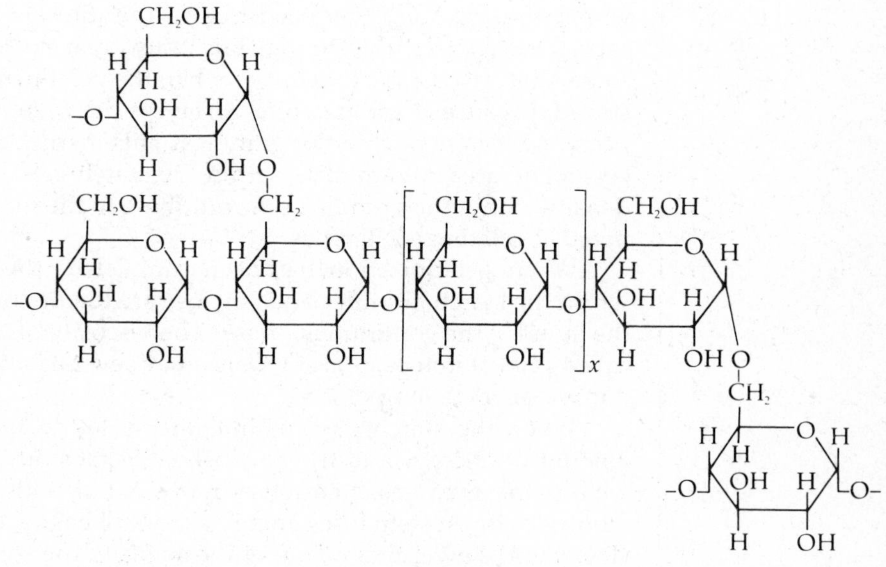

Amylopectin

Starch granules are the organized units in which starch, actually amylose and amylopectin, molecules are deposited in the leucoplasts in plants. The shape of the granules varies with the type of plant, but the basic features are the same in all starch granules. Most commonly the ratio of amylose to amylopectin is about one molecule of amylose to four amylopectin molecules, but this varies.

The molecules are arranged in concentric spheres, much like the organization of a child's toy in which a ball is contained within a ball within a ball, and so forth until finally the central, very tiny ball is reached. However, the layers of the granule are composed of regions where amylose molecules are aligned quite neatly, creating some crystalline areas, while the amylopectin molecules are random in their associations. All of the molecules are held to each other in the concentric layers by hydrogen bonds. There is no skin or other protective coating surrounding the assembled granule. It is this granule that can be gelatinized.

With this picture in mind, gelatinization can be visualized and appreciated. The energy in the system is increased by the heat being applied during gelatinization. This energy causes some of the hydrogen bonds to break within the granule, thus allowing some water to move into the voids created. This water keeps moving in toward the center of the granule as continuing heating breaks more and more of the hydrogen bonds responsible for the original rather tight granular structure. The solution of some of the freed amylose molecules causes them to begin to leave the granule, but the water continues to enter the granule and to be bound there. As more and more water enters the granule, the granule gets larger and larger, but the density of the starch molecules within the granule is reduced due to the dilution by the water. This causes the desired thickening, but it also makes the swollen granules somewhat susceptible to damage when the gelatinizing mixture is being stirred, because of the potential distances between amylose and amylopectin molecules within the granules. This disruption of the somewhat crystalline areas of amylose within the starch granule and the reduced density within the granule both contribute to the increased translucency noted in gelatinized starches.

When gelatinization has been completed, the system is a sol in which the starch granules and amylose are the discontinuous phase and the liquid is the continuous phase. The viscosity of this starch sol (often called a hot starch paste) is influenced by several factors, one of the most important being temperature.

When the starch paste is hot, the system contains a considerable amount of energy, and the amylose molecules outside the granules as well as the granules themselves move about within the total system. However, the system loses energy as the sol begins to cool. The result is slower and slower movement of the solids in the sol. Gradually, hydrogen bonds will begin to form between the various amylose molecules outside the granules, making a random network in which the swollen

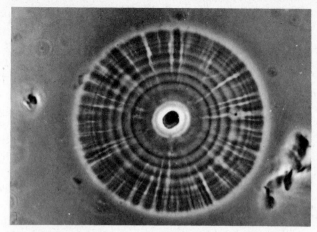

Photomicrograph of a starch granule that has been treated with alpha-amylase to break down the amylose fraction and reveal the radial cracks and concentric layers characterizing the granular structure.

starch granules become enmeshed. The ultimate result is that a continuous network of the solid develops, and the liquid becomes the discontinuous or disperse phase. In other words, the system becomes just the opposite of the sol that was formed originally. The new colloidal system is a gel.

Factors Influencing Properties

The type of starch undergoing gelatinization influences the properties of the starch system. One of the differences is the amount of water that can be absorbed into the starch granule before it ruptures. The cereal starches have a limited ability to absorb water compared with root starches. Corn and wheat starch granules will rupture when the equivalent of about 40 percent of their weight in water has been absorbed; that is, rupturing is likely to occur if 100 grams of either of these starches absorbs 40 grams of water. Remarkably, potato starch can absorb considerably more water per weight (as much as 100 grams of water per 100 grams starch) before the granules disintegrate!

The temperature ranges over which gelatinization occurs also vary with the type of starch. The root starches begin to swell at about 150° to 160°F, and gelatinization is completed at temperatures well below boiling, forming quite clear pastes. In fact, the root starches will tend to disintegrate when they are heated to temperatures just below boiling. However, the cereal starches are quite resistant to water penetration in the early phases of gelatinization and these types of starch must be heated to temperatures ranging from 200° to 212°F for gelatinization to be completed. Even when gelatinization has been finished, the cereal starches will be less translucent than the root starches. These characteristics are summarized in Table 7.1.

Several factors determine the viscosity of starch sols and gels: (1) the concentration of starch, (2) the type of starch, (3) the addition of acid or sugar, (4) the extent of dextrinization, and (5) the thoroughness of the dispersion of the starch.

The concentration of starch, as would be expected, has a great influence on the viscosity of gelatinized starch products. The higher the starch concentration, the greater will be the potential viscosity of the pastes, and resulting gels will be increasingly firm as the starch content is increased. The modification of a recipe by increasing the liquid or decreasing it will have an opposing effect on the concentration of starch; an increase in liquid dilutes the concentration of starch, for example.

The type of starch used in thickening products also influences the viscosity of the gelatinized mixture. There is not only a distinct difference between the thickening ability of the cereal starches (more effective) and the root starches, but there also are differences within the groups. Rice starch has less thickening ability than does cornstarch or wheat starch. Wheat flour has only

Table 7.1 Commonly Used Starches and Their Characteristics

Starch	Classification	Comparative Thickening Ability	Characteristics of the Paste
Cornstarch	Cereal starch	Great	Optimum thickening by heating to 200–212°F; moderately translucent
Flour (contains wheat starch and protein)	Cereal starch	Half as great as cornstarch	Optimum thickening by heating to 200–212°F; more opaque than cornstarch
Rice starch	Cereal starch	Moderate	Optimum thickening by heating to 200–212°F; moderately translucent
Potato starch	Root starch	Less than cereals	Optimum thickening by heating to 160°F; thins when boiled; tendency to become gummy; quite translucent
Tapioca	Root starch	Less than cereals	Optimum thickening by heating to 185°F; thins when boiled; tendency to become gummy; quite translucent

about half as much thickening ability as cornstarch, a reflection of the difference in the thickening ability of wheat versus cornstarch and also the replacement of starch by some protein in the flour, which means that flour actually has less starch per measure than does cornstarch. If flour is to be substituted for cornstarch in a recipe, the measure of flour should be increased to twice the amount of cornstarch indicated. Conversely, half as much cornstarch can replace the amount of flour indicated as the thickening agent in a recipe. The substitution of root starches for cereal starches will result in even more tender gels than are produced with rice starch. This means that potato and arrowroot starches will need to be used in increased quantities if they are to be substituted for cereal starches.

The final temperature to which a starch paste is heated has an important influence on the viscosity. To obtain maximum thickening from any specific starch, the starch sol must be heated to a high enough temperature to ensure complete gelatinization. For the cereal starches, this means essentially reaching boiling. However, the root starches require less severe heat treatment. In fact, tapioca and potato starches reach maximum viscosity at a comparatively low temperature (see Table 7.1) and will actually begin to thin as the mixture approaches boiling.

Many cookbooks suggest cooking a starch mixture in a double boiler over boiling water, but this arrangement requires a considerable amount of time to bring the starch mixture to a high enough temperature for maximum gelatinization of cereal starches. At high elevations, it is physically impossible to heat the starch mixture to a high enough heat when heating in a double boiler. With the exception of potato and tapioca, the common starches used in cooking can be heated fairly quickly to achieve maximum gelatinization over direct heat; the double boiler is helpful in avoiding overheating root starch products. If starch mixtures also have eggs being used as a thickening agent, the starch should be gelatinized first just by heating to the boiling point, and then the protein should be added carefully and the entire mixture heated over boiling water to coagulate the protein.

Sugar has a significant effect on several aspects in gelatinized starch products, including a tenderizing effect on the starch gel. The very hygroscopic nature of sugar enables it to compete with starch for the water in the recipe, which means that less water will be available to aid in gelatinizing the starch as the sugar level is increased. Because of this competition for water, sugar in starch mixtures causes the following changes:

1. The temperatures at which the initial swelling and maximum swelling occur are higher for the sugar-starch mixture than for a starch product without sugar.
2. The maximum viscosity of the starch paste is reduced when sugar is present because the sugar competes for the water and reduces the uptake of water into the starch granules.
3. Less disintegration of starch grains occurs when sugar is present because there is less swelling of the granules.

Syneresis Separation of liquid from a gel.

4. The resulting gel is less rigid because less amylose is released into the liquid to form the gel network when sugar is present.

5. *Syneresis* (loss of liquid from the gel) is increased as the level of sugar in the starch product increases.

6. Increased sugar increases translucency.

If the concentration of sugar exceeds 20 percent by weight in the product, the foregoing effects are quite pronounced.

Lumping in a gelatinizing starch mixture can be the cause of reduced viscosity in the product because there will be dry starch granules trapped inside the lumps. Since these dry granules cannot obtain water for gelatinization, they will remain in their original, ungelatinized state. In effect, lumpy starch products contain less gelatinized starch to thicken the paste than they were expected to contain. Aside from the detrimental characteristic of being a little too thin, lumpy products are unattractive in appearance and do not feel good in the mouth. These are all important reasons for following one or more of the procedures described earlier for dispersing the starch with the other ingredients.

The addition of acid prior to heating a starch mixture causes a thinning of the product during gelatinization due to acid hydrolysis of some of the starch. So for preparing such acid-containing gelatinized starch products as Harvard beets or lemon meringue pie filling, the starch should be gelatinized before adding the acid. The lemon juice or vinegar can be stirred in following gelatinization without having a significant amount of acid hydrolysis occurring.

Reduced thickening ability also occurs when flour is dextrinized or browned; the darker the flour has been browned, the less will be the thickening ability of the browned flour. A practical solution to the reduced thickening ability is to add some nondextrinized flour to augment the thickening ability of the browned product and achieve the desired viscosity in a brown sauce.

Starch Gels

Gelation Formation of a colloidal dispersion in which the solid forms a continuous phase and liquid forms the discontinuous or disperse phase; a gelatinized starch system that does not flow is an example of a gel.

Gelation Most gelatinized starch pastes lose their ability to flow when they become cool. This formation of a gel is called *gelation*, a term unfortunately similar to gelatinization, yet meaning something very different. In the preparation of cream pie fillings and in puddings and some other desserts, starch is the ingredient used to achieve the desired firmness. These products are expected to hold their shape and not flow, yet they are supposed to be sufficiently tender to sag just a bit or to bulge out very slightly when cut, without actually moving at the base of the cut. Too much starch causes such a stiff texture that the pie or other product will remain absolutely rigid when cut rather than bulge. It also will have an excessively firm feeling in the mouth. Conversely, too little starch, too much sugar, lumping, or acid hydrolysis can cause too thin a product to serve easily.

Not all gelatinized starch systems will undergo gelation. For this transition to a gel to occur, there must be a sufficient concentration of gelatinized

SCIENCE NOTE: Chemical Degradation

Acid Hydrolysis
Cleavage of a molecule by utilizing a molecule of water in the presence of an acid, which serves as a catalyst.

The linkages between the glucose units comprising starch molecules are covalent bonds, but they still are susceptible to cleavage by acid or intense dry heat. When starch is being gelatinized, the presence of acid results in some *acid hydrolysis* of the molecules, particularly of the amylose molecules released from the swelling granules. The reaction involves the uptake of a molecule of water to form hydroxyl groups on the carbon atoms involved in this reaction. The result is two fragments, each of which is shorter than the original molecule. These fragments are more soluble and have less thickening ability than the original, longer-chain molecule. In prolonged heating, this reaction can be repeated many times, to produce quite short fragments. The reaction of hydrolysis is

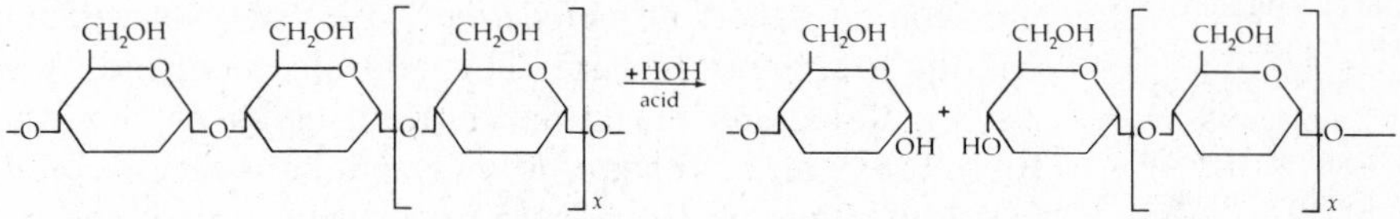

Dextrinization is another means of degrading starch molecules. In this instance, dry starch is heated to temperatures well above the boiling temperature possible when water is the cooking medium. This intense energy from the heat enables some of the linkages between glucose units in starch molecules to split, with the uptake of a molecule of water. This water is available from the very limited moisture content naturally present in flour and other starch-containing foods. In effect, the chemical change occurring during dextrinization results in the same type of products that are liberated in acid hydrolysis, and the actual reaction involves the formation of a hydroxyl group on each carbon involved in the linkage between glucose units, just as is shown here. The difference between the two reactions is the amount of energy required; without acid as a catalyst, a great deal of energy is required, which is provided by heat in the dextrinization process.

starch, with a reasonable amount of free amylose molecules. Without the free amylose, the necessary interlocking structure will not form. Also, if there has been too much hydrolysis of the amylose molecules, the molecular strands will be too short to form an entrapping network, and the gelatinized system will remain a sol.

Syneresis   Gels appear to be solids, with little propensity for change, but in fact the amylose network is held in place by hydrogen bonds between molecules, and these bonds are constantly breaking and reforming. The result is molecular movement within the gel. The liquid (the disperse phase) in the gel is trapped within the interstices of the amylose network. However, the constant rearranging of the amylose provides opportunity for liquid to escape from the gel. This draining of liquid from a gel is called syneresis. By cutting through a starch gel, many trapped pockets of liquid will be revealed, and syneresis will begin to be noticeable.

Frozen starch gels that have been thawed exhibit very obvious syneresis. The liquid in the gel freezes into sharp crystals, and these crystals interfere with the maintenance of a strong amylose network during thawing. Syneresis can be a problem in frozen pie fillings but not for gravies or other types of sauces that have been frozen, for the reheating and stirring prior to service causes the separated liquid to recombine. Rice starch exhibits less syneresis after frozen storage than is true for some other types of starches.

Retrogradation Formation of crystalline areas due to aggregation of amylose and amylopectin molecules in a starch gel; a physical process that can be reversed by heating.

Retrogradation   When starch gels are established, they will undergo a gradual change called *retrogradation*. The effect of retrogradation is a noticeable change to a gritty texture. This change is caused by the amylose and amylopectin molecules rearranging themselves as the hydrogen bonds between them break and subsequently reform between various molecules of the starch fractions. The tendency is to group closer and closer together in a somewhat organized, crystalline relationship. It is this crystalline aggregation that is perceived as a grittiness. Retrogradation is a reversible process. Simply by heating the starch gel, the hydrogen bonds will begin to break, allowing the amylose to move freely once again. However, the crystalline areas will form again. The formation of crystalline areas in bread is noted in stale bread, which becomes seemingly fresh and soft when the bread is heated. Another example is gravy or a white sauce that has been stored in the refrigerator. The retrograded starch sauce will lose its crystalline character when reheated.

Starch products

Waxy Starches Starches from plants bred to produce a starch that is virtually all amylopectin and is free of amylose; valued for use in products where a gel is not desirable.

Special Starches   Selective breeding is being done to produce new varieties of starch-yielding plants with the desired physical characteristics. A particularly important product has been the development of strains of plants that produce starches comprised virtually entirely of amylopectin. These starches, which are almost 100 percent amylopectin, are called *waxy starches*. Amioca, also called waxy cornstarch, is the result of genetic research aimed at providing useful variations in starch. These waxy starches are valued because they will thicken but will not form a gel, due to the absence of amylose. This type of starch sol is ideal for use in fruit pie fillings, as well as in some salad dressings and instant puddings. These waxy starches produce pastes comparable in viscosity to pastes made with potato starch in low concentrations, but in high concentrations and with longer cooking, the paste from amioca will be slightly thicker than tapioca and distinctly less viscous than a comparable potato starch paste. A nice feature of waxy starches is that they do not form a scum or skin on top because there is no amylose present to retorgrade on the surface.

Edible Starch Films
Films made from special starches containing about 80 percent amylose.

Edible starch films are gaining in interest, partially as a novelty and partly because of their utility. Geneticists in 1957 developed a corn that deposited starch with about 20 percent amylopectin and 80 percent amylose, a ratio just about the reverse of regular cornstarch. The interesting feature of this special high-amylose starch is that the high concentration of amylose makes it possible to produce thin, edible films of this starch when it has been gelatinized. These films can be used as wrappers for candies, and the wrappers can be consumed with the candy, since the starch wrapper is chewable and digestible. Japanese candies wrapped in ''rice paper'' are familiar examples of this application of high-amylose starch products. Casings for meat products and soluble packets for foods to be boiled are other possible applications.

Precooked Starches   The first of the treated starch products was minute rice, a product of five years of research, which was first marketed in 1946. This product is cooked to gelatinize the starch until the process is about 60 percent complete and then is dried. Minute tapioca is another precooked starch product. Instant puddings are yet other examples of the types of special precooked starch products on the market. These products require rehydration before being served, but they do not need the boiling or other heating ordinarily required to gelatinize the starch.

Perhaps the most popular of the precooked starch products is instant mashed potatoes. The advantages of these potatoes include an excellent shelf life, reduced shipping costs because of the light weight of the dehydrated product, and appreciable saving in preparation time. These and other dehydrated potato products have carved out a sizable niche for themselves in the marketplace. Preparation at the factory involves cooking the potatoes in very small pieces, freezing the cooked product at 9°F followed by thawing at 35°F, and ultimately dehydrating to 8 percent moisture. These conditions must be controlled carefully to avoid producing products that are sticky and gummy when rehydrated and served.

Frozen Products   A crunchy candy can be made by gelatinizing a 5 percent starch paste, cooling, and then freezing it to produce a fragile starch sponge that can be dipped in chocolate.

Some frozen puddings and pie fillings are made using waxy rice flour as a replacement for egg and cornstarch thickeners. Use of waxy rice flour and gelatin in frozen commercial puddings causes the thawed product to have a desirable consistency, with little syneresis in comparison with related products made with other starches. Puddings made with waxy rice flour (sometimes called glutinous rice) can be stored at 0°F for up to nine months and still have satisfactory characteristics when thawed. The chief objection to the waxy rice flour is the raw starch flavor that persists.

Modified Starches   An approach to producing frozen starch-thickened products is to use a starch with phosphate cross-linkages. Phosphate or acetyl can be esterified on the carbon atoms external to the rings of glucose comprising

Stabilized Starches
Starches resistant to retrogradation and syneresis because of formation of phosphate or acetyl esters of starch; often called modified starches.

Cross-linked Starches
Starches treated with various phosphate compounds prior to gelatinization to reduce rupturing of the starch granules.

Thin-boiling Starch
Starch that has undergone limited acid hydrolysis, resulting in a product that is fluid when the gelatinized mixture is hot, but forms a rigid gel when cooled.

the starch molecules. This arrangement helps to minimize the tendency to retrograde and to exhibit syneresis. These cross-linked starches with their esters are sometimes called *stabilized or modified starches.*

One complaint about starch-thickened products is the pasty or stringy quality that occurs sometimes due to fragile starch granules. Various phosphorous-containing compounds (metaphosphate, for example) can be used to cross-link starch molecules within the uncooked starch granules. This change in the chemical nature of the granules results in resistance to rupturing during the gelatinization process, which reduces the pasty quality of the gelatinized product. These *cross-linked starches* have undergone less processing than the stabilized starches, for they do not undergo sufficient treatment to form the ester linkages typical of the stabilized starches.

Thin-boiling starches are useful in some commercial applications, such as making gum drops, where their thin, fluid nature allows the gelatinized starch to be poured easily. However, these starches form desirably stiff gels when cooled after gelatinization. These unique starches are made by allowing limited acid hydrolysis to occur when the raw starch is heated gently in a dilute acid.

Cream of vegetable soups are basically a thin white sauce, with a variety of vegetables added for color and flavor.

STARCH COOKERY

White Sauces

Starch-thickened sauces are used widely in cooking, and the ability to prepare a smooth sauce of the appropriate viscosity for the desired end use is key to making such diverse products as soufflés and cream soups. Basic white sauces and their variations can be prepared successfully if certain basic knowledge has been acquired. One of the key pieces of information is the appropriate viscosity of white sauce for different applications. The four viscosities of white sauces and their suggested uses are

1. *Thin sauce.* Cream soups.
2. *Medium sauce.* Creamed vegetables, cheese sauce, and gravy.
3. *Thick sauce.* Soufflés.
4. *Very thick sauce.* Binding agent for croquettes.

These sauces vary in the proportion of flour and fat they contain in relation to the milk. The fat used may be butter, margarine, shortening, or salad oil, depending upon the flavor and color characteristics desired in the finished product. The proportions for making the different white sauces are presented in Table 7.2.

White sauces utilize two of the techniques mentioned previously to disperse starch uniformly prior to gelatinization. First, the starch is blended thoroughly with fat that has been melted or with oil to help separate the starch granules. Then this fat-starch slurry is blended with cold liquid to disperse the starch still more before any heat is available to start gelatinization. When making large quantities of white sauce, about a fourth of the milk is used cold to disperse the starch, while the remainder is scalded before being added. This helps to shorten the cooking time without causing the lumping that would result if the scalded milk were added all at once directly to the starch-fat mixture. An absolutely smooth product must be achieved before any heat is applied to the starch mixture. Any lumps present prior to heating will remain throughout the preparation for the starch on the outside of the lumps will gelatinize and trap dry starch within each of the lumps, resulting in a poor texture and a product that is slightly thinner than desirable.

When the sauce is completely smooth, heating is initiated at a moderate rate. Constant stirring throughout the heating period is essential if a smooth

Table 7.2   Proportions for White Sauces

Type of Sauce	Flour	Fat	Milk	Salt
Thin	1 T	1 T	1 c	¼ tsp
Medium	2 T	2 T	1 c	¼ tsp
Thick	3 T	3 T	1 c	¼ tsp
Very thick	4 T	4 T	1 c	¼ tsp

sauce is to be produced. Stirring with a wooden spoon helps to maintain a uniform rate of heating. Otherwise, the starch will start to gelatinize rather quickly along the edges and across the bottom of the pan where the mixture heats most quickly; and when these areas are stirred, some of the thickened portions will be scraped free, becoming large lumps in the thickening sauce.

Evaluation of white sauces is based on their consistency, texture, flavor, and surface appearance. Consistency varies with the type of sauce being prepared. A *thin sauce* should be thickened very slightly, but should have a definitely fluid nature. In contrast to the thin sauce, the *medium sauce* should flow rather slowly so that a creamed dish will not flow all around a plate quickly. Since a *thick sauce* needs to be able to be folded into beaten egg whites, it needs to be spreadable, but should flow extremely slowly. Pastelike is a reasonable description of the desired consistency of a *very thick sauce*; remember, this is the sauce used to hold ingredients together for deep-fat frying.

Regardless of the viscosity of the sauce, the product should be perfectly smooth. Lumps may result from inadequate mixing of the starch with other ingredients prior to gelatinization. They may also result from too little stirring in all areas of the pan during gelatinization. If a sauce starts to get lumpy during cooking, the heat should be reduced to allow time for the stirring to keep up with the gelatinization process.

Flavor of a white sauce ordinarily is quite uncomplicated. There should be no trace of a raw starch flavor. Adequate gelatinization should eliminate this problem. Also there should be no suggestion of scorching. Use of a heavy pan for preparing a white sauce can be invaluable in helping to eliminate scorching, because the combination of sugar and protein in milk can scorch very easily if any hot areas develop in a pan. The type of fat selected for use in making the sauce may make a positive contribution to the flavor, and the salt (plus possibly some other seasonings) will help to create a flavorful sauce.

An undesirable fat film sometimes appears on a white sauce, the cause on a thin or medium white sauce usually is failure to gelatinize the starch completely or using too little starch in relation to the amount of fat used. If a film is evident, the first corrective measure is to bring the sauce to a boil to ensure that gelatinization has been completed. Often this treatment will solve the problem. If not, a smooth slurry of some starch and cold liquid needs to be made and added to the sauce with stirring, followed by adequate heating to gelatinize the newly added starch and bind the fat.

In thick or very thick white sauces, a fat film usually is the result of excessive evaporation of liquid from the sauce. This is particularly likely to happen if a small amount of sauce is being prepared and the heating is being done very cautiously. The very rapid thickening that occurs when thick and very thick sauces are being prepared can result in lumping unless the heat is reduced drastically. It is this circumstance that often results in loss of so much liquid through evaporation that the sauce breaks, releasing a very noticeable layer of fat in the sauce. Although this looks terrible, the problem is remedied easily by slowly stirring in a small amount of liquid to help reform the emulsion and bind the fat in. Before thick sauces can be utilized in soufflé preparation, the separated fat must be recombined with the sauce.

Gravies

Gravies are medium white sauces in which the drippings from the meat serve as the fat for the sauce. The technique for preparing the gravy depends upon the cookery method used for the meat. The drippings from fried or roasted meat are essentially all fat and can be used to combine directly with the flour to help separate the starch granules before adding liquid and gelatinizing the sauce. In these cases, the drippings must be measured, using two tablespoons of drippings for each cup of gravy desired (the proportions for a medium white sauce), and removing the remainder of the drippings from the pan. Failure to do this will result in a gravy with a fat layer because there will be too much fat to be bound by the flour or starch in the gravy. This method of stirring the starch directly into the measured drippings of fat is called the *roux method* for making gravies.

Roux Method Preparation of gravy by stirring starch into the measured drippings from fried or roasted meats.

Braised and stewed meats are cooked in liquid, which means that the liquid in the pan from braised or stewed meats can cause gelatinization of the starch to begin as soon as the hot liquid comes in contact with the dry starch. A lumpy gravy almost inevitably results unless a smooth slurry of starch and cold water or milk is made and then added slowly, with stirring, to the hot liquid. This method sometimes is called the ''kettle'' method of making gravy.

Regardless of the technique used for making the gravy, the desired result is a pleasingly flavored and colored sauce with a perfectly smooth texture and the consistency of a medium white sauce. There should be no fat film. The most likely cause of a fat film is failure to measure the fat accurately for the amount of gravy being prepared. Lumpiness may be the result of failure to disperse the starch uniformly before gelatinization or of inadequate stirring during thickening. The problem of adequate stirring is exaggerated when gravy is made in a skillet or other pan with a very large surface.

Cream Soups

Cream soups basically are simply thin white sauces with pureed vegetables or other food added for color, flavor, and general interest. Various seasonings appropriate to the type of cream soup being prepared ordinarily are added to heighten the appeal of the soup. Although by strict definition, cream soups should contain only pureed foods, many people precook the foods to be added and chop rather than puree them so that the soup acquires textural interest. The one exception to using the proportions for a thin sauce in making cream soups is cream of potato soup. The starch in the potatoes will add to the viscosity of the soup, making it necessary to reduce the amount of starch used in making the thin white sauce itself.

Preference regarding the amount of pureed vegetable to use in cream soups varies with individual taste and also with the vegetable, but usually ranges between 2 and 4 tablespoons per cup of soup. Spinach, for instance, is used in the smaller measure to produce the desired color and flavor, for the large measure would be overpowering. On the other hand, celery is so bland and has such a subtle color that the large amount produces a more appealing soup than is made using the small measure.

Most cream soups require careful attention to correct measurements, proper dispersion of the starch, and uniform gelatinization with stirring to prepare an excellent product. However, cream of tomato soup adds another dimension because of the acidity of the tomatoes. The milk proteins in the cream soup will curdle if they are placed in too acidic a medium, and tomatoes have the potential for causing curdling. The acidic tomato must be added slowly and with stirring to the white sauce so that the milk will never become acidic enough to precipitate the proteins. By also being sure to use milk that is fresh (but pasteurized) and by keeping the heating period as short as possible, the tendency to curdle is minimized. In other words, add the tomato puree to the soup just in time to heat to the desired temperature and serve immediately.

The color of homemade cream of tomato soup is very important for palatability. If only tomato juice is used, the product will have a sickly, orangish color and will lack appeal. However, if the pulp is pressed vigorously through the mesh used for pureeing, this pulp will result in a pleasingly red color and wholesome flavor, as well.

Well-prepared cream soups should be perfectly smooth, free of any trace of a fat film, well seasoned, and an appropriate color and flavor for the type of soup being prepared. All cream soups should be the viscosity of a thin white sauce.

Cornstarch Puddings

Whether called blanc mange or simply cornstarch pudding, these puddings are nourishing, simple ways of providing a considerable amount of milk. The preparation follows that for many other starch-thickened products. Since cornstarch puddings have very little fat, actually just enough butter to provide a flavor highlight, the starch is dispersed through mixing it thoroughly with the sugar in the recipe and then blending in about a fourth of the milk, cold, to form a slurry. Through these two steps, the cornstarch should be dispersed uniformly, thus eliminating much of the potential for lumping. Then the scalded milk can be added with stirring to assure uniform heat distribution. By scalding three-fourths of the milk, the actual heating period for gelatinizing the starch is kept reasonably short, which reduces the labor involved and also helps to minimize the sticky texture that can develop when starch granules begin to rupture due to excessive stirring. Stirring must be done throughout the gelatinization process to avoid lumps—as is true in making any starch-thickened product. A moderate rate of heating is recommended, for that allows control of the gelatinization in a smooth, uniform fashion without injuring the starch from prolonged stirring. Gelatinization is done when a spoon pulled through the pudding leaves a distinct path, but not a barren freeway.

A well-prepared cornstarch pudding will be perfectly smooth, with a light, rather delicate mouthfeel and an appealing flavor with no hint of raw starch. When the pudding has been chilled, the edge should soften slightly when cut with a spoon, but should not actually flow. The flavor should not indicate any evidence of scorching.

CEREALS

Cereals in the Diet

Cereals of various types (named after the Roman goddess of grain, Ceres) have been the mainstay of people's diets for countless centuries since the very earliest efforts at cultivating crops. Depending upon the land and climatic conditions, the staple cereal crop may be corn, wheat, rice, oats, rye, or millet; rice and wheat are of particular importance. Interestingly, about equal amounts of calories are provided for feeding the world by both wheat and rice, but the farming of rice is done so intensively that only half as much land is used to raise the world's rice as is used to raise the wheat. When all grain crops are considered together, more than 70 percent of the total cultivated land on earth is used for growing cereals.

The relative abundance of cereals and their nutrient contribution have caused them to occupy a prominent spot in the diets of people with limited incomes. However, the pattern of cereal consumption in the United States has shown a downward trend for the past three quarters of a century as incomes have risen and physical activity and requirements for energy have decreased. The exception to this pattern has been rice, which has increased quite modestly, partly as a consequence of increased immigration by people from regions where rice has been the traditional cereal and partly due to a developing image of rice as a special or gourmet cereal. Wheat, long the traditional cereal grain in the United States, is being purchased increasingly in baked products and ready-to-eat cereals rather than in flour or cereals requiring cooking.

Corn, unlike many of our foods that originated in other parts of the world, is considered to be a rather special American crop, with its ancestor (maize) flourishing here when the ships of Columbus arrived. In fact, corn spread to Europe from the American continent when explorers took seeds back to the European continent. Presently, a large percentage of the corn consumed by people and also by livestock in the United States is grown in the Midwest, an area of the country often referred to as the Corn Belt. There are three basic types of corn: sweet corn for human consumption, field corn for feeding animals, and popcorn, a popular snack item.

Rice is the staple grain in the Far East, ranging from Japan and China through India, and has been the number one grain for centuries there. In the United States, rice is growing in popularity, but still lags very far behind wheat in its consumption. Although rice is spoken of as a single cereal, there really are three different types available—short, medium, and long grain. The short (sometimes called ''sticky'') rice is particularly popular in Japan, while the long grain rice is preferred in the United States. Production of rice in the United States is limited, with the states of Missouri, Arkansas, Mississippi, Louisiana, Texas, and California accounting for most of the rice grown here.

Wheat, the staple grain in the U.S. diet, includes several different types: hard red spring, hard red winter, soft red winter, white, and durum. The hard red spring and hard red winter wheats are grown intensively in Kansas, Montana, Nebraska, Minnesota, and Texas. Soft red winter wheat is grown in the states primarily south and east of Illinois, while the white wheat is the product of the Pacific Northwest.

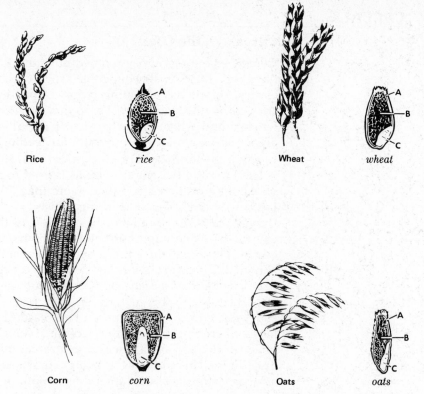

Four vital cereals. The grain itself is divided into the bran layers (A), the endosperm (B), and the germ (C).

Durum Wheat A very hard, high-protein wheat grown primarily in North Dakota and particularly well suited to the production of pastas.

Pasta Various dough pastes containing durum wheat and water and sometimes egg and shaped in a variety of flat and rounded or twisted shapes.

Durum wheat is a unique, amber-colored wheat of a different species and is valued for making macaroni, spaghetti, and the various other alimentary pastes or *pastas*. This variety is the very hardest of all of the wheats. Since it was first imported from the Crimea in the middle of the nineteenth century, this crop has been bred for high protein content and resistance to disease. Remarkably, 13 counties in North Dakota (in the northeastern part of the state) produce about 85 percent of the durum wheat grown in the United States, with the remainder being primarily from Minnesota and Montana.

Oats are grown along the northern tiers of states, from the Dakotas and Nebraska to Pennsylvania and New York, plus Texas. Barley, a somewhat less familiar cereal grain, is grown in the northern tier of states from Washington to Minnesota and in California. Oats and barley are used primarily for breakfast cereals and have limited use in baked products. Rye is another cereal valued for its flavor and also for its structural capability in baked products, sometimes being used in combination with wheat flour to make bread. Triticale, a comparatively new type of cereal, is a cross between wheat and rye that has been developed by geneticists. The supply of triticale is somewhat limited, but it has considerable promise as an interesting grain for use in baked products.

Grain Structure

All cereal grains are comprised of three distinct parts: bran, endosperm, and germ (also called the embryo). The bran portion actually consists of several outer protective layers covering the endosperm and germ (Figure 7.1). These bran layers are high in cellulose and hence valued as good sources of fiber, as well as providing useful amounts of several of the B vitamins (see Table 7.3).

The endosperm is the region of the kernel where starch is deposited in a protein matrix. This area, comprising the large majority of the kernel, is a source of both starch and protein, plus rather limited amounts of the B vitamins. This is the fraction utilized primarily in the milling of wheat flours.

By far the smallest portion of the grain is the germ or embryo, for it constitutes only about 2.5 percent of the kernel. However, this is the portion that will produce the viable sprouts. A unique feature of the germ is that it contains fat. It also is a rich source of thiamin. The presence of fat in the germ limits the storage life of whole grains because the fat will become rancid over a period of time, particularly if the storage temperature is not cold.

Nutritional Contribution

Cereals undergo varying degrees of processing, resulting in some variations in nutrient content from one cereal product to another. However, some generalizations can be drawn. The protein content of cereals is modest, but very important amounts of protein are provided when cereals occupy a prominent part of the diet. For example, a person eating 4 cups of rice daily would obtain 16 grams of protein, which is almost 30 percent of the protein needed in a day by an adult man. This protein is classified as being incomplete, because it does not provide adequate amounts of all the essential amino acids. However, the protein from cereals is utilized quite well when combined with animal protein, which is the case when cereals are eaten with milk added. They also complement the protein from legumes and nuts, enabling these plant protein sources to be utilized with increased efficiency.

Table 7.3   Distribution of Nutrients in the Kernel of Wheat

Nutrient	Bran (%)	Endosperm (%)	Germ (%)
Protein	19	70–75	8
B vitamins			
Thiamin	33	3	64
Riboflavin	42	32	26
Niacin	86	12	2
Pyridoxine	73	6	21
Pantothenic acid	50	43	7

Source: Adapted from *From wheat to flour.* Wheat Flour Institute. Chicago, Ill. 1966. P. 38.

Kernel of Wheat

The kernel of wheat is a storehouse of nutrients needed and used by man since the dawn of civilization.

This cross section shows the nutrients in each part of the kernel. They are considered essential in the human diet.

ENDOSPERM

... about 83% of the kernel

Source of white flour. Of the nutrients in the whole kernel the endosperm contains about:

70-75% of the protein
43% of the pantothenic acid
32% of the riboflavin   } B-complex
12% of the niacin   } vitamins
6% of the pyridoxine
3% of the thiamine

Enriched flour products contain added quantities of riboflavin, niacin and thiamine, plus iron, in amounts equal to or exceeding whole wheat — according to a formula established on the basis of popular need of those nutrients.

BRAN ... about 14½% of the kernel

Included in whole wheat flour.
Of the nutrients in whole wheat, the bran, in addition to indigestible cellulose material contains about:

86% of the niacin
73% of the pyridoxine
50% of the pantothenic acid
42% of the riboflavin
33% of the thiamine
19% of the protein

GERM ... about 2½% of the kernel

The embryo or sprouting section of the seed, usually separated because it contains fat which limits the keeping quality of flours. Available separately as human food. Of the nutrients in whole wheat, the germ contains about:

64% of the thiamine
26% of the riboflavin
21% of the pyridoxine
8% of the protein
7% of the pantothenic acid
2% of the niacin

A Grain of Wheat
(enlarged approximately 35 times)

kansas
wheat
commission
1021 North Main Street
Hutchinson, Kansas 67501

Kansas is the largest wheat state in the United States.

Approximately 300 million bushels of hard red winter wheat are harvested annually. This wheat is planted in the fall. The seeds root; shoots and leaves emerge. In the spring, the wheat plants which have been dormant during the winter, begin to grow again to reach maturity in June and July. Hard red winter wheat is used in bread and all-purpose flours.

Figure 7.1 Cross-sectional diagram of a wheat kernel.

All cereals are excellent sources of starch, which makes them useful as inexpensive sources of energy. Thiamin, riboflavin, and niacin occur naturally in cereal grains in abundance; the bran and germ are appreciably higher in their vitamin content than the endosperm is, while the protein is most abundant in the endosperm (Table 7.3).

Table 7.4 contains information about the actual nutrient content of many different cereals and cereal products. In addition to the nutrients mentioned, cereals contain small amounts of other vitamins and trace minerals. However, these may be lost during processing, particularly if refined cereal products are being maufactured, for the bran and embryo often are removed.

Commercial Processing

Of the many different techniques used in processing cereals, refining, or fractionation, is most common. Fractionation may be done by hulling (as is done with popcorn), milling (used in making flour), and polishing (rice); the purpose is to remove the bran, germ, or endosperm to facilitate cooking and/or

Table 7.4 Nutrient Content of Selected Cereals[1]

Food	Energy (kcal)	Protein (g)	Iron (mg)	Thiamin (mg)	Riboflavin (mg)	Niacin (mg)
Bran flakes	105	4	12.3	0.14	0.06	2.2
Bread, slice cracked wheat	65	2	0.3	0.03	0.02	0.3
rye	60	2	0.4	0.05	0.02	0.4
white, enriched	70	2	0.6	0.06	0.05	0.6
whole wheat	65	3	0.8	0.09	0.03	0.8
Bulgur	245	8	1.9	0.08	0.05	4.1
Corn flakes	100	2	0.4	0.11	0.02	0.5
Corn grits enriched	125	3	0.7	0.10	0.07	1.0
Farina	105	3	0.7	0.12	0.07	1.0
Macaroni enriched	190	6	1.4	0.23	0.14	1.8
Noodles enriched	200	7	1.4	0.22	0.13	1.9
Oatmeal	130	5	1.4	0.19	0.05	0.2
Rice, white enriched	225	4	1.8	0.23	0.02	2.1

Source: Adapted from Nutritive values of the edible part of foods. *Home and Garden Bulletin* No. 72. U.S. Dept. Agriculture. Washington, D.C. 1981.

[1]All items are reported as cooked or ready to eat. Portions are 1 cup (1 slice for breads).

enhance storage life. When wheat is refined in making white flour, the bran and germ are removed, resulting in the white color, a product with enhanced shelf life (due to removal of lipids in the germ) and loss of fiber and some of the vitamins. Refined cereal products clearly have advantages as well as disadvantages.

To compensate for the loss of vitamins resulting from refining cereal products, enrichment is often done to replace thiamin, riboflavin, niacin, and iron at a required level, with the addition of calcium and vitamin D being optional. *Enriched cereals* must indicate this information on the label and must have the specified amounts of the three B vitamins and iron added (see Table 7.5). Although a number of states require that refined cereals be enriched, this is not a legal requirement in all states, which makes it important for consumers to read labels to be sure to purchase the enriched product when selecting refined cereals.

Some cereal products are fortified with various nutrients that are not normally present in the food, with some products having so many nutrients added that much of the day's total nutrient requirement is provided by a bowl of the cereal. These are usually quite expensive and are not mandatory for good nutrition.

In addition to enrichment, cereals may undergo a variety of changes as a result of technology. Whole-grain cereals often are broken by various means into smaller particles to facilitate cooking. Cracked wheat and rolled oats are whole-grain cereals that are broken mechanically into smaller pieces to facilitate softening of the cellulose (see Chapter 3) and gelatinizing of the starch during preparation.

New breakfast cereals, both ready-to-eat and hot, enter the marketplace in a seemingly constant stream. The wide variety of types, flavors, and shapes represents a vast investment in creativity and resources in attempts to capture significant shares of this highly competitive market. The products basically fit into one of six basic categories of processed cereals: extruded, flaked, granulated, puffed, rolled, or shredded. Additional variety is available

Enriched Cereals Refined cereals to which thiamin, riboflavin, niacin, and iron have been added at specified levels.

Table 7.5 Federal Standards for Enriched Rice and Enriched Macaroni Products

Nutrient	Macaroni Products (Ingredients/pound of flour)	Rice (Ingredients/pound)
Required		
Thiamin	4.0– 5.0 mg	2.0– 4.0 mg
Riboflavin	1.7– 2.2 mg	1.2– 2.4 mg
Niacin	27.0–34.0 mg	16.0–32.0 mg
Iron	13.0–16.5 mg	13.0–26.0 mg
Optional		
Calcium	500–625 mg	
Vitamin D	250–1000 USP units[1]	

[1]One USP unit equals one International Unit (I.U.).

by combining products from more than one cereal grain and by adding varying levels of fiber.

Among the hot cereals, quick cooking or instant products compete with the untreated cereals. Disodium phosphate is added to produce *quick-cooking cereals* and rice. This addition does speed softening by reducing the heat energy needed for water to penetrate starch granules. On the negative side, the resulting product is more gummy and sticky than the untreated cereal. The *instant* hot *cereals* have undergone gelatinization prior to being dehydrated and packaged; hence these need only to be rehydrated with boiling water before being served.

Quick-cooking Cereals Cereals treated with disodium phosphate to hasten softening during cooking.

Instant Cereals Cereals which have been precooked to gelatinize the starch and then dehydrated to produce a product requiring only rehydration to serve.

Corn and Barley

Although corn is popular as sweet corn in various forms, fresh, frozen, and canned sweet corn represent only a portion of the food items that may be processed from corn. Hominy and grits are two processed corn items popular among many people, particularly in the South. *Hominy* is made by removing the bran and germ of the corn kernel, utilizing a lye treatment, to yield a unique form of corn endosperm. Closely related to hominy is another lye-treated corn product called *grits*. Actually, grits are simply coarsely chopped hominy. Hominy and grits can be made from either white or yellow corn, the white being traditional in the South and the yellow being common in the northern states. Another familiar cereal product from corn that is often an ingredient in cooking is cornmeal. Cornmeal is simply finely ground corn from which the germ has been removed to enhance shelf life. Cornmeal and hominy grits, regardless of whether they are produced from white or yellow corn, usually are marketed as the enriched products because of the loss of nutrients during their manufacturing.

Hominy Endosperm product made by soaking corn in lye.

Grits Coarsely chopped hominy.

Cornstarch, an interesting product derived from corn, is a popular thickening agent in food preparation. The endosperm, separated from the remainder of the corn kernel by wet milling, serves as the source of cornstarch and corn syrup. Production of cornstarch requires separation of the starch from protein and other extraneous compounds in the endosperm. Corn syrup then may be produced from the cornstarch by acid hydrolysis and/or enzymes appropriate to the desired end product.

Barley is used to only a very limited extent in the United States. The customary form in which it is marketed for use as a food ingredient is as pearl barley, which is the portion remaining after the bran has been removed. It also is used in malted products and in making whiskey.

Rice

Rice is enjoying a popularity in this country never known before. The combination of increased interest in creative cookery and the marketing of rice in various forms as gourmet items has contributed to a growing market for this cereal. Several types of rice are found in most markets. Brown rice is whole-grain rice containing the bran and germ, as well as the endosperm; despite the fact that brown rice takes about twice as long to cook as polished rice, brown rice is quite popular, particularly among people who are seeking the fiber and vitamin and mineral content provided by this whole-grain cereal. Instant brown rice is available for those who wish to avoid the 40-minute cooking period usually required to prepare brown rice. A distinctive nutty flavor, slightly crisp texture, and light brown color are characteristic of brown rice that has been prepared carefully.

At one time, and in some circles, polished rice was a status symbol. The snowy white of boiled, polished rice was considered to be far more desirable than the slightly brown color of brown rice. The fact that polished rice can be ready to serve in 20 minutes (half the time needed for brown rice) doubtless added to the appeal of polished rice. However, the removal of the bran and germ during polishing or milling also meant the removal of many of the nutrients present in useful quantities in the whole-grain brown rice. The enrichment of polished rice often is done to replace the thiamin, riboflavin, niacin and iron lost during milling, making enriched polished rice only slightly less nourishing than brown rice. If polished rice is the form of rice selected, it is important to be sure that it has been enriched, a fact that will be identified on the label.

Parboiled rice is another choice in the market. This rice is slightly more yellow than polished rice, but otherwise is very similar in appearance. To produce parboiled rice, the rice grains are steamed under pressure and then are dried prior to being polished. This steaming period drives the water-soluble B vitamins from the bran into the endosperm of the grains, where these vitamins remain following milling. It is the yellowish color of riboflavin that contributes the yellow cast to parboiled rice. By this process, about 92 percent of the thiamin, 70 percent of the riboflavin, and almost 78 percent of the niacin present in the bran will be retained in the grains of parboiled rice after polishing. This processing adds significantly to the cost of this form of rice, but it still is well below the price of the instant or dehydrated, pregelatinized rice.

SCIENCE NOTE: Characteristics of Rice Grains

The previous discussion has focused on the merits of different methods of processing rice to influence color, textural characteristics, and cooking time. However, the type of rice selected for the processing is also of great importance in influencing the characteristics of the cooked rice. The length of the rice grain is the means commonly used for differentiating types of rice—the types being short-grain, medium-grain, and long-grain rice. Their cooking characteristics vary because of the general differences in the ratios of amylose to amylopectin.

Long-grain rice is the type of rice preferred by U.S consumers because it cooks into well-defined grains and has a fluffy character. Properly prepared, long-grain rice has a pleasing, nonsticky character when being chewed. This type of rice absorbs a considerable amount of water

Long-grain rice, characterized by being long and slender, becomes a fluffy rice when cooked; short-grain rice is easily distinguished by its fat and stubby shape and sticky quality when cooked; while medium-grain rice is intermediate between the long- and the short-grain varieties.

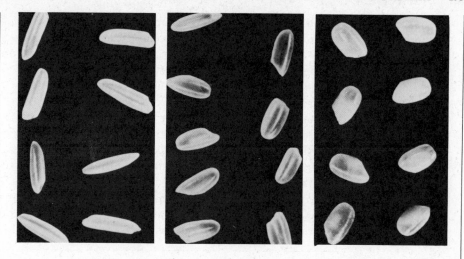

To mold rice, as is done in preparing this Sonora-style soup, short-grain rice is recommended. Its adhesive quality has caused short-grain rice to be called ''sticky rice.''

during boiling, when compared with the amount absorbed by the medium- or the short-grain rices. These characteristics of long-grain rice appear to be the result of the comparatively high proportion of amylose in the starch granules in this type of rice grain.

The short-grain rices have a rather cohesive, sticky quality when properly prepared. These characteristics are valued when using rice to make a molded rice ring or when the rice will be eaten using chopsticks. The stickiness is thought to be due to the tendency of short-grain rice to split on the ends during cooking, thus releasing some starch into the cooking water and also disrupting the general structure of the individual grains. Both the medium- and the short-grain rices have a reduced content of amylose in comparison with the long-grain variety. The gelatinization process takes place at a somewhat lower temperature in the short-grain than in the long-grain rices.

There is another "rice" product on the market—wild rice—but wild rice is not truly a rice. Instead, it is the seeds of a wild grass grown in cold marshlands in northern Minnesota and southern Canada. Harvesting of this crop is restricted by law to the Indians who live in the area. Harvesting is done by pushing canoes through the marshes and shaking the mature seeds from the grasses into the canoes—not exactly a modern harvesting technique. The limitations on harvesting wild rice have caused the price to remain very high. However, the distinctive flavor, crisp texture, and excellent nutritive value of wild rice make this a pleasing, healthful, yet costly item when used in menus.

Wheat

Wheat is an extremely versatile cereal grain adaptable to many uses. Its importance as the source of the principal flour used in baked products accounts for much of the wheat consumed in this country (see Chapters 12–14). However, there are other wheat products of merit in the diet. Wheat is utilized in both hot and cold cereals. Farina, a traditional hot cereal, is made of small pieces of the endosperm of wheat and contains no bran and a maximum of 3 percent flour. Rolled wheat can be purchased as wheat flakes for use as a ready-to-eat cereal or as an ingredient in baked products and casseroles.

Bulgur Parboiled, cracked wheat; chewy and nutlike.

Bulgur is an ancient form of wheat that has been popular for centuries in Middle Eastern cuisines and that recently has been gaining in popularity in the United States as a substitute for rice or potatoes. The cooked product has a distinctly chewy texture and a nutlike flavor. To produce bulgur from wheat, the wheat grains are parboiled and dried before part of the bran layer is removed. Although bulgur with whole kernels is available, the more common form is cracked bulgur.

Pastas of numerous shapes and formulations are also wheat products, but these are ordinarily made only from durum wheat. The doughs used in making the three forms of pastas (spaghetti, macaroni, and noodles) contain a large proportion of semolina, which is a granular product produced by milling durum wheat and restricted to a maximum of 3 percent flour. Macaroni and spaghetti and their variations are extruded from doughs containing *semolina*, granulars (milled durum with more flour than is allowed in semolina), and water. Noodles differ in that they also contain more than 5 percent egg solids or yolks in their doughs.

Semolina Granular, milled durum wheat, with a maximum of three percent flour.

Pasta variations include the green noodles, which feature spinach as an ingredient. Green noodles are particularly appealing when served topped with grated cheese or sesame seeds. A popular trend is the use of fresh pastas rather than the familiar dehydrated products. Fresh pastas require refrigeration and must be boiled and used promptly before any fermentation occurs in the dough. Fresh pastas are available in some markets. Pasta makers are becoming an increasingly popular piece of equipment in U.S. kitchens where people have gained an appreciation for the high quality of the fresh pastas.

Kasha Buckwheat groats (hulled and fragmented particles).

Buckwheat, a relative of wheat, is the source of *kasha*, which is similar to bulgur. The hull of the grain is removed before the kernel is fragmented to produce kasha.

Large pasta shells, linguini, and lasagna noodles are just some of the huge array of pastas made using durum wheat, a type of wheat noted for its comparatively high content of strong protein.

Storage

There are two basic problems in the storage of cereals and pastas in the home: possible hatching of larvae and potential uptake of moisture and off-flavors. Desirable storage conditions are a cool, dry cupboard, for these conditions delay deteriorative changes. Under these conditions, the maximum storage time for unopened or tightly reclosed packages of cereals ranges between two months and a year (Table 7.6). Whole-grain products are limited in their shelf life by the onset of rancidity of the fat in the germ. Occasionally, refrigerated or frozen storage of cereals may be desirable, for these temperatures prevent the hatching of larvae during extended storage and also greatly retard onset of rancidity. Of course, such cold storage is more costly than is use of a cool kitchen cabinet. Counterbalancing that cost may be the prevention of spoilage losses and the opportunity to take advantage of low sale prices. If dry cereals have lost their crispness because of absorbing moisture from the air, they may be heated in a 350°F oven until they have lost their excess moisture.

Preparation of Cereals

The objectives for cooking the various types of cereals are (1) to soften the cellulose and (2) to gelatinize the starch. Specific directions for preparation usually are provided on the packages, and these often are the best guide for preparing the cereal. Variations may include using milk as the cooking medium rather than water, a change that modifies the flavor and increases the nutritive value of the prepared cereal. Well-prepared hot cereals will be free of lumps, will be light on the tongue (not pasty), will have a pleasing flavor with no suggestion of a raw starch flavor, and will pile softly when hot.

Hot Breakfast Cereals One of the basic problems in preparing hot cereals is avoiding lumps when the cereal and water are combined and then heated to gelatinize the starch. The technique used for adding cereals to the boiling,

Table 7.6 Approximate Storage Time for Cereals and Pastas

Product	Maximum Storage Recommended (months)
Breakfast cereals	2–3
Bulgur	6
Cornmeal and grits	4–6
Pasta	
Macaroni and spaghetti products	12
Egg noodles	6
Rice	
White, parboiled, packaged, and precooked	12
Brown and wild	6

Source: Maximum storage periods for maintaining the best quality are adapted from Cereals and pasta in family meals. *Home and Garden Bulletin* No. 150. U.S. Dept. of Agriculture. Washington, D.C. 1968.

salted water varies with the size of the cereal particles. Fine cereals, such as cornmeal, will lump badly if they are added directly to boiling water. To avoid this problem, cornmeal and similar products should be mixed with some cold water before being stirred into boiling water. Other cereals may be stirred in as the dry particles. Cereals are added when the water has already reached a boil to help reduce the cooking time, which reduces the amount of stirring required. Since boiling granular cereals need to be stirred while being cooked in order to achieve uniform gelatinization of the starch and a smooth product, there will be some tendency toward a sticky product if the cooking time (and consequently the stirring time) is long.

The actual length of time required to reach the desired end point in a cooked cereal is determined by (1) size of the cereal particles (large particles take longer), (2) the amount of cellulose present, (3) previous treatment of the cereal, and (4) the elevation of the cooking site. Since cellulose softens comparatively slowly, the more cellulose in a cereal, the longer will be the cooking time. Previous treatment might include gelatinization and dehydration, a circumstance requiring merely the addition of boiling water prior to service. Disodium phosphate may have been incorporated as an additive, and this speeds the gelatinization process. The discussion in Chapter 1 about boiling points indicated that water boils at a lower temperature at high elevations, which means that cereals will require a longer boiling time in the mountains than they do at sea level.

Cereals usually are added to a measured amount of boiling, salted water and are boiled over direct heat (with stirring, if a granular product) until the desired end point is reached. The amount of water to use varies with the type of cereal being prepared and is dependent on the character of the particles, as can be seen in Table 7.7. When available, package directions should be followed. To reduce problems of foaming and possible boiling over, a small amount of margarine, butter, or oil may be added to the boiling water. If milk is being used as the liquid medium, use of a double boiler is recommended, because its moderate heat will prevent scorching the milk and avoid the likelihood of boiling over, both being common problems when using direct heat with milk. If a cooked cereal needs to be held at all after it has been prepared, the pan should be covered to prevent or at least minimize formation of a skin on the surface.

Table 7.7 Proportions for Preparing Cereals[1]

Type of Cereal	Quantity of		
	Cereal	Salt	Water
Rolled, flaked	1 c	½ tsp	2–3 c
Coarse or cracked	1 c	1 tsp	3–4 c
Fine granules	1 c	1¼ tsp	4–5 c

[1]Package directions are a better guide to preparing specific cereals. This table is a general guide to cereal cookery.

Rice Cookery   Unless otherwise specified on the package, polished rice should be boiled in 2 to 2¼ cups of salted water per cup of rice. Ideally, all the water will have been absorbed just when the rice is done. This eliminates the problem of losing water-soluble B vitamins into the cooking medium, but it does mean that enough water must be provided to allow the starch to be gelatinized. Otherwise, the rice will not soften adequately. If the rice is not done when the cooking water is gone, more water will need to be added to complete the gelatinization process. The average time for boiling polished rice is about 20 minutes, while brown rice requires about 40 minutes, and some wild rice takes as long as 60 minutes. Minute rice and quick-cooking brown rice require significantly less time than their conventional counterparts. The tests for doneness vary with the type of rice: polished rice should be soft when rubbed between the fingers; brown rice should be tender, yet somewhat crisp; and wild rice will start to curl open on the ends of the grains.

Washing of rice is not recommended after cooking because of the resulting loss of the B vitamins. This is true for brown, enriched polished, parboiled, or wild rice. If desired, the cooked rice can be spread in a thin layer on a large baking sheet, covered with a layer of cheesecloth, and heated briefly in the oven to help fluff the finished rice.

Other variations for preparing rice include baking rice. This is done by pouring either boiling water or scalded milk over the rice in a baking dish, covering tightly, and baking for about 35 minutes at 350°F until the rice tests done. Another variation, sometimes referred to as the pilaf method, is to saute the raw rice grains lightly and then to add water or other cooking liquid and boil or simmer until done. Bouillon often is used as the liquid in this method.

Bulgur and Other Cereals   The methods used for preparing rice are equally applicable to the preparation of bulgur. Like rice, bulgur takes about 20 minutes of boiling in a covered pan to reach the desired degree of doneness. Both rice and bulgur swell appreciably due to the gelatinization of the starch in them, actually about tripling the original uncooked volume.

Kasha (buckwheat groats) will boil to the desired degree of doneness in about 15 minutes following a brief period of sauteing in butter or oil. Only twice as much water as kasha is usually an adequate ratio for preparing this cereal product. Preparation of pearl barley also is similar, although more time is required to complete the softening of pearl barley than is required for rice.

Hominy grits require five times as much water as dry grits when they are being prepared. This is more than double the amount of water required for preparing rice and bulgur. Therefore, it is not surprising that grits expand to about four times their original volume after cooking (in contrast to rice expanding about three times). Grits become softened and ready to eat after about 15 minutes of boiling.

Pasta   Directions for preparing pastas usually are provided on the packages, but the following are some general suggestions that can be used if specific guidelines are not provided. About 6 cups of water should be brought to a boil before half a pound of pasta is added. For this amount, 1 teaspoon of salt and 1 teaspoon of oil generally are added, the latter being helpful in reducing foaming and preventing pieces from sticking readily to each other. Long pieces of pasta need to be added by pushing them slowly into the boiling water as the first portion softens and bends. All of the pasta must be immersed in the boiling water so that cooking will be uniform. The time required to reach the desired *al dente* ("to the tooth") stage varies with the type of pasta and usually is close to the length of time indicated on the package. The pasta can be checked for doneness by pressing a piece with a fork against the side of the pan or by sampling a piece. The piece should feel firm and chewy, yet have just the tiniest suggestion of a firm core. An important part of pasta preparation is thorough draining of the pasta before serving. A colander or strainer works well for this task. Unless this is done carefully, a plate of pasta may turn into a small lake with an island of pasta.

SUMMARY

Although much of the starch used in cooking is obtained from cereals, some root and tree starches are also used in thickening a number of food products. Starch is composed of two fractions—amylose and amylopectin; these fractions are deposited in an organized fashion in granules. When heated to extremely high temperatures by dry heat, dextrinization occurs, and the ability to thicken is reduced somewhat. When starch is heated in the presence of water, gelatinization of the uptake of water into the starch granules and the resultant swelling cause a noticeable thickening. Some of the somewhat soluble, linear amylose will leave the granules and move freely in the water, while some of the water will enter the granule and become bound inside. A dispersion of gelatinized starch that flows is called a sol; if the flow properties are lost upon cooling, the dispersion is termed a gel.

The concentration, type of starch, final temperature during cooking, amount of sugar, presence of lumps, addition of acid prior to gelatinization (causing acid hydrolysis), and the extent of dextrinization (if dextrinized starch is used) all influence the viscosity of the starch sols and the firmness of their resulting gels. Gels undergo changes during storage. Syneresis is the loss of some of the liquid from a gel and occurs particularly where there is a cut surface. The amylose molecules that are outside the granules gradually rearrange themselves into somewhat more organized arrangements than existed when the gel first formed. This rearrangement, called retrogradation, results in a tendency toward some crystalline areas, causing a gritty character.

Starches bred to contain almost entirely amylopectin are called waxy starches and are useful when gels are not desired, yet the product needs some thickening. High-amylose starches are bred to provide edible thin films. Regular starches (about 20 percent amylose and 80 percent amylopectin) may be precooked and then dehydrated to make "instant" starch products. Waxy rice starch or other starches with phosphate cross-linkages are stabilized sufficiently to undergo frozen storage with little retrogradation occurring. Thin-boiling starches for use in making candies containing starch gels undergo some acid hydrolysis, but not enough to interfere with the ability to form a strong gel.

Examples of products using starch as the thickener include white sauces (thin, medium, thick, and very thick), gravies, cream soups, and cornstarch puddings. Thorough dispersion of the starch using a fluid fat, a cold liquid, or dry ingredients must be done before the starch comes in contact with hot liquid if lumps are to be avoided. Stirring is necessary throughout the gelatinization period to make a smooth product. Layers of fat on top are not desirable and may be the result of (1) incomplete gelatinization, (2) too little starch or too much fat, or (3) excessive moisture loss when making thick and very thick products.

Cereals occupying important places in the diet as sources of starch, energy, and the B vitamins include corn, wheat, rice, oats, and millet. Wheat is particularly important in the United States because its flour is used in most baked products, and durum wheat is the main ingredient in pastas. All cereal grains are comprised of the bran (rich in nutrients), the germ (a source of B vitamins and fat), and endosperm (high in starch and some protein). In cereals the bran and embryo are often removed to give the refined product a longer shelf life (without the fat) and a reduced cooking time (removal of the fibrous bran). Enrichment frequently is done to replace some of the nutrients removed from refined cereals. Parboiling is done in processing some rice as a means of shifting nutrients into the endosperm before polishing the grains.

Storage of grains is limited by the possibility of insect infestation and by development of rancidity in whole-grain products. A cool, dry storage area and possibly even refrigerator or freezer storage extend shelf life.

The preparation of cereals is directed toward softening the cellulose and gelatinizing the starch. Lumping may be a problem in some hot breakfast cereals, but rice and other individual grain products do not present this problem, hence do not require stirring during cooking. When done, there should be no trace of a raw starch flavor, and grains should be tender. Rice and other cereals and their products expand significantly (usually three or even four times, in the case of hominy grits) as a result of the gelatinization of their starch. Pasta is usually added to boiling water containing salt and a little oil and boiled until tenderized to the *al dente* stage.

Selected References

Anderson, R. H. et al. Effects of processing and storage on micronutrients in breakfast cereals. *Food Tech.* 30 (5): 1976.

Banks, W. and C. T. Greenwood. *Starch and its Components.* John Wiley. New York. 1975.

Bean, M. L. and E. M. Osman. Behavior of starch during food preparation. II. Effects of different sugars on the viscosity and gel strength of starch pastes. *Food Res.* 24: 665. 1959.

Bechtel, B. O. and Y. Pomeranz. Rice Kernel. *Adv. Cereal Sci. Tech* 3: 73. 1980.

Biliaderis, C. G. et al. Starch gelatinization phenomena studied by differential scanning calorimetry. *J. Food Sci.* 45(6): 1669. 1980.

Casey, J. P. Future for corn wet milling. *Food Tech. 32(1):* 72. 1978.

Chabot, J. F. et al. Freeze-etch ultrastructure of waxy maize and acid hydrolyzed waxy maize starch granules. *J. Food Sci. 43:* 727. 1978.

Derby, R. E. et al. Visual observation of wheat-starch gelatinization in limited water systems. *Cereal Chem. 52:* 702. 1975.

Elbert, E. M. Starch: changes during heating in the presence of moisture. *J. Home Econ. 57:* 197. 1965.

Engstrom, A. and M. Kern. Analysis of sugar content of ready-to-eat cereals. *Cereal Foods World 25(4):* 150. 1980.

Ghiasi, K. et al. Gelatinization of wheat starch. II. Starch-surfactant interaction. *Cereal Chem. 59(2):* 86. 1982.

Greenwood, C. T. Structure, properties, and amylolytic degradation of starch. *Food Tech. 18:* 138. 1964.

Hellman, N. N. et al. Bread staling problem. *Cereal Chem. 31:* 495. 1954.

Hester, E. E. et al. Effect of sucrose on properties of some starches and flours. *Cereal Chem. 33:* 91. 1956.

Hullinger, C. H. et al. Food applications of high amylose starches. *Food Tech. 27(3):* 22. 1973.

Hulse, J. H. and D. Spurgeon. Triticale. *Sci. Ameri. 231(2):* 72. 1974.

Inglett, G. E., ed. *Corn: Culture, Processing, Products.* Avi Publishing Co., Westport, Conn. 1970.

Inglett, G. E., ed *Wheat: Production and Utilization.* Avi Publishing Co., Westport, Conn. 1974.

Katz, S. H. et al. Traditional maize processing techniques in the new world. *Science 184:* 765. 1974.

Keller, R. L. Soy flour and grits for use in food products. *J. Am. Oil Chem. Soc. 48:* 481. 1971.

Kent, N. L. *Technology of Cereals.* Pergamon. New York. 2nd ed. 1975.

Kies, C. et al. Triticale, soy-TVP, and millet-based diets as protein sources for humnan adults. *J. Food Sci. 40:* 90. 1975.

Leach, H. W. et al. Structure of the starch granule. I. Swelling and solubility patterns of various starches. *Cereal Chem. 36:* 534. 1959.

Linebock, D. R. and G. E. Inglett. *Food Carbohydrates.* Avi Publishing Co. Westport, Conn. 1982.

Little, R. R. and E. H. Dawson. Histology and histochemistry of raw and cooked rice kernels. *Food Res. 25:* 611. 1960.

Lorenz, K. Triticale. *Baker's Digest 48 (June):* 24. 1974.

Lorenz, K. and W. Dilsaver, Buckwheat starch—physiochemical properties and functional characteristics. *Starch/Stärke 34(7):* 217. 1982.

Matthews, R. H. and E. A. Bechtel. Viscosity of white sauces made with wheat flours from different U.S. regions. *J. Home Econ. 58:* 392. 1966.

Miller, B. S. et al. Pictorial explanation for the increase in viscosity of a heated starch-water suspension. *Cereal Chem. 50:* 271. 1973.

Mitsuda, H. and K. Nakajima. Storage of cooked rice. *J. Food Sci. 42:* 1439. 1977.

Osman, E. Interaction of starch with other components of food systems. *Food Tech. 29:* 4. 1975.

Parrott, M. E. and B. E. Thrall. Functional properties of various fibers: Physical properties. *J. Food Sci. 43:* 759. 1978.

Pisesookbunterng, W. et al. Bread staling studies. II. Role of refreshing. *Cereal Chem. 60(4):* 301. 1983.

Pomeranz. Y. ed. *Wheat Chemistry and Technology.* Amer. Assoc. Cereal Chem. St. Paul, Minn. 1971.

Pomeranz, Y. ed. *Advances in Cereal Science and Technology*. Amer. Assoc. Cereal Chem. St. Paul, Minn. 1976.

Pomeranz, Y. Grain structures and end use products. *Food Microstruc. 1(2)*: 107. 1982.

Sanderson, G. R. Polysaccharides in foods. *Food Tech. 35(7)*: 50. 1981.

Sandstedt, R. M. Fifty years of progress in starch chemistry. *Cereal Sci. Today 10*: 305. 1965.

Savage, H. L. and E. M. Osman. Effects of certain sugars and sugar alcohols on the swelling of cornstarch granules. *Cereal Chem. 55*: 447. 1978.

Sikka, K. C. et al. Comparative nutritive value and amino acid content of triticale, wheat, and rye. *J. Ag. Food Chem. 26(4)*: 788. 1978.

Snow, P. Factors affecting the rate of hydrolysis of starch in food. *Am. J. Clin. Nutr. 34(12)*: 2721. 1981.

Spies, R. D. and R. C. Hoseney. Effect of sugars on starch gelatinization. *Cereal Chem. 59(2)*: 128. 1982.

Trimbo, H. B. and B. S. Miller. Factors affecting quality of sauces (gravies). *J. Home Econ. 63*: 48. 1971.

Williams, M. R. Gelatinization of starch. *Starch/Stärke 34(7)*: 112. 1982.

Wurzberg, O. B. and C. D. Szymanski. Modified starches for the food industry. *J. Ag. Food Chem. 18*: 997. 1970.

Zeringer, H. J., Jr., et al. Triticale lipids: Composition and bread making characteristics of triticale flours. *Cereal Chem. 58(1)*: 351. 1981.

Study Questions

1. What is the relationship between glucose and starch? Between amylose and amylopectin?
2. Describe a starch granule and the changes it undergoes during gelatinization.
3. What is the difference between a starch sol and gel? What are some uses of both of these forms in foods?
4. What factors influence the viscosity of starch sols and gels?
5. What are the ways in which starch can be dispersed uniformly without introducing lumps into starch-thickened products?
6. Explain each of the following and indicate why each is important in working with starch: dextrinization, hydrolysis, retrogradation.
7. Describe the differences between instant and quick-cooking starch products.
8. What kinds of rice are available? How does the type of rice influence its preparation?

Detail of illumination from the Flemish "Hours of The Virgin," Pierpont Morgan Library.

CHAPTER 8

PROTEINS: MILK AND CHEESE

INTRODUCTION

Milk, the fluid secreted by lactating mammals, conjures different mental pictures in various countries around the world. In the United States, milk is assumed to be milk from cows, unless the product is specified to be from a different source. However, in some countries milk may be from goats, ewes, or such exotic sources as water buffalo.

The composition of milk varies with the source, but the merits of milk from the nutritional standpoint as well as from the culinary perspective are appreciated widely. Actually, milk is a complex fluid containing protein, fat, and carbohydrate (in the unique form of lactose). Its high nutrient value has made milk an important food for people, and it has also made it a nourishing medium for microorganisms that may invade milk.

This chapter examines the nutritional merits of milk and its various products, the control of microorganisms during milk storage, processing techniques to produce the desired products, and the cookery principles involved

Milk is extremely versatile, used not only as a beverage, but also being made into ice cream, whipped cream, butter, and many types of cheeses.

in preparing foods using the various milk products, with their protein content. In fact, much of the discussion on milk and cheese cookery is based on the behavior of protein under various circumstances in foods.

NUTRITIONAL VALUE OF MILK

Whole milk is about 87 percent water, with the remainder being about 4.9 percent carbohydrate, 3.5 percent fat, 3.5 percent protein, and a residue of ash. The carbohydrate in milk is lactose, which accounts for the sweet taste of milk. Lactose, like other metabolizable carbohydrates, serves as a source of energy (4 calories per gram). Milk is the major source of lactose in the food supply, and it is this sugar that is responsible for the abdominal discomfort a few people experience from milk if they have a deficiency of lactase, the enzyme needed to digest lactose.

Milk fat, like many animal fats, is relatively low in polyunsaturated fatty acids. The most abundant fatty acids in milk fat are oleic, palmitic, and stearic acids; butyric and other fairly short-chain fatty acids contribute to the flavor of milk, as well as to its energy value.

Casein Chief protein in milk and is precipitated in the manufacturing of cheese from milk.

Milk is a useful source of complete protein. In fact, milk contains a variety of proteins, some of which are water soluble, others of which may precipitate under conditions employed in cooking or in manufacturing cheese. *Casein* is the chief protein fraction in milk. Whey proteins, the water-soluble proteins that are part of the *whey* formed in the production of cheese, include lactalbumin and lactoglobulin. The various milk proteins are utilized very well by the body.

Whey Liquid removed from clotted milk in cheese manufacturing.

The nutritive merits of milk are so high that milk almost seems to possess a halo. Certainly, the useful amounts of protein, carbohydrate, and fat are significant to good nutrition, but these nutrients alone do not explain the significance of milk in the diet. The levels of most vitamins and many minerals are quite high in milk, with the exceptions of iron and vitamin C (see Table 8.1). The low levels of these two nutrients make it important to include a range of other foods to ensure good nutrition.

Riboflavin, one of the B vitamins, is present in significant amounts in milk. Since this vitamin is very sensitive to light and it is present in abundance in milk, careful packaging and storage to prevent exposing milk to sunlight are important to the level of riboflavin when the milk is consumed. Cardboard or brown-tinted glass containers are important devices for conserving riboflavin during marketing. Milk also contributes useful amounts of thiamin and vitamin A (if the milk is whole milk or has been fortified with vitamin A in the case of nonfat milk). Milk ordinarily is fortified with vitamin D at the level of 400 I.U. (International Units; 10 micrograms) per quart so that a quart of milk daily provides all of the vitamin D a child requires.

Among the minerals contained in milk, calcium and phosphorus are present in particularly significant amounts. In fact, milk serves as such an important source of these two key minerals that it is extremely difficult to get enough of either of them (particularly enough calcium) without using milk

Table 8.1 Nutrient Contributions of 1 Cup (8 fl oz) Milk

Nutrient	Percent of U.S. Recommended Dietary Allowance
Protein	20
Vitamin A	4
Vitamin C	4
Thiamine	8
Riboflavin	25
Niacin	*1
Calcium	30
Iron	*1
Vitamin D	25
Vitamin B_6	4
Vitamin B_{12}	15
Phosphorus	20
Magnesium	8
Zinc	4
Pantothenic acid	6

Source: Adapted from Lecos, C. Milk: Cows produce it; man improves it. *FDA Consumer 36(5):* 16. 1982.
[1]Less than 2 percent of the U.S. RDA (Recommended Dietary Allowance).

generously in the diet. The favorable ratio of calcium to phosphorus and the addition of vitamin D make the utilization of calcium and phosphorus particularly effective.

KEEPING MILK SAFE

Milk and foods containing milk require careful handling to avoid the possibility of food-borne illnesses. Some of the microorganisms that can thrive in milk are capable of causing tuberculosis, undulant fever, scarlet fever, septic sore throat, typhoid fever, gastroenteritis, and diphtheria. Some of these microorganisms are transmitted by the cow directly into the milk, while others may be introduced by persons handling the milk. Thus, the point of contamination may be the dairy, or it may be the home.

To reduce the possibility of milk-borne infections in dairies, efforts are made to ensure that the herd and the handlers are all in good health. All dairy cattle are tested for bovine tuberculosis, and many are tested for *Brucella abortus*, the cause of undulant fever in humans. Adequate housing for the cows and high sanitation standards are essential in maintaining dairy herds in excellent health. Dairies also have a significant responsibility for being sure that all equipment used in handling the milk is absolutely clean. Rapid cooling of milk is essential to helping to keep the microorganismal growth to a minimum before milk can be pasteurized.

Because milk affords such a good medium for growth of microorganisms, sanitary handling throughout the marketing chain from the cow to the consumer is essential. Pasteurization is a key aspect of this sequence, even when sanitation and storage temperatures are monitored carefully.

Pasteurization Heat treatment to kill disease-producing microorganisms in milk.

An extremely important treatment in assuring the safety of milk is *pasteurization*. This process is a heat treatment developed by Louis Pasteur as a method for inactivating disease-producing microorganisms. There is no way to prevent the presence of some microorganisms in the raw milk obtained from the cow. Even when very high levels of sanitation are maintained in a dairy, there will be live microorganisms in the milk, and some of these microorganisms may be harmful. It is for this reason that pasteurization is so vital.

Various heat treatments can be used for pasteurizing milk. The hold method is done by heating milk to 145°F, holding it at that temperature for 30 minutes, and then cooling it rapidly to at least 45°F or cooler. The method used most commonly today is the high-temperature short-time (sometimes called HTST) method, in which milk is heated to 161°F and is held there for at least 15 seconds before being cooled to 50°F or below. Other temperature treatments also are authorized and include 191°F for 1 second, 204°F for 0.05 second, or 212°F for 0.01 second.

UHT Ultra-high-temperature pasteurization of milk (280°F for 2 seconds) to make the milk sterile, permitting storage at room temperature when UHT-treated milk is aseptically packaged.

A fairly new development is ultra-high-temperature (*UHT*) pasteurization. This process involves rapid heating to 280°F for at least 2 seconds, an extreme treatment that makes it possible for the milk to be stored in a sterile container at room temperature until it is opened. This aseptically packaged product can be stored up to six months on the shelf if it is not opened. Once opened, the contents must be refrigerated to avoid spoilage. Creams of various fat percentages are sometimes prepared for marketing by use of UHT. The high temperature involved in processing milk and cream by UHT results in a slight "cooked" flavor, but the convenience of unrefrigerated storage makes this treatment a useful one for some applications.

MODIFYING MILK

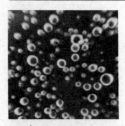

By forcing milk through tiny apertures under pressure, the large fat globules of non-homogenized milk (a) are split into very tiny ones, which remain suspended in homogenized milk (b). The smallest gradations on the scale are 2 microns. Dark-field illumination was used to make these photomicrographs.

Homogenization

The cream in milk, because of its low specific gravity, naturally floats to the top, where a layer of cream can be observed and even poured off or separated from the rest of the milk. Although this milk, often referred to as "cream-top" milk, used to be the only type available, consumers found that their milk often tended to vary in richness because of inadequate shaking of the bottle. Researchers responding to this complaint developed a technique in which heated milk is forced through tiny apertures at a pressure between 500 and 2500 pounds per square inch. This force causes the fat globules to be broken up into droplets so small that they remain suspended and distributed uniformly throughout the milk. This homogenization process also causes some denaturation of the milk proteins (notably casein) as they are being forced through the tiny openings, a change that makes homogenized milk somewhat more digestible than its nonhomogenized counterpart.

Fortification

The addition of vitamin D to milk is a measure that has been invaluable in helping to reduce the incidence of rickets among young children in this country. Milk was chosen as the vehicle for vitamin D fortification because of the abundance of calcium in milk and the role of vitamin D in promoting calcium utilization. There are three different ways in which the specified 400 I.U. of vitamin D per quart may be added: feeding irradiated yeast to the cows, irradiating milk by letting a thin stream of milk run under an ultraviolet light prior to pasteurizing, and adding a vitamin D concentrate to milk prior to pasteurization. The impracticality of the first two methods basically mandates that the third method—that of adding a vitamin D concentrate—be the technique used.

MILK PRODUCTS

Fluid Milks

Whole Milk   Whole milk marketed today generally has been homogenized and pasteurized, and these processes are indicated on the label. By definition, whole milk must contain a minimum of 3.25 percent fat and at least 8.25 percent nonfat milk solids. Usually, the milk also is fortified with 400 I.U. of vitamin D per quart. This is the type of milk generally assumed when the term ''milk'' is used. Its level of richness provides a flavor pleasing to many and also contributes some fat to products prepared using whole milk.

Low-Fat Milk Milk from which part of the fat has been skimmed, resulting in a product with fat usually at the level of 1 or 2 percent.

Low-Fat Milk   The national interest in reducing fat in the diet and in losing weight has resulted in an increasing market for *lowfat milk*, the milk produced when some of the cream is removed from whole milk. The amount of fat permitted in low-fat milks ranges from 0.5 to 2.0 percent. In some regions, the milk may be marketed as 1 percent or 2 percent milk. Pasteurization and homogenization ordinarily are key parts of the preparation of these milks for market. The nonfat milk solids content must be at least 8.25 percent. Since vitamin A is lost when the fat is being removed, it is mandatory to add 2000 I.U. of vitamin A; the addition of vitamin D is optional. The retention of the low level of fat in these milks makes the flavor basically acceptable to many people who are interested in reducing their calorie intake without giving up much flavor pleasure.

Skim or Nonfat Milk Milk resulting when almost all of the fat has been removed, leaving a maximum fat content of 0.5 percent and usually 0.1 percent or less.

Nonfat or Skim Milk   Specifications require that milk marketed as *skim or nonfat milk* have a maximum fat content of less than 0.5 percent (often 0.1 percent or less) and a minimum of 8.25 percent nonfat milk solids. Usually this type of milk is homogenized, despite its minimal fat content; it also is pasteurized and fortified with 2000 I.U. of vitamin A and 400 I.U. of vitamin D per quart. The virtual elimination of the fat results in a reduction of calories by almost half when skim milk is compared with whole milk. This removal of fat is attractive to dieters and to people who are trying to lower their intake of fat, particularly animal fats. The reduced fat level results in a loss of the richness

Among the many milk products on the market are fluid, evaporated, and dried milks with varying fat levels. Sweetened condensed milk differs from whole evaporated milk because of the added sugar. Flavored and cultured milks and yogurt also are found in the dairy case.

of flavor preferred by many people. However, nutritionally, nonfat milk is an excellent choice. In fact, the concentration of nutrients is very slightly higher (with the exception of fat) in nonfat milk than in whole milk, and the protein content of milk identified as "protein fortified" is at least 10 percent nonfat milk solids.

Flavored Milks Chocolate milk, available as the whole milk product or at lesser fat levels, is flavored with a chocolate syrup or a cocoa powder, with the chocolate solids ranging from 1.0 to 1.5 percent. The sucrose or other sugar, added at a level of between 5 and 7 percent, adds to the calorie content of such milks. The fat level (whole, low-fat, or nonfat) is indicated on the label, and so are such processing steps as pasteurizing, homogenizing, and fortifying the milk with vitamins A and D.

Cultured Milks *Acidophilus milk* has had the bacterium *Lactobacillus acidophilus* added to it. This results in the production of lactic acid from lactose as the bacterial colony metabolizes the carbohydrate. Nutritionally, acidophilus milk is comparable to the nonfat milk from which it is made, although the price will be significantly higher than the ordinary nonfat milk. However, this cost may be very acceptable to people who ordinarily have trouble digesting milk because of lactose intolerance. The flavor of acidophilus milk also is appealing to a moderate-sized audience.

.   Cultured *buttermilk* is made by adding a lactic acid bacterial culture to fresh, pasteurized fluid nonfat milk, whole milk, concentrated fluid milk, or reconstituted nonfat dry milk. Usually, nonfat milk is used to make cultured buttermilk, so that buttermilk, despite its name, is actually a milk low in fat. Sometimes flecks of butter are added to increase the palatability of cultured buttermilk, with the result that buttermilk may have as much as 1 percent fat.

Yogurt is not a fluid milk product, but because it is is marketed in its fresh state and is a cultured product, it is discussed here. The consistency of yogurt is custardlike rather than fluid. This texture is the result of the fermentation of milk, either whole or skim, by an inoculum of *Streptococcus thermophilus*, *Bacterium bulgaricus*, and *Placamo-bacterium yoghourti*. The acid produced by these lactose-digesting bacteria results in precipitation of the protein in the milk to form the familiar soft curd of *yogurt*. Fruits and other flavorings often are added to provide a variety of flavors to yogurt in the marketplace. These products have gained popularity as dressings for fruit salads, as dessert items, and as snack foods. Those made from skim milk can be useful in weight reduction diets.

Frozen yogurt, basically a sweetened, flavored yogurt that has been frozen, is a popular dessert item. The high sugar content often found in frozen yogurts adds significantly to the calorie content of this dessert, which is viewed as being competitive with ice cream.

Canned Milks

Evaporated Milks About 60 percent of the water in fluid milk is evaporated in the production of *evaporated milk*, leaving a concentrated product with a

Acidophilus Milk Milk containing a culture of *Lactobacillus acidophilus*, which metabolizes the lactose in milk.

Buttermilk Skim milk sometimes containing flecks of butter and a bacterial culture.

Yogurt Milk-based food produced when milk is clotted by lactic acid-producing bacteria.

Evaporated Milk Canned milk product in which about half of the water content has been evaporated prior to canning; available in varying levels of fat, that is, ranging from nonfat to whole.

minimum fat content of 7.5 percent and a milk solids content of at least 25 percent if evaporated whole milk is being processed. The milk is homogenized and fortified with vitamin D prior to canning. The heat of the canning process sterilizes the milk so that it remains unspoiled during storage at room temperature in its airtight can. The advantages of evaporated milk are the reduced volume and weight in the marketing process because of the removal of so much water and the ability to be stored at room temperature as long as the can has not been opened. The disadvantages are the somewhat altered color (a creamy color) and cooked flavor, both the result of the heat processing required in canning. The cost usually is quite competitive.

Although evaporated whole milk was, for years, the only type of evaporated milk on the market, the growth of acceptance of low-fat and nonfat fluid milks made it feasible to consider producing evaporated milks with these reduced fat levels. These have found a satisfactory place in the market. Regulations regarding composition of evaporated skim milk stipulate a fat content of not more than 0.5 percent and a milk solids content of at least 20 percent. Vitamins A and D must be added. Evaporated milks sometimes are used undiluted and sometimes reconstituted with an equal amount of water. The undiluted milk can be whipped and used as a topping.

Sweetened Condensed Milk Canned milk product made by evaporating about half of the water and adding a high percentage (44 percent) of sugar.

Sweetened Condensed Milk Since both evaporated milk and *sweetened condensed milks* are marketed in cans, confusion about the two types of milk exists for some consumers. They have a significant feature in common—a bit more than half of the water has been evaporated from the milk. However, sweetened condensed milk, as the name suggests, contains a high percentage of sucrose and/or glucose (actually 44 percent) to help retard bacterial growth. Thus, canned sweetened condensed milk can be stored very satisfactorily at a cool room temperature for as much as a year or more if the can is not opened. The high sugar content adds to the viscosity of sweetened condensed milk as well as to the browning of this milk when heated slowly for a period of two hours or more; the very sweet taste of this type of milk makes the major application as a liquid ingredient in desserts. The high concentration of milk protein, combined with the tendency to precipitate and thicken fairly readily with the addition of acid or the application of heat, makes sweetened condensed milk a useful ingredient in some dessert preparations.

Dry Milks

Nonfat dry milk solids are the most common of the powdered milk products. This type of milk usually is prepared by evaporating part of the water from pasteurized nonfat milk with the use of a vacuum. This concentrated product then is sprayed into a drying chamber to remove the remainder of the water. The solids are collected and then instantized by moistening the dried milk with steam so that it clumps into aggregates that disperse readily when reconstituted in water. Vitamins A and D may be added to enhance the nutritive value. Often nonfat dry milk is the least expensive form of milk available in the store. This type of milk can be stored at room temperature, and, of course, it is much less bulky and heavy than the original skim milk from which it was produced. Although there is a slight "processed" flavor in this type of milk when reconstituted, thorough chilling of the reconstituted milk and/or mixing some fluid milk with the reconstituted milk may make nonfat dry milk acceptable as a beverage. This milk, when only partially reconstituted (equal amounts of solids and water) can be whipped to provide a low-calorie, low-cost whipped cream alternative.

Whole milk and low-fat milk also can be dehydrated to produce their dried milk counterparts. Unfortunately, the fat in these products limits their shelf life owing to potential rancidity. Therefore, these forms of dried milk are not always available in the retail market. They are used in commercial chocolate and candy manufacturing as well as in infant feeding formulas in some instances, however.

Creams

Creams with varying concentrations of fat are available for various applications. The fat content of various creams is presented in Table 8.2. These creams may have various designations, which tend to be confusing if you are selecting a cream for whipping. Half-and-half, the cream with the lowest fat content, usually is used as the cream on cereals or in coffee and other beverages. Light cream, also called coffee cream or table cream, is preferred by some people who like a richer addition to their cereals and coffee. Light whipping cream is sometimes simply labeled as *whipping cream*, which indicates its ability to be beaten into a foam. Heavy whipping cream, with its slightly higher fat content, whips into the stiffest of the cream foams. Unless the fat content of a cream is at least 30 percent, the cream will not whip into a useful foam. There are also whipped toppings marketed commercially, often with stabilizers added to them, and their fat content may vary significantly from one product to another.

Sour cream is a popular cream for use in making dips and salad dressings, as well as in some baked products. The fat content is at least 18 percent, which makes it well below the fat content of butter and therefore a comparatively low-calorie topping for baked potatoes. Pasteurization is done for 30 minutes at temperatures between 165 and 180°F, a procedure not only ade-

Whipping Cream Cream capable of being whipped into a foam because of its fat content of at least 30 percent.

Sour Cream Viscous, acidic cream containing at least 18 percent fat; acidified by action of lactic acid bacteria on lactose.

Table 8.2 Fat Content of Creams[1]

Type of Cream	Percent Fat
Half-and-half	10.5–18.0
Light cream (coffee or table)	18.0–30.0
Light whipping cream (whipping)	30.0–36.0
Heavy cream (heavy whipping)	36.0
Sour cream (cultured sour)	18.0

Source: Adapted from Lecos, C. Milk: Cows produce it; man improves it. *FDA Consumer 16(5):* 19. 1982.
[1]Terms in parentheses are alternative names under which the cream may be marketed.

quate for killing harmful bacteria, but also helpful in producing the desired firm body characteristic of sour cream. A controlled culture of lactic acid bacteria is added to develop the desired acidic tang and promote firmness of the sour cream. Since sour cream curdles rather readily with heat, it should be added to heated sauces or meats just long enough to be heated to the desired temperature.

Butter

Butter is unique among milk products, for it is primarily a fat (at least 80 percent) and is not useful as a source of calcium and the other nutrients for which milk and milk products often are recommended. Nevertheless, butter is popular as a fat in food preparation for its color and flavor. Either sweet or sour cream may be churned to make butter, with the buttermilk being drained from the fat to concentrate the butter to its required fat content of at least 80 percent. Other steps in the production of most butter include washing, salting, working (squeezing some water out), and cutting into blocks. Some recipes call for sweet butter or unsalted butter. If a recipe requiring unsalted butter also specifies the addition of salt, there is little reason to purchase the sweet butter when the added salt can be reduced or eliminated and regular butter or margarine be utilized.

Whipped butter is a variation of the solid butter. This ordinarily is used as a table spread by people who wish to reduce the amount of fat and the calories in their diets. Substitution of whipped butter for regular butter in recipes should be done on the basis of weight rather than volume.

Frozen Milk Products

Frozen milk products of various composition are available in today's markets. Ice cream is a sweetened, often flavored, frozen milk product with a minimum fat content of 10 percent, unless the flavoring is a bulky substance, in which case the minimum fat level is 8 percent. Ice milk is lower in calories than ice cream because its fat content is between 2 and 7 percent. Sherbets contain so little milk solids (limited to between 2 and 5 percent) that they are really not considered milk products. They also have only 1 to 2 percent milkfat, giving a granular texture. Even ice milk has at least 11 percent milk solids, and ice creams range as low as 16 percent for bulky-flavored ice creams and 20 percent or more in other ice creams.

Mellorine Frozen ice cream–like dessert in which the fat is not the original milkfat.

Parevine Frozen imitation ice cream made without any dairy products.

Some markets sell an imitation ice cream. This product must be labeled "imitation." Some of these imitations are called *mellorine*, indicating that the original milkfat has been replaced by another fat. Others are of the type known as *parevine*, which indicates that no dairy ingredients are contained in this frozen dessert. Tofutti, a frozen tofu-based (soybean curd) food, is another nondairy "ice cream."

In addition to the milkfat, ice creams and related products contain varying amounts of sugar, milk solids, stabilizers, flavorings, and coloring to achieve the desired characteristics. These ingredients are mixed and pasteurized before being frozen either in a batch process or continuous freezer. Agitation in the batch freezer permits incorporation of air, whereas the continuous freezer introduces fixed amounts of air as the ice cream moves through the freezer section. Either method increases the volume through the addition of air; this addition and the expansion due to freezing water into ice result in the phenomenon known as *overrun*. Some overrun is desirable in promoting a pleasingly light consistency and smooth texture, but too much results in an unpleasantly airy, fluffy ice cream. Stabilizers contribute to the texture of the frozen product by facilitating development of small ice crystals. They also aid in retarding the melting of ice creams when they are served.

Overrun The increase in volume of ice creams during freezing as a result of expansion as water turns into ice and the incorporation of air during freezing.

Imitation Milk and Whiteners

Certain foods in the marketplace must be labeled as imitations. Imitation milks can be manufactured to resemble milk and be used in place of milk. However, their formulations may be quite different from milk. For example, vegetable fat may replace milkfat in some products; dextrose or corn syrup may replace lactose in others; sodium caseinate, which is derived from milk, often serves as the protein source. No standards have been established for these imitation milks; hence, label reading is necessary if someone decides to use an imitation milk.

Filled milk was defined in the Filled Milk Act (PL-513) of 1923 as follows:

> . . . any milk, cream, or skimmed milk whether or not condensed, evaporated, concentrated, powdered, dried, or desiccated, to which has been added or which has been blended or compounded with any fat or oil other than milkfat, so that the resulting product is an imitation or semblance of milk, cream, or skimmed milk whether or not condensed, evaporated, concentrated, powdered, dried, or desiccated.

Under this definition, coconut oil, a vegetable oil with more than 90 percent saturated fatty acids, may be used as the replacement for milk fat; this substitution clearly provides no advantage over the saturated fatty acid content of about 60 percent in milk fat.

Interest in imitation milks today is so low that there is little concern over regulating the production of these types of products. However, coffee whiteners or lighteners are popular among consumers because of their excellent storage life (six months when stored at 100°F or two years when stored at 70°F). Such longevity is a distinct advantage to people who usually only serve cream to company. Although whiteners may vary somewhat in their ingredients, they generally are a combination of a vegetable fat (often coconut oil), a protein (sodium caseinate), corn syrup or other sweetener, emulsifiers, stabilizers, coloring, and flavoring. These products generally can be added directly into a hot beverage or reconstituted with hot water and chilled for service as the fluid cream imitation. The caloric content of coffee whiteners and light cream is about comparable.

INSPECTION AND GRADING

Grade shields (top to bottom) for: butter, instant nonfat dry milk, and cottage and process cheeses.

The Agricultural Marketing Service of the U.S. Department of Agriculture is the agency responsible for maintaining surveillance of milk and other dairy products entering interstate commerce. Individual states are responsible for control within their boundaries, although their regulations for intrastate inspection must conform, as a minimum, to federal guidelines. Included in the monitoring responsibilities are inspection of the dairy plant and surrounding areas to ensure clean, orderly, and well-maintained physical facilities for production. Incoming raw materials are checked regularly for safety, and all products produced in the plant are subjected to rigorous quality control standards. The top grade of milk, the grade reaching consumers, is Grade A.

Butter is graded according to U.S. grade standards as U.S. Grade AA (highest quality), U.S. Grade A, or U.S. Grade B. U.S. Grade B usually is made from sour cream, causing it to have a slightly acidic, but generally acceptable, flavor.

U.S. Extra Grade is the designation on instant nonfat dry milk of optimal quality, having a sweet and pleasing flavor, a natural color, and the ability to dissolve immediately in water. Instant nonfat dry milk bearing the shield stating "U.S.D.A. Quality Approved" has been processed under sanitary conditions and is of good quality.

Cheddar cheese may be graded AA, the top grade, with A being just slightly lower in quality. A shield stating "USDA" and "Quality Approved" is placed on cottage cheese and pasteurized process cheese that meet U.S. Department of Agriculture standards for quality and production.

STORAGE OF MILK AND CREAM

The perishability of milk and milk products makes it important that fluid products be kept in refrigerated storage to extend shelf life. This is true not only for fluid milks, but also for the canned and reconstituted dry products. The practice of removing milk from the refrigerator just long enough to pour the amount needed is a useful one in preventing spoilage of milk before it is used. Suggestions regarding home storage of various milk products are presented in Table 8.3.

PROBLEMS IN MILK COOKERY

Milk is a valued ingredient in many different food products, but certain precautions must be observed when heating milk. The changes in milk of particular concern are those associated with scum formation, curdling, and scorching. These outcomes are attributable to the proteins in milk, and they are undesirable because they detract from the quality of the finished product. Since proteins in milk are at the root of these difficulties, the avoidance of problems will be more understandable if the nature of proteins is discussed.

Table 8.3 Home Storage of Dairy Products

Product	Storage Conditions	Duration of Safe Storage
Fresh whole milk	Covered, refrigerator	3–5 days
Fresh skim milk	Covered, refrigerator	3–5 days
Reconstituted nonfat dry milk	Covered, refrigerator	3–5 days
Evaporated milk		
Unopened can	Room temperature	6 months
Opened can	Covered, refrigerator	3–5 days
Sweetened condensed milk		
Unopened can	Room temperature	Several months
Opened can	Covered, refrigerator	3–5 days
Dry milks		
Whole	Refrigerator	Few weeks
Nonfat	Room temperature	Few months
Cream, table and whipping	Covered, refrigerator	3–5 days
Whipped cream (aerosol can)	Refrigerator	Few weeks

Source: Adapted from Milk in family meals. *Home and Garden Bulletin* No. 127. U.S. Dept. Agriculture. Washington, D.C. Rev. 1972. P. 5. Open dating is a guide to freshness at store.

SCIENCE NOTE: Proteins and Denaturation

Proteins are organic compounds containing two unique structural features—an amino group ($-NH_2$) and an organic acid radical ($-C\!\!\diagup^{\displaystyle O}_{\diagdown OH}$).

These features are found in each of the basic units of a protein; these units are called *amino acids* and have the following basic structure, with R representing a range of different structures, from simply a hydrogen atom in glycine to quite a complex double-ring structure in tryptophan (an amino acid). The R group for each amino acid differs, giving the unique quality to each specific amino acid (see Table 8.4).

$$R-C-C\!\!\diagup^{\displaystyle O}_{\diagdown OH}$$
$$|$$
$$HNH$$

Amino acid

Amino Acid Subunit of protein; contains an amino ($-NH_2$) group and an organic acid group ($-C\!\!\diagup^{\displaystyle O}_{\diagdown OH}$).

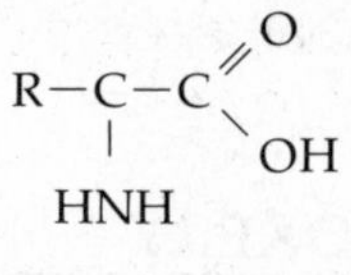

Proteins are made up of many, many amino acids joined together by a linkage called a peptide linkage or *peptide bond*. The peptide linkage is a covalent, very strong bond between the acid (carboxyl) group of one amino acid and the amino group of another amino acid, a linkage that is formed with the loss of a molecule of water. An example of the peptide bond and the union of two amino acids to form a dipeptide is given be-

Peptide Bond Bond formed between the carboxyl of one amino acid and the amino group of a second amino acid with loss of water.

Table 8.4 The R Groups of Some Amino Acids

Amino Acid	Formula of R Group
Glycine	$-H$
Alanine	$-CH_3$
Phenylalanine	$-CH_2-$  ⬡
Cystine	$-CH_2-S-S-CH_2-$
Methionine	$-CH_2-CH_2-S-CH_3$
Lysine	$-CH_2-CH_2-CH_2-CH_2-NH_2$
Histidine	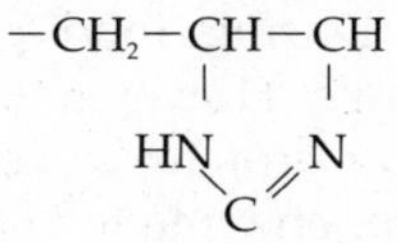 $-CH_2-CH-CH$

with Histidine showing the imidazole ring structure:

$$-CH_2-CH{-}CH$$

HN   N
    C

Tryptophan

$$-CH_2-C$$ with an indole ring structure (C, C, N-H, and fused benzene ring)

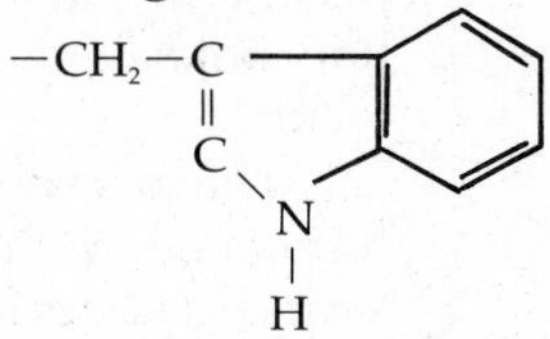

low. This is repeated again and again to form protein molecules, all of which are extremely large.

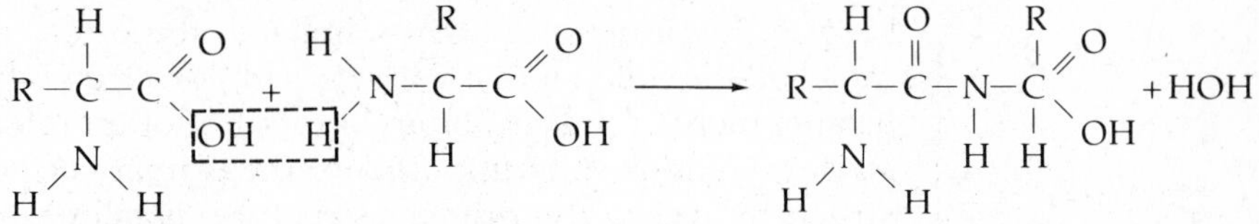

Amino acid   Amino acid   Dipeptide

Primary Structure

The linkage of one amino acid to another and then to another creates a backbone chain consisting of a repeating pattern of a carbon atom (with the R group attached) joined to a second carbon atom (with an oxygen attached to make a carbonyl or $-C{=}O$) and then attached to a nitrogen atom (with a hydrogen atom). Thus, the repeating pattern of the basic chain of a protein is $-C-C-N-C-C-N-C-C-N-$ throughout the extremely large molecule. Note that throughout the long molecule, all of the linkages in the backbone chain are covalent, which gives this basic structure a linear structure with considerable strength. This basic backbone chain is called the primary structure of protein, and it is formed entirely by covalent bonding. The general appearance of the primary structure is shown below, with one of the peptide bonds indicated by a dashed line.

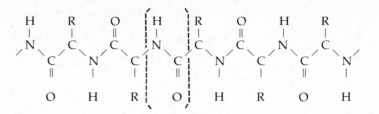

Primary structure

Proteolytic Enzyme
Enzyme capable of cat-
alyzing a break in a
protein at a peptide
linkage.

During food preparation, this primary structure is resistant to change. However, some enzymes (called *proteolytic enzymes* because they attack protein) can cause a cleavage along this backbone. When this happens, enzymatic hydrolysis will result in an uptake of water at the peptide linkage, and two shorter peptides (chains of amino acids) will result.

This backbone or primary structure is the same in all proteins. The difference in individual proteins is due to the R groups of the various amino acids comprising the specific protein molecule. The amino acid sequence of individual proteins varies with the specific protein and with the species synthesizing the protein.

Secondary Structure

Proteins in nature are found in a more complex arrangement than that seen in the primary structure. Instead, the primary structure of protein molecules is coiled into a less strained, lower-energy state in nature; this arrangement is the secondary structure, often referred to as the helical structure and is superimposed on the primary structure. The secondary structure, unlike the primary structure, is held in position only by secondary bonding forces in most instances. The arrangement for this secondary (helical) structure is in a right-handed alpha helix, which is quite a stable, nonstressed form. The bonding forces operating within the secondary structure are hydrogen bonding, van der Waals forces, and disulfide bridges (covalent bonding). The hydrogen bonds and van der Waals forces are the predominant bonds, and they are secondary bonding forces, which makes them more susceptible to alteration than the covalent bonding comprising the primary structure. The spherical configuration is strengthened by hydrogen bonding between the oxygen of the carbonyl in one amino acid and the hydrogen linked to a nitrogen in an amino acid at a comparable position on the adjacent coil of the helix.

Secondary
structure

The coiled secondary structure resembles a spring in which the primary structure corresponds to the wire of the spring, representing the continuous covalently bonded chain. This appears in the next diagram. The linkage between portions of the protein molecule is illustrated by the hydrogen bonding in the diagram showing a small portion of the protein structure in its secondary configuration.

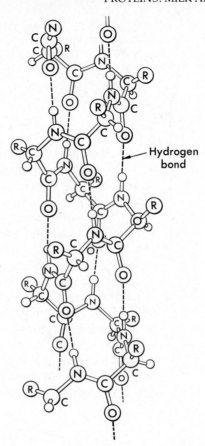

Hydrogen bond

A drawing of a portion of an alpha-helix of a protein molecule. (From R. B. Corey and L. Pauling, ''The Configuration of Polypeptide Chains of Proteins'' in *Proceedings of the International Wool Textile Research Conference*, Volume B. *Chemical Physics and Physical Chemistry of Wool and Proteins.* Copyright © 1955 by the Commonwealth Scientific and Industrial Research Organization, Melbourne, Australia. Reprinted by permission.)

This secondary structure is quite a low energy state and is further stabilized by the hydrogen bonding occurring between every fourth amino acid residue.

A few proteins are categorized as fibrous proteins, which assume a somewhat different structure, usually referred to as the pleated sheet structure. In these fibrous proteins, the rather tightly coiled alpha helix is extended distinctly into a zigzag extension known as the beta configuration. This pleated sheet structure is found in wool and hair, both of which meet the requirement of being rather stretchy because of the pleated arrangement. This configuration is of limited importance in food products.

A unique fibrous protein of importance in food preparation is the connective tissue known as collagen. Proline and hydroxyproline are repeated with frequency in collagen, but these amino acids provide a distinctly rigid character wherever they occur along the amino acid chain. This is explored in the context of the connective tissue in meat in Chapter 9.

Tertiary Structure

Yet another level of organization is found in protein molecules, referred to as the tertiary structure. A distortion of the helical structure appears to exist in some protein molecules in nature, causing the molecules to be convoluted into a spatial arrangement resembling a globe or globular shape, with some parts of the coiled helix becoming a bit compressed, while other areas may be quite stretched out. This tertiary arrangement can be visualized by taking a spring and twisting it into a globular (spherical) shape. Note that some areas of the helical spring become compressed; others are stretched. This tertiary arrangement of proteins in nature is held in place by secondary bonding forces, but the greater distortion of low-energy bond angles in this tertiary structure causes it to be susceptible to change more readily than is true for the nonstressed secondary structure. A possible visualization of the tertiary structure of protein is shown in the diagram, with the line itself representing the primary structure, the recognizable helical coils showing the secondary structure, and the overall configuration being the tertiary structure.

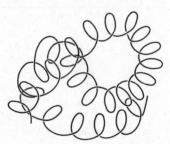

Tertiary structure

Quaternary Structure

Some very large protein molecules, with molecular weights exceeding 50,000, may have more than one peptide chain associated together. This association is referred to as the quaternary structure. An example of this is seen in meats (see Chapter 9).

Denaturation

Proteins in foods as they are harvested are referred to as native proteins. Their structures conform to the previous levels of organization and arrangements just described. However, these native proteins are capable

Denaturation A physical change in proteins, resulting in a change from native to denatured protein to decrease the solubility and alter the flow properties of food proteins.

of undergoing some physical changes during certain treatments used commonly in preparing foods. A key change is that of *denaturation*, a physical change altering the behavior of proteins from native protein to denatured protein.

Denaturation is the unfolding of the tertiary structure of the protein as heating or beating supplies enough energy to break the secondary bonding forces responsible for holding the native protein in its convoluted, usually globular, shape. The physical shape of the protein molecule begins to resemble the helical secondary structure, exemplified by a coiled spring. When this happens to many protein molecules, it is possible for some of these ''coiled springs'' to align themselves sufficiently to begin to form hydrogen bonds between molecules. This binding together of molecules reduces the flow properties of the system because these large aggregates or clumps of protein present considerable resistance to movement. In other words, the protein becomes less soluble and tends to precipitate or to resist movement. This protein then is said to be denatured.

In addition to the larger aggregates that are formed, proteins are also altered in their behavior because of the different R groups exposed by the changes in the physical contours of the individual molecules. The various R groups will have the ability to be attracted to or to be repelled by other protein molecules as the result of the types of substances comprising the individual R groups. Thus, electrical charges on protein molecules are subject to change during the denaturation process as the physical shape and conformation of the molecule change.

Coagulation The clumping together of partially denatured protein molecules to make a relatively insoluble protein mass.

Another term often associated with physical changes in protein is *coagulation*. Often coagulation is used interchangeably with denaturation. However, there actually is a fine distinction between these two terms. Technically, coagulation refers only to the second step of the process of denaturation; specifically, coagulation is the clumping together of the partially denatured molecules.

Scum Formation

When milk is heated, a scum or a skin tends to form over its surface, particularly when the pan is not covered. The skin effectively traps steam, creating pressure and causing milk to boil over. This scum appears to be the result of evaporation from the surface of the milk, which concentrates the protein (particularly casein) at the surface. The skin traps milk solids, including proteins and calcium salts, all of which can be removed by spooning the skin off frequently. Unfortunately, this spooning off is not a cure for scum formation, for a new scum begins to form as soon as the existing skin is removed. Covering a pan in which a hot cream soup is being held for a time or placing a cover of foil or plastic wrap directly on the surface of a cooling milk-based pudding keeps scum formation on these products to a minimum.

Cocoa and hot chocolate are notorious for forming scums. To reduce the problem for these drinks, beat the product until a foam is formed on the surface. Another approach is to add a marshmallow or a topping of whipped cream, both of which form barrier that prevents air from coming in contact with the surface of the beverage.

Scorching

Use of a heavy pan or double boiler for heating milk helps eliminate scorching, which is caused by overheating the serum proteins that precipitate during cooking. These proteins are altered by heat and rapidly undergo denaturation. The denaturation of the serum proteins also carries some calcium phosphate to the bottom of the pan, trapped in the protein precipitate. The sugar in milk interacts with the precipitated protein on the bottom of the pan to cause a browning (*Maillard*) *reaction*. Along with the precipitation of the serum proteins, a cooked milk flavor also develops. This is the result of the formation of sulfur-containing compounds, notably hydrogen sulfide.

Scorching can be alleviated by keeping the heating time to a minimum and by stirring frequently to keep the precipitated serum proteins from sticking to the bottom of the pan and overheating. A double boiler is particularly effective in preventing scorching because the water beneath the pan of milk provides a slow rate of heating, allowing excellent heat distribution throughout the milk.

Maillard Reaction Browning reaction in food caused by reaction between protein and a sugar.

Curdling

A significant problem in working with milk is the formation of unsightly curdled products. These curds are precipitated protein aggregates and may be caused by various factors. Some foods are more likely to curdle than others containing milk because the foods may contain acidic ingredients or may be rather high in salt; either of these characteristics can cause curdling, although for different reasons.

When fruits are combined with milk, the milk tends to curdle. As acidic fruits are added, the milk protein becomes less soluble. These precipitated proteins, notably casein, form the curds so distracting to the eye. One way of helping to reduce the likelihood of curdling occurring when milk and fruits or tomatoes will be heated together is to be sure that the milk is fresh, because milk gradually may become more acidic as it ages. This acidity enhances the action of the acidic ingredients being added, and curdling is quite likely to occur. When working with milk, keep heating times as short as possible, for heating tends to destabilize the protein, making curdling somewhat more likely to occur after heating has been continuing for many minutes than when the ingredients are first combined.

The effect of salt on curdling can be seen when scalloped potatoes are baked with generous amounts of salty ham cubes. The more salty the ham, the greater is the prospect the milk-based sauce will curdle. This curdling is attributed to the fact that the ions of sodium and chloride from the salt interact with the electrical charges on the surface of the milk proteins. When the normally repulsive (similar charges causing molecules to be prevented from approaching each other) charges on the protein molecules are canceled by the ions from the salt, the protein molecules can hydrogen-bond between molecules to form aggregates. These molecular aggregates of milk protein are seen as curdled sauce in the scalloped potatoes.

SCIENCE NOTE: pH and Protein Denaturation

pH

The effect of acids and bases on such food components as pigments and carbohydrates has been pointed out in preceding chapters. Proteins undergo particularly dramatic changes as a result of acids. The acidity or alkalinity of a food or other substance is expressed in terms of its *pH*, which is defined as the negative logarithm of the hydrogen ion potential. This pH scale ranges from 0 to 14, with pH 7 representing neutral, that is, neither acidic nor alkaline. The range between 0 and 7 is acidic, and the smaller the number, the more acidic the substance. Between pH 7 and 14, the food is alkaline, becoming increasingly alkaline as the number gets larger.

Isoelectric Point

Amphoteric Ability to act as an acid (carrying a + charge) or as a base (a − charge). Their carboxyl and amino groups permit proteins to do this.

Proteins are *amphoteric* compounds; that is, they are capable of behaving either as acids or bases, depending upon the medium in which they are found. This dual nature is the result of the presence of both the carboxylic acid and the amino groups in the molecules of proteins. At varying pH values, the carboxylic acid groups may ionize (COO^-), resulting in an overall negative charge on the protein molecules, while under other conditions, the amino groups may ionize to form NH_3^+, thus giving an overall positive charge. Because of this ability to ionize at the carboxyl or amino group (and also because of their various R groups), proteins will carry different electrical charges, depending upon the pH of the medium.

At a specific pH (which differs for each protein), the electrical charge on a protein will be neutralized (neither plus nor minus) on the surface of the molecule. When this electrical charge is at its minimum or neutral point, the protein is said to be at its *isoelectric point*. At this point, the protein molecules are very unstable or insoluble; they precipitate or form curds because the molecules get close enough to each other to form hydrogen bonds that hold them in clumps. Sometimes this is the action being sought (as is true in the making of cheese); other times the curdling is a culinary catastrophe.

Isoelectric Point pH at which the electrical charge of a protein molecule is essentially neutral (neither positive nor negative), resulting in easy aggregation of protein molecules to form curds.

The isoelectric point of casein in milk is pH 4.6. Milk pH will vary with its freshness, but usually will be 6.5 or higher. If milk is added to a fruit with a pH of maybe 3.5, the combination of the two foods will clearly result in a pH approaching the isoelectric point of casein. In fact, if a small amount of milk is blended with the fruit or with tomatoes, that milk will pass through the range of the isoelectric point of casein, and curds will form. If the converse is done, that is, if some fruit is stirred into a quantity of milk, the acid will gradually reduce the pH of the mixture as more and more fruit is added, but none of the milk protein will be in the pH of the isoelectric point of casein unless enough fruit is added to reduce the whole system to a pH approaching 5 or lower.

When working with protein, be it milk proteins or other foods with a significant quantity of protein, it is important to consider the isoelectric point of the specific protein system if the pH of the system is going to be modified by any ingredients. Techniques of preparation or ratios of ingredients can be modified to achieve the desired results if the likelihood of precipitation of protein at the isoelectric point is kept in mind.

Clotting of Milk

In most milk products, the goal is to avoid curdling the milk protein so that the result will be the desired smooth, fluid texture. However, sometimes the ability of casein to form a precipitate is utilized to produce clotted (clabbered) milk products. In fact, cheeses are clotted milk products that are subjected to a variety of techniques following the actual clotting process. Cheeses are such an important part of the diet that these are treated in a separate section of this chapter.

Rennin Protein-digesting enzyme from calves' stomachs.

There are two types of clotted milk products that sometimes are produced in the home—*rennin* (rennet) puddings and yogurt. These two products are of interest because different clotting mechanisms are used for each of them.

Rennin puddings are made by the addition of an enzyme, rennin, the protein-digesting enzyme from the lining of calves' stomachs. The action of this enzyme results in the formation of a soft gel in which the precipitated protein serves as the continuous solid network. The water of the milk is trapped within this protein network, making a delicate, tender gel that, with suitable flavorings, is an easily digested, nourishing dessert. Although this clotting procedure is not complex, temperature control at about 100°F is essential. If the rennin is subjected to too high a temperature, the enzyme will denature because it is a protein; unfortunately, the denatured protein no longer has the capability of catalyzing the digestive process. Too cool a temperature delays the gel formation, the extent of delay being dependent on how cool the mixture is.

Yogurt relies on the growth of a bacterial culture of special lactic acid bacteria that are inoculated into the milk. Temperature well above room temperature (about 115°F) is maintained to promote the digestion of lactose to lactic acid by the bacteria. As lactic acid accumulates, the pH of the milk decreases until the fluid begins to approach the isoelectric point of casein, at which point the casein begins to precipitate to begin to form the soft gel structure characteristic of yogurt. As is true in making rennin puddings, temperature control is vital, although the reason is different. In the case of yogurt, too high a temperature would kill the microorganisms, and no more lactic acid would be produced. Electric yogurt makers provide the controlled temperature needed for producing the desired quality.

A few people make cottage cheese in the home. This process can be accomplished by use of rennin or by acid coagulation. Regardless of the clotting mechanism used, the gel structure formed will trap the large quantity of water normally found in milk. In order to produce cottage cheese at home, it is necessary to cut through the gel structure in a number of places to allow the liquid (called whey) to drain from the curd. A modest amount of heating of the curd or squeezing the cut curd in cheesecloth helps to concentrate the protein curd.

DAIRY FOAMS

Protein-containing foods often are capable of forming foams (see Chapter 10), and some of these are quite useful in food preparation. The dairy products used for foams include whipping cream, evaporated milk, and nonfat dry milk solids. The ease of forming such foams and the stability of the resulting foams are qualities of particular interest when deciding which type of foam to use.

Whipped Cream

Whipped cream is the dairy foam with the highest fat content; in fact, at least 30 percent fat is required for this type of milk product to foam satisfactorily. The stability of whipped cream is excellent, providing that the cream is kept chilled, for the foam is stabilized by the aggregation of very small fat particles in the films of liquid that form the confining walls of the air bubbles. If the foam is slightly warm, the fat begins to soften, and the foam loses the strength originally contributed by the clumps of solid fat in the chilled foam. The protein in whipping cream is of some assistance in forming whipped cream foams, but this is quite insufficient to form the desired foam without the high fat content.

One of the precautions (in addition to being sure that the cream to be whipped is well chilled) important in preparing whipped cream from whipping cream is to stop beating before the emulsion reverses itself. Cream is an oil-in-water emulsion, but the beating involved in making whipped cream is sufficient to begin to make the emulsion somewhat less stable. If beating is not stopped at the right point, the emulsion will break, and clumps of butter (a water-in-oil emulsion) quickly result. Unfortunately, no reversal is possible if cream has been beaten beyond the desirable stage for whipped cream.

Often sugar is added to whipped cream to provide a touch of sweetness. This addition makes it somewhat more difficult for the fat to clump within the films surrounding the air bubbles, thus requiring additional beating if the sugar is added before the desired end point. Overbeating is less likely to occur if sugar has been added to the foam while whipping is being done than is the situation when the foam is finished before the sugar is folded in. However, sugar may be added satisfactorily at either time.

Evaporated Milk Foams

Evaporated milk can be used to make a less expensive, lower-calorie foam than is available when whipping cream is the starting material. However, stability in evaporated milk foams can be a real challenge. The undiluted evaporated milk makes the most stable foam when the milk has been chilled in an ice cube tray to the point where some ice crystals are forming in it. Chilling the bowl and beater blades to be used in whipping the evaporated milk also is an aid in keeping the developing foam as cold as possible. An evaporated milk foam is stabilized primarily by the viscous nature of the concentrated milk protein dispersion. The fat content is only about 7.5 percent, well below the 30 to 35 percent found in whipping cream; the protein content is about three times that in whipping cream. The composition of an evaporated milk foam clearly is quite different from that of whipped cream.

The protein is not nearly as effective at providing stability to the evaporated milk foam as is the fat in whipped cream. This limited stability of evaporated milk foams makes it necessary to refrigerate them immediately and to serve them quite soon after the foam is completed unless gelatin or some other stabilizing agent is added. Lemon juice (2 tablespoons per cup of undiluted evaporated milk) also aids with stabilization because it helps to bring the milk toward the isoelectric point of casein, thus promoting some denaturation of the protein to help strengthen the cell walls of the foam.

Nonfat Dried Milk Foams

Nonfat dried milk solids, when diluted with an absolute maximum of an equal quantity of cold water (preferably a ratio of 1.5 parts solids to 1.0 part chilled water), can be beaten into a fine foam that can be held in the refrigerator for a few hours. This type of foam has the distinct advantage of being much lower in calories than the other types of foams because of the lack of fat. The disadvantage related to the lack of fat content is the lack of richness of flavor.

The stability of this type of foam, while somewhat limited, is adequate for use as a topping. The addition of lemon juice helps to bring the mixture closer to the isoelectric point of casein, thus helping to denature the protein to add some stability to the resulting foam. Nonfat dried milk solid foams are stabilized by the denaturation of part of the protein during beating. The protein concentration varies with the amount of water added to the solids, but often will be 20 percent or even higher, which far exceeds the less than 3 percent found in whipping cream. This large amount of protein facilitates stabilization of the foam by protein denaturation. Of course, the fat content is essentially nil, making the stabilizing effect of the protein vital to nonfat dried milk solid foams.

ICE CREAMS AND OTHER FROZEN DESSERTS

Ice cream and related frozen desserts are enjoyed by many people for their pleasing flavors, refreshing coolness, and smoothness in the mouth. An important aspect of these desserts is the presence of very small ice crystals, along with a somewhat light feeling on the tongue. Much of the technology associated with ice creams and other frozen desserts is focused on the factors influencing crystal size. Important among these factors is the role of the various ingredients included in the mixture to be frozen.

Ingredients and Their Influence

Sugar The obvious role of sugar in ice cream is to sweeten the product. However, sugar also plays a role in determining the textural characteristics of the frozen ice cream, because sugar causes the freezing temperature of the mixture to drop. In fact, a cup of sugar in a quart of the ice cream mixture will decrease the freezing point approximately 2°F. This means that the ice cream must be chilled below the normal freezing temperature of water if ice crystals are to form. The greater the content of sugar in an ice cream, the lower the freezing point. This delayed freezing helps to keep the size of crystals in the ice cream very small because a reasonable amount of stirring can be done during the freezing process to help break up any ice crystal aggregates as they slowly form. There is a counterbalancing negative role of sugar in ice cream. Very sweet ice creams will melt more quickly when served than will those with very little sugar in them, a direct result of the effect of sugar on freezing (and, conversely, melting) points.

Dairy Ingredients Cream of various weights often will be used as the liquid in making ice cream, not too surprising a fact in view of the name of the products. The cream is valued for its fullness of flavor, a contribution of the fat in the cream. The fat also helps to interfere with aggregation of ice crystals in the freezing mixture, a desirable influence in obtaining velvety smooth ice cream. Homogenized creams are even more effective in promoting a smooth texture than are nonhomogenized creams because of the greater number of very small fat globules in the homogenized form.

Some milk solids may be added to help promote the desired texture. These solids help to develop a smooth texture because they increase the viscosity of the mixture to be frozen. They also contribute a bit to lightness in the mouth because of the tendency toward foaming introduced by the added protein content. The action of evaporated milk, when the milk is used without adding water to dilute it to normal strength, is similar to that of the nonfat dried milk solids. However, both these products introduce added lactose, which adds not only to the sweetness, but may contribute to some sandy character in the frozen product. This textural problem is a good indication of the fact that lactose is comparatively poorly dissolved and tends to precipitate in coarse crystalline aggregates when the content of lactose is increased much beyond the normal concentration in cream.

Juices The liquid in sherbets and ices is primarily fruit juices. These juices contribute delightful flavors, but their acidity may necessitate using an increased amount of sugar, which adds to the calories and tends to create problems about melting during service. In the event that both fruit juices and milk are to be used, curdling of the cream mixture is likely to be a problem, although prompt freezing of such a mixture can keep curdling to a minimum. Interestingly, because these tart mixtures need more sugar for adequate sweetening, the added sugar increases the viscosity of the mixture, thus helping to promote the formation of small crystals rather than large aggregates.

Freezing the Mixture

With Agitation Commercial ice creams are pasteurized, homogenized, and often allowed to be refrigerated for a short period of time to allow blending of flavors and hydration of any added stabilizers before freezing. However, home-prepared ice cream mixtures frequently are not heated prior to being frozen. If mixtures are heated first, they should be allowed to cool to refrigerator temperature before placing them in the container for freezing. The freezing process at home may be done either with or without agitation, although agitation usually is considered desirable whenever possible because of the modifications in texture accomplished through the use of some type of mixer.

Designs for ice cream freezers vary somewhat, but most are composed of a bucket with a small drain in which a container holding the ice cream and a rotating dasher are suspended, with a motor or a mechanical crank being attached to the dasher. A variation of this device is a small container with a motorized agitator that can be operated within the freezer unit of a refrigerator, thus eliminating the need for a large bucket and ice. Although this freezer device is small and convenient, the rate of freezing is considerably slower than is that possible in the conventional bucket assembly.

The conventional ice cream freezer is designed to permit rapid cooling of the ice cream mixture while agitating the freezing dessert. This rapid freezing is accomplished by packing the bucket surrounding the ice cream container with a mixture of ice and rock salt, the usual ratio being 1 part rock salt (a coarse ice cream salt) to 8 parts ice. The freezing process involves the removal of heat from the ice cream mixture until the product becomes so cool that ice crystals start to form. Removal of heat is facilitated by the use of a metal container to hold the ice cream because the metal helps to conduct the heat out of the ice cream and transfers the energy into melting the ice. As the ice melts, a

The dasher rotating through an ice cream mixture during freezing helps to lighten the texture by incorporating air and also helps to create small ice crystals. The metal can containing the ice cream mixture is able to be cooled rapidly by surrounding it in the freezer with a mixture of chipped ice and rock salt. The dasher is removed after the ice cream is frozen to the point where cranking is very difficult.

salt brine is formed, with the salt dissolving into the brine. The presence of the sodium and chloride ions from the dissolved salt lowers the freezing (or the melting) point progressively as the amount of salt used is increased.

The recommended ratio results in a rate of freezing sufficiently slow to permit some air to be incorporated into the increasingly viscous mixture and also breaks up large aggregates of ice crystals that might be starting to gather. Sherbets, which have a lower freezing point than ice creams, require a ratio of 1 part salt to only 6 parts ice so that the melting ice-salt brine will be sufficiently cold to freeze even these foods. The coldest temperature that can be reached by this technique is $-6°F$, the result of using a ratio of 29 percent salt and 71 percent ice (by weight). This approach to freezing ice cream is unsatisfactory, however, because the ice cream will cool so rapidly that not enough air will be incorporated to give the desired smooth texture before the mass freezes.

The rate of cranking the freezing mixture needs to be varied, depending upon the stage in the freezing process. To start, rather slow cranking is appropriate to help keep the entire mixture a relatively uniform temperature, rather than having freezing starting to take place around the edges of the container while the center is still comparatively warm. As the mixture begins to freeze, the rate of cranking should be increased to help maintain small crystals of ice and avoid the coarse, large aggregates that cause the finished ice cream to feel rough. As more and more ice crystals form, the mixture becomes increasingly viscous, making it necessary to crank more slowly until further agitation is too difficult. The ice cream then is allowed to chill, covered, without further agitation while still standing in the brine solution for about half an hour. During this standing period, the ice cream becomes the desired firm consistency. Removal of the dasher from the ice cream as soon as agitation is stopped is advised because its removal after the ripened ice cream has become hard enough to serve is extremely difficult.

The key to preparing frozen desserts is maintaining the agitation at the appropriate rate throughout the freezing process. Very rapid cranking before ice crystals begin to form may cause the butterfat to clump together in the ice cream and contribute to a curdled look in the ice cream. Insufficient agitation during active formation of ice crystals contributes to the rough texture characteristic of ice cream containing large aggregates of sugar crystals. These aggregates will occur unless the dasher or other device regularly passes through the freezing ice cream to break up developing clusters before they solidify.

Without Agitation   Desserts also may be frozen without agitation, a process often referred to as *still freezing*. This method of freezing ice cream can be done in any freezer with no other special equipment. Sometimes these mixtures are removed briefly from the freezer as the ice crystals start to form and are stirred a bit. This method helps to lighten and smooth the texture, but it still results in a product that has a rather heavy consistency and a suggestion of grittiness. To help overcome these drawbacks, recipes for still frozen ice creams frequently contain interfering substances to help minimize the tendency of ice crystals to congregate. A recipe high in fat, using whipping cream or other source of fat, increases the viscosity of the mixture and reduces the likelihood of coarse crystals of ice forming. If the cream is whipped or if some other type of foam (perhaps beaten egg whites, whipped gelatin, or whipped undiluted evaporated milk) is used, the frozen product will have a reasonably light texture, albeit not as pleasing as ice cream made with agitation.

Evaluating Ice Creams

Ideally, frozen desserts of all types should have a rather light, yet not frothy, feel on the tongue and should feel extremely smooth when eaten. The texture should be free of curdling and grittiness. Both flavor and color should be pleasing, yet distinctive. These frozen desserts should be able to be served and consumed without softening very much.

CHEESES

Origins and Applications

Cheese making is a skill known to have existed as long ago as 9000 B.C. and possibly earlier than that. As far as is known, cheese production began in Arabia and flourished in Europe during the Middle Ages, especially in the monasteries. Cheese was typically made in the home in the United States until the middle of the nineteenth century, when a cheese factory was built in New York State. Most of the cheese consumed in the United States today is commercial cheese.

Cheese and milk have many nutritional attributes in common, although the actual amounts of the various nutrients in cheese depend on the type of cheese. Most cheeses are high in fat and calories, as well as good sources of complete protein; cottage cheese and other cheeses from skim milk are low in fat. The nutrients generally are fairly concentrated in cheeses as a result of the removal of a great deal of the water from in the milk used to produce the cheeses. Thus, calcium, phosphorus, and vitamin A are abundant in many cheeses.

In the following sections, the types of cheeses will be discussed.

Types of Cheese

The two principal divisions in categorizing cheeses are natural and process. Natural cheeses may be classified on the basis of the following criteria: means of clotting (lactic acid or rennin), amount of ripening (cured or uncured), firmness, and source of the milk (cow, goat, or sheep). Process cheese products are differentiated into categories on the basis of moisture and fat content.

Natural Cheeses

Natural Cheese Concentrated curd of milk; ripening is optional.

Production of *natural cheeses* begins with the clotting of milk proteins to form a curd, which then is cut and worked to force much of the liquid from the gel. The liquid separated from the curd is whey, a distinctly fluid product with a yellowish-green tint caused by riboflavin and a rather sweet taste due to its lactose content. The curd is pressed into a compact mass and then is subjected to any of several treatments to achieve the desired end product. Some cheeses will have coloring added, while others may be inoculated with bacteria and/or molds to modify the flavor and texture. At this point, some natural cheeses are marketed as unripened cheeses, but many are stored to allow various changes to take place, resulting in ripened cheeses with characteristics unique to the particular type of cheese being ripened.

The ripening of cheeses may be very brief, or it may be a matter of many months to achieve the desired changes typical of a particular variety of cheese. Ripened natural cheeses lose some of their naturally tough and rubbery characteristics, which makes them easy to blend with other ingredients in recipes. Textures of ripened natural cheeses vary, depending upon the treatment. Some become very soft, whereas others may become quite hard and even a bit crumbly; some become distinctly porous, with Swiss cheese being a particularly good example of this. Another important area of change is in flavor, which usually becomes increasingly distinctive and full as the aging process continues. The actual extent of these various changes during ripening depends on storage time and temperature, with warm storage temperatures accelerating flavor development.

Table 8.5 provides an overview of many of the popular cheeses available to consumers. Included is information about the type of milk used and the ripening process (or lack of ripening). The firmness of the cheese is a common way of differentiating between the various natural cheeses. Ripening is another distinction often made in cheese classifications. These characteristics were used to provide the classifications in Table 8.5: soft, unripened; firm,

This display of ripened and unripened natural cheeses is but a portion of the many different cheeses and cheese products that can be manufactured from clotted milk.

Table 8.5 Characteristics of Some Popular Varieties of Natural Cheeses

Kind or Name Place of Origin	Kind of Milk Used in Manufacture	Ripening or Curing Time	Flavor	Body and Texture	Uses
Soft, Unripened Varieties					
Cottage, plain or creamed (Unknown)	Cow's milk skimmed; plain curd, or plain curd with cream added	Unripened	Mild, acid	Soft, curd particles of varying size	Salads, with fruits, vegetables, sandwiches, dips, cheese cake
Cream, plain (United States)	Cream from cow's milk	Unripened	Mild, acid	Soft and smooth	Salads, dips, sandwiches, snacks, cheese cake, desserts
Neufchatel (Nŭ-shä-tĕl') (France)	Cow's milk	Unripened	Mild, acid	Soft, smooth similar to cream cheese but lower in milk fat	Salads, dips, sandwiches, snacks, cheese cake, desserts
Ricotta (Rĭ-co'-ta) (Italy)	Cow's milk, whole or partly skimmed, or whey from cow's milk with whole or skim milk added; in Italy, whey from sheep's milk	Unripened	Sweet, nutlike	Soft, moist or dry	Appetizers, salads, snacks, lasagne, ravioli, noodles and other cooked dishes, grating, desserts
Firm, Unripened Varieties					
Mysost (Mūs-ôst), also called Primost (Prem'-ôst) (Norway)	Whey from cow's milk	Unripened	Sweetish, caramel	Firm, buttery consistency	Snacks, desserts; served with dark bread
Mozzarella (Italy)	Whole or partly skimmed cow's milk	Unripened	Delicate, mild	Slightly firm, plastic	Snacks, pizza, lasagne, casseroles
Soft, Ripened Varieties					
Brie (Brē) (France)	Cow's milk	4–8 weeks	Mild to pungent	Soft, smooth when ripened	Appetizers, sandwiches, snacks; good with crackers and fruit, dessert

Table 8.5 Continued

Kind or Name Place of Origin	Kind of Milk Used in Manufacture	Ripening or Curing Time	Flavor	Body and Texture	Uses
Camembert (Kăm′ĕm-bâr) (France)	Cow's milk	4–8 weeks	Mild to pungent	Soft, smooth; very soft when fully ripened	Appetizers, sandwiches, snacks; good with crackers, and fruit such as pears and apples, dessert
Limburger (Belgium)	Cow's milk	4–8 weeks	Highly pungent, very strong	Soft, smooth when ripened; usually contains small irregular openings	Appetizers, snacks; good with crackers, rye or other dark breads, dessert
Semisoft, Ripened Varieties					
Muenster (Mŭn′stēr) (Germany)	Cow's milk	1–8 weeks	Mild to mellow	Semisoft, numerous small mechanical openings; contains more moisture than brick	Appetizers, sandwiches, snacks, dessert
Firm Ripened Varieties					
Cheddar (England)	Cow's milk	1–12 months or more	Mild to very sharp	Firm, smooth, some mechanical openings	Appetizers, sandwiches, sauces, on vegetables, in hot dishes, toasted sandwiches, grating, cheeseburgers, dessert
Edam (Ē′dăm) (Netherlands)	Cow's milk, partly skimmed	2–3 months	Mellow, nutlike	Semisoft to firm, smooth; small irregularly shaped or round holes; lower milk fat than Gouda	Appetizers, snacks, salads, sandwiches, seafood sauces, dessert
Swiss, also called Emmentaler (Switzerland)	Cow's milk	3–9 months	Sweet, nutlike	Firm, smooth with large round eyes	Sandwiches, snacks, sauces, fondue, cheeseburgers

Very Hard Ripened Varieties					
Parmesan (Pärme-zän), also called Reggiano (Italy)	Partly skimmed cow's milk	14 months to 2 years	Sharp, piquant	Very hard, granular, lower moisture and milk fat than Romano	Grated for seasoning in soups, or vegetables, spaghetti, ravioli, breads, popcorn; used extensively in pizza and lasagne
Romano (Ro-ma'-no), also called Sardo Romano, Pecorino Romano (Italy)	Cow's milk; in Italy, sheep's milk (Italian law)	5–12 months	Sharp, piquant	Very hard, granular	Seasoning in soups, casserole dishes, ravioli, sauces, breads; suitable for grating when cured for about 1 year
Blue-Vein Mold Ripened Varieties					
Blue, spelled Bleu on imported cheese (France)	Cow's milk	2–6 months	Tangy, peppery	Semisoft, pasty, sometimes crumbly	Appetizers, salads, dips, salad dressing, sandwich spreads; good with crackers, dessert
Gorgonzola (Gôr-gŏn-zo'-la) (Italy)	Cow's milk; in Italy, cow's milk or goat's milk or mixtures of these	3–12 months	Tangy, peppery	Semisoft, pasty, sometimes crumbly, lower moisture than Blue	Appetizers, snacks, salads, dips, sandwich spread; good with crackers, dessert
Roquefort (Rok'-fĕrt) or (Rôk-fôr') (France)	Sheep's milk	2–5 months or more	Sharp, slightly peppery	Semisoft, pasty, sometimes crumbly	Appetizers, snacks, salads, dips, sandwich spreads; good with crackers, dessert
Stilton[1] (England)	Cow's milk	2–6 months	Piquant, milder than Gorgonzola or Roquefort	Semisoft, flaky; slightly more crumbly than Blue	Appetizers, snacks, salads, dessert

Source: Adapted from Fenton, F. E. How to buy cheese. *Home and Garden Bulletin* No. 193. U.S. Dept. Agriculture. Washington, D.C. 1971. PP. 8–17.
[1]Imported only.

237

unripened; soft, ripened; semisoft, ripened; firm, ripened; very hard, ripened; and blue-vein mold ripened.

Soft Natural Cheeses   Cottage cheese is made commercially or at home from skim milk clotted by rennin and/or lactic acid. *Streptococcus lactis*, lactic acid–producing bacteria, will convert lactose to lactic acid when milk is allowed to stand at a moderately warm temperature for a period of time, causing the milk to begin to approach the isoelectric point of casein. Under these conditions, the casein precipitates, leaving much of the calcium in the milk in the whey in the form of calcium lactate, a soluble calcium salt. This explains why cottage cheese made by precipitating casein with acid is lower in calcium than the milk was from which it was made.

Rennin provides another means of clotting milk for making cheese. When rennin is the mechanism for clotting the milk to make cheese, the calcium will be retained in the curd rather than being lost in the whey, because the calcium forms an insoluble salt with casein (calcium caseinate). Although cottage cheese ordinarily does not contain fat in the curd because of the absence of fat in the skim milk being clotted, some cottage cheese has cream added back to the cheese. When this is done, the fat content is 4 percent, and the cheese is identified as creamed cottage cheese.

Cream cheese is another soft natural cheese, but it is made from whole milk with some cream added, which explains its name. Lactic acid is the agent responsible for curd formation. Neufchatel is quite similar to cream cheese, the difference being that this type of cheese has somewhat less cream in it than is used in making cream cheese.

Camembert is a soft, ripened cheese cured with *Penicillium camemberti*. Characteristically, the center of camembert is rather fluid when fully ripened. Brie is closely related to camembert, but is firmer. Two popular dessert cheeses classified as soft cheeses—limburger and liederkranz—are noted for their highly developed aromas and flavors, the result of the ripening process.

Semisoft Natural Cheeses   There are three similar cheeses laced with a characteristic blue-green color and a distinctive flavor. These rennin-clotted cheeses, which are distinctly firmer than the soft cheeses, include Gorgonzola, Roquefort, and blue (or bleu). *Penicillium roqueforti* or a similar mold injected into the cheese will grow impressively during the ripening period of between 2 and 12 months to develop the desired textural and flavor changes. Gorgonzola and blue are produced using cow's milk, while Roquefort is made from sheep's milk. The other distinctive requirement for a cheese to be called Roquefort is that it be ripened in the caves near Roquefort, France, where the atmospheric conditions are quite uniform and uniquely suited to accomplish the desired ripening.

Muenster is a cheese reflecting the locale where it has been produced. The Muenster from the United States is mild in comparison with the well-developed flavor of Muensters from Europe.

Brick gets its name from the ability of this cheese to be formed into brick-like shapes. The flavor is mild and comparatively sweet.

Hard Natural Cheeses Cheddar cheese, named for the town in England where it was first made, is produced by using lactic acid bacteria to acidify the milk to the pH where rennin will be effective in bringing about curd formation. Anatto (an extract from the seed pods of a Central American tree) usually is added to produce the characteristic yellow-orange color often associated with cheddar cheese. The repeated cutting of the curd and draining of the whey, a process called cheddaring, is done to achieve the desired moisture content before salting and ripening are done. Commonly, cheddar cheese will be found in the market in various stages of ripening, ranging from mild to very sharp. The cost of extended storage for ripening cheddar long enough to produce the distinctive and permeating flavor of very sharp cheddar is reflected in the comparatively higher cost of cheddar cheeses, with mild being the least costly.

Edam and Gouda are hard dessert cheeses that gain distinction by sporting colorful wax coatings. Holland is the home of these two types of hard cheeses. Another popular cheese sometimes used for dessert (as well as for many other occasions) is Swiss cheese, or Emmentaler. *Streptococcus thermophilus* and *Lactobacillus bulgaricus* are the microorganisms used to precipitate the curd. However, it is the gas production stemming from the inclusion of *Propionibacterium shermanii* that causes the impressive holes in ripened Swiss cheese.

Parmesan cheese, developed in Italy, is virtually synonymous with Italian cookery. To help this very hard cheese ripen satisfactorily over a period of between 16 months and several years, the exterior is rubbed with an oily mixture that gradually causes a dark green to black exterior to develop.

Process Cheese

Process Cheese Blend of natural cheeses heated to at least 145°F, with the addition of an emulsifying agent and water; cheese that will not ripen.

Process cheese is made from a mixture of natural cheeses and an emulsifier blended together with controlled heating. The various flavors of process cheeses are the result of the natural cheeses selected for making a particular process cheese. The emulsifier added is sodium citrate, disodium phosphate, or other additive that will be effective in binding the high fat content of the natural cheese ingredients with the water that is added to the process cheese to produce the desired consistency. By heating this mixture to at least 145°F and no hotter than 165°F and stirring to achieve a homogeneous mixture, a cheese with excellent keeping qualities and usually a bland flavor is produced. The heat enhances shelf life because bacterial and enzymatic action are halted, thus preventing ripening. This process produces a pasteurized product, the accurate name being *pasteurized process cheese*.

Process Cheese Food Process cheese product with about 4 percent more water than in process cheese.

For some purposes, cheese products with varying textural characteristics may be useful. Pasteurized process cheese products have a very slightly higher moisture content than do the natural cheeses used to manufacture the process cheese, which makes process cheeses a bit softer. However, variations of the process cheese are made with even a higher moisture content and a lower fat content. *Process cheese food* contains about 4 percent more water than does the comparable process cheese, while process cheese spreads have

Process Cheese Spread Process cheese product with about 4 percent more water than in process cheese food, or about 8 percent more water than in process cheese.

Coldpack (Club) Cheese Mixture of natural cheeses with an added emulsifier, but without heating.

more than 4 percent more water than does the process cheese food. This additional water in the *process cheese spreads* results in excellent spreading characteristics.

Although process cheese products do not undergo flavor changes due to ripening, some variation in flavor is possible through the addition of such ingredients as pimiento, crushed pineapple, or bacon bits. Added seasonings are used in various process cheese spreads to heighten the flavor of these basically bland products.

Coldpack cheese is not a process cheese despite its similar formulation, for no heat is applied in manufacturing the coldpack cheese, hence its name. (Coldpack is also known as club cheese.) The lack of heat in coldpack cheese processing results in flavors similar to the natural cheeses used in the product, but with enhanced spreading qualities due to the addition of the emulsifier.

Packaging and technological advances have resulted in the availability of a wide choice of process cheeses, process cheese foods, and process cheese spreads, a number of which can be stored in their packaging without refrigeration until they are opened.

Cheese Cookery

The process cheeses and related products are simple ingredients to use in cooking because they melt and blend readily with other ingredients. The emulsifier in them helps to prevent oil from separating and forming a greasy product. Performance also is enhanced by the somewhat lower fat content of process cheeses. The disadvantage of these types of cheeses is the lack of distinctive flavors.

The natural cheeses afford a pleasing and exciting range of flavors for use in different foods. Ripened natural cheeses will melt and combine well with other foods because the casein in the cheese is modified by the action of molds or bacteria to make this protein easier to disperse. A natural cheese that has not been ripened very much will be difficult to disperse and will lack the well-developed flavor of the fully ripened cheese.

The exciting flavors of ripened natural cheeses explain why many people select these cheeses over process cheeses in cooking. As just noted, unripened natural cheeses blend less readily than do ripened counterparts, but even the ripened counterparts tend to separate more readily than the process cheeses. Natural cheeses also may become tough and rubbery when held at serving temperatures for a period of time or when heated to too high a temperature.

Success in cooking with natural cheeses is achieved when attention is paid to certain factors, beginning with careful selection of well-ripened natural cheeses because of their ease in blending with other ingredients. Moreover during the actual heating process, remember to

1. Avoid high temperatures.
2. Keep the heating period as short as possible.

By grating the cheese and then sprinkling it on the surface of the finished product, the heating time in the oven required to melt the cheese is very short. This avoids toughening the cheese and separating the oil from the cheese.

These precautions are consistent with the fact that natural cheeses are high in protein and in fat content. The low temperatures and short heating periods are designed to keep the denaturation changes of protein to a desirable level. If protein is subjected to too much heat, the protein molecules will clump together very tightly, squeezing out considerable fat and making a tough, stringy protein curd. The longer the heating period and/or the higher the temperature, the more severe these changes will be. A cheese pizza that is baked at too high temperature is a familiar example of these deteriorative changes. The toughening of the cheese proteins is evident when removing a piece of the pizza from the pie is accompanied by seemingly endless strands of cheese and an oily residue where the piece had been.

Often cheese-containing products are thickened by starch. The best results are obtained when the starch mixture is gelatinized prior to the addition of the cheese. Basically, the cheese only needs to be added long enough to be melted completely before the fondue, cheese soup, rarebit, or other dish is served. Clearly, such items should not be boiled once the cheese is incorporated; grainy and stringy sauces will be the result when cheese is overheated.

When making casseroles and other baked products containing cheese, oven temperatures should be as low as feasible for the overall quality, and the baking time should be kept short. When possible, the cheese should be protected from the direct oven heat by a protective layer of buttered bread crumbs, a sauce, or other insulation. The sides and bottom of a casserole, such as macaroni and cheese, can be protected by placing the casserole dish in a pan of hot water, thus insulating the cheese in the casserole from some of the intensity of the oven heat. In some instances, cheese is used to garnish the top of casseroles. This can be added just long enough before the end of the baking period to allow the cheese to melt.

SUMMARY

Milk is a key food nutritionally, being a particularly valuable source of calcium, phosphorus, vitamin D, riboflavin, protein, along with other nutrients. Pasteurization and refrigeration are invaluable in helping to maintain the safety of milk. Homogenization and fortification are valued for their contributions to convenience, palatability, and nutrient content. These processes are used in fluid milks of varying fat content, as well as a part of the processing of canned and dry milks. Butter, creams, ice creams, and imitation products, as well as the various milk products, are handled and stored under rigorous state and federal controls.

Protein structure (from the amino acid units comprising a single molecule through the primary to even the quaternary structure) is very complex and is subject to change when various forms of energy are applied, notably when heat or mechanical agitation are used during food preparation. Denaturation involves physical changes, particularly in the tertiary structure of proteins, and a clumping together of molecules.

Proteins are of concern in food preparation because of their participation in such changes as scum formation, scorching, curdling, and clotting of milk. Control of the acidity of protein-containing mixtures can help to keep the protein away from the isoelectric point, thus reducing the likelihood of detrimental changes in the protein.

Whipping cream with a fat content of 30 percent or more will whip readily to a foam with reasonable stability. Evaporated milk foams can be made if the undiluted milk is chilled until crystals start to form on the edges. Stability of evaporated milk foams is very limited unless gelatin or other stabilizer is used. Dried milk foams can be made when the solids are diluted with water in a 3:2 ratio.

Natural cheeses are valued for their distinctive flavors and wide range of textures. However, in food preparation, the toughening of the protein and the tendency for the fat to separate are potential problems that can be minimized by keeping temperatures low and heating times short. Process cheese (pasteurized), process cheese food, and process cheese spread are mixtures of natural cheeses blended with an emulsifier and water and then pasteurized to produce rather bland cheeses that are easy to use without becoming unduly tough or exhibiting fat separation. Coldpack cheese is virtually the same as process cheese except that heating is not involved.

Selected References

American Home Economics Association, *Handbook of Food Preparation*. AHEA Washington, D.C. 8th ed. 1980. PP. 48–53.

Andrews, A. T. and G. C. Cheeseman. Properties of aseptically packed UHT milk: Casein modification during storage and studies with model systems. *J. Dairy Res. 38*: 193. 1971.

Bloomfield, V. A. and R. J. Mead, Jr. Structure and stability of casein micelles. *J. Dairy Sci. 58*: 592. 1975.

Brunner, J. R. Physical equilibria in milk: Lipid phase. In *Fundamentals of Dairy Chemistry*. Ed. B. H. Webb, et al., Avi Publishing Co. Westport, Conn. 1974. P. 487.

Brunner, J. R. Homogenization. In *Principles of Food Science. Part I*. Ed. O. R. Fennema. Marcel Dekker. New York. 1976. P. 648.

Cheryan M. et al. Secondary phase of enzymatic milk coagulation. *J. Dairy Sci. 58*: 477. 1975.

Clifford, A. J. et al. Homogenized bovine milk xanthine oxidase: A critique of the hypothesis relating to plasmalogen depletion and cardiovascular disease. *Am. J. Clin. Nutr. 38*: 327. 1983.

Crick, F. H. C. and J. C. Kendrew. X-ray analysis and protein structure. *Adv. Prot. Chem. 12*: 133. 1957.

Doty, P. Proteins. *Sci. Am. 197(3)*: 173. 1957.

Kroger, M. Quality of yogurt. *J. Dairy Sci. 59*: 344. 1976.

Lecos, C. Milk: Cows produce it; man improves it. *FDA Consumer 16(5)*: 16. 1982.

Lockie, B. Acidophilus products. *Dairy Prod. 8(2)*: 3. 1980.

Mettler, A. E. Fortified milk and supplements. *J. Soc. Dairy Tech. 33(4)*: 1980.

Morr, C. V. Chemistry of milk proteins in food processing. *J. Dairy Sci. 58*: 977. 1975.

Morr, C. V. Whey protein concentrates: An update. *Food Tech. 30(3)*: 18. 1976.

Nelson, J. H. Impact of milk clotting enzymes on cheese technology. *J. Dairy Sci. 58*: 1739. 1975.

Newberry, R. E. Infant formula act of 1980. *J. Assoc. Offic. Anal. Anal. Chem. 65(6)*: 1472. 1983.

O'Leary, V. S. and J. H. Woychik. Comparison of some chemical properties of yogurts made from control and lactase-treated milks. *J. Food Sci. 41*: 791. 1976.

Schmidt, R. H. Gelation and coagulation. *ACS Symposium Series 7*: 131. 1981.

Speck, M. L. Use of microbial cultures: Dairy products. *Food Tech. 35(1)*: 71. 1981.

Swartz, R. Maillard reaction in milk and milk products. *S. African J. Dairy Tech. 14(1)*: 11. 1982.

Thakur, M. K. et al. Changes during ripening of unsalted cheddar cheese. *J. Dairy Sci. 58*: 175. 1975.

Study Questions

1. What useful changes occur in milk as a result of the homogenization process?
2. Compare the ease of formation and stability of foams made from whipping cream, coffee cream, evaporated milk, and nonfat dried milk solids. What contributes stability to the different foams?

3. Why is the calcium content of cottage cheese clotted with acid lower than that clotted with rennin?

4. Describe the result of using a process cheese versus a well-ripened natural cheese in a grilled cheese sandwich. What advantages and disadvantages can you cite for the two types of cheeses used in this preparation?

5. Compare ice cream made without agitation and the same recipe made with agitation. Explain the differences.

6. Why is the cranking of an ice cream freezer done slowly at first? What may happen if the cranking is much faster than recommended?

7. Why is salt added to the ice used in an ice cream freezer?

8. Diagram the (a) primary, (b) secondary, and (c) tertiary structures of a protein.

9. Why is the isoelectric point of a protein important?

10. Why does heat cause denaturation of protein?

Edward Hicks, ''The Residence of David Twining.'' Abby Aldrich Rockefeller Folk Art Collection, Williamsburg, Virginia.

CHAPTER 9

PROTEINS: MEATS, POULTRY, AND FISH

MEATS

Meat is defined in food preparation as the edible flesh of domesticated animals. According to this definition, the meats commonly utilized in the United States include beef, veal, pork, and lamb. These "red meats" are cornerstones of the diets of many Americans and are prominent not only for the portion of the food dollar spent for them, but also because of the quantity consumed. Other types of protein foods (poultry, fish, eggs, and cheese) are eaten in much smaller quantities than are the red meats, although there is an increasing consumption of these other protein sources. Of the red meats, beef clearly is the favorite; in fact, approximately half again as much beef is eaten as the total of the other red meats consumed annually by Americans.

The expense of protein-rich foods and particularly of meat makes the entree selection a logical place to start when planning a menu. All aspects of meats, from selection, through storage, preparation, and service, deserve careful attention because meat serves as the focal point of a meal as well as the focal point of the food budget. A thorough understanding of all aspects of meat in the menu will enable the consumer to obtain maximum pleasure and effectiveness from tender, flavorful, and juicy meats.

This chapter is divided into three main sections—meats, poultry, and fish—the three major categories of muscle-type foods. The underlying principles for handling and preparing these various types of protein foods are essentially the same, although there are specifics that require emphasis.

Definition of Meats

Various terms are used to designate particular animals and particular types of meat. These designations are helpful in indicating what characteristics might be expected in these meats, because the color, flavor, and tenderness vary with the age of the animal. As animals mature and age, the color of the muscles becomes darker. The flavor becomes a bit more intense with the age of any of the animals and is particularly noticeable in sheep. Similarly, beef also has a richer, fuller flavor than does veal. The designations for meats from animals at different ages are presented in Table 9.1.

Cross-sectional view of raw beef semitendinosus (small muscle of bottom-round), as shown in scanning electron micrograph. The endomysium (E) is the connective tissue surrounding the fascicules; the perimysium (P) surrounds the whole muscle.

Muscle

Structure   Meats are composed of muscle, connective tissue, fat, and bone. The bone is peripheral to the portions that are consumed and hence is of interest because of the type and amount of bone associated with a particular meat cut. Whereas bone is cut from the muscle either at the market or at the table, the muscle, connective tissue, and some of the fat may be eaten. The changes occurring in these components of meat are of special interest.

Muscle is the reason that people eat meats. The muscle is approximately 75 percent water and 20 percent protein, with the remaining 5 percent representing a combination of fat, carbohydrate, and minerals. The percentage of water in meat varies with the type of muscle, the kind of meat, the season of

Table 9.1 Overview of Meat Classifications[1]

Name	Age	Description
Cattle		
Veal	3 to 14 weeks	Very light in color, delicate flavor
Calf (baby beef)	14 to 52 weeks	Medium color, moderate flavor, high proportion of connective tissue
Beef	Over 1 year	Bright red, full flavor
Swine		
Pork	5 to 12 months	Greyish-pink, some marbling, full flavor
Sheep		
Lamb	To 1 year	Cherry-red, delicate flavor, tender
Mutton	Over 1 year	Deep-cherry-red, strong flavor, less tender than lamb

[1]The classification of animals is based on the sex, age, and sexual condition of cattle and swine. These classes are:

Beef—Steer, male castrated at a young age; heifer, female that has never borne a calf; cow, female that has borne a calf; bull, male; stag, male castrated after reaching maturity

Swine—Barrows, young males; gilts, young females; sows, females that have borne young; boars, mature uncastrated males; stags, mature castrated males

Sheep—Lambs, less than a year old; yearling, a year old; mutton, older sheep

the year, and the pH of the meat. The ability of meat to hold water is termed its *water-holding capacity*; this ability is important to the juiciness of the meat.

The structure of muscle is much more complex than it appears to the naked eye, for it consists of several levels of organization. The basic structure begins with a protein sol called the sarcoplasm being bound by a very fine membrane, the sarcolemma, to make a muscle fiber. Within the structure of these fibers are units called myofibrils. To break this structure down still farther in exploring the structure of muscle, the myofibrils are comprised of thick and thin myofilaments. These myofilaments give a striated or striped appearance to muscle tissue when viewed under magnification. Apparently the number of these muscle fibers ceases to increase following birth of the animal, but the existing fibers grow, resulting in the observable growth of young animals.

The fibers are held into bundles of fibers, fasciculi, by connective tissue. These fasciculi are large enough to be seen by the naked eye, and they are what are perceived as strands within muscles. The connective tissue surrounding each of the fasciculi in a muscle is called the endomysium. The total muscle is comprised of many of these fasciculi plus some fatty deposits, all arranged in an orderly fashion and held in position by a surrounding sheath of connective tissue, the perimysium. Clearly, a great deal of organization is involved in the complex arrangement, from the thick and thin myofilaments of the myofibrils, to the fibers, fasciculi, and the total muscle.

Muscle Proteins The muscle proteins found within the individual fibers are dominated by *myosin*, the most abundant of the muscle proteins. Myosin is an

Water-holding Capacity Ability of muscles to hold water; an important contribution to juiciness of meats.

Myosin Key elongated and large protein molecule in muscle.

elongated molecule with a molecular weight of about 480,000; when heated, it forms a gel, which increases the toughness of the muscle fibers. Tropomyosin, another muscle protein with properties similar to myosin, has a molecular weight of only about 50,000, which is essentially the same size as actin. Actin is a globular protein important in muscle fibers. Muscle contraction is theorized to be due to a complexing of actin and myosin to form actomyosin.

The colors in meats are the result of the presence of some other proteins. *Myoglobin* is the central pigment in meat coloration. This pigment, a protein similar in structure to hemoglobin, is capable of combining with several different substances, including oxygen. With oxygen, oxymyoglobin is formed, which gives meat a particularly bright red color. In combination with water, a brownish-red color develops as metmyoglobin is formed. The central iron atom in myoglobin can change valence, resulting in color changes.

Myoglobin Pigment in meat; compound similar to hemoglobin and capable of reacting with various substances to effect color changes in muscle.

Cured meats have nitrates added to form nitric oxide myochrome, a change accounting for the permanent pinkish color of cured meats. Sometimes in cured meats, the porphyrin ring of heme is oxidized, causing an irridescent, greenish color on the surface of ham or other cured meats. Exposure to oxygen and ultraviolet light hasten the development of this condition.

Problems with discoloration of meat can be retarded by wrapping meat cuts in relatively airtight packages and storing them away from light. Ordinarily, discoloration should be minimal for as long as three days when displayed in a refrigerated meat case in a store. Freezing causes some fading, although the change in color is minimized by a careful wrapping to exclude most of the air.

Connective Tissue

The two types of connective tissue proteins in meat cuts are collagen and elastin. *Collagen* is of particular significance in meat cookery, for this is the structural protein for the connective tissue sheaths throughout the muscles. Sometimes, collagen is called simply "white connective tissue." Collagen molecules are elongated, fibrous molecules and are arranged sometimes randomly, sometimes in parallel.

Collagen White connective tissue in meats; fibrous structural protein encasing muscle proteins.

Elastin is found in rather concentrated deposits, where this type of connective tissue appears as a yellow, almost rubbery mass. This type of connective tissue protein usually is discarded as "gristle" because it essentially remains unchanged and tough throughout any type of cookery technique.

Elastin Extremely strong connective tissue; a yellow-colored protein in meat that is not tenderized by cooking.

SCIENCE NOTE: Collagen and Gelatin

Collagen is the connective tissue that forms the sheaths encasing muscle proteins in muscles. The fibrous nature of collagen derives from the fact that two somewhat unusual amino (actually imino) acids—proline and hydroxyproline—are repeated frequently in the amino acid chain constituting the primary organization of the molecules. These two acids (shown below) interfere with the helical coiling as collagen attempts to assume the normal helical (secondary) structure of most proteins. The difficulty in achieving a helix is due to the fact that the nitrogen needed for the peptide linkage between amino acids is actually part of a ring structure of the two acids, which limits the ability of the backbone chain of the protein to bend.

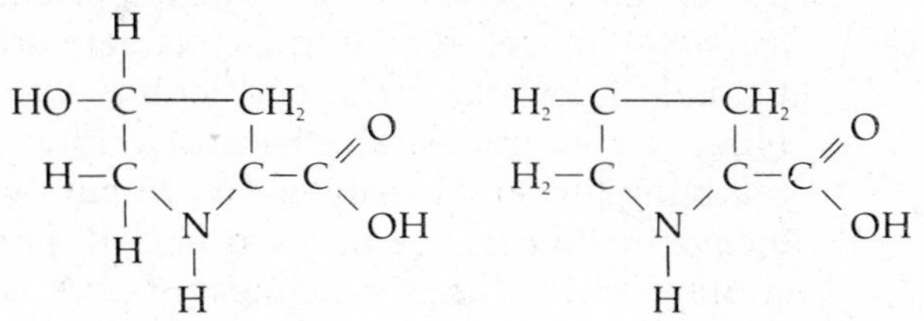

$$
\underset{\text{Hydroxyproline}}{
\begin{array}{c}
\text{H} \\
| \\
\text{HO} - \text{C} -\!\!-\!\!- \text{CH}_2 \\
| \qquad\qquad | \\
\text{H} - \text{C} \diagdown \quad \diagup \text{C} - \text{C} \diagup^{\text{O}} \\
| \qquad \text{N} \qquad\qquad \diagdown \text{OH} \\
\text{H} \quad | \\
\text{H}
\end{array}}
\qquad
\underset{\text{Proline}}{
\begin{array}{c}
\text{H}_2 - \text{C} -\!\!-\!\!- \text{CH}_2 \\
| \qquad\qquad | \\
\text{H}_2 - \text{C} \diagdown \quad \diagup \text{C} - \text{C} \diagup^{\text{O}} \\
\text{N} \qquad\qquad \diagdown \text{OH} \\
| \\
\text{H}
\end{array}}
$$

These elongated chains are somewhat more complex than is suggested by simply examining the unique linearity caused by the hydroxyproline and proline. In collagen, usually three of these chains are twisted together loosely in an arrangement comparable to that of a three-ply cord. The chains are held together by hydrogen bonding between the individual strands to make a collagen molecule. The association of the strands in this way makes collagen quite a tough fiber and contributes significantly to the apparent toughness of meat in which collagen is abundant. The analogy of the three-ply cord can be used to demonstrate the increased strength resulting from the three-ply arrangement rather than testing single strands.

These three-ply molecules of collagen are instrumental in holding the muscles of meat together in an organized fashion. Their fibrous nature, however, is susceptible to some change when heat is supplied to begin to allow the hydrogen bonds holding the three strands together to break. When heat, particularly moist heat, is applied, these bonds start to break. Over an extended period of time, enough of these hydrogen bonds will break to cause these loosely twisted chains to start to pull away from each other. No chemical breakdown is occurring within a single chain; rather, the change is a dissociation between chains. Gradually, single strands will begin to drift individually, resulting in a distinct, tenderizing effect in the meat. These individual strands that separate from collagen are gelatin. Since they represent strands with only a third the cross section of collagen, these gelatin molecules present much less resistance to cutting than does the native collagen. For this reason, meats braised for an extended period of time become literally "fork tender" and can be cut without using a knife.

Fat

Fat in meats is found between muscles and within muscles, and in both locations, fat contributes to the overall flavor and juiciness of meats. These fatty deposits in animals consist of many aggregates of fat cells that are formed early in life and then enlarged. Fat first is laid down subcutaneously as a protective layer around the organs in the abdominal cavity, and then it begins to accumulate around and between muscles, with the intramuscular fatty deposits being laid down last. The deposition of fat within muscles is known as *marbling*. In beef, marbling is considered desirable if a person is seeking a particularly juicy, flavorful, and tender cut. However, in pork, abundant marbling is rated undesirable because of the greasy quality imparted by excessive marbling (pork naturally has a comparatively large amount of marbling). Selective breeding is being used in pork production to attempt to minimize fat content and reduce the richness of pork, an effort that has met with considerable success in the last few years.

Marbling Deposition of fat within the muscles of meats.

Nutritional Contributions

All red meats are significant sources of complete protein, with the actual contribution ranging between 9 and 19 percent, depending upon the particular species (beef is higher than pork) and cut. This protein is utilized efficiently within the body unless extreme heat is used in preparing the meat.

The fat in meats is a source of calories and of saturated fatty acids, with beef being criticized particularly for its content of saturated fatty acids. In fact, it is because of the abundance of fat, particularly saturated fatty acids, that Americans have been encouraged to shift meat consumption patterns to reduce the amount of red meats and increase poultry and fish. However, with judicious removal of fatty deposits around muscles and servings of appropriate size, red meats can be utilized as a nourishing food at least three or four times a week by most people.

Red meats are excellent sources of iron and copper, as well as some other minerals, and for this reason, beef and other red meats are important components of the diet. In fact, people who avoid red meats often have difficulty in meeting the Recommended Dietary Allowance for iron. The organ meats, particularly liver, are especially rich sources of the various minerals, although all of the red meats are useful sources.

Thiamin, riboflavin, and niacin are vitamins that are particularly abundant in red meats. Of the meats, pork is the highest in thiamin content, although all the red meats are good sources of thiamin. Vitamin B_{12} also is provided by red meats. Since the liver is the storage area for vitamin A, it is not surprising that liver from any type of meat animal is a useful source of this vitamin.

When meat is prepared by dry heat cookery methods, the retention of vitamins is quite good. However, moist heat cookery methods cause some of the B vitamins (thiamin, riboflavin, and niacin) to migrate into the cooking liquid. If the liquid is consumed with the meat, this does not present a problem, but if the liquid is discarded, some of the B vitamins will be lost.

Preparing Meat for the Market

Production Practices   One of the major concerns among meat producers is the cost of getting the meat animals to the meat packers. The longer an animal is fed prior to marketing, the more costly is the production of the animal. Feed costs, feedlot space, and labor are all involved in fattening an animal for slaughter. By the administration of sex hormones either orally or as implants, animals can be brought to maturity and to market more rapidly than if no hormones are provided. Testosterone (a male hormone) and diethylstilbestrol (DES), which is a female hormone, have been shown to accelerate maturation. The specific effects of DES vary with the species: cattle grow more rapidly and produce meat with a higher meat-to-bone ratio; chickens deposit more fat; and turkeys fight less and mature more quickly. Only pigs appear to be unaffected by the use of DES.

There has been a considerable controversy over the wisdom of using DES, however, although DES will clear from the carcasses if the hormone is removed from the feed an adequate length of time prior to slaughter. Regulations requiring that DES pellets, if they are being allowed at all, must be implanted in inedible parts of the carcass have been enforced as a protective

Beef cattle being fed on the range. Many cattle are fattened subsequently in feedlots, often with corn or other grain.

measure to ensure that residues of DES do not enter the human food supply. Use of DES in poultry production is banned, and the authority to use this hormone in beef production vacillates from time to time.

Rigor   Progressive chemical changes occur following the slaughtering of an animal, with these changes leading to the onset and ultimately the passing of *rigor mortis*. The live animal will have some *glycogen* (carbohydrate) stored, but this source of energy varies considerably in quantity and is particularly dependent upon the circumstances at the time of slaughter. A comparatively high level of glycogen at slaughter is desired. To help to achieve this, a calm, quick dispatch is very helpful. Any exercise, nervous exhaustion, insulin release, or fasting prior to slaughter will reduce the amount of glycogen in reserve.

The level of glycogen in the animal is important because this carbohydrate is the source of energy for chemical reactions and also for the formation of lactic acid in the carcass during rigor. With an adequate supply of glycogen at the time of slaughter, the acidity of the carcass will drop to a pH of about 5.3. When meat reaches this acidic pH, the color of the meat, its tenderness, and juiciness will be optimal. However, if there is little glycogen in reserve at slaughter, the pH of the carcass will not drop sufficiently low. The resulting meat will be an undesirable, dark color and sticky and gummy in character. Beef in which the pH has remained too high is designated as *dark-cutting beef* and is considered lower in quality.

Rigor mortis, the stiffening of the muscles in the carcass, appears to be due to the formation of actomyosin from actin and myosin as the glycogen breaks down and ATP (adenosine triphosphate, a high-energy compound) and lactic acid form. First the trend is toward the reduced pH due to lactic acid formation, but then ammonia ultimately is liberated when ATP breaks down. Ammonia production causes the pH of the carcass to rise a bit, and the stiffening of the muscles passes. Rigor mortis usually reaches its peak in cattle in about 24 hours, with softening of the muscles occurring gradually after that.

Cold Storage   High standards of sanitation and maintenance of a low relative humidity and constant low temperature are essential during the initial chilling of carcasses and storage of meats until they reach the consumer. Meats, like other protein-rich foods, are very susceptible to spoilage by microorganisms unless storage conditions are controlled carefully. Since spoilage takes place on the surfaces, storage problems can be kept to a minimum if the carcasses are cut to yield the largest possible pieces that can be handled. At the packing houses, this ordinarily means splitting the carcasses in half to allow for thorough cleaning of the region formerly in the interior. The introduction of ozone or carbon dioxide into the chilling and holding rooms at packing plants, as well as the maintenance of temperatures just above freezing, help to extend the length of time that carcasses can be held in packing houses before being shipped and sold to as long as 10 days.

All meats are held in cold storage until rigor passes before they are marketed or frozen. The holding of meat until the muscles relax again is impor-

Rigor Mortis Series of chemical changes occurring in the carcass following slaughtering.

Glycogen Polysaccharide in muscle, which breaks down to produce energy and lactic acid in the carcass following slaughter.

Dark-cutting Beef Darkly colored beef with a sticky, gummy character, the result of too little glycogen at slaughter, usually due to exhaustion or inadequate feeding at dispatch.

tant in achieving optimal water-holding capacity. If meat is frozen before a carcass passes through rigor, the water-holding capacity will be minimal, with the result that there will be considerable drip loss when the meat is thawed. In contrast, meat frozen after rigor has passed will have a high water-holding capacity so that much of the water will be bound when the meat is frozen, and this bound water will continue to be held in the meat following thawing, thus allowing only limited drip loss.

Aging   A small amount of top-grade (prime) beef is held in cold storage for a ripening period of 15 to 40 days before being marketed. During this holding period, mold grows on the outer surface of the side of beef, but the layer of fat on the surface is so thick in prime beef that the mold and some of the fat can be trimmed easily from the *aged beef* as the carcass enters the marketing chain. Lower-quality beef and also veal do not have enough fat to permit ripening or aging. Pork cannot be aged even though it has a thick coating of fat, because the fat will start to become rancid during the storage period.

Aged Beef Prime beef that has been held in very cold storage for 15 to 40 days to intensify flavor, darken the color, and tenderize the muscles.

Beef aged or ripened for a period between 10 and 29 days will become increasingly tender due to the action of proteolytic enzymes on the various proteins in the muscles. There also is increased hydration of the protein during ripening. Connective tissue remains unchanged during the aging process. Color and flavor changes of significance occur during aging of beef. The fresh red color gives way to a gray-brown at lower cooking temperatures than are required for color change in unripened beef. Even before cooking, ripened beef is noticeably darker than unripened beef. The flavor of beef becomes increasingly distinctive and intense as aging progresses, with the flavor usually being judged to be best when beef is ripened for 20 to 40 days. All these changes occur more slowly at temperatures just above freezing than they do at warmer temperatures, but the microbiological problems at warmer temperatures make very cold (not frozen) storage important.

Curing Treating of meats with salt, sodium nitrate, and heat to achieve color and flavor changes and to promote shelf life and reduce spoilage.

Curing   Both beef and pork may be preserved by *curing*, the former product being called corned beef and the latter ham. The permanent reddish color is the result of treatment by a combination of salt, sodium nitrate, and heat. During the brining period, the original nitrate is reduced to nitrite, which then reacts with myoglobin in the meat to produce the familiar red color.

The possible carcinogenicity of nitrates and nitrites has generated a good bit of dialogue regarding the allowance of these chemicals in curing meat products. Although there is apparently an extremely small risk of nitrates contributing to the development of cancer, the risk (if indeed there really is one) is so very small that cured meats continue to be permitted. The risk of botulism in sausages and some other cured meats is far, far greater than any possible cancer hazard if nitrates were to be banned in the maufacturing of cured meat products. The controversy over the use of nitrates resulted in a flurry of research activities, which culminated in a reduction in the level of nitrates used for curing, but not an elimination of these important preservatives.

The extent of penetration of curing agents varies with the pH of the meat being cured, with meat at about pH 5.2 achieving far higher penetration than that at the less acidic pH 6.6. The meats that are not very acidic are more susceptible to spoilage than are those approaching pH 5.2. However, heating of the meats at the higher pH levels is a help in reducing spoilage because heating enhances the penetration of the curing agents. Sage, black pepper, and salt hasten rancidity of fats on cured meats, whereas other spices retard this problem.

Smoking Means of helping to promote shelf life of meat by hanging it in a smokehouse to dry out the surface and add flavor to the meat.

Smoking *Smoking* of ham and sometimes other meats is done to enhance flavors and to promote shelf life. The smoking, preferably done using sawdust from hard woods, dries the surface and also adds distinctive flavors, depending upon the type of wood being used as fuel for the smoking process. Not only does the surface become dry, but the proteins in the meat are denatured slowly by the heat from the smoking fuel.

Freezing Meats may be frozen by sharp freezing or by quick freezing. Sharp freezing is done by holding meat in a storage room with rapidly moving air and a temperature of $-10°F$. This method is slow in comparison with quick freezing. As a result, the ice crystals in meats that have been sharp frozen tend to be quite large (see Chapter 16).

Quick freezing is a term for any technique that results in extremely fast freezing. The methods may be (1) immersion, (2) contact, and (3) convection. Immersion freezing employs use of a brine solution to achieve temperatures below the point of freezing water. A blast of cold air is the technique used in convection freezing. Any of the quick-freezing methods will result in a frozen meat with small ice crystals and with extremely low bacterial, yeast, or mold growth because of the rapid cooling to unfavorable temperatures for microbiological activity.

Drip loss will be comparatively less for thin pieces of frozen meat than for thicker cuts because thick pieces will freeze slowly in the center. This means that moisture will tend to be drawn out and frozen between the fibers, while the thin pieces will freeze so rapidly that the moisture is trapped within the fibers. Beef should be held at least 48 hours after slaughter before being frozen; the other meats need to be held at least 24 hours to allow the changes necessary to keep drip loss of frozen meats to a minimum.

In frozen storage, meats can be held for several weeks without serious loss of quality, whereas the fresh meat would need to be consumed within a matter of very few days. Another advantage of freezing meats is that the meats are made more tender by freezing. The meats should be held in frozen storage at $-10°$ to $0°F$ to achieve a satisfactorily long, safe storage period. The packaging used for the frozen meat is another important factor in determining how long the frozen meat can be held. A packaging material resistant to damage and yet capable of being fitted tightly around the meat is needed. The packaging should keep air from reaching the meat. If the package has any tears or other openings, the very dry environment of the freezer will result in formation of a dried, tough area because of desiccation on the surface of the cut, a circumstance termed *freezer burn*. Once freezer burn has occurred, the

Freezer Burn Desiccation of part of the surface of frozen meat, a result of improper packaging, which allows air to be in contact with the meat surface.

area will never return to its former rehydrated state, regardless of the treatment applied.

Freeze-Drying Drying has long been a means of preserving meats, but the addition of a second process, freezing, makes a unique and effective way of preserving meat. *Freeze-drying*, as the name suggests, involves freezing of the meat and then sublimating the ice from the meat to produce a very lightweight product that does not require refrigeration for storage. This preservation method has proven to be particularly useful in the formulation of dehydrated soups with meat.

Inspection

Meat's potential for carrying harmful microorganisms prompted legislation for inspection as far back as 1890 when the Meat Inspection Act was passed. Since that time, other laws governing inspection have been passed by the federal government and cover the sanitation standards required for meat and poultry entering interstate commerce. In fact, the Wholesome Meat Act of 1967 and the Wholesome Poultry Products Act of 1968 mandated that meats and poultry, respectively, involved in intrastate commerce be inspected under state programs at least as rigorous as the standards required for interstate marketing. This legislation effectively ensured that any meat reaching consumers would have been slaughtered under sanitary conditions and would be from animals free of disease at the time of slaughter.

Inspection of meat and poultry must be done by authorized inspectors. States can elect to have their own inspectors for meat being marketed within the state, or they can utilize federal inspectors. Only federal inspectors are authorized to inspect meat for interstate commerce. The inspection includes assessment of the entire slaughtering and packing operation, from checking the healthiness of the animal through all packing plant patterns of sanitation and refrigeration. The fact that a meat carcass bears the inspection stamp on each primal cut means only that the meat was safe for consumption at the time of inspection. This stamp carries no guarantee that subsequent handling has met the same standards of cleanliness. No statement of the palatability or eating quality of the meat is suggested by the inspection stamp.

Consumers may often buy retail cuts that show no sign of the inspection stamp, for only one small stamp is imprinted with a safe (usually red or yellow) vegetable dye on each primal cut. The inspection stamp simply indicates that the meat has been inspected and passed and identifies the packer by number.

The one potential hazard in meat that is not revealed by inspection is *Trichinella spiralis* (see Chapter 2). This is a parasitic worm sometimes found in pork if hogs have been fed on uncooked garbage. Despite the requirement by all states that any garbage fed to hogs must be cooked, inadequate heat treatment is still a possibility. If viable trichinae are present in pork, the parasite can infect humans, too, resulting in the condition called *trichinosis*. Trichinae usually can be killed by holding frozen meats in storage at temperatures no higher than 5°F for 20 days, by heating fresh pork to 170°F or hams to 160°F, or by heat processing for a period of time at 137°F internal temperature.

Freeze-drying Process of drying frozen foods.

Inspection of all meat carcasses crossing state lines is required by law. The round inspections stamp, bearing the number of the inspector and the message "U.S. Inspected and Passed," is imprinted on each primal cut.

Trichinosis Illness caused by the presence of viable *Trichinella spiralis*, a parasite sometimes found in pork and transmitted to humans if pork is heated inadequately.

Grading by federal personnel is optional, but meat indicating USDA Prime or other federal grade must be graded by federal personnel and meet the criteria established for the imprinted grade.

Grading

Unlike inspection, which is mandatory, grading is done at the discretion of meat packers who may elect any of three options: (1) federal grading, (2) packer grading, or (3) no grading. If federal grading is the choice, federal graders are hired by the packers to classify the meat according to government specifications into the appropriate federal grade. Occasionally, packers may wish to use their own grading system, a practice seen most commonly in the marketing of hams under the packers' grade names. The chief value of grading for the consumer is as a guide to meat quality. However, the range of quality in some grade categories still makes it useful to be able to make educated choices within the grade.

Beef The grades for beef have been established by the U.S. Department of Agriculture, the federal unit also responsible for administration and enforcement of federal meat grading standards. The descriptions of the characteristics required in each grade have been altered occasionally, with the result that the U.S. Choice grade, the grade commonly available to consumers in the markets, encompasses a wide range of quality. Although the grade designation is helpful in this case, consumer knowledge of quality is essential to making the best choices within the grade.

The top grade of beef is U.S. Prime (Table 9.2); restaurants are the primary market for this grade. If beef achieves this grade, the shield-shaped grade marker will show this in a continuously repeating pattern imprinted by a roller, which repeats the grade stamp along the entire length of the carcass. A similar stamping is done for the USDA Choice and other grades. Because of the continuous strip of grading symbols, many retail cuts will have at least a portion of the shield showing on the outer side of the cuts.

The regulations for establishing beef grades were revised most recently by the U.S. Department of Agriculture in 1976, with the regulations stipulating quality and yield as the criteria for grading. The quality is assessed on the following factors: texture of the lean, marbling, and overall palatability. The yield evaluation is an assessment of the usable meat in relation to the waste from fatty deposits and the ratio of muscle to bone. The overall grade established for a specific carcass is based on a composite score for quality and yield.

Table 9.2 U.S. Department of Agriculture Grades for Beef, Veal, Lamb, and Pork

Beef	Veal	Lamb	Pork
Prime	Prime	Prime	U.S. No. 1
Choice	Choice	Choice	U.S. No. 2
Good	Good	Good	U.S. No. 3
Standard	Standard	Utility	U.S. No. 4
Commercial	Utility	Cull	Utility
Utility	Cull		
Cutter			
Canner			

Sides of beef inspected and graded by federal personnel carry the round inspection stamp at points that will mark each of the prime cuts. The shield-shaped grade stamp is imprinted in a continuous strip by running an inked roller down the carcass.

Approximately 6.5 percent of the carcasses now receive a grade of USDA Prime, and 68.5 percent are graded USDA Choice. Obviously, there is a wide range of quality and yield within the USDA Choice grade because it involves such a large share of the total carcasses brought to market.

Occasionally, USDA Good beef may be found in retail outlets. The carcasses graded in this category, as well as USDA Prime, USDA Choice, and the lower grade, USDA Standard, are from animals considered by graders to be satisfactorily young, while USDA Commercial is a grade reserved for very mature animals. Usually, the carcasses graded USDA Standard or lower are used in the production of various meat products by the meat processing industry. These meats are as nourishing as higher grades of beef, but they are better suited for consumption when incorporated in ground meat products, such as frankfurters and cold cuts, rather than being prepared in meat recipes commonly used in the home.

Pork Pork considered to be acceptable for the consumer market is graded from the high U.S. No. 1 to U.S. No. 4, grades that are based more on yield than on quality distinctions, because there are only minimal differences between carcasses for palatability. The grade is of use in the wholesale market because it indicates the relative yield of the four major lean cuts, but the grade designation is not evident in the retail meat case. Soft and watery pork is rated only as USDA Utility, considered to be an unacceptable rating for the consumer market.

Lamb The quality of lamb varies far more than pork does, despite the fact that both species generally are marketed at a much younger age than beef.

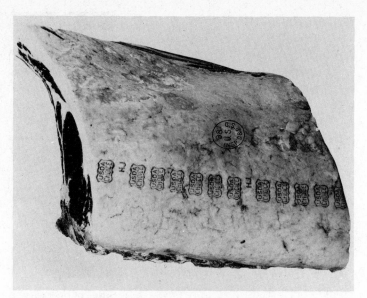

Beef rib (primal cut) is graded as U.S. Choice because of its relatively heavy covering of fat, as well as marbling within the muscles. Note the single inspection stamp on the primal cut and the repeating shield-shaped imprint for the grade.

Lamb has five quality grades (USDA Prime through USDA Cull), as shown in Table 9.2. Mutton begins with USDA Choice as the top grade. The yield designations range from 1 to 5, with the rating being determined by the amount of fat covering the outside of the carcass and the fat deposited inside.

Selection and Care

Decisions regarding choice of meat cuts begin with the planning of the menu. The amount of time available for preparation and the amount of money for meat in the food budget are two important concerns when selecting meats. A general way of looking at meats in relation to these two factors is to classify meats into tender and less tender cuts. The tender cuts often require little preparation time, but usually are comparatively costly; the less tender cuts are best when prepared using a long cooking period, but they usually cost less than the tender cuts. Persons working outside the home may decide against buying less tender cuts unless they can use a slow cooker or they can cook the meat on the weekend or other times when at home.

The classification of a particular cut is dependent upon the location on the carcass, the type of meat, and the grade. Generally, portions of the animal that receive little exercise will be more tender than will the cuts from areas that are used extensively by the animal. In fact, the tenderloin muscle receives almost no exercise, regardless of the type of animal, and is tender regardless of the grade of the carcass. In beef, the cuts from the shoulder, rump, and belly are classified as less tender, while the rib, short loin, and sirloin primal cuts are the sources of the tender cuts of beef. However, the rump of USDA

Prime beef is classified as tender, while USDA Choice and lower grades yield a rump classified as less tender.

The designation of tender or less tender for a particular part of the animal differs with the type of animal. Whereas the rump of beef usually is classified as less tender, the rump of pork is tender. In fact, pork usually is classified as tender, regardless of the cut. Veal, although it is from a very young animal, is only moderately tender because there is a reasonably high proportion of connective tissue in relation to the muscle proteins. There also is very little fat deposited in veal. Lamb, from the leg primal cut (with the exception of the shank) through the rib, is classified as tender. However, the shank of the leg, the neck, shoulder, and the breast of lamb are all considered to be less tender cuts, reflecting the heavy exercise in these areas.

Identification of Cuts Recognition of the various cuts is a tremendous help in making selections at the meat counter. The first point is to determine the type of meat, which can be done by looking at the size of the cuts, the color of the muscles, and the character of the fat. Beef cuts are the largest of the meats in the meat case, with veal being somewhat smaller, followed by pork, and finally lamb. The muscle color adds more information because beef is red, while veal is an extremely light to moderate pink, pork is a grayish-pink, and lamb is a dark red. Even the fat serves as a means of distinguishing between the meats. Beef has a hard fat, which usually is white, but may begin to assume a yellowish overtone in very mature beef. Veal has very little fat, and what fat there is will have a pink overtone. Pork fat is the softest of the fats, and it has a somewhat pink color. Lamb fat is the hardest of the fats and is quite white.

Primal Cuts First cuts (wholesale cuts) to provide large sections, yet small enough to be handled by the butcher.

Recognition of cuts needs to be developed at two levels—the primal cuts and the retail cuts. The *primal cuts* are the first cuts made on each half of the carcass. Primal cuts are designated for the various meat animals in Figures 9.1 through 9.4. Note that more primal cuts are made in beef than are made in the smaller animals. This is done so that the butcher can handle a primal cut; beef cuts comparable to those in pork would be so heavy that they would be very difficult for the butcher to manage.

The National Live Stock and Meat Board has assumed the responsibility for developing the terminology for the primal cuts and also for standardizing the retail cuts. The terms for the primal cuts are

Beef	*Veal*	*Pork*	*Lamb*
Chuck	Shoulder	Jowl	Shoulder
Rib	Rib	Boston shoulder	Rib (hotel rack)
Short loin	Loin	Loin	Loin
Sirloin	Sirloin	Leg	Sirloin
Round	Round	Spare ribs	Leg
Tip	Breast	Picnic shoulder	Breast
Flank	Shank	Foot	Shank
Short plate			
Brisket			
Fore shank			

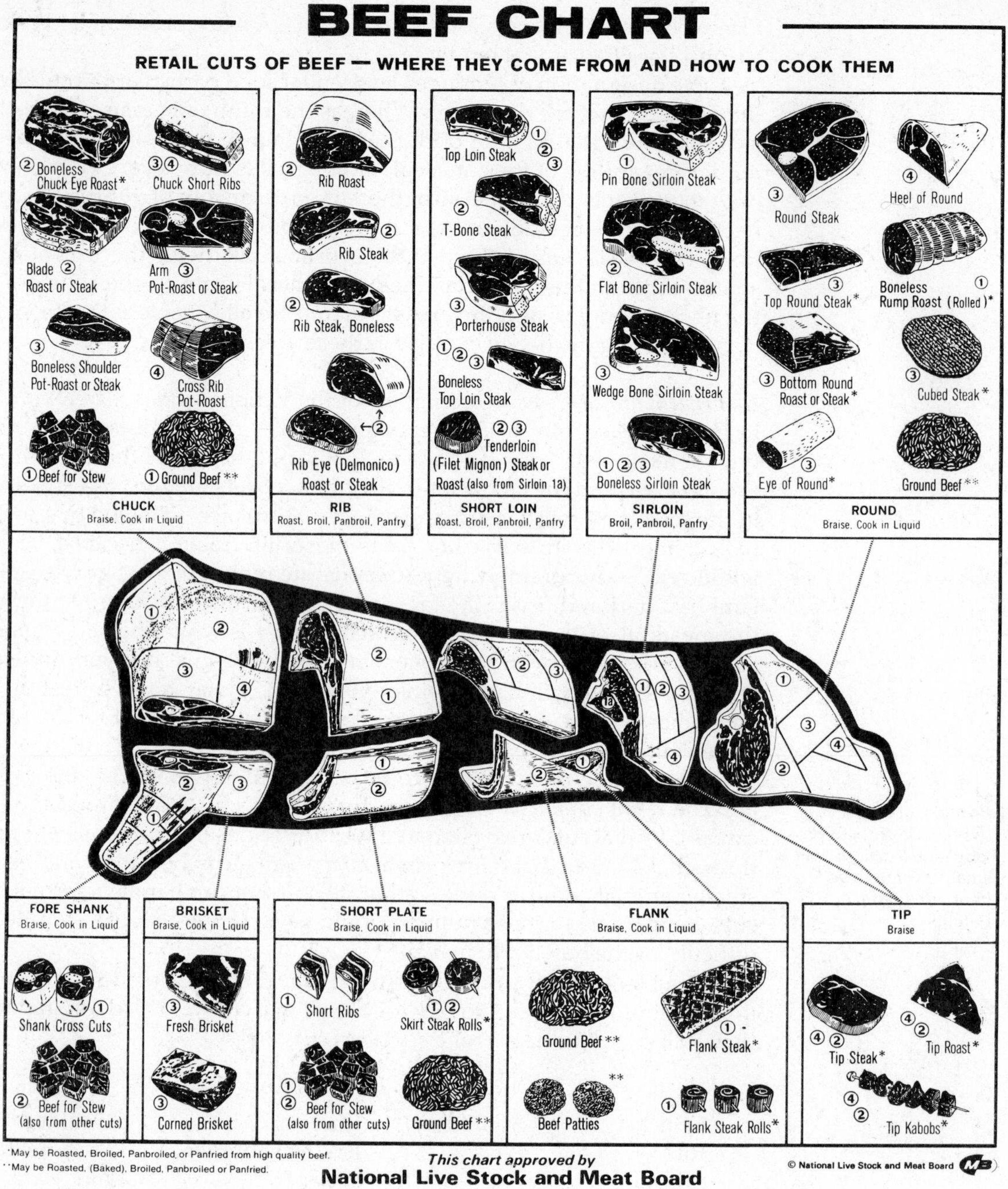

BEEF CHART

RETAIL CUTS OF BEEF — WHERE THEY COME FROM AND HOW TO COOK THEM

Figure 9.1 Primal and retail beef cuts.

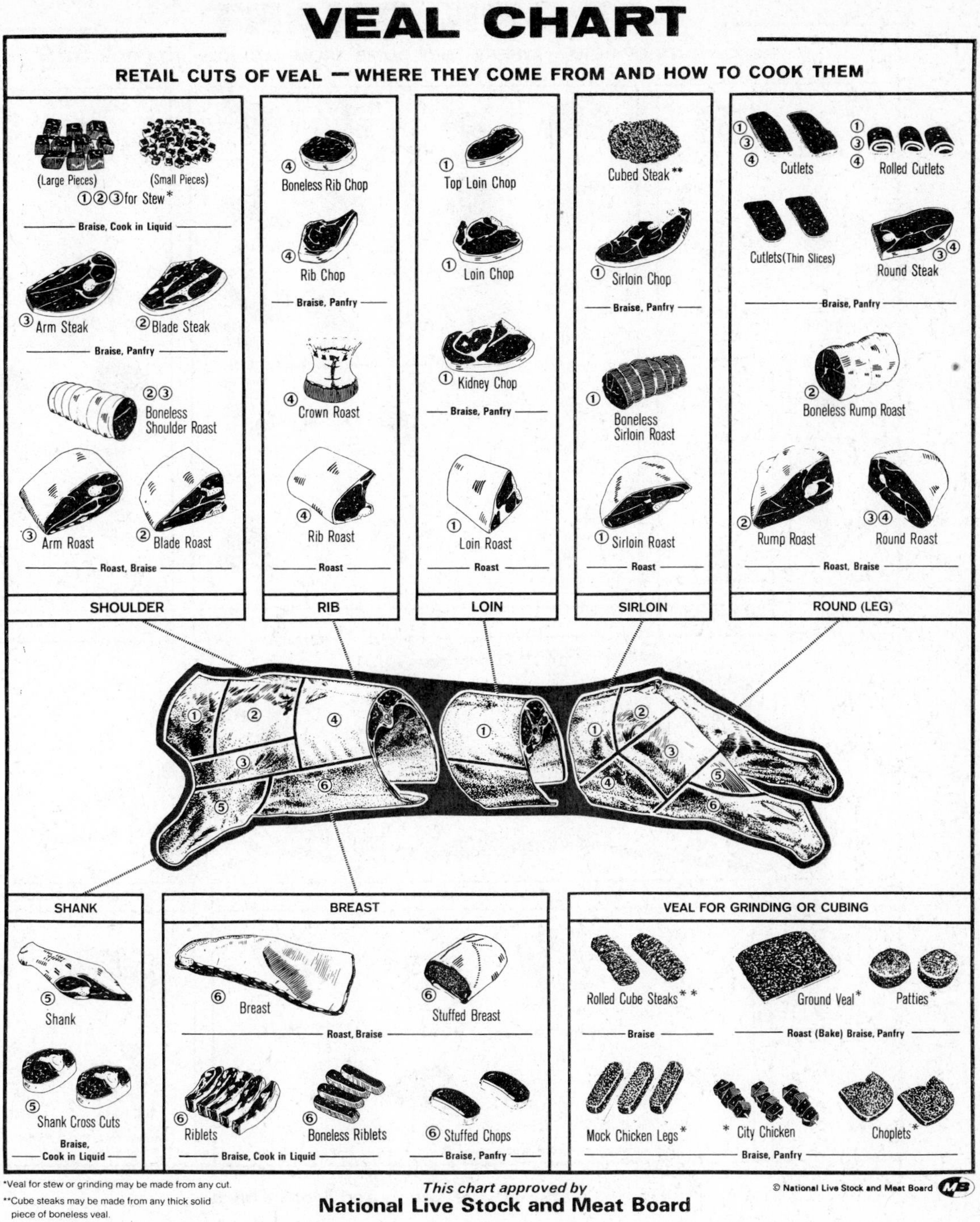

VEAL CHART

RETAIL CUTS OF VEAL — WHERE THEY COME FROM AND HOW TO COOK THEM

SHOULDER

(Large Pieces)   (Small Pieces)
①②③ for Stew*

— Braise, Cook in Liquid —

③ Arm Steak   ② Blade Steak

— Braise, Panfry —

②③ Boneless Shoulder Roast

③ Arm Roast   ② Blade Roast

— Roast, Braise —

RIB

④ Boneless Rib Chop

④ Rib Chop

— Braise, Panfry —

④ Crown Roast

④ Rib Roast

— Roast —

LOIN

① Top Loin Chop

① Loin Chop

① Kidney Chop

— Braise, Panfry —

① Loin Roast

— Roast —

SIRLOIN

Cubed Steak **

① Sirloin Chop

— Braise, Panfry —

① Boneless Sirloin Roast

① Sirloin Roast

— Roast —

ROUND (LEG)

① ③ Cutlets   ① ③ ④ Rolled Cutlets

Cutlets (Thin Slices)   ④ Round Steak

— Braise, Panfry —

② Boneless Rump Roast

② Rump Roast   ③④ Round Roast

— Roast, Braise —

SHANK

⑤ Shank

⑤ Shank Cross Cuts

Braise, Cook in Liquid

BREAST

⑥ Breast   ⑥ Stuffed Breast

— Roast, Braise —

⑥ Riblets   ⑥ Boneless Riblets   ⑥ Stuffed Chops

— Braise, Cook in Liquid —   — Braise, Panfry —

VEAL FOR GRINDING OR CUBING

Rolled Cube Steaks **   Ground Veal*   Patties*

— Braise —   — Roast (Bake) Braise, Panfry —

Mock Chicken Legs*   * City Chicken   Choplets*

— Braise, Panfry —

*Veal for stew or grinding may be made from any cut.

**Cube steaks may be made from any thick solid piece of boneless veal.

This chart approved by
National Live Stock and Meat Board

© National Live Stock and Meat Board (MB)

Figure 9.2 Primal and retail cuts of veal.

PORK CHART

RETAIL CUTS OF PORK — WHERE THEY COME FROM AND HOW TO COOK THEM

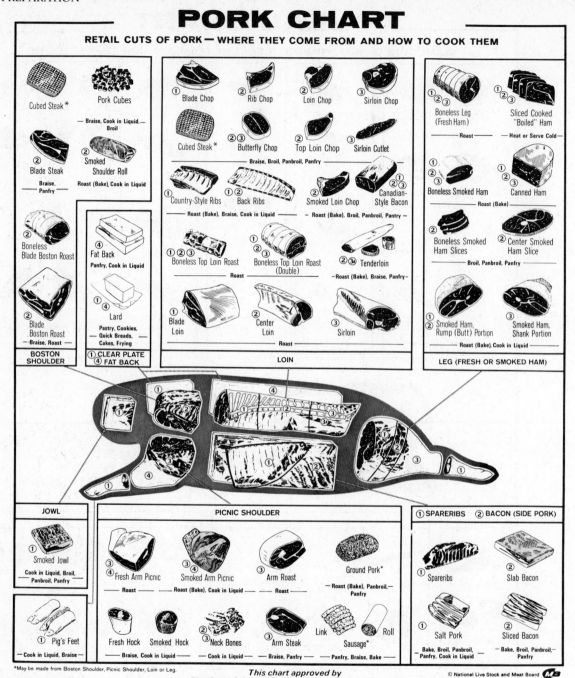

BOSTON SHOULDER

Cubed Steak*

Pork Cubes

— Braise, Cook in Liquid,— Broil

② Blade Steak

Braise, Panfry

Smoked Shoulder Roll

Roast (Bake), Cook in Liquid

② Boneless Blade Boston Roast

② Blade Boston Roast

—Braise, Roast—

① CLEAR PLATE ④ FAT BACK

④ Fat Back

Panfry, Cook in Liquid

①④ Lard

Pastry, Cookies, Quick Breads, Cakes, Frying

LOIN

① Blade Chop

② Rib Chop

② Loin Chop

③ Sirloin Chop

Cubed Steak*

② ③ Butterfly Chop

② ③ Top Loin Chop

③ Sirloin Cutlet

— Braise, Broil, Panbroil, Panfry —

① Country-Style Ribs

① ② Back Ribs

② ③ Smoked Loin Chop

② ③ Canadian-Style Bacon

— Roast (Bake), Braise, Cook in Liquid —   — Roast (Bake), Broil, Panbroil, Pantry —

① ② ③ Boneless Top Loin Roast

① ② ③ Boneless Top Loin Roast (Double)

② ③④ Tenderloin

—Roast—   —Roast (Bake), Braise, Panfry—

① Blade Loin

① ② Center Loin

③ Sirloin

—Roast—

LEG (FRESH OR SMOKED HAM)

① ② ③ Boneless Leg (Fresh Ham)

① ② ③ Sliced Cooked "Boiled" Ham

—Roast—   —Heat or Serve Cold—

① ② ③ Boneless Smoked Ham

① ② ③ Canned Ham

— Roast (Bake) —

② Boneless Smoked Ham Slices

② Center Smoked Ham Slice

— Broil, Panbroil, Panfry —

① ② Smoked Ham, Rump (Butt) Portion

③ Smoked Ham, Shank Portion

— Roast (Bake), Cook in Liquid —

JOWL

Smoked Jowl

Cook in Liquid, Broil, Panbroil, Panfry

① Pig's Feet

— Cook in Liquid, Braise —

PICNIC SHOULDER

④ Fresh Arm Picnic

③④ Smoked Arm Picnic

③ Arm Roast

Ground Pork*

— Roast —   — Roast (Bake), Cook in Liquid —   — Roast —   — Roast (Bake), Panbroil,— Panfry

Fresh Hock

Smoked Hock

② ③ Neck Bones

③ Arm Steak

Link / Roll Sausage*

— Braise, Cook in Liquid —   — Cook in Liquid —   — Braise, Panfry —   — Panfry, Braise, Bake —

① SPARERIBS ② BACON (SIDE PORK)

① Spareribs

② Slab Bacon

① Salt Pork

② Sliced Bacon

— Bake, Broil, Panbroil, Panfry, Cook in Liquid —   — Bake, Broil, Panbroil, Panfry —

*May be made from Boston Shoulder, Picnic Shoulder, Loin or Leg.

This chart approved by
National Live Stock and Meat Board

© National Live Stock and Meat Board

Figure 9.3 Primal and retail cuts of pork.

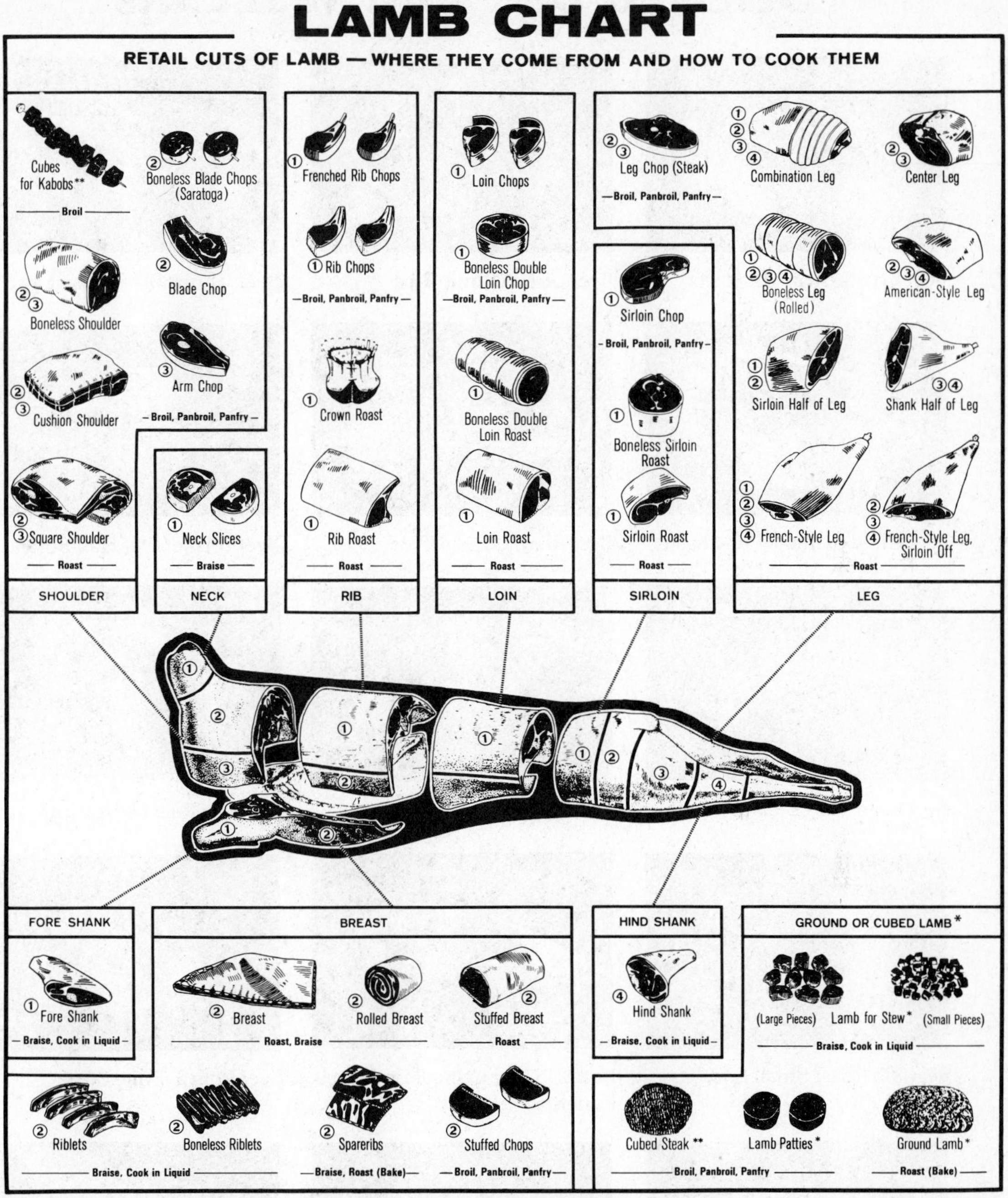

LAMB CHART

RETAIL CUTS OF LAMB — WHERE THEY COME FROM AND HOW TO COOK THEM

SHOULDER

Cubes for Kabobs**

Boneless Blade Chops (Saratoga)

Blade Chop

Arm Chop

— Broil, Panbroil, Panfry —

Boneless Shoulder

Cushion Shoulder

Square Shoulder

— Roast —

NECK

Neck Slices

— Braise —

RIB

Frenched Rib Chops

Rib Chops

— Broil, Panbroil, Panfry —

Crown Roast

Rib Roast

— Roast —

LOIN

Loin Chops

Boneless Double Loin Chop

— Broil, Panbroil, Panfry —

Boneless Double Loin Roast

Loin Roast

— Roast —

SIRLOIN

Sirloin Chop

— Broil, Panbroil, Panfry —

Boneless Sirloin Roast

Sirloin Roast

— Roast —

LEG

Leg Chop (Steak)

— Broil, Panbroil, Panfry —

Combination Leg

Center Leg

Boneless Leg (Rolled)

American-Style Leg

Sirloin Half of Leg

Shank Half of Leg

French-Style Leg

French-Style Leg, Sirloin Off

— Roast —

FORE SHANK

Fore Shank

— Braise, Cook in Liquid —

Riblets

— Braise, Cook in Liquid —

BREAST

Breast

Rolled Breast

Stuffed Breast

— Roast, Braise —   — Roast —

Boneless Riblets

— Braise, Cook in Liquid —

Spareribs

Stuffed Chops

— Braise, Roast (Bake) —   — Broil, Panbroil, Panfry —

HIND SHANK

Hind Shank

— Braise, Cook in Liquid —

GROUND OR CUBED LAMB*

(Large Pieces)   Lamb for Stew*   (Small Pieces)

— Braise, Cook in Liquid —

Cubed Steak**

Lamb Patties*

Ground Lamb*

— Broil, Panbroil, Panfry —   — Roast (Bake) —

* Lamb for stew or grinding may be made from any cut.

**Kabobs or cube steaks may be made from any thick solid piece of boneless Lamb.

This chart approved by
National Live Stock and Meat Board

© National Live Stock and Meat Board

Figure 9.4 Primal and retail cuts of lamb.

Selected Beef and Veal Cuts

Beef Chuck-Arm Pot-Roast

Beef Chuck Short Ribs

Beef Chuck Blade Roast

Beef Chuck 7-Bone Pot-Roast

Beef Shank Cross Cuts

Beef Brisket Flat Half Boneless

Beef Plate Skirt Steak Boneless

Beef Flank Steak

Beef Rib Roast Large End

Beef Rib Roast Small End

Beef Rib Steak Small End
Boneless

Beef Loin T-Bone Steak

Beef Loin Porterhouse Steak

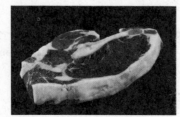
Beef Loin Flat Bone Sirloin
Steak

Beef Loin Tenderloin Roast

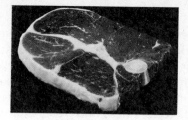

Beef Round Steak

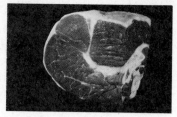

Beef Round Rump Roast

Veal Loin Chops

Pork and Lamb Cuts

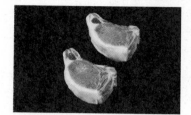

Pork Loin Rib Chops

Pork Loin Chops

Pork Spareribs

Pork Leg (Fresh Ham) Shank Portion

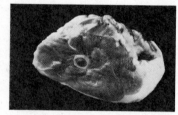

Pork Leg (Fresh Ham) Rump Portion

Smoked Pork Shoulder Picnic Whole

Lamb Shoulder Blade Chops

Lamb Shoulder Arm Chops

Lamb Breast

Lamb Loin Chops

Lamb Leg Sirloin Chops

Lamb Leg Frenched Style Roast

Retail Cuts Meat cuts available to consumers.

Within each of the primal cuts, a number of *retail cuts* will be made to provide the cuts of meat available at the market. The bones in these cuts can serve as aids in identifying a specific meat cut, for the bones from various parts of the carcass have unique and readily recognizable shapes. For example, the presence of a round bone clearly indicates that the cut is from either a front or back leg, and the ''T-bone'' is a backbone. These and other examples are presented in Table 9.3. When the location of the cut is known and the type of meat has been identified, the classification of the cut as a tender or less tender cut can be made readily. This classification is very important, for selection of a cooking technique appropriate to the tenderness of the cut is essential to success in meat cookery. Tender and less tender cuts can be very pleasing to eat when they are prepared correctly, while even the most tender of cuts can be disappointing when cooked improperly.

Making the Selection In most markets, decisions may be made between two or more packages of the same cut of meat. One obvious guide in making the

Table 9.3 Identification of Retail Cuts by Bone Shape

Name	Bone Shape			Cuts
Arm bone				Shoulder, arm cuts
Blade bone	(Near neck)	(Center)	(Near rib) 	Shoulder blade cuts
Back bone and rib bone				Rib cuts
Back bone (T-bone)				Short loin cuts
Hip bone	(Pin bone)	(Flat bone)[1]	(Wedge bone)[2] 	Hip (sirloin) cuts
Leg or round bone				Leg or round cuts
Breast and rib bones				Breast or brisket cuts

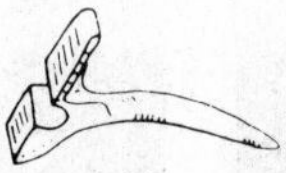

Source: Adapted from *Lessons on Meat*. National Live Stock and Meat Board. Chicago, Ill. 4th ed. 1974.
[1]Formerly part of ''double bone,'' but today the back bone usually is removed, leaving only the ''flat bone'' (also called ''pin bone'') in the sirloin steak.
[2]Wedge bone, which is near the round, may be wedge shaped on one side of sirloin steak while on the other side the same bone may be round.

selection is whether or not a specific package contains the approximate amount of meat needed to serve those to be fed. The following figures are a general guideline for the amount of meat to purchase, although individuals vary rather widely in just how much they eat at a meal:

Boneless cuts	¼ lb
Small bone	⅓ lb
Average bone	½ lb
Large bone	¾–1 lb

Look for packages with the smallest amount of bone in relation to meat when you are selecting among packages of the same cuts. Also note the size of the fatty deposits surrounding the edible portion of the cut being considered. Since both bone and fatty deposits generally are discarded, they can represent significant waste and expense in comparison with possibly a similar cut that has been trimmed more sparingly. Check the texture of the meat cuts you are considering. The finer the texture appears to be for a specific cut, generally the more tender will be the cut. A bright color characteristic of the particular type of meat is yet another clue to selecting optimum quality and freshness. However, sometimes real savings can be made by purchasing a package that has been marked down because it was cut the day before. This is recommended only when the meat will be cooked and served the same day it is purchased, for such meat will spoil more quickly than will freshly cut meats.

Storage   Meat is a highly perishable food unless it is kept refrigerated. The time elapsing between removal from the refrigerated meat counter in the store until the meat is refrigerated in the home should be kept to minimum to reduce the potential for spoilage by microorganisms. Also loosening the plastic wrap or even removing it to allow some air to contact the meat rather than creating an anaerobic, potentially dangerous storage situation is recommended. A loose covering over the surface of the meat prevents excessive drying in the refrigerator while allowing a small amount of drying of the surface to help in reducing microorganismal growth. The exception to this recommendation is the prepackaged, ready-to-eat cured and smoked products from meat processors. Even canned hams should be refrigerated unopened in their containers unless the package indicates refrigeration is not necessary. This precaution is needed because some canned hams have not undergone sufficient heat treatment during canning to permit safe storage at room temperature.

Many refrigerators have a special meat compartment that should be maintained at between 35° and 40°F, preferably 35°F. If this is not available, the meat should be stored in the coldest part of the refrigerator for short-term storage (see Table 9.4). For somewhat longer periods, meats can be stored in the freezer section of the refrigerator. However, the freezer of a refrigerator does not sustain a temperature uniformly low enough for extended freezer storage. A separate freezer must be maintained at a maximum temperature of 0°F if meat is to be stored for the extended times suggested in Table 9.4.

Table 9.4 Storage Guide for Fresh, Processed, and Cooked Meats

Product	Storage Period to Maintain Quality	
	Refrigerator 35°–40°F (days)	Freezer 0°F (months)
Fresh Meats		
Roasts (beef and lamb)	3–5	8–12
Roasts (pork and veal)	3–5	4–8
Steaks (beef)	3–5	8–12
Chops (lamb and pork)	3–5	3–4
Ground and stew meats	1–2	2–3
Variety meats	1–2	3–4
Sausage (pork)	1–2	1–2
Processed Meats		
Bacon	7	1
Frankfurters	7	½
Ham (whole)	7	1–2
Ham (half)	3–5	1–2
Ham (slices)	3	1–2
Luncheon meats	3–4	Not recommended
Sausage (smoked)	7	Not recommended
Sausage (dry and semidry)	14–21	Not recommended
Cooked Meats		
Cooked meats and meat dishes	1–2	2–3
Gravy and meat broth	1–2	2–3

Source: Adapted from Meat and poultry care tips for you. *Home and Garden Bulletin* No. 174. U.S. Department of Agriculture. Washington, D.C. 1970. P. 7.

Selecting an Appropriate Cookery Method

The first decision to make in cooking is whether to use a dry heat or a moist heat method. For tender cuts of meat, dry heat is preferred, whereas less tender cuts need the long, slow cookery provided by moist heat methods. This distinction is based on the major protein components found in the tender versus the less tender cuts.

In tender cuts, the muscle proteins are the dominant consideration. Since muscle proteins are fairly soluble and tender prior to cooking, the heat will only serve to toughen the overall character of the meat by denaturing the muscle proteins. As a result, tender cuts of meat will become progressively less tender the longer they are cooked, because the muscle proteins draw closer and closer together as they denature. Roasting, broiling, pan broiling, pan frying, and deep-fat frying are the methods for dry heat cookery of meat.

On the other hand, the less tender cuts are dominated by a comparatively high content of collagen. A cookery technique that proceeds slowly and takes an extended period of time provides just the right circumstance for the collagen molecules to relax and release the individual gelatin strands. The extremely tender results of moist heat cookery on less tender cuts emphasize the merits of selecting this type of preparation. The two basic types of moist heat cookery are braising and cooking in liquid (also called stewing).

Regardless of the type of cookery method selected, tests for doneness are important guides to achieving a high-quality product. Tender cuts of meat are tested most accurately by using a meat thermometer to indicate the temperature on the interior of the meat. The final temperature for beef is dependent on personal preference. For rare beef, the internal temperature should be 140°F; for medium, 160°F; and for well done, the center of the meat should measure 170°F. Variations in doneness are also recommended for lamb, although the range is higher than for beef. Rare for lamb is recommended as being 170°F, for medium is 175°F, and well done is 180°F. The potential risk of viable trichinae mandates that pork should be cooked to an interior temperature of 170°F to allow a margin of safety. Hams that have not been heat treated during processing should be heated to at least 165°F and preferably 170°F.

Less tender cuts of meat are done when a fork can be inserted into them and removed easily. In all instances, this will mean that the meat has been cooked to well done. However, a thermometer is not necessary to determine this; the fork test is a convenient and sufficiently accurate means of determining doneness in home cookery.

The rate at which various meats will reach the desired end point varies somewhat from one piece of meat to another. Variations are due to the amount of bone, the amount of fat, and the dimensions of the cut. Of course, minor variations in temperature control during the cooking period will add to the possible variations in time needed for meat to be ready to serve. Despite these many influences, some guide is needed to help decide when the meat should be started for a meal. Timetables have been worked out for various meats, various cuts, and different cookery methods. These timetables are intended merely as guides. The foregoing tests for doneness should be applied (by using a thermometer or fork, depending on the cookery method being used) to ensure that the desired end result is achieved.

Dry Heat Methods

Roasting Roasting is an appropriate technique for large cuts of tender meat, such as a rib roast. Preparation by roasting is a very simple process, beginning with assembling the roast on a rack in a shallow pan and then inserting the thermometer so that the sensing portion is in the center of the roast, but touching neither bone nor fat. Rib roasts with the bone in can stand on their own bone structure rather than needing a rack to hold them out of the drippings, hence, the name "standing rib roast." The assembled meat, with its thermometer and roasting pan, is placed *without any cover* in the center of the oven and positioned so that the meat thermometer can be read quickly and easily while the meat is roasting. Since this is a dry heat method, no covering, not even an aluminum foil covering, should be used.

Roasting, a dry-heat method, requires that the meat be placed on a rack to keep the cut out of the collecting drippings while the meat is being roasted without a cover in the oven. Meats should be roasted until the thermometer inserted into the center of the roast indicates the degree of doneness desired.

The temperature used for roasting is influenced by the size of the roast. Small roasts ordinarily are roasted at 325°F, while large roasts are placed in ovens set at 300°F, the lower temperature being used to provide more uniform heat penetration through the large mass of muscle. When these comparatively low oven temperatures are used, meats show less drip loss, less shrinkage, increased juiciness, and more uniformity in heat penetration than are noted if meats are roasted in ovens between 425° and 450°F. The low temperatures also cause less spattering and burning, which eases the cleaning of the oven and roasting pan. Basting can be done during roasting, but this step is not at all necessary.

Roasting times can be calculated, based on the figures indicated in the timetable shown in Table 9.5. In addition to the actual roasting time, a standing time of between 10 and 20 minutes should be allowed at room temperature to allow the meat to become slightly firm for ease in carving.

Some people start to roast meat by searing the roast or browning it quickly on the surface in a 500°F oven, followed by roasting to done at 300°F. There is no apparent advantage to this technique; the disadvantages are greater fuel consumption and high drip and evaporative losses. This method is not recommended for these reasons.

Broiling Cooking by direct heat, usually at a distance of about 3 inches; fat is allowed to drain away from the meat.

Broiling *Broiling* is the only preparation utilizing direct heat to cook meat. Broiling may be done on a charcoal broiling unit or hibachi in which the heat comes from beneath, or it may take place in an oven or special broiler compartment. In either of these types of compartments, the heat comes from the top onto the upper surface of the meat. In a sense, charcoal broiling may be considered as "upside down" broiling.

Both approaches to broiling require tender cuts of meat an inch or more in thickness with the the thickness being uniform throughout the cut to be

Table 9.5 Timetable for Roasting

Cut	Weight (lb)	Oven Temperature (°F)	Interior Temperature When Removed from Oven (°F)	Approximate Cooking Time (min/lb)
Beef				
Standing rib	6–8	300–325	140 (rare)	23–25
			160 (medium)	27–30
			170 (well done)	32–35
	4–6	300–325	140 (rare)	26–32
			160 (medium)	34–38
			170 (well done)	40–42
Rolled rib	5–7	300–325	140 (rare)	32
			160 (medium)	38
			170 (well done)	48
Veal				
Leg	5–8	300–325	170 (well done)	25–35
Loin	4–6	300–325	170 (well done)	30–35
Rib (rack)	3–5	300–325	170 (well done)	35–40
Pork (fresh)				
Loin	5–8	325–350	170 (well done)	30–35
Shoulder, rolled	3–5	325–350	170 (well done)	40–45
Leg (ham), bone in	10–14	325–350	170 (well done)	25–30
Pork (cured)				
Ham (cook before eating)	10–14	300–325	160 (well done)	18–20
Ham (fully cooked)	10–14	325	130 (well done)	15
Lamb				
Leg	5–8	300–325	175–180 (well done)	30–35
Shoulder, rolled	3–5	300–325	175–180 (well done)	40–45

Source: Adapted from *Lessons on Meat*. National Live Stock and Meat Board. Chicago. 2nd ed. 1968.

broiled. Cuts thinner than this will become unpleasantly dry during broiling. Porterhouse, T-bone, club, and rib steaks of beef, cured ham slices, lamb chops, and bacon all broil well.

Oven broiling requires a special broiler pan that allows the fat to collect on the bottom, below a rack that serves the dual function of keeping the meat out of the drippings and also protects the collecting fat from the intense heat of the broiler unit. This type of broiler pan minimizes smoking of fat during

Broiling is done by placing the meat on a broiler pan directly under the broiler heat source in a range or on a rack directly above the coals when broiling over charcoal on a grill. This dry-heat method drains the fat from the meat constantly during the entire time this direct-heat method is being used.

broiling, and what is more important, sharply reduces the hazard of a fire in the broiler.

Since broiling is done by means of a rather intense, continuous heat, it is important that the entire surface of the meat remain at a uniform distance from the heat source. In other words, meats being broiled need to remain flat during the broiling period rather than curling up. When meat curls during broiling, pockets of fat collect on the surface and present a fire hazard; furthermore, the meat nearest the heat source is likely to burn, while the remainder will not yet be done. This entire problem can be avoided by *scoring* the edges of the steak at intervals of about an inch, being sure to cut entirely through the connective tissue surrounding the muscle without making a cut into the meat itself. These breaks in the connective tissue prevent the meat from curling due to the shrinkage of the connective tissue at the perimeter of muscle during broiling, and the meat remains flat.

Scoring Cutting the fat and connective tissue at intervals of about an inch to prevent curling of meat during broiling.

Usually the top surface of meat to be broiled is positioned about 3 inches from the heat source. However, if the meat is to be broiled until well done, the meat should be lowered a little to allow more time for heat to penetrate through the meat before the surface becomes too done. The meat is broiled on the first side until about half done, at which time the top surface is salted, if desired, and the cut is turned over. Then the second side is broiled until the desired degree of doneness is reached. The meat is not turned a second time during broiling. To maintain constant direct heat, most broilers must be operated with the door ajar.

When the cut being broiled is thick enough, a thermometer should be inserted from the side and parallel to the two cut surfaces so that the temperature in the center of the cut can be measured. However, this often is not feasible. The timetable for broiling (Table 9.6) serves as a guide in such instances, but the actual degree of doneness can be determined by making a small incision in the finished piece of meat.

To add flavor interest to meats to be broiled, the meat can be marinated for at least an hour before broiling. Acid fruit juices in a marinade can also

Table 9.6 Timetable for Broiling

Cut	Thickness (in.)	Approximate Total Cooking Time (min)	
		Rare	Medium
Beef			
Rib steak	1	15	20
	1½	25	30
	2	35	45
Club steak	1	15	20
	1½	25	30
	2	35	45
Sirloin steak	1	20	25
	1½	30	35
	2	40	45
Porterhouse steak	1	20	25
	1½	30	35
	2	40	45
Ground beef patties	1	15	25
Lamb			
Shoulder chops	1		12
	1½		18
	2		22
Rib chops	1		12
	1½		18
	2		22
Loin chops	1		12
	1½		18
	2		22
Ground patties	1		18

Source: Adapted from *Lessons on Meat.* National Live Stock and Meat Board. Chicago, Ill. 2nd ed. 1968.

Papain, a proteolytic enzyme obtained from papaya, is sometimes used to help tenderize less tender cuts of meat.

help to promote tenderness. Another treatment prior to broiling is adding meat tenderizer according to the package directions to less tender, less expensive cuts of meats. Papain, a proteolytic enzyme from papaya, often is the enzyme used. Unfortunately, this enzymatic digestion frequently results in a powdery surface texture.

Pan Broiling Both broiling and *pan broiling* are cookery methods resulting in a comparatively low fat content in the finished product, for in both these methods, the fat is removed from the meat as it drains out. Cuts that can be broiled can also be pan broiled. In addition, tender cuts of meat too thin for broiling can be pan broiled satisfactorily.

Success in pan broiling requires a heavy ungreased skillet so that the pan broiling can be done relatively slowly without burning the meat. During the preparation of meat by pan broiling, fat is removed from the pan as it drains from the meat. It is this removal of the collecting fat that differentiates pan broiling from pan frying. Unlike broiling, pan broiling is done by turning the meat several times with tongs to help achieve the desired degree of doneness without overheating the exterior surface and drying out the meat.

Pan Broiling Cooking meat in a skillet, being careful to keep removing the fat as it drains from the meat.

Pan Frying Cooking meat in a frying pan and allowing the fat to accumulate in the pan.

Pan Frying   Tender cuts of meat half an inch to an inch in thickness are suitable for *pan frying*. The requisite for successful pan frying is a heavy skillet with uniform heat conduction. This allow the meat to be fried uniformly and without burning before it is done to the desired end point. Preparation of meat for pan frying requires scoring the fat and connective tissue in the same fashion as is done for broiling and pan broiling. Then the meat is placed in the skillet containing just enough fat to keep the meat from sticking. Careful control of the temperature during frying is important to the quality of the fried product. If the heat is too intense, the fat draining from the meat will begin to smoke, irritating the eyes and leading to a burned flavor in the meat.

The principal difference between pan broiling and pan frying is the treatment of the fat released from the meat. In pan frying the fat is allowed to collect in the pan throughout the frying period. This results in the development of a suggestion of crispness on the surface of the fried meat and also a higher fat and calorie content in the meat when it is served. For persons concerned with reducing fat intake, pan frying is not as suitable for preparing tender cuts of meats as are broiling, pan broiling, or roasting.

Deep-Fat Frying   Deep-fat frying is the dry heat method employing enough fat to immerse the frying food completely in hot fat. Often this is done using a deep-fat fryer, but a deep pan on a thermostatically controlled heating element also may be used satisfactorily. Careful control of the temperature in deep-fat frying is very important, for if the fat is too hot, the food will be burned on the outside before the center is done. Fat that is too cool results in a prolonged cooking time, and the absorption of extra fat will give a greasy feel to the food. The temperature can be maintained reasonably well once the correct frying temperature (usually 350° to 375°F) has been reached if only a small amount of food is added at a time. If a large quantity is added, the cold food will cause the temperature to drop considerably, and it will require several minutes to reheat the fat to the correct frying temperature.

Deep-fat frying is used fairly commonly for frying chickens and fish. Only rarely are the red meats prepared in this fashion. However, bite-sized pieces of beef tenderloin or other tender beef steak sometimes are prepared in this general fashion as a beef fondue.

Care should be taken to blot food to eliminate extra water if chunks of beef or other items are to be deep-fat fried. This will reduce the foaming and splattering that can occur if hot fat and cool water come in contact. The quality of deep-fat fried foods is also enhanced by draining fried foods well and blotting on a paper towel before serving. This technique will also reduce the amount of fat consumed when deep-fat fried foods are served.

Moist Heat Methods

Braising Cooking meat slowly in a small amount of liquid in a covered pan until the meat is fork tender, usually a matter of 2 hours or more.

Braising   *Braising* is used very frequently in preparing less tender cuts of meat. This moist heat method sometimes is begun by browning the cut of meat thoroughly on all sides before adding a small amount of liquid and covering the pan for an extended period of simmering. The initial fast browning

Less tender cuts, such as round steak, short ribs, and chuck roast, become very tender when cooked for a long period of time by moist heat methods (braising or stewing).

gives the meat a pleasing color and develops a full flavor, both of which add to the palatability of the liquid as well as to the meat itself. Sometimes this initial browning is omitted which results in a satisfactory product, but one lacking the heightened color and flavor obtained by the browning.

During the simmering period, the liquid level needs to be checked occasionally and more liquid added to compensate for evaporation that has taken place. If the simmering is being done on the range top, the heat needs to be adjusted very low, and the pan should be equipped with a lid that fits snugly. Even with these precautions, evaporation will occur during the 2 or 3 hours of simmering needed to achieve the desired degree of tenderness. Braising is continued until a fork can be inserted and removed easily, which means that braised meats always are at the well-done stage.

One of the nice features of braising is that a variety of flavors can be introduced to add interest to the entree for the meal. For instance, tomatoes, such seasonings as thyme and basil, onions, and numerous other flavorful ingredients may be added to intermingle with the flavors of the meat during the long period of simmering. Also the acidity of tomatoes or other ingredients helps to promote the tenderizing of the meat. However, an extended simmering period still is necessary for the meat to reach the desired degree of tenderness.

Many different types of meat cuts are well suited to braising. Any cuts classified as less tender can be prepared very satisfactorily in this way. Veal, regardless of the cut, benefits from braising because the comparatively high proportion of collagen in the meat will be converted to gelatin, making veal that is extremely tender. The other benefit to veal that is braised is the added flavor, for veal itself has an extremely delicate, if not bland, flavor. Thick pork chops also should be braised to ensure that the interior reaches the necessary 170°F in the center before the chops are too dark and dry on the exterior.

Stewing (cooking in liquid). The other method categorized as moist heat cookery is stewing or cooking in liquid. Basically, braising and stewing are very similar methods, the primary difference being that stewed meats have enough liquid added to cover them, while braised meats have only enough liquid added to cover the bottom of the pan and keep the meat from sticking. The browning of meats to be stewed is optional, although often meats being made into stews are browned on all sides of the cubes prior to adding the water or other liquid. In most instances, the liquid used in stewing is water, often with a bouquet garni or selected seasoning being added to the water. Once the liquid is added, the temperature needs to be controlled to maintain a simmering temperature. Boiling will promote production of a slightly tougher product than will be the result of simmering. Somewhat less energy will be required to maintain the simmering temperature than is needed for boiling, which is an added advantage of temperature control.

Stewed meats are tested in the same way that they are for braising, that is, by inserting a fork and removing it to be sure that this can be done easily. Although the time will vary somewhat with the size of the piece(s) of meat being stewed, the usual stewing period is about 3 hours.

Often vegetables are added to meats being stewed. The size of the vegetables and types of vegetables will influence the time required to achieve the

Stewing, a moist-heat method, requires usually at least two hours to tenderize the meat, but this method permits imaginative use of herbs and spices.

desired degree of tenderness, but always the length of time for the vegetables will be far less than that for the meats. Therefore, the vegetables are added to the stewing meats fairly near the end of the stewing period to avoid overcooking the vegetables. Stews may be thickened, if desired. This is done by blending the thickening agent (usually flour) with some cold water until perfectly smooth before stirring this slurry into the stew containing the tender meat and vegetables. The entire stew then is heated, with thorough stirring, until the starch is gelatinized (see Chapter 7).

In addition to cubed stew meats, several of the variety meats are well suited to cooking in liquid. Tongue, kidney, heart, tripe, sweetbreads, and brains are all appropriate for this cookery technique. The times range from as long as 3 to 4 hours for beef heart and tongue to as little as 15 to 20 minutes for sweetbreads and brains. Smoked country hams and picnics, as well as corned beef, are suitable for cooking in liquid, the time required for the hams being approximately 20 to 30 minutes per pound. Smoked picnics and corned beef require about 45 minutes per pound.

POULTRY

Interest in reducing serum cholesterol levels, and possibly the incidence of heart attacks, and also the desire to reduce fat intake have spurred considerable gains in poultry consumption. From the standpoint of nutrition, poultry of all types can be recommended highly. Food budgets also benefit from the use of poultry, particularly chicken and turkey.

Classification

The types of poultry available most commonly in the United States include chickens, turkeys, ducks, and geese. Chickens are popular throughout the year, but turkeys are beginning to augment chickens in the markets at times far removed from the traditional holiday feasts. Each type of poultry has specific classes, and these are listed as follows:

Chickens

1. *Cornish game hen or Rock Cornish game hen.* Young chicken (either Cornish chicken or a cross between a Cornish and another breed) usually 5–7 weeks old and weighing a maximum of 2 pounds.
2. *Broiler or fryer.* Usually 9–12 weeks old.
3. *Roaster.* From 3–5 months old.
4. *Capon.* Castrated male, usually under 8 months old.
5. *Stag.* Male under 10 months old.
6. *Hen or stewing chicken.* Mature female less than 10 months old.
7. *Cock.* Mature male having coarse skin and toughened, darkened meat.

Chicken and other types of poultry are wise choices nutritionally because of their excellent protein and comparatively low fat content. The flavor blends well with many ingredients, including fruits, artichoke hearts, olives, or various nuts.

Turkeys

1. *Fryer-roaster turkey.* Usually under 16 weeks old.
2. *Young hen turkey.* Female, usually 5–7 months old.
3. *Young tom turkey.* Male, usually 5–7 months old.
4. *Yearling hen turkey.* Female under 15 months old.
5. *Yearling tom turkey.* Male under 15 months old.
6. *Mature or old turkey.* More than 15 months old.

Ducks

1. *Broiler or fryer duckling.* Usually under 8 weeks old.
2. *Roaster duckling.* Usually under 16 weeks old.
3. *Mature or old duck.* Usually over 6 months old.

Geese

1. *Young goose.* Tender flesh, windpipe easily dented.
2. *Mature or old goose.* Toughened flesh, hardened windpipe.

Shopping for Poultry

Poultry must be inspected by the appropriate federal or state inspectors before interstate and intrastate marketing can commence. These inspectors check according to the guidelines for wholesomeness of poultry outlined in the Wholesome Poultry Products Act of 1968. Grading often follows inspection, with the federal grade standards serving as the usual basis for evaluating quality. Under federal guidelines, poultry may be graded as U.S. Grade A, U.S. Grade B, and U.S. Grade C. However, the U.S. Grade A is the grade commonly seen in the markets. This grade is based on a good overall appearance denoting good conformation and meatiness, a well-developed layer of fat in the skin, and skin virtually free of defects. The lower two grades sometimes may be sold on the retail market, but their grade usually is not displayed. Common use of the lower grades is in processed poultry products.

Shoppers must decide whether to buy whole fowl or part(s). In the case of chickens, those that have been cut up cost more than do those that are purchased whole. However, some time is saved by not having to cut the pieces. For people who have a strong preference for certain parts, the purchase of only those parts may be satisfactory, though more costly than buying the entire fowl. The breast is the most expensive part, followed in decreasing order by the thighs, drumsticks, and wings.

The ratio of muscle to bone varies a good deal with the type of poultry being selected, which makes the amount of poultry to purchase sometimes puzzling. Usually, a whole Cornish hen is served as a single portion, which may be really more than some people desire unless the hen is quite small. For people with light appetites, half a Cornish hen is quite adequate. Similarly, other types of poultry may require a fairly heavy portion to provide enough meat if the fowl has a high ratio of bone to meat. Examples of the amount to allow per serving of various poultry choices are given in Table 9.7.

Table 9.7 Suggested Quantities of Poultry Needed per Serving

Type	Purchasing Guide
Turkey	Just less than ½ lb
Duckling	More than ½ lb
Goose	More than ½ lb
Chicken	
Barbecuing or broiling	¼ chicken (2½-lb chicken)
Frying	½ lb

Storage

Particular care is necessary when storing poultry because microorganisms grow readily, particularly on the surfaces of the body cavity. Refrigeration just as soon as possible after purchase is extremely important to keep potential hazards to an absolute minimum. Table 9.8 outlines satisfactory storage periods in the refrigerator and the freezer.

Much of the poultry purchased is in the frozen form. Ideally, this poultry will be thawed completely just when preparation is ready to begin. For a small bird, thawing can be done within a reasonable length of time in the refrigerator, although room temperature is significantly faster, as can be seen in Table 9.9. A convenient thawing technique used in many homes today is intermittent heating and standing time provided by use of a microwave oven. Other methods involve immersing the poultry (in a watertight bag) in cold water, making frequent changes of water to help promote thawing. When it is possible to separate pieces and to remove the giblets and neck from the interior body cavity of whole fowl, thawing will be accelerated. A concern with room temperature thawing of very large birds is that the exterior portions will be at a temperature conducive to microorganismal growth before the interior is thawed. However, the heat during roasting or frying will be sufficient to kill these microorganisms.

Cookery

The various cookery methods described for meats also are utilized in preparing poultry. Whole fowl, particularly turkey and other large birds, frequently are roasted. In preparation for roasting, the giblets and neck are removed

Table 9.8   Refrigerator and Freezer Storage Periods for Poultry

Type of Poultry	Storage Period	
	Refrigerator 35–40° F (days)	Freezer 0° F (months)
Fresh Poultry		
Chicken	1–2	12
Turkey	1–2	12
Duck	1–2	6
Goose	1–2	6
Giblets	1–2	3
Cooked Poultry		
Pieces covered with broth	1–2	6
Pieces not covered	1–2	1
Cooked poultry dishes	1–2	6
Fried chicken	1–2	4

Source: Adapted from *Inspection, Labeling, and Care of Meat and Poultry.* Agriculture Handbook 416. U.S. Dept. Agriculture. Washington, D.C. 1971.

Table 9.9 Estimated Thawing Time for Chicken and Turkey

Frozen Poultry to Be Thawed	Time Required		
	Refrigerator[1]	Cold Water[2]	Cool Room[3]
Chickens			
Less than 4 pounds	12–16 hours	1–1½ hours	8–10 hours
4 pounds or more	1–1½ days	2 hours	12 hours
Turkeys			
4–12 pounds	1–2 days	4–6 hours	12–15 hours
12–20 pounds	2–3 days	6–8 hours	15–17 hours
20–24 pounds	3–4 days	8–12 hours	17–20 hours

Source: Based on Poultry in Family Meals. *Home and Garden Bulletin* No. 110. U.S. Dept. Agriculture. Washington, D.C. Rev. 1971. P. 7.
[1]Leave in original wrapping with poultry resting on a tray.
[2]Cover poultry, wrapped in watertight bag, with cold water. Change water frequently.
[3]Wrap bird in a least two thicknesses of heavy paper or two sacks and thaw at ambient temperature no warmer than 70° F.

from the interior cavity, and the carcass is scrubbed carefully on the outside and the interior. Any remaining pinfeathers or other feathers should be removed. Just before roasting is to begin, the body and neck cavities are stuffed, if desired, and roasting is started to avoid an opportunity for potentially hazardous development of microorganisms. Clearly, a turkey should not be stuffed and then refrigerated overnight before roasting. The stuffing should not be packed into the cavities vigorously, for dressing needs some room to expand. The skin flap is pulled over the neck cavity and skewered to hold the dressing inside.

The trussed turkey can be roasted particularly satisfactorily if it is held inverted in a V-shaped rack placed in a shallow pan to catch the drippings. The turkey and pan are placed on the oven rack, located usually at the bottom position so that the turkey will be fairly well centered for good heat circulation. A meat thermometer placed in the dressing makes it easy to tell when the turkey is done, for the temperature in the dressing should reach 165°F. In roasting unstuffed turkeys, the thermometer needs to be positioned with the sensing device in the center of the thigh, at which position the temperature indicating doneness is 185°F. Timing of meals featuring roast turkey can be facilitated by calculating the approximate time required for roasting, according to weight. Guidelines are presented in Table. 9.10

Since roasting is a dry heat method, no cover is placed over the turkey, despite the fact that turkey roasting pans traditionally have a cover. Use of aluminum foil surrounding a turkey results in a moist heat approach to preparing the fowl, a situation in which the skin assumes a grayish pallor rather than the golden brown traditionally visualized with roast turkey. Even when the oven temperature is increased to 425°F to compensate for the insulating effect of the foil, this poor color remains a problem, and the energy required for roasting is increased significantly. The advantage is that oven splattering

The thermometer is placed in the thigh, but away from the bone, when a turkey is roasted without stuffing. The thigh temperature should reach 185°F. When stuffed, the thermometer is inserted into the middle of the dressing; roasting is continued until a temperature of 165°F is reached in the dressing.

is minimal, although splattering will occur if the foil is opened for the final phase of roasting as a means of achieving some browning. Fowl can also be prepared in a special clay pot that has a relatively tight lid. Again, this device steams rather than roasts.

One reason given by people electing to these moist heat cookery methods is that they feel that turkey is too dry when roasted. Indeed, turkey meat will be quite dry when roasted—if, and only if the turkey is roasted too long. When roasted to the correct final temperature, turkey is a very juicy meat. When overheated, the meat will be dry—even when moist heat is used.

Other dry heat meat cookery methods also may be used very successfully to prepare poultry unless the fowl is too mature and tough. Suitable methods include deep-fat frying, broiling, and frying. Oven frying is a variation of frying deserving mention as a means of saving time when preparing chicken. Pieces of chicken are prepared by washing them carefully, rolling in flour or crumbs, and then coating very lightly with oil or melted fat before placing them in a shallow baking dish. Baking is done at 400°F until done, with the pieces being turned once to promote uniform browning.

Very mature poultry needs to be prepared by moist heat methods. Although braising can be done, stewing is more common. Poultry for stewing may be left whole if a container sufficiently large is available; an option is to cut individual pieces before stewing. Use of a pressure saucepan or cooker

Table 9.10 Timetable for Roasting Poultry

Poultry Type	Ready-to-Roast Weight (lb)	Estimated Roasting Time at 325° F (hr)
Chickens		
Whole broilers, fryers,	1½–2½	1–2
roasters	2½–4½	2–3
Capons	5–8	2½–3½
Ducks	4–6	2–3
Geese	6–8	3½–4½
Turkeys	6–8	3–3½
	8–12	3½–4½
	12–16	4½–5½
	16–20	5½–6½
	20–24	6½–7½
Halves, quarters,		
pieces	3–8	2–3
Boneless roasts	3–10	3–4

Source: Adapted from Poultry in Family Meals. *Home and Garden Bulletin* No. 110. U.S. Dept. Agriculture. Washington, D.C. Rev. 1971. P. 10.

saves considerable time in stewing. Stewed poultry will be done when they are tender enough for a fork to be inserted easily. This usually requires about 2 hours.

FISH

Fish Cold-blooded aquatic animal, usually used as a term to designate those with fins, a backbone, skull, and gills.

Shellfish Subcategory of fish; equipped with shell or horny outer covering.

Mollusks Shellfish protected by an outer shell; scallops, clams, and oysters are common examples.

Crustaceans Shellfish covered by a horny protective layer; shrimp, lobsters, and crabs are familiar examples.

Fish have been swimming upstream for years in an attempt to gain a reasonable place in the nation's menus. Today the publicity encouraging the increased use of fish to replace meats, with the latter's high saturated fat and cholesterol content, has enhanced consumption of fish significantly. Nutritionally, fish generally are much lower in fat than the red meats and, consequently, are also lower in calories. The fat they do contain is high in polyunsaturates. From the perspective of cookery, fish have the advantage of usually being quick and easy to prepare.

Kinds of Fish

More than 240 varieties of fish and shellfish are available to consumers in different parts of the United States. In differentiating *fish* from *shellfish*, the former are defined as a cold-blooded aquatic animal equipped with fins, a backbone, skull, and gills for removing air from water, whereas the latter are equipped with a shell or horny outer covering. Fish are categorized according to their oil content (see Table 9.11); shellfish are divided into *mollusks* with shells (oysters, scallops, mussels, and clams) and *crustaceans* with horny outer coverings (shrimps, lobsters, and crabs).

Table 9.11 Approximate Fat Content of Selected Common Fish

Oily Species (6–20% oil or more)	Intermediate (2–6% oil)	Nonoily Species (less than 2% oil)
Chub, lake	Bass	Clams
Herring, sea	Buffalo fish	Cod
Mackerel	Carp	Haddock
Salmon, king	Crab	Halibut
Salmon, silver (medium red)	Oysters	Lobster
Salmon, sockeye (red)	Salmon, chum	Mullet
Sardines	Salmon, pink	Ocean perch
Smelt	Shrimp	Pike, lake
Swordfish		Pollock
Tuna, canned		Rockfish
Whitefish, lake		Scallops
		Sole
		Flounder
		Whiting

Source: Fisheries Marketing Bulletin. Bureau of Commercial Fisheries. FMB35-20M-61. P. 8. n.d.

Anadromous Fish living part of their lives in fresh water and part in salt water.

Fish may be obtained from fresh water or salt water, or they may spend part of their lives in fresh water and part in salt water (*anadromous*). Because of their differences in habitat, fish frequently are labeled as freshwater fish or saltwater fish. Both these water sources have the potential for being polluted, which can influence the safety of the fish obtained from them. Such pollution may be from natural causes, such as the red tide (see Chapter 17), which can cause paralytic shellfish poisoning at certain times of year. Industrial waste or improper sewage treatment may be prominent among the sources of contamination of both fresh and salt water.

Increasing consumption of fish for health reasons and concern for developing all possible food sources to meet the food needs of the burgeoning world population have stimulated considerable activity in developing food from the sea and also from fresh water. Fish farming is resulting in controlled production of selected fish, such as trout and salmon. However, this type of farming is in its infancy compared with the sophisticated approaches that have been developed for farming crops on land.

Inspection and Grading

The U.S. Department of Interior, through its Bureau of Commercial Fisheries, is the governmental unit responsible for the inspection and grading of fish (in contrast to the U.S. Department of Agriculture, which assumes these roles for meat and poultry). Inspection encompasses surveillance of the condition of the fish prior to processing and the conditions throughout the plant handling the fish. Since fish are very susceptible to spoilage, sanitation and temperature control are absolutely vital to maintaining acceptable microbiological limits. Inspection standards are directed toward these types of controls.

Grading of fish is done to identify whether the quality meets Grade A, B, or C standards. The top quality is Grade A. Grade B is of very acceptable quality, but more variation in size and more blemishes are acceptable in Grade B than in the higher grade. Grade C fish are nourishing and wholesome, but are of lesser quality than the two higher grades. Fish monitored and graded by the standards of the U.S. Department of the Interior will have a shield printed on their packaging stating U.S. Grade A or a shield announcing that the fish were packed under continuous inspection of the U.S. Department of the Interior.

Selection and Care

Fish can be very costly or quite inexpensive, depending on the type selected. Live lobsters air freighted to market are at the top end of the scale, while local catches usually are comparatively inexpensive. The difficulty of maintaining high quality in fresh fish has resulted in a broad frozen fish market as a means of maintaining excellent and safe fish during the marketing process. Because of the significant reduction in waste effected by freezing, frozen fish can be marketed at very competitive prices.

Dressed Fish Fish from which the gills, fins, head, tail, and entrails have been removed.

Filets Lengthwise pieces of fish free of the backbone and associated bones.

To select fresh fish, look for a shiny and unfaded skin, red gills, and clear eyes. The odor should be mild. If the fish has cut surfaces, these should look fresh and not dry. Frozen fish should be encased in airtight packaging and frozen solidly. If the fish can be seen in the package, look for a plump appearance rather than a spongy, somewhat desiccated look.

Fish may be prepared for market in several ways. *Dressed fish* are fish that have had the heads and tails, the scales, and the entrails removed, but the bones are still present. Filleting of fish to produce fish *filets* is done by strip-

CRITERIA FOR SELECTING FISH

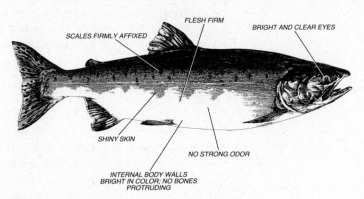

Visible criteria for selecting fish.

Fish filets are made by cutting along the backbone and lifting off the flesh intact.

Steak Cross-sectional slice of a uniform thickness.

ping the flesh lengthwise from the backbone. Fish *steaks* are simply cross-sectional slices from a large dressed fish, such as salmon. The recommended portion size for a serving of fish prepared in these various ways is

Dressed	½ lb
Filet	⅓ lb
Steaks	⅓ lb
Sticks	¼ lb
Canned	⅙ lb

For optimal quality, fresh fish should be refrigerated immediately after purchase and prepared the same day or at least the next day. If fresh fish is not to be used in three days, the fish should be frozen as soon as it is brought into the kitchen from the market. Frozen storage should be limited to an absolute maximum of six months, but the quality will be best if used within a pe-

Fish may be purchased whole (dressed), as a filet (upper row, left to right), as a roast, or as a steak (bone in).

riod of about three months. During storage, whether on shipboard when the fish is first caught or in the home, contamination begins in the slime of the skin, causing loss of firmness and color in the flesh beneath. Trimethylamine, a compound contributing heavily to the smelly odor of fish, is formed during storage unless great care is taken to regulate sanitation and temperature.

Fish Cookery

Fish have a limited amount of connective tissue, and even this connective tissue is more tender than that found in land animals. As a result, fish cookery basically becomes a problem of heating to a desirable serving temperature without causing the fish to become dry and tough. The protein will coagulate when the fish is hot enough to serve, and the flesh will tend to flake apart when cut with a fork. Beyond this point, continued heating will reduce the quality of the fish dish because the protein will continue to draw together

Fish, because of the limited quantity of connective tissue, can be cooked by dry-heat methods and heated just long enough to coagulate the flesh in the center. The addition of dill weed, green onion, and sesame seeds adds pleasing contrasts in flavor and texture.

more tightly, causing the flesh to be tougher and forcing liquid out, which reduces the juiciness. Optimum juiciness and tenderness are achieved by brief cooking.

Fish cookery is unusual in that either moist heat or dry heat methods can be used successfully. Baking requires the longest time of the various methods, possibly up to an hour, depending upon the size of the fish being baked. Broiling and oven frying (at 500°F) require approximately 15 minutes, assuming that the fish is close to an inch thick. Pan frying is slightly faster because of the efficiency of heating with the very hot fat. In fact, deep-fat frying usually requires between 3 and 5 minutes to achieve the desired end point when frying fish. Although sauce or seasonings can be placed on fish being baked, the other dry heat methods do not add flavors.

One of the reasons for using moist heat cookery is the possibility of adding a subtle flavoring to the fish. Poaching and steaming are favorite moist heat methods. Poaching is done by placing a single layer of fish in a large frying pan and barely covering them with a liquid, such as milk, water, or white wine. The fish are simmered until the flesh flakes readily when tested with a fork, which usually requires about 5 to 10 minutes. Steaming is done by placing the fish on a rack above boiling water and then covering the pan tightly to trap the steam around the fish. The test for doneness also is flaking with a

Shrimp (classified as crustaceans) and all types of fish can be prepared using moist-heat cookery methods to introduce flavor variations. Cooking times must be short to avoid toughening the flesh.

fork, and the steaming time is essentially the same as that required for poaching. Poaching is preferred by some people over steaming because of its potential for adding flavor, whereas steaming simply heats the fish and coagulates the protein without adding flavors.

TEXTURED VEGETABLE PROTEINS

Interest in developing textured vegetable proteins has been spurred in the past few years by a combination of factors, including the vegetarian movement, the comparatively high cost of meat, and anticipated food shortages in feeding the world's soaring population. The vegetable source of protein that has proven to have excellent potential for processing successfully in a variety of ways is the soybean. The amino acid profile of soy protein is the most complete of the vegetable proteins, which makes this bean a particularly appropriate choice from the standpoint of nutrition. Farmers find this a good cash crop because of its ease of growth and its ability to put nitrogen back into the soil, leaving the soil more fertile than before the soybeans were planted.

Several different types of products have been developed by food technologists from soybeans. Textured vegetable protein, also referred to by such synonyms as TVP and TSP (textured soy protein), can be used with considerable success as a meat extender to save meaningfully in the meat budget. Carlin et al. (1978) tested the levels of substitution that might be acceptable and found that up to 30 percent substitution of ground beef by TVP was ac-

Soybeans are a type of legume which, when dried and processed, can be made into a wide array of edible products, including textured meat extenders.

ceptable to consumers. In fact, substitution at this level is authorized in the school lunch program. Use of TVP in meat loaf resulted in increased thiamin content, reduced drip losses, and retention of fat. Although the soy protein does not contain as much fat as ground beef, the ability of TVP to absorb fat during the baking period resulted in comparable fat levels in substituted and unsubstituted baked meat loaves. It is this ability to absorb fat that contributes to the pleasing juiciness of ground beef products containing TVP.

Among the various commercial items developed with TVP, imitation bacon is one of the most successful. TVP ''bacon'' bits are popular additions to salads because of their crisp texture and baconlike flavor. Some fabricated meats have been made from TVP, but although these have found a market among people avoiding meats, the general public has not been very receptive to these items in their present level of development.

SUMMARY

Red meats (beef, veal, pork, and lamb), poultry, and fish are very important sources of protein in the diet. Meat cuts are comprised of muscle, connective tissue, fat, and bone. In muscle, the sarcoplasm is bound by the sarcolemma to make a muscle fiber in which are found myofibrils and their thick and thin myofilaments. The fibers are in bundles (fasciculi), each of which is encased in connective tissue (endomysium), and fasciculi are clustered and surrounded by the perimysium. Myosin, actin, actomyosin (in contracted muscle), and tropomyosin are important muscle proteins. Myoglobin and related pigments provide the color in meats. Connective tissue may be elastin or collagen; collagen can be converted to gelatin by a slow, long cooking period to tenderize meats. Fats add to the flavor and juiciness of meats. In addition to the fat and protein in meats, meats are excellent sources or iron and copper, as well as providing thiamin, riboflavin, and niacin.

Meat passes through rigor following slaughter, with the conditions at slaughter influencing the drop in pH occurring during rigor. The ease of spoilage of meats requires that careful sanitation and refrigeration be provided for all meats, but prime beef being aged for two to more than five weeks to heighten the flavor needs particularly well-controlled conditions. Curing, smoking, freezing, and even freeze-drying are techniques used for extending the shelf life of meats. Inspection by government inspectors is used to monitor meat packing to assure safety of meat supplies. *Trichinella spiralis,* a parasite for which pigs sometimes are hosts, is not detected by inspection and, hence, requires that pork be heated to 170°F internal temperature to assure the safety of the pork.

Grading of carcasses of beef, pork, and lamb can be done as an optional aid to consumers, whereas the inspection is legally mandatory. Beef is the most likely type of meat to be graded. This grading is based on palatability, texture, and marbling, factors that are considered to be quality, and upon yield.

Identification of cuts is important to consumers so that they will be knowledgeable about how the cut should be prepared. Carcasses are cut into primal cuts, and these large cuts are cut into the retail cuts. Consumers can deduce much about the identity of a cut by examining the color of the meat, the size and shape of the bone, and the type of fat. Meat can be stored up to about five days (depending on the cut) in the refrigerator, but cuts should be frozen if they will be held longer than the recommended storage time.

The first decision in meat cookery is whether to use one of the moist heat or one of the dry heat methods, the former being recommended specifically for less tender cuts of meat, most veal cuts, and thick pork chops. Dry heat cookery is the appropriate category for most other cuts. Dry heat cookery methods include roasting, broiling, pan broiling, pan frying, and deep-fat frying. Braising and stewing (cooking in liquid) are the two moist heat methods. These moist heat methods require an extended cooking period to form gelatin from collagen and thus achieve the desired, tender entree.

Poultry (chickens, turkeys, ducks, and geese) are generally tender, although old fowl may be quite tough. Inspection divides poultry into U.S. Grades A, B, or C. Excellent refrigeration and thorough cleaning and rinsing of carcasses of poultry are other important measures to assure safety when poultry reaches consumers.

Roasting is an appropriate method for preparing turkeys and other fowl, with the exception of less tender, old poultry, such as stewing hens. Stewing or cooking in liquid is necessary to tenderize these fowl. Roasting should be done without any type of covering until the thermometer indicates 165°F in the dressing or 185°F in the thigh.

Fish (fresh water, salt water, or anadromous) may be categorized as fish (fins and gills) or shellfish, which are subdivided further into mollusks and crustaceans. Inspection and grading are the responsibility of the U.S. Department of the Interior's Bureau of Commercial Fisheries. Three grades (A, B, or C) of fish have been established.

Fish are dressed and marketed usually as the fresh or frozen product, sometimes being cut into steaks or into filets. Careful cleaning and controlled temperature storage are vital to the quality and safety of fish as they reach the marketplace and the consumer. The minimal amount of connective tissue in fish dictates that fish need to be heated just enough to reach the desired serving temperature; longer heating toughens fish. Either moist heat or dry heat methods can be used to prepare fish.

Textured vegetable proteins (TVP) can be spun using soy protein. Several acceptable products have been developed, one of these being imitation bacon bits and another being the TVP used as a meat extender with ground beef at levels up to 30 percent.

Selected References

Agricultural Research Service. *Meat Research*. Agriculture Information Bulletin. No. 375. U.S. Dept. Agriculture. Washington, D.C. 1976.

Asghar, A. and R. L. Henrickson. Chemical, biochemical, functional, and nutritional characteristics of collagen in food systems. *Adv. Food Res. 28:* 231. 1982

Bloch, B. *Meat Board Meat Book*. McGraw-Hill. New York. 1977.

Bramblett, V. D. et al. Effect of temperature and cut on quality of pork roast. *J. Am. Diet. Assoc. 57:* 132. 1970.

Bramblett, V. D. and G. E. Vail. Further studies on qualities of beef as affected by cooking at very low temperatures for long periods. *Food Tech. 18:* 245. 1964.

Carlin, A. F. et al. Destruction of trichina larvae in cooked pork roasts. *J. Food Sci. 34:* 210. 1969.

Carlin, F. et al. Texturized soy protein in beef loaves: Cooking losses, flavor, juiciness, and chemical composition. *J. Food Sci. 43:* 830. 1978.

Chang, S. S. and R. J. Peterson. Recent developments in flavor of meat. *J. Food Sci. 42:* 298. 1977.

Chant, J. L. et al. Composition and palatability of mechanically deboned meat and mechanically separated tissue. *J. Food Sci. 42:* 306. 1977.

Cornforth, J. F. et al. Evaluation of various methods for roasting frozen turkeys. *J. Food Sci. 47(4):* 1108. 1982.

Cunha, T. J. Eliminating excess fat in meat animals. In *Symposium on Fat Content and Composition of Animal Products.* NRC-NAS. Washington, D.C. 1976.

Deethardt, D. et al. Effect of electronic, convection, and conventional oven roasting on the acceptability of pork loin roasts. *J. Food Sci. 38:* 1076. 1973.

Dutson, T. R. and M. W. Orcutt. Chemical changes in proteins produced by thermal processing. *J. Chem. Ed. 61(4):* 303. 1984.

Fulton, L. and C. Davis. Cooking chicken and turkeys from the frozen and thawed states. *J. Am. Diet. Assoc. 64:* 505. 1974.

Forrest, J. C. et al. *Principles of Meat Science.* W. H. Freeman. San Francisco. 1975.

Giddings, G. G. Basis of color in muscle foods. *J. Food Sci. 42:* 288. 1977.

Glick, N. Bringing home (nitriteless) bacon. *FDA Cons. 13(4):* 25. 1979.

Holmes, Z. A. Factors affecting the acceptability of beef: Clues from bibliographic research. *J. Am. Diet. Assoc. 72:* 622. 1978.

Hultin H. O. Postmortem biochemistry of meat and fish. *J. Chem. Ed. 61 (4):* 289. 1984.

Jennings, T. G. et al. Influences of thickness, marbling, and length of aging on beef palatability and shelf-life characteristics. *J. Animal Sci. 46:* 658. 1978.

Kang, C. K. and E. E. Rice. Degradation of various meat fractions by tenderizing enzymes. *J. Food Sci. 35:* 563. 1970.

Khan, A. W. and W. W. Ballantyne. Post-slaughter pH variation in beef. *J. Food Sci. 38:* 710. 1973.

Korschgen, B. M. et al. Quality factors in beef, pork, and lamb cooked by microwaves. *J. Am. Diet. Assoc. 69:* 635. 1976.

Lechowich, R. V. et al. Role of nitrite in production of canned cured meat products. *Food Tech. 32(5):* 45. 1978.

Lee, Y. B. Modified sample preparation method for measuring meat tenderness by Kramer shear press. *J. Food Sci. 48(1):* 304. 1983.

Marsh, B. B. Basis of tenderness in muscle foods. *J. Food Sci. 42:* 295. 1977.

Moody, W. G. et al. Beef thawing and cookery methods. *J. Food Sci. 43:* 834. 1978.

National Academy of Sciences. *Effects on Human Health of Subtherapeutic Use of Antimicrobials in Animal Feeds.* National Academy Press. Washington, D.C. 1980.

National Live Stock and Meat Board. *Lessons on Meat.* National Live Stock and Meat Board. Chicago, 4th ed. 1975.

Odland, D. and C. Adams. Textured soy protein as a ground beef extender. *Family Econ. Review (Summer):* 3. 1976.

Shults, G. W. et al. Effects of sodium nitrate and sodium nitrite additions and irradiation processing variables on color and acceptability of corned beef briskets. *J. Food Sci. 42:* 1506. 1977.

Stadelman, W. J. Some factors influencing tenderness, flavor, and nutritive value of chickens. *Food Tech. 32(6):* 80. 1978.

Viser, R. Y. et al. Effect of degree of doneness on tenderness and juiciness of beef cooked in the oven and in deep fat. *Food Tech. 14:* 193. 1960.

Wang, P. L. et al. Characteristics of frozen fried chicken products obtained from a retail store. *J. Food Sci. 41:* 453. 1976.

Weatherley, A. H. and B. M. Cogger. Fish culture: Problems and prospects. *Sci. 197:* 427. 1977.

Wekell, J. C. et al. Implications of reduced sodium usage and problems in fish and shellfish. *Food Tech. 37(9):* 51. 1983.

Study Questions

1. What federal departments are responsible for inspecting the following when they enter interstate commerce: (a) beef, (b) pork, (c) lamb, (d) veal, (e) poultry, (f) fish, and (g) shellfish?
2. Identify the types of connective tissue. What means can be employed for tenderizing meats containing a high percentage of connective tissue? What is the significance of connective tissue in fish cookery?
3. Describe the process of aging meat, including the suitability of various meats for aging.
4. Why is inspection of meat mandatory and what types of characteristics are inspected?
5. Describe the grading process and what is meant by the grades for various types of meats.
6. Outline the process of preparing meats by each of the following cookery methods and identify several cuts that can be cooked appropriately by each: (a) broiling, (b) braising, (c) frying, (d) roasting, (e) pan broiling, (f) stewing, (g) deep-fat frying.
7. Compare the results of cooking fish a very long time with the braising of a pot roast for the same length of time. Why are the results so different?

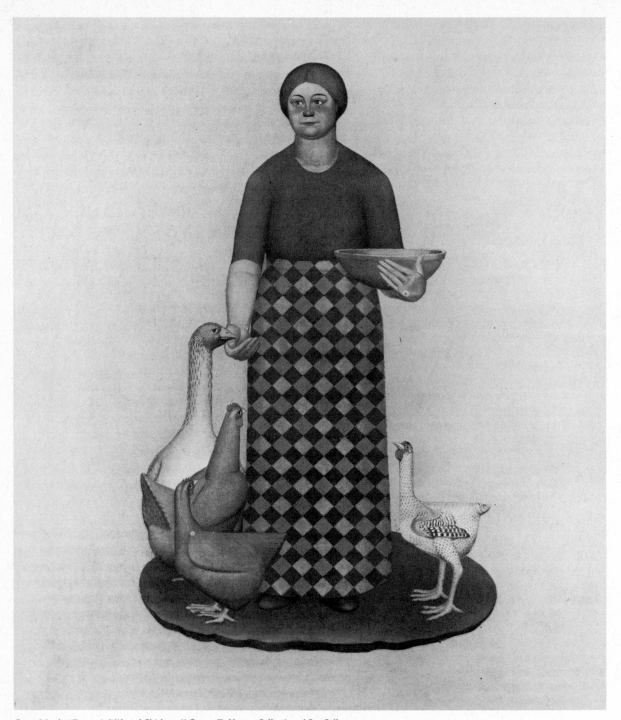

Grant Wood, "Farmer's Wife and Chickens." George T. Henry, Collection of Coe College.

CHAPTER 10

PROTEINS: EGGS

INTRODUCTION

If only one word could be used to describe eggs in food preparation, that word well could be "versatile," for eggs are used not only in simple egg dishes, but also in many other complex food systems. Often eggs are prepared alone, perhaps fried, poached, baked, scrambled, or cooked in the shell. In addition, soufflés, omelets, angel cakes, and sponge cakes are just some of the familiar foods relying on large proportions of eggs.

In food preparation, eggs are valued for their ability to

1. Emulsify.
2. Thicken.
3. Foam.
4. Bind.

Food systems containing both fat and a liquid can be emulsified with the aid of eggs, particularly egg yolks. This emulsifying property is used in stabilizing salad dressings, cream puffs, cake batters, and many other foods. The thickening ability of eggs is of importance in preparing such items as custards and some sauces. Egg white foams add to the volume and texture of such food products as sponge cakes and angel cakes, as well as being baked as meringues. Yolk foams are also used occasionally. The batter used in deep-fat frying vegetables illustrates the use of egg as a binding agent.

NUTRITIONAL VALUE

Eggs are one of the most cost-effective means of obtaining complete protein, because they each provide about 6 grams of animal protein, and the price per serving is quite low in comparison with beef and other animal protein foods. The fat content of eggs (6 grams) is entirely in the yolk, the amount being equal to the amount of protein in the whole egg (3 grams in the yolk and 3 grams in the white). The combination of the protein and fat adds up to a calorie content of approximately 80 calories per egg. Most vegetarian diets permit generous use of eggs as a means of ensuring adequate protein intake and also providing other nutrients.

The yolk is a source of other nutrients as well as fat. For instance, the iron in the yolk (0.9 milligrams) is valuable in helping to meet the required intake of this key mineral. Another positive nutritional benefit of the egg yolk is the presence of useful amounts of vitamin A, even though the actual level varies somewhat with the diet of the hen. A negative contribution of the yolk is cholesterol, a substance to be avoided or minimized by people who are deemed by physicians to be at risk of a heart attack. The yolk of single egg provides 252 milligrams of cholesterol. The significance of this high level is clear when compared with the average dietary intake of cholesterol per day of between 0.5 and 1.0 grams, which is about equal to the cholesterol provided by two to four eggs. Eggs marketed as being high in polyunsaturated fats and some egg substitutes developed in response to the concern over cholesterol are rather costly alternatives to fresh eggs.

STRUCTURE

The various structural features of eggs are all of importance, because of their contributions toward the practical aspects of marketing and storage, as well as to the functional roles played in food preparation. The shell, made up largely of calcium carbonate, serves as a protection for the contents of the eggs, despite the fact that it is perforated with innumerable tiny holes. These holes hold the potential for bacterial contamination and infiltration into the interior and also provide the avenue for the loss of some water and carbon dioxide from the egg. A mucin layer, called the bloom, coats the exterior of the shell until the egg is washed or buffed.

Inside the shell, yet another protective device is found. In fact, there are two protective membranes, the inner and the outer membranes; both membranes aid in blocking passage of materials through the shell. An air cell is situated between the two membranes at the end of the egg. Immediately inside the inner membrane (see Figure 10.1) there is a layer of thin white. Sandwiched between this first layer of thin white and another layer of thin white is the thick white. Trapped by the three-layered white is the yolk, which is contained within the *vitelline membrane*. The *chalazae*, two fibrous tissues, extend on either side of the yolk, helping to keep the yolk centered within the egg and restricting its movement. The germ spot or *blastoderm* is seen as an indistinct spot on the yolk. The latebra is the white column extending under the blastoderm to the center of the yolk. Although difficult to see, the yolk actually is composed of layered sections of white and yellow yolk.

The composition of the white is quite different from that of the yolk. The white is very high in water (87 percent) and contains essentially no fat. In contrast, the yolk is about 35 percent fat and only about 50 percent water, differences that help to explain the distinctive behavior of the yolk and the white in food preparation.

Vitelline Membrane Membrane surrounding the yolk.

Chalaza A fibrous structure at the side of the yolk, aiding in centering the yolk within the egg.

Blastoderm Germ spot in the egg yolk.

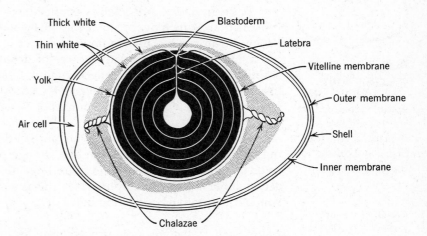

Figure 10.1 Cross-sectional diagram of an egg.

SELECTION AND STORAGE

Deteriorative Changes

Although all eggs have the same structural features, the quality will vary as a result of storage conditions and deteriorative changes. One obvious change in eggs as they lose quality is the increasing size of the air cell. This is the consequence of the loss of some moisture and carbon dioxide from the egg through the pores in the shell. The rate at which this happens is dependent upon the storage conditions and the retention of the protective covering on the shell. The loss of carbon dioxide stems from the white, a loss that causes the egg white to become increasingly alkaline as deterioration proceeds.

Accompanying this loss of carbon dioxide and increase in alkalinity is a thinning of the thick white. As the thick white decreases, the yolk is able to move through the white more readily than through the original thick state, and the yolk tends to float toward the upper surface within the white. This movement within the white is possible despite the impedance provided by the chalazae. In addition, the vitelline membrane weakens.

When eggs are broken from the shell, these changes can be noted. The white spreads over a large surface area and fails to pile up around the yolk. The yolk is flattened on the surface, rather than being held in a rounded shape, a consequence of the weakening of the vitelline membrane. There also is considerable likelihood of the yolk breaking. These changes are the basis for the grading of eggs.

Grading

Federal grading of eggs is done under the direction of the U.S. Department of Agriculture. Since this grading often is done in concert with state programs, the joint program is referred to as the Federal-State Grading Program. The grades for eggs reaching retail markets are U.S. Grade AA (the top grade), U.S. Grade A, and U.S. Grade B.

To be graded as AA, shell eggs must have a clean, unbroken shell, an air cell less than ⅛ inch deep, and a yolk that is well centered and free of defects. When the air cell is a maximum of a quarter of an inch deep, the yolk is centered fairly well and is relatively free of defects, and the shell is clean and sound, the egg is of U.S. Grade A quality. Grade B, the lowest-quality grade for consumers, is assigned if the yolk is somewhat mobile with a flattened appearance, if the air cell is a maximum of ¾ inch deep, and the shell is only slightly stained.

The grades are established in advance of the marketing process, often being determined prior to an extended storage period. Hence, the grade indicated on eggs tells the condition at grading and may not necessarily reflect the actual grade at the time of purchase. This is a problem for consumers, but no suitable alternative has been found.

In the Shell *Candling* is the process used for grading eggs in the shell before eggs enter the consumer market. This process is a simple one in which eggs

Examples of shell egg grade marks. U.S. AA is the top grade. Note that the size is indicated on the label on the top. Size is not related to the grade.

Candling Grading procedure based on silhouetting eggs in the shell.

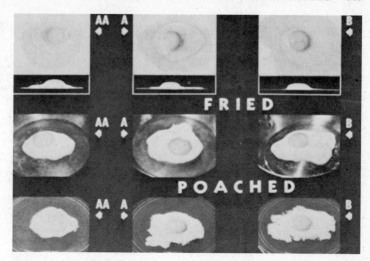

Grading standards for eggs are based on the comparative deteriorative changes that may have occurred. Grades range from top quality, Grade AA to Grades A and B. Note the greater surface area covered by the white and the reduced height of the yolk with each grade reduction.

are rotated as they pass in front of a light. The size of the air cell, the position and mobility of the yolk, and the possible presence of such foreign substances as rots, molds, and blood spots can be seen as silhouettes. The viscous nature of the white in high-quality egg will prevent the yolk from moving readily, and the yolk will appear as an indistinct, dark silhouette in the center of the egg, while a Grade B egg will be marked by a yolk that reveals a rather distinct silhouette moving near the edge of the egg.

A blood spot on the yolk is not graded down, for it can be removed easily, but blood in the white is not acceptable, since this condition causes rapid spoilage. Eggs with a porous shell are graded down because of the increased ease of moisture and carbon dioxide loss. The color of the shell is ignored in determining egg grades, for this characteristic has absolutely no influence on the quality of the egg or its nutritive value. The shell color is simply a characteristic determined by heredity.

Out of the Shell For the commercial food industry, eggs often are sold in bulk after being shelled. These shelled eggs are graded by various methods. One system uses the *yolk index*, a figure derived by measuring and dividing the height by the diameter of the yolk. Another measurement is the height of the thick albumen (thick white), expressed in arbitrary units called Haugh units. In this system, Grade AA whites have a minimum value of 72 Haugh units; Grade A, 60–71; and Grade B, 31–59. The color of the yolk is ignored in establishing egg grades out of the shell, for the color is merely an indication of the hen's diet, not the quality.

Yolk Index Measure of egg quality out of the shell; height of yolk divided by diameter.

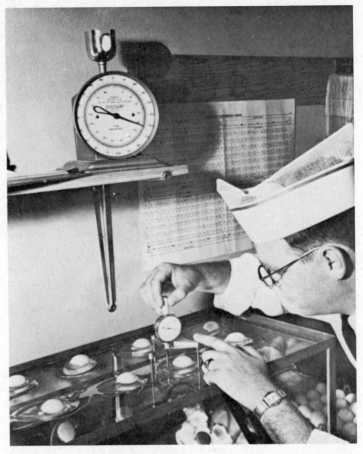

A micrometer can be used to grade quality when eggs are graded out of the shell. The height of the thick albumen, measured in Haugh units, is progressively less from Grade AA to Grade B.

Weight Classes

Egg cartons in the retail market identify not only the grade quality, but also the weight class (on the basis of a dozen eggs). Jumbo (the largest) eggs weigh 30 ounces per dozen, and the smallest (peewee) weigh only 15 ounces per dozen. The weight classes are as follows (per dozen):

Jumbo	30 oz
Extra large	27 oz
Large	24 oz
Medium	21 oz
Small	18 oz
Peewee	15 oz

These weight designations provide an indication of the general size of the eggs within the container, but the actual size of individual eggs may vary considerably within a single carton. For example, a particularly large egg may be offset by including a small one, yet the weight of the dozen will average out appropriately.

Standardized recipes are based on the use of medium eggs, although most recipes have sufficient tolerance to permit the use of large or even extra large eggs. In fact, recipes relying on egg white foams often are superior when made using extra large eggs.

Grade and weight classes are two independent features of egg marketing. Grade clearly designates quality at the time the candling was done. Weight denotes only size and carries no implication of the quality of the egg. Most markets offer choices between sizes and between grades, the most common being extra large and large for sizes and AA and A for grades. If the difference in price between sizes is less than 9 cents per dozen, the larger size is less costly than the smaller size. Conversely, a price difference of more than 9 cents makes the smaller size the more economical buy. For many egg dishes, including frying and poaching, U.S. Grade AA is the wise choice, but U.S. Grade A or even B can be used satisfactorily in puddings and many baked products. Angel cakes and other foam products are best when prepared with high-quality eggs.

Storage

One of the remarkable features of eggs is their capability of undergoing storage for even longer than six months if the conditions are controlled carefully. By utilizing such storage, the supply of eggs to markets can be kept quite constant throughout the year, thus helping to keep eggs comparatively low in cost. Eggs naturally have an excellent protection in the form of the shell, but certain techniques are utilized to enhance the maintenance of quality during storage. Appropriate storage conditions include a controlled atmosphere of carbon dioxide and very cool temperatures (between 29° and 31°F). These conditions reduce carbon dioxide loss and inhibit enzymatic and microbiological action. The humidity must be sufficiently low to inhibit mold formation on the shells.

Since the pores in the shells represent the potential for deteriorative mechanisms to function, eggs needing cleaning before storage will be washed, which removes the bloom as well as the dirty material. The pores are resealed by coating the shells, usually simply by dipping them in mineral oil held at 110°F, a temperature high enough to keep the oil from being drawn into the egg through the pores during dipping.

A crucial aspect of maintaining quality during storage is the control of temperature, for eggs lose quality rapidly when they are not chilled. At no time during the marketing process should eggs reach even 60°F, and preferably the temperature will be maintained just above freezing. Unless eggs are shipped and marketed under refrigeration, their quality will be something less than their grade classification indicates.

Consumers have no visibility of much of the storage and marketing process, but they do have an opportunity to observe how eggs are handled in the display area of the market. Clearly, eggs displayed in the market aisles, with no refrigeration, will be of lower quality than will those kept properly chilled. Even display cases that are overflowing with egg cartons do not afford adequate refrigeration for optimal maintenance of quality. The adequacy of refrigeration of eggs in the back of the store and in all previous phases of the marketing process can only be assessed by the actual quality of the eggs when they are used. Egg selection needs to be based on the known quality of eggs purchased from a store as well as on the grade indicated on the carton, because of the many opportunities for inadequate refrigeration and loss of quality. In other words, shopping for egg quality is based on selecting a store with high standards for maintaining good control of temperature for eggs.

EGG COOKERY

Functional Roles

Coloring and Flavoring Agent When egg yolks are included in products, they add a pleasing, richness of color in addition to enhancing flavors. For instance, in a lemon meringue pie filling, it is the egg yolk and not the lemon that contributes the expected yellow color. Cream fillings and cream puddings gain their creamy color from the egg yolks they contain.

Emulsifying Agent The ability of egg yolk to act as an emulsifying agent is due, at least in part, to lecithin, a phospholipid in the yolk. Lecithin is attracted to the interface between the aqueous and lipid phase of an emulsion. In essence, lecithin helps to form a protective, monomolecular layer around the droplets in an emulsion. This layer prevents the droplets from coalescing and breaking the emulsion, because the lecithin blocks direct contact of the oil droplets with each other in most food emulsions. Hollandaise sauce and cream puffs are two classic examples of foods that rely heavily on their egg yolk content for successful emulsions.

Thickening Agent The ability to serve as a thickening agent or a binding agent depends upon the change in solubility occurring when proteins are denatured by heat. Proteins in the yolk are different from those in the white, which results in slightly different behaviors of these two portions of egg when heated. However, both the white and the yolk are capable of thickening when heated. The heating of egg-thickened mixtures requires much more careful attention to temperature control than is necessary for gelatinizing starch in preparing starch-thickened mixtures. Egg mixtures should be heated just to the point where they achieve maximum thickening without any sign of curdling, and then they should be served immediately or cooled to prevent curdling due to the residual heat in the mixture. Such precautions are not necessary when thickening with most starches. Novices in egg cookery often overheat products when learning to use egg as a thickening agent, because they expect the same dramatic thickening with egg as occurs with starch. In fact, the thickening occurring with egg is fairly subtle.

SCIENCE NOTE: FACTORS INFLUENCING DENATURATION

There are several proteins in egg whites of interest in studying denaturation. *Ovalbumin*, the most abundant of these proteins, is a protein that can be denatured by mechanical agitation and by heat. *Ovomucin* and lysozyme are two other proteins that have been studied in relation to heat denaturation. Ovomucin is responsible for much of the structure of the thick white and is about four times as abundant in the thick as in the thin white. Initiation of the actual coagulation of egg white is thought to be the result of the formation of a complex between the ovomucin and lysozyme molecules in the white, a change that causes an increasing opacity as denaturation progresses.

Egg yolks contain a mixture of proteins. The water-soluble protein fraction in egg yolk is called livetin. Two other proteins contribute to the emulsifying ability of the yolk, as well as adding to the thickening power of yolks. These proteins, lipovitellin and lipovitellinin, are lipoproteins; the combination of protein and lipid in their structures accounts for their emulsifying power.

Type of Protein

Proteins in egg white are more responsive to heat denaturation than are those in the yolk. Denaturation begins at about 125°F under extremely controlled laboratory conditions. Under ordinary conditions of heating, whites will start to coagulate perceptibly at about 140°F and will cease to flow at about 149°F. The yolk starts to coagulate at just about the temperature where the whites cease flowing (149°F). The flow character of the yolks is lost at about 158°F.

Since there is a difference in coagulation temperatures between the yolks and the whites, it is not surprising that the use of whites, yolks, or whole egg will cause a small difference in the temperature to which egg-thickened products will need to be heated to achieve optimum thickening. A product containing only egg whites will thicken more readily than will one thickened only with yolks, while whole egg mixtures will thicken over an extended temperature range.

Rate of Heating

A slow rate of heating permits coagulation to be completed at the lower end of the temperature range for the type of protein being heated because there is adequate time for the necessary unwinding of the tertiary structure and aggregating of several of these relaxed molecules before the temperature rises very much. When heat input is great and the tem-

---

Ovalbumin Heat-sensitive, abundant protein in egg white.

Ovomucin Structural protein abundant in thick egg white.

perature is rising rapidly, there is very little time for the relaxation and subsequent aggregation of protein molecules to occur before the temperature is at the upper end of the range for denaturation.

Time is an important factor to consider when denaturing egg proteins, for it is interwoven intimately with temperature and possible curdling of products. The very gradual temperature rise resulting from a slow rate of heating provides adequate time to assess the progress of the denaturation process and to remove the product from the heat before curdling can occur. An intense heat input causes denaturation to occur at a comparatively high temperature, but there is almost no time between reaching the desired degree of denaturation and the onset of curdling, which is, unfortunately, an irreversible and unattractive condition.

Added Ingredients

The addition of acids, such as lemon juice and cream of tartar, lowers the coagulation temperature because they help to reduce the alkalinity of the egg, bringing the proteins toward their isoelectric points. Since the electrical charges on the surface of the protein molecules are reduced as the isoelectric point is approached, the electrical repulsion of the molecules will be reduced on the surface, and the clumping together of molecules will be facilitated by the addition of acid ingredients. Although it is possible theoretically to add so much acid to a food system that the pH drops below the isoelectric point of the protein, this does not occur in normal food products. Thus, it is realistic to say that the addition of acid reduces the temperature for coagulating egg proteins.

Sugar has the opposite effect of acid on the coagulation temperature of egg-thickened products. When sugar is added, the coagulation temperature rises too. The effect of sugar is due, at least in part, to the dilution of the protein concentration by the added sugar. The dilution of protein, whether by sugar or other ingredient in a reasonable quantity, will cause a detectable rise in the coagulation temperature of the protein system. This is even true when milk is added, despite the fact that adding milk is adding some protein. The overall effect of adding milk is to dilute the protein, because milk contains mostly water. The reverse arises if the concentration of egg protein is increased by increasing the amount of egg used or decreasing the level of sugar, milk, or other significant ingredient. The increased concentration of protein causes the denaturation temperature range to drop and resemble rather closely the range for concentrated egg white, whole egg, or yolk.

The effects of the rate of heating, the type of protein, and the concentration of the protein, as well as the pH of the medium, are important to recognize, for they clearly influence the preparation of successful products. Salts (because of their ability to ionize) are recognized as being involved in denaturation of egg proteins. However, this is not of practical significance since virtually any food being prepared will have sufficient salts to permit denaturation. This can be demonstrated by baking a custard prepared with distilled water rather than milk. This water custard will fail to gel properly until a salt is added to provide the electrical ions needed to interact with the electrical charges on the surface of the protein molecules. Once the ions are available, the complete coagulation process can be observed. Milk and other ingredients commonly used in egg-thickened products provide adequate ions for normal denaturation to occur; hence, salts need not be added.

Structural and Textural Agent   When egg proteins are denatured, they become rather rigid and are capable of providing structural strength and texture to food products, particularly if the concentration of egg is high. Perhaps the best example of the importance of eggs as a structural agent is in the preparation of popovers. The high concentration of egg explains the rigid, yet somewhat elastic quality of the cell walls in popovers, a texture quite different from the usual character of breads. Similarly, the walls of sponge cakes and angel cakes gain much of their character from the egg foams they contain.

Divinity is a candy that illustrates a unique contribution of egg white protein to texture. In this case, the egg white foam and the hot, concentrated sugar syrup are beaten together. The egg white proteins are denatured by the combination of beating and the heat from the hot syrup. These denatured proteins aid in separating sugar crystals in the divinity, thus blocking the aggregation of crystals that would result in a gritty candy.

Foams, particularly egg white foams, are both structural and textural aids in several different types of products. Fluffy omelets, soufflés, and foam cakes (sponge, angel, and chiffon) are familiar examples of the use of foams to attain a large volume and a light, somewhat porous texture. Skillful preparation and careful incorporation of these foams with other ingredients are necessary if a high-quality product is to result. Foams can be prepared using egg whites, egg yolks, or even a mixture of the two, but the largest volume by far is obtained using only egg whites to make the foam. Foams need to be beaten to the correct point and then incorporated very gently with any other ingredients to avoid as much loss of air as possible. Finally, the product containing the foam usually is baked to help stabilize the foam by denaturing the protein to strengthen the cell walls. Immediate baking in a preheated oven reduces the time available for cells to collapse and for volume to be lost from the foam.

In the Shell

Eggs may be prepared as soft-cooked or hard-cooked by placing them gently in boiling water and then maintaining a simmering temperature (185°F) until the desired stage of doneness is reached. For soft-cooked, between 3 and 5 minutes will be sufficient to thicken the white and perceptibly thicken the yolk without hardening it; about 18 minutes will complete the coagulation of the yolk of a hard-cooked egg if the egg is at room temperature before being

SCIENCE NOTE: EGG FOAMS

Foams are colloidal dispersions in which bubbles of air are surrounded by thin layers of liquid, which sometimes contain protein. Egg foams are but one example of foams found in foods. Other types of foams are formed with gelatin and with some dairy products. All these foams gain their stability from the protein. These foams can be formed because the protein-containing liquid has a relatively low *surface tension*, which allows the liquid to increase its surface area around the gas bubbles without squeezing out the air too quickly. Another important characteristic besides low surface tension is low vapor pressure of the liquid; low vapor pressure assures that the liquid will not evaporate quickly.

Egg proteins have excellent foaming qualities because of their low surface tension and low vapor pressure. With a limited amount of effort, the liquid can be stretched out into thin films encompassing air to form the desired, high-volume foams. This is particularly true of egg white proteins. Ovomucin in thick egg white is sheared by the beater blades into comparatively short fibers, which can be spread by additional beating into monomolecular films to help stabilize the forming foam. Ovalbumin and the other proteins in the whites also are spread into thin films to aid in forming the egg white foam. The comparatively low surface tension of these proteins explains their capability in being able to be spread into thin films with the aid of an egg beater. The fact that the foams have some degree of stability is attributed to some denaturation of the protein during beating but, more important is the fact that the vapor pressure of egg protein liquids utilized in the foams is quite low, showing limited tendency to evaporate.

Stability and ease of formation are two characteristics of interest when preparing egg foams. The *ease of formation* is decreased when sugar or acid ingredients are added to the foam during its preparation. Presumably, the delay in forming a foam when sugar is added is due largely to the dilution of the protein by the sugar. This addition appears to inhibit the denaturation of the protein by agitation, although eventually a fine-textured, stable foam results. The fine texture is achieved because of the increased amount of agitation required. The continuing beating constantly stretches and modifies the size of the individual cell walls into finer and finer cells with thinner walls.

The delay in foam formation noted when cream of tartar or other acid ingredient is added appears to be due to the fact that the egg white is being carried increasingly away from the isoelectric point of *lysozyme*, one of its proteins involved in foam formation. This delay in foaming is beneficial to the formation of a fine-textured foam, for the extended period of agitation permits continuing stretching into thinner cell walls and smaller cells.

The temperature of egg whites influences the ease of foam formation; whites at room temperature can be beaten easily into a foam of fine

Surface Tension Tendency of a liquid to present the least possible surface area (to form a sphere rather than to spread into a film); low surface tension is essential to foam formation and stability.

Lysozyme Protein involved in egg white foams; isoelectric point is pH 10.7.

texture, while chilled egg whites are more viscous and difficult to beat, requiring more beating to form a foam of lesser volume and coarser texture.

Other factors influencing ease of foam formation of whites are the presence of fat and the use of dried egg whites. The presence of even a trace of fat greatly retards foam formation of egg whites. This is the reason that absolutely none of the yolk, with its content of fat, should contaminate whites that have been separated to make a foam.

Stability of egg foams is determined by several factors: quality of the egg (amount of thick white), concentration of the protein; pH of the system, the presence of sugar, and the extent of beating. Eggs of comparatively low quality foam readily because of their abundance of thin white, but this foam is less stable than is one created with more effort using high-quality eggs with abundant thick white. The addition of water or other liquid to egg whites or egg yolks increases initial foam volume, but has a marked negative effect on the stability of such foams, due to the reduced concentration of protein. The proteins, which are denatured by the mechanical action of beating, are essential to the strength and stability of cell walls in foams. The addition of an acid provides a stabilizing influence on egg foams, and so does the use of sugar. In addition, sugar imparts a somewhat elastic, resilient quality to foams, enabling these foams to be folded into other ingredients with a minimum loss of air. Egg white foams are beaten to different stages for specific applications, but foams are less stable when underbeaten than they are when beaten to the point where the peaks will just bend over.

simmered, but somewhat more time will be needed if the egg is colder at the start of heating. The use of a simmering temperature during egg cookery is recommended to avoid toughening the protein of the white before the heat has had sufficient time to penetrate and coagulate the yolk. To reduce the likelihood of cracking the eggs when they are being added to the boiling water, a gentle dunking of each egg with the aid of a slotted spoon allows an opportunity for the expanding gas in the air cell to escape through the pores at a moderate, rather than at an explosive rate. When simmering is completed, hard-cooked eggs should be immersed immediately in cold water and then peeled to cool them rapidly.

A well-prepared soft-cooked egg will possess a white that is tender, yet completely coagulated, while the yolk will flow somewhat lazily when cut. The flavor should be pleasingly fresh. Hard-cooked eggs of high quality should have a firm and tender white surrounding a well-centered, completely coagulated, nonwaxy yolk with no discoloration surrounding the yolk.

Success in preparing soft-cooked eggs depends upon using an egg of acceptable quality and accurate timing. Hard-cooked eggs present similar requirements, but the quality of the egg is of greater importance than is true for

Ferrous Sulfide Iron-sulfur compound formed on the surface of the yolk of hard-cooked eggs if eggs are of low quality or are held at high temperatures too long a time.

soft-cooked eggs. The hard-cooking of eggs immortalizes the quality so that a portrait of that quality can be seen when the egg is peeled and sliced in half. If the yolk is close to one side and the air cell is large, the egg was of low quality. Additional evidence of low quality is the formation of a dark ring of *ferrous sulfide* on the surface of the yolk. This combination of iron and sulfur from the yolk and the white, respectively, is unattractive evidence of a low-quality egg, poor control of simmering and cooling conditions, or both. The comparatively high alkalinity of a low-quality egg promotes formation of ferrous sulfide, but this compound will form even in an egg of high quality if the cooking period is extremely long or if the egg is not cooled rapidly following the simmering period.

Hard-cooked eggs sometimes are resistant to peeling. The problem of having some of the white peel off with the shell leaves a distressing topographic outline, yet this is the sign that the egg is of high quality. Ease of peeling is associated with eggs having whites with a pH of at least 8.9, which means that carbon dioxide has been lost from the egg and that quality is deteriorating. The only eggs having a pH lower than 8.9 are those less than two days old or those that have been dipped to seal their pores and prevent loss of carbon dioxide.

Out of the Shell

Fried Eggs prepared in very simple ways are included frequently in meals, especially at breakfast. Fried eggs are a favorite way of preparing eggs out of the shell. Basically, fried eggs simply are eggs heated in fat in a shallow frying pan using either of the following methods. One technique is to fry eggs slowly in an excess amount of fat, with the hot fat being spooned over the upper surface to baste the egg and coagulate the protein fairly uniformly, including the thin layer of white coating the yolk surface. In the other method, just enough fat is used to keep the eggs from sticking, and a small amount of water is added to form steam within the tightly covered frying pan. The steam aids in coagulating the upper surface. Either method should result in an egg that has a tender white and a slightly thickened, unbroken yolk covered by a film of coagulated white. There should be no evidence of crisp browning on the white, for this is an indication of extreme overheating of the proteins in the white and results in unnecessary toughness. Careful control of the heat is needed for either method of frying to avoid making the egg tough. High-quality eggs should be used for frying.

Poached With the emphasis on weight control and keeping the fat content of the diet low, poaching is an appropriate way of preparing eggs. Only eggs of high quality will be satisfactory when poached, because low-quality eggs will spread badly when slipped into the simmering water. A high-quality egg, with its abundance of thick white, will have little tendency to spread away from the yolk.

Poaching is done by heating water almost to boiling before slipping the egg in very gently, directing it toward the side of the pan to help retain the desired shape. Water is retained at simmering to coagulate the egg without unduly toughening the protein. The turbulence associated with boiling would also tend to fragment the structure of the egg, resulting in a less attractive egg than can be achieved in simmering water. Simmering should be continued only until the white has coagulated into a solid mass, and the yolk is very slightly denatured to a honeylike consistency. Just as soon as this point is reached, the egg should be removed gently with a slotted spoon to allow any extra water to drain.

A poached egg should have a firm, tender white piling well around a slightly thickened, unbroken yolk. No part of the yolk should be coagulated to the point where it begins to solidify. The white should be in a single mass and not display streamers of denatured thin white. The problem of spreading of poached eggs can be eliminated by using an egg poacher to contain the egg while it is being poached.

Baked   Baking is another way of preparing eggs with little or no fat. They are prepared by breaking eggs and placing them in individual ramekins or cus-

Pleasing poached eggs are prepared by sliding a high quality egg very gently into simmering water and removing carefully with a slotted spoon when the white is completely coagulated and the yolk is thickened very slightly.

tard cups and baking in a 325°F oven until the desired degree of doneness has been reached. Although butter and salt and pepper sometimes are added to the surface of the egg before baking, this is not necessary for those who are watching fat and salt intake. High-quality eggs are desirable for baking because they will have a fresher flavor than will eggs of lesser quality.

Well-prepared baked eggs will have a tender white, which is completely coagulated, and the yolk will be viscous, but not set when it is cut. There should be no trace of browning around the edge.

Scrambled Scrambling is a good way of preparing eggs below U.S. Grade AA, for the eggs are beaten gently to blend the whites and yolks completely before they are heated. A weak yolk and a limited amount of thick white are not particular problems when scrambling eggs, and the usual addition of milk to tenderize the product by diluting the egg protein has the added benefit of enhancing flavor, which might otherwise be dull. Of course, high-quality eggs can be used to make scrambled eggs, too.

When the ingredients have been blended completely, but without creating a foam, the mixture is poured into a greased or nonstick skillet and heated slowly. Continuous, slow stirring is done during the entire cooking period to scrape moderately large pieces of coagulated egg from the skillet bottom and allow the undenatured fluid egg to reach the heat of the pan. This procedure is continued until no more egg mixture actually flows, but the large pieces of scrambled egg are still quite shiny on their surfaces. For best results, the eggs are served immediately; holding scrambled eggs increases toughness of the product and may lead to syneresis (liquid separating from the coagulated masses).

Evaluation of scrambled eggs is done on the basis of appearance and eating qualities. The pieces should be solid (not porous), moderately large, and a uniform, yellow color throughout. There should be no trace of browning, for that is an evidence of too intense a heat. The surfaces should be just slightly shiny, but there should not be any evidence of a tendency to flow. In the mouth, the eggs should be tender, and the flavor should be pleasing.

French Omelet A French omelet could be described as a golden brown half-moon of a cooked egg mixture. Actually, the mixture cooked for scrambled eggs is the same as that used in making a French omelet; only the cooking method is different. However, the results are startlingly different.

The eggs are blended thoroughly with a tablespoon of milk (the same as is used for scrambled eggs) for each egg and a bit of salt for flavor; care is taken in making both products to avoid beating air into the mixture so that the finished products will not be porous. Unlike the preparation of scrambled eggs in a rather cool skillet, butter is heated in the skillet until it is sizzling before the egg mixture is added when a French omelet is being prepared. This rather intense heat is desired so that the egg in contact with the pan will begin to coagulate almost immediately and will start to develop the desired golden brown color and smooth surface desired on the outside of the finished omelet. As the egg is cooking, the omelet is lifted in places with a narrow spatula

A French omelet, unlike scrambled eggs, should be browned pleasingly before being folded and served. Browning is promoted by having the butter sizzling when the egg mixture is added.

to allow uncooked egg to flow to the bottom of the skillet. When no more uncooked egg can be tipped to flow to the bottom, lifting of the omelet ceases, except for a quick examination to be sure the desired golden brown color has been achieved. If not, the heat is turned up briefly to finish browning. Then the omelet filling is scattered on half the omelet, and the omelet is folded over or rolled so that the browned bottom surface is on the outside of the omelet.

A French omelet should have a pleasing, golden brown exterior surface, and the interior should be a uniform, yellow color with no evidence of streaks of white or of porosity. The center should be glossy, but not runny. The flavor should be pleasing, and the omelet should be tender, except for the slightly toughened crust.

Custards

Stirred Custard In contrast to the egg products already discussed—and made with only egg and perhaps a very small amount of diluent—a stirred custard is a mixture of a comparatively large amount of milk, flavored with sugar and extract and thickened with a rather small amount of egg. When prepared carefully, a stirred custard will be a very smooth, delicately flavored sauce with a viscosity about that of heavy cream. The content of milk and egg makes a stirred custard a very nourishing sauce to serve over fresh fruit, gingerbread, or other baked desserts.

Preparation of stirred custard requires some patience and diligence to achieve the desired viscosity without curdling. First, the ingredients are beaten gently together and then strained to remove the chalazae. Then, very gentle heating is done in a double boiler over simmering water or over very

A stirred custard must be cooled very rapidly as soon as it is heated enough to coagulate the mixture just to the point where a silver spoon dipped in will be coated. Otherwise, the custard will curdle as a result of the residual heat in the hot custard.

low direct heat. Stirring is done slowly and constantly to assure uniform heating and denaturation of the egg protein. Slowly, the mixture will approach the temperature range at which denaturation will occur.

Heating is continued until a silver spoon is coated evenly when dipped in the custard. Just as soon as this test is noted, the custard is poured immediately into a shallow dish resting on a bed of ice for very rapid cooling. This is necessary to avoid having the residual heat curdle the mixture by overheating the denaturing protein. Once the egg proteins have been overheated and the custard has curdled, there is no way of reversing the process, although judicious use of an egg beater will make the texture somewhat more acceptable than the curdled custard. The recommended slow rate of heating not only helps to obtain uniform denaturation, but also provides a somewhat extended period of time to determine when the desired end point has been reached and to initiate cooling before curdling can happen. Regardless of the rate of heating, residual heat can cause curdling of the custard after it has been removed from the heat unless cooling is done very rapidly.

Baked Custard   Either a baked or a stirred custard can be prepared from the same milk-egg mixture, the difference being only in the method by which they are heated. The stirred custard retains its flow properties because the constant stirring prevents the formation of a gel structure. However, a baked custard is heated quiescently in the oven at 350°F until a thin knife can be inserted halfway between the center and the edge of the custard and come out clean. The center of the custard still will shake a bit when the custard is moved at this point, but the residual heat in the hot custard will be sufficient to set the custard by denaturing the egg protein even in the center of the dish. This test is not performed at the center of the custard because the residual heat will be sufficient to overheat the protein severely if the custard is baked until a knife comes out clean in the center. Overbaking causes a porous texture in a baked custard and syneresis. On the other hand, an underbaked custard will fail to set (form a gel) in the center, and the product will be rather soft and runny.

The ideal baked custard will be tender enough to shake just a tiny bit in the center, but will hold a sharp edge when sliced. The interior texture is perfectly smooth, with no holes, and there will be no evidence of syneresis. The upper surface may have a touch of golden brown, but will not have even a trace of burning. No traces of white will interrupt the golden yellow of the interior. Creme brulée, with its topping of caramelized sugar, is but one of the variations that can be made utilizing a custard base.

Custard pies and quiches also are popular. These pies should be tested with a knife halfway between the center and the edge to determine whether they have been baked sufficiently. Overbaking of pumpkin, pecan, or plain

Quiches are based on a foundation of baked custard. Consequently, they should be baked only until a knife inserted halfway between the center and edge comes out clean. Overbaking will result in considerable syneresis and a soggy crust.

custard pies is the most common reason for a soggy crust in these types of pies. Another means of helping to avoid a soggy crust is to bake the crust partially (but not enough to brown it) before adding the filling. For the adventurous, the crust can be baked in one pie pan and the filling in another. After cooling the filling, the filling is slipped cautiously into the crust.

Cream Puddings and Pies

Nourishing and pleasing desserts can be made by combining egg yolk with cornstarch-thickened puddings to enrich the color and flavor. Cream puddings (like the cornstarch pudding described in Chapter 7) are prepared by gelatinizing the starch completely over direct heat. Then the pudding is removed from the heat, and a spoonful of the hot pudding is stirred vigorously into the beaten yolks to be sure that the hot pudding is dispersed immediately throughout the yolks, gradually causing the yolks to approach coagulation temperature. This process is repeated three more times to dilute the egg yolks and help to raise the coagulation temperature of their proteins before they are stirred into the hot pudding. The warm, diluted egg-protein mixture is stirred into the cream pudding, and heating is continued gently for about 5 minutes to ensure that the yolk proteins are coagulated. This heating is imperative, for upon standing, uncoagulated yolks will cause the pudding to become quite thin. The coagulation of the yolks is evidenced by a subtle increase in the viscosity of the hot pudding and a slight loss of glossiness. Overheating of the yolk-containing pudding by boiling or by heating too long a time should be avoided so that the pudding will not develop a curdled texture. Use of a double boiler or a very low heat setting will aid in avoiding this problem. It should be noted that the starch gelatinization process, with its extended period of intense heating, is completed before the egg is added to assist in preventing overheating of the egg proteins.

Whether preparing a cream pudding or a cream pie, the procedure just outlined is the technique used. Puddings are usually poured into appropriate serving dishes and chilled before being served. Cream pie fillings are poured into baked pie shells and then are usually topped with a meringue and baked. Both cream puddings and cream pies need to be held in refrigerated storage as soon as they have had an opportunity to cool a bit, as their content (egg and milk) can support strong growth of microorganisms if they should happen to contaminate the product. Refrigeration is important to food safety.

A well-prepared cream pudding or pie filling will be perfectly smooth, showing neither lumps from the starch nor from overheated egg protein. When chilled and cut, the product should soften very slightly, but should not flow. In other words, it is just a bit softer than a baked custard. Cream puddings should have a rather light feel on the tongue, with no trace of stickiness or pastiness. Overstirring, often the result of too slow a rate of cooking during gelatinization, often leads to a pasty quality. The flavor should be pleasing and appropriate for the specific type of product being prepared; scorching should not have occurred.

Meringues

Stages of Beating Egg white foams form the basis of hard and soft meringues, as well as being utilized in many cakes and other baked products. The characteristics of the foams vary with the extent of beating, and these stages need to be recognized if optimum quality is to be obtained in products utilizing them. Egg whites are beaten to the *foamy stage* before other ingredients are added. The foamy stage is characterized by quite a porous texture, with large, uneven air cells, and a transparent appearance. At the foamy stage, cream of tartar or lemon juice may be added to aid in stabilizing the foam. Sugar also is added, but very gradually, at the foamy stage.

Continuation of beating beyond the foamy stage gradually increases the viscosity and also the opacity of the foam. The texture becomes increasingly fine and more uniform with beating beyond the foamy stage. Sugar continues to be added gradually during this period, if sugar is a part of the recipe. For most recipes, beating should be continued until the beater can be pulled slowly out of the foam, and the resulting peaks will just bend over. This is often referred to as the *soft peak stage*. At this point, the foam will have some elasticity if it is used immediately, yet will be sufficiently stable to maintain a good volume while being blended with other ingredients and baking in the oven. The soft peak stage is the stage used most frequently in cookery. This stage is reached rather rapidly if whites are beaten without adding sugar or

Foamy Stage Transparent, coarse, somewhat fluid foam; stage appropriate for adding the acid and starting to add the sugar, but not suitable for use in food mixtures.

Soft Peak Stage Egg white foam beaten until the peaks just bend over, a point noted for ease of blending with other ingredients and for stability during mixing and baking.

The foamy stage, the point at which acid often is added to stabilize the foam, is characterized by large bubbles throughout the egg white.

When the peaks just bend over when the spatula is withdrawn slowly from beaten egg whites, the foam is at the soft peak stage. This is the point at which most egg whites foams are used or incorporated into other ingredients.

acid, but is delayed significantly when either of these ingredients is used, making use of an electric mixer convenient for forming these latter foams.

With a bit more beating, the egg white foam will continue to get even stiffer than it is at the soft peak stage. The peaks will stand up straight when the beater is withdrawn at this point, yet the surface has a sheen to the foam, and the foam remains intact. This stage, called the *stiff peak stage*, is used in making hard meringues and chiffon cakes.

If beating is continued beyond the stiff peak stage, a very few revolutions of the beater will result in the whites being overbeaten and so stiff that they become brittle and the foam breaks apart. This *dry stage* is unsuitable for any application in food preparation. The rigidity of the cell walls is due to considerable denaturation of the protein by mechanical action. Care should be taken to be sure that beating is stopped at the correct point. However, if this dry stage is reached, a partial reversal can be accomplished by beating in some sugar, which helps in softening the foam and facilitating folding in of ingredients. Unfortunately, this will result in too much sugar in the product. Avoidance of overbeating is the best solution.

Soft Meringues Egg whites, beaten with an acid and sugar beginning at the foamy stage, can be whipped to the soft peak stage and then spread on a pie filling or other suitable dessert item in preparation for baking. The usual amount of sugar added in making soft meringues is 2 to 2½ tablespoons of

Stiff Peak Stage Point at which egg white peaks stand up straight, but the foam does not break apart; used in making hard meringues and chiffon cakes.

Dry Stage Point at which beaten egg white foam becomes brittle and loses the sheen normally seen on an egg white foam.

Egg whites need to be beaten until the peaks stand up straight when tested if they are to be used in making chiffon cakes. This extra stiffness is necessary to keep the rather fluid batter from draining out of the meringue before the cake structure is set.

sugar per egg white, the latter producing a sweeter, higher-calorie product that cuts better than the one with less sugar. Addition of sugar needs to be started at the foamy stage; the texture and volume will not be as nice if the foam is beaten beyond this point before the sugar addition is initiated. Adequate beating to achieve the soft peak stage where the peaks just bend over is essential to obtaining the desired fine texture and volume. Underbeaten soft meringues have poor volume and will tend to shrink because they start to collapse during baking. Overbeaten whites are difficult to spread attractively, and the surface looks quite dry after baking.

Soft meringues should be spread on their appropriate substrate and baked immediately in a preheated oven (350°F) until the surface is a pleasing, golden brown (about 15 minutes or slightly longer). Baking should result in coagulation of the protein throughout the soft meringue. However, this is somewhat difficult to do without overbaking the upper surface because of the insulating effect of the air in the foam. When possible, the meringue should be placed on the filling in the pie shell while the filling is still in the temperature range of 140° to 170°F and baked immediately. The heat of the filling will help to begin to denature the protein in the meringue from beneath, while the oven heat exerts its effect from above. The motivation for this haste in baking the meringue on a hot filling is to produce a pie with less leakage or *weeping*, terms used to describe the collection of liquid between the meringue and the filling. Leakage apparently is caused by inadequate denaturation of the protein in the meringue.

Spreading a meringue a comparatively uniform thickness over the entire surface of the pie facilitates adequate heating of the entire meringue. This means that high peaks should be avoided, for they will be overbaked and may even burn before the rest of the meringue has been baked enough. For a pleasing appearance, make a shallow, swirling pattern with a rubber spatula without pulling up any points. This spatula also can be used effectively to seal the meringue tightly to the crust all around the edge. This is useful in helping to keep the meringue from shrinking and pulling away from the crust. By reducing the possibility of overbaking and burning of peaks with the simple technique of the shallow undulations, another problem is alleviated. That problem is the formation of golden brown droplets of syrupy liquid on the surface of baked meringues, a problem termed *beading*. Beading occurs when protein is overcoagulated during the baking of meringues, which seems to force out some of the sweetened liquid in the form of little beads resembling beads of perspiration. Beading is particularly obvious if meringues are placed on hot fillings and then the meringues are overbaked to quite a brown color; the heat from the filling as well as from the oven means that more total heat has entered the meringue than would be true if the filling had been cold and the pie baked the same length of time. Because of the problem with weeping, the recommendation still must be to use a hot filling, but also to bake meringues only to a golden brown. Even with these precautions, leakage and weeping can occur if a meringue pie has to stand more than a very few hours before being served.

Weeping Leakage or collection of fluid between the filling and meringue due to failure to denature the protein in the egg white.

Beading Droplets of moisture on a meringue due to overbaking.

Soft meringues, prepared by beating two tablespoons of sugar per egg white, are beaten to the soft peak stage, spread on a cream pie or other dessert, and baked until a light golden brown.

Ideally, a soft meringue will be of excellent volume and fine texture, with no evidence of leakage between the filling and meringue and no beading on the surface. The color will be a pleasing golden brown. Cutting can be done easily without the meringue clinging to the knife. An underbaked meringue will have considerable leakage; an overbaked one will exhibit beading and will stick to the knife when cut.

A unique use of the soft meringue is the preparation of a Baked Alaska. In this dessert, the oven is preheated to 450°F while the meringue is being prepared and the Alaska is being assembled by arranging a hard block of ice cream on a bottom layer of cake and then frosting with a thick coating of soft meringue on all sides and the top. An immediate baking at 450°F quickly browns the meringue before the heat has a chance to penetrate the meringue and soften the ice cream. The temperature contrast between the hot meringue and the very cold ice cream makes this a seemingly magical, yet simple, dessert to prepare. Since this meringue is eaten right after baking, there is no concern about the formation of beads despite the fact that the very intense heat of the oven actually causes some overbaking.

Hard meringues contain twice as much sugar as soft meringues, which results in the need for very extensive beating to reach the soft peak stage. By baking at no more than 250°F, it is possible to achieve the desired dry, crisp meringue without browning.

Hard Meringues   Hard meringues need to be made with the aid of an electric mixer; the high sugar content (almost twice as much as is recommended for soft meringues) delays foam formation significantly. The easiest technique is to add half of the sugar in the same manner used for making soft meringues and then to continue beating vigorously while adding the final half. Beating should be continued until the peaks stand up absolutely straight. Even then, the large amount of sugar makes it possible to shape the very stiff mixture into the desired shells or drop cookies on a nonstick baking sheet or brown paper. Baking basically is done to dry out the whites and to denature the protein. There is no need to be hasty about the duration of the baking period, for the foam is extremely stable as a result of the large amount of sugar. The baking is done at the low setting of about 200°F or slightly higher to avoid browning while the meringues are being dried to the point of becoming crisp, but not brittle.

A desirable hard meringue is an appropriate size, easy to cut, not sticky, and is white, with no more than a trace of browning. Sticky meringues are due to underbaking or underbeating. Hard, tough meringues are the result of overbaking. Browning is the result of using too high an oven temperature for baking.

Fluffy Omelets

Fluffy omelets are an example of a product utilizing both yolk foams and white foams. After separation, the yolks need to be beaten until they are very thick and will pile, a process requiring extended, energetic beating. Then the whites are beaten (with added liquid) to the soft peak stage. Immediately, the

A fluffy omelet, when compared with a French omelet, clearly illustrates the importance of egg foams as leavening agents. A high quality fluffy omelet will be a pleasing golden brown, but there will be no trace of a layer of yolk.

yolks are poured gently over the whites and are folded in until absolutely no streaks of yellow show and no yolk is at the bottom of the bowl. While this folding is being done, butter is heated until bubbling in a heavy skillet, and the oven is preheated to 325°F. Just as soon as folding is completed, the omelet is transferred gently onto the bubbling butter and is heated half a minute to brown the bottom surface of the omelet and begin the denaturation process. Then the skillet containing the omelet is transferred to the hot oven and baked until the upper surface is dry and the protein is coagulated, as evidenced by inserting a knife in the center and finding it clean when it is withdrawn. For service, the omelet is folded in half and served with or without a sauce.

There is a strong tendency for a layer of the yolk mixture to collect in the bottom of a fluffy omelet because of the comparative instability of the egg white foam, which has been diluted with added liquid. However, by beating to the correct end point, folding until all of the yolk foam is completely blended with the whites, and then immediately heating at a fairly rapid rate, little drainage can occur before the foam and its contents are denatured and held in position. A person who works quickly is more likely to be successful than is one who works slowly. However, even very slow workers can make excellent fluffy omelets if they use acid to help stabilize the egg white foam and if they are sure to beat the yolk foam long enough to get the yolks very thick. Tomato juice, lemon juice, or cream of tartar effectively can be used to reduce drainage and help stabilize the egg white foam. Also to be avoided are underbeating or overbeating the egg whites, inadequate folding, and allowing the foams or omelet to stand *at all* before completing the mixing and baking.

Maximum volume is achieved by beating the yolks and whites to just the right stages, efficiently and gently folding the two foams together just until they are blended, baking immediately, and avoiding too little or too much baking. Underbeaten foams of yolks or whites lack stability and do not have the maximum amount of air incorporated in them, thus contributing to poor volume. Overbeaten whites lack the extensibility needed for stretching a little in the oven. In addition, they are difficult to fold into the yolks because they break into pieces. This problem requires additional folding to eliminate the white chunks and causes loss of volume even before baking. An underbaked omelet will tend to collapse when removed from the oven, while an overbaked one will start to lose volume because the protein will become overcoagulated and will tend to shrink.

A well-prepared fluffy omelet will be light, tender, and of good volume, with a pleasingly golden-brown exterior. There will be absolutely no suggestion of a layer, nor will there be any streaks of unblended white or yolk. Only slight shrinkage will be evident when the omelet is removed from the oven.

Soufflés

Soufflés and fluffy omelets have many features in common, for they both are products in which a viscous yolk mixture is combined with an egg white foam and baked. However, there are several differences. To begin, the yolk mixture in a soufflé actually is a thick white sauce in which yolks are incorporated. The starch in this thick sauce must be gelatinized (see Chapter 7) by bringing the sauce to a boil, after which the yolks are combined in the same fashion described in the discussion of cream puddings earlier in this chapter, that is, by stirring a spoonful of the gelatinized starch sauce into the beaten yolks, followed by three more additions prior to stirring the yolk mixture into the sauce. This sauce is set aside, covered, while the whites are beaten to the soft peak stage. The foam is formed most effectively by adding cream of tartar or some other acid at the foamy stage and beating with an electric mixer until the soft peak stage is reached. Gently, but quickly the warm yolk mixture is poured down the side of the bowl containing the egg white foam, and the two are folded together efficiently and gently just until there are no streaks and no yolk mixture remains on the bottom. Then the soufflé is transferred to a deep

Soufflés have such a high volume that the foam is stretched to the maximum. They must be served promptly after being removed from the oven before the cooling foam structure begins to sag.

soufflé dish, a circle is traced around the surface about an inch away from the edge of the dish, and the dish is placed in the oven that has been preheated to 350°F. About an hour usually is needed for the soufflé to be set enough so that a thin knife inserted in the center will come out clean. Soufflés need to be served just as soon as they are removed from the oven because they will settle a bit even when they are done and will look less dramatic than when they first emerge. Holding in the oven after baking is completed is not satisfactory, because the overheating will cause the protein to begin to shrink together and much volume will be lost.

One of the problems sometimes encountered in preparing a soufflé is the breaking of the emulsion in the thick sauce. This is likely to happen when a cheese or chocolate soufflé is being prepared because of the added fat from either of these ingredients. The usual cause is too much evaporation of liquid during gelatinization. Although the sauce looks dreadful when the emulsion is broken, the addition of only a very small amount of milk or water and some stirring will return the sauce to its original smooth state, and preparation of the soufflé can be continued. This remedy must be applied before the sauce is combined with the egg yolks or with the white foam so that the soufflé will be able to be folded together easily.

Soufflés should be very high and light, pleasingly browned, and well blended, with no suggestion of a layer on the bottom. A good soufflé is tender and flavorful. The impression of a particularly light soufflé can be created by baking the soufflé in a dish that is a bit too small and putting an aluminum foil collar around the rim to contain the soufflé as it rises until it sets. When baking is completed, the collar is removed, leaving a soufflé rising well above the dish. This has dramatic psychological benefit, but is a little difficult to do successfully.

Volume and the possible presence of a layer are the two concerns to be addressed when preparing a soufflé. Proper beating of the egg white foam to the soft peak stage and appropriate folding of the yolk mixture into the whites are two aids in achieving maximum volume. Immediate baking at the desired temperature to just the correct end point also helps. Note that the position for testing a soufflé is the center rather than the point midway between the center and edge used in testing custards. The center of a soufflé must be set before the product is removed from the oven. Otherwise, the cool room temperature will cause the expanded hot gas in the soufflé to contract; the undenatured egg foam will not have the strength to hold itself up, and the soufflé will fall.

A layer in a soufflé can be the result of a sauce that is too thin, so that the sauce drains toward the bottom of the soufflé before the structure is set. Inadequate folding of the sauce into the whites may cause a similar problem. As would be expected, allowing the completed soufflé to stand before it is baked in a preheated oven or failing to preheat the oven can cause even a properly prepared soufflé to undergo some drainage so that the sauce begins to form a layer.

Some soufflés contain vegetables and are served as the main course for a luncheon or as a side dish in a dinner, while sweet ones are used as desserts. Sauces sometimes are served on soufflés. Spoon bread is a cornmeal soufflé (originating in the South) that is enjoyed with butter as a substitute for mashed potatoes at a meal.

Foam Cakes

Foam cakes are special types of cakes using a large proportion of egg white foam to provide high volume and a comparatively open structure. The foams for these are prepared according to the principles discussed in this chapter. However, there are additional ingredients and principles involved in cakes. This discussion is presented in Chapter 14. The problems of foam formation and possible settling of layers during baking are of concern in making foam cakes, just as they have been in the preparation of soufflés and other egg dishes utilizing foams.

ALTERNATIVES TO FRESH EGGS

Frozen Eggs

In institutional feeding operations, frozen eggs represent a valuable time saver because of the great deal of time required to break eggs in quantity and the even greater amount of time required to separate the yolks and whites after they are broken. Add to that labor cost the fact that yolks may be dropped into the whites when eggs are being separated, and it is obvious that alternatives to fresh eggs are of interest in quantity work. Frozen egg products are alternatives.

One of the important problems in freezing eggs is the control of microorganisms. To reduce contamination, the shells are washed just before the eggs are broken from the shell. Freezing then is done just as quickly as possible, with attention being directed throughout the processing to eliminating any contamination. Pasteurization of the white, yolk, or whole egg is an aid in reducing microorganism counts. The heat treatment of pasteurization has only a very slight effect on the baked products made with pasteurized frozen egg products.

Frozen whole egg and egg white are more satisfactory than the frozen yolks because the yolks begin to thicken during frozen storage and then do not blend well with other ingredients after being thawed. The addition of salt or sugar to yolks or whole eggs prior to freezing reduces this tendency, however. It is important to consider the end use intended for frozen yolks or whole eggs, because those containing sugar can be used very satisfactorily in dessert items, but are not acceptable in scrambled eggs and similar items.

Whites can be frozen commercially or in the home without adding other ingredients. They can be thawed and used just as fresh whites would be used.

Dried Eggs

Packaged mixes provide a familiar example of the use of dried eggs, with angel cake mix being a popular one. Institutional feeding operations also are customers for dried eggs. Spray drying is done by forcing liquid egg through an atomizer as a fine spray, which then is dried quickly, cooled, and packaged. Bacterial control is vital to the production of a high-quality dried egg. Eggs may be dried as the yolk, the white, or the whole egg, but objectionable changes in color, flavor, odor, and solubility occur when either dried yolks or whole eggs are held at storage temperatures above 40°F. Commercial bakeries using dried egg products are able to incorporate them with other ingredients quite satisfactorily if mixing is done at high temperatures (as high as 154° to 176°F).

Egg Substitutes

As a response to the public concern over the cholesterol content of egg yolks, egg substitutes are now on the market. Formulas in different brands vary, but basically the egg white is retained and the yolk is replaced with vegetable oil products and carotenoids (as coloring agents) and a nutritional additive. Other substances also are added to make the final product simulate fresh whole egg. These substitutes are available in both frozen and fluid (refrigerated) forms. The nutritional analyses vary with the product, with the calorie value ranging from higher to lower than fresh whole egg. All egg substitutes are alike in that they do not contain cholesterol, and they are significantly more expensive than eggs. Their use in various recipes where whole fresh egg is an ingredient is suggested by the manufacturers, but the results frequently are not identical to those made with eggs. Nevertheless, most products are quite acceptable to those who have been instructed to curtail cholesterol intake because of diagnosed health problems. Use of egg substitutes in scrambled eggs and French omelets has been more satisfactory than in some more elaborate egg preparations. Consumers do need to be aware of the fact that cartons of egg substitutes usually contain less than the equivalent of a dozen eggs.

SUMMARY

Eggs are used alone or in food combinations to perform several different functions in cookery. They are valued for their ability to emulsify ingredients, thicken products, form foams, and bind ingredients. They are able to perform these various roles because they contain a useful amount of proteins in both the yolk and white. They are also sources of other nutrients; the yolk is a source of vitamin A, cholesterol, and some fat, as well as some other vitamins and minerals.

The egg is packaged in a slightly porous, protective shell, which encompasses the white (thick and thin whites), as well as the yolk, with its vitelline membrane and chalazae extending on either side. Key changes when eggs are not stored under good, cold storage conditions are a weakening of the vitelline membrane, an increase in alkalinity, increased space in the air cell, an increase in thin white, and a decrease in thick white. These changes can be assessed by candling eggs in the shell to classify them as U.S. Grade AA through U.S. Grade B. Weights range from jumbo to peewee, with extra large and large being the most common sizes in the retail market.

Eggs are important ingredients in omelets (French and fluffy), custards (stirred and baked), cream puddings and pies, meringues (hard and soft), soflés, and foam cakes. They also are prepared individually in the shell (soft or hard cooked) and out of the shell as fried, poached, baked, and scrambled. In several of these products, egg foams are important for volume and texture. The coagulation temperature of eggs is influenced by the type and concentration of protein, rate of heating, and added ingredients.

Eggs, particularly the whites, are used often to form foams to enhance volume and modify texture of food products. The low surface tension and vapor pressure of egg whites are important characteristics in forming stable foams. Sugar and acid stabilize foams, but delay foam formation. Dilution of protein and inadequate beating reduce foam stability. The presence of fat interferes with formation of egg white foams.

The desirable characteristics and techniques for achieving these qualities for several different egg preparations are included in this chapter. Products and appropriate tests for doneness are presented for eggs cooked in the shell (hard and softcooked), out of the shell (fried, poached, baked, and scrambled), omelets (French and fluffy), stirred and baked custards, cream puddings and pie fillings, hard and soft meringues, soufflés, and foam cakes (sponge, angel, and chiffon). Foams are stabilized by adding acid at the foamy stage and continuing beating until the soft peak stage is reached. For hard meringues and chiffon cakes, beating is continued to the stiff peak stage. Overbeating foams reduces final volume and quality.

Dried and frozen eggs are utilized commercially. Frozen yolks and whole eggs need some added salt or sugar to prevent the development of an extremely gummy texture. Egg substitutes are available in frozen and liquid form to provide a product simulating eggs, but without the cholesterol of egg yolks. These are more costly than regular eggs, but may be important for people on restricted diets since they can be substituted satisfactorily in some products for fresh eggs.

Selected References

Baldwin, R. E. et al. Effects of microwaves on egg whites. I. Characteristics of coagulation. *J. Food Sci. 32:* 305. 1967.

Baker, R. C. et al. Factors affecting discoloration of hard-cooked egg yolks. *Poultry Sci. 46:* 664. 1967.

Beveridge, T. and S. Nakai. Effects of sulfhydryl blocking on thinning of egg white. *J. Food Sci. 40:* 864. 1975.

Chang, C. H. et al. Studies on gelation of egg. *J. Food Sci. 42:* 1658. 1977. (a)

Chang, C. H. et al. Microstructure of egg yolk. *J. Food Sci. 42:* 1193–1200. 1977. (b)

Childs, M. T. and J. Ostrander. Egg substitutes: Chemical and biologic evaluations. *J. Am. Diet. Assoc. 68:* 229. 1976.

Consumer and Food Economics Institute. *Eggs in Family Meals: Guide to Consumers.* Science and Education Administration. U.S. Dept. Agriculture. Washington, D.C. 1975.

Consumer and Marketing Service. *USDA Egg Products Inspection.* U.S. Dept. Agriculture. Washington, D.C. 1968.

Cunningham, F. E. Properties of egg white drainage. *Poultry Sci. 55:* 738. 1976.

Cunningham, F. E. and O. J. Cotterill. Performance of egg white in the presence of yolk proteins. *Poultry Sci. 51:* 712. 1972.

Fennema, O. R. *Principles of Food Science. I. Food Chemistry.* Marcel Dekker. New York. 1976. P. 665.

Fromm, D. Some physical and chemical changes in the vitelline membrane of the hen's egg during storage. *J. Food Sci. 32:* 52. 1967.

Garland, J. D. and W. D. Powrie. Chemical characterization of egg yolk myelin figures and low-density lipoproteins isolated from egg yolk granules. *J. Food Sci. 43:* 1210. 1978.

Grange, G. R. *Regulations Governing Grading and Inspection of Egg Products.* U.S. Dept. Agriculture. Agr. Marketing Service. Poultry Div. Washington, D.C. 1964.

Grange, G. R. *Regulations Governing the Grading of Shell Eggs and United States Standards, Grades, and Weight Classes for Shell Eggs.* U.S. Dept. Agriculture. Agr. Marketing Service. Poultry Div. Washington, D.C. 1965.

Heath, J. L. and S. L. Owens. Effect of oiling variables on storage of shell eggs at elevated temperatures. *Poultry Sci. 57:* 930. 1978.

Helwig, L. R. et al. Effects of varied zinc/copper ratios on egg and plasma cholesterol level in white leghorn hens. *J. Food Sci. 43:* 666. 1978.

Hester, E. E. and C. J. Personius. Factors affecting beading and leakage of soft meringues. *Food Tech. 3:* 236. 1949.

Irmiter, T. F. et al. Methods of preparing hard cooked eggs. *Poultry Sci. 49:* 1232. 1970.

Johnson, T. M. and M. E. Zabik. Gelation properties of albumen protein singly and in combination. *Poultry Sci. 60:* 2071. 1981.

Meehan, J. J. et al. Relation between internal egg quality stabilization methods and peeling difficulty. *Poultry Sci. 40:* 1430. 1961.

Moats, W. A. Egg washing—a review. *J. Food Protection 41(11):* 919. 1978.

Robinson, D. S., and J. B. Monsey. Changes in composition of ovomucin during liquefaction of egg white: Effects of ionic strength and magnesium salts. *J. Sci. Food Agri. 23:* 893. 1972.

Romanoff, A. L. and A. J. Romanoff. *Avian Egg.* John Wiley. New York. 1949.

Sauter, E. A. and J. E. Montoure. Relation of lysozyme content of egg white to volume and stability of foam. *J. Food Sci. 37:* 918. 1972.

Schmidt, R. H. *Gelation and coagulation.* ACS Symposium Series 147. 1981. P. 131.

Stadelman, W. et al. Thermally processed hard cooked eggs. *Poultry Sci. 61(2):* 388. 1982.

Wang, A. C. et al. Effects of sucrose on quality characteristics of baked custard. *Poultry Sci. 53:* 807. 1974.

Whitaker, J. R. and S. R. Tannenbaum. *Food Proteins.* Avi Publishing Co. Westport, Conn. 1977.

Study Questions

1. How are eggs graded in and out of the shell? What changes take place in eggs as they gradually deteriorate?
2. What factors determine the coagulation temperature of an egg mixture?
3. Compare the causes of a layer in the bottom of a fluffy omelet with the causes in a soufflé.
4. What, if anything, can be done to remedy the separation of fat from the thick white sauce used in making a soufflé?
5. Compare the tests for doneness of a baked custard and a soufflé. Why is each tested the way it is?
6. Describe the results of overbaking a baked custard. A stirred custard.
7. What are four functions eggs can perform in food preparation? Cite an example of each in a food prepared in the home.
8. Compare the size of package and the cost of equivalent amounts between fresh eggs and egg substitutes.

Pablo Picasso, detail from "La Gourmet." National Gallery of Art, Washington/Art Resource.

CHAPTER 11

LEAVENING AGENTS

OVERVIEW

Most baked products undergo some rather remarkable changes during baking, one of the most dramatic often being a large increase in volume. Sometimes the increase triples the volume of the original mixture, and frequently, there is at least a doubling of the size during baking. Although this growth may be like an act of magic, tricks are not the secret. The key lies in the formation and expansion of gases with heat. This chapter explores the development and expansion of these gases in baked products.

Air, carbon dioxide, and steam are the gaseous components causing these impressive increases in volume. The sources of these gases are rather varied in foods, yet they all are important because gases expand when they are heated. When the oven heat begins to reach the gases in the interior of a food, pressure starts to build within each cell as the gas pushes with increasing force. The pressure causes elastic, undenatured, protein-containing cells to stretch ever thinner and occupy a larger and larger volume. When this protein in the cell walls denatures from the heat, the cell walls lose their elasticity and become fixed in their extended position. Clearly, leavening of a baked product is a very dynamic occurrence, one with tremendous potential for expansion, but also one carrying the possibility of potential problems in quality control. The problems are to generate the desired amount of pressure within the cells of the product and to set the cell walls permanently at the maximum volume.

AIR

Any baked product will receive at least some leavening action from air. Even pastry, a seemingly compact dough, undergoes some increase in volume during baking because of air trapped in the stiff mixture. At the opposite end of the spectrum of leavened baked items is a soufflé. The lightness of the egg white foam in the soufflé mixture prior to baking provides ample evidence of the fact that air is present in abundance in a soufflé and that this air expands in the heat of the oven to contribute to the leavening.

The importance of air as a leavening agent can be demonstrated by evacuating the air from a cake batter and baking the cake; that is, without the air to provide the necessary pressure within each cell, rising fails to occur during baking, even when steam is generated. The air-lightened cells are needed as spaces in which steam and carbon dioxide can collect and expand. Although air frequently is not the most effective of the gases in increasing volume, it must be present, even if only in small quantities. The actual contribution of air to the total volume of leavening is influenced by several factors: (1) the amount of manipulation, (2) the viscosity of the batter, (3) the nature of the ingredients, and (4) the length of time elapsing before baking.

Amount of Manipulation

Frequently, increased mixing increases the amount of air incorporated into a product, but this is not always true. Perhaps the best example of the use of manipulation to incorporate air is the beating of egg whites into foams. In-

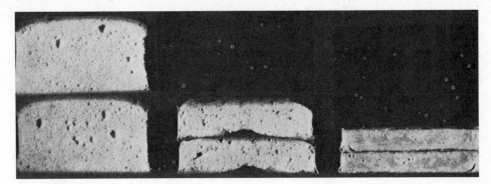

Air is essential to the leavening of pound cake (left), in which the creaming of butter and sugar creates a foam that traps air in the batter. The volume of a cake made with the same ingredients, but without creaming and trapping air (center), is only about half as great as the control on the left. Air was removed from the batter before the same cake formula was baked (right), resulting in a still smaller volume.

creasing the amount of beating increases the volume of the foam up to an optimum point, after which the egg white proteins begin to lose some of their extensibility. The rigidity of an overbeaten egg white foam makes the incorporation of other ingredients difficult, and increased folding is required to distribute the white foam uniformly. With each stroke during folding, air is lost from the foam. In other words, overbeating of egg whites results in reduced leavening from air because of the loss of air from the foam during folding.

Quick, skillful folding of ingredients into a foam can make a significant difference in the volume of a foam-containing product because of the variation in the amount of air lost from a foam with careless, slow, or excessive folding. Experience is an important factor in getting maximum leavening from air, particularly from air in a baked product based largely on the presence of an egg white foam.

Viscosity of the Batter

One of the most viscous mixtures containing air is a creamed combination of shortening and sugar, such as that prepared in making conventional cakes. Directions optimistically say to cream the fat and sugar until they are light and fluffy. Although it is true that vigorous action results in digging little air pockets in the fat, using the sharp crystals of sugar to cut into the fat is ineffective in making a foam that even remotely resembles the light foam available with egg whites. The viscous nature of the fat, however, traps most of the air within this very heavy foam, providing the vital and numerous small cells needed as the basic structure within which the leavening gases can collect and expand during baking. The air itself in this foam contributes a proportionately small, but highly significant, leavening action.

The temperature of the ingredients, as well as the proportion, will play an important role in determining how much air is incorporated in a mixture. To illustrate, a chilled fat is so hard that only a little air can be trapped within it to make a fat-air foam. At the opposite extreme is a melted fat or oil, which is so fluid that any air caught within it by mixing is not held, because the liquid fat quickly forces the air out as it flows to minimize its surface area. Plastic fats (those that can be creamed easily without becoming excessively soft) are optimal for trapping air to provide leavening, and this characteristic is obtained at approximately room temperature for most solid fats.

The ingredients and the temperature of the batter itself also influence the amount of air held within the batter. A cool batter will be more viscous than a warm batter; consequently, air will be held within the cool batter more readily than in the warm batter. If a batter has sufficient flour to make a stiff dough or so little flour that the batter flows readily, air will be held less well than in a batter that can be beaten with some difficulty or stirred fairly vigorously to add air during mixing.

Nature of the Ingredients

Foams are the effective way of introducing air into baked products, and egg foams are the lightest of the foams. Egg foams may be of three types: yolk, whole egg, and white. Yolks can be beaten, with considerable expenditure of energy, into moderate foams that are reasonably stable for blending with other ingredients. If enough patience is exercised in beating a yolk foam, sponge cakes and fluffy omelets can gain a moderate amount of their leavening from the air incorporated in the yolk foam. Whole egg foams ordinarily represent a very modest incorporation of air, yet they do introduce some air into the cakes in which they are used. The most significant source of air for leavening is egg white foams. The whites are able to be extended rather easily into fine-textured, thin-walled foams trapping large amounts of air, and properly beaten whites are elastic enough to be able to be folded into other ingredients with only a modest loss of air.

The type of fat selected is another factor influencing the amount of air that might be held within a batter or dough. Oils are detrimental to the inclusion of air because they increase fluidity of the mixture. Fats that are spread with moderate ease at room temperature are good choices when air leavening is of considerable importance, as is true in shortened cakes.

Bench Time

Air is an elusive commodity in batters and doughs. Just because air has been trapped in a foam or in the mixture itself at one point, there is no guarantee that the air will still be there when the product is being baked. Time is the enemy of air leavening. Mixing times need to be kept relatively short after the air has been introduced, and standing time prior to baking following completion of mixing should be avoided. The period of time the mixture is either being mixed or is standing prior to baking is referred to as bench time. Air will provide its maximum leavening in baked products if bench time is kept short by mixing efficiently and avoiding any delays between mixing and baking.

STEAM

The heat of the oven causes some water to be converted to steam in any baking product, and this steam provides a remarkable increase in volume—actually an expansion of 1600 times from the original volume of the water! Even a

The combination of a highly fluid batter and an extremely hot oven generates so much steam in a baking popover that the volume is about tripled during baking.

comparatively dry cooky dough contains enough water to gain some leavening from steam. In fact, steam, like air, is a source of leavening in all baked products. The most dramatic examples of steam as a leavening agent are provided by popovers, puff pastry, and cream puffs. These products rely on an extremely hot oven at the beginning of baking to generate steam rapidly before the structure becomes set by the denatured proteins. The large amount of steam almost seems to explode these items. Popovers, puff pastry, and cream puffs get so much leavening from steam and a little air that no additional leavening needs to be provided. In most other products, steam and air are augmented by other leavening agents to achieve the desired volume.

CARBON DIOXIDE

Carbon dioxide is a gas that can be generated within batters and doughs by either biological or chemical means. Yeasts are microbiological sources of carbon dioxide, and these one-celled plants produce carbon dioxide for leavening when they are allowed to grow within a dough. Bacteria in batters and doughs can contribute indirectly to leavening by producing acids (lactic and acetic) that can react with alkaline ingredients in a chemical reaction to yield carbon dioxide or that can promote the growth of certain yeast. The yeast, in turn, produces the carbon dioxide.

Chemical reactions to produce carbon dioxide occur in a batter or dough when an acid ingredient and an alkaline substance both are present. These may be separate ingredients in a recipe, as was often the case in the past. Formulated baking powders are the most common source of carbon dioxide today.

Biological Agents

Saccharomyces Cerevisiae Strain of yeast used to produce carbon dioxide in yeast-leavened products.

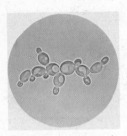

Saccharomyces cerevisiae (shown under a magnification of 1200×) is the yeast used in yeast-leavened baked products to generate carbon dioxide during the fermentation period.

Quick-Rise Active Dry Yeast New strain of yeast capable of reducing rising time by half in yeast-leavened products.

Yeast *Saccharomyces cerevisiae*, the strain of yeast used in yeast-leavened batters and doughs, produces the carbon dioxide needed for achieving the desired volume. This one-celled plant uses various sugars as sources of energy for growth and survival. In the course of metabolizing the sugars, carbon dioxide and ethyl alcohol are released into the batter or dough. Of course, this reaction is dependent upon the survival of the yeast until an adequate amount of carbon dioxide has been produced.

Yeast can be purchased in compressed form as cornstarch-containing cakes, which are preferred by some people because of their rapid action. These cakes, with their high moisture content of about 72 percent, require refrigerated storage and have a maximum viable shelf life of only about five weeks. Even with careful storage, the yeast cakes tend to dry out around the edges within their foil-wrapped packages, limiting their viability to close to the expiration date stamped on the package.

Active dry yeast is a popular form of yeast because of its long shelf life. If stored at 90°F, the expected shelf life of active dry yeast is six months, but when stored at 40°F, active dry yeast will be active even after a period of two years. This type of yeast, like compressed yeast, can even be frozen without harm. The expiration date stamped on an envelope of active dry yeast is based on storage at room temperature.

In late 1983, a new strain of active dry yeast was announced. This strain, produced through careful genetic research, purportedly reduces the time required for adequate carbon dioxide production by half. For persons desiring to make yeast-leavened products, but who have only limited time available for making them, the *quick-rise active dry yeast* may represent a saving of about an hour in the total time required for making bread.

Production of active dry yeast begins with a propagation period on dilute molasses at 86°F, after which the yeast is recovered and made into press cake. This press cake is extruded to facilitate dehydration to a moisture content of only about 8 percent before the product finally is ground to produce the granular active dry yeast contained in the individual packets in the market. The biggest drawback to using active dry yeast is the need to rehydrate the yeast, although this can be done very quickly in water at 100° to 115°F. The granules of active dry yeast also can be combined directly with flour for incorporation into batters and doughs. When using this method, the liquid being added to the mixture should be at a temperature of between 120° and 130°F so that the batter or dough will be warmed sufficiently for adequate hydration to occur. Quick-rise active dry yeast should be hydrated at the same temperatures used for the traditional active dry yeast.

The production of carbon dioxide and alcohol from sugar in yeast-containing doughs is termed the fermentation period. For the fermentation to take place, the yeast mixture must contain a fermentable sugar. Sucrose (granulated sugar) often is added to batters and doughs to provide food for the yeast. An enzyme in the yeast, *sucrase,* catalyzes the breakdown of sucrose to its two component sugars, glucose and fructose. These two sugars, in turn, are metabolized into the desired carbon dioxide, plus ethyl alcohol.

Sucrase Enzyme in yeast that catalyzes breakdown of sucrose to glucose and fructose to initiate the production of carbon dioxide in batters and doughs containing yeast.

In addition to the sugar that may be added to batters and doughs, there naturally is some sugar available from the flour. About 1 to 2 percent of flour is glucose, which can be used immediately by the yeast to start fermentation. The starch in flour is a rich potential source of glucose for fermentation. The first step in this breakdown process is catalyzed by *beta-amylase,* which progressively attacks the long starch chains until maltose is produced, and then maltose is split into two molecules of glucose. Other enzymes aiding beta-amylase in this extensive breakdown are R-enzyme, Z-enzyme, and limit dextrinase.

Beta-Amylase Enzyme prominent in the catalytic release of maltose and glucose from starch to provide food for yeast.

The production of carbon dioxide by yeast by the fermentation process requires time, but the precise length of time needed is variable, depending largely on the temperature of the medium. Yeast can grow at 50°F, but they multiply far more rapidly when in a medium at 85° to 95°F, the range considered optimal for the proofing of batters and doughs with yeast. Fermentation, the period when alcohol, acids, and carbon dioxide are being generated to double the volume of a yeast-leavened batter or dough, ordinarily requires about 1 hour for the first rising when the surrounding temperature is between 85° and 95°F, but about 8 hours will be required if the mixture is fermented in the refrigerator. *Proofing,* the rising period following shaping and placing in the baking pan, takes only about half as long to double the volume as the time required for the initial fermentation period.

Proofing Fermentation of a yeast-leavened batter or dough in the baking pan to produce the necessary carbon dioxide to double the volume: usually controlled at a temperature between 85° and 95°F.

Too warm a temperature during fermentation and proofing is detrimental to the quality of the finished product, for the flavor and texture may be less pleasing as a result of too much alcohol and carbon dioxide production. If the temperature rises to 110°F, the yeast will be killed by the heat in about an hour, and dead yeast no longer can produce carbon dioxide. At 140°F, yeast will be killed in about 5 minutes. However, carbon dioxide production undergoes considerable stimulus when the yeast temperature is first elevated to warm oven temperatures. In fact, the increase in volume in the preliminary phase of baking is recognized as *oven spring,* a phenomenon that is expected prior to the killing of the yeast.

Oven Spring Sharp increase in volume in early phase of baking due to accelerated carbon dioxide production in a hot oven.

Sugar is added as an ingredient to many batter and dough products to promote the desired fermentation reaction and produce carbon dioxide. As a regulatory measure to counteract partially the effect of sugar, salt also is added in the recipe. Salt has an inhibitory regulatory function in moderating the growth of yeast and, hence, the production of carbon dioxide.

Although yeast must be maintained within a comparatively narrow temperature range for optimal production of carbon dioxide, frozen storage of yeast-containing doughs is not detrimental to the yeast activity upon thawing and warming to normal fermentation temperatures. This capability of yeast to remain viable during frozen storage in batters and doughs has led to the development of unbaked frozen bread doughs that, upon thawing and baking, are accepted widely as a satisfactory replacement for home-baked breads.

Saccharomyces Exigus Yeast primarily responsible for the production of carbon dioxide in acidic, sourdough breads.

Bacteria and Yeast *Saccharomyces cerevisiae* produce carbon dioxide readily at the comparatively neutral reaction of most batters and doughs. However, two other yeasts are involved in the popular sourdough breads. These yeasts, *Saccharomyces exigus* and *Saccharomyces inusitatus,* are active in a distinctly acidic medium. In fact, *S. exigus* can grow very well at the distinctly acidic pH of 4.5, a pH where *S. cerevisiae* cannot thrive.

The acidity needed for the sharp flavor and the growth activity of *S. exigus* and *S. inusitatus* is the result of bacterial action in the mixture. The type of bacteria capable of producing acid in the batter or dough is *Lactobacillus sanfrancisco,* the strain bearing the name of the city of its origin. Happily, *L. sanfrancisco* ferments maltose to produce the acid responsible for the decline in the pH of the proofing mixture to the comparatively low pH range where *S. exigus* and *S. inusitatus* become active in producing the desired carbon dioxide.

This combination of bacteria and yeast needed to produce sourdough bread (often referred to as San Francisco sourdough) requires an extensive incubation period for the necessary acid formation (about 8 hours) and reproduction of yeast to maintain the starter and another very slightly shorter proofing period for the dough prior to baking. Careful maintenance of the starter is essential to quality control, with care being required to avoid contamination of the culture with undesirable bacteria or yeast.

Chemical Agents

Baking Soda Bicarbonate of soda, an alkaline ingredient ($NaHCO_3$).

Separate Ingredients Recipes may obtain part of their leavening from the reaction of acid and alkaline ingredients when both are present. The alkaline ingredient in recipes is *baking soda,* also called sodium bicarbonate or bicarbonate of soda. Baking soda alone is not able to produce carbon dioxide for leavening. However, when this white powder is dissolved and placed in contact with an acid, a chemical reaction occurs, and carbon dioxide is produced. It is this gas that is responsible for the actual leavening.

Several familiar ingredients can be used to provide the acidic reaction needed to combine with soda to produce carbon dioxide. Sour milk and sour cream, as their names indicate, are acidic ingredients. If sour milk is not available, the addition of vinegar or lemon juice (1 to 1½ tablespoons per cup) to milk is sufficient to produce the desired acidity. This acidic milk, when combined with about ½ teaspoon soda per cup of milk, will be neutralized, and carbon dioxide will be released in appropriate quantities to leaven quick breads and cakes containing about 2 cups of flour. Cream of tartar is another acid often available in the home. Honey, molasses, and fruit juices are also acidic ingredients that can produce carbon dioxide when combined with soda.

A couple of limitations are noted when carbon dioxide is to be produced as a result of combining acid and alkaline ingredients. Reasonable speed in completing the mixing and initiating the baking is necessary if an adequate volume is to be achieved using this approach to leavening, for the chemical reaction begins as soon as the dissolved soda and acid are combined. A delay in finishing the mixing and starting baking will permit much of the carbon dioxide to escape from the batter or dough, which results in a poor volume in the finished product. The other problem is that the varying acidity of the acid ingredients makes it difficult to know just exactly how much soda is needed to neutralize the batter. If too much soda is used, the alkaline reaction will contribute a soapy flavor and a yellowish color. If too little soda is used, too little carbon dioxide will be produced. In short, the volume of products leavened with soda and an acid ingredient will vary from time to time and will be influenced significantly by the experience of the chef.

Baking Powder   Baking powder was developed more than a century ago (by a Dr. Price) in Illinois. This invention was lauded because it provided reliable and consistent leavening in baked products. Dr. Price's baking powder was made by combining 60 parts of cream of tartar, 30 parts of baking soda, and 10 parts of potato starch. In this mixture, the cream of tartar provided the acid salt, the baking soda contributed the alkaline salt, and the potato starch served as an absorbent to take up any moisture that might be present and prevent interaction of the two active components. Following this formulation, other acid salts were used to produce baking powders with varying characteristics.

Today's baking powders for the home market are surprisingly similar to the baking powder of Dr. Price's day. Basically, they still are composed of baking soda, starch, and acid salts. The chief difference is that the baking powders on the grocery store shelves contain two acid salts. It is these two salts that cause these powders to be dubbed *double-acting baking powders.* These powders contain a phosphate salt capable of reacting at room temperature when dissolved and a sulfate salt requiring oven temperatures for reaction.

Double-acting Baking Powder Baking powder containing two acid salts: an acid salt that reacts at room temperature (phosphate salt) and one requiring heat for reaction (sulfate salt); common type of baking powder in the retail market.

By law, these powders must provide 12 percent carbon dioxide; by practice, they usually provide 14 percent. Cornstarch is added to protect the viability of the baking powder by absorbing moisture entering the can and preventing reaction of the acid and base during storage. The other function of cornstarch is to serve as a filler so that a measure of the powder will generate the required 12 percent or slightly more carbon dioxide.

SCIENCE NOTE: ACID SALTS

When an acid reacts with baking soda, a salt residue remains after the carbon dioxide has been released. The taste of some of these salt residues sometimes can be noted as an aftertaste. Since these residue flavors may be objectionable to some people, baking powders are judged on the basis of strength of aftertaste as well as such other characteristics as ease of reaction and cost.

Tartrate Salts

On the basis of the lack of aftertaste, tartrate baking powders are deemed to be very desirable, for they can be used at adequate levels with little or no aftertaste. Two of the forms of tartrate salts that are used in making tartrate baking powders are tartaric acid and cream of tartar (properly termed acid potassium tartrate). The reaction of tartaric acid with baking soda is as follows:

$$2\,NaHCO_3 + H_2C_4H_4O_6 \rightarrow Na_2C_4H_4O_6 + 2\,H_2O + 2\,CO_2\uparrow$$

Cream of tartar in baking powder produces carbon dioxide according to the following reaction:

$$NaHCO_3 + KHC_4H_4O_6 \rightarrow NaKC_4H_4O_6 + H_2O + CO_2\uparrow$$

The disadvantages of tartrate baking powders are their completeness of reaction at room temperature and their comparatively high cost. Although people who are experienced and efficient in preparing baked products are able to obtain excellent baked goods using tartrate baking powders, the volume obtained by slower workers may be disappointing. As a result, the tartrate baking powders generally have disappeared from the marketplace. However, ½ teaspoon cream of tartar may be blended thoroughly with ¼ teaspoon soda and used in place of 1 teaspoon of commercial baking powder if a tartrate powder is desired.

Phosphate Salts

Sodium acid pyrophosphate (SAPP) and monocalcium phosphate (MCP) are two phosphate salts that can be used to combine with baking soda in making a baking powder. Although it is true that the phosphate salts react a little slower than the tartrate, the phosphates are capable of reacting almost completely at room temperature. The reaction of monocalcium phosphate with baking soda is

$$8\,NaHCO_3 + 3\,CaH_4(PO_4)_2 \rightarrow Ca_3(PO_4)_2 + 4\,Na_2HPO_4 + 8\,H_2O + 8\,CO_2\uparrow$$

The ready reaction of both the tartrates and the phosphates at room temperature helps to develop a fairly fine texture in baked products as long as the mixing and baking proceed rapidly enough to denature the protein and set the structure of the product before the carbon dioxide all escapes from the baking product. A poor volume can result if delays occur or if mixing is unduly long.

Sulfate Salt

Sodium aluminum sulfate is a salt that, when combined with water, forms sulfuric acid and then reacts with soda to form carbon dioxide primarily at oven temperatures; when the reaction does occur, it leaves a residue with a penetrating, bitter taste. When used as the sole acid in a baking powder, sodium aluminum sulfate (often referred to simply as SAS) generates carbon dioxide so late in the baking period that the crust may set before very much volume has developed. The reaction of this somewhat reluctant sulfate salt occurs in two steps:

$$Na_2Al_2(SO_4)_4 + 6\,H_2O \rightarrow 2\,Al(OH)_3 + Na_2SO_4 + 3\,H_2SO_4$$

$$3\,H_2SO_4 + 6\,NaHCO_3 \rightarrow 3\,Na_2SO_4 + 6\,H_2O + 2\,CO_2\uparrow$$

Sulfate-Phospate Salts

To obtain the desired release of some carbon dioxide during mixing to help promote a fine and uniform texture and also to have sufficient gas available in the baking period, a combination of two acid salts was selected for incorporation with baking soda. The two salts chosen were a sulfate salt for gas generation in the oven and a phosphate salt for the necessary production of gas during the mixing of a batter or dough. To indicate these two different contributions, the resulting powder was dubbed a double-acting or sulfate-phosphate baking powder. The approximate ratio of the two types of acid salts is 1 part SAS (sulfate) to 4 parts phosphate. The reactions from the two salts are those already presented for the respective salts.

Commercial Leavening Agents

Food processors have choices in leavening that are not available to the consumer. Various acid salts are used to combine with soda in the commercial mixes presently being marketed. There even is a flour for consumers in which the baking powder and salt (for flavoring) are already added so that no additional leavening is used in making the product. This type of flour is marketed as *self-rising flour*.

Self-rising Flour Flour containing the necessary amounts of baking powder and salt for preparing batters and doughs, making it necessary to eliminate these two ingredients from recipes using self-rising flour.

Commercial food manufacturers select the specific acid salts needed to optimize the quality of the particular product being prepared. These salts and the baking soda are added as separate ingredients, but in amounts calculated to react completely and thus to avoid changes in the acidity or alkalinity of the batter or dough. By keeping the acid salts separated from the soda until mixing is being done, the production of carbon dioxide is not a problem during shelf storage. Among the acid salts used commercially, there are several phosphate salts. Sodium acid pyrophosphate (SAPP), monocalcium phosphate (MCP), and sodium aluminum phosphate (SAP) are common ones in the baking industry. Glucono-delta-lactone is another type of acid salt of importance as an acidic ingredient for leavening.

SUMMARY

Leavening of baked products is achieved by the inclusion of air and water (to produce steam), often augmented by carbon dioxide. The contribution of air in leavening baked products is influenced by the amount of manipulation, the viscosity of the batter, the nature of the ingredients, and the length of time elapsing before baking. Steam is particularly important in leavening popovers, puff pastry, and cream puffs, but it is of some significance in leavening any baked product.

Carbon dioxide is a very effective gas in promoting leavening. It is the result of the reaction of an alkaline ingredient (baking soda) with an acid ingredient or an acid salt in a baking powder mixture. Acid ingredients in foods include sour milk, sour cream, cream of tartar, molasses, honey, and fruit juices. Baking powders in the retail market are double-acting baking powders containing a sulfate and a phosphate salt as acid ingredients. Baking soda is the alkaline ingredient.

Carbon dioxide is available in a more leisurely fashion when *Saccharomyces cerevisiae* (baker's yeast) are included in the batter or dough and are allowed to ferment until enough carbon dioxide is produced to double the volume. Sugar is used as food for the yeast to metabolize and produce the desired carbon dioxide. Salt serves as a means of controlling the rate of yeast growth in yeast-leavened products. Temperature control is vital to maintaining viable yeast for the desired gas production at a reasonable fermentation rate. Sourdough bread provides another example of the use of microorganisms as sources of carbon dioxide: *L. sanfrancisco* produces acid from maltose, and *S. exigus* and *S. inusitatus* thrive in the acidic environment and generate carbon dioxide for leavening.

Selected References

Ayres, J. C. et al. *Microbiology of Foods*. W. H. Freeman. San Francisco. 1980. pp. 187–190.

Cooper, E. J. and G. Reed. Yeast fermentation—effect of temperature, pH, ethanol, sugars, salt, and osmotic pressure. *Baker's Digest 42(6):* 22. 1968.

Dunn, J. A. and J. R. White. Leavening action of air included in cake batter. *Cereal Chem 16:* 93. 1939.

Golal, A. M. et al. Lactic acid and volatile (C_2—C_5) organic acids of San Francisco sourdough French bread. *Cereal Chem. 55:* 461. 1978.

Hood, M. P. and B. Lowe. Air, water vapor, and carbon dioxide as leavening gases in cakes made with different types of fats. *Cereal Chem. 25:* 244. 1948.

Oszlanyi, A. G. Instant yeast. *Baker's Digest 54(4):* 16. 1980.

Pomper, S. Biochemistry of yeast fermentation. *Baker's Digest 42(2):* 32. 1969.

Ponte, J. G., Jr. et al. Studies on the behavior of active dry yeast in breadmaking. *Cereal Chem. 37: 263.* 1960.

Saunders, R. M. et al. Sugars of flour and their involvement in the San Francisco sour dough French bread process. *Cereal Chem. 49: 86.* 1972.

Sugihara, T. F. et al. Nature of the San Francisco sour dough French bread process. II. Microbiological aspects. *Baker's Digest 44(2): 51.* 1970.

Reiman, H. M. Chemical leavening systems. *Baker's Digest 51(4): 33.* 1977.

White, J. W., Jr. Honey. *Adv. Food Res. 24: 304.* 1978.

Study Questions

1. Identify and explain the factors that influence the leavening contribution of air in various batters and doughs.
2. Will yeast be able to produce carbon dioxide in a dough that does not contain sugar as an ingredient? Explain your answer. Describe the leavening developing in a yeast-leavened dough with added sugar and in one made without added sugar.
3. What are the three basic constituents of baking powder? Explain the function of each.
4. What are the pros and cons for using a double-acting baking powder?

Pieter Breugel, detail from "Peasant Wedding." Kunsthistorisches Museum, Vienna.

CHAPTER 12

BASICS OF BATTERS AND DOUGHS

INTRODUCING FLOUR MIXTURES

Batters and doughs, when baked, add considerable interest as well as nutrition to the diet. These products range from a wide variety of breads to numerous desserts, including cakes, pastries, and cookies, and have served as a mainstay of the diet for many civilizations over the centuries. In fact, the ancient Egyptians apparently had the ability to make leavened bread more than 5000 years ago! Breads take many different shapes and include diverse ingredients, depending upon the particular staple foods available and the cultural preferences of consumers.

Interest in bread has undergone a resurgence in the past few years as the nation has become aware of the nutritional merits of eating complex carbohydrates and fiber. The enthusiasm for natural foods without preservatives has prompted the baking industry to market breads containing a variety of whole-grain cereals. Consequently, the standards that people formerly used for selecting breads in the market have undergone some significant changes from the ''balloon'' loaves of earlier years. This same movement is reflected in the increase in baking bread at home, particularly breads made with mixtures of different flours.

Baked products have certain ingredients in common, but these ingredients can be combined in varying ratios and with diverse techniques to make many different foods to be used from appetizers to desserts in meals. All these products possess a structural network, a combination of protein and starch, responsible for holding the baked item together. Much of the study of batters and doughs is directed toward the development and solidification of this network. Wheat, with its unique proteins, is the basis of high-quality batter and dough products. No other cereal or other type of food possesses the specific characteristics that can be developed when wheat flour is used in mixing and baking batters and doughs. The nature of wheat flour and its contributions to batters and doughs, as well as the roles of other ingredients of batters and doughs, are discussed in this chapter.

WHEAT FLOUR

Flour Finely ground cereal grains; often used to imply wheat as the grain.

Flour is the name applied to any finely ground cereal grain, although many people use the term to mean specifically the product resulting from grinding wheat. It is the protein in wheat that makes it possible to produce breads capable of withstanding the force involved in spreading butter or margarine on them. Protein also is responsible for the fact that cakes and pastries made with wheat flour can be cut and served without disintegrating. The key protein complex in wheat flour is called gluten, and this gluten is responsible for the elastic and cohesive nature of batters and doughs made with this type of flour. The starch in that same flour is of value in strengthening structure and absorbing the extra liquid during baking. However, the starch from any type of flour can perform these functions. It is the protein in wheat that is so distinctive.

The mature wheat plant forms seeds or kernels, the portion of the plant used for making flour.

Milling

Milling Grinding and separating of the desired fractions of the cereal kernel to produce flour.

To obtain the flour used in making baked products, the wheat grains undergo a grinding and refining procedure, a process called *milling*. Milling begins with the grinding of whole wheat kernels after a very brief preliminary steam (tempering) treatment, which facilitates separation of the outer bran layers and the germ from the endosperm (see Chapter 7). Grinding shatters the endosperm and splits off the bran coating, although the bran tends to remain intact. At the same time, the fat content in the germ allows the germ to be pressed into flakes, and these separate readily from the endosperm.

Separation of the various fractions of the kernel is done by using air currents. The differing weights of the various fractions cause them to be tossed with varying ease by the currents. The different fractions can be directed in streams and collected to give the blend desired for a particular flour product. The flour streams can be selected to range from whole wheat flour to very refined or selective products.

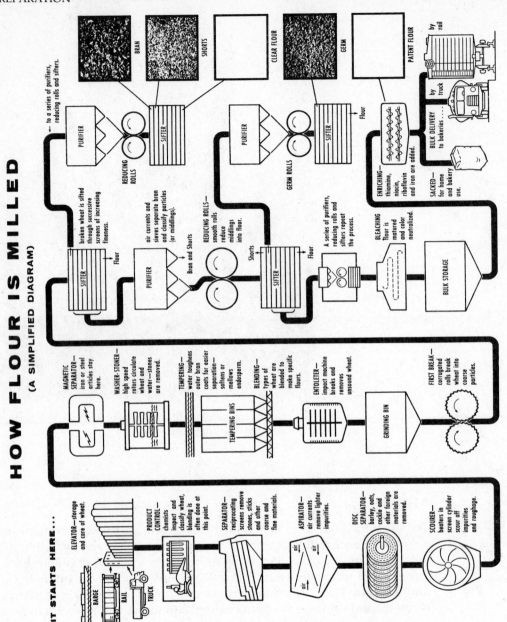

HOW FLOUR IS MILLED
(A SIMPLIFIED DIAGRAM)

IT STARTS HERE...

ELEVATOR—storage and care of wheat.

PRODUCT CONTROL—chemists inspect and classify wheat, blending is often done at this point.

SEPARATOR—reciprocating screens remove stones, sticks and other coarse and fine materials.

ASPIRATOR—air currents remove lighter impurities.

DISC SEPARATOR—barley, oats, cockle and other foreign materials are removed.

SCOURER—beaters in screen cylinder scour off impurities and roughage.

MAGNETIC SEPARATOR—iron or steel articles stay here.

WASHER-STONER—high speed rotors circulate wheat and water—stones are removed.

TEMPERING—water toughens outer bran coats for easier separation—softens or mellows endosperm.

BLENDING—types of wheat are blended to make specific flours.

ENTOLETER—impact machine breaks and removes unsound wheat.

FIRST BREAK—corrugated rolls break wheat into coarse particles.

BRAN

SHORTS

CLEAR FLOUR

GERM

PATENT FLOUR

PURIFIER

REDUCING ROLLS

SIFTER

PURIFIER

GERM ROLLS

SIFTER

Flour

ENRICHING—thiamine, niacin, riboflavin and iron are added.

SACKED—for home and bakery use.

BULK DELIVERY to bakeries.....

by rail

by truck

— to a series of purifiers, reducing rolls and sifters.

SIFTER

Flour

broken wheat is sifted through successive screens of increasing fineness.

PURIFIER

air currents and sieves separate bran and classify particles (or middlings).

Bran and Shorts

REDUCING ROLLS—smooth rolls reduce middlings into flour.

Shorts

SIFTER

Flour

A series of purifiers, reducing rolls and sifters repeat the process.

BLEACHING Flour is matured and color neutralized.

BULK STORAGE

Schematic diagram of the milling of flour.

NOTE: This chart is greatly simplified. The sequence, number and complexity of different operations vary in different mills.

Bleaching and Maturing

Freshly milled wheat flour tends to produce products with reduced volume and rather sticky doughs, characteristics that do not exist if a mature flour is used. Unfortunately, maturing or aging is costly because of the cost of the storage space and also because of prospective loss due to insects or rodents during prolonged storage. To overcome the performance objections and to shorten the storage times, the milling industry adds bleaching and maturing agents to the freshly milled flour. The additives approved for use include chlorine dioxide gas, acetone peroxides, and oxides of nitrogen. Soft wheat flours may be matured and bleached with chlorine gas and nitrosyl chloride. These bleaching agents lighten the pigments (xanthophyll and anthoxan-thins) in the flour. The improved baking performance is attributed to a change in the chemical structure of the protein (see ''Science Note—Flour Proteins and Lipids'').

Enrichment

Since the milling of flour splits the vitamin- and mineral-rich bran and germ from the endosperm and removes these fractions in refined flours, much of the nutritive value of flour is lost. The advantage of milling is that the keeping quality of the refined flour is raised due to the removal of the germ and its fat (with its potential for becoming rancid). To compensate for the removal of important nutrients, a federal enrichment program has been developed to add three B vitamins (thiamin, riboflavin, and niacin) and iron back into a pound of flour at levels of 2.9 milligrams of thiamin, 1.8 milligrams of riboflavin, 24.0 milligrams of niacin, and 13.0 to 16.5 miligrams of iron. Calcium is an optional additive, but if added, it is to be added at the rate of 960 milligrams per pound of flour. Flour that has been enriched must bear a label indicating this, but there is no federal legislation requiring that enrichment of refined flour be done. Most states now have legislation mandating that all refined flour and bakery products made with refined flour must be enriched. Although the enriched flours are not enriched with all of the nutrients lost in milling and refining wheat, they are very wholesome and nourishing, and they do provide important sources of three B vitamins and iron. Enriched, refined flour produces lighter baked products with finer textures and volume than can be made using the whole-grain flour or blends of whole-grain wheat flour with other cereal flours. However, the nutritive value of the whole-grain products is slightly higher, and their ranges of flavor, color, and textural character are greater than in products made of enriched, refined flour. The choice can be based on personal preference, for either flour represents an intelligent approach to good nutrition.

Types of Flour

Bread Flour   Bakers utilize bread flour to bake breads because of the strong structure provided by the gluten in this type of flour. The comparatively high protein in this hard wheat flour is ideal for developing the cohesive crumb quality needed in breads. Bread flour ordinarily is not available for home use.

All Purpose Flour
Flour from hard or hard and soft wheat blended; protein content of about 10.5 percent and suitable for making most baked products.

All-Purpose Flour All-purpose flour is made from hard wheat or a blend of hard and soft wheat. These wheats, commonly grown in the central part of the nation, usually result in a flour with a protein content of about 10.5 percent. The protein content is sufficient to make satisfactory breads, yet is is not so strong that cakes will be unpleasantly tough. Consequently, all-purpose flour can be used with reasonable success to make any type of baked product for families, which explains its other names—family flour.

All-purpose flour is available bleached and unbleached, to suit individual consumer preferences. The unbleached version is preferred by people who are concerned about additives in food and who are willing to accept baked goods of somewhat reduced quality in preference to consuming additives. This clearly is a matter of individual choice, for evidence of harm from the use of approved additives for bleaching flour is lacking.

Cake Flour Flour from soft wheat; contains about 7.5 percent protein.

Cake Flour The desired tenderness and fine texture in cakes are promoted by the use of *cake flour*. This type of flour, made from soft wheat, has a protein content of only about 7.5 percent. Not only is it significantly lower in protein than all-purpose flour, but the protein structure resulting from use of cake flour is more tender and finer than the comparable all-purpose product is.

Pastry Flour Pastry flour is quite similar to cake flour in that it contains about 7.5 percent protein and also is made from soft wheat. However, it is not ground to as fine a particle size as is cake flour. This is the type of flour preferred by commercial bakers for making cookies and pastries, but it is not commonly available to home bakers.

Whole Wheat Flour
Flour containing the bran and germ, as well as the endosperm.

Whole Wheat Flour As the name implies, the entire wheat grain is used in making whole wheat flour. The presence of the bran adds a slightly crunchy texture and a light brown color. Unfortunately, the presence of the germ limits the shelf life of *whole wheat flour*, because of the fat present in this portion of the grain. The products made with whole wheat flour are a bit more compact, lower in volume, and more chewy than are those made with refined all-purpose flour.

Self-Rising Flour Self-rising flour is, in a sense, a partial mix for baking. It contains not only flour, but also an acid salt (usually monocalcium phosphate), baking soda, and salt (sodium chloride), the amounts of these providing the equivalent of half a tablespoon of baking powder and a half a teaspoon of salt per cup of the self-rising flour. Recipes stipulating self-rising flour have already been adjusted to compensate for these additions, but the salt and baking powder need to be omitted if using self-rising flour in recipes based on use of all-purpose flour. Similarly, self-rising flour is not well suited for use in yeast-leavened products. The wheat used in producing self-rising flour is a blend of hard and soft wheats to give a total protein content of about 9.3 percent, somewhat lower than the usual level in all-purpose flour. Self-rising flour is particularly popular in the South, where it is often preferred for making biscuits.

Gluten Flour The protein level in gluten flour is raised to about 41 percent by the addition of vital wheat gluten, a dry form of gluten. This gives a distinctly chewy texture to breads made with this type of flour. From the perspective of nutrition, there is no need to use this type of flour, for the average American diet contains far more protein than is needed. However, gluten flour does add variety to the types of breads in the diet and clearly is an appropriate choice for those who like it.

Other Flours Rye flour is used in conjunction with wheat flour in making rye bread. Although rye flour has some capability in contributing to structure because of its protein, the protein in rye is less cohesive and elastic than is that comprising the gluten in wheat.

Triticale Grain produced by crossing rye and wheat; its flour has a protein mixture with some potential for making good baked products.

Triticale is a comparatively new grain, having been developed through cross breeding of wheat and rye. It carries some of the characteristics of both parent grains, but it cannot be used in place of wheat in achieving optimum quality in baked products. However, continuing research efforts exploring the utilization of triticale in baking may eventually make triticale products quite acceptable without the addition of wheat flours. The somewhat higher level of lysine in triticale, in comparison with wheat proteins, makes triticale of interest nutritionally. Partial substitution of wheat flour with triticale in breads and other baked products can be done with good results.

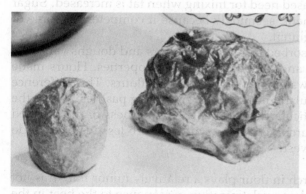

Gluten ball from cake flour (left) and from all-purpose flour (right). The smaller content of protein in cake flour is evident when compared with the all-purpose flour product. The balls are essentially all protein, the starch having been removed by washing under running water to prepare this demonstration.

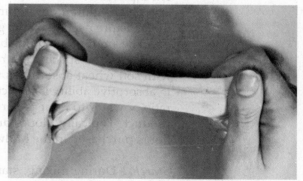

Gluten, an elastic protein complex formed when wheat flour and liquid are mixed together, is able to stretch during baking until the temperature becomes so hot that the protein denatures. This denatured gluten is responsible for much of the structure of baked products.

Use of Flour in Baked Products

Gluten   When water and wheat flour are mixed together, a cohesive quality begins to develop in the dough or batter, leading to increased resistance to mixing and an elasticity. These characteristics are the result of an association between insoluble proteins in the flour to form a complex known collectively as *gluten*. Gluten can be stretched into fairly thin strands to form cell walls in batters and doughs during the early phase of baking and then to become rigid in the extended conformation as heat denatures the protein. In essence, this describes the significance of wheat gluten in providing the structure to baked products.

Gluten Protein complex formed in batters and doughs when wheat flour is mixed with water (or other aqueous liquid).

Development of the optimum gluten network is central to making batter and dough products of excellent quality. Too little gluten development is evidenced by a crumbly baked product that is difficult to serve. Too much gluten development results in a tough, chewy product with slightly reduced volume. The amount of mixing actually needed to develop gluten depends upon the presence of other ingredients. When the ratio of liquid to flour is high (1:1), as it is in popover batter, gluten is developed with difficulty. However, in muffins, which have a liquid to flour ratio of about 1:2, the batter is so sticky that the gluten strands tend to adhere to each other during mixing, causing them to develop readily. A similar situation is found in the somewhat more viscous 1:3 ratio of liquid to flour in biscuits, although the increased viscosity makes it possible to do somewhat more mixing in biscuits than in muffins before a tough product results.

The presence of added fat interferes with gluten development, making it necessary to increase the amount of mixing as the amount of fat in a recipe increases. The coating provided by the fat, coupled with the difficulty that water has in penetrating the fat coating to interact with the gluten, is the apparent explanation for the increased need for mixing when fat is increased. Sugar also delays gluten development, seemingly because it competes for some of the moisture needed by the gluten.

The amount of liquid absorbed by gluten in batters and doughs varies according to the specific flour and its gluten-forming properties. Flours made with soft wheat absorb less water than do hard wheat flours. This difference in absorptive ability is particularly noticeable in preparing pastries, where the ratio of water to flour is particularly critical to the tenderness of the finished product. Typically, flours purchased in the South absorb less water than do flours purchased in the Midwest.

Starch.   During mixing, starch in flour plays a relatively minor role. It is not until the starch begins to undergo gelatinization in response to the heat in the oven that much water is absorbed into the granules. During baking, starch aggressively absorbs water in an attempt to gelatinize the granules. In very fluid batters, considerable swelling and gelatinization occur, because there is sufficient liquid there for this physical change to progress smoothly. The gelatinized starch contributes meaningfully to the strength of the cell walls in which the granules are imbedded. In fact, moderately acceptable cakes can be made using pure starch as the primary structural ingredient when gluten-free baked goods are needed for special diets. This is in contrast to the high-quality cakes that can be prepared when flour, with both its protein and starch, is the principal structural agent.

SCIENCE NOTE: FLOUR PROTEINS AND LIPIDS

Soluble Proteins—Albumins and Globulins

To help clarify the various proteins found in flour, these often are classified according to solubility. On the basis of solubility, two types of proteins—the albumins and globulins—are classified as soluble proteins. The comparatively small amount of these proteins (only about 15 percent) and the seemingly minimal significance of either of these globular proteins in relation to structure have caused the globulins and albumins in flour to gain little research attention.

Gluten

Gliadin Sticky fraction of gluten.

Gliadin The remaining 85 percent of the flour protein is said to be insoluble, although about half is soluble in alcohol. This protein, which is soluble in 70 percent alcohol, is called *gliadin*. When isolated from the other proteins, gliadin (molecular weight of 50,000) is a viscous liquid. The gliadin molecules, which are polypeptide chains in an apparently fairly spherical, compact shape, contribute to the sticky, flowing character of the gluten complex, partly because of their high glutamic acid content and consequent ability to form secondary bonds between molecules.

Glutenin Very large, elastic component of gluten.

Glutenin Glutenin (molecular weight of 2–3 million) is considered to be the protein fraction responsible for the elastic quality of the gluten complex. Actually, glutenin is not a single protein, but consists of two and probably more fractions that have a somewhat fibrous character. Proline is abundant, which limits the physical, spatial configurations the molecules may assume. Cystine, another amino acid occurring in glutenin, contributes disulfide bonds. In fact, the presence of sulfhydryl groups and disulfide bonds (both of which are subject to change from oxidation and reduction) is involved in the elasticity of the gluten complex, a characteristic of considerable importance in achieving the desired volume.

The Complex For gliadin and glutenin to form an elastic and cohesive complex, manipulation is needed to bring these two fractions together in a complicated and intimate association. It is probable that the glutenin molecules associate to form a loose network of these elongated molecules, with the more compact gliadin molecules being trapped in this network in a somewhat random fashion. The fluid nature of the gliadin probably permits some slippage of the glutenin fibers over each other during mixing.

Lipids

Surprisingly, the elaborate combination of gliadin and glutenin to make gluten is not adequate alone to produce the familiar elastic and tenacious qualities seen in batters and doughs. The lipids naturally present in flour also are important, even though their quantity (less than 2 percent) may seem rather insignificant. The fats are present primarily as phospholipids and glycolipids. The glycolipids are primarily galactose combined with fat, giving molecules that can use hydrogen bonds and van der Waals forces effectively to bind with the proteins in the flour. It is hypothesized that the glycolipids in flour act almost like a sandwich filling between layers of the gluten complex.

Although the importance of lipids and of the two principal fractions of gluten (gliadin and glutenin) have been studied extensively, there still is much to be learned about the complex formation of the structure in baked products. Research is ongoing in this field of proteins and lipids and their interactions.

FUNCTIONS OF OTHER INGREDIENTS

Eggs

Eggs, depending on the quantity used and the treatment prior to inclusion in the batter, may fulfill a variety of important functions in addition to adding to the nutritive value of the product. During the mixing of a batter or dough, eggs act as a liquid to help moisten dry ingredients and to assist in developing the gluten. The coagulation of egg proteins during baking adds to the stability of the structure of baked products, with the actual importance of this added strength being dependent on the amount of egg used. In popovers and angel cakes, for example, the amount of protein provided by the eggs is an important adjunct to the structure provided by the flour. Additionally, eggs contribute flavor, and, when the yolks are used, color also is enhanced.

Beaten eggs add to the leavening of baked products because of the air they hold trapped within the foam. Egg white foams are particularly important in aiding with leavening. However, the egg yolk foam used in sponge cakes is a particularly good example of the fact that yolks can also be significant sources of air.

The emulsifying ability of egg yolks is an important factor in producing smooth cake batters. Another example of the use of egg yolks as emulsifying agents is in the preparation of cream puffs, for they contain a very large proportion of fat, which would separate from the flour and liquid were it not for the binding ability of the egg yolks, with their content of lecithin (a noted emulsifying agent).

Sugar

The obvious function of sugar in baked products is to provide a sweet taste. If light or dark brown sugar is used in place of refined sugar, additional flavors are added. Honey is yet another source of sweetness and accompanying flavor variations. Sugar substitutes afford an alternative means of sweetening baked products. However, these variations in the form of sweetening, when substituted in batters and doughs for refined sugar, quickly reveal that sugar does far more than merely sweeten baked products.

One of the important contributions of sugar is to aid in the browning of the crust of baking products. Although the sucrose (refined sugar) itself does not participate in the Maillard reaction, glucose and fructose liberated by hydrolysis from the original sucrose can react with protein to cause the surface browning. In fact, when honey or fructose is substituted for refined sugar in batters and doughs, the Maillard reaction is much more intense because of the abundance of reducing sugar available from either of these sources to participate.

Tenderness and volume of baked products are important characteristics influenced by the amount of sugar in relation to other ingredients in batters and doughs. The strongly hygroscopic (water-attracting) nature of sugar introduces a strong competition with flour for the liquid, which means that sugar will decrease the amount of liquid actually available to the developing gluten complex. This change means that additional mixing is needed to develop the gluten satisfactorily in products containing sugar, and the amount of mixing needed increases directly with the increase in the quantity of sugar. This can be illustrated by comparing the preparation of muffins and shortened cakes. Muffins have a very small amount of sugar added, and a minimal amount of mixing is required to develop the gluten appropriately. On the other hand, shortened cakes have a comparatively large amount of sugar (and other interfering ingredients, too), necessitating a considerable amount of manipulation to develop the desired gluten network. Actually, sugar is a helpful ingredient during mixing because it allows sufficient time for adequate blending of the ingredients before the gluten is developed too much.

Sugar also has a tenderizing effect, due to two actions. As just noted, gluten development is delayed by sugar, and this delay helps to keep gluten from becoming so developed that it is tough and chewy. The second action to help tenderize products by adding sugar is involved in the baking period. An increase in the amount of sugar in a recipe results in a somewhat higher coagulation temperature of the protein present. If a baking flour mixture has to be heated to an elevated temperature before the gluten denatures and sets the structure, the elastic nature of the gluten will be maintained for a longer time than if no sugar is present. During this extended period of time when the glutten remains elastic, the pressure of the hot gases within the cells keeps stretching the cell walls thinner and thinner. Thin cell walls are more tender than thick cell walls. In short, the sugar causes a higher coagulation temperature and longer period of time for stretching the gluten into thin cell walls before denaturation occurs; this is the second reason for regarding sugar as a tenderizing ingredient.

The increased temperature of denaturation of the gluten when sugar is increased also explains the way in which sugar influences volume. Up to a certain critical point, increasing sugar will increase volume because of the extended period of stretching cell walls. However, if cell walls get stretched too thin before the gluten denatures, the cells will explode because the gluten strands will break from the pressure generated by the hot gases. This situation is analogous to blowing up a balloon until it is stretched so thin that the material simply cannot stretch enough to accommodate the pressure of the enclosed air. When the cells in baking products reach the point of exploding, the product falls and remains extremely compact.

Sugar substitutes do not have effects comparable to sugar on the tenderness and volume of baked products, because they have little influence on the development and coagulation temperature of the gluten. Even the use of sugars other than sucrose will give somewhat different results in tenderness and volume.

Salt

Salt is used to enhance flavors in baked products. Its other function is to regulate the growth of yeast in yeast doughs, where it serves to counterbalance the stimulating effect of sugar and to help tighten the gluten, both of which aid in avoiding a coarse texture.

Leavening Agents

Leavening agents, as discussed in Chapter 11, are necessary to increase the volume and promote development of the desired texture in baked products. They need to be included in amounts adequate to achieve the desired volume without imparting an undesirable flavor or aftertaste. The American Home Economics Association (1980) recommends between 1 and 2 teaspoons of baking powder per cup of flour for most baked products.

Liquids

Milk is the liquid used most commonly in batters and doughs, though water, sour milk, sour cream, or fruit juices sometimes serve as the liquid. Liquid aids in the development of the gluten. Without liquid to help hydrate the mixture, gluten does not develop. Liquid also is needed to gelatinize starch during the baking period; gelatinized starch adds rigidity and strength to cell walls. Fruit juices and the other liquids with distinctive flavors add to the flavor of the baked product, but they may affect the denaturation of protein and the gelatinization of starch.

Leavening action is provided by liquids when they are converted to steam during baking. They also serve as a solvent to activate the reaction of baking powder to produce carbon dioxide. Unless baking powder is dissolved, the reaction between the soda and acid salt will not occur. Similarly, baking soda must be dissolved if it is being used in conjunction with an acid ingredient. For example, the liquid in sour milk dissolves the soda, and the acid in the milk then reacts with the soda to generate carbon dioxide for leavening.

Fats and Oils

An important function of fats and oils is to tenderize baked products by impeding gluten development. The coating of fat that develops on gluten strands tends to block water from the flour proteins needing the liquid for gluten development. This coating of fat also has a lubricating effect.

The texture of various baked products reflects the type of fat used, particularly in recipes where the fat content is comparatively high. For instance, pastry made with oil tends to have a granular texture in contrast to the flaky, layered texture of a pastry made with a firm fat, such as shortening. Fats also promote a soft crumb in breads and cakes.

Fats contribute to the flavor of baked goods, particularly when a flavorful one (butter or margarine) is used. Even when the fat itself has little apparent flavor, there is a richness of flavor that is promoted by the presence of the fat. Yellow margarine, butter, or other colored fat adds to the creamy color of breads, cakes, and other items in which they are used. The color often is perceived as indicating a particularly rich product, possibly causing improved flavor acceptance by some people.

The specific contributions made by a fat are dependent, in part, upon the type of fat being used (See Chapter 5). Selection of the appropriate fat for making a specific batter or dough can result in a product with optimum characteristics. Since the physical properties and composition vary from one type of fat to another, it is necessary to modify recipes when substitutions of fat are being made.

MIXING TECHNIQUES

Individual technique in preparing batters and doughs can have a very significant effect on the final volume, texture, and tenderness of baked products. Certain key words are used in recipe instructions to indicate the operations to be used during preparation. Each of the following terms has a specific meaning in relation to preparing batters and doughs. These need to be understood and then practiced until quality products are prepared each time.

Creaming Mixing fat and sugar together vigorously to create an air-in-fat foam.

Creaming is the creation of a heavy, air-in-fat foam by agitating solid fat and sugar together until the mixture is somewhat light and fluffy. This may be done with the aid of an electric mixer or by mixing fairly vigorously with a wooden spoon or paddle. Creaming should be discontinued if the mixture begins to lose volume and become soft.

Beating Very vigorous agitation of food mixtures using an electric mixer at high speed or a wooden spoon to trap air and/or to develop gluten.

Stirring Gentle blending of ingredients when trapping of air and development of gluten are not necessary.

Folding Very gentle manipulation with a rubber spatula, narrow metal spatula, wire whisk, or whip to bring ingredients up from the bottom and spread them over the upper surface to aid in blending them uniformly.

Cutting In Process of cutting solid fats into small pieces with the use of a pastry blender or two table knives.

Kneading Folding over of a ball of dough and pressing it with either the fingertips or the heels of both hands, depending upon the amount of gluten needing to be developed and the ratio of ingredients.

Beating is rapid agitation of a mixture of foods with the aid of an electric mixer or a wooden spoon. This action is more vigorous than creaming and is applied on a wide range of ingredients. Usually the purposes are to beat in air and to develop gluten.

Stirring is gentle mixing of ingredients to blend them thoroughly. This technique is used when trapping of air is not necessary and when excessive gluten development needs to be avoided.

Folding is a gentle motion designed to bring ingredients up from the bottom of the mixing bowl and spread them across the upper portion of a foam or batter with minimum disruption. This process is repeated, with every fifth stroke coming up through the middle to facilitate uniform blending, until the entire mixture is homogenous. A rubber spatula is particularly well suited for folding, because it scrapes the ingredients up from the bottom efficiently. Other utensils suitable for folding include a narrow metal spatula or a wire whip or whisk. The important action in folding is to blend ingredients thoroughly with a minimum development of gluten or loss of air from the foam.

Cutting in is the technique used to cut solid fats into small particles in the preparation of pastries and biscuits. A pastry blender is designed specifically for doing this task efficiently, but two table knives can be used in a cross-cutting motion to accomplish the desired result. A light, tossing motion with the pastry blender is important in avoiding packing the fat into a solid mass while the cutting in is being done.

Kneading is the mixing together of ingredients with the hands or a dough hook on a mixer. Techniques for kneading vary, depending upon the amount of gluten needing to be developed. In yeast breads, considerable gluten needs to be developed, so the kneading technique involves a folding over of the dough and then a vigorous push with the heel of both hands simultaneously. The dough is turned a quarter of a turn, and the process is repeated in a rhythmic pattern until the gluten is developed to the point where blisters can be seen under the surface of the dough, but the dough itself has a smooth surface. Since gluten develops very readily in preparing biscuit dough, the folded dough is pushed gently with just the fingertips of both hands, after which the dough is turned a quarter of a turn, and the process is repeated. Only a brief kneading period with this gentle kneading stroke is used for making biscuits to avoid causing them to become tough. Kneading not only mixes ingredients, it also develops the necessary gluten network and contributes to the desired flaky quality of biscuits. The extensive amount of kneading in yeast bread doughs is done so much that the layers of the folded dough tend to merge together into a continuous gluten network, and layering or flakiness is not present.

BAKING

Preparation of pans for baking varies with the product and with the container selected. Breads being baked in pans with sides can be removed easily if the sides and bottom of the pans are greased lightly (unless the pan has a nonstick coating). Layer cakes can be removed easily from pans if the bottom of the pan is lined with a layer of wax paper or is greased. The sides are not greased, which helps the cake cling to the sides and pull upward during baking. Foam cakes (angel, sponge, and chiffon) can be removed easily when baked in ungreased tube pans of two-part construction. Nonstick coatings on tube pans are not recommended when foam cakes are being prepared, because the cakes are likely to fall out when the pan is inverted to maintain the cake at maximum volume during cooling. Usually, cookies are baked on nonstick cooky sheets or jelly roll pans or simply on ungreased sheets. A spatula is used to remove the cookies from the baking sheet when they come out of the oven before they stick hard and tend to break easily. Avoiding greasing cooky sheets saves the problem of burning and polymerizing fat in all of the areas where the bare pan is exposed between the cookies.

Before turning on an oven, check the rack position and shift the rack if necessary. When baking in a preheated oven, baking pans should be baked in the center rack position, with sufficient space between pans and between pans and the oven edges to permit good air circulation and achieve relatively uniform browning. Pans should not be placed directly underneath one another; the top pan will not bake adequately on the bottom, and the bottom pan will be too done on the bottom and very pale on the top. Preheating allows baking to begin immediately at the desired temperature, but this practice wastes energy. Yeast breads should be baked in a preheated oven when volume has doubled, or else they should be started in a cold oven before they have doubled in volume. Too much oven spring occurs, and a coarse texture results if a cold start is used on rolls that already have doubled.

When starting cakes, quick breads, or other baked products in a cold oven, the oven rack should be positioned just above the center. This added distance from the heating element at the bottom of the oven will eliminate excessive browning (or possibly burning) while the oven is being heated to the appropriate temperature. When baking from a cold start, more time is necessary than is indicated in the recipe to reach the desired end point because of the low temperature during the early phase of baking. Foam cakes have the potential to lose gas from the foams and for the heavier ingredients to begin to drain toward the bottom to form a layer if baking is delayed, including starting in a cold oven.

Tests for doneness need to be made for baked products to be sure that the product structure has been set throughout. Tests in the center of the product give information about the exact state of affairs at the coolest point. The delicate nature of the structure of baked goods immediately prior to the setting of the structure with the denaturation of gluten requires that the product be kept pressurized in the oven until coagulation has been accomplished. Then the reduced pressure in the cells as the gases in them cool will not create a problem, for the cell walls will be strong enough to support themselves. Shortened cakes and loaves of quick breads are tested by inserting a toothpick in them and checking to be sure that no batter is clinging to it when it is withdrawn. Foam cakes are done when they spring back after being touched lightly on the surface. Yeast breads, pastries, cookies, and many quick breads are checked on the basis of elapsed time and appropriate browning.

TREATMENT FOLLOWING BAKING

The strength of the structure immediately after baking determines the way in which a specific product will be cooled. Drop cookies, for example, usually are strong enough to be lifted off the baking sheet gently with a spatula when they come from the oven, whereas they will tend to break if allowed to cool on the sheet before they are loosened. Cakes, with the exception of foam cakes, are placed upright on a rack to permit air to circulate under the pan and hasten the cooling. Layers can be cut loose from the edges of the pan, covered with an inverted plate, and then turned over abruptly to unmold them onto the plate while the pan feels warm, but not hot to the hand.

Foam cakes have weak structures when they first come from the oven, and the weight of the cake pushing down on itself in the pan will cause loss of volume while the cake is cooling. This problem is avoided by inverting the tube pan as soon as the cake is taken from the oven and letting the cake hang suspended until the pan is cool. This stretches out the cells during the cooling period, resulting in maximum volume. Once the foam cakes have cooled, they can be removed from the tube pans by cutting the cakes loose around the outer edge and the tube, removing the tube with the cake, and then cutting the cake loose from the bottom of the pan before inverting the tube and cake onto a suitable plate.

Quick breads and yeast breads are quite strong even when first removed from the oven. Therefore, there is no reason to delay taking them from their pans. In fact, breads should be transferred from pans onto cooling racks immediately, unless they are being served at once. Otherwise, the crusts will become soggy from condensing steam.

Breads have a strong structure even when first taken from the oven. To avoid soggy crusts, breads should be removed immediately from baking pans and cooled on a rack.

ADJUSTMENTS FOR ALTITUDE

The decreased atmospheric pressure at elevations of 3000 feet or more causes detectable changes in the quality of baked products unless some modifications in the formula are made. The recommended changes are based on the fact that expansion occurs more readily at high altitudes than at sea level, where the atmospheric pressure is greater. This creates greater resistance to expansion at low elevations than in the mountains. To avoid having cell walls rupture, recipes are modified in the mountains to strengthen cell walls and decrease pressure within the cells. (see ''Science Note—High-Altitude Baking'' in Chapter 14).

SUMMARY

Wheat flour is the basic ingredient in most baked products because of its unique combination of insoluble proteins. When water is added and the mixture is manipulated, these proteins can be worked into a cohesive, elastic complex called gluten. To obtain wheat flour suitable for the consumer market, the wheat grain is milled, bleached and matured, and enriched if the bran and germ have been removed to make a refined flour.

Bread flour is a high-protein flour available primarily to commercial bakers. All-purpose flour, made from hard wheat or a blend of hard and soft wheat to give a protein content of about 10.5 percent, is well suited to the preparation of breads, cookies, pastries, and even some cakes. Cake flour has a protein content of only about 7.5 percent; the rather tender protein from this soft wheat flour is well suited to making cakes. Pastry flour is similar, but a bit coarser than cake flour. Other flours on the market include whole wheat flour, self-rising flour (contains an acid salt, soda, and salt), gluten flour, and flours from other cereals (rye and triticale, for example).

Wheat flour is able to provide the basic structure of baked products because of the protein strands that are developed during the mixing of batters and doughs. Gluten (the protein complex) is a combination of gliadin, a sticky and viscous protein, and glutenin. Glutenin contributes the necessary elasticity of the unbaked protein complex. Lipids in flour are also involved in the formation of the structure during mixing and baking. The presence of sugar and fat delay the development of gluten; the ratio of liquid to flour also influences how readily gluten develops appropriately during mixing. Gluten needs to be developed sufficiently to hold the baked product together, but not so much that it becomes tough. When properly developed, gluten will be able to stretch into appropriately thin cell walls during baking, yielding a good volume and a tender product.

Starch is another important structural component of flour. During the baking period, starch absorbs water as gelatinization occurs. The gelatinized starch granules are imbedded in the gluten matrix to help add rigidity to the structure after baking.

Eggs are another element of the structure of baked products. They also contribute air for leavening when they are beaten into a foam. Other contributions are flavor, color, and emulsifying ability.

The pleasing golden-brown crust on baked products is due in large measure to the Maillard reaction, a combination of sugar with protein. Of course, sugar contributes a sweet taste, too. Sugar promotes volume and tenderness by modifying the rate of gluten development during mixing and raising the coagulation temperature of gluten during baking. Sugar substitutes do not have these effects.

Salt is primarily a flavoring substance, although it does serve to retard carbon dioxide production by yeast appropriately. Leavening agents are valued primarily because of their influence on volume. Between 1 and 2 teaspoons of baking powder per cup of flour usually is sufficient to leaven products appropriately without leaving an objectionable aftertaste.

Liquids are needed to develop gluten and to gelatinize starch. They aid leavening by dissolving baking powder and baking soda as well as by providing steam during baking. Most liquids also contribute some flavor.

Tenderness and fullness of flavor are two characteristics promoted by the appropriate use of fats or oils. By interfering somewhat with gluten development, they aid in producing a tender product. The form of fat used and the way in which it is incorporated often influence the texture. Flavor and color may also be a reflection of the type of fat used.

For production of high-quality baked products, it is important to know and to practice the basic mixing techniques (creaming, beating, stirring, folding, cutting in, and kneading) and to follow appropriate baking guidelines. Optimal results are obtained when the correct pans are prepared appropriately and when the panned product is arranged in the correct position in the oven and baked until the correct end point is reached.

Selected References

American Home Economics Association. *Handbook of Food preparation.* AHEA. Washington, D.C. 8th ed. 1980.

Bernardin, J. E. and D. D. Kasarda. Microstructure of wheat protein fibrils. *Cereal Chem.* 50: 735. 1973.

Bloksma, A. H. Thiol and disulfide groups in dough rheology. *Cereal Chem.* 52: 170. 1975.

Bushuk, W., and E. N. Larter, Triticale: Production, chemistry, and technology. *Adv. Cereal Sci. & Tech.* 3: 115. 1980.

Carlson, W. A. and E. M. Ziegenfuss. Functional properties of vital gluten. *Food Tech.* 12: 629. 1958.

Chung, O, K. and Y. Pomeranz. Recent research on wheat lipids. *Baker's Digest* 55(5): 38. 1981.

Danno, G. and M. Natake. Susceptibility of wheat glutenin to enzymatic hydrolysis. *Ag. Biol. Chem.* 44(9): 2155. 1980.

Ewart, J. A. D. Recent research in dough visco-elasticity. *Baker's Digest* 46(4): 22. 1972.

Haber, T. et al. Hard red winter wheat, rye, and triticale. *Baker's Digest* 50(6): 24. 1976.

Hashiba, H. Browning reaction of Amadori compounds derived from various sugars. *Ag. Biol. Chem.* 46(2): 547. 1982.

Hoseney, R. C. et al. Functional (breadmaking) and biochemical properties of wheat flour components. VIII. Starch. *Cereal Chem. 48*: 191. 1971.

Hoseney, R. C. Dough forming properties. *J. Am. Oil Chem. Soc. 56*: 78A. 1979.

Huebner, F. R. Wheat flour proteins and their functionality in baking. *Baker's Digest 51(5)*: 25. 1977.

Hulse, J. H. and D. Spurgeon. Triticale. *Sci. Amer. 231(2)*: 72. 1974.

Kahn, K. and W. Bushuk. Glutenin: Structure and functionality in breadmaking. *Baker's Digest 52(2)*: 14. 1978.

Knorr, D. Potato protein as partial replacement of wheat flour in bread. *J. Food Sci. 42*: 1425. 1977.

Leung, H. K. et al. Water binding of wheat flour doughs and breads as studied by the deuteron method. *J. Food Sci. 48(1)*: 95. 1983.

Magnuson, K. Vital wheat gluten update '77. *Baker's Digest 51(10)*: 108. 1977.

Nursten, H. E. Recent developments in studies of the Maillard reaction. *Food Chem. 6(3)*: 263. 1981.

Pomeranz, Y. What? how much? where? what function? in bread making. *Cereal Foods World 25(10)*: 656. 1980.

Rice, E. W. *Baking and Cooking at High Altitudes*. Author. Laramie, Wyo. 1972.

Ryadchikov, V. G. et al. Study of glutenins and gliadins of wheat flour. *Appl. Biochem. Microbiol. 17(1)*: 18. 1981.

Sikka, K. C. et al. Comparative nutritive value and amino acid content of triticale, wheat, and rye. *J. Ag. Food Chem. 26(4)*: 788. 1978.

Tu, C. C. and C. C. Tsen. Effects of mixing and surfactants on microscopic structure of wheat glutenin. *Cereal Chem. 55*: 87. 1978.

Vetter, J. I. Technology of sodium in bakery products. *Cereal Foods World 26(2)*: 64. 1981.

Wall, J. S. Properties of proteins contributing to functionality of cereal foods. *Cereal Foods World 24(7)*: 288. 1979.

Zabik, M. E. et al. Dietary fiber sources for baked products. *J. Food Sci. 42*: 1428. 1977.

Zeringer, H. J., Jr., et al. Triticale lipids: Composition and bread making characteristics of triticale flours. *Cereal Chem. 58(1)*: 351. 1981.

Study Questions

1. What are the differences among all-purpose flour, cake flour, and whole wheat flour? What are the effects of using each of these types of flour in making batter and dough products?
2. What factors influence the rate of gluten development in batters and doughs?
3. What adjustments are needed if self-rising flour is to be substituted for all-purpose flour in a recipe?
4. Why is the starch content of flour important in baked products?
5. In baked products, what are the functions of (a) eggs, (b) sugar, (c) butter, (d) shortening, (e) liquids?

Ogden Pleissner, "The Reapers." The Minneapolis Institute of Arts, Julia Bigelow Fund.

CHAPTER 13

BREADS—QUICK AND YEAST

THE WORLD OF BREAD

Bread A baked mixture containing a flour or meal (usually wheat) as its primary ingredient.

Around the globe, most cultures have at least one *bread*like product filling a major, vital role in the cuisine. These breads range from the chapatis of India and the pita (also called pocket bread) of Middle Eastern cuisines to the familiar sliced loaves of bread and English muffins that are staples of the U.S. diet. Although the "breads" of the world assume many different shapes and flavors, they generally can be characterized as being prepared from a cereal flour (usually wheat) and possessing a structure sufficiently strong to permit butter or other soft product to be spread over the surface without disintegrating into crumbs.

Generally, breads are classified according to the type of leavening action used. If yeast is used to produce carbon dioxide, the bread is classified as a yeast bread, whereas breads leavened with steam primarily or with carbon dioxide produced from the chemical reaction of soda and an acid salt are termed quick breads. Actually, the designation "quick breads" is a key to the sharp distinction between the two categories of breads. Yeast-leavened breads take much longer to make than do quick breads because of the time required for fermentation and proofing (producing carbon dioxide) of the dough before baking. Conversely, quick breads can be made quickly, for they do not have to wait for living organisms (the yeast) to generate carbon dioxide.

QUICK BREADS

Ingredients for Variety

Quick Bread Bread leavened with steam or carbon dioxide produced by a chemical reaction; a bread that does not require time for biological agents to generate carbon dioxide.

Considerable variety is found among the *quick breads*. They vary in their ingredients and their ratios of liquid to flour as well as in their mode of cooking. The quick breads popular in the United States usually have wheat flour as the principal ingredient, but there may be other grains combined with all-purpose flour to add flavor and textural contrasts. Corn bread is a familiar example of the use of another cereal being combined with all-purpose, refined wheat flour to obtain a different flavor, texture, and even a distinctive color. Buckwheat is a popular grain added to some pancake batters to make buckwheat pancakes. These are but a couple of examples of the use of different grains for variety.

Although flour and an occasional use of other cereal grains would seem to dominate the quick bread scene, other ingredients add to the assortment of breads classified as quick breads. For instance, the use of butter, shortening, or oil can make quite a difference in the textural characteristics and the flavor of the baked breads. The use or absence of eggs, as well as the use of only the yolks or only the whites, provides other modifications in quick breads. Sugar adds sweetness and color to some quick breads, although most of these breads usually are rather low in this sweetener.

The type of liquid and the amount of liquid used in making quick breads can also vary. Ordinarily, milk is used, but occasionally orange juice, water, or other liquid may be chosen. Flavor, texture, and browning are influenced by the liquid used.

Comparison of Quick Breads

The range of products classified as quick breads is indeed impressive. Popovers and cream puffs are quick breads that rise so dramatically during baking that they appear to have literally exploded. Muffins are baked from a rather soft batter dropped into individual containers or cups in a special pan, the muffin pan. Biscuits are rolled and cut from a dough that is stiff enough to be baked in individual shapes on a cooky sheet. Cake doughnuts are cut from a dough rolled into a thickness of about half an inch and then fried in deep fat. Loaves of fruit and nut breads basically are a viscous drop batter and are fairly similar to muffins in their consistency. In contrast, waffle and pancake batters flow. The most important distinction between waffles and pancakes is their method of baking.

Quick breads are comparatively complex mixtures in which the accuracy of measuring ingredients begins to be evident in the finished product. For instance, the thickness and the spread of a pancake are determined primarily by the ratio of liquid to flour in the batter. Even small variations in the measure of either of these key ingredients will cause noticeable changes in quality of the baked pancake. The same is true of other types of quick breads, too.

The diversity of batters and doughs comprising the array of quick breads is interesting to review. A comparison between common types of quick breads is given in Table 13.1. Typical ratios of ingredients are but a part of the study of ingredients. The physical state of the fat, whether liquid or solid, the use of egg, baking powder, and sugar and the method of mixing are all of importance in determining the properties of the final product.

Muffins

Muffins Quick bread with a cauliflowerlike, rounded surface resulting from careful mixing and baking of a batter with a 2:1 ratio of flour to liquid.

Muffins can be a tender, flavorful quick bread, but they may turn out to be crumbly or even very tough. Technique in preparing muffins will have a particularly important effect on the quality of the baked product, largely because the sticky ratio of flour to liquid (2:1) causes considerable gluten development with each stroke used in mixing. A small miscalculation in mixing can make a significant difference in the baked muffin.

Table 13.1 Typical Formulas for Quick Breads

Type	Flour (cups)	Milk (T)	Shortening State	Shortening Amount (T)	Egg	Sugar (T)	Baking Powder (tsp)
Muffins	1	7	Liquid	2	½	1⅓	1½
Biscuits	1	5½–6	Solid	2	—	—	1½
Popovers	1	16	Liquid	½	1	—	—
Cream puffs	1	16[1]	Liquid	8	4	—	—
Waffles	1	11½	Liquid	4½	1+	—	1¾
Pancakes	1	13	Liquid	1⅔	1	1	2½
Doughnuts	1	3½	Liquid	1	1	3½	1½

[1]Liquid is water.

SCIENCE NOTE: FLOUR/LIQUID RATIOS

The ratio of flour to liquid is perhaps the most critical component of quick bread formulas. A quick, but useful, preliminary evaluation of quick bread recipes can be done by comparing the amount of flour with the amount of liquid when both ingredients are expressed in the same units of measure. This comparison is simplified arithmetically to gauge whether the mixture will be a pourable batter, a batter capable of being dropped onto a flat surface for baking, or a dough to be rolled.

The thinnest batter ordinarily made will have a ratio of 1:1, that is, 1 part flour to 1 part liquid. When equal amounts of liquid and flour are used, the mixture will be fluid or very pourable, as is the case in the preparation of popovers. In fact, the 1:1 ratio is so fluid that gluten fails to form well because of the limited interaction between individual gluten strands during mixing.

A very different product with this 1:1 ratio is cream puffs. Anyone who has made cream puffs will recognize that the dough must be viscous enough to stand up in almost a ball when dropped from the spoon onto the baking sheet. Although the 1:1 ratio of flour to liquid makes this sound impossible, the egg yolks that are used in the puff dough are such effective emulsifying agents that they, augmented by starch in the flour, are able to bind all of the fat and liquid in an emulsion within the dough.

Muffins are a batter product capable of being spooned into cups or a baking pan and flowing a bit to conform to the shape of the container. This viscosity is achieved by using a flour/liquid ratio of approximately 2:1, that is, 2 parts flour to 1 part liquid. This ratio is a very sticky combination in which the gluten strands receive enough liquid to cause gluten to begin to develop and to tend to cling to each other and stretch during mixing. This 2:1 ratio results in very rapid gluten development; overmixing quickly becomes a problem.

Biscuits are a good example of a 3:1 ratio of flour to liquid. This large amount of flour in relation to liquid means that the flour proteins hydrate more slowly and develop into gluten with greater difficulty than is found in working with the 2:1 ratio of muffins. Somewhat more manipulation of the mixture is necessary to develop gluten appropriately in biscuits than is needed in muffins. Nevertheless, overmixing in biscuits can be a problem, albeit less of a problem than in muffins. This 3:1 ratio results in a dough that can be handled with reasonable ease, being neither so sticky that it would be impossible to knead with the hands or so stiff that it would be hard to keep in a cohesive, yet tender, mass. Occasionally, a quick bread will be stiffer than biscuit dough. Cake doughnuts may have a ratio of 4:1, that is, only a ¼ cup of liquid to 1 cup of flour.

In addition to the sticky ratio of flour to liquid, muffins contain only a moderate amount of fat and little sugar to help retard the effect of mixing. If either of these ingredients were increased, muffins would be far less likely to be overmixed than they are in the typical muffin recipe, but then they would lose their breadlike quality and begin to assume the characteristics of a cake. Consequently, the preparation of muffins focuses primarily on achieving just the right amount of gluten development—neither too much nor too little.

Muffin Method of Mixing Method in which all the dry ingredients are sifted together in one bowl and all the liquid ingredients (including melted fat) are combined in a second bowl before the liquid ingredients are poured into the dry ingredients and stirred together just enough to moisten the dry ingredients completely.

The technique for preparing muffins is termed the *muffin method of mixing*. The muffin method begins with the thorough blending of dry ingredients by sifting them together into a bowl. A second bowl is used to blend all of the liquid ingredients together completely. The fat is melted and treated as a liquid ingredient in the muffin method of mixing. The method is completed by pouring the liquid ingredients all at once into a well in the dry ingredients and then stirring just enough to moisten the dry ingredients. This results in a lumpy batter, but one with no areas with dry flour. It is the lumpy batter that produces the cauliflowerlike surface of muffins, but this is the desirable product. If mixing is continued until the lumps are removed, the baked muffin will be tough and full of tunnels.

Surprisingly, gluten develops so readily in muffins that it is necessary even to avoid extra manipulation of the batter while spooning the batter into the greased muffin cups. Care must be taken to get a large spoonful of batter, enough to fill a muffin cup half full, so that a single spoonful will make one muffin. This gives the desired surface appearance, whereas the addition of a bit more batter to the batter in a muffin cup frequently produces a misshapen, lopsided muffin.

Evaluation of muffins involves careful examination of the top surface and also a close look at the cross section of the interior, for these areas reveal quickly the quality of preparation. The upper surface of muffins should be rounded and have a cauliflowerlike appearance and a golden-brown color. The cross section inside should reveal a moderately coarse texture, which is comparatively uniform throughout and does not show any pockets or tunnels. Cell walls should be of moderate thickness and should not show any trace of a waxy appearance. The structure should be sufficiently strong to make it possible to spread butter or margarine on its surface with only a little crumbling, yet the muffin should be able to be bitten and chewed with ease.

Undermixed muffins will have a poor volume and flat surface, perhaps with even some flecks of dry flour showing. Some sharp points also seem to erupt from the surface, rather than being rounded. The poor volume is due to failure to moisten all the baking powder so that not all of the gas needed for leavening is released. Undermixing also causes muffins to be very crumbly, because the gluten has not been developed sufficiently to give the amount of structure required. Cell walls also usually are quite thick, and the cells range from very small to some that are quite large within the same muffin.

Overmixing develops the gluten more than is desirable. This can be spotted readily simply by looking at the contour and texture of the upper crust. When a muffin is fairly pointed, and the texture of the crust has the smooth appearance of a yeast bread, the muffin batter has been overmixed. In fact,

Undermixed muffin (left) exhibits poor volume and a crumbly texture; proper mixing develops a slightly rounded, cauliflower-like top and a fairly uniform, rather coarse texture; excessive mixing causes a peaked top and a smooth exterior surface with tunnels inside. These characteristics demonstrate the development of gluten throughout the mixing of muffin batter.

the top of an overmixed muffin often resembles the shape of a lopsided miniature mountain, the peak being the point where the last of the batter was pushed from the spoon into the muffin pan. The interior of an overmixed muffin will reveal tunnels leading toward the peak of the muffin. These tunnels are passageways in which the expanding carbon dioxide pushed its way toward the surface of the muffin, with the overdeveloped gluten directing its movement upward. The visual message of overmixing is accompanied by a detectable toughness. These various symptoms of overmixing develop so rapidly that it often is possible to examine a batch of muffins and tell by their surface appearance the sequence in which they were spooned into the pan, the small amount of manipulation in spooning the batter being sufficient to cause overmixing in the last ones.

Fruit and Nut Breads

Date nut bread, banana bread, and certain other fruit or nut-containing breads represent quick breads. Often these are made by the muffin method, although a few of them contain so much fat and sugar that they resemble cakes more closely than muffins and, consequently, are prepared by the same method used for making shortened cakes (see Chapter 14). These breads are baked in loaf pans until a toothpick inserted in the center of the loaf comes out clean. This test ensures that the batter in the center has had an opportunity to become hot enough for the gluten to denature and the starch to gelatinize. The visual test of a golden-brown exterior used in muffins cannot be used for these breads because of the potential for inadequate heating of the interior of these rather large volumes. Elapsed baking time is a good guide to knowing when to test with the toothpick, for the volume of the bread loaf will be affected if the oven is opened and the bread is tested when the structure is stretched to its maximum but has not yet been denatured.

Ideally, the loaf will be gently rounded on the top and with a slightly cauliflowerlike surface, and the interior will be tender and a little coarse, but not crumbly. The volume should be good, and without tunnels. The amount

Fruit and nut breads often contain more sugar and fat than muffins, thus requiring somewhat more mixing to develop the gluten enough for easy slicing. Excessive mixing will cause tunnels.

of mixing and its effect on fruit and nut breads made by the muffin method is similar to that on muffins. Overbaking dries out the loaf and may cause an overly brown crust. Underbaking causes the loaf to fall as a consequence of allowing the expanded gases to cool and contract before the structure sets.

As soon as baked loaves are removed from the oven, they should be eased from the pan onto a wire rack to cool. This avoids the problems of condensed moisture on the bottom and side crusts. The structure of these breads is strong enough to allow this type of handling without losing volume. However, slicing is done more readily the day after baking than when the loaves are fresh, because the structure will become increasingly rigid and will hold the sliced edge with ease.

Biscuits

Biscuit Quick bread made by cutting in the solid shortening and using a ratio of flour to liquid of 3:1, which results in a dough that is able to be kneaded, rolled, and cut into the desired round disk for baking.

The ingredients in *biscuits* are combined in a totally different way to achieve this unique type of quick bread. An important feature of biscuits is that the fat is used in a solid form, being cut into pieces. These pieces are partially responsible for the flaky texture desired in biscuits, a texture totally unlike that of muffins. To make these flour-covered fat particles, a pastry blender usually is used with a light flipping motion that coats each piece of fat with a layer of flour while slicing the fat into progressively smaller particles. The coating of flour helps to keep the fat particles separated while the dough is being mixed. During baking, these pieces of fat melt, leaving little pockets where the carbon dioxide and steam can expand and create a flaky texture.

After the fat has been cut into the dry ingredients, all of the liquid is added at once. This mixture is stirred briefly with a fork to moisten all of the ingredients, using an occasional cutting motion to penetrate the thick dough and help to moisten the dry ingredients that may not be contacting the liquid. Gluten develops a little less readily in biscuit dough than in muffin batter, because the flour/liquid ratio in biscuits is about 3:1, which is not as sticky as the 2:1 ratio in muffins. This slight inhibition of gluten development in biscuit dough makes it possible to stir the ingredients about 20 strokes and then to knead the dough. The kneading for biscuits is done by folding the dough in half and pressing lightly in a rhythmic motion with the finger tips, a technique that is repeated 10 to 20 times to promote the development of flaky layers as the gluten develops in the dough. As kneading progresses, the dough tightens noticeably and becomes smooth. Kneading must be stopped before the dough starts to spring back or take on a rubberlike character.

After kneading, the dough is rolled to a thickness about half that of the desired height of the baked biscuit, for biscuits will just about double in height during baking. They expand upward, but not sideways. Thin biscuits (only about half an inch high when baked) will be crusty and dry. Usually, biscuits are rolled about half an inch thick, which results in a biscuit with a pleasing crispness on the surface and a breadlike, flaky interior. The rolled dough is cut with a sharp cutter pressed evenly downward through the dough to help produce biscuits that stand up straight during baking. For crisp-sided biscuits, the unbaked biscuits are positioned at least an inch apart on the baking sheet. Placing biscuits so that their sides touch helps to hold biscuits in position and prevents their leaning over during baking. Since the oven heat does not reach the sides of biscuits arranged so that they touch, these biscuits will be soft on the sides, rather than crisp. By brushing milk lightly on the surface of the biscuits before baking, the top surface will develop a shiny, golden brown crust free of the tiny brown "freckles" of undissolved baking powder that show on the crust of biscuits not brushed with milk.

Evaluation of biscuits involves the appearance of the exterior and also the palatability characteristics of the interior. A high-quality baking powder biscuit will have straight sides, a flat top, and a pleasingly browned crust. Some horizontal cracks will show in the sides, clear indications of the flaky texture within. The top surface should be crisp, and the interior crumb should be tender.

If biscuits have a somewhat rough surface and poor volume, the dough was not kneaded sufficiently before being rolled out and baked. On the other hand, too much kneading develops the gluten too much, resulting in a smooth surface, tough crumb, and small volume. Tough biscuits may be the result of too much stirring or kneading, or they may be due to using too little liquid. Optimal results are obtained when the dough is just slightly sticky, but still able to be kneaded. At this moisture level, the edge of the biscuit right at the bottom crust will curl up ever so slightly.

Drop biscuits are a variation of rolled biscuits. Although the ingredients are the same, drop biscuit recipes include too much liquid for the resulting mixture to be kneaded. The biscuits are dropped from a spoon onto the baking sheet, rather than being rolled and cut with a biscuit cutter. The result is a rather casual appearance—a rough surface and a poorly defined shape. However, they are quick to make and are often enjoyed for their crisp crust. A close relative is the dumpling, which simply is dropped on a bubbling gravy or other liquid and steamed until cooked throughout. Dumplings, because of their steaming, do not have a crisp exterior.

Cake Doughnuts

Cake doughnuts are a quick bread that is fried rather than baked. The dough for doughnuts is made with a small amount of liquid fat and with only a little over half as much liquid as is used in biscuits. Doughnut dough is toughened with excessive handling. The key to making tender cake doughnuts is to avoid working in any extra flour, and using just enough to be able to roll the dough with ease. The dough should be chilled before being rolled or extruded, as the increased viscosity and reduced stickiness result in less toughening of the dough during this phase.

Careful control of the temperature of the fat during the frying of doughnuts is important to the quality of the finished product. When fat is too hot, the doughnuts will brown very rapidly on the surface, but the interior will not be hot enough to denature the protein and gelatinize the starch until the exterior is practically burning. This leads to undercooked doughnuts with gummy interiors. An even greater problem involves the rapid breakdown of the overheated fat to acrolein (an eye irritant) and free fatty acids, which together impair flavor of the doughnuts and aggravate the cook. Conversely, frying at too low a temperature extends the length of time required to achieve the desired internal temperature and exterior browning. Moreover, the dough absorbs fat from the frying medium, which results in a greasy doughnut. Maintaining the hot fat at 375°F results in the best doughnuts.

Waffles and Pancakes

Unlike many of the other quick breads, waffles and pancakes are eaten with a fork and are often topped with syrup or sauce. The proportions of flour to liquid vary slightly between different recipes for pancakes and waffles, but generally pancake batters are slightly more fluid mixtures than are waffle batters. Waffles contain not quite 3/4 cup of milk to 1 cup of flour, while pancakes are made with a little over 3/4 cup of milk to the same amount of flour. Although neither of these batters is quite a 1:1 ratio, they both are very fluid mixtures that can be beaten vigorously to make a smooth batter without developing the gluten extensively. Waffle batter, although leavened with baking powder, sometimes is made by folding an egg white foam into the batter to help introduce additional air and promote lightness.

Temperature control on waffle irons and pancake griddles is a tremendous aid to making products of high quality. If there is no temperature control, the iron or griddle should be preheated until drops of cold water seem to dance, rather than sizzle, when they touch the surface. Pancakes are poured to make a circle of the desired size on the griddle and then are allowed to bake on the first side until bubbles rise through the batter and burst at the surface and the bottom is a pleasing brown, at which time they are flipped to brown the second side. They should be served with the surface that was browned first on top. Waffles are poured onto a preheated iron and are baked without opening the iron until the steam stops issuing from the iron. Attempts to open the iron sooner usually tear the waffle because the batter will stick to the iron.

Pancakes should be a picture-perfect golden brown on the surface and should be shaped as circles. The size is strictly a matter of personal preference. They should be light and tender. Overmixing of the batter or too much flour in relation to the milk can cause pancakes to be tough.

Waffles should be crisp and golden brown on the exterior and tender to chew. The waffle should fill the grid pattern of the iron completely. In case appetites and amounts of batter for waffles do not match, the remaining batter can be baked, and the cooled waffles can be frozen for subsequent reheating in a toaster. Commercially produced frozen waffles have gained a reasonable market segment because of their convenience. Moreover, they can be enjoyed by people who do not have a waffle iron.

Variations of both waffles and pancakes are popular items. Pecans and blueberries are typical of the ingredients that can be added to batters to create intriguing variations of these products. Additional variety is gained by using fruits and sauces for toppings. Crepes are pancakes with extra liquid added to the batter, creating a very fluid mixture that produces very thin pancakes. Crepes are often made using a special crepe pan that is heated and then dipped into a shallow bowl of batter. A small frying pan is recommended as a suitable substitute for a crepe pan. Crepes can be rolled with fillings of chicken, fish, or other protein foods in sauces to serve as an entree, or they may have sweet fillings or be cooked in sweet sauces to create an exotic dessert. Waffles also have their sophisticated gadgetry. A Belgian waffle iron permits the preparation of waffles with a very crisp texture and deep squares that effectively trap any of a wide variety of syrups and toppings.

Popovers

Popovers Quick bread made with a flour/liquid ratio of 1:1 and egg and baked in deep cups in an oven heated to at least 425°F to generate steam for leavening.

One of the most exciting quick breads to make is *popovers*, a steam-leavened product that can be characterized as "wonder bread," for popovers often triple in volume during baking. The explanation is that steam is generated very rapidly in this fluid batter as it is heated in a very hot oven, and this steam forcefully expands the gluten from the flour and the protein from the egg, particularly the protein from the white. Then the proteins denature in this very extended position and the starch gelatinizes, resulting in the familiar shell-like structure of popovers.

Preparation of popovers is simple and quick, merely involving beating milk, flour, eggs, and salt together until the batter is smooth. This very fluid

Popovers are a dramatic quick bread leavened primarily by steam, the result of a very fluid batter (1:1 ratio of liquid and flour) and baking in a very hot oven.

batter, with its ratio of equal amounts of milk and flour, permits fairly extensive beating without overdeveloping the gluten. Actually, the gluten and starch of the flour are augmented considerably in popovers by the protein of the egg white; adequate egg white is essential to obtain the desired degree of popping during baking. The extensibility of egg white proteins during the early part of baking and the strength contributed to the structure by the denatured egg white protein in the finished product are vital to the success of popovers. In short, popovers with an inadequate amount of egg white protein fail to ''pop.'' Popovers are definitely one product for which extra large eggs are a real asset.

Ideally, popovers are poured directly into lightly oiled, preheated custard cups or popover pans and are baked immediately in an oven preheated to at least 425°F. Under these conditions, a large volume of steam will be generated quickly, causing the essential rapid expansion of the batter. This high temperature causes rather rapid browning, gelatinization of the starch, and setting of the structure, but the interior may not be dried out sufficiently unless the baking time is extended to about 45 minutes total time. If browning starts to become excessive, the oven temperature can be lowered to 350°F after the first 15 minutes of baking.

The ideal popover will have a crisp texture and a pleasingly browned exterior. The volume will be very large, with a large central cavity being surrounded by reasonably thin walls defining the total popover. There should be no sogginess in the cavity, although the walls will be slightly moist. The most vexing problem in making popovers is failure to pop. This difficulty is due most likely to having too little egg white in the batter. However, too cool an oven can also be the fault.

Cream Puffs

Technically, *cream puffs* are quick breads that are served as a base for an entree or a dessert rather than as an accompanying bread product. Cream puffs are of special interest because of their similarities and dissimilarities with popovers. Both are steam-leavened quick breads and, hence, must be baked in a very hot oven to generate sufficient steam to create the desired volume and large cavity. The cavity is the unique feature of both of these quick breads. In the case of cream puffs, this cavity is essential so that it can serve as the site for holding various fillings.

The intriguing aspect of cream puffs is that their unbaked state is a dough, not a fluid batter, despite the fact that equal amounts of liquid and flour are used. Since popovers contain the same flour/liquid ratio, it would be natural to expect that cream puffs would also form a batter. However, cream puffs contain not only starch gelatinized in a boiling water-butter mixture, but also a large amount of eggs—enough to emulsify the butter in the cream puff mixture (see Table 13.1), forming an oil-in-water emulsion that very significantly modifies the flow properties of the system to create a dough. Sometimes too much water may be evaporated during the preparation of cream puff dough, causing the oil-in-water emulsion to break. If the dough begins to look curdled, and fat oozes from the mixture, a small amount of water must be stirred in to reestablish the emulsion and provide the water needed for leavening by steam during the baking period. Just enough water is added to produce a smooth dough in which the fat is emulsified; too much water causes so much thinning that the baking cream puff cannot contain the steam and the puff then fails to live up to its name.

Cream puffs should be large, pleasingly golden-brown puffs with a large interior cavity and somewhat crisp walls. The puff is accomplished by baking a properly emulsified dough containing sufficient egg protein in a very hot oven to generate enough steam to stretch the gluten network and create the large cavity. If too little butter, egg, or water is present, the desired large volume and cavity will not be achieved. Other causes of failure to puff are too cool an oven or too much water.

YEAST BREADS

Yeast breads take time to make because of the time required for the yeast to produce adequate amounts of carbon dioxide for leavening the dough as it bakes. The generation of carbon dioxide requires careful control of fermentation conditions to maintain viable yeast within an optimal temperature range (see Chapter 11). The level of sugar and of salt must be consistent with the conditions needed by the yeast for normal metabolic reactions to take place. Regardless of whether yeast breads are intended to become loaves of bread, bread sticks, or other types of rolls, the doughs generally are prepared by the straight dough method, although the sponge method sometimes is used. These methods are examined next.

Straight Dough Method

Straight Dough**Straight Dough
Method** Method of
making a yeast bread
dough by combining
the ingredients
(scalded milk, sugar,
salt, butter, and egg,
with softened yeast
added after mixture is
sufficiently cool, and
the flour) and knead-
ing prior to the proof-
ing period.

The initial step in preparing the dough by the *straight dough method* is to soften the yeast; compressed yeast cakes are placed in lukewarm water (about 104°F), while active dry yeast should be rehydrated in water at a temperature of between 100° and 115°F. While the yeast is softening, the milk is scalded by holding it at almost 200°F for a minute and then is poured into a bowl containing the fat, sugar, and salt. The heat of the milk should be sufficient to melt the butter, which helps to cool the milk to around 100°F or slightly cooler so that the softened yeast can be added safely. If eggs are being used, they are added just before the yeast so that their cool temperature will provide additional security against killing the yeast by exposing them to too high a temperature during mixing.

The addition of approximately a third of the flour creates a batter that can be beaten vigorously to help initiate development of a strong gluten network. Then, additional flour is stirred in to create a soft dough, one that can be kneaded vigorously without becoming too sticky. The kneading process for yeast breads is a far more vigorous technique than is that used in kneading biscuits. Although the dough is folded in half and then pushed with the hands, this type of kneading involves using the heels of both hands rather than a gentle push with the fingertips. However, kneading in yeast breads should not be done so vigorously that gluten strands are torn by the force of the push. By rotating the dough a quarter of a turn each time the kneading motion is done, folding over the dough, and pressing with the heels of the hands, a rhythm can be developed to facilitate the development of the necessary amount of gluten in the dough. Kneading can be done with a mixer or food processor, if desired. When blisters begin to show just under the surface of the dough when it is folded over gently, an adequate amount of gluten has been developed. The ball of dough then is oiled on its surface and is placed in

Vigorous kneading, accomplished using the heels of both hands in a rhythmic motion while rotating the dough, is necessary for the development of an adequate amount of gluten. The appearance of the dough will progress from a rough surface (left), to undermixed gluten with gluten strands beginning to show (center), and finally to a satin-like surface when sufficient gluten has been developed (right).

a bowl, where it is covered and then held for fermentation, preferably at a temperature of about 80°F.

Fermentation is allowed to proceed until the dough has doubled in volume, a process that helps to promote extensibility of gluten, as well as produce acids and alcohol. When doubled, the fist is used to push the dough down in preparation for the proofing period. Unlike the fermentation period, which is completed in a covered bowl in about an hour's time, the proofing period is done with the dough shaped into the desired form and placed on the baking pan, where rising is allowed to continue without a cover until the dough has again doubled in volume, a process requiring about half as much time as was needed for the initial fermentation.

Baking is done in a preheated oven, usually at about 400°F, until the bread is a pleasing golden brown and the appropriate amount of time has elapsed. Breads high in sugar or containing raisins or other sweet ingredients need to be baked at about 350°F to avoid scorching or burning. The baking period is marked by the phenomenon called oven spring which is an obvious increase in volume due to volatilization of alcohol and to rapid carbon dioxide production by yeast in the warm environment until the yeast are killed by the heat.

The straight dough method is the method commonly used in the home for making yeast breads, because mixing is relatively quick. The resulting product is excellent, but a good bit of physical effort is needed to develop the gluten sufficiently by the straight dough method. Some people enjoy the task of kneading the dough; others use food processors.

Sponge Method

Sponge Method
Method of preparing a yeast dough, in which the salt and part of the flour are withheld until the batter has generated enough carbon dioxide to give a sponge-like quality to the mixture: addition of the rest of the flour and the salt precedes the completion of the kneading and subsequent steps.

The other traditional method of mixing yeast doughs is the *sponge method*. Much of this method is comparable to the straight dough method. The principal difference is that part of the flour and all of the salt are withheld until after an initial fermentation period. During this fermentation of the fairly fluid batter, the carbon dioxide being formed causes the mixture to begin to develop a spongelike appearance, hence, the name of the sponge method of mixing. Following the first rising period, the salt and remaining flour are added, and the remaining preparation steps are the same as in the straight dough method, that is, kneading, rising, shaping, rising, and baking. This method used to be necessary some years ago because the yeast that was available at that time required a long rehydration and activation period, a problem no longer encountered today. Consequently, only a few recipes now are made using the sponge method. The time required for the development of the sponge is a real disadvantage of the sponge method.

Rapidmix Method

Some time can be saved when preparing yeast breads at home by using the rapidmix method—by mixing the active dry yeast pellets directly with 2 cups of flour before pouring in warm milk or very hot tap water and the fat. This mixture is beaten vigorously with an electric mixer to develop the gluten before the remaining flour is stirred in. The subsequent handling of the dough is the same as in the straight dough method. Some time is saved in the early steps of mixing. The very warm liquid in the rapidmix method does not harm the yeast because the mixture cools to a safe temperature for the yeast before the yeast becomes hydrated.

Factors in Yeast Bread Quality

The amount of flour incorporated into the yeast doughs has a significant influence on the quality of the finished product, but there is no simple way of communicating to the novice just how much flour is needed in a specific recipe. The vague indication of how much flour to use in a yeast dough can be disconcerting, for exact measurements when preparing new recipes help to generate a feeling of confidence. Some yeast bread recipes do indicate a measure of sifted flour to use, but this may not prove to be the optimal amount. The problem stems from the fact that the absorptive qualities of flour vary among lots, and they vary particularly among different parts of the country. The goal is to add enough flour to allow the dough to be kneaded without sticking to the hands. The dough should have an alive, springy feel and should sag a little when resting on the bread board after kneading. If dough appears rigid and feels resistant to kneading, the dough contains too much flour and will be tough and somewhat dry when baked.

Control of fermentation is absolutely essential to production of high-quality yeast breads. Temperatures must be kept below 115°F any time hydrated yeast is present. Temperatures above this will kill yeast quickly, resulting in poor volume. The most likely points where the system may be too hot are when the yeast is being combined with scalded milk mixtures and when fermentation may be taking place in an oven that is too warm, which may be the case if a gas oven has a high pilot light. In addition to temperature regulation, fermentation can be controlled partially by the amount of sugar contained in the formulation. Sugar needs to be available throughout the fermentation period to serve as food for the yeast. When this situation exists, carbon dioxide will continue to be generated until the structure has stretched and set. To counterbalance the effect of sugar, some salt is necessary to act as an inhibitor on the metabolism of yeast, thus regulating carbon dioxide production and helping to prevent formation of too much of this gas.

Baking of bread loaves and rolls is best done in a preheated oven when the shaped dough has just doubled in volume. The oven spring occurring when baking is initiated will add the finishing touch to the desired volume. The texture will become too porous and may even fall if the proofing time is extended to permit too much carbon dioxide production to occur before baking kills the yeast. To save energy and time, the oven rack can be shifted to the next position above the center, and the bread pan can be placed at that level for baking from a cold start; this avoids the excessive browning of the lower crust because of excessive heat from the lower unit during oven preheating.

Yeast bread doughs can be formed into many different shapes and topped with various seeds, dried herbs, or icings to create appealing breads that will highlight a meal or a snack. Care in shaping is essential to achieving products of high quality.

Elapsed time is one of the key tests for doneness of breads and rolls. A golden brown crust color is a misleading guide to doneness, for a pleasing crust color usually develops prior to the time the bread actually is denatured inside. An underbaked loaf of bread or roll will have a doughy center. When done, most breads should be removed immediately from the baking pan and transferred to a cooling rack or to a bread basket for prompt service to diners. The structure of yeast breads is tenacious and more than strong enough to hold its original volume and shape when handled while hot, which is fortunate, for crusts become soggy from condensed moisture if products are allowed to cool in their baking pans. However, sweet rolls baked in a syrup coating the bottom of the pan should be cooled in the baking pan until the syrup has started to cool and become viscous. At that point, the pan should be inverted and the syrup allowed to drip onto the rolls until most of the topping has been transferred onto the rolls.

Quality of yeast breads is assessed by examining the exterior and interior carefully. The product should be shaped pleasingly and be appropriate in size for the occasion. The crust should be a tempting golden brown and have a sheen. This sheen is created by brushing melted butter or margarine over the crust immediately after the product is removed from the oven. The crust should not be soggy; breads made without milk or fat should have a crisp crust. The interior of the bread should be uniform, with cells of moderate size and cell walls of medium thickness, characteristics clearly coarser than the texture in cakes. An extremely coarse texture, however, is a clear sign of excessive fermentation. Bread and rolls should be easy to chew, but should not be so tender that butter or other spreads cannot be spread without creating a large quantity of crumbs. Attention should be directed toward shaping rolls into a uniform size, a means of enhancing the beauty of home-baked rolls.

Managing Yeast Bread Preparation

Time management in making yeast breads sometimes is critical. Although not a great deal of time is required to mix and knead a bread dough, the two periods required for fermentation and proofing and the subsequent baking period dictate the need for a comparatively long time span for completing the project, usually about 3 hours. However, the fermentation and proofing times can be shortened by increasing the amount of yeast added to the dough. Another technique used by some is to prepare the dough in the evening, covering it and allowing it to proof in the refrigerator during the night. By morning, the dough will have doubled, and the remainder of the preparation can proceed. It also is possible to shape rolls on the baking sheet and let them rise in the refrigerator. The baking time will need to be extended a little to offset the cold temperature of the dough at the start of baking.

Sourdough

Sourdough breads conjure up vivid images of bearded prospectors joining in the Gold Rush, but this popular type of bread is also very familiar today.

Sourdough breads are leavened by use of a starter containing microorganisms to produce carbon dioxide. Consequently, sourdough breads, like yeast-leavened breads, require fermentation and proofing.

Many colorful stories have been spun about the miners who slept with their sourdough starter placed right next to their guns so that nothing could happen to the starter. Actually, the care and feeding of sourdough starter are vital to bakers today, too, just as in the past, for maintenance of the proper strain requires proper feeding of the desired microorganisms and avoidance of new, undesirable strains. A sourdough starter is made with flour, sugar, yeast, and water and is stored at room temperature. A portion of this starter is saved for making the next product, and flour and water are added to feed the starter before storing this sponge in the refrigerator. Uses for sour dough starter are rather varied and include bread, pancakes, waffles, biscuits, muffins, and cakes. The flavor of this sour dough starter adds a distinctive quality to products in which the starter is used.

SUMMARY

Breads are baked products containing a large proportion of flour (usually wheat) and a liquid with leavening agents, eggs, and flavoring agents rounding out the list of ingredients. On the basis of the type of leavening they contain, baked bread products are divided into quick breads and yeast breads. Quick breads are leavened by air, steam, and/or carbon dioxide provided from a chemical reaction between an acid and an alkaline ingredient. Although carbon dioxide, air, and steam also serve as the leavening agents in yeast breads, the carbon dioxide is generated slowly by the metabolic reactions of yeast (*Saccharomyces cerevisiae*, a one-celled plant) during proofing at a controlled temperature.

Quick breads contain a variety of ingredients, but one of the most significant aspects of ingredients in influencing the characteristics of quick breads is the flour/liquid ratio, which has considerable impact on gluten development. Muffins, with a ratio of two parts flour to one part liquid (2:1), can be easily overmixed because of the very sticky nature of the dough and its gluten. On the other hand, the very fluid nature of a 1:1 ratio, which is found in popovers and cream puffs, permits considerable mixing without overdeveloping the gluten. The 3:1 ratio used in biscuits can be handled somewhat more than muffins without becoming tough.

Overmixed muffins will have pointed peaks, with interior tunnels leading up toward the peak; they also will be tough. Undermixed muffins will have some areas of dry ingredients, which have not been moistened with any liquid. The baking powder in these dry areas will not be able to react because it is not dissolved. The crust will appear somewhat rough or jagged, and the muffins will be quite crumbly when they have not been mixed enough. With the proper amount of mixing, the surface of muffins will have a cauliflowerlike look, be somewhat rounded, and have a golden-brown color. The interior will be slightly coarse, but will not have tunnels.

In addition to muffins, quick breads include fruit and nut breads, biscuits (kneaded and drop), cake doughnuts, waffles, pancakes, popovers, and cream puffs. Some of these are batters of an appropriate viscosity for dropping or baking in a loaf pan or muffin pan; others are doughs capable of beings rolled out and cut. Although baking is the usual method of cooking quick breads, cake doughnuts are fried in deep fat.

Yeast breads usually contain enough flour to enable the dough to be kneaded, either by hand or machine. Proofing ordinarily is done twice, once after mixing and once after shaping into the baking container. Each time, the dough is allowed to double in volume as the yeast generates carbon dioxide. During baking, an initial oven spring increases the volume due to the stimulating effect of the heat on the yeast. However, the yeast is killed quickly, thus limiting the leavening action. Baking is done until the appropriate baking time has elapsed and the crust is a pleasing golden brown. As soon as the bread is removed from the oven, loaves are taken from their baking pans and are placed on racks to cool, just as is done with quick breads, to avoid developing soggy crusts.

Sourdough breads are popular because of their tart flavor. This tartness is due to the development of acid by bacteria introduced into the dough via a sour dough starter. This acidic medium promotes the development of yeast, which serves as the source of the carbon dioxide for leavening.

Selected References

D'Appolonia, B. L. and M. M. Morad. Bread staling. *Cereal Chem. 58(3):* 186. 1981

American Home Economic Association. *Handbook of food Preparation.* AHEA. Washington, D.C. 8th ed. 1980.

Biltcliffe, D. O. Active dried baker's yeast. II. Factors involved in the fermentation of flour. *J. Food Tech. 7:* 63. 1972.

Consumer and Food Economics Research Division. Breads, Cakes, and Pies in Family Meals. *Home and Garden Bulletin* No. 186. U.S. Dept. Agriculture. Washington, D.C. 1976.

Golal, A. M. et al. Lactic and volatile (C_2-C_5) organic acids of San Francisco sourdough French bread. *Cereal Chem. 55:* 461. 1978.

Hoseney, R. C. et al. Functional (breadmaking) and biochemical properties of wheat flour components. VIII. Starch. *Cereal Chem. 48:* 191. 1971.

Knightly, W. H. Evolution of softeners and conditions used in baked foods. *Baker's Digest 47(5):* 64. 1973.

Knightly, W. H. Staling of bread. *Baker's Digest 51(5):* 52. 1977.

Magoffin, D. C. and R. C. Hoseney. Review of fermentation. *Baker's Digest 48(6):* 22. 1974.

Martson, P. E. and T. L. Wannan. Bread baking—transformation from dough into bread. *Baker's Digest 50(4):* 24. 1976.

Morrison, W. R. Lipids in flour, dough, and bread. *Baker's Digest 50(4):* 29. 1976.

Nursten, H. E. Recent developments in studies of the Maillard reaction. *Food Chem. 6(3):* 263. 1981.

Oszlanyi, A. G. Instant yeast. *Baker's Digest 54(4):* 16. 1980.

Pomeranz, Y. Fiber in breadmaking. *Baker's Digest 51(5):* 1977.

Schoch, T. J. and D. French. Studies on bread staling. *Cereal Chem. 24:* 231. 1947.

Vetter, J. I. Technology of sodium in bakery products. *Cereal Foods World 26(2):* 64. 1981.

Zeringer, H. J., Jr., et al. Triticale lipids: Composition and breadmaking characteristics of triticale flours. *Cereal Chem. 58(1):* 351. 1981.

Study Questions

1. Compare the method of preparing muffins with that used in making biscuits.
2. Why does gluten develop so easily in muffins? Describe the changes in the appearance of the batter and the baked muffins with different amounts of mixing.
3. What differences can be identified between popover batters and cream puff pastes? Why are the physical properties of the two so different when their flour/liquid ratios are comparable?
4. Contrast the straight dough, rapidmix, and sponge methods of making yeast breads.
5. What precautions are necessary when making yeast breads of good volume?

15th century French illumination/The Granger Collection.

CHAPTER 14

CAKES, COOKIES, AND PASTRIES

THE "SHORT AND SWEET" OF IT

Although breads are increasing in popularity, the study of quick breads and yeast breads actually represents but a fraction of the total possibilities in flour-based mixtures. Many cake recipes are very similar to quick bread recipes, except that they contain appreciably more sugar and fat than quick breads do. Because of this sweet richness, cakes are served as the finale to a meal or as a snack. Cakes of this type are classified as shortened cakes, a term signifying their fat content, and foam cakes, so named to indicate the egg foams that contribute so significantly to their structure.

Cookies comprise yet another category of baked product. The physical characteristics vary rather widely; some doughs are dropped, while others can be rolled and cut, and still others are baked as a sheet or layer and cut into bars. They range in texture from crisp and chewy to tender and fairly light.

Pastries most commonly are used as the crusts for pies. However, puff pastries form the basis for patty shells and French pastries. Other pastries are made utilizing very thin sheets of dough; for example, baklava is a popular Middle Eastern dessert made of numerous layers of filo dough. These different pastries usually are dessert items. Recently, the popularity of quiche has brought pastry to the fore for the main course. In addition, meat pies, chicken à la king in patty shells, and spanakopita (spinach in layers of filo dough) expand the use of pastries in the main course.

These baked products certainly cover a broad range of characteristics and applications. Nevertheless, they all have in common the fact that they are dependent on gluten for much of their structural integrity. The variety is a result of varying proportions and kinds of ingredients combined and baked in different ways. Imagination and careful culinary techniques are important ingredients in preparing any baked product. In addition, a good basic knowledge of the various types of cakes, cookies, and pastries helps to ensure success.

CAKES

The two basic categories of cakes—foam and shortened—are distinctly different in their preparation and problems. The ratios of ingredients and procedures for mixing and baking are related to quick breads, yet each type of cake has certain unique features that need to be identified and respected in preparing either a foam or a shortened cake.

Foam Cakes

Foam cakes gain their name from the fact that much of their basic structure is due to the use of an egg foam into which other ingredients are blended. The foams used may be egg white, egg yolk, or both; foams of whites are the most common basis of foam cake recipes. Regardless of the type of foam used, the structure of foam cakes is quite weak, usually requiring use of a tube cake pan to help the batter pull itself upward to achieve maximum volume during baking. Additional assistance is provided by cooling the baked cake in an inverted position to help stretch out the foam cell walls until they gain strength by cooling. These foam cakes are categorized as angel, sponge, and chiffon. Although all are foam cakes, there are certain unique features of each type. These features are explored in the paragraphs that follow.

Angel Cake Foam cake consisting primarily of egg white foam, sugar, and cake flour, with no fat or baking powder.

Angel Cake *Angel cakes* are the simplest of the foam cakes to make for they really are just an egg white foam stabilized with some sugar and combined with cake flour to strengthen the cake structure. Persons on weight reduction diets or on low cholesterol diets particularly appreciate angel cakes because of their lack of fat and cholesterol. Formulas for angel cake contain neither shortening nor baking powder.

Not surprisingly, the key to a successful angel cake is the preparation and handling of an optimal egg white foam (see Chapter 10). This challenge is met, in part, by the use of cream of tartar and part of the sugar, beginning at the foamy stage of beating the whites. The whites are beaten until the peaks just bend over, a point at which the foam maintains reasonable elasticity and stability. Use of eggs with a large amount of thick white is a further aid in achieving optimal quality.

The other half of the sugar is combined with the cake flour before these dry ingredients are added, a fourth at a time, and folded into the egg white foam. By mixing the cake flour with the sugar, the tendency of the cake flour to ball up in the mixture is reduced, and the sugar-flour combination blends readily with the foam, allowing the folding operation to be reduced to a minimum. Even though it tends to ball up because of its fine texture, cake flour is the flour of choice in making angel cake. The tender gluten and somewhat reduced amount of protein in cake flour are pluses in making angel cakes, for the flour is needed only as a supplemental aid to the egg white protein for the necessary structural strength of the baked cake. Folding in of the flour-sugar mixture is done as efficiently as possible, with the process beginning just as soon as the egg white foam has been formed. The goal is to keep as much of the air trapped in the foam as possible, for it is this air (in combination with moisture from the egg whites) that is responsible for the leavening of the cake.

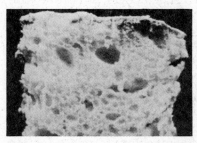  

Inadequate manipulation of flour and sugar into angel cake batter results in an uneven and coarse texture with low volume (left) in comparison with angel cake made with the correct amount of folding (center). Too much folding (right) develops the gluten so much that the texture becomes rather compact and tough.

After the batter has been transferred very gently into an ungreased tube pan, a knife is used to cut through the batter once to eliminate any large pockets of air that might have been trapped as the batter was eased into the tube pan. The pan is not greased, thus helping the cake cling and pull itself up. Immediately, baking should be initiated, preferably in a preheated oven to avoid loss of air from the batter while the oven is heating. The test for doneness of an angel cake is to touch the cake lightly with a finger when the appropriate length of time has elapsed. If done, the cake will spring back, but a cake that is not quite done will retain the indentation from the finger and may even fall. Such testing needs to be done quickly to avoid cooling the cake if it is not done, for cool air will cause the air within the cake to contract; this reduces the pressure within the cells and causes the cake to shrink or even fall.

When the cake is done, the pan should be removed from the oven and inverted immediately to allow the fragile cake structure to hang and stretch to maximum volume while cooling. Ideally, the tube pan has legs to keep the surface of the cake from contacting the counter while cooling. If this is not available, the pan should rest on a rack to allow air to circulate under the cake, thus avoiding condensation on the surface. An underbaked angel cake will fall from the pan when inverted, whereas an overbaked cake will be slightly dry and tough due to loss of moisture and overcoagulation of the egg white and gluten proteins in the cell walls.

An angel cake of high quality is very tender, seeming to virtually "melt in the mouth." It will have an excellent volume, and the air cells will be rather uniform, of moderate size, and with thin walls. The crumb should be slightly moist, and there should not be any dry flour. The crust should be a pleasing brown.

Angel cake mixes are popular because they eliminate the problem of what to do with the egg yolks left when making an angel cake "from scratch." They are also something of a time saver. The dried egg whites used in angel cake mixes require extensive beating, preferably with an electric mixer, to achieve the correct end point. The peaks need to just barely stand up straight when the beater is extracted from a foam of dried egg whites, which is an extension of beating beyond that required for fresh egg whites. Volume is affected adversely if dried egg whites are not beaten sufficiently, that is, if they are only beaten so that the peaks just bend over, as is done with fresh whites.

Sponge Cake Foam cake comprised of an egg yolk foam and an egg white foam, plus a small amount of cake flour, water, lemon, and sugar, and usually baked in a tube pan.

Sponge Cake   *Sponge cakes* are similar to angel cakes—with some unique features. Perhaps the most apparent distinction is that sponge cakes have an egg yolk foam as well as an egg white foam. In fact, the egg yolk foam is unique because of the extensive amount of beating that is done to obtain a foam that is almost thick enough to pile, despite the addition of a small amount of water. Stability of the egg yolk foam is enhanced by the addition of a small amount of lemon. This foam is combined with the cake flour by gentle folding and then allowed to stand briefly while the egg white foam is being prepared, for the egg yolk foam retains its volume and elasticity better than the foam of the whites. The whites are whipped into a comparatively stable foam, with the stabilizing effect of added cream of tartar and sugar. The two foams are folded together gently, but quickly, just until a completely homogeneous batter develops, and no streaks of the yolk or white foam can be found. Extra folding should be avoided because it will cause excessive gluten development and also will release air from the foams unnecessarily.

The baking of sponge cakes usually is done in an ungreased tube pan so that the batter will cling to the pan and will help to increase the volume during baking. The tube permits air to circulate in the center area as well as around the outside edge of the cake; it also has the advantage of reducing the total distance that heat has to travel to reach the center of the cake and coagulate the proteins. If a sponge cake is to be used as a jelly roll, the batter is spread over the entire surface of a jelly roll pan in an even layer. The baking time for a jelly role is fairly short, due to the thinness of the cake layer.

The use of yolks, as well as the whites, in making sponge cakes results in the somewhat elastic quality of the baked cake. In fact, a layer baked in a jelly roll pan can be rolled in a kitchen towel sprinkled with powdered sugar, spread with a filling, and then rerolled to make a jelly roll which can be served in slices.

Sponge cakes are tested in the same manner as angel cakes, that is, by touching them gently and having them spring back, leaving no indentation in the surface. Unless being baked as a jelly roll, sponge cakes should be inverted to cool before being removed from the pan. A jelly roll needs to be removed and rolled in a towel while still warm so that the layer can be rolled without cracking.

A high-quality sponge cake has fairly fine, uniform cells and thin cell walls. When examined in cross section from top to bottom, the color should be a uniform yellow, with no streaks of yellow or pieces of egg white and no tendency toward formation of a layer toward the bottom. The exterior should be a pleasing, golden brown, and the volume should be very high.

Technique is important in preparing a sponge cake, for inadequate beating of the egg yolks can cause thick cell walls, poor volume, and a tendency for a layer to form in the bottom of the cake. Underbeating of whites causes similar problems: the whites will not contain enough air in them, and they will tend to be a little fluid and drain from the yolk foam before the structure is set. Inadequate folding of the yolk and white foams can also cause a layer to begin to form, because the yolk foam is fairly heavy and will start to move toward the bottom. Overbeating of whites avoids this problem, but it will reduce volume due to some loss of extensibility of the white foam and also the increased amount of folding needed to blend the stiff white foam with the yolks. Toughness is due to too much development of gluten which occurs fairly easily if extra folding is needed to blend the yolk and white foams.

Chiffon Cake Foam cake containing oil and baking powder, as well as the ingredients used in other foam cakes combined together and folded into an egg white foam beaten until the peaks just stand up straight.

Chiffon Cakes In some ways, *chiffon cakes* represent a transition between foam cakes and shortened cakes, although they are classified as foam cakes. The formula for chiffon cakes includes oil and baking powder, neither of which is found in true sponge cakes or angel cakes. Baking powder commonly is used as a source of leavening in shortened cakes, and shortened cakes also have fat, albeit usually not oil. The presence of these two ingredients promotes distinct differences between chiffon cakes and either angel or sponge cakes. Chiffon cakes typically have the greatest volume of the foam cakes, are a bit finer in texture, and more tender than angel or sponge cakes.

Preparation of chiffon cakes begins by combining all of the ingredients (including the yolks) except the egg white, part of the sugar, and the cream of tartar in a large bowl and then beating until the batter is smooth. Since this batter is quite fluid, extensive beating can be done without developing the gluten excessively. The whites then are beaten in a separate bowl until they reach the foamy stage, at which time the cream of tartar is added all at once, and the sugar is added gradually. Beating of whites for chiffon cakes needs to be continued until the foam is stiff enough that the whites just barely stand up straight when the beater is pulled upward from them gently. This slightly exceeds the stage of beating for other egg white foam uses, but is necessary because of the distinctly fluid nature of the yolk-flour mixture that needs to be folded into the beaten whites.

The folding of the whites and the yolk-flour mixture must be done with careful attention to be sure that all of the fluid mixture gets blended uniformly throughout the whites. Unless total homogeneity is achieved, there will be a tendency for the yolk-flour mixture to drain toward the bottom before the structure sets. Chiffon cakes are much more likely to have evidence of a layer starting to form toward the bottom of the cake than are sponge cakes, because of the fluidity of the yolk-flour mixture. This layer not only is unattractive to the eye, but it has a rather rubbery texture as a result of the egg yolk. The problem of separation is reduced considerably by being sure to use part of the sugar in the recipe (2 tablespoons per white) to form a stable egg white foam rather than placing all the sugar in the yolk-flour mixture. This use of the sugar creates quite a stable egg white meringue with the elasticity necessary to permit the blending and folding of the yolk-flour mixture with the whites.

A chiffon cake of excellent quality is rather imposing to see, for its volume usually is greater than either angel or sponge cakes. When well prepared, a chiffon cake will be tender, slightly moist, and uniform in texture from top to bottom, with no evidence of separation of a layer. The cells will be moderate in size and uniform, and the cell walls will be just a little thicker than those seen in shortened cakes. A chiffon cake is detectably more tender than a sponge cake, due in large measure to the oil in the chiffon cake and the extensive stretching of the cell walls, making them thinner and, therefore, more tender than sponge cake cells.

Comparison of the Foam Cakes The foam cakes all contain an egg white foam to help promote volume and a pleasing, uniform texture. They also all utilize cake flour. Beyond these similarities, there are crucial differences in the various foam cakes. For example, in the use of eggs, angel cake contains no yolk, whereas sponge cake uses a well-developed, fairly viscous yolk foam, and chiffon cake merely has the yolks beaten in with the other ingredients to make a satin-smooth batter to be folded ultimately with the whites. As can be seen in Table 14.1, chiffon cakes are the only type of foam cake using a fat (actually oil) and baking powder.

Stable egg foams, particularly stable egg white foams, are fundamental to successful foam cakes, even to chiffon cakes that contain baking powder for leavening. The use of sugar and cream of tartar is almost like an insurance policy, helping to assure good volume and a desirable texture in foam cakes. In Chapter 10, the action of sugar in promoting elasticity and a fine texture due to delaying foam formation was discussed; the shift toward the isoelectric point of a key egg white protein that results when cream of tartar is added also is of importance.

Shortened Cakes

Shortened Cake Cake containing a solid fat (commonly creamed with sugar), sugar, usually leavening agent, flour, and liquid.

Usually, the word ''cake'' conjures up visual images of a cake baked as a sheet or a layer in a round or rectangular pan approximately 2 inches deep. Such cakes have a finer texture, more tender crumb, and a richer flavor than characteristically will be found in foam cakes. These cakes are often called *shortened cakes*, a term denoting their comparatively high fat content. Variations are great within the category identified as shortened cakes. The liquid

Table 14.1 A Comparison of Four Basic Types of Cakes

Type of Cake	Flour	Liquid	Eggs		Fat		Leavening Agent
			Number, Part	Method of Adding	Type	Amount	
Angel	1 c	—	12 whites	Foam, folded in	—	—	Air (egg white foam stabilized with sugar and acid), steam
Sponge	1 c	5 T water	4 yolks and whites	Foams, folded in	—	—	Air (egg white and yolk foams stabilized with acid and sugar), steam
Chiffon	1⅓ c	6 T water	2 yolks 4 whites	Yolks added with liquid, white foam folded in	Oil	⅔ c	Baking powder (1¼ tsp), air (egg white foam stabilized with sugar), steam
Shortened	1 c	¼ c milk	1 whole	Creamed with the fat and sugar foam	Plastic fat	⅔ c	Baking powder (¾ tsp), air, steam

used may vary, the portion of egg and its treatment may differ, flavoring agents may cover a wide range, and even the leavening agents my be somewhat diverse.

The simplest of the shortened cakes often is referred to simply as a plain cake. This term designates a cake made with whole egg and just the basic ingredients for a cake (fat, sugar, cake flour, liquid, baking powder, and flavoring). White cakes are very similar, with the exception that only the egg white is used, usually in the form of a foam. Chocolate or *devil's food cakes* are a very popular form of shortened cake. The color range in chocolate cakes is quite remarkable, depending upon the pH of the cake batter. If extra soda is added to bring the batter well within the alkaline range, the chocolate cake will become a rich red, deep mahogany color. Such a cake usually is called a devil's food cake. Chocolate cakes with a definitely brown color tone are neutral or even slightly acidic. Variations in color are the result of using an acidic ingredient (sour milk or cream, for example) and soda to react and form carbon dioxide.

The shortened cakes can be combined in a variety of ways to achieve varying results. The methods are based on the conventional method, but also include variations to meet special requirements. In addition to the conventional method, the modified conventional, conventional sponge, muffin, and single-stage methods are suited to certain shortened cake formulas.

Conventional Method   The *conventional method* of making shortened cakes begins with a thorough creaming to create a very heavy fat-sugar foam, one in

Devil's Food Cake Shortened cake made with some excess of soda to achieve the desired deep mahogany color.

Conventional Method Method of preparing shortened cakes, in which the fat and sugar are creamed, the beaten eggs added, and the sifted dry ingredients added (in thirds) alternately with the liquid (in halves).

which the crystals of sugar actually dig tiny air pockets to create the cells entrapping air. This foam provides the framework of the cake's structure, helping to create a uniform, fine texture as the air starts to expand during baking. Creaming should be terminated if the fat starts to melt at all from the physical action, for a very soft fat is unable to trap air effectively.

During the latter part of creaming, vanilla or any other flavoring agent should be added to the creamed mixture. This step is recommended because fats retain the flavor and aroma of extracts effectively and carry that flavor throughout the batter uniformly.

When creaming has been completed, the beaten eggs are blended into the creamed mixture to establish an emulsion, with the yolks serving as the primary emulsifying agent. Formation of an emulsion in the cake batter is important to helping to produce a shortened cake with a fine texture. The combined manipulation involved in the creaming process and the blending in of the eggs should be stopped before the butter or other fat in the mixture becomes extremely soft. This precaution needs to be observed to avoid producing a curdled-looking batter, the result of breaking the emulsion. The texture of a cake batter containing a broken emulsion will be somewhat more coarse than will a cake produced with an emulsified batter.

The dry ingredients (flour, salt, and baking powder, plus cinnamon or other spices being used in certain recipes) should be sifted together prior to beginning the actual mixing of the cake so that the preparation of the batter can proceed without delay. Approximately a third of the dry ingredients is stirred carefully into the creamed mixture containing the eggs. This addition thickens the batter, which helps to avoid curdling or breaking of the emulsion when the first half of the liquid is added and stirred in. The second third of the dry ingredients is added and stirred until no dry flour is evident. At this point, the rest of the liquid is added, with stirring; finally, the last third of the dry ingredients is added and stirred. The best results are obtained when a cake recipe has been standardized, with a given number of strokes to be stirred after each of the dry ingredient and the liquid additions if mixing by hand or a specified number of minutes at a designated speed on the electric mixer.

The conventional method frequently is chosen as the method for making shortened cakes because this will produce a cake with a tender crumb, a fine texture, and excellent keeping qualities. The disadvantages of the comparatively long mixing time and the energy demands deter some individuals from using the conventional method.

Modified Conventional Method Method of mixing a cake utilizing the conventional method, but separating the eggs and adding the whites as a foam folded in at the end of mixing.

Modified Conventional Method The *modified conventional method* of making shortened cakes differs from the conventional method only in the way that the eggs are incorporated. In this instance, the eggs are separated, and the yolks are beaten together and added to the creamed mixture (rather than the whole eggs added in the conventional method). When the other ingredients have been combined, the egg whites are beaten until the peaks just bend over and then folded gently into the batter. By using the egg whites as a foam, additional air is incorporated into the batter to help promote a light cake.

Conventional Sponge Method Method of mixing shortened cakes, differing from the conventional method by separating the eggs and using part of the sugar to make a meringue to fold in at the end of mixing.

Conventional Sponge Method Yet another variation of the conventional method is the conventional sponge method, a technique particularly good for cakes low in fat. For the *conventional sponge method*, the eggs are separated. Part of the sugar (2 tablespoons per egg white) is reserved for making a meringue with the egg whites at the end of the mixing period, while the rest of the sugar is used for creaming with the fat as the first step in the mixing process. The yolks are added in the same fashion as in the modified conventional method, and the remainder of the mixing generally is comparable to the modified conventional method. The only difference is that the egg white foam is prepared by gradually adding the reserved sugar, beginning at the foamy stage. The added stability of the egg white foam as a result of the sugar is valuable in preparing a light cake with good volume and a fine texture.

Muffin Method The muffin method of making cakes is the same as that used in making muffins (see Chapter 13). To utilize this method, the fat must either be melted or an oil must be used so that the fat can be blended with the other liquid ingredients, including the beaten whole eggs. All the dry ingredients are sifted together to blend them thoroughly before the liquid ingredients are added all at once and stirred in. This method of making a cake is very fast compared with the rather deliberate techniques required in the conventional method and its variations. However, the lack of creaming of the solid fat and sugar causes cakes made by the muffin method to be rather coarse in texture. This method also results in rapid staling, as contrasted to the conventional method. For instances when the quality of the finished product is somewhat less important than the time required to prepare it, the muffin method may be acceptable.

Single-Stage Method Method combining all of the ingredients except the egg and possibly part of the liquid, mixing, and then adding the egg and any remaining liquid with beating.

Single-Stage Method The *single-stage method* of making shortened cakes is basically the method used in making cake mixes; that is, the dry ingredients (sifted together) are combined all at once with the soft shortening and most or all of the milk. Usually a mixer is used for a designated length of time to combine these ingredients. Then the egg and any remaining liquid are added and are mixed into the batter for a specified period. This method is very fast, but it does produce a fairly coarse texture, and the cake stales rapidly.

These five variations of preparing the batter for a shortened cake are compared in Table 14.2.

Baking Prior to starting mixing of the batter, the pans for shortened cakes can be lined on the bottom with wax paper if the cake is to be removed after baking. The sides do not need to be greased, for the cake can be released easily from the edges with a spatula or a knife. If a shortened cake is to be stored in the pan, the bottom of the pan is greased lightly, but wax paper is not used.

As soon as mixing has been completed, the batter should be poured gently into the prepared cake pan(s), and the pan should be placed in the center of a preheated oven. The oven temperature for shortened cakes usually is about 365°F, for this temperature is sufficiently hot to generate carbon dioxide

Table 14.2 Comparison of Methods for Making Shortened Cakes

Method	Method of Adding		
	Eggs	*Fat*	*Liquid and Flour*
Conventional	Whole, beaten, blended into creamed mixture	Creamed with sugar	Alternately (⅓ flour, ½ liquid, ⅓ flour, ½ liquid, ⅓ flour)
Modified conventional	Yolks, beaten and blended with creamed mixture; whites, beaten with no sugar, folded in at end	Same as conventional method	Same as conventional method
Conventional sponge	Same as modified conventional except ½ of sugar used to make white foam	Same as conventional method	Same as conventional method
Muffin	Whole, beaten and added with liquid ingredients	Oil or melted shortening added with liquid ingredients	All of liquid and dry ingredients combined at one time
Single stage	Whole, near end of mixing when last liquid added	With all dry ingredients and most of liquid	Dry ingredients and most of liquid added at same time as shortening; remainder of liquid added with egg after initial mixing period

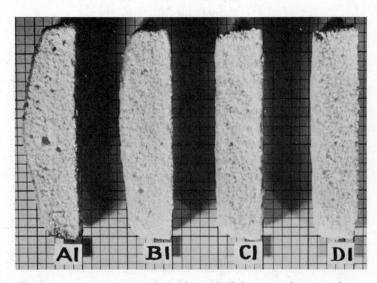

The humping seen in A1 (baked at 425°F) happens because the structure sets at the sides firmly while the center portion is still elastic; the surface becomes flatter due to more uniform heat penetration at 375°F (B1) and 325°F (C1). Some loss of volume occurs at 300°F (D1).

When a toothpick inserted in the center comes out clean, the structure of a shortened cake is set, and the cake should be removed from the oven.

rather rapidly from baking powder and to promote leavening from steam and air, too, yet it is not so hot that the structure sets before the cake has expanded to a desirable volume. Shortened cakes are baked until a toothpick inserted in the center comes out clean, a quick and easy means of being sure that the protein had denatured. They are overbaked if the cake is pulling away from the pan.

The cakes are cooled in the pan until the pan feels warm, but not hot, on the bottom. It is at this point that layer cakes are removed from the pan by inverting the cake and pan onto a plate and then carefully removing the pan and peeling the warm wax paper away. Shortened cakes are not inverted to cool; their fat content weakens the cell walls to the point where the cake would fall out of the pan.

The changes occurring in a cake during baking are indeed remarkable. What starts as a fluid batter of small dimensions emerges from the oven as a light and tender, yet rigid, structure that can be cut and served easily. The cells have grown in size, and their walls have stretched and become considerably thinner than in the original batter. The liquid responsible for the flowing character of the batter has been used to gelatinize the starch in the flour. The combination of the binding of water in gelatinizing the starch and in developing the gluten and the evaporation occurring during baking explains the shifts in water occurring during the transition of the batter from the liquid state into a rigid structure.

The growth in volume during the baking process results from the expansion of air and carbon dioxide and the development of steam from water in the batter. Gases expand tremendously when heated, and these expanding gases push against the cell walls. These cell walls are able to stretch because of their content of gluten. The elasticity of gluten permits the cell walls to keep stretching and stretching as the gases and steam within the cells push against the walls. Ideally, these cell walls will be quite thin, yet still strong enough to support the weight of the cake when the protein in the walls has denatured and cooled.

The transition from elastic protein to the rigid, denatured gluten occurs as a result of adequate heating during baking. This transformation occurs rather slowly in most cakes, but it will take place first at the edges and the top and bottom of the cake where the oven heat first contacts the batter. If the oven heat is too hot, the crust will set well in advance of the denaturation of the protein on the interior. Since the interior will still have elastic gluten and gases pushing against it, considerable pressure to expand builds up inside the cake until there is so much pressure that the cake crust breaks open. Then the interior batter will push upward through the break, resulting in a cracked, humped cake.

The converse occurs if the oven heat is somewhat below 365°F, for the fat in the batter will melt, and the cells in the cake will start to move around and bump into each other, sometimes coalescing into larger cells. Ultimately, the baked cake will have a coarse cell structure and thick cell walls because of this migratory mode. Some of these changes will occur in cakes started in a cold oven while the oven is preheating to its correct temperature. This is why pre-heating the oven is recommended for baking shortened cakes.

Evaluation Shortened cakes should be very tender and have a fine, velvety texture, a pleasing flavor, and good volume. The texture should be uniform, with no evidence of tunneling. The crust should be pleasingly browned and gently rounded, being neither humped nor sunken.

Deviations Variations from this ideal cake may result from several factors. Good volume is achieved by a proper balance of ingredients and a good technique, which traps air in the batter. Volume and tenderness are factors that are closely related; an increase in the volume of a given amount of batter means thinner cell walls, as the same amount of solid material is stretched to cover a larger total surface area. An appropriate amount of baking powder promotes the desired volume. Too much baking powder can contribute so much carbon dioxide that the cake will collapse from the pressure generated (Table 14.3). There also likely will be an objectionable residue flavor when an appreciable excess of baking powder is used. On the other hand, too little baking powder results in a very heavy cake.

Sugar has a tenderizing effect by promoting an increased volume. One effect of increasing the sugar is the need for an increased amount of mixing to develop the gluten. Of course, sugar influences the sweet taste of a cake; sugar also promotes browning of the crust. Small increases in the amount of sugar in many cake recipes will be acceptable, but large increases are likely to cause the cake to fall because of excessively high temperatures for the gluten to denature and set the structure.

Too much fat can cause a cake to fall and to have a greasy crumb. Increased fat also enhances browning. The tenderizing effect of fat in interfering with gluten development can be offset, in part, by increasing the mixing.

Table 14.3 Possible Causes of Loss of Quality in Cakes

Problem	Possible Cause
Too dark a crust	Too hot an oven; use of fructose or honey; position too near the top or bottom of the oven
Fallen center	Too much sugar; too much fat; too much baking powder; inadequate baking; too cool an oven; oven door opened during baking
Peaked or humped	Too much flour; too little sugar, fat, or milk; too hot an oven; overstirring (too much gluten developed); too deep a pan
Poor volume	Not enough leavening; too cool an oven; too much fat or liquid
Large cells and tunnels	Too much baking powder; excessive mixing
Dry, tough crumb	Too much flour; too much egg; too little fat; too little sugar; too little liquid
Sticky, sugary crust	Too much sugar
Overflowing pan	Too small a pan; too much sugar; too much baking powder

Most shortened cakes are made with cake flour to take advantage of the tender, less abundant gluten in this type of flour. If all-purpose flour is used, the cake will be less tender than if cake flour is used.

Eggs are valuable in shortened cakes because of their emulsifying ability, as well as their capacity to form foams. However, too much egg is a toughening factor in shortened cakes and can cause the crumb to have a somewhat waxy character.

All these ingredients clearly contribute to the characteristics of a specific cake. In addition to the factors noted, the extent of mixing is a vital influence on cake quality. There must be sufficient gluten developed to hold the cake together, but extra stirring will promote the development of very strong gluten strands. The manifestation of too much mixing will be the formation of tunnels and a tough cake.

COOKIES

Cookies generally are somewhat less delicate and sensitive than shortened or foam cakes. Nevertheless, there are guidelines to preparing and evaluating this type of baked product. In fact, cookies usually are categorized into three groups: drop, bar, or rolled cookies. Usually, these cookies are mixed by about the same method used for making shortened cakes, that is, the conventional method. The proportions of the ingredients are quite different from those in shortened cakes, with the limited amount of liquid being the most obvious difference. Cookies frequently have special textural and flavoring ingredients, such as raisins, chocolate chips, and nuts.

Drop cookies, compared with shortened cakes, are richer, and the dough is stiffer, which is necessary to keep them from flowing on the baking sheet. The added stiffness is achieved by reducing the liquid. Ordinarily, drop cook-

SCIENCE NOTE: HIGH-ALTITUDE BAKING

The greatly reduced atmospheric pressure experienced at altitudes exceeding 3000 feet influences the preparation of many different foods. For example, water boils at temperatures significantly below the 212°F characteristic of sea level, which means that boiled foods require more cooking time as altitudes increase. Similarly, baked products, particularly cakes, are influenced significantly by the altitude at which the product is prepared. Water will also evaporate more readily at high altitudes than at sea level.

Of particular importance at high elevations is the reduced pressure of the atmosphere bearing down on the surface. This means that the expanding gases and stretching cell walls in a shortened cake or other baked product will have reduced opposition to their stretching. This can cause cakes to fall before the structure is set.

To avoid having cakes fall when being baked in the mountains, bake them at a temperature of 400°F to help set the structure rapidly. The baking powder should be decreased by between an eighth and a fourth, with the smaller reduction being used at elevations of between 3000 and 5000 feet and the larger figure being followed at between 5000 and 7000 feet. A decrease of 1 tablespoon of sugar per cup of sugar up to 5000 and of as much as 3 tablespoons between 5000 and 7000 feet also helps to strengthen the structure and prevent the cake from falling. To compensate for the increased loss of moisture, liquid can be increased by about 1 tablespoon at 3000 feet and up to 4 tablespoons per cup of liquid at 7000 feet. Fat may need to be reduced by between 1 and 2 tablespoons per cup of fat to help strengthen the structure. When using foams, the egg whites should be beaten slightly less than normal to avoid trapping too much air if the cake is being prepared at a high elevation.

Cakes are very sensitive in their balance between ingredients and the pressures that they can withstand within their cells during baking. Therefore, these suggestions are merely guidelines. Experimentation is necessary to determine just what the ratio of the various ingredients will need to be to achieve the optimal product at different elevations. The general approach is to reduce the pressure within the cells and to strengthen the cell walls by modifying the amounts of the appropriate ingredients, specifically, by reducing baking powder and sugar (and probably fat), and by increasing liquid to compensate for excessive moisture loss.

ies are dropped from a spoon onto the baking sheet, but they also can be forced through a cooky press to create special shapes. Baking usually requires between 10 and 15 minutes at 375°F to achieve the desired golden-brown color. The appearance is the criterion for determining that drop cookies are done.

Bar cookies usually are slightly softer in their consistency than drop cookies are before baking. This permits the dough to be spread into a fairly uniform thickness in a rectangular baking pan. After baking, bar cookies are cut into the desired size and are removed from the pan. Sometimes they are frosted before they are cut and served. Their structure is strong enough that they can be cut while still warm.

Rolled cookies require a dough sufficiently stiff to be able to be rolled, cut, and transferred to a baking sheet. Usually, rolled cooky doughs are refrigerated to chill them thoroughly so that they can be rolled out with a minimum of flour. Extra flour adds to the toughness of the baked cookies and should be avoided as much as possible in rolled cookies. Stiff cooky doughs can also be made into logs, refrigerated, and sliced and baked even several days after mixing the dough if the logs are wrapped tightly to prevent loss of moisture.

The texture of cookies varies considerably, depending upon the specific type of cooky being prepared. Some are quite crisp, while others may be chewy, or even soft. In general, cookies should spread only a little, and they definitely should not be burned or underbaked. Cookies with too much fat in relation to the flour in the mixture will tend to spread too much, brown too quickly, and be greasy. On the other hand, cookies with too much flour will be tough and dry.

To preserve quality after baking, drop and rolled cookies should be removed from the baking sheet while they are still warm but not so hot that they tend to fall apart when lifted with a spatula. The warm cookies can be placed in a single layer on paper toweling to finish cooling. When completely cooled, the cookies can be transferred to an airtight container for storage. Brief storage can be very satisfactory at room temperature, but excellent quality can be maintained for an extended storage period when baked cookies are frozen carefully in tightly sealed containers.

PASTRY

Pastry is the simplest of the baked products in terms of ingredients, but may be the most difficult to prepare well. The simplicity explains the confounding difficulties that may arise during the preparation of a pie crust, for only the necessary materials are there—water and flour to provide for the gluten development necessary for the structure and some fat to promote flaky texture. The gluten develops very easily in pastry, both because of the limited amount of water and because of the poor use of the fat. Water has to be provided at a level that allows the tenacious gluten to develop and hold the product together without making the dough too sticky and fluid to handle and roll out. This ratio is approximately 6 parts flour to 1 part water. Such a 6:1 ratio promotes gluten development readily, even with only a little handling.

Ordinarily, a flour product with an abundance of fat will be extremely tender because the fat coats gluten very effectively and blocks some of the water from interacting with the flour proteins easily. This happens to an extent in pastry, but the fat is not used to its maximum advantage. Instead, fat is cut into pieces, leaving much of it encapsulated and unable to interact with the flour. In essence, the net effect of the fat in a pastry dough is comparable to using a much smaller amount of fat effectively by completely coating the flour with the fat. The inefficient use of fat in a pastry dough is responsible for much of the problem of tough pastries when people are learning to make pie crusts. Fortunately, tender and flaky pastries can be made with practice and understanding of the process.

Ingredients

In the home, pastry ordinarily is prepared using all-purpose flour that has been sifted once before being measured carefully. Commercially, pastry flour is used because of its lower protein content and consequent tenderizing effect, but pastry flour is not generally available to consumers in retail markets. All-purpose flour can be used quite satisfactorily as long as it is measured carefully and the dough is handled delicately and skillfully. The ratio of flour to liquid is extremely critical in preparing pastry doughs; hence, the need for careful measuring of sifted flour.

Salt in pastry dough is there simply for flavor. In fact, omission of salt is consistent with the recommendation today that salt intake should be reduced where feasible. Since pastry ordinarily is the foundation of a dessert or main dish with a flavorful filling, deletion of salt in the pastry is likely to go unnoticed.

Fat contributes flavor and tenderness. It also promotes flakiness and browning. Interestingly, although fat is included primarily for its tenderizing effect, its inclusion by being cut into small pieces is productive in promoting flakiness but counterproductive to tenderness. However, so much fat is used in pastry that it is possible to make an extremely tender crust despite the limited surface area of the fat. The ratio of flour to fat can be varied considerably, depending upon the skill of the person making the dough. Practically anyone can make a tender pie crust using a ratio of 2 parts flour to 1 part fat (2:1). This ratio provides a considerable amount of surface area of fat, even when the fat is left in small pieces, and protects the flour rather effectively from the water. Of course, the calorie content of such a rich pastry is very high. Consequently, the somewhat leaner ratio of 3 parts flour to 1 part fat (3:1) is the ratio used most commonly. This reduced amount of fat requires more skill on the part of the baker than is needed with the 2:1 ratio, but a tender crust can be prepared with a little practice. For those who are intent on reducing fat as much as possible and still making pastry, a ratio of 4 part flour to 1 part fat (4:1) is the answer. However, this lean mixture is something of a challenge to handle without overdeveloping the gluten.

Water is added as sparsely as possible, yet it must be included to develop the gluten sufficiently to bind the crust together. With the proper amount of water, pastry dough will feel slightly dry, but the dough will stick together when pressed firmly. If too little water is used, the dough will crumble at the edges when being rolled. Even a small excess of water needs to be avoided, for water promotes toughness.

Preparation

Technique is fundamental to the quality of pastry, and this technique begins with extremely careful measuring of the ingredients. The ratio of flour to water is particularly crucial to the ease of handling and the tenderness of the final product. Both of these ingredients require especially careful measurements to ensure correct quantities. The actual preparation begins with a careful mixing of the salt and the flour, followed by cutting in of the fat. The cutting in process is done most efficiently using a pastry blender, wielded with a light, tossing motion to help maintain the fat in the small, discrete pieces desired to promote flakiness. A relaxed flick of the wrist helps to avoid pressing the dough mixture into a compact mass. If a pastry blender is not available, a couple of table knives can be used in a cross-cutting motion. Cutting in should be done until the fat is in pieces about the size of rice grains.

The addition of the water is a critical process in making a tender, high-quality pastry, because this is when the gluten development begins. The goal is to get uniform distribution of the water with an absolute minimum of manipulation of the dough mass. This goal can be reached by adding the water, only a drop at a time, while lightly tossing the flour-coated fat particles with a table fork. This action requires considerable coordination, for one hand is doing a flipping motion with the fork while the other is controlling the dropwise addition of the water all around the mixing bowl. Care must be taken to add water throughout the dough, not just in a small area. The most effective distribution of water in the dough is done at the time the water is being dropped into the dough. By moving around so that water is being dropped into a dry area at all times, the problem of having a soggy dough in one area and a crumbly section in another part of the dough can be avoided. Ideally, the entire dough mass will be moistened slightly but not really adhering when the water has all been added. At this point, the back of a table fork is used to mash the dough together just enough to make it stick together in a ball. Minimum action should be used for this, for gluten develops very easily at this point.

In preparation for rolling, enough dough for one crust should be removed and worked very gently and quickly with the hands to form a ball. Then this ball is crafted quickly, on a lightly floured pastry cloth, into a flattened disk with a smooth circumference and no indication of cracks. In other words, this shaping prepares the dough to be rolled easily into the desired round shape needed for lining the pie plate. Gentle pressure is needed in rolling out the crust so that the gluten strands in the dough will be eased into position and not be torn or stretched unduly. The pressure is eased toward the edge of the dough to help achieve a uniform thickness throughout the dough. Maintenance of the desired circular shape is helped by continually changing the angle of the strokes of the rolling pin. Rolling is completed when the dough shows only a slight imprint when the dough is touched lightly with the finger and when the dough is large enough to fit into the pan with an extra half-inch margin for the edging.

Care must be exercised to avoid stretching or tearing when transferring the pastry from the cloth into the pie plate. An easy way to accomplish the transfer is to fold the pastry delicately in half and then into quarters. This permits easy handling and allows the dough to be unfolded and gently eased into the pie plate. The pastry needs to be fitted into the pan by letting the weight of the crust pull the crust down to the junction between the side and bottom of the pan, being careful to avoid stretching the dough to make it go into this portion of the pan.

For a one-crust pie shell that is to be baked before filling, a number of holes should be perforated in the crust before baking. This can be done quickly using a table fork. These holes allow steam to escape during baking and help to prevent the development of pressure in pockets, which would form large blisters in the baked crust. Also, these holes help the crust to retain the shape of the pie plate. Another technique for helping the crust to retain its desired shape is to trim the crust about half an inch beyond the edge of the pie plate, fold the edge under so that it stands on the lip of the plate, and then flute or do other trim finishing so that the edge continues to rest firmly on the lip. This avoids having the edge fall into the pie plate during baking.

Baking of unfilled pie shells is done in an oven at 425°F until the crust is a light golden brown. The baked crust should be a uniform, golden brown, should conform to the pie plate shape, and should be tender and flaky. The quality of rolling and handling of the dough into the pie plate is evident in the finished crust, for a crust that has been rolled unevenly will brown unevenly, with the thin areas being much darker than the thicker areas. A stretched crust will pull away from the sides of the pan and may be almost bowl-shaped rather than have an angular junction between the sides and bottoms. Flakiness is judged by looking at a cross section and is seen most easily by examining the edge trim area. The desired appearance is one of fine layers of dough so that the crust almost shatters or flakes when cut. Tenderness also is evaluated most easily at the trim area because the extra layer adds to the difficulty of cutting with a fork. This makes differences in tenderness apparent between pastry samples.

Factors Influencing Tenderness

The efficiency with which fat is protecting gluten from water in a pastry dough is a key factor in influencing the tenderness of a pastry. A soft, warm fat coats the gluten strands very effectively. In fact, in one method of making pastry, the fat is whipped into boiling water before combining with the dry ingredients. This melts the fat and gives a very thorough protective coating. Oils, because of their very fluid nature, are particularly effective in coating gluten strands to develop a very tender crust. Even very soft, but not fluid, fats are able to provide a reasonably good covering. Clearly, to make the most tender crust possible, fat needs to be sufficiently warm to be able to be spread easily. Chilled fats lack the ability to be spread enough to be very effective in promoting tenderness.

Tenderness also is promoted by keeping all manipulation to a minimum after the water has been added. The dropwise addition of water, rather than the pouring in of all of the water at one time, is very helpful in maintaining tenderness in a pastry, because the amount of mixing required to finish distributing the water uniformly is reduced greatly by this technique. Only enough mixing should be done to get the dough to stick together and to roll it out. Beyond this minimal mixing, the gluten will become too developed, and the crust will be unpleasantly tough.

The amount of water used is vital to the tenderness of the pastry when baked. Extra water means extra toughness as a result of increased gluten development. Increased flour or decreased fat also will have a toughening effect. Substitution of margarine or butter for shortening in pastry also results in a tougher product, for both of these table fats have water comprising about 15 percent of their total, which also means that the fat level is reduced. Therefore, the actual content of such a pastry includes an excess of water and a deficiency of fat. Although table fats can be used satisfactorily to make pastry with a pleasing golden color and a distinctive flavor, it is necessary to modify the usual formulation to increase the fat measure, decrease the water, and eliminate the salt.

Flakiness in Pastry

Flakiness is the layered texture in a pastry when thin layers of cells are interspersed with flat holes between the layers. To achieve this, the flour, with its gluten strands, must provide a network incorporating small pieces of fat and some air pockets. During baking, the fat particles melt and flow a bit, often being adsorbed by the gluten strands. Moisture in the dough is converted into steam during baking, and this steam can collect in the little spaces left by the melting fat. Quickly, the steam expands, creating an even larger space between the gluten strands, and a flaky pastry is the result. Flakiness is promoted by using a firm fat rather than very soft one or an oil, for these latter fats tend to be spread into thin layers throughout the dough. A mealy or grainy texture is the result of this type of fat distribution.

Flakiness and tenderness are two desirable characteristics in pastry, but they are not necessarily going to be developed simultaneously. For instance, an oil in a pastry surely will provide the most tender pastry, but such a pastry usually is mealy, not flaky. On the other hand, a hard fat can be cut in just until fairly large particles of fat are achieved. This circumstance will give a distinctly flaky quality, but the ineffective distribution of fat will promote a tough pastry. Fortunately, a reasonable compromise is achieved by using a firm, yet slightly soft, fat and cutting it in until the size of rice grains. This situation provides the potential for steam to collect in little pockets to create the flaky character and also distributes the fat fairly extensively so that the gluten will be inhibited reasonably in its development.

Flakiness in these three layers of pastry is evidenced by the numerous cavities formed when the cells trap steam and air during baking and stretch the walls until the gluten denatures, and the structure sets.

The choice of flour also influences flakiness versus tenderness. Pastry or cake flour reduces flakiness because of the weak gluten but promotes tenderness; the gluten in hard wheat flours is sufficiently strong to promote the desired flaky quality but reduces tenderness.

Evaluation of Pies

One-Crust Pies Custard, chiffon, and meringue or cream pies are familiar one-crust pies. The crust for chiffon and meringue pies always is baked before filling, and often the custard pies also are made with baked or partially baked shells to help reduce the soaking of the crusts of custard-type pies. These pies are evaluated in relation to the quality of their crusts and their fillings. The problems of cream fillings and meringues are presented in Chapter 12.

Chiffon pies require the thickening of egg yolk protein, forming a stable egg white foam, and folding a partially congealed protein mixture with the egg white foam to form a light gelatin-containing foam filling capable of being sliced and served. Chiffon fillings should be rigid when they are cut, yet not rubbery. They should hold a straight line along the cut edge, but should not be difficult to cut. The fillings should be light, airy, flavorful, tender, and uniform in appearance and texture, with no rubbery bits of gelatin present. Due to the airy nature and the large volume of the foam, it is important to make the flavoring strong enough to present the desired result.

Custard pies are basically simply a custard with a pastry base. Evaluation of the filling is the same as was outlined in Chapter 10 for baked custards. Perhaps the greatest difficulty in preparing a custard pie is avoiding a soggy bottom crust. If the filling is baked in the crust, a fairly long time passes before the liquid filling coagulates, which permits a fair amount of liquid to be absorbed by the crust as it is baking.

One solution is to bake the crust without the filling until the crust just begins to get a bit crisp, but is not browned before adding the filling. Thus, the crust can be baked adequately without overbaking the filling. Also, the hot crust begins to warm the filling from the bottom, which facilitates the baking of the filling. Overbaking the filling is to be avoided, for the syneresis resulting from overbaking causes the crust to become quite soggy after baking. The filling is done when a knife inserted half-way between the center and the edge comes out clean. This test should be applied to any custard-type pie, including pumpkin and pecan pies.

One-crust pies should be made the same day they are to be served. The crust of even a well-prepared custard pie will gradually become a bit soggy if the pie must be held until the following day. Chiffon fillings and meringues are very difficult to cut and are rather tough the second day (see Chapter 10). The fillings used in one-crust pies do not freeze well (Chapter 7); they should be made fresh when they are planned on a menu.

Two-Crust Pies Two-crust pies are evaluated on the basis of both the crust and the filling. The top and bottom crusts should have no suggestion of sogginess. The crust should be about an eighth of an inch thick and should be flaky and tender. The appearance should be very attractive. By baking the pie as soon as the filling has been added and the top crust has been completed, the amount of time available for the juiciness of the filling to soak the bottom crust is kept to a minimum. Another way of helping to keep the crusts crisp is

Pecan is categorized as a custard pie because it is thickened with eggs. When a knife inserted half way between the center and edge of the filling comes out clean, the pie should be removed from the oven to avoid overbaking. The residual heat will set the center portion.

to be sure to cut an adequate steam vent in the upper crust. This permits the steam from the filling to escape in the oven during baking, which prevents a soggy upper crust and also helps to keep the top crust from being pushed way above the filling.

The filling of a two-crust pie should have a pleasing flavor and be somewhat thickened, yet not have a pasty character. The upper crust should be very close to, or resting on the surface of the filling. In fresh fruit pies, this is facilitated by being careful to pack the fruit quite firmly before baking to help eliminate wasted air spaced between pieces. The pie should be beautiful to look at and boast a beautiful, golden-brown color. The crusts should be crisp and tender, preferably with a flaky texture. Although these pies usually can be held overnight without the tremendous loss of quality seen in one-crust pies, two-crust pies do lose desirable characteristics when held more than a few hours. If at all possible, two-crust pies should be served the same day they are made. If necessary, they can be prepared and frozen without baking until the day they are to be served. Two-crust pies generally freeze quite satisfactorily in their unbaked state. Then the baking period restores the desirable qualities of these pies.

Puff Pastry

Although the pastry used for pies is far more common than puff pastry, puff pastry is used with sufficient frequency to warrant at least passing mention here. Puff pastries actually are very flaky, rich pastries comprised of many layers of thin pastry rolled with butter spread generously between layers. These pastries provide a graphic illustration of the fact that tenderness and flakiness are not necessarily parallel characteristics, for puff pastries always are extremely flaky, voluminous pastries, but they often are rather tough to cut.

A well-prepared puff pastry is very flaky and high in volume, because of the puffed up layers of dough. It will be only moderately tender. There will be numerous layers of dough that have a rich flavor as a result of the butter used to form layers between the dough layers. The high volume in puff pastry is promoted by baking in a hot oven, which generates generous amounts of steam quickly and almost seems to levitate the layers. These pastries form the foundation of such famous French pastries as Napoleons and patty shells, the latter being used as a base for various creamed entrees as well as for desserts.

MIXES

Vast amounts of time, energy, and resources have been invested by food companies in developing mixes and convenience foods. There are frozen cakes, cookies, and pies, some being ready to eat, while others still need to be baked. The bakery section provides other items that are ready to eat, and the packaged mixes afford yet another alternative for people who do not wish to bake their own items. Some mixes offer only a limited saving of time, while other products such as frozen patty shells, are tremendous time savers. An angel cake mix saves having to separate a dozen eggs and resolves the dilemma of what to do with the remaining 12 yolks! Refrigerated biscuit doughs and cooky doughs afford quick solutions to preparing something hot and fresh when an unexpected food need emerges.

With the large numbers of two-income families and the increasing pressures on time, the presence of mixes and convenience foods clearly is here to stay. These items not only save time, but often provide quality superior to the product that can be prepared by inexperienced people. Price comparisons between mixes and comparable products prepared in the home need to be made on an individual basis, for circumstances vary widely among products and among people.

Many people find food preparation is an exciting outlet for their creativity. Mixes may tend to stifle their creativity, but certainly it is possible to invent new applications of the mixes if creativity is a high priority. Even then, some people clearly will prefer to start with the basic ingredients, either because of possible savings or because of creative satisfactions.

Mixes contain additives that enable them to survive the rigorous demands imposed by the extended marketing period. These additives are listed in the ingredient label on each package, often with the explanation of the reason for their inclusion. Extensive testing has been done on the safety of the various additives, and the general agreement is that our food supply is very safe and that the additives used in mixes are safe in the amounts used. Nevertheless, people who wish to avoid additives where possible can prepare baked products from the basic ingredients.

The flurry of concern over the ethylene dibromide (EDB) residues contained in numerous mixes for baked products and the resultant recalls associated with the high residual levels of this fumigant in 1984 is a sober reminder of the potential concerns associated with a complex food supply. The level of EDB in the basic ingredient (flour) available to consumers was far lower than that measured in the various mixes recalled. This episode adds emphasis to the possible merits of making the foods in the home rather than relying exclusively on food manufacturers for sustenance.

Actually, the decision regarding the use of mixes versus preparation in the home is a very individual matter. There is no simple answer applicable to all people and all situations. The one clear fact is that either approach can provide wholesome and nourishing food for consumers.

SUMMARY

Cakes, cookies, and pastries are desserts using flour as the basic structural ingredient, with sugar, fat, and other ingredients being added to produce a wide range of products. The foam cakes include angel cake (which contains only the egg whites and no baking powder or fat), sponge cake (made with both yolk and white foams, but with no baking powder or fat), and chiffon cakes (made with baking powder, oil, yolks, and an egg white foam). These cakes are baked in tube pans and are inverted to stretch out their weak structures while they cool. Technique is important in each of the foam cakes to achieve a high volume and a tender product with a pleasing texture.

Shortened cakes are more tender and finer in texture than foam cakes because shortened cakes contain a solid fat that is creamed with sugar to provide a very fine cellular framework. The basic method for making shortened cakes is the conventional method, in which the fat and sugar are creamed together, the eggs are added, and the dry ingredients and liquid are added in alternating order. Variations include the modified conventional method, the conventional sponge method, and the single-stage method. The ratios of ingredients and the baking conditions can cause variations in the finished products. For high-altitude baking, cake recipes need to have the baking powder and sugar reduced, and the liquid increased slightly.

The types of cookies are divided into drop, bar, and rolled cookies. These formulas are far less critical than the formulas used for making cakes. However, proper proportions of ingredients, careful mixing, and appropriate baking techniques still are important in obtaining products of high quality.

Technique is particularly important in making pastry, for its simple formula of flour, fat, liquid, and salt has the potential for making tender or tough products. A ratio of 3 parts flour to 1 part fat usually makes a satisfactory pastry, and a ratio of 6 parts flour to 1 part water produces a tender product when manipulation is done properly. Flakiness is promoted by cutting a solid fat into pieces the size of rice grains. Tenderness is promoted by keeping the water content to a minimum and by limiting handling of the dough as much as possible. These doughs need to be rolled to a thickness of about an eighth of an inch and then fitted carefully into pie plates. Either one- or two-crust pies can be made. The fillings should be prepared carefully to meet the criteria for the specific type of pie being prepared. In general, pies need to be eaten the same day that they are made.

Puff pastry is a very rich dough with fat lavished between layers. By baking at a high temperature, the pastry is puffed up by the steam within the dough. Although very flaky, puff pastry generally is not as tender as pie pastry.

Mixes are available for quick preparation of baked products. Their use needs to be considered on an individual basis. For some people, mixes are a very important part of the diet, while other people prefer to make products from the basic ingredients because of the possibly improved quality, the creative experience, the possible saving in money, and the reduced problem of food additives and contaminants.

Selected References

American Home Economics Association. *Handbook of Food Preparation*. AHEA. Washington, D.C. 8th ed. 1980.

Arlin, M. L. et al. Effect of different methods of flour measurement on the quality of plain two-egg cakes. *J. Home Econ. 56:* 399. 1964.

Ash, D. J. and J. C. Colmey. Role of pH in cake baking. *Baker's Digest 47(1):* 36. 1973.

Bean, M. M. et al. Wheat-starch gelatinization in sugar solutions. 2. Fructose, glucose, and sucrose. Cake performance. *Cereal Chem. 55:* 945. 1978.

Birnbaum, H. Surfactants and shortening in cake making. *Baker's Digest 52(1):* 28. 1978.

Consumer and Food Economics Institute. *Baking for People with Food Allergies.* U.S. Dept. Agriculture. Washington, D.C. 1975.

Consumer and Food Economics Institute. *Breads, Cakes, and Pies in Family Meals.* U.S. Dept. Agriculture. Washington, D.C. 1976.

Elgidaily, D. A. et al. Baking temperature and quality of angel cakes. *J. Am. Dietet. Assoc. 54:* 401. 1969.

Howard, N. B. Role of some essential ingredients in formation of layer cake structure. *Baker's Digest 46(5):* 28. 1972.

Howard, N. B. et al. Function of starch granule in the formation of layer cake structure. *Cereal Chem. 45:* 329. 1968.

Kamat, V. B. et al. Contribution of egg yolk lipoproteins to cake structure. *J. Sci. Food Agr. 24:* 77. 1973.

Lagendijk, J. and J. van Dolfsen. Classification of puff-pastry fats and margarines based on dough firmness. *Cereal Chem. 42:* 255. 1965.

Matthews, R. H. and O. M. Batcher. Sifted versus unsifted flour: Weight variations and results of some baking tests. *J. Home Econ. 55:* 123. 1963.

Matthews, R. H. and E. H. Dawson. Performance of fats and oils in pastry and biscuits. *Cereal Chem. 40:* 291. 1963.

Peart, V. et al. Optimizing oven radiant energy use. *Home Econ. Research J. 8:* 242. 1980.

Volpe, T. and C. Meres. Use of high fructose syrups in white layer cake. *Baker's Digest 50(2):* 38. 1976.

Study Questions

1. What differences are found among the ingredients used in angel, sponge, and chiffon cakes? How does each of the differences influence the characteristics of the baked cakes?
2. Prepare similar cakes from mixes and from recipes using the basic ingredients. Compare the time of preparation, cost, and palatability. When is a mix the best choice? When is a homemade cake preferred?
3. What ingredients are used ordinarily in making a shortened cake? What are the functions of each of these ingredients?
4. Why are modifications needed in a recipe for a cake being prepared at an elevation of 5000 feet? What changes probably need to be made?
5. Describe the conventional method for making cakes. What is the reason behind each procedure?
6. Prepare three samples of pastry, one with butter as the fat, one with hydrogenated shortening, and one with salad oil. Evaluate each baked sample and explain how the fat influenced the quality of each pastry.
7. Compare the preparation of a puff pastry using the frozen ready-to-bake product and one made from the basic ingredients. Considering both cost and the value of time, which product suits your needs better?

Ferdnand Toussaint, ''Cafe Jacqmotte.'' © Sotheby Parke Bernet.

CHAPTER 15

BEVERAGES

THE SYMBOL OF HOSPITALITY

Beverages, more than any other food item, are the symbol of hospitality among people. Whether meeting in an office or informally in a home, a beverage of some type frequently is served to welcome the visitor and set a friendly mood. Often coffee or tea will be prepared, depending upon the time of day and the cultural heritage of the host.

In recent years, a vast array of beverages began arriving in markets across the country, until now the choices are almost overwhelming. Bottled beverages are popular for use in the form in which they come from the container. However, coffee, tea, and hot chocolate or cocoa require preparation. This chapter focuses primarily on these beverages and their preparation, for the ability to prepare these hallmarks of hospitality is a very important part of the study of foods in the context of the social aspects of food.

COFFEE

In the United States, coffee generally is considered to be the national symbol of hospitality, despite the fact that large numbers of people also consume other beverages, such as tea, particularly in the evenings. The tempting aroma and stimulating flavor of coffee are catalysts to help get conversations and ideas flowing, especially in the early morning hours. In business offices and industrial settings across the nation, the coffee break has become a respected tradition. In the home, coffee is synonymous with friendship and relaxation; students, however, often use the stimulating properties of coffee to help them stay awake while cramming for exams.

Around the world, coffee is served in many different ways to suit different national palates. Greeks and Turks savor a very strong, sweet, almost syruplike coffee that is boiled, while Syrians add cracked cardamom seed and rose water or orange blossom water to boiled coffee. The distinctive coffee served by Italians is prepared from darkly roasted coffee beans, which are ground very finely. Cafe au lait, the French way of serving coffee, is a combination of equal parts of strong coffee and hot milk. The Spanish version uses boiled milk to brew the coffee. And it comes as no surprise that coffee is served with a generous dollop of whipped cream in Vienna. Even in the United States, various versions of coffee are prepared, including the distinctive coffee in the South, which combines chicory with coffee. These are but some of the ways coffee is prepared and served around the world.

Production

The coffee available in orderly cans in the supermarket has come a long ways from its original habitat. Much of the coffee is from Brazil and other South American countries; however, the African country of Kenya, the East and West Indies, and Hawaii also contribute to the national supply of coffee. The varieties of coffee differ from one locale to another, but the climate generally

Coffee cherries require about six months to achieve their mature, purple to red appearance so that they can be picked from the trees.

particularly favorable to raising coffee is warm and moist, with the temperature hovering around 70°F, the result of daily sun and frequent showers.

Coffee beans are produced on trees; the total process starts with the blooming of the tree, followed by the development of the fruit (a cherry). When the cherry is about six months old, it turns to a deep purple or red color, a sign that it is ready to be harvested. It is inside the cherry that the desired product, the coffee bean, is found. The coffee beans have to be separated from the cherry pulp before being dried and shipped to the countries desiring to import coffee.

Nations import green coffee beans from many different locales in order to obtain the desired characteristics that will be popular within that country. The primary varieties of beans presently being imported are *Coffea arabicas*, *Coffea liberica*, and *Coffea canephora*, although limited amounts of other varieties also are imported. From these different varieties of coffee, blends of the beans will be made to achieve the desired mix of characteristics.

Following blending, the green beans are roasted to the extent preferred in the country where the coffee will be sold. The roasting is done in the country where the roasted coffee will be used to ensure that the flavor will be appropriate to the palates of the nation. For example, Brazilians and Italians prefer a darkly roasted coffee bean, whereas many Americans prefer a much lighter roast, a preference found particularly on the West Coast. A medium roast is used commonly in the East, while the people in the South choose a darker roast. This is why roasting needs to be done near the specific market.

Roasting accomplishes far more than simply a change in the color of the coffee beans. The browning of the beans is a sign of the chemical breakdown or caramelizing of some of the sugars and dextrinizing of some of the starch.

These chemical reactions produce not only color changes, but also flavor changes and a distinctive aroma of the beans. Roasting also causes an appreciable loss of moisture (about 16 percent) and a limited loss of other volatile compounds. These combined changes create the desired flavor in coffee, a flavor that is at its peak immediately after roasting.

Before the beans can be used effectively to brew the beverage, it is necessary to expose a considerable surface area. This is accomplished by grinding the roasted beans. Grinding creates a good bit of surface to facilitate the extraction of flavoring compounds during brewing, but it also creates the opportunity for loss of the volatile flavoring compounds during storage and prior to the brewing of the beverage. Particular attention must be devoted to airtight packaging once the coffee has been ground. Although there is some loss of volatile substances even from the whole roasted beans, the loss is really quite small compared with the extreme losses occurring if ground beans are not stored carefully. Flavor retention is maximized and oxidative changes are minimized by quickly packaging the ground coffee in hermetically sealed cans. An even fresher quality can be obtained by buying the roasted beans at the market and then simply grinding as much coffee as needed for each brewing at home. The desire to have coffee just as fresh as it possibly can be has led to an active market in electric coffee grinders for home use.

Constituents of Coffee

One of the reasons that coffee has such a full, pleasing flavor is its natural oils, which carry and hold the volatile flavoring compounds. Unfortunately, the oils can become rancid during prolonged storage, particularly if oxygen is present. The stale flavor of coffee that has been stored carelessly or too long is partially the result of oxidized oils, a change that can begin as soon as the surfaces of the ground coffee beans are exposed to the air. Fortunately, vacuum packaging of the ground coffee is an effective deterrent. If unsealed coffee cans are kept tightly closed, the shelf life of coffee will be enhanced. Storage at a cool temperature, either in the refrigerator or the freezer if the coffee will be used only occasionally, also extends shelf life.

Caffeine Compound in coffee credited with contributing the stimulating effect of the beverage and a touch of bitterness.

Caffeine, the stimulating substance in coffee, is found in abundance in the green coffee bean, but roasting volatilizes some of it. Nevertheless, brewing the beverage extracts a considerable amount of caffeine from the ground coffee into the actual beverage. It is the caffeine that is credited with creating the stimulating quality of coffee. The actual amount of caffeine in a specific cup of coffee will be influenced by the type of coffee maker used. Coffee brewed in a dripolator contains appreciably more caffeine per cup than does coffee prepared in a percolator (see Table 15.1). Caffeine contributes to the somewhat bitter flavor of coffee.

The flavor of coffee is extremely complex and is derived from many compounds in addition to caffeine. Chromatographic analyses have revealed the presence of more than a hundred compounds contributing to the aroma and flavor of the beverage. Among these are sulfur-containing compounds, including hydrogen sulfide, dimethyl sulfide, and several others. Various or-

Table 15.1 Caffeine Content of Coffee and Other Beverages

Beverage	Serving Size (ml)[2]	Mean Caffeine Content[1] (mg)	Caffeine per 100 ml
Coffee			
Percolator			
Nonautomatic			
5 min.	150	107	70
10 min.	150	118	77
Automatic	150	104	69
Dripolator,			
Nonautomatic	150	142	95
Automatic	150	151	100
Instant	150	66	44
Tea[3]			
Bagged			
Black	140	28	20
Oolong	140	13	9
Green	140	14	10
Leaf			
Black	140	31	22
Oolong	140	17	12
Green	140	28	20
Cocoa			
Dutch process	150	14	10
Carbonated Beverages			
Coca Cola	360	65	18
Pepsi Cola	360	43	12

Source: Bunker, M. L. and M. McWilliams. Caffeine content of common beverages. *J. Am. Dietet. Assoc.* 74: 28. 1979.

[1]Means of coffees represent seven brands; of bagged black teas, three brands; of bagged green teas, two brands; and of cocoa, two brands. All other data are for single brands.
[2]Coffee and tea measures are about ⅔ of a measuring cup; cola beverages are about 1½ cups.
[3]Brewed 1 minute.

ganic acids and phenolic compounds also are credited with contributing to the flavor. Chlorogenic acid is the most abundant of the acids. Carbon dioxide also is found in freshly brewed coffee, which accounts for part of the sparkling quality of the beverage. Some of the flavoring and aromatic substances are very volatile and can be noted when coffee is ground or when a sealed can is opened. However, the polyphenols are extracted from the grounds, along with the caffeine and many other compounds when boiling water is present. By using temperatures slightly below boiling, the astringent quality of the polyphenols can be kept to a minimum.

The techniques for brewing influence the flavor of the beverage. Generally, the methods for brewing coffee used in the United States are directed toward minimizing the extraction of the polyphenols and optimizing some of the other delicate and pleasing volatiles. However, the preparation of Italian espresso is designed specifically to extract the bitter phenols by forcing steam through finely ground, dark-roasted coffee.

SCIENCE NOTE: CHEMICAL CONSTITUENTS IN BEVERAGES

Although there are far too many compounds contributing to the flavor and aroma of coffee and other brewed beverages to permit an in-depth study of all of them, there are some key substances to be examined. Caffeine heads the list of substances of possible concern. The stimulating effect of caffeine has been known a long time. Recently, the possible involvement of caffeine in heart disease, hypertension, bladder cancer, cancer of the pancreas, breast disease, and peptic ulcers has been the subject of considerable research. Concern has also been expressed about the possible teratogenic effects of caffeine when consumed by pregnant women because of the ease of passage through the placenta to the infant, who metabolizes caffeine quite slowly. Sensitivity to caffeine appears to vary considerably between individuals, but consumption of four or more cups of coffee can cause such symptoms as sleeplessness, an upset stomach, feelings of anxiety and depression, or even a rapid heart beat. Probably pregnant and lactating women should restrict their intake of caffeine to avoid transmitting the stimulant to their offspring. However, proof of definite correlations between serious health problems and caffeine intake is still lacking.

Theobromine Stimulant prominent in cocoa and chocolate.

The formula for caffeine and the formula for theobromine are given below. Note that the two compounds actually are quite similar. *Theobromine* is the primary stimulant in cocoa and chocolate, while caffeine is more abundant in coffee and tea, as well as in cola beverages.

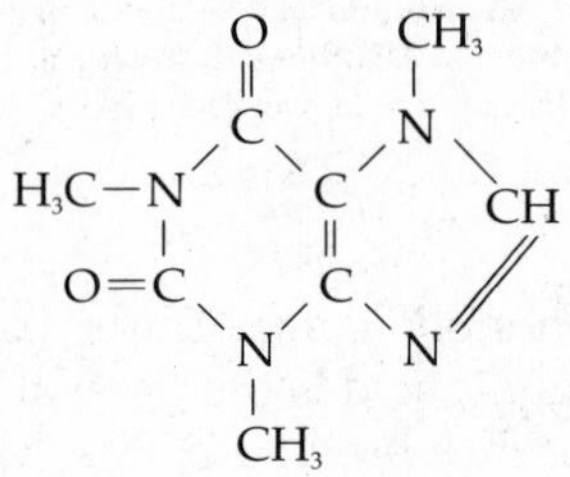

Caffeine 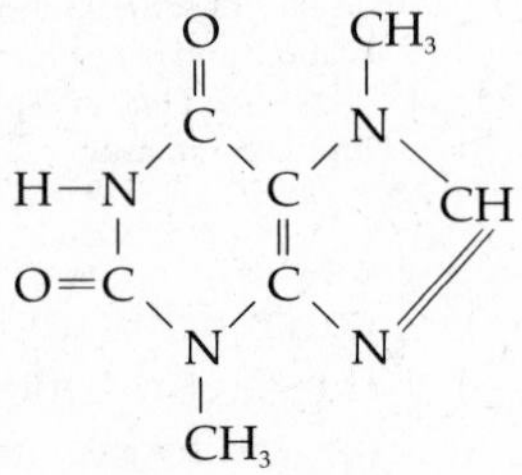   Theobromine

Chlorogenic Acid Most abundant acid in coffee; contributes some of the sour and bitter quality to coffee flavor.

Acids are important constituents in coffee. The most abundant acid is *chlorogenic acid*, but there are other organic acids, including formic acid, acetic acid, propionic acid, and butyric acid. The flavor contributions of chlorogenic acid are of particular importance because the abundance of this particular acid (shown below) adds to the bitter and slightly sour characteristics in the coffee beverage.

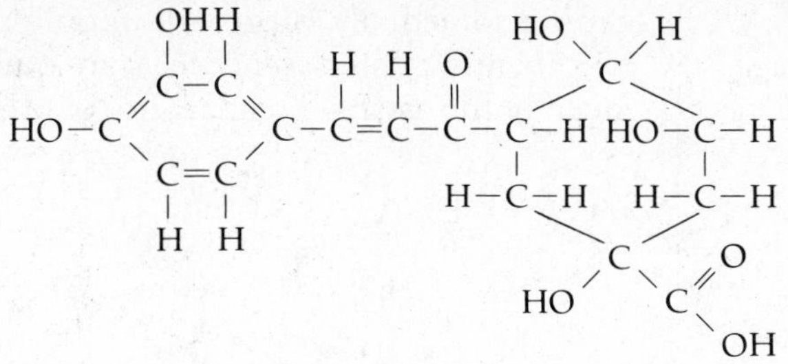

Chlorogenic acid

Chlorogenic acid also is the parent of some key aromatic compounds contributing to the characteristic aroma and flavor of coffee. Among these compounds are furfural and many related compounds, such as 5-methylfuran, 5-methylfurfural, to name just a couple. Guiacol is yet another derivative of chlorogenic acid. As can be seen from the structures of furfural and guiacol, the furfural is a five-membered ring, while the guiacol is a six-membered ring.

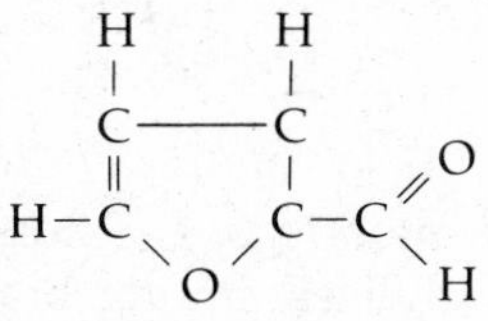

Furfural

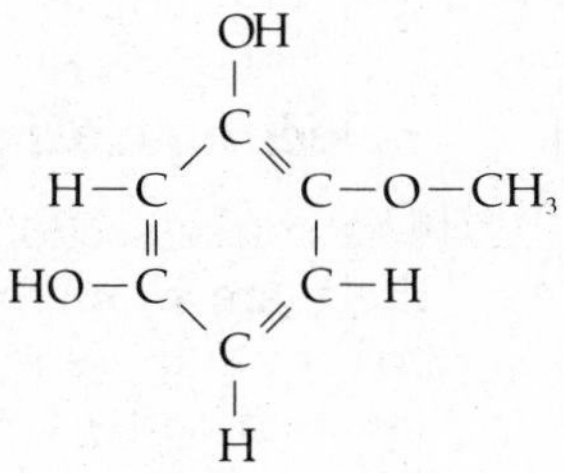

Guaiacol

Another abundant bitter compound in coffee is trigonelline. Trigonelline can be converted to niacin, which accounts for the fact that coffee does contain a bit of this B vitamin. Pyridine and pyridinic substances are apparently derived from trigonelline when coffee is roasted.

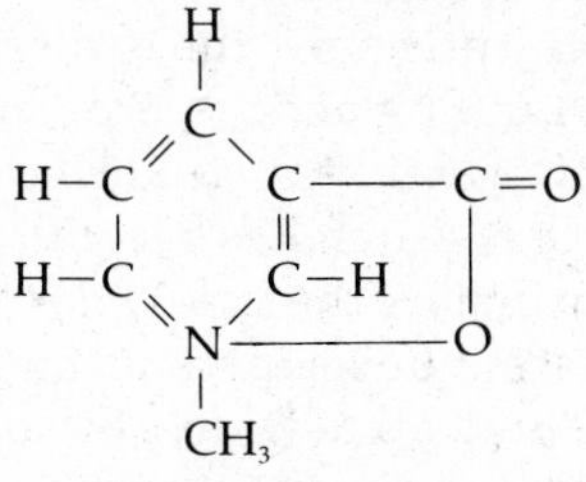

Trigonelline

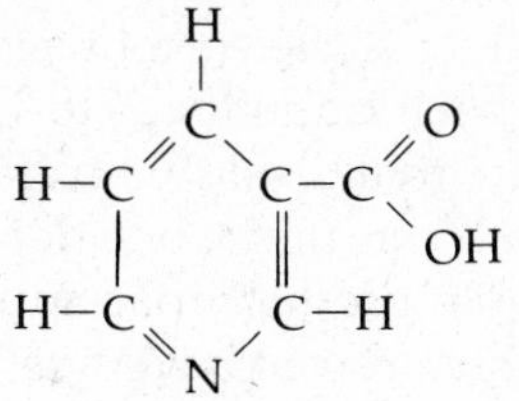

Niacin

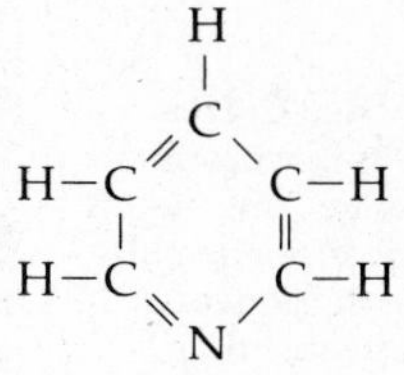

Pyridine

In tea, some other polyphenolic compounds occur in significant amounts, contributing to the characteristics of the beverage. Chloro-

Catechin A prominent polyphenol in green tea.

Polyphenols Compounds containing more than one six-membered phenolic ring; contribute astringency to tea.

Polyphenolase Enzyme active in converting polyphenols into theaflavins during fermentation of black tea leaves.

Theaflavins Extremely astringent compounds in black tea, which, in combination with caffeine, provide the brisk quality to black tea.

Instant Coffee Soluble coffee solids remaining after the water vapor has been removed from brewed coffee; often made by spray drying.

Freeze-dried Coffee Soluble coffee product made by freezing brewed coffee and sublimating the aqueous portion to obtain dry solids.

Sublimation Change of state from ice directly to water vapor without passing through the liquid water state.

genic acid actually is present in only rather minor quantities in tea, but *catechin* and related *polyphenols* are quite abundant in tea, accounting for much of the astringent character of brewed green tea.

Catechin

An important enzyme, *polyphenolase*, is active during the fermentation of black tea leaves; the *theaflavins* resulting from the action of polyphenolase, although very astringent, apparently combine with caffeine in black tea to produce the pleasing briskness associated with this fermented type of tea.

Selecting Coffee

The coffee section in most grocery stores now is quite an exciting spot, for there are numerous choices among brands, among grinds, among ground coffees and soluble coffees, and even among caffeine-containing and decaffeinated coffees. Start by making the decision between soluble coffees and coffees that need to be brewed. The soluble coffees have the advantages of not requiring any special equipment and also of saving time. However, the ground coffees that require brewing time and equipment for brewing still have a fuller flavor than the soluble products, despite significant improvements in the soluble coffees.

Soluble Coffees The flurry of developments in soluble coffees to develop flakes, crystals, and powders suggests that soluble coffees are a very recent product of the current age. Surprisingly, the earliest version of soluble coffees has been traced back to 1771 in England; records in the United States also indicate that a soluble coffee was field tested during the Civil War in the nineteenth century. Considerable research has been directed toward developing a soluble product that approximates the color, flavor, and appearance of the freshly brewed beverage. Recent developments have resulted in some soluble coffee products that are accepted quite widely by consumers.

Soluble coffees are marketed as *instant* and *freeze-dried coffees*. Until about 20 years ago, spray drying was the method used for producing soluble coffees, which were labeled instant coffee. Then the process of freeze-drying was developed. Basically a four-step process, freeze-drying begins with freezing, followed by heat transfer of the heat of *sublimation*, movement of water vapor through the dried portions from the subliming ice crystals, and finally, taking away the water vapor that emerges above the surface.

One of the problems encountered in developing a soluble coffee product was to attain a product that was dissolved very easily in hot water when being reconstituted. Fine particles presented a solubility problem because of the tendency to lump rather than dissolve readily. This problem was overcome by producing the soluble coffee in large particles that sank toward the bottom of a cup, dissolving on the way. These large particles are the result of agglomeration, or the clustering together of the fine particles of coffee solids.

Retention of the volatile flavoring components in soluble coffees has been a subject of considerable effort by researchers. Now techniques have been developed to recover many of the aromatic volatiles lost during processing and then add them to freeze-dried coffee. By this technique, a freeze-dried product can be produced that approaches the flavor characteristics of the freshly brewed beverage.

Decaffeinated soluble coffees are being marketed for people who want to reduce their intake of caffeine but still enjoy the flavor of the beverage. Caffeine is removed either from the green beans or from the liquid beverage prior to the drying of soluble coffees. The extraction process is so effective that only 2 percent or less of the original caffeine remains in the final product. Some loss of volatile flavoring components occurs during this step, however.

Public taste in coffee is becoming increasingly cosmopolitan, a fact that is reflected in the types of soluble coffees seen in markets today. Special flavors of soluble coffees can be purchased for those who like the flavor of almond or other overtone blended with coffee. These soluble coffees gain their inspiration from the beverages served in Vienna and many other exotic locations where food specialties are noteworthy.

Ground Coffees Coffee connoisseurs often prefer to brew their beverage rather than consume the soluble coffees. They may buy the roasted coffee beans and grind them themselves, or they may purchase coffee that has been ground already. Specialty shops often display a wide choice of coffee varieties, the beans being representative of many coffee-producing regions of the world and of various degree of roasting. Although the range is not nearly as dazzling in the supermarket as in the gourmet shops, the consumer can still choose among brands and among grinds. The grinds vary in particle size to meet specific brewing conditions in different types of coffee pots. For instance, regular grind is designed for use in percolators, while drip grind is intended for use in dripolators. The fairly coarse grind of the regular grind coffee provides a slightly limited surface area, which is compatible with the extensive recirculation of water in the grinds during percolation. The rather small particle size of drip grind provides an extensive surface area, thus permitting adequate extraction during the limited contact time between water and coffee grounds. Manufacturers also are providing electric perk and electric drip grinds for use in the automatic coffee makers, as well as fine grind coffee.

Preparing the Beverage

There are four requirements for making an excellent cup of coffee: (1) fresh coffee of the grind appropriate for the pot being used, (2) water with a pleasing flavor that is not hard, (3) a clean coffee maker, and (4) controlled heat. If any of these essentials is missing, the quality of the finished beverage will be adversely affected. Fortunately, these conditions can be controlled.

Coffee beans or ground coffee may suffer flavor impairment by two routes of particular significance. In the first case, since much of the flavor in coffee is contributed by volatile flavor constituents, flavor loss may occur during storage, simply because of vaporization of key components from the dry coffee. The second problem with flavor concerns the fact that coffee contains some oils, and oils become rancid as they take up oxygen. Fortunately, both these adversities can be reduced by careful storage practices. To prevent loss of the volatiles and entry of oxygen into the storage container, coffee needs to be stored in a tightly sealed container. The plastic closure provided with metal coffee cans meets this description admirably and inexpensively. By keeping the plastic cover tightly in position except when actually measuring coffee out of the can, the original flavor can be maintained satisfactorily for at least two weeks after the can has been opened. Changes can be retarded and quality maintained for a reasonably extended period if the closed can is stored in the refrigerator or freezer.

Not surprisingly, the flavor of water used to brew coffee influences the flavor of the brewed beverage. Sulfur overtones or other distinctive characteristics of the water are transmitted to the beverage, despite the rather strong flavor of the coffee itself; water with heavy mineral content affects the clarity of the beverage; and hard water causes precipitation of the polyphenols extracted from the coffee during the brewing period. The murky appearance of the coffee is undesirable. If tap water is not of sufficient quality to produce a good cup of coffee, bottled water may be used. However, most commercial water supplies are satisfactory for making coffee of excellent quality.

Coffee pots must not only look clean, but also smell clean if a beverage of high quality is to be produced. Coffee makers need to be washed with soapy water to remove any of the oils from the beverage that are clinging to the pot. Of course, a very thorough rinsing is needed after the washing has been completed. This eliminates the soaplike flavor overtones that come from traces of soap or detergent. Particular attention during washing needs to be directed toward the pouring spout and any seams or joints in the pot where the oily film might collect. To be sure a coffee pot is clean enough to make a quality cup of coffee, check the aroma just as the cover is being removed. A stale aroma is a clear indication that additional cleaning should be done before the pot is used. Special coffee pot cleaners can eliminate the oily film in spots that are difficult to reach.

The optimum temperature range for brewing coffee is between 185° and 203°F. At temperatures slightly below boiling, the bitter polyphenols are extracted less readily than when the brew actually is boiling. This circumstance exists in a dripolator, but not in a percolator.

Yet another aid to producing an excellent cup of coffee is to use a filter paper for holding the grounds. Filter papers designed for specific coffee makers will prevent even the finest particles of the ground coffee from collecting in the beverage and affecting the desired clarity.

The amount of coffee to use in brewing coffee is a subject open to debate, because people's tastes in the strength they desire cover quite a wide range. Cookbooks suggest using 2 tablespoons of coffee grounds per cup of the brewed beverage (¾ cup of water). However, some people prefer the weaker beverage that results from using 1 tablespoon per cup. Less than 2 tablespoons of grounds per cup probably will be appropriate when coffee is being prepared in large quantities, but the exact amount to use will be determined by the strength preferred in the beverage and by the type of equipment being used (see Table 15.2) Whether making coffee in quantity or in a small pot, the best results usually are obtained if the pot is filled to at least three-fourths of its capacity.

In making coffee, two basic designs of pots are available to consumers: percolators and dripolators. When no coffee pot is available, a simple kettle can be used to make steeped (also called "boiled") coffee. The various ways of preparing coffee are described in the paragraphs that follow.

Dripolator Coffee maker with a unit for the heated water, a section for the coffee grounds, and a pot to collect the coffee.

Dripolator The traditional design of a *dripolator* is composed of three parts: a pot to collect the beverage, a center container for holding the coffee grounds, and an upper unit to hold the heated water. An automatic variation of the dripolator is used extensively for brewing coffee today. This unit differs in that it has a compartment to hold the water while it is being heated to the brewing temperature, at which time the water exits into the coffee grounds en route to the collecting pot. Another version of the dripolator has a conical-shaped upper unit, which is lined with filter paper to contain the coffee grounds and prevent them from falling into the pot below.

Preparation of dripolator coffee begins with heating the water for the beverage to the boiling point. Meanwhile, the coffee grounds are placed in

Table 15.2 Proportions Suitable for Making Coffee in Large Quantities

Number of People	Number of Servings[1] (5½ oz)	Coffee Needed (lb)	Water Needed (gal)
25	40	1	2
50	80	2	4
75	120	3	6
100	160	4	8
125	200	5	10
150	240	6	12

Source: From the Pan-American Coffee Bureau.
[1]Based on the average number of servings consumed by a given number of people.

the perforated basket designed for them. The upper unit and the drip grind coffee grounds are measured and positioned above the pot in readiness for brewing the beverage. Just as soon as the water comes to a rolling boil, the measured amount of water is poured into the top unit of the assembled pot. If available, a cover should be placed on the unit containing the water to help retain the heat while the water is being held and passed through the grounds. When all the water has drained through the coffee grounds, the upper assembly and the grounds are removed, and the cover is placed on the pot containing the beverage. If necessary, the beverage is reheated to bring it to the desired serving temperature.

Dripolator coffee is stimulating because of the high caffeine content and is flavorful without being bitter. The pleasing flavor is developed because the water passing through the grounds is a little cooler than boiling and has been in contact with the grounds only briefly. This combination extracts the desirable flavor components and only a minimal bitterness.

Cone-topped dripolators in which the coffee grounds are placed in the same unit with the boiling water permit a longer contact period between water and the coffee grounds than occurs in the standard dripolator. In this pot design, the entire quantity of water is in contact with the grounds until it drains through. This permits extraction of the bitter components. There also will be loss of some of the volatile desirable flavor compounds unless the pot has a cover. Although these pots have been marketed as the gourmet version of the dripolator, they can produce a less desirable product than is obtained with the traditional dripolator.

Percolator Coffee pot containing a basket for coffee grounds that is suspended on a hollow stem above the water in the pot.

Percolator *Percolators* consist of a single unit in which a perforated basket containing the measured regular grind coffee is placed, suspended on a hollow stem. The water is measured into the pot, the lid is placed firmly on the assembly, and heat is applied rapidly until water begins to pass up through the stem, hitting the lid and falling onto the basket containing the coffee grounds. When this ''perking'' action begins, the heat is adjusted to maintain a slow, but continuing, action. This form of brewing circulates water continuously through the grounds at a very hot temperature, with the result that bitter compounds are extracted to a greater extent than ordinarily occurs in making dripolator coffee. The longer the period of percolation, the stronger the brewed beverage will be. Often coffee is percolated for 5 minutes, but some people prefer the beverage resulting from a brewing period of as little as 3 minutes. When the desired strength has been achieved, the basket with the coffee grounds and the stem holding the basket are removed from the pot, and the lid is replaced on the pot to help retain heat. If desired, the pot may be heated at a low setting to maintain a serving temperature for up to an hour without an undue loss of quality.

Automatic percolators can be set to the desired length of percolating time, thus eliminating the need for careful timing during brewing. Most automatic percolators need to be started with cold water so that the high heat needed for the percolation will be triggered to brew the beverage.

Percolator coffee has slightly different flavor characteristics from dripolator coffee as a result of the differences in the brewing techniques. The circulat-

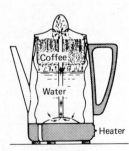

Diagram of a percolator. The grind of coffee should be regular grind.

ing action in a percolator introduces air into the beverage to a far greater extent than occurs in a dripolator, and this causes some loss of flavor in percolator coffee. The recirculation of water through the grounds over and over again during the brewing period enhances the bitter overtones of coffee made in a percolator, while dripolator coffee has only a limited opportunity to extract these components. Generally, dripolator coffee will be superior to percolator coffee. However, percolator coffee is less trouble to make because the water is heated right in the pot where the coffee will be brewed, while another container is needed to heat the water for making dripolator coffee.

Steeped Coffee   Even when a coffee pot is not available, it is possible to make coffee by placing the coffee grounds directly in water heated almost to boiling. The grounds should be tied in a cloth bag so that they can be removed following the steeping period. Optimal quality of steeped coffee is achieved by being careful not to boil the water during the steeping period and by being sure to keep the grounds in the pot only as long as is needed to achieve the desired strength and flavor. The fact that this version of coffee frequently is called ''boiled coffee'' reveals that such temperature control often is not maintained during the brewing period. When regular coffee is measured into a bag and allowed to steep with the appropriate amount of water just under boiling for 5 minutes, steeped coffee should be of acceptable quality. However, if boiled or if allowed to steep too long, steeped coffee can be distinctly inferior to either percolator or dripolator coffee.

Evaluating Coffee

The diverse cultural patterns influencing coffee brews around the world make it difficult to define a ''good'' cup of coffee. U.S. consumers generally prefer a clear beverage with a delightful, full aroma and a rich flavor free of any bitterness. The color desired is a deep, lively brown, and the beverage should be free of any suggestion of sediment or particles of grounds. For optimum enjoyment, hot coffee should be served steaming. Freshly made coffee is at its peak of flavor and aroma. When held at serving temperature for an extended period of time, the flavor gradually will be lost, due to the volatilization of some of the key aromatic compounds. To alleviate this problem when coffee is desired throughout the day, simply heat a cup of coffee in a microwave oven as needed, leaving the remainder of the pot at room temperature.

Espresso

Espresso Extremely strong and rather bitter Italian coffee resulting from brewing finely ground, dark-roasted coffee with steam.

As people have had increasing opportunities for experiencing specialties from other countries, the variety available in food products has mushroomed, and variety in coffee reflects this trend. A particularly popular version of coffee that has been adopted from Europe is *espresso*, a strong coffee with its roots in Italy. Some people are certain that espresso is only for the hardy, the adventurous, and the mechanically competent. This last requirement stems from the need to be able to operate an espresso machine, complete with its pressurized steam. Between the use of a finely ground coffee that has been roasted to a very dark color and the vigorous application of steam to these grounds, espresso is a very strong and somewhat bitter beverage. The fact that it is served black heightens the intense impact of espresso.

Iced Coffee

Sometimes coffee is served iced rather than hot. The preparation of iced coffee involves simply brewing a strong pot of coffee and then pouring the hot beverage over an excess of ice, part of which melts and dilutes the beverage to the normal strength. Preferences regarding the strength of iced coffee vary, but the usual practice is to prepare the hot coffee half again or even twice as strong as the beverage. This increased strength is achieved by extra grounds, not extra brewing time. In other words, coffee to be iced should be made with 3 to 4 tablespoons of ground coffee per cup of the hot beverage desired. The iced coffee resulting from this level of grounds should have a pleasing flavor, with no bitterness and with a deep color.

Iced coffee can also be prepared by pouring coffee of regular strength into ice cube trays and freezing them. For use, these cubes are placed in a glass, and then coffee of regular strength is poured over the coffee cubes. When these melt, the coffee still maintains its desired strength. A convenient variation involves dissolving instant or freeze-dried coffee in hot water and pouring this mixture over ice.

Regardless of the technique used in making iced coffee, the end product should have a distinct, coffeelike flavor, and the beverage should be sparklingly translucent.

TEA

Camellia sinensis
Shrub in the *Theaceae* family, the leaves of which are plucked and used in making tea.

The leaves from a shrub (*Camellia sinensis*) in the *Theaceae* family serve as the base for a beverage that has been popular since about 350 A. D., at which time the Chinese were known to have included this brewed product in the diet. The spread of the knowledge of this brew touched key points throughout the world, beginning with adoption of the drink in Japan and then spreading to the Arabs, Venetians, English, and Portuguese. By the midseventeenth century, tea had even made its way to the United States. Perhaps the most notable mention of tea was in America, when the Colonists angrily staged the Boston Tea Party, a party quite different from the traditional high tea found in the British Commonwealth!

Tea bushes thrive in a topical climate and at altitudes up to about 6000 feet, conditions found in Japan, India, Sri Lanka, and the East Indies as well as in part of China. Surprisingly, tea research on the agricultural and production problems of tea is being conducted in the United States to determine the feasibility of producing tea here. Although *Camellia sinensis* bushes thrive on a rainfall of up to 68 inches annually, irrigation appears to be a satisfactory substitute for rain.

A pound of tea may appear insignificant when held in the hand, but considerable human labor is required to produce even this small quantity. The

Tea bushes are kept short for convenience in plucking only the buds and next two leaves tipping the branches, the portions most desirable for tea of high quality.

bushes have to be cultivated and pruned carefully for 3 years before the first crop can even be harvested. Fortunately, the shrubs may remain productive for as long as 50 years if they are kept pruned to a height of between 3 and 5 feet. Plucking of the tea leaves is done exclusively by hand, a slow task yielding at the most only about 9 pounds of marketable leaves a day per picker. Only the bud and next two leaves are picked from the tips of the branches when high-quality tea is the goal.

Types of Tea

Teas are marketed under many different, often romantic-sounding names, but all of these are categorized under three main types: green, oolong, and black. All three can be produced from the same tea leaves—the difference being created in the processing of the leaves. Black tea is the most popular of the three types in the United States, but green and oolong teas also are available in most markets.

Orange Pekoe Top grade of black tea.

The grades of tea are indicated by names familiar and meaningful to people in the business, but which carry little meaning to consumers. For example, the top grade of black tea leaves is designated as *orange pekoe*. In descending order, the other grades of black tea leaves are pekoe, souchong, broken orange pekoe, broken pekoe, broken pekoe souchong, fannings, and dust. The tea found in markets in the United States usually is a blend of more than one grade. However, in Darjeeling in northern India or in other regions famous for their tea, it is possible to purchase the desired single grade.

Specialty teas are other choices available in the market. A familiar illustration is jasmine tea, so named because of the dried jasmine petals added to the tea leaves to modify the flavor. Orange rind and cinnamon are other flavoring agents. These are only a few of the dried food and spice ingredients that are included in special tea blends. Choices are available to please any palate and to suit any occasion.

Green Tea Somewhat astringent tea that has not been fermented.

Green Tea *Green tea* is the simplest of the three types of tea to produce. The initial step in processing the freshly picked tea leaves to make green tea is to steam the leaves. The heat involved in steaming is sufficient to inactivate the enzymes in the leaves so that chemical changes are halted. Following steaming, green tea leaves are rolled to break the leaves and then are fired. Firing is the drying process in which the leaves are subjected first to a temperature of 200°F and finally to a lower temperature of about 120°F. This results in a moisture level of only about 3 percent in the tea leaves, which makes it possible to store the leaves for extended periods of time when packaged properly. Green tea leaves have a soft, greenish-gray color. Green tea is produced in Japan, and it is particularly popular there. The beverage characteristics of green tea, notably the very delicate green color and slightly astringent quality, complement the foods of Japan particularly well.

Oolong Tea Tea that has undergone limited fermentation, resulting in characteristics intermediate between green and black tea.

Oolong Tea Production of *oolong tea* begins by allowing the leaves to wither slowly until they are ready to be rolled to release some of the fluid and enzymes from the cells in the leaves. During the subsequent fermentation period, the enzymes begin to catalyze chemical changes, the result of which is a darkening of the leaf and a milder, less astringent, flavor in the brewed beverage. This fermentation period is quite brief and is done on the tea farms where the leaves are harvested. The subsequent firing to halt the enzymatic changes is done in towns. Taiwan is recognized as a producer of particularly fine oolong tea.

Black Tea Brisk, rather mild, deep amber–colored tea produced by an extended fermentation period during the processing of tea leaves.

Black Tea The production of *black tea* begins just like that of oolong tea, namely, by spreading the leaves on racks to wither slowly before being rolled to break open the cells and release the juices and enzymes. As soon as rolling is completed, the leaves are sifted and spread thinly on trays to ferment. During the fermentation process, the various polyphenols are oxidized to produce the dark color of the leaves and the rich, deep amber color characteristic of the brewed beverage. Oxidation of the polyphenols gives rise to theaflavins, which are *astringent* alone, but simply provide briskness to the brewed beverage when in the presence of caffeine. The fermentation of black tea is done at a moderate temperature (between 70° and 80°F) for a long period of time. Finally, the fermented leaves are fired to dry them for packaging and storage. Some caramelization occurs during the drying, a chemical change contributing to the characteristic color and flavor of black tea.

Astringent Characteristic of drawing together or puckering; green tea is noted for making the mouth feel a bit puckered and almost dry, particularly if the leaves have steeped more than 5 minutes.

Quality in black tea is related directly to the polyphenol content and the enzyme activity upon the polyphenols during processing. The importance attached to using the buds and next two leaves derives from the fact that these are higher in both polyphenol content and the copper-containing polyphenolase needed for optimum flavor development in black tea. The other leaves, being lower in the polyphenols and polyphenolase, develop slightly less de-

After being rolled to release juices and enzymes in the leaves, black tea leaves are allowed to ferment in a humid environment (above) to alter the color and flavor characteristics of the beverage brewed from the fired and dried leaves. Oolong tea is fermented briefly, while green tea has no fermentation during the processing of the leaves.

sirable qualities in black tea than can be achieved by using orange pekoe (the desired bud and two leaves) to produce black tea.

Preparing the Beverage

Tea is prepared in different ways and is intended to meet the preferences of the group being served. In Japan and China, tea is intended primarily as a thirst quencher. The tea leaves are allowed to steep in the pot with the water until all of the beverage has been poured, which results in increasing astringency as the pot sits. In comparison with the U.S. version of tea, the British and nations that have been under the influence of England brew a very strong and stimulating beverage by using a longer and hotter steeping period than is used in the United States.

Tea of high quality is needed for brewing a beverage of excellence. This means buying a high grade of tea and then handling it appropriately after purchase. Fortunately, tea does not contain oils, nor does it rely heavily on volatile components for its flavor; this is quite a different circumstance from that of coffee. Storage of tea can be quite long in the home if the package is fairly airtight to keep volatile losses reduced and prevent entry of moisture. Refrigerated storage is not necessary, even when the tea will be held on the shelf for many weeks.

Tea preparation by American practices is quite simple, requiring only a high quality of tea, good water, and a china or glass teapot with a lid. The best appearance can be obtained by using distilled water, but the flavor of distilled water creates a less interesting tea than can be prepared with water possess-

Tannins Previous
term for polyphenols.

ing a pleasing flavor. Water should not be hard, for the resulting beverage will be cloudly and form a film on the cup due to precipitated polyphenols (sometimes called *tannins*). The water selected should be brought to a rolling boil and then used immediately to avoid loss of oxygen from the water. This helps to promote the desired fresh flavor of the beverage.

While the tea water is being brought to a boil, the pot should be filled with very hot water to warm the pot, and the tea leaves should be measured into a tea ball or bagged tea should be readied. Only 1 teaspoon of the dry tea leaves is needed for each cup of brewed tea (actually ¾ cup of water). As soon as the water starts to boil, the teapot is drained of the water used to preheat it, the tea ball or bag(s) inserted, and the boiling water is poured over the tea. By quickly replacing the lid, the preheated teapot should be able to maintain the steeping tea within the desired temperature range of 180° to 211°F during the 3- to 5-minute brewing period. At these temperatures, the tea leaves open out, exposing a maximum surface area for extraction of the flavor components.

A 3-minute extraction period is sufficient to obtain maximum caffeine extraction, while keeping the undesirable polyphenols at a minimum level. This results in a tea with a brisk and stimulating quality, but without astringency. However, more flavor is developed by a 5-minute than by a 3-minute steeping period. The choice really is an individual matter, either time being acceptable for a quality product.

Evaluating Tea

A cup of tea of high quality will be sparklingly clear, with no suggestion of a film. Black tea will be a deep amber color, oolong will be only slightly lighter, and green tea will have a rather pale greenish-yellow color. "Full," "rich," and "brisk" are adjectives describing the desired flavor of black tea. There should be no trace of bitterness or astringency. The aroma is mild, yet tempting. Oolong tea is similar to black tea, and although the characteristics should parallel those of black tea, oolong does carry overtones of the character of green tea. Green tea has little aroma, and its flavor is slightly bitter, lacking the fullness associated with the fermented teas (black and oolong). The astringency of green tea should be kept to a minimum, although there always will be some astringency associated with green tea.

Iced Tea

Iced tea is a very popular beverage in warm weather, far exceeding the consumption of iced coffee in the United States. To prepare a high-quality iced tea, two different methods may be used. Hot tea may be prepared and allowed to cool thoroughly before being poured over ice. For this method, the normal concentration of tea leaves (1 teaspoon per cup) is brewed 3 to 5 minutes, just as in the preparation of hot tea. The other method of preparing iced tea begins with the preparation of a tea of double strength and then pouring this strong infusion of hot tea directly over ice. The double strength is achieved by using twice as many tea leaves (2 teaspoons per cup) and maintaining the 3 to 5 minutes of brewing time. The strong, hot tea is diluted by the melting ice to produce iced tea of the desired strength. This is a quick method, but the quickest iced tea is made by stirring instant tea into water and then adding ice cubes.

Cloudiness often is something of a problem in making iced tea, for the polyphenols tend to precipitate in an iced product, causing the cloudy appearance. Soft water in brewing the tea helps to reduce this problem, and distilled water usually avoids the difficulty. The addition of lemon juice helps to eliminate cloudiness, while lightening the color and altering the flavor a bit.

In some locales, the water simply is inappropriate for making a high-quality iced tea. However, sun tea (also called sunshine tea) can be prepared, usually with considerable success. Sun tea is made by adding the tea leaves directly to tap water and allowing the product to steep in the sun for an hour or at room temperature for 12 hours or slightly longer. At the comparatively low temperature of this brewing technique, there is greatly reduced extraction of the polyphenols, which virtually eliminates the problems with a cloudy tea.

Instant Tea

Instant tea is rather widely utilized for hot tea as well as for iced tea, the treatment for manufacturing instant tea being comparable to the technology used in making instant coffee. It is marketed as a powder soluble in either hot or cold water, for the very fine particles of the tea solids are quite soluble even in cold water. Because of its convenience, instant tea has attracted a broad consumer base.

Herb Teas

Herb Tea Beverage made by steeping herbs and other ingredients in water; chosen by some people because of absence of caffeine.

Technically, tea is a term used to designate a beverage brewed by steeping a substance in water. Of course, the beverage called simply "tea" fits this definition, but so do several other products found in the marketplace today. For example, *herb teas* fit the broad definition of tea, although they do not include leaves from the *Camellia sinensis,* as do the traditional teas. Instead, herb teas containing such diverse items as roasted carob, malted barley, cinnamon bark, orange peel, orange petals, fennel seeds, chamomile, rose hips, licorice root, roasted chicory root, and many other ingredients are blended to make products for consumers who are seeking hot beverages free of caffeine. These beverages have no known curative powers, nor do they appear to have nutritional benefits over tea, aside from the possible benefit of not containing caffeine. However, regular teas are not very high in caffeine and do not seem to be any more harmful or unsafe than the herbal teas. In fact, some question has been raised regarding the occasional inclusion of some desert plants in herb teas that could cause harm. At the present time, there are more accusations than facts regarding the safety of tea versus that of the herb teas. This issue may indeed be the proverbial tempest in a teapot.

Cacao pod from the *Theobroma cacao* tree is the source of the chocolate products so popular in the United States and around the world. These trees are cultivated in Sri Lanka, Java, and Samoa.

Dutch Process Chocolate Chocolate manufactured with the addition of alkali to produce a pH between 6.0 and 8.8, causing the chocolate to be dark in color, less acidic, and less susceptible to settling out than is true of chocolate made without adding alkali.

Processing of Cocoa and Chocolate

Cocoa and hot chocolate are popular beverages, particularly in the cold winter months. The main ingredient in these beverages is obtained from the beans contained in the pods that form on the *Theobroma cacao* tree. Sri Lanka, Java, and Samoa are leading sources of the cacao beans. After the beans have been removed from the mature cacao pods, roasting is done to develop the characteristic aroma of the nibs, the fleshy part of the beans. The heat during roasting is effective in driving off some of the moisture and in developing compounds with minimum astringency. The roasted nibs from various lots of chocolate are blended together and then are stone ground to produce a chocolate liquor in preparation for further processing. Ultimately, the chocolate may be made into not only bitter chocolate, but also semisweet, sweet, or milk chocolate can be produced by adding varying amounts of sugar, fat, and even milk solids, as outlined in Table 15.3.

Nibs contain cocoa butter, starch, theobromine, caffeine, and pigments of the anthocyanin group identified as cocoa red and cocoa purple. Four fatty acids (oleic, stearic, palmitic, and linoleic acid) are particularly prominent in products from the roasted nibs, the concentration ranging from a mere 2 percent of linoleic acid to about 38 percent in the case of oleic acid.

The pressed ground nibs are used to make both cocoa and chocolate products. Cocoa is made by removing much of the cocoa butter, resulting in a fat content of at least 22 percent in breakfast cocoa; some of the surplus cocoa butter remaining after making cocoa is added to chocolate to raise the fat content of bitter chocolate to between 50 and 56 percent. Milk and sugar are added when milk chocolate is the end product.

Any of these chocolate derivatives can be made into either natural or *Dutch process chocolates*. The addition of alkali produces a pH of 6.0 to 8.8 in Dutch process chocolates. In contrast, the pH range without the Dutching process is about 5.2 to 6.9. This low pH is the result of not adding an alkaline ingredient; hence, chocolate products without added alkali are referred to as natural chocolate. One of the benefits of Dutch cocoa or chocolate is its reduced tendency to settle out when combined with liquids. Dutch chocolate is less tart and also is a darker color than the chocolate made without added alkali.

Table 15.3 Composition of Four Types of Chocolate

Type of Chocolate	White Milk Solids (%)	Sugar (%)	Fat (%)
Bitter	0	0	50–56
Semisweet	0	5–20	40–50
Sweet	0	40–55	32–42
Milk	12	35–55	28–39

Source: Fiene, F. and S. Blumenthal. *Handbook of Food Manufacture.* Chemical Publishing Co. New York. 1942.

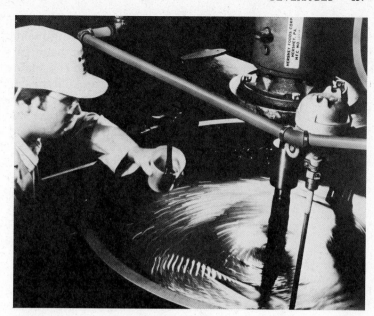

Conching is the process of holding chocolate at a temperature controlled between 210° and 110°F while stirring slowly for 36 to 72 hours; a technician checks the physical characteristics of the batch in the conch.

Conching Processing step in making chocolate in which the melted chocolate is held in constant motion for between 36 and 72 hours at temperatures ranging from 110° to 210°F, a process helpful in avoiding bloom during storage.

Tempering Carefully controlled cooling of conched chocolate to develop extremely fine fat crystals, thus helping to minimize the possibility of the development of bloom during storage.

Bloom White or light gray discoloration on chocolate where the chocolate has softened and moisture has collected during storage; tempering is helpful in avoiding the development of bloom.

The appearance and texture of chocolate are important characteristics that influence consumer acceptance. To enhance the physical appearance of chocolate and its acceptability following storage, chocolate is subjected to two processing steps: *conching* and *tempering*. These steps involve keeping melted chocolate in continuous, slow movement for between 36 and 72 hours in machines called conches that hold the chocolate within the temperature range of 110° and 210°F. Then the chocolate is tempered by cooling the chocolate very gradually, with agitation, to help to maintain a chocolate containing very fine crystals of cooled fat. The end result is a chocolate capable of resisting modest temperature changes during storage, leading to *bloom* on the chocolate. When chocolate is exposed to warm temperatures, the fat softens in untempered chocolate, causing light gray or white areas on the surface of the chocolate where moisture has collected. By tempering chocolate, much of this problem is avoided.

Preparing the Beverage

The preparation of cocoa and hot chocolate is designed to minimize the tendency to sedimentation. Since chocolate and cocoa contain starch, it is possible to get some leverage against sedimentation by gelatinizing the starch in the chocolate products. When chocolate is being used, the solid chocolate must first be melted carefully to avoid scorching. This can be done easily by placing the chocolate in the top of a double boiler over boiling water, a step appropriate any time chocolate is being melted. Melting chocolate without scorching can also be accomplished in the microwave oven, although this requires accurate timing. Packets of fluid chocolate afford yet another alternative to obtaining liquid chocolate for making the beverage.

When the chocolate is melted, the sugar, salt, and water are mixed together and are heated to boiling while stirring. This gelatinizes the starch in preparation for adding the milk. The milk is added gradually to the gelatinized chocolate mixture and stirred while being heated to serving temperature. This procedure eliminates the undesirable raw starch flavor, minimizes sedimentation in the finished beverage, and produces a minimum amount of scum from the precipitation of milk proteins. The shorter the length of time the hot beverage must be held before serving, the less scum will form. The problem can be alleviated still more by whipping up some foam on the surface with a rotary egg beater just prior to serving.

Evaluating the Beverage

Ideally, hot chocolate or cocoa will have a pleasing flavor entirely free of any suggestion of scorching. The minimum amount of sediment is achieved by the gelatinization of the starch, thus helping to achieve suspension of the chocolate or cocoa particles in the beverage. Sediment is considered undesirable in these beverages. Extensive scum formation can be caused by an extended heating period or by too high a temperature. This problem always is present, but by avoiding a long heating period and by beating with a rotary beater, the difficulty is not a problem. When hot chocolate or cocoa is garnished with either a dollop of whipped cream or a marshmallow, the topping provides a protective coating, thus removing the problem of scum formation.

Substitutions

Cocoa can be substituted for chocolate in a recipe, providing that fat is added in an appropriate amount. An ounce (a square) of chocolate can be replaced by 3½ tablespoons of cocoa plus ½ tablespoon margarine or butter.

FRUIT BEVERAGES

Fruit juices and combinations of juices are popular beverages at meal and snack times. Often these are purchases ready to drink, although they may require reconstituting with water to the normal strength. The various concentrations of juices and the use of real or synthetic juice components are covered by federal regulations and are discussed in Chapter 3.

The main concern in combining various juices to make a mixed fruit beverage is the effect on color. Although orange and yellow fruit juices do not undergo significant color changes when combined with other juices, the juices containing anthocyanin pigments can and do create some surprising colors in mixtures. The inclusion of lemon juice or other rather acidic juice helps to re-

Lemons, limes, and mangoes are but some of the fruits that can provide juice for flavorful beverages. Many fruit juices are excellent sources of vitamin C.

tain the desired reddish tone in anthocyanins rather than promote a muddy blue tone.

If fruit juices are being served with ice, they may get quite dilute as a result of the water introduced from the melting ice. This problem can be avoided by planning ahead and freezing some of the juice in a ring mold or ice cube trays so that the frozen juice can be used to chill the rest of the juice at the time it is served.

SUMMARY

Coffee and other beverages are symbols of hospitality, providing social pleasure and stimulation. Coffee gains its flavor and aroma from a wide array of volatile substances and oils found in coffee following roasting. Caffeine is the stimulant in coffee, and it is present most abundantly in coffee made by the dripolator method, although percolator coffee also has significantly more caffeine than tea or hot chocolate.

Coffee may be purchased in a soluble form (usually freeze-dried) or in grounds (and sometimes as roasted beans). The recommended amount of ground coffee for preparing the beverage is 2 tablespoons of grounds per beverage cup, although many people prefer a weaker brew than this makes. Dripolators (using drip grind) are recommended for the mild, full-flavored coffee they produce; water circulates only once through the grounds, and this water is not quite boiling by the time it has filtered through. Caffeine extraction from coffees is greatest when brewing is done by the drip method. Percolators extract less caffeine than dripolators, but the flavor of percolator coffee tends to have a somewhat bitter aftertaste, a consequence of the repeated recycling of the boiling hot water through the coffee (regular grind) grounds. Steeped coffee is made in a large kettle by maintaining the temperature of the water in the kettle just below boiling while steeping the regular grind coffee. Coffee grounds are removed when the steeping period is over. Coffee should be clear and sparkling. Espresso and iced coffee are but a couple of the variations afforded by creative marketing today.

Tea ranges from rather astringent to brisk and full in flavor, depending on the quality of the tea leaves themselves, as well as on their preparation into the beverage. Green tea is steamed to halt possible enzyme action and quickly moved through the processing steps to drying without having fermentation occur. This results in a delicately colored, very slightly astringent beverage. Oolong tea has been allowed to ferment briefly, resulting in a rather dark leaf and a somewhat mild flavor. Black tea has a long fermentation period, which permits the development of numerous flavoring compounds to heighten the flavor interest in black tea and to develop a relatively dark amber color. Only 1 teaspoon of tea per cup of beverage being brewed is necessary for brewing tea. Unlike coffee, tea contains essentially no oils; the flavoring compounds in tea are less likely to be lost during storage than are those of coffee. Instant teas and iced teas are popular variations of the brewed beverage. Although not tea from *Camellia sinensis*, the herb teas, with their mainstays of chamomile and other herbs, are becoming quite popular among people striving to reduce their intake of caffeine, for the herb teas usually contain no caffeine.

Cocoa and hot chocolate are prepared from the roasted beans contained in the pods of the *Theobroma cacao* tree. Both regular and Dutch process cocoa or chocolate contain some starch, which is gelatinized during the early part of the preparation. The increased viscosity of the gelatinized starch aids in preventing the formation of sediment in the bottom of a cup of cocoa or hot chocolate. A short heating period just long enough to bring the beverage to serving temperature, is appropriate after the milk has been added; this measure helps to minimize scum formation.

Fruit juices in combination or alone are served as beverages, too. The main concerns are to avoid diluting the juice with melting ice and to prevent unfortunate color changes when mixing juices containing anthocyanins with other juices.

Selected References

Bunker, M. L. and M. McWilliams. Caffeine content of common beverages. *J. Am. Dietet. Assoc. 74:* 28. 1979.

Charalambous, G. and G. Inglett. *Chemistry of Food and Beverages: Recent Developments.* Academic Press. New York. 1982.

Co, H. and G. W. Sanderson. Biochemistry of tea fermentation: Conversion of amino acids to black tea aroma constituents. *J. Food Sci. 35:* 160. 1970.

Eden, T. *Tea.* Longmans, Greens. New York. 1958.

Gianturco, M. A. Coffee flavor. In *Chemistry and Physiology of Flavors.* Ed. H. W. Schultz. Avi Publishing Co. Westport, Conn. 1967. P. 431.

Konigsbacher, K. S. and M. E. Donworth. Beverage flavors. In *Flavor Chemistry.* Ed. R. F. Gould. American Chemical Society. Washington, D.C. 1966. P. 174.

Leviton, A. Caffeine: Behavioral effects. *Food Tech. 37(9):* 44. 1983.

McWilliams, M. *Illustrated Guide to Food Preparation.* Plycon Press. Redondo Beach, Calif. 4th ed. 1982.

Miles, C. I. Caffeine: FDA status. *Food Tech. 37(9):* 48. 1983.

Mosher, B. A. *Health Effects of Caffeine.* American Council on Science and Health. Summit, N.J. 2nd ed. 1983.

Nagy, M. Caffeine content of beverages and chocolate. *J. Am. Med. Assoc. 229:* 337. 1974.

Pintauro, N. *Soluble Coffee Manufacturing Processes.* Noyes Development Corp. Park Ridge, N.J. 1969.

Pintauro, N. *Soluble Tea Production Processes.* Noyes Development Corp. Park Ridge, N.J. 1970.

Roberts, H. W. and J. J. Barone. Caffeine: History and use. *Food Tech. 37(9):* 32. 1983.

Stagg, G. V. Chemical changes during the storage of black tea. *J. Sci. Food Agr. 25:* 1015. 1974.

Timble, D. J. et al. Application of high-pressure liquid chromatography to the study of variables affecting theobromine and caffeine concentrations in cocoa beans. *J. Food Sci. 43:* 560. 1978.

Von Borstel, R. W. Caffeine: Metabolism. *Food Tech. 37(9):* 40. 1983.

Zoumas, B. L. et al. Theobromine and caffeine content of chocolate products. *J. Food Sci. 45:* 314. 1980.

Study Questions

1. Describe the preparation of coffee using a dripolator and a percolator. What grind should be used in each pot? Why?
2. What are the advantages and disadvantages of a dripolator? Of a percolator?
3. Which method of making coffee results in the highest caffeine? Compare the caffeine levels of various types of tea with coffee.
4. What is the stimulant predominating in cocoa? In coffee? In tea?
5. Compare the color, flavor, and aroma of black, oolong, and green teas. Explain the reasons for these differences.
6. Compare the methods for storing coffee and tea. Why are they stored differently?
7. What is the difference between Dutch process and plain cocoa?
8. Why is it necessary to be concerned about combining fruit juices containing anthocyanin pigments? Are the same problems encountered when combining juices containing carotenoid pigments? If not, why not?

Joachim Beuckelaer, detail from ''La Fruttivendola.'' Alinari/Art Resource.

CHAPTER 16

PRESERVING FOOD AT HOME

RATIONALE

Anyone who cooks doubtless has been involved in food preservation, whether consciously or unconsciously. At the very least, some leftovers have been packaged and placed in the freezer; at the other extreme, entire days have been devoted to canning seemingly endless jars of produce or tending grapes that were drying to become raisins. Home food preservation is an important aspect of managing the family's food supply for some people; for others, the primary responsibility for preserving food is given willingly to the food industry.

A basic goal of preserving food is to avoid future hunger, a motivating force that is centuries old. Food preservation also affords a means of having favorite foods available to eat when they are not in season. This is not basic to survival, but it does enhance food pleasures. For instance, a person who is very fond of the flavor of fresh strawberries may be highly motivated to have frozen strawberries to eat when the fresh berries are not available. Despite the drastic textural changes resulting from freezing, the flavor of frozen strawberries remains quite similar to the fresh berries. Other illustrations abound.

Saving money also may be a motivating force for preserving food. If fresh produce is available for the picking, a considerable amount of food can be preserved for future use at very little, if any, cost. Even if foods to be preserved need to be purchased, wise food buying can translate into real savings in the food budget because of the comparatively low cost of foods in the height of their harvest season.

PRESERVATION METHODS

Food preservation can be done very satisfactorily in the home if the methods are known and followed carefully. Drying is the oldest means of preserving food, but interest in this form of preservation has been low until the past few years. The growing numbers of people who go backpacking and camping account for much of the growth in popularity of dried foods.

The emphasis on "natural" foods and the heritage of the past have encouraged home gardening and the associated need for preserving the harvest in some form—most commonly by canning or freezing. Whereas drying preserves foods by providing too little moisture for microorganisms to survive, canning uses heat to kill microorganisms in the container, and freezing kills some microorganisms and *slows* other deteriorative changes greatly. Yet another technique, that of preserving with sugar, creates an unfavorable osmotic pressure condition for microorganisms, thus preventing their survival in jams and jellies. The addition of acid in the form of vinegar enables pickles to be kept for long periods because the environment is too acidic for microorganisms to reproduce readily; heating in canning and sometimes added salt augment this action.

Food spoilage can be caused by many different types of bacteria, molds, and yeasts. In most instances, the greatest problems stem from bacteria, although molds are the microorganisms causing the primary losses in dried foods. Interestingly, all three types of microorganisms are added deliberately to certain foods to create such popular products as yogurt, Roquefort cheese, and sourdough bread. The important fact is that the growth of microorganisms must be recognized as a potential risk in food, although some microorganisms may be desirable in specific foods.

Canning

There are two basic ways in which foods may be canned in the home, the choice between the two being based on the food being canned. Foods high in acids, which include fruits of all types and usually tomatoes, are canned by processing in a boiling water bath. Foods low in acids cannot be processed to a high enough temperature by this technique to ensure a product safe for human consumption after extended room temperature storage. Pressure canning is needed for these low-acid foods so that the contents of the jars can be heated to a high enough temperature to assure the destruction of even the spores of *Clostridium botulinum*. Unless processing times are controlled carefully and the right equipment is used, canned foods (particularly low-acid foods) may spoil and can even be fatal to eat. The importance of careful attention to processing techniques during canning cannot be overstated, particularly for vegetables, meats, and other low-acid foods. The danger from inadequate processing of these foods is due to the toxin produced by *Cl. botulinum*, which is discussed in Chapter 17.

Boiling Water Bath (Water Bath Canning) Preservation by packing high-acid foods, including fruits and tomatoes, into canning jars, covering closed jars with water, and heat processing for the appropriate length of time.

Boiling Water Bath.   Processing using the *boiling water bath* is suitable only for canning fruits, pickles, and tomatoes because the temperature is inadequate to destroy bacterial spores that may be present in foods with comparatively low acidity. Actually, some comparatively new varieties of tomatoes are not as acidic as their forerunners so that ½ teaspoon of citric acid per quart of tomatoes or 2 teaspoons of vinegar or lemon juice in each quart should be added to the tomatoes to ensure that they are sufficiently acidic to be processed safely by the boiling water bath method.

The equipment needed for canning with a boiling water bath includes a large kettle, with a cover and a rack, as well as canning jars with smooth glass all around the lip of the jar and appropriate closures. The kettle must be at least an inch and a half deeper than the height of the jars. The rack to hold the jars needs to keep the jars at least a quarter of an inch above the bottom of the pan so that the boiling water can circulate easily.

In preparation for the actual canning process, enough water is brought to a boil in the boiling water bath canner to rise an inch above the jars when they are placed on the rack in the water bath canner. This water is brought to a boil while the jars are being washed and rinsed thoroughly and the fruit is being prepared for placement in the jars, according to the directions in Table 16.1.

After their preliminary preparation, fruits and tomatoes are packed efficiently into jars to a level no higher than half an inch below the top of the jar. Boiling syrup, juice, or water then is poured to within an inch and a half of the top if the fruit has not been heated prior to being placed in the jar or to

A water bath canner equipped with a rack is recommended for processing fruits and tomatoes by boiling water bath canning.

Table 16.1 Canning Recommendations for Selected Fruits and Tomatoes

| Food | Preparation Instructions | Time in Boiling Water Bath (min)[1] | |
		Pints	Quarts
Apples	Wash, pare, core, cut in pieces. Drop in slightly salted water. Drain. Boil 3 to 5 minutes in syrup.	20	25
Apricots	Wash, halve, and pit.	20	25
Berries	Wash, stem.	15	20
Cherries	Wash, stem, and pit.	20	20
Cranberries	Wash, remove stems, boil 3 minutes in heavy syrup.	10	10
Peaches	Peel after immersing in boiling water, add syrup and boil 3 minutes.	20	25
Pears	Using not overripe pears, pare, halve, and boil in syrup 3 to 5 minutes.	25	30
Plums	Wash, prick skins.	20	25
Tomatoes[2]	Scald 1 minute. Cold dip, peel, core, quarter.	35	45

Source: Adapted from *Kerr Home Canning Book*. Kerr Glass Manufacturing Corp. Sand Springs, Okla. 1971. P. 8.
[1]At altitudes above sea level, add 1 minute for each 1000 feet if the time indicated above is less than 20 minutes; add 2 minutes for each 1000 feet if more than 20 minutes is recommended.
[2]For safety, 2 teaspoons of lemon juice per quart assures sufficient acidity for water bath canning (see Science Note).

within half an inch of the top if the fruit is packed hot. The syrup may be thin, medium, or heavy, depending on preference. The various viscosities of syrups are made by boiling the following solutions a maximum of 5 minutes:

Thin syrup	2 cups sugar:4 cups water
Medium syrup	3 cups sugar:4 cups water
Heavy syrup	4¾ cups sugar:4 cups water

A narrow rubber spatula is moved gently through the jar to release any pockets of air that may be trapped, and additional syrup is added if necessary. Then the lid is tightened firmly by hand. Tightening more than this may damage the sealing compound in the rim of the lid and interfere with achieving a good seal.

The closed jars are lifted with tongs and are placed in the boiling water bath. When the designated processing period in boiling water is completed, the jars are removed and cooled upright on several thicknesses of cloth so that they cool slowly to room temperature. The following day the seal should be checked before the jars are placed in the cupboard for extended storage. Two-piece closures are checked by pressing the center of the lid to see that it is flexed downward. Zinc closures are checked by turning the jars around while tilted and noting evidence of any leakage. If the seal is not good, canned foods should be reprocessed or else stored in the refrigerator and served within a day or two. In the event that the closures being used are different in design from the ones mentioned here, the manufacturer's directions should be followed for that specific closure design. The instructions given here are general in nature.

Pressure Canner
Large, heavy kettle with tight-fitting lid capable of withstanding internal pressure of at least 20 pounds; used for canning low-acid foods.

Pressure Canning The spores formed by *Cl. botulinum* are extremely heat resistant, and these can thrive in canned low-acid foods, such as meats and vegetables. Fortunately, the high temperature (about 240°F) achieved in a *pressure canner* at 10 pounds of pressure is sufficient to inactivate the spores of *Cl. botulinum* in a reasonable length of time.

The preparation of the food to be canned by pressure canning is done as indicated in Table 16.2. While the vegetables or other foods are being prepared, 2 inches of water needs to be heated to boiling in the pressure canner. The vegetables are packed into jars to within an inch of the top of the jar and boiling water is added, leaving half an inch of headspace in the jar. Immediately, the filled jar is closed according to the manufacturer's instructions and is placed on the rack in the pressure canner.

When the pressure canner is full of jars, the cover of the canner is fastened securely, and the petcock is left open for 7 to 10 minutes to exhaust the canner. Then the petcock is closed, which causes pressure to begin to mount in the canner. High heat is maintained while developing the desired 10 pounds of pressure (or more if at higher elevations, as noted in Table 16.2). The heat is adjusted then to maintain the desired pressure, and the processing time is begun. When the processing has been completed, the heat is turned off, and the pressure canner is allowed to cool at room temperature without disturbance until the pressure has been reduced to atmospheric pressure. Then the petcock is opened gradually to allow the steam to escape before the lid is removed. The jars are held in the canner until the liquid in them stops boiling to avoid unnecessary thermal shock to the jars. The cooling and

A pressure canner, with its strong construction and pressurized seal, is appropriate for canning low-acid foods (vegetables and meats, for example) because the high temperatures reached as a result of the pressure are effective in killing the spores of *Cl. botulinum*.

Table 16.2 Canning Recommendations for Selected Vegetables

Food	Preparation Instructions	Time at 10 pounds Pressure[1]	
		Pints	Quarts
Asparagus	Wash, pack raw or boil 3 minutes.	25	30
Beans, wax or green	Wash, string, cut and pack raw or boil 5 minutes.	20	25
Beets	Wash, boil 15 minutes, and skin.	30	40
Corn	Remove shucks, cut from cob, pack raw, or bring to boil.	55	85
Okra	Wash, boil 1 minute.	25	40
Peas	Shell, wash, and grade for tenderness. Pack raw or bring to boil.	40	40
Spinach	Wash, steam, or boil to wilt.	70	90

Source: Adapted from *Kerr Home Canning Book*. Kerr Glass Manufacturing Corp. Sand Springs, Okla. 1971. P. 9.
[1]At altitudes above 2000 feet, the pressure must be increased 1 pound for each 2000 feet of additional altitude.

Processing time when pressure canning is being done should begin when the correct pressure is achieved. Use of a timer is recommended for timing. The processing time needs to be increased when canning is being done at high elevations.

checking for sealing then follow the same routine used for jars processed in the boiling water bath.

In preparing to serve home-canned vegetables and meats, it is vital to boil these foods actively for at least 15 minutes before even tasting. This precaution is sufficient to eliminate the risk of botulism, which can result in death if viable toxin from the spores of *Cl. botulinum* is ingested even in extremely tiny amounts! This procedure is necessary even when jars look normal. Furthermore, any jars with bulging lids should be discarded without even being opened.

SCIENCE NOTE: ACIDITY AND CANNING METHODS

The pH of a food is very important in determining the viability of microorganisms during the heat processing used in canning. The break point for using water bath or pressure canning is a pH of 4.5. Below pH 4.5, a safe canning technique is provided by the use of a water bath canner, with its maximum processing temperature of 212°F. However, at pH 4.5 and higher, an unreasonably long processing time is required to ensure against botulism unless a higher processing temperature is used. This increase in temperature can only be obtained by increasing the pressure in the canner. At 10 pounds of pressure, the processing temperature is increased to 240°F, an adequate temperature for safe processing.

Since knowledge of the pH of a food is essential to determining the processing technique to use, some appreciation of the approximate pH of some of the foods commonly canned is helpful. The accompanying chart indicates the approximate pH's of many different types of foods. The fruits range from very tart plums at a pH of less than 3 to pears, which have a pH approaching 4.

Tomatoes are generally in the critical area around a pH of 4.5, with the actual pH being influenced considerably by the variety of tomato. Beefsteak tomatoes are one of the most acidic varieties; their average pH of 4.23 is safely in the pH range for water bath canning. However, several other varieties of tomatoes are in the pH range requiring pressure canning. Fireball tomatoes have an average pH of 4.50, and Royal Chico (pH 4.58) and San Marzano (pH 4.68) have even higher pH values. Since the pH of tomatoes usually is not known in the home, the addition of acid to any tomatoes being canned is recommended at the level of 2 teaspoons of lemon juice per quart of tomatoes or ½ teaspoon of citric acid (U.S.P.) per quart.

The pH of vegetables other than tomatoes ranges from the high 4 range for okra and pumpkin to peas and corn with values over 6. With these high pH values, it is easy to see why pressure canning is needed for all vegetables.

Tomatoes often are canned with other ingredients, as is done when stewed tomatoes are canned with added green pepper and onion. The addition of vegetables causes the pH of the combined food mixture to rise a little. When tomatoes already are at the pH critical to the decision about pressure canning, the added vegetables make a crucial difference. For instance, chili sauce needs pressure canning and so do salsa-type products. If there is any doubt about pH, pressure canning should be the method chosen.

pH	
2.5	Plums
	Gooseberries
	Prunes
	Dill pickles, rhubarb, apricots
3.0	Apples, blackberries
	Sour cherries, strawberries
	Peaches
	Sauerkraut, raspberries
	Blueberries
	Sweet cherries
	Pears
4.0	
	Tomatoes
	Okra
5.0	Pumpkin, carrots
	Pimiento (lye peeled)
	Turnips, cabbage
	Parsnips, beets, string beans, green peppers
	Sweet potatoes, baked beans
	Spinach
	Asparagus, cauliflower
	Red kidney beans
	Lima beans
	Succotash, meats, poultry
6.0	
	Peas
	Corn, hominy, salmon
	White fish
	Shrimp, wet pack
7.0	Lye hominy

Freezing

Freezing is a food preservation technique used in almost all homes in the United States today as a means of preserving food at least for very-short-term storage, even a matter of a few days. Many cooked foods can be frozen with the simple step of wrapping them tightly in a plastic or aluminum foil cover and placing them in the freezer. No special equipment (except for the usual freezer in a refrigerator) is needed, and only the time required for wrapping is necessary. Simply stated, freezing is the simplest way possible to preserve food. However, the length of time that extremely high quality is maintained in automatically defrosting freezers in refrigerators is limited in comparison with the storage time possible in free-standing freezers or in foods preserved by canning or drying.

Packaging is an important aspect of successful freezing, for the surface of frozen foods needs to be protected from the extremely dry atmosphere in the freezer unit. Extreme desiccation or drying occurs as ice crystals are sublimated wherever air comes in contact with frozen surfaces. This leaves unattractive, tough, and dry areas on the surface, a defect referred to as freezer burn. A clear illustration of freezer burn can be seen on the breast of frozen turkeys if the freezer bag has even a small tear in the bag covering the turkey.

Plastic freezer cartons that are stackable and have lids that fit tightly are excellent for freezer storage. Other alternatives are plastic bags or aluminum foil that are closed securely. Glass jars with wide mouths can be used if there is no shoulder on the jar. Otherwise, the contents of the jar may be very difficult to remove before being thawed completely. The possibility of breakage is another disadvantage of using glass jars.

Vegetables Foods following freezing are never any better than the food that is frozen. Therefore, only vegetables or other foods of highest quality are suggested for freezing and frozen storage. Freezing as a means of preserving foods requires adequate maintenance of cold temperatures to assure that deteriorative changes are kept to an absolute minimum throughout the storage period, and this method of storage carries some cost because of the power needed to maintain the necessary storage temperature of 0°F or lower. Comparatively warm temperatures in the freezer during storage (20°F) may allow quality to deteriorate within only five weeks, while storage at −10°F permits high quality to be maintained during a storage period of six months.

The slow deterioration of the quality of frozen foods during storage is an indication of the fact that freezing is not an effective means of completely preventing food losses due to spoilage; it merely retards losses. Enzymatic reactions and growth of microorganisms account for the deterioration over time. Vegetables are fairly susceptible to enzymatic changes unless they are blanched prior to freezing. Blanching, a short heating period in boiling water or steam, inactivates enzymes as well as helps to reduce the final volume of the food being frozen. Only a short blanching period (see Table 16.3) is needed to accomplish the necessary inactivation and appropriately retard enzyme action in frozen vegetables. In fact, the short blanching period is preferable to a

Table 16.3 Procedures for Preparing Selected Vegetables for Freezing

Vegetable	Preparation Procedures	Scalding Time[1] (min)
Asparagus	Wash, drain, and trim.	3
Beans, lima	Shell, wash, and drain.	3
Beans, green and wax	Wash, drain, and cut if desired.	3
Broccoli	Cut into sections, wash, and drain.	3
Brussels sprouts	Trim, wash, and drain.	3
Cauliflower	Cut into sections, wash, and drain.	3
Peas	Shell, wash, and drain.	2
Spinach	Wash and drain.	2
Corn	Boil 3 to 4 minutes, dip in cold water, cut from cob, rinse in cold water. Drain.	Done in preparation

Source: Adapted from McWilliams, M. and H. Paine. *Modern food preservation.* Plycon Press. Redondo Beach, Calif. 1977.
[1]For altitudes above 5000 feet, increase the scalding time 1 minute.

longer cooking period because of the better texture in the finished product with the short blanching period compared with vegetables cooked until done before being frozen.

Since overcooking during blanching is detrimental to the final texture, blanched vegetables are immersed in ice water directly from the blanching water to halt the cooking immediately. As soon as the food has been cooled in this way, vegetables are drained thoroughly, packaged, labeled, and placed immediately in the freezer. Best results are obtained when only a small amount of food is frozen at any one time. This permits the freezer to maintain a temperature sufficiently cold to freeze the package of food very fast. This rapid freezing results in the formation of very small ice crystals and helps to avoid serious disruption of the cell walls in vegetables, that results in improved texture in the final product.

Fruits Best results in freezing fruit are obtained when only a small quantity is being frozen at one time, just as is true in freezing vegetables. The preparation of fruits for freezing actually is even easier and faster than is the time required to prepare vegetables. Fruits are washed, sorted, and cut (if desired), but they are not blanched. They are packed plain, sprinkled with dry sugar, or packed in syrup in most instances, with ascorbic acid or vitamin C sometimes being added to help retard discoloration.

Fruits (such as pineapple, plums, raspberries, rhubarb, strawberries, blackberries, blueberries, and gooseberries) can be frozen immediately after they are cleaned thoroughly and packaged without sugar or syrup, although use of sugar or syrup often is the method chosen (see Table 16.4). A sugar pack is done simply by sprinkling about ¾ cup of sugar on each quart of tart fruit or ½ cup on sweet fruits per quart of fruit. Fruits susceptible to browning should be combined with a solution of ¼ teaspoon of vitamin C or ascorbic

Table 16.4 Procedures for Freezing Fruits

Fruit	Preparation	Type of Pack	Vitamin C
Apricots	Scald apricot halves 30 seconds, chill in ice water.	Syrup or dry sugar	Yes
Blackberries	Sort, wash, drain.	Syrup, dry sugar, or no sugar	No
Cherries	Sort and wash.	Syrup or dry sugar	Yes
Peaches	Wash and peel, halve or slice.	Syrup or dry sugar	Yes
Raspberries	Sort, wash, drain.	Syrup, dry sugar, or no sugar	No
Rhubarb	Wash, cut into short pieces, blanch 1 minute, cool in ice water.	Syrup	No
Strawberries	Sort, wash, remove cap, drain.	Syrup, dry sugar, or no sugar	No

acid in ¼ cup of water to coat the surface and prevent enzymatic oxidation and browning.

Syrups of varying sweetness can be used to pack fruits for freezing. Most fruits are satisfactory when the syrup contains 3 cups of sugar to 4 cups of water; very tart fruits need 4 ¾ cups of sugar to 1 quart of water. After the fruit and any sugar or syrup to be used have been added, the lid is positioned and secured snugly to keep deteriorative changes to a minimum, and the product is labeled carefully, with the date being a prominent part of the label. Careful and thorough labeling helps to ensure maximum maintenance of quality in storage and proper inventory control. Frozen fruits held at a steady temperature of 0°F or colder can be stored for a year.

Other Foods Meats, poultry, and fish freeze well when wrapped tightly in airtight packaging. As with fruits and vegetables, meats will maintain structural integrity best when the rate of freezing is very fast, thus minimizing drip loss upon thawing. When meats are frozen very slowly, large ice crystals form and break through some of the cell walls. It is these breaks in the walls that permit considerable drip loss when some meats are thawed.

Casseroles and stews can be frozen after they are prepared. The major problem with the freezing of starch-thickened mixtures is the retrogradation of the starch that occurs during frozen storage. This can be reversed by heating stews and stirring them. However, puddings thickened with starch and other comparable items that cannot be reheated and stirred do not freeze well because of the retrogradation of the starch and the somewhat gritty texture of the thawed product. The use of waxy rice flour in place of wheat or cornstarch minimizes the problem of retrogradation, which helps to produce an acceptable frozen pudding (see Chapter 7).

Typically, baked products freeze well. Rolls and breads of all types may be baked, cooled, and then frozen in plastic or other airtight wrap. Cakes, cookies, cream puffs, and doughnuts also are baked and cooled before being frozen. Powdered sugar icings freeze reasonably well, but more elaborate icings on cakes may be poor following frozen storage. The best method with frozen fruit pies is to freeze the unbaked pie and then bake it close to the time it will be served. Soft meringues do not freeze well, but hard meringues can be frozen following baking.

Preserving with Sugar

Jelly Pectin gel made with fruit juice to yield a clear gel.

Jam Pectin gel with pieces of fruit plus the juice.

Preserves Pectin gel with juice and fruit pieces larger than the pieces used in jam.

Conserves Preserves with nuts added.

Marmalade Citrus preserves.

Fruit Butter Cooked fruit puree with spices.

Pectin Pectic substances in barely ripe fruit; capable of forming a gel.

Pectinic Acid A form of the pectic substance, pectin.

Protopectin Pectic substance in very green fruit; incapable of forming a gel.

Pectic Acid Pectic substance in overly ripe fruit; incapable of forming a gel.

Sugar can be an effective preservative for foods, its action being the result of the disturbance of osmotic pressure and the consequent loss of necessary fluid from microorganisms. Several different products can be made using fruit and sugar. *Jelly* is the pectin gel made using fruit juice to produce a clear product. *Jams* and preserves are two virtual synonyms for pectin gels containing both juice and pieces of fruit. *Preserves* are pectin gels consisting of some juice and very large pieces of fruit. *Conserves* are merely preserves with nuts added. *Marmalades* are preserves made with citrus fruits. *Fruit butters* are semisolid, somewhat viscous purées of fruit cooked with spices.

Fruit Selection The best fruits for making *pectin* gels are those with a high pectin content and a rather low (acidic) pH. Tart apples, berries, citrus fruits, and grapes are fruits that contain a useful level of acid. Citrus fruits and apples are good sources of pectin.

Fortunately, pectin can be purchased to help in making gels that are sufficiently strong to be served easily. Pectin is prepared for commercial sale from the skins and cores of apples and from the albedo (white portion) of the skin of citrus fruits. This pectin is marketed as the fluid pectin or as a powdered pectin, either one being effective in forming an appropriate gel structure.

The pectic substances (various chemical relatives of pectin) undergo some changes during the ripening of fruit, and these changes determine the effectiveness of pectic substances in achieving gelation. The desired form of pectic substances for making gels is *pectinic acid* or pectin, the form found in fruit that is barely ripe. Of the various pectic substances, only pectin is capable of participating in the formation of a gel in combination with fruit juices. The *protopectin* in very green fruit and the *pectic acid* that forms as fruits become overly ripe are not able to form a gel. For this reason, only barely ripe fruit is recommended for making jams, jellies, and preserves.

Fruits for Jams and Jellies Select the type of fruit desired for making jams and jellies and then pick fruits of this type that are barely ripe. This gives the maximum pectin content. However, many fruits are not high enough in pectin to form a gel. For this reason, commercial pectins ordinarily are added to the mixture to ensure that a gel will result.

Acid also is important in the gel-forming process. Some fruits are quite acidic, but others need added acids to achieve the necessary acidic pH for gel formation.

Preparation Jelly is prepared by boiling the ingredients rapidly to bring the sugar to a concentration of 60 to 65 percent. During this boiling period, some breakdown of the sugar occurs, the extent being determined by the length of

SCIENCE NOTE: THE PECTIC SUBSTANCES

The pectic substances are a family of polysaccharides that are a part of the cellular composition of fruits, being found in cell walls and also between cells. The form of the pectic substances changes during the ripening of fruits. However, they all have the same underlying structure composed of repeating units of galacturonic acid. Galacturonic acid is the uronic acid derived from galactose and is present when the external (sixth) carbon of galactose is an acid functional group rather than the hydroxyl group of galactose.

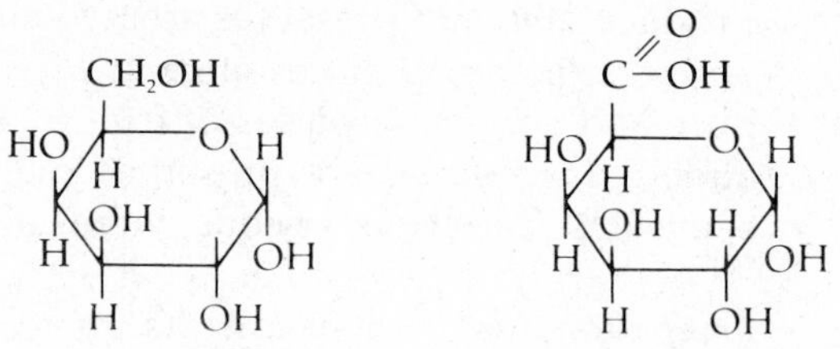

Galactose

Galacturonic acid

Protopectin is a polysaccharide in which very long polymers or chains of galacturonic acid units are linked together. These cumbersome molecules contribute considerable rigidity to immature fruits. However, the acid radical on the sixth carbon is capable of forming an ester with methanol, a reaction that is catalyzed by enzymes during the ripening process.

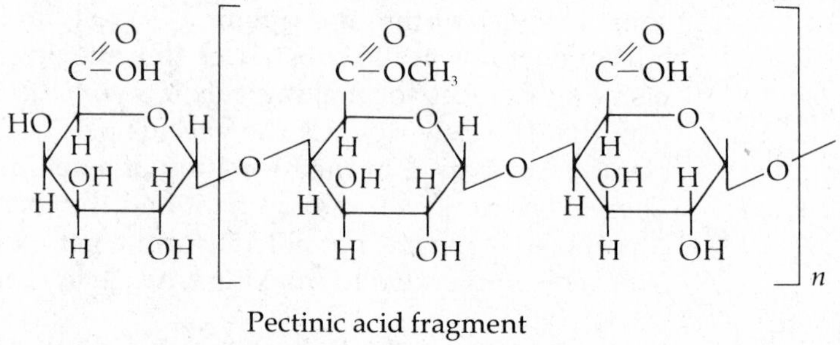

Pectinic acid fragment

Pectin molecules vary a bit, but basically they are pectinic acid and/or pectinates, which are salts of pectinic acid. Pectin molecules that are particularly effective in forming gels are derived from apples and citrus. The molecular weight of apple pectin is approximately 280,000 and that of citrus fruit pectin is about 229,000. The concentration of pectin is greatest in fast-growing surface tissues. Polygalacturonase and pectin esterases are the enzymes catalyzing the transformation from protopectin to pectin. As this reaction gradually occurs, the texture of the fruits begins to soften. In the barely ripe fruit, enough methylation has occurred to produce pectinic acids and pectinates capable of forming gels.

However, chemical reactions continue to occur in fruits, and pectin gradually changes to pectic acid, another pectic substance. Pectic acids are characterized by having fewer methyl groups esterified on the sixth carbon than are found on pectinic acids. This change in structure results in loss of gel-forming properties.

Pectin is capable of forming a gel because its colloidal-sized molecules are able to hydrogen bond to each other, forming a continuous network of pectin molecules linked to each other in a random fashion. Acid facilitates this cross-linking; at a pH of about 3.3, pectin molecules will be hydrated very little. When the usual protective coating of water on pectin is absent, the actual molecules of pectin can approach each other rather easily and form the hydrogen bonds needed for gelling. The presence of sugar in jellies also aids in gel formation because of the excellent hygroscopic nature of sugar. Sugar is quite effective in helping to bind some of the water that would otherwise tend to interfere with the formation of the gel.

A pectin gel can be visualized as being a system in which the pectin molecules, which are hydrogen bonded together, form a complex brushlike structure somewhat similar to the structure of a tumbleweed. The acid in the mixture allowed the water to be freed from the pectin sufficiently for hydrogen bonding to occur. However, the water in the fruit juice is able to be held in the pectin gel when the mixture is cold because the spaces between the various pectin molecules in the structural framework are quite small. This makes it possible for sugar to bind much of the water and to aid in trapping the water so that the gel structure becomes rigid.

time the mixture is boiled. Some of the sugar is changed by acid hydrolysis to invert sugar, which is an aid in preventing the formation of sugar crystals in the finished product during storage. The other change is the caramelizing of sugar, which can occur if the cooking period is too long. This is evidenced by a darkening of the color and a change in odor. Caramelizing should be avoided.

For both maximum yield and general desirability of a jelly, sufficient sugar needs to be used in the recipe so that long boiling will not be required to reach the necessary concentration of sugar to 60 or 65 percent. Unnecessary loss of volatile flavors is circumvented by using a short boiling time. The short boiling period possible when adequate sugar is used helps to avoid getting the rubbery texture that results if the pectin becomes too concentrated as water is boiled away. The short boiling period also prevents much hydrolysis of pectin. Some breakdown (hydrolysis) of pectin will occur while the jelly mixture is boiling, but the amount of change is not significant unless boiling is extended. With considerable chemical change in pectin, the final jelly will be softer than it should be because of loss of some of the gel-forming capability of the original pectin.

Various tests for doneness are possible when making jellies. A thermometer can be used to determine when the right concentration of sugar has been reached. The temperature should be 9 F° higher than the boiling point of water when cooking stops, for this indicates a sugar concentration of 65 percent. A visual test for this is to let the hot jelly flow from a spoon. At the correct end point, the jelly will "sheet off" the spoon because of its viscosity. Commercial jelly makers use the refractive index of the boiling liquid to determine when the correct end point has been reached.

As soon as jelly is removed from the heat, it should be poured into the glasses. This achieves the maximum gel structure. Pouring after gelation begins causes disruption of the gel structure and weakens the final product. A good jelly is strong enough to retain the outline of the glass when it is unmolded, yet is flexible enough to sway when the dish is moved. When spread with a knife, jelly breaks into pieces that yield under pressure. The flavor should be fresh and characteristic of the fruit, and the color should be bright. No sugar crystals should be evident, and there should not be any mold.

A very soft or fluid jelly can be caused by several errors. An imbalance in the ratio of pectin, sugar, or acid and the liquid can be the result of an error in the recipe or too little evaporation of water during cooking. Too little pectin in the fruit itself can be corrected by the addition of commercial pectin; too little acid can be corrected by adding citric or tartaric acid to reach the desired pH of 3.3.

Overcooked jellies often contain some sugar crystal aggregates that give a distinctly gritty character to the product. This usually is accompanied by a rubbery texture because of the excessive concentration of the pectin molecules. Darkening of jellies also occurs in overcooking as a result of the caramelization of some of the sugar.

Syneresis is a problem in some very acidic jellies. Cranberry jelly is particularly notorious for this problem. The loss of some of the liquid out of the gel occurs when the pH of the jelly is less than 3.3.

Drying

Drying, the original method of food preservation, was used by people many centuries ago, but this technique was not used much in recent times in the home until it benefited from a renewed interest in the mid-1970s. Heightened participation in camping and backpacking and the interest in "natural foods" contributed to the swelling sales of dehydrators for drying foods at home. Although many dehydrators have been sold, there is no requirement that fancy or elaborate equipment be available for drying foods. The equipment can be as simple as some cheesecloth stretched over the rack in the oven. In addition to the appeal of being able to preserve food without investing in equipment, drying of food is appealing because the finished product can be stored in tightly closed plastic bags at room temperature; campers appreciate the reduced weight and bulk of the dried foods, too.

Vegetables, fruits, and meats can be dried satisfactorily in the home. Vegetables that can be dried without blanching include chives, herbs, mushrooms, okra, onions, parsley, peppers, and tomatoes. Blanching is done to asparagus, broccoli, Brussels sprouts, cabbage, carrots, cauliflower, corn, celery, greens, peas, potatoes, and squash before they are dried. Fruits that tend to brown upon standing will have a better color when dipped in an acidic fruit juice or a solution of ascorbic acid before before being dried; peaches and apricots will have a brighter color if they are sulfured before drying. Meats may be marinated prior to drying, if desired.

Foods for drying are sliced thinly, with the exception of a few fruits, such as grapes, that are left whole, but are punctured with a fork. Only very lean cuts of meat are suitable for drying because rancidity can be a problem if fat content is very high. Moreover, the meat must be sliced very thinly so that the interior can be dried satisfactorily. The thin slices of food are placed on racks outdoors, in a dehydrator, or in the oven (maintained at 200°F). If sun drying is being done, the food must be protected from insects and animals. The food is dried until it is dry, yet pliable. Then it is placed in plastic bags that are closed tightly and labeled. Storage should be in a cool, dry, dark closet.

COMMERCIAL METHODS OF FOOD PRESERVATION

Commercial methods of food preservation include the same techniques used for home food preservation—canning, freezing, drying, pickling, and preserving with sugar—but the equipment used and the formulations vary from those used at home. For example, nitrogen spray can be used to freeze berries commercially to minimize the damage to the cell walls that results from normal rates of freezing. Freeze-drying and aseptic canning are other techniques of importance in industry, but which are not available in the home. In freeze-drying, foods are frozen and then the frozen food is dehydrated under a high vacuum. This circumstance causes the ice to be sublimed rather than to melt before evaporation occurs. Freeze-dried coffee is a well-known commercial application of this technique.

Irradiation offers another possible way of preserving foods. When foods are subjected to gamma rays from cobalt[60] or cesium[137], microorganisms and insects are killed, thus enhancing the storage qualities of the food. Storage of grains and potatoes in particular can be extended by the use of irradiation. The safety of this preservation technique is the subject of some controversy at the present time. In 1984, the Food and Drug Administration proposed permitting fresh fruits and vegetables to be treated with a maximum radiation dosage of a kilogray (Table 16.5), an amount equivalent to 100 kilorads or 100,000 rads (radiation absorbed dose). A low dosage for food irradiation is considered to be up to 100 kilorads; a medium level is 100 to 1000 kilorads (1 megarad); a high level is 1000 to 5000 kilorads (1 to 5 megarads). The FDA at the same time proposed that spices be treated at levels up to 30 kilograys because the spices often have high levels of contaminants and are eaten in extremely small quantities. These levels are designed to kill insects and other agents that could cause spoilage during room temperature storage.

Table 16.5 Units Used in Expressing Radiation Energy

Term	Definition
Rad	Radiation absorbed dose
Gray	100 rads
Kilorad	1000 rads
Kilogray	1000 grays or 100 kilorads or 100,000 rads
Megarad	1000 kilorads or 1,000,000 rads

SUMMARY

Foods may be preserved by canning, freezing, drying, freeze-drying, adding preservatives such as salt and sugar, and irradiation. In the home, food preservation has enjoyed a resurgence as more people have resumed canning, pickling, freezing, drying, and jam and jelly making. All preservation techniques are directed toward preventing the growth of yeasts, molds, and bacteria that will cause food spoilage or illness. Canning utilizes high temperatures to kill microorganisms. Freezing significantly retards the growth of microorganisms. Drying promotes long storage life because microorganisms fail to thrive in an extremely low-moisture environment. Irradiation kills microorganisms, and high concentrations of salt or sugar prevent their growth. Whether preservation is done commercially or in the home, processing must be controlled conscientiously to insure safety and long storage life of the food.

Although all canning needs to be done carefully, particular attention must be given to the processing of vegetables and meats because of their low acid content. These foods must be canned in a pressure canner or pressure saucepan so that the food will reach a high enough temperature to inactivate spores of *Cl. botulinum*. The toxin that this bacterium can produce in these foods often is lethal to humans, even in infinitesimal amounts. If such foods are boiled for 15 minutes, they will be safe to eat.

Freezing is a quick method of preserving food. Fruits may be packed without sugar, with sugar, or with a syrup pack. Vegetables are blanched before freezing to inactivate the enzymes. Drying may be done in the oven, by sun drying, or in a dehydrator. Some fruits require sulfuring to prevent discoloration; some vegetables are blanched prior to drying.

Jams and jellies are made by using levels of pectin and sugar to gel fruits and juices at a pH of about 3.3. The high level of sugar in the cooked product prevents spoilage. Pectin and acid levels are appropriate in some fruits for making jams and jellies, but often the addition of either pectin and/or acid may be essential to the formation of a gel of satisfactory strength. Small batches should be prepared to avoid unnecessary breakdown in the sugar or pectin during the boiling period.

Pectin is the methylated galacturonic acid polymer found in the cell walls and intercellular spaces of fruits that has the ability to form gels. Protopectin (the pectic substance in unripened fruits) and pectic acids (the pectic substances in overly ripe fruits) lack the gel-forming properties of pectin. These changes in pectic substances occur as a result of enzymatic action in the maturing fruit.

Selected References

Beacham, L. M. Shelf life of canned foods. *Assoc. Food Drug Official Quarterly Bull. 41(3):* 213. 1977.

Consumer and Food Economics Institute. How to Make Jellies, Jams, and Preserves at home. *Home and Garden Bulletin* No. 56. U.S. Dept. Agriculture. Washington, D.C. 1975.

Desrosier, N. W. and J. N. Desrosier. *Technology of Food Preservation.* Avi Publishing Co. Westport, Conn. 4th ed. 1977.

Drew, F. and K. S. Rhee. Energy use, cost and product quality in preserving vegetables at home by canning, freezing, and dehydration. *J. Food Sci. 45(6):* 1561. 1980.

Feinberg, B. Vegetables. In *Food Dehydration.* Vol. 2. Ed. W. B. Van Arsdel et al. Avi Publishing Co. Westport, Conn. 1973.

Foster, E. M. Food safety: Problems of the past and perspectives of the future. *J. Food Protection 45(7):* 658. 1982.

Giddings, G. G. and M. A. Welt. Radiation preservation of food. *Cereal Foods World 27(1):* 17. 1982.

Harris, H. and L. M. Davis. *Use of Low Water Level in Boiling Water Bath Canning.* Ag. Experiment Sta. Auburn University, Auburn, Ala. 1976.

Kennedy, S. O. *How to Dry Food for the Home.* Bull. C166. Coop. Extension U. of Nevada. Reno, Nev. 1975.

Kerr Glass Manufacturing Co. *Kerr Home Canning and Freezing Book.* Sand Springs, Okla. 1974.

Kory, J. V. Food preservation by irradiation. *International Atomic Energy Agency Bull. 23(3):* 33. 1981.

Kuhn, G. D. and L. W. Hamilton. *Sealing Performance of Jar Lids for Home Canning.* Ag. Experiment Sta. University Park, Penn. 1976.

Lecos, C. Irradiation proposed to treat food. *FDA Consumer 18(4):* 10. 1984.

McWilliams, M. and H. Paine. *Modern Food Preservation.* Plycon Press. Redondo Beach, Calif. 1977.

Miller, M. W. et al. Drying Foods at Home. *Home and Garden Bulletin* No. 217. U.S. Dept. Agriculture. Washington, D.C. 1977.

Shibasaki, G. Food preservation with nontraditional antimicrobial agents. *J. Food Safety 4(1):* 35. 1982.

Skelton, M. M. and C. W. Marr. Ascorbic acid content, pH, and acceptability of tomatoes processed by different home canning methods. *H. Ec. Research J. 6:* 305. 1978.

Takeguchi, C. A. Regulatory aspects of food irradiation. *Food Tech. 37(2):* 44. 1983.

Thomas, M. W. et al. Effect of radiation and conventional processing on the thiamin content of pork. *J. Food Sci. 46:* 824. 1981.

York, G. K. *Home Canning of Fruits.* HXT-32. No. 2269. Coop. Extension. U. of Calif. Berkely, Calif. 1975. (a)

York, G. K. *Home Canning of Vegetables.* HXT-54. No. 2270. Coop. Extension. U. of Calif. Berkeley, Calif. 1975. (b)

Study Questions

1. What is the oldest method of food preservation? Why do you think this method was used first?
2. Compare the advantages of canning with the advantages of freezing as preservation methods. Then contrast the disadvantages of each method. When might you decide to can foods? To freeze them?
3. Why is dried food popular with hikers and backpackers?

4. Outline the method for drying apples in the home.
5. Explain the role of each of the following in making jelly: (a) pectin, (b) sugar, (c) acid.
6. What is the general chemical structure of pectin? Describe the changes occurring as protopectin is transformed to pectin.
7. What foods need to be canned in a pressure canner? Why must a pressure canner be used for them?
8. What is the effect of a very slow rate of freezing on the quality of frozen foods?
9. What breads and desserts may be frozen satisfactorily after baking? Which ones should be frozen without being baked?

Carl Larssen, detail from ''The Kitchen.'' National Museum, Stockholm/Art Resource.

CHAPTER 17

FOOD SAFETY AND QUALITY

Food safety can be viewed from two perspectives: the immediate consequences of eating a food and the long-term consequences. Attacks often dubbed simply "food poisoning" usually are noted within a matter of hours after the offending food is eaten. Physicians and public health authorities are likely to be involved in these situations because of the violent symptoms commonly associated with such episodes. If the problem relates to food being served to the public, the newspapers and television may seize the initiative to spread the word their audiences, sometimes for the protection of the public, occasionally only for something to add spice to the day's events.

On the other hand, substances in foods that may cause serious health problems in the future may not be made widely known until researchers or even self-appointed ombudsmen of the public's welfare bring possible hazards into public view. Contaminants in the food supply, such as mercury in swordfish, have been pinpointed as potential problems for humans, and evidence of the potential for harm is being gathered.

There also are many imagined hazards in the food supply, risks for which no physical evidence presently exists. Consider, for example, the instance of a consumer who barged into our office recently and proceeded to announce that we were all being poisoned by toxic levels of additives in commercial bread. Her mission, it seems, was to spread the word far and wide that we will all die soon if we continue to eat the "poisoned" bread the food processors are forcing upon us. Although this woman represents an extreme example of public fear and distrust of the food supply, her attitude can be found to varying degrees throughout the land.

There is no question that the food we, as individuals, choose to eat represents the potential for good or ill. Present knowledge of the possible effects of some minute components in foods upon health is not complete. However, humankind has been surviving for countless centuries and has even flourished, which is proof of at least some degree of safety in the food supply. Whether you elect to eat many processed foods containing an array of additives or whether you decide to prepare most of your foods from basic ingredients, you are responsible for the choice. Present evidence would suggest that either choice is a nourishing and healthful way to eat.

Probably far more people will encounter food poisoning episodes from unsanitary food handling than will ever be harmed by additives in foods. Not surprisingly, the food that is so helpful in supporting life and growth for humans also can be just what microorganisms also need to flourish. When studying food preparation, some basic knowledge of food microbiology is extremely important in helping to ensure that the food you prepare will be safe to eat.

POTENTIAL MICROORGANISMS IN FOODS

Sources and Control of Microorganisms

Many varieties of bacteria, yeasts, and molds may appear in foods being marketed to the consumer. These microorganisms are present as a result of numerous possibilities: the soil in which plant foods are grown may contain microorganisms; crops may be fertilized with natural fertilizers containing viable microorganisms; the storage containers or trucks or other conveyances may have microorganisms remaining from previous loads; even the air may transport microorganisms into the food supply. These are not the only possible sources of contamination, for people handling food from field to market are yet another significant source of contamination. In short, there is little possibility that a food will not encounter some form of microorganism at some point before it reaches the consumer.

Fortunately, consumers can protect themselves from possible harm from food-borne microorganisms by paying attention to the way in which food is handled and prepared for the table. Thorough washing of fresh produce before storage and before preparation removes many of the microorganisms clinging to these items. Similarly, thorough washing of hands with soap and water before handling food is an effective way of reducing the contamination of food by food handlers. Being sure that food is not handled by people with tuberculosis, colds, flu, and other contagious diseases adds to the safety of the food you eat.

Adequate temperature control of protein-containing foods is essential to retarding the growth of microorganisms in milk, egg products, meats, fish, poultry, gelatin, mayonnaise, and other foods of this type. By keeping these foods in the temperature range below 40°F and above 140°F, the reproduction of many microorganisms will be kept to an absolute minimum, which is vital to food safety (see Figure 17.1).

High temperatures are important to kill viable microorganisms present in foods before the food is eaten. For instance, pasteurizing milk or cooking pork to a uniform interior temperature of 170°F will ensure that these foods are perfectly safe to eat, even though they may have contained microorganisms before being heated.

Even when foods have been heated enough to kill microorganisms in them, careful attention to temperature control is essential for protein-containing foods. These types of food may be recontaminated by food handlers or other agents, and the new microorganisms will flourish unless the food is stored at refrigerator or steam table temperatures, that is, below 40°F or above 140°F.

Types of Microorganisms

Three types of microorganisms—yeasts, bacteria, and molds—represent the range of microbiological contaminants that can cause food spoilage and/or food-borne illnesses. The food substrates each of these types prefers varies from one to another. Consequently, the care of food during storage and preparation varies with the type of food and its likely contaminants.

Yeast Single-celled fungus that reproduces by budding.

Yeasts usually grow well in a slightly acidic medium and in the presence of some source of energy, such as sugar, plus water. The ideal conditions for yeasts to flourish are approximately room temperature and a moist atmosphere. Yeasts need at least 20 percent moisture in foods to remain viable.

Molds Multiple-celled microorganisms capable of forming heads with spores that scatter and are viable even in moisture levels as low as 13 percent.

Molds generally represent a far greater potential for food spoilage than do yeasts. Molds, in contrast to the usual single cell of yeasts, usually have sev-

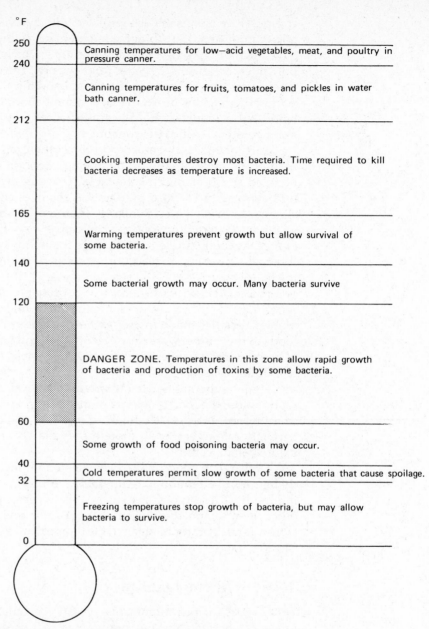

°F

250 — Canning temperatures for low–acid vegetables, meat, and poultry in pressure canner.
240 —

Canning temperatures for fruits, tomatoes, and pickles in water bath canner.

212 —

Cooking temperatures destroy most bacteria. Time required to kill bacteria decreases as temperature is increased.

165 —

Warming temperatures prevent growth but allow survival of some bacteria.

140 —

Some bacterial growth may occur. Many bacteria survive

120 —

DANGER ZONE. Temperatures in this zone allow rapid growth of bacteria and production of toxins by some bacteria.

60 —

Some growth of food poisoning bacteria may occur.

40 —
Cold temperatures permit slow growth of some bacteria that cause spoilage.
32 —

Freezing temperatures stop growth of bacteria, but may allow bacteria to survive.

0 —

Figure 17.1 Storage temperatures for controlling bacterial growth.

eral cells and often form a filament topped by a head with spores that scatter when the food containing a colony of mold is moved. Molds can be seen frequently on loaves of breads made without preservatives if the loaves have been stored at room temperature for only a very few days. The moisture level maintained in a tightly wrapped loaf of bread is just right for molds to flour-

Mycotoxin Poisonous substance produced by the growth of some molds.

Aflatoxin Mycotoxin produced by the growth of *Aspergillus flavus* or *Aspergillus parasiticus*, molds sometimes growing on peanuts, corn, seeds, or nuts that are not stored in a dry enough environment or are grown in mold-containing soil.

Bacteria Microscopic plants, often single-celled and of varied shapes (filamentous, rodlike, round, or spiral), some of which are causes of food-borne illnesses.

Anaerobic Capable of surviving in an oxygen-free environment.

Aerobic Needing oxygen for survival and reproduction.

ish. However, molds can remain viable even if a food has been stored at moisture levels as low as 13 percent, a characteristic that makes molds the most troublesome of the microorganisms to control in the storage of dried foods.

The visibility of molds on foods helps to avoid the problem of food poisoning from molds. However, a few molds produce *mycotoxins* that are poisonous. Perhaps the most familiar example of the problem of mycotoxins from molds is *aflatoxin*, the mycotoxin sometimes found in moldy peanuts that are stored, a problem particularly in some parts of Africa.

Bacteria are the type of microorganism most commonly causing foodborne illnesses. These microscopic plants often are single-celled and vary in shape, being possibly filamentlike, rod-shaped, round, or spiral. When live colonies or groups of bacteria are consumed, they may create symptoms ranging from general discomfort to nausea, vomiting, and even death. Although many bacteria grow well in a wide range of foods, sugar and salt concentrations that create an unfavorable osmotic pressure can destroy bacteria by dehydration.

Classification of bacteria sometimes is done on the basis of adaptability to oxygen requirements or temperature levels. On the former basis, bacteria are *aerobic* or *anaerobic*, depending on their need for oxygen for survival. Aerobic bacteria will die if they lack an adequate supply of oxygen. Conversely, anaerobic bacteria flourish in an oxygen-free system. Bacteria that are able to reproduce rapidly at temperatures well above room temperature are classified as *thermophilic* (heat loving), while those that reproduce well at very cold temperatures are termed *cryophilic* (cold loving). Clearly, there are some bacteria capable of adapting to many of the conditions employed in storing foods.

FOOD POISONING

Thermophilic Thriving at temperatures above room temperature.

Cryophilic Thriving at temperatures well below room temperature.

Salmonellae Bacteria capable of causing severe gastrointestinal upset when ingested in large quantities in food.

Salmonellosis Condition characterized by fever, nausea, abdominal cramps, and diarrhea resulting from ingestion of viable salmonellae.

Bacterial Poisoning

Salmonellosis When present in food, several different microorganisms classified as bacteria are capable of causing illness among people. Among the comparatively common bacteria capable of causing illness when they are eaten are strains of salmonellae, streptococci, clostridia, staphylococci, and botulina. Illness is the direct result of ingesting streptococci, salmonellae, or clostridia, whereas it is the toxins produced by staphylococci and botulina that are responsible for their potent effects.

Salmonella is the name of a type of bacteria capable of causing the illness called *salmonellosis*. (The nomenclature recognizes the research of D. E. Salmon.) The symptoms of salmonellosis develop between 6 and 72 hours after eating the infected food, with 12 hours being the customary incubation period prior to evidence of symptoms. Evidence of salmonella infection includes abdominal cramps, fever, nausea, and diarrhea. Susceptibility to developing salmonellosis varies from one individual to another, but infants and people who already are sick are likely candidates. However, even healthy adults can develop salmonellosis if they eat a food with a high count of viable salmonellae. The increasing numbers of cases of salmonellosis being diagnosed may be the result of increased problems of food sanitation, or it may simply mean that diagnosis is being done with increased accuracy, resulting in identification of the cause of the problem rather than the vague description of "something he ate." Salmonellae and other food-borne bacterial poisonings are identified in Table 17.1.

Salmonellae are found commonly in protein foods such as pork, poultry, and eggs. To prevent serious episodes of intoxication by salmonellae, keep foods containing these items at refrigerator temperatures or above the danger zone (above 140°F) and minimize storage in the danger zone (40° to 140°F). Frozen storage does not kill all salmonellae in a food; even a storage period of six months at 0°F still is not sufficient to kill all salmonellae. To ensure safety from salmonellae infection, heat foods that might contain these bacteria to at least 140°F and hold for 10 minutes or use a somewhat higher temperature for a shorter period.

Streptococcal Infection Infections from eating food contaminated with a few strains of streptococci have been diagnosed in humans, although the incidence appears to be far less than the numbers of cases attributed to infection by salmonellae. A prominent symptom is a sore throat, which may develop into a comparatively serious health hazard in people with weakened resistance, notably the very young and the elderly. These bacteria are found sometimes in poultry and in unpasteurized (raw) milk. Heat treatment to at least 165°F is an adequate measure to destroy any viable streptococci that might be present in the uncooked food.

Perfringens Poisoning This type of food poisoning is the result of the presence of an anaerobic bacterium, *Clostridium perfringens*. *Clostridium perfringens*, found in meats and meat dishes, can form spores that are extremely resistant to heat. The obvious means of protecting against this type of food contamination is to avoid infecting the meat and to prevent rapid reproduction and increase in population. By avoiding storage at room temperature, this hazard can be reduced.

Meats and meat-containing dishes should be served soon after they are prepared, or held for service at 140°F, and leftovers should be refrigerated promptly, not allowed to sit on the kitchen counter for hours while cooling. Careful temperature control minimizes the reproductive capacity of these bacteria, which is very important because of the strong resistance to heat exhibited by the spores when they have formed. The usual practice of simply heating foods to a temperature of 165°F or more is not effective in killing *Clostridium perfringens*. Avoidance of growth is the key to reducing the possibility of contracting perfringens poisoning.

Clostridium perfringens Anaerobic, spore-forming bacteria that multiply readily at room temperature; ingestion can result in perfringens poisoning.

Nausea is a key symptom of perfringens poisoning. Vomiting does not occur, but there is a general feeling of discomfort due to irritation of both the stomach and the intestines.

Staphylococcal Infection Staphylococcal *toxin* infections (also referred to as staph) are particularly common, a fact due in large measure to the ease with

Toxin Poisonous substance produced by metabolic reactions; *S. aureus* and *Cl. botulinum* are the bacteria most commonly responsible for food poisoning from toxins.

Staphylococcal Poisoning Food poisoning due to ingestion of the enterotoxin produced by *Staphylococcus aureus;* violent disturbance of gastrointestinal tract for one to two days and occurring usually within 8 hours of eating the contaminated food.

Botulism Food poisoning caused by eating the toxin produced by *Cl. botulinum;* most commonly may be type A, B, or E.

Clostridium botulinum Type of bacteria producing a toxin that is highly poisonous and frequently fatal to humans when consumed.

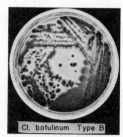

Cl. botulinum Type B

Culture of *Clostridium boltulinum* Type B. Canned meats and vegetables can be lethal sources of the toxin from this type of bacteria if heat processing during canning is inadequate.

which staphylococci can be transmitted by food handlers. The signs prominently displayed in restrooms cautioning people to be sure to wash their hands well with soap are a public effort to help eliminate staph infections. The infection is evidenced by vomiting, diarrhea, and stomach cramps and is due to eating food containing the toxin produced by *Staphylococcus aureus.* This strain of bacteria reproduces with vigor in the danger zone between 44° and 115°F, resulting in a dangerous level of toxin in a matter of hours. Symptoms are evident within 3 to 8 hours after ingestion and last for a day or two (although to the victim it seems more like an eternity).

Staphylococcal poisoning is thought to be the cause of between 75 and 80 percent of all diagnosed cases of food poisoning in the United States despite the frequent warnings issued on the safe handling of food. The foods that are particularly vulnerable to invasion and production of staphylococcal toxin include baked ham, creamed foods, poultry, cream pies, and milk and cheese products of all types. These types of foods are the ones requiring particularly careful attention to adequate refrigeration or to control of temperatures above 140°F to retard growth of staph and development of the toxin.

The toxin, once formed, is very resistant to heat, requiring boiling for several hours or cooking under pressure at 15 pounds per square inch (psi) for 30 minutes to render the toxin harmless to humans. Such extreme treatment decreases food quality; clearly, prevention of toxin formation is the important measure in preventing staphylococcal poisoning.

Botulism The other familiar type of bacterial poisoning from a toxin is *botulism,* a type of food poisoning that frequently may be fatal. The cause is ingestion of the toxin produced by any of several strains of *Clostridium botulinum.* The problem originates when foods contaminated with *Cl. botulinum* are not heat-processed adequately to kill the spores prior to anaerobic storage for a period of time.

Since these bacteria can survive nicely in an oxygen-free environment, some canned products may be subject to toxin production because the very heat-resistant spores of *Cl. botulinum* may not have been killed during the canning process. The problem is found most commonly in canned, low-acid foods such as vegetables and meats, poultry, or fish. Fruits, because of their acidity, are not receptive to the survival of *Cl. botulinum,* and an adequate heat treatment during canning is not difficult to accomplish.

Ingestion of the toxin is not always fatal, but it often is; the approximate statistic is that two out of three people who are infected will die. An idea of the potency of the toxin is gained when you know that a mere 0.35 micrograms of toxin will kill an adult.

The symptoms of botulism generally are related to the functioning of the nervous system, with the most severe reactions occurring in the respiratory system. Death, if it occurs, is caused ultimately by paralysis of the respiratory muscles. The initial symptoms are observed 12 to 36 hours after ingestion of the food containing the toxin. If a patient survives until the ninth day, the prognosis for recovery is good, although the recuperative process may be quite slow.

Table 17.1 Some Food-Borne Illnesses from Bacteria

Name of Illness	What Causes It	Symptoms	Characteristics of Illness	Control Measures
Salmonellosis	*Salmonellae.* Bacteria widespread in nature, live and grow in intestinal tracts of human beings and animals. About 1200 species are known; 1 species causes typhoid fever. Bacteria grow and multiply at temperatures between 44° and 115°F.	Severe headache, followed by vomiting, diarrhea, abdominal cramps, and fever. Infants, elderly, and persons with low resistance are most susceptible. Severe infections cause high fever and may even cause death.	Transmitted by eating contaminated food, or by contact with infected persons or carriers of the infection. Also transmitted by insects, rodents, and pets. Onset: usually within 12 to 36 hours. Duration: 2 to 7 days.	*Salmonellae* in food are destroyed by heating the food to a temperature of 140°F and holding for 10 minutes or to higher temperatures for less time. Refrigeration at 45°F inhibits the increase of *Salmonellae,* but they remain alive in the refrigerator or freezer, and even in dried foods.
Perfringens poisoning	*Clostridium perfringens.* Spore-forming bacteria that grow in the absence of oxygen. Spores can withstand temperatures usually reached in cooking most foods. Surviving bacteria continue to grow in cooked meats, gravies, and meat dishes held without proper refrigeration.	Nausea without vomiting, diarrhea, acute inflammation of stomach and intestines.	Transmitted by eating food contaminated with abnormally large numbers of the bacteria. Onset: usually within 8 to 20 hours. Duration: may persist for 24 hours.	To control growth of surviving bacteria on cooked meats that are to be eaten later, cool meats rapidly and refrigerate promptly at 40°F or below.
Streptococcal infections	*Streptococci.* Bacteria common in poultry; also in raw milk.	Sore throat	Transmitted by consuming raw milk.	Adequate heating, usually to at least 165°F.

			Onset: varies. Duration: usually several days.	
Staphylococcal poisoning (frequently called staph)	*Staphylococcus aureus.* Bacteria fairly resistant to heat. Bacteria growing in food produce a toxin that is extremely resistant to heat. Bacteria grow profusely with production of toxin at temperatures between 44° and 115°F.	Vomiting, diarrhea, prostration, abdominal cramps. Generally mild and often attributed to other causes.	Transmitted by food handlers who carry the bacteria and by eating food containing the toxin. Onset: usually within 3 to 8 hours. Duration: 1 or 2 days.	Growth of bacteria that produce toxin is inhibited by keeping hot foods above 140°F and cold foods at or below 40°F. Toxin is destroyed by boiling for several hours or heating the food in pressure cooker at 240°F for 30 minutes.
Botulism	*Clostridium botulinum.* Spore-forming organisms that grow and produce toxin in the absence of oxygen, such as in a sealed container. The bacteria can produce a toxin in low-acid foods that have been held in the refrigerator for 2 weeks or longer. Spores are extremely heat resistant. Spores are harmless, but the toxin is a deadly poison.	Double vision, inability to swallow, speech difficulty, progressive respiratory paralysis. Fatality rate is high, in the United States about 65 percent.	Transmitted by eating food containing the toxin. Onset: usually within 12 to 36 hours or longer. Duration: 3 to 6 days.	Bacterial spores in food are destroyed by high temperatures obtained only in the pressure canner. More than 6 hours is needed to kill the spores at boiling temperature (212°F). The toxin is destroyed by boiling for 10 or 20 minutes; time required depends on kind of food.

Occasional instances of botulism result from home-canned foods that have been processed inadequately, with the result that some spores of *Cl. botulinum* survived and the toxin was generated within the can. Although similar problems can occur in commercial canning, standards of quality control generally are far in excess to ensure avoiding this potential risk. Even so, an occasional "scare" does develop. Such episodes are publicized extensively in the media, and potentially hazardous items (cans from the problem lot) are recalled and removed from all markets.

To avoid problems, home-canned vegetables, meat, poultry, and fish should be boiled actively for 15 minutes prior even to tasting them. This is not necessary with fruits, because their acid generally is sufficient to discourage *Cl. botulinum* growth.

An important requisite for home canning any vegetables, fish, poultry, or meat is a pressure canner, for this is the only way that the food can be brought to a temperature high enough to ensure inactivation of the spores. In a pressure canner, the temperature will reach 240°F if the food is processed at a pressure of 15 pounds per square inch, which allows adequate heat processing for safety within a reasonable period of time.

People processing these low-acid foods must maintain pressure at the appropriate 15 psi throughout the required processing time. The safe processing period ordinarily is at least 25 minutes at 15 psi, but the number of containers being processed and the size of the containers will influence the recommendation. Since the time-temperature relationships are so critical to achieving safety in canned vegetables and meats, very careful timing for the number of minutes indicated at the correct pressure in a pressure canner must be done.

Animal Parasites

Sometimes foods are contaminated with small living organisms, occasionally in the egg or larval stages. If consumed in a viable state, these organisms (called *parasites*) may remain in the body and proceed through the reproductive and total life phases, relying on a parasitic relationship with the host. Such foreign organisms can pose serious health hazards.

Trichinosis is the most familiar parasitic disease in this country. The problem stems from eating meat, notably pork, which contains larvae of *Trichinella spiralis*. The presence of these larvae is fairly rare today, but the feeding of uncooked garbage to pigs (the most likely source of parasitic contamination) still occurs occasionally.

Since the potential exists for pork to be contaminated with *Trichinella spiralis* and since there is no way of detecting them by governmental inspection, appropriate cooking precautions need to be taken to kill any parasites that might be present. The heating of pork to an internal temperature of 170°F is the recommended way of ensuring against eating viable trichinae. Actually, the parasites are killed when the internal temperature of a cut of pork reaches at least 140°F, but the higher temperature (170°F) is recommended to ensure a suitable margin of safety without impairing the palatability of the meat. A meat thermometer is a convenient tool for measuring the degree of doneness

Parasite Organism living within another organism and deriving its sustenance from the host; worms, such as *Trichinella spiralis,* can cause weight loss and other health problems in people.

Trichinella spiralis larva encapsulated in muscle. This parasite occasionally may be found in pork. For safety, all pork should be heated to an internal temperature of 170°F.

in the center of the cut. Another means of killing trichinae is by freezing at 0°F for a minimum of one day or at 5°F for at least 20 days.

Although rarely fatal, trichinosis can be debilitating over an extended period. The larvae first are confined to the intestinal region, but they soon mature and produce larvae within the host before they die. Ultimately, the trichinae invade the muscular areas of the body only to become encapsulated in cystlike formations that may be viable as long as 10 years in the host. Symptoms in severe infestations may include diarrhea, nausea, and vomiting, but such reactions are intermittent. Over a period of weeks, recurring fever and muscular pains accompany the migration of larvae within the body. Treatment with thibenzole aids in controlling the course of the illness.

Parasitic invasions are not limited to *Trichinella spiralis.* Other worms may be introduced from a variety of sources, but the most common route is via the water supply. Filtering of water is necessary when the water supply is unsafe. Potable water also should be used to wash all fresh fruits and vegetables carefully to help avoid possible parasites. The other source of contamination may be food handlers who are careless about keeping their hands and their working areas in the kitchen clean.

Chemicals

Occasionally, a food may be contaminated with a heavy metal or other chemical substance that is toxic to the body. Perhaps the greatest source of accidental contamination with metals occurs in the kitchen when metal equipment becomes worn, exposing the core metal. For instance, copper or other base metal may reach unusually high levels in foods prepared with utensils so worn that the base metal reaches the food. Worn equipment should be thrown away.

Pesticides and other harmful chemicals should not be kept in the vicinity of food. Another important precaution is to be sure that any toxic compounds are labeled clearly and stored in cupboards away from the food preparation areas.

Contaminants in Fish

Shellfish Poisoning
Life-threatening poisoning from saxitoxin produced in shellfish feeding on *Gonyaulax catanella;* characterized by loss of strength and respiratory failure.

Gonyaulax catanella
One-celled organism in "red tide" that produces saxitoxin in infected shellfish.

Possible problems with environmental contaminants are certainly not a phenomenon of the past couple of decades. The maxim to eat oysters only in months with a "R" in their names emerged long before the current concern over detrimental changes in the environment, apparently because some people eating oysters in the summer months became ill. This illness, called *shellfish poisoning,* was and still is transmitted through clams and mussels, as well as oysters, at certain times of the year.

During the summer months and early fall, a one-celled organism, *Gonyaulax catanella,* is an abundant food for shellfish. In extremely large concentrations, this organism actually causes the fluorescence and reddish coloring of ocean water known familiarly as "red tide." However, somewhat lesser concentrations (insufficient to cause "red tide") still have the potential for causing shellfish poisoning when contaminated oysters or other shellfish are eaten.

The substance secreted by *Gonyaulax catanella* that actually causes the poisoning is *saxitoxin*, which is toxic enough to kill people but is not poisonous to the shellfish host. Saxitoxin accumulates in the digestive gland of the shellfish and may increase within a matter of three or four days from barely detectable to lethal levels.

Saxitoxin Poison secreted by *Gonyaulax catanella* within a shellfish host; capable of being concentrated enough to kill a person.

If a shellfish containing saxitoxin is eaten, the poison acts with startling rapidity, for death can ensue in as little as two hours after ingestion. Symptoms begin with a loss of strength in the extremities and the neck, followed by failure of the respiratory system. The quantity of poison ingested is a factor in determining whether or not the patient will survive. If the shellfish has been fried in oil and eaten as a part of a large meal, the toxic effects will be less than in other circumstances. Artificial respiration is an important aid in treating cases involving the respiratory system.

The most obvious means of avoiding this poisoning is to avoid shellfish from uncontrolled areas during times of possible problems. The risk can also be reduced by holding shellfish in clear water for a period of time to provide the opportunity for the shellfish to eliminate some of the poison. Oysters dissipate the saxitoxin relatively quickly, mussels are rather slow in eliminating saxitoxin, while butter clams are extremely slow.

The potential for shellfish poisoning can be reduced still further after the holding period in clear water by frying the shellfish meat or using steam or boiling water to help destroy the potency of the saxitoxin. Very high cooking temperatures and plenty of water to leach out the toxin are two effective devices to help reduce potential risk of shellfish poisoning.

Commercial fish canneries heat shellfish in steam to reduce greatly the amount of poison that might be present. Chemical tests provide yet another check against the toxin. In addition, the commercial harvesting of clams and mussels is done under the control of the government to reduce the hazard further.

Although shellfish poisoning is particularly dramatic, both ocean and freshwater fish are subject to other possible environmental hazards. Contaminated waters can cause contaminated fish. The presence of mercury, the result of uncontrolled effluents from factories into local waters, has been responsible for episodes of mercury poisoning from fish (swordfish, for example) and other seafood, such as some oysters harvested off the coast of Japan. Protests about such contamination and improved monitoring have helped to reduce the problem.

Fish are extremely susceptible to spoilage during the marketing process because the enzyme systems in fish are active at somewhat lower temperatures than are optimal for land animals, which makes appropriate handling imperative. Icing of fish helps to keep the temperature low enough to retard spoilage. Special attention is needed in handling oysters or other fish that might be consumed raw and in storing shrimp, for they may be eaten whole, digestive tract and all. Even with such precautions, fish will spoil quickly, necessitating either consumption within a day or two or else prompt processing (freezing, canning, or drying).

Fish spoil even more quickly than any other protein-rich foods, making cooking or icing (or freezing) soon after catching essential to food safety.

Why the Concern?

Microbiological contamination is a concern throughout the world, for contamination results in both economic and human losses. Considerable loss of food occurs due to spoilage either before reaching the consumer or while being stored by the consumer. Spoilage at any time represents an economic loss, whether to the farmer, the middlemen in the marketing chain, the retailer, or the consumer. Losses incurred prior to sale to the consumer ultimately will be reflected in increased costs to the purchaser at the point of sale. Unfortunately, losses do not stop here. Foods stored in the home also are susceptible to spoilage by microorganisms. For instance, if some potatoes spoil while being held in a bag in the home, they are thrown away—clearly adding to the cost of food in the home.

With the worldwide concern about adequate supplies, food spoilage translates dramatically into human terms. For instance, grain that ferments before distribution represents a tragic loss to those needing the food simply for survival. And when food is scarce, even contaminated food may be eaten, causing serious health problems, as sometimes is the case when moldy peanuts are distributed for consumption.

Although not life threatening, anyone who has endured a food-borne illness will certainly wish to avoid a recurrence of the discomfort. Often, too, such episodes represent not only an unpleasant period for the person afflicted but also an economic loss because of the person's inability to work during that time. No good figures are available to tell accurately the cost of food-borne illnesses, but the problem is all too common, particularly when most episodes could be avoided with improved food handling practices.

MAINTAINING FOOD SAFELY

Even when food is safe from harmful levels of microorganisms when brought into the kitchen, the potential for food-borne illnesses still exists. Whether in a commercial food establishment or in the home, standards of hygiene need to be maintained in all aspects of food preparation. There are three key areas to check when monitoring food safety: (1) personal hygiene of the food handler, (2) kitchen sanitation, and (3) storage conditions and practices.

The Food Handler

Habits that may prevent transport of microorganisms from the food handler to the food are vital to maintaining high standards of sanitation. As a starting point, all people handling food should be sure to wash their hands thoroughly with soap and hot water before beginning preparation and again at any time that the hands are used to touch hair or blow the nose. Any restroom stop should end with a thorough hand washing before returning to the kitchen or laboratory. Personal habits, such as licking fingers or playing with a lock of hair, need to be recognized and corrected.

Although tasting is necessary to be sure that seasonings are right, only clean utensils should be used for tasting. Tasting utensils should be used only once in a food. Otherwise, the taster's saliva will contaminate the food.

Kitchen Sanitation

Clean food can only be prepared in a clean kitchen. All dishes need to be scrubbed thoroughly, washed in soap or detergent and hot water, and rinsed thoroughly in very hot water. Both the heat of the water and the sanitizing afforded by the detergent and a good rinsing are valuable in killing microorganisms that might otherwise remain and contaminate food subsequently.

All surfaces in the food preparation area should be washed carefully with soap and water after each use, with particular attention being given to such difficult areas as the rim around the sink and grouting between tiles. This also includes the top of the range.

Cutting boards require special attention, for they can easily be a source of contamination, particularly for foods that are going to be served without additional heating after being cut on the cutting board. Ideally, cutting boards are made of plastic because of their easy maintenance in a sanitary condition. Wooden cutting boards need to be scrubbed vigorously with soap and hot water or chlorine solution and then rinsed thoroughly to be certain to eliminate microorganisms that might tend to collect in the cuts in the surface.

Storage Conditions and Practices

Because of the tremendous impact of temperature on the survival and growth of microorganisms, careful attention to food temperatures is of great importance in assuring the safety of protein-rich foods. Refrigerator should be monitored to be certain that they are maintaining a temperature no higher than 40°F, the range needed to retard reproduction and growth of most microorganisms that might be present. Cold foods should be kept refrigerated, removing them from the refrigerator only for efficient preparation and service. Extended periods standing at room temperature should be avoided.

Leftovers should be cared for promptly after the meal. Hot foods should be cooled as quickly as possible to the point where they can be placed in the refrigerator without raising the temperature of the refrigerator above 45°F. The refrigerator will be able to return quickly to its desired cool temperature while also completing the rapid chilling of the leftover. By stripping the meat from the bones of turkeys and scooping the dressing from the cavity, this bulky and potentially hazardous type of leftover can be cooled and refrigerated very quickly after roasting and serving.

After preparation, protein-containing foods that are to be served cold should be chilled until serving time. Meringue and custard pies should be refrigerated when the pan has cooled sufficiently to be held comfortably in the hand. Cakes with cream fillings can be refrigerated as soon as the icing has been added. Potato salad, egg salad, tuna salad, and other protein-rich salads should be kept refrigerated at all times except when being served. Their abundance of cut surfaces makes them prime targets for microorganisms.

CONTROL OF FOOD WASTE

Short Term

Many foods can be moved through the marketing chain and consumed in the home without spoiling if attention is given to the handling of food during this comparatively short interval of time. One of the keys to successful control of food waste of fresh foods is to handle the food carefully at all stages. Fresh produce contains enzymes that are capable of catalyzing chemical changes in fresh fruits and vegetables. These changes shorten the length of time these foods can be held in the marketing process. If bruising can be avoided, enzyme changes will not occur as readily as they do in bruised tissues of fruits and vegetables. A particularly important means of controlling enzyme-catalyzed spoilage is to chill most fresh produce as soon as it is harvested and to continue to keep it at refrigerator temperatures during all phases of marketing and storage. Such treatment also helps to keep microorganisms under control.

In addition to controlling temperatures when handling fresh produce, control of the atmosphere is important. Some moisture is needed in the air to prevent dehydration during storage, but too much moisture can encourage growth of molds. Some storage units have controlled atmospheres, with the levels of both carbon dioxide and moisture being regulated carefully. Sometimes other gases, such as ethylene gas, may be introduced at controlled levels to help achieve optimal quality of bananas and other fresh produce. Related to the control of gases and moisture is the need for some circulation of air among the stored foods.

Some foods, particularly the cereal grains, are attractive to mice and other rodents. To avoid food waste of this nature, rodents and insects must be eliminated from storage areas.

In the home, hydrator drawers need to be kept clean in refrigerators to avoid contaminating newly purchased produce with microorganisms remaining from previous produce. A cool, dry area is needed for storage of such items as potatoes and winter squash. In addition, these items should be checked regularly to be sure that no spoiling items are being held to contaminate the remainder of the lot. In addition, purchase of all fresh produce (whether intended for storage in the refrigerator or at cool room temperature), of all protein-rich foods (meats, milk, and similar foods), and of cereal products (including flour and pastas) should be planned to avoid long storage periods. Purchase of just the amounts that will be used before they spoil can be the key to preventing food spoilage.

Long Term

Storage of foods for extended periods will require special processing to avoid spoilage. Fortunately, through various means, foods are now available virtually all year long in one form or another. The methods commonly used for making foods resistant to spoilage during long-term storage include canning, freezing, preserving with sugar, pickling, and drying. The mechanisms of destroying the microorganisms in foods differ for these various methods (see Chapter 16).

ADDITIVES

What Are Additives?

Additives Substances added by intent or by accident into foods.

FDA Food and Drug Administration; the federal agency regulating food additives.

Food Additives Amendment of 1958 Amendment to the Food, Drug, and Cosmetic Act of 1938; regulates food additive usage.

GRAS List List of over 680 additives considered to be safe and legal to use while testing of the numerous additives was being conducted.

Additives are substances added either by intent or by accident into foods. The former are termed intentional additives, and the latter are incidental additives. The incidental additives are the result of carelessness in food processing or preparation and are to be avoided. This section of the chapter will focus on intentional additives. These substances are regulated by the Food and Drug Administration (*FDA*) in the Department of Health and Human Services; legal authority stems from the *Food Additives Amendment of 1958* and the Food, Drug, and Cosmetic Act of 1938.

Hundreds of substances are potential ingredients in food products today; many have been in use for many years, in fact, well before the Food Additives Amendment of 1958. The amendment called for a review of the safety of the various additives in use at that time or being proposed for use in the future. To approach this assignment, the FDA appointed a group of experts to identify the additives it considered to be safe for use, based on previous use in foods for many years. The result of the work of this group was the development of the *GRAS list,* a list of over 680 additives that were "Generally Recognized as Safe." Substances on the GRAS list were permitted to be used while vast series of tests were conducted over a period of years to prove that the various additives actually are safe for humans.

Carcinogens Capable of causing cancer.

Delaney Clause Clause in the Food Additives Amendment mandating that additives shown to cause cancer at any level must be removed from the marketplace.

Work to test the safety of the various additives, particularly to identify any potential *carcinogens*, has been proceeding in laboratories across the country. If an additive is found to cause cancer at any level (regardless of whether or not that level would be consumed by a person), the *Delaney clause* of the Food Additives Amendment requires that the additive not be permitted to be used. This clause was the basis for the banning of cyclamates. However, the Delaney clause is being challenged, with the result that saccharin (also shown to be carcinogenic in a study challenged by some authorities) is still on the market through special authorization.

Why Are Additives Used?

A very general answer to the question of using additives is that additives improve food quality. Actually, this answer barely skims the surface, for various additives may improve food quality in many different ways. The specific reasons for using an additive may include one or more of the following:

1. Extend shelf life.
2. Improve nutritive value.
3. Improve color.
4. Improve flavor.
5. Improve texture.
6. Control pH.
7. Leaven.
8. Bleaching and maturing.
9. Facilitate food preparation.

Extending shelf life can mean a saving in money and in food. Risks of food-borne illnesses can be reduced by the use of some additives. Similarly, the other reasons for adding various substances influence consumer food choices by enhancing the sensory appeal of foods, increasing nutrient value, or providing some other function valued by consumers. Although some people prefer to avoid food additives by preparing almost all their foods from the basic ingredients, many prefer to buy at least some items that contain additives in their formulations. These consumers may be attracted by the nutritive merits, convenience, and time saving or by such quality attributes as color, texture, and flavor. Regardless of the reasons a consumer cites, the decision to buy an item containing food additives is evidence that many people feel that the benefits clearly outweigh any possible risk associated with the use of additives.

How Are Additives Categorized?

Since additives can do so many things, it is not surprising that additives are classified according to their specific qualities. The *Federal Register 39(185): 34175 (1974)* has classified additives according to technical functions:

1. Anticaking agents (free-flowing agents).

2. Antimicrobial agents.

3. Antioxidants (prevent oxidation of fats and nutrients).

4. Colors, coloring adjuncts (including color stabilizers, color fixatives, color-retentive agents, etc.).

5. Curing, pickling agents.

6. Dough strengtheners.

7. Drying agents.

8. Emulsifiers, emulsifier salts.

9. Enzymes.

10. Flavor enhancers.

11. Firming agents.

12. Flavoring agents, adjuvants.

13. Flour-treating agents (including bleaching and maturing agents).

14. Formulation aids (including carriers, binders, fillers, plasticizers, film-formers, etc.).

15. Fumigants.

16. Humectants (moisture-retention agents), antidusting agents.

17. Leavening agents.

18. Lubricants, release agents.

19. Nonnutritive sweeteners.

20. Nutrient supplements.

21. Nutritive sweeteners.

22. Oxidizing and reducing agents.

23. pH control agents (including buffers, acids, alkalies, neutralizing agents).

24. Processing aids (including clarifying agents, clouding agents, catalysts, flocculents, filter aids, etc.).

25. Propellants (aerating agents), gases.

26. Sequestrants (binding of metal ions).

27. Solvents, vehicles.

28. Stabilizers, thickeners (including suspending and bodying agents, setting agents, gelling agents, bulking agents, etc.).

29. Surface-active agents (other than emulsifiers, including solubilizing agents, dispersants, detergents, wetting agents, rehydration enhancers, whipping agents, foaming agents, defoaming agents, etc.).

30. Surface-finishing agents (including glazes, polishes, waxes, protective coatings).

31. Synergists (enhancers of other additives).

32. Texturizers.

This extensive list outlines many specific roles of the various types of additives in modifying food products to make them successful commercially, both from the perspective of quality maintenance throughout marketing and the quality characteristics the consumer is presumed to desire. Manufacturers use many of the additives to give their products increased consumer appeal. The importance of such an obvious characteristic as food color has a tremendous impact on consumer acceptance, a fact that was illustrated dramatically in the years when oleomargarine manufacturers were not permitted to color their naturally white product a butter-yellow color. Sales of margarine were distinctly sluggish until legislation changed and the product could be colored. Clearly, a white spread on bread lacked appeal. Too, people tend to pick the cherry pie with the cherry-red filling rather than the subdued canned cherry color. Illustrations of this type abound throughout the food marketplace. The use of additives to enhance the appeal of a food is done by manufacturers because consumers respond by buying the modified food products.

Federal regulations aid consumers in their desire to know what is in the foods they eat by requiring that additives be listed in the ingredient label on each package. Ingredient labeling lists all ingredients in decreasing order of the amount (by weight) in the product. Since most additives are used in comparatively small quantities, they often are toward the end of the label. The chemical name of an ingredient or additive is not terribly informative to the average consumer, so many food processors now are providing a very brief explanation of the reason for the various additives listed on the label. This is being done to help relieve consumer anxiety about additives.

There are so many different additives that it is not reasonable to expect people to recognize the reasons for their inclusion in a food. However, it is useful at times to be able to identify the reason for using a particular additive. Appendix A provides this information about some of the additives used commonly in the American food supply.

Incidental Contaminants

The additives identified in the preceding section—intentional additives—are used in formulating the food for a specific purpose. These substances are legal when used according to the regulations mandated through the FDA. The other type of additives—incidental contaminants—is not desirable and should not be found in foods, for example, a stem from a pea plant or a rodent hair. Fortunately, the heat treatment utilized in canning foods makes these contaminants safe, if not very pleasing. In addition, the size of such items makes them readily apparent to anyone preparing the food, and they can be removed without harm.

Insect infestations, particularly of grain products, represent a range of incidental contaminants that might be introduced to the food during storage. Detection presents some difficulties, although considerable effort has been expended to attempt to develop good tests for insects. Visual observation tests are only moderately successful because the eggs of insects may be buried within kernels. A staining technique aids detection by staining the plugs covering the holes where insects have laid eggs. Other useful tests include flotation tests, density differences, and X-ray radiography.

Insects create problems in the various stages from larva, to pupa, and the adult stage, as well as in the egg phase. For example, some beetles have been found to shed more than 10 skins. Beetles and cockroaches are highly visible; mites are so small that they are very difficult to see in grains. However, it is clear that when any type of insect invades a food, other insects are likely to follow.

Serious economic losses can be the result of insect invasions into foods. Entire carloads of grain may be declared to be filthy and unfit for human use. The original contamination can be controlled somewhat by avoiding storing any infested grains and by thoroughly cleaning any storage area before introducing fresh grain for storage. Storage in a cool, dry environment retards the life cycle and reproduction of many of the pests. The presence of these uninvited guests is not limited to granaries and warehouses, for insects may hatch while being stored in the home. Storage in metal or glass containers helps to prevent insect infestation into uncontaminated foods.

Rodent control is another important line of defense in protecting food from incidental contaminants. Well-constructed warehouses and granaries represent a good line of defense, but careful monitoring and elimination of any rodents in the vicinity must be maintained to avoid this source of contamination.

NATURAL TOXICANTS

The additives used in producing foods commercially are tested for their safety. However, no such testing occurs as nature synthesizes foods. For the most part, the foods normally eaten are quite free of harmful substances. Some compounds tend to block utilization of nutrients; certain others have physiological effects, particularly in sensitive people. A listing of some of the toxicants found in foods is given in Table 17.2.

Herb teas represent an interesting dilemma to persons seeking to avoid the possible harm of caffeine. Herb teas do not contain caffeine; on the other hand, their various chemical constituents have not been analyzed or studied for possible harm. The process of brewing herbal teas does extract water-soluble components into the beverage. With the increased consumption of the many types of herb teas, there is need to increase the research on the safety of these products. In the meantime, there may be some wisdom in avoiding a high intake of any one particular type of herbal tea.

SUMMARY

Food safety is a vital concern of all consumers, whether the food being eaten is prepared from basic ingredients in the home or whether it is produced in factories or large food service facilities. A key part of maintaining safe food is to control contamination by microorganisms (bacteria, yeast, and molds), as

Table 17.2 Some Natural Toxicants Found in Foods

Toxicant	Food Source	Characteristics
Unidentified	Fava beans	Hemolysis, vomiting, dizziness, prostration
Aflatoxin	Moldy peanuts contaminated with *A. flavus*	Liver damage, chronic consumption may lead to cancer.
Ergot	Moldy rye	Severe muscle contraction, serious to fatal nervous system involvement
Antitrypsin	Legumes (raw)	Blocks protein digestion; inactivated by heat
Goitrogen	Cabbage	Blocks thyroxin synthesis
Phytin	Cereals	Restricts absorption of calcium and iron
Solanine	Sun-burned potatoes	Vomiting and diarrhea
Oxalic acid	Rhubarb, spinach	Restricts calcium absorption
Caffeine	Coffee	Possible carcinogen and teratogen
Benzopyrene	Charcoal-broiled meats	Carcinogen
Nitrates and nitrites	Cured meats, some vegetables	Potential carcinogen
Gossypol	Cottonseed	Toxic to animals
Cyanogens (amygdalin)	Almonds, peach and apricot pits	Headache, heart palpitations, weakness; can be fatal

well as parasites, which can cause food-borne illnesses. Salmonellosis, perfringens poisoning, and streptococcal infections are familiar examples of bacterial infections causing sickness in people. The toxins produced by staphylococci and by *Clostridium botulinum* are other causes of illness. Botulism is particularly serious because of its potential for being fatal.

Control of these types of food-borne illnesses can be effected by careful use of heat in cooking and processing and by appropriate cold storage. The danger zone for reproduction of many microorganisms is between 40° and 140°F, necessitating refrigerated storage or cooking and holding protein-rich foods at temperatures above the danger zone. High standards of sanitation in maintaining the kitchen and among people handling food are important to keep microorganismal contamination to a minimum. Thorough washing of fresh produce with safe water is an important means of avoiding animal parasites; trichinosis, usually traced to contaminated pork, can be controlled by cooking pork to a uniform internal temperature of 170°F. Shellfish poisoning due to saxitoxin produced by *Gonyaulax catanella* is a particular problem in the summer months.

Food can be kept safe for later consumption by a variety of preserving methods, including canning, freezing, drying, and preserving with sugar. Vegetables and meats need to be canned in a pressure canner to reach the high temperature needed for killing the spores of *Cl. botulinum* that might be present and flourish in these low-acid foods. Water bath canning is adequate for fruits. Freezing is a successful and simple technique for preserving food if frozen storage is available. Drying is the oldest of the preserving methods and is useful, despite the significant changes it causes in color, and texture.

Food additives, monitored by the FDA, are of two types: incidental and intentional. Intentional additives are used to extend the shelf life of foods, to improve nutritive value, and to enhance food quality. Many additives were originally placed on the GRAS list and have subsequently been tested for safety. New substances being proposed for use as additives must be approved by the FDA before they can be included in foods. Incidental contaminants, notably insect and rodent contaminants, need to be kept to an absolute minimum through careful storage and monitoring techniques.

Some natural toxicants are found in foods. The severity of the problem ranges from the possibly fatal result of consuming cyanogens in almonds and the pits of apricots and peaches to a minor influence in restricting mineral absorption. Herb teas generally are safe, but the toxicants they may contain have not been studied.

Selected References

Anderson, A. W. Significance of yeasts and molds in foods. *Food Tech. 31(2)*: 47. 1977.

Anonymous. Yesterday's additives = generally safe. *FDA Consumer 15(2)*: 14. 1981.

Asner, M. Worms that turn good food into bad. *FDA Consumer 16(7)*: 4. 1982.

Ayres, J. C. et al. *Microbiology of Foods*. W. H. Freeman. San Francisco. 1980.

Ballentine, C. L. and M. L. Herndon. Who, why, when and where of food poisons. *FDA Consumer 16(6)*: 24. 1982.

Clydesdale, F. *Food Science and Nutrition*. Prentice-Hall. Englewood Cliffs, N.J. 1979.

Engel, R. E. Status of USDA microbiological criteria. *Food Tech. 32(1)*: 61. 1978.

Fruin, J. T. and L. S. Gutherlz, Survival of bacteria in food cooked by microwave oven, conventional oven, and slow cookers. *J. Food Protection 45(8)*: 695. 1982.

Getoff, M. M. Unsafe food practices in the kitchen. *J. Home Econ. 70(1)*: 45. 1978.

Hall, R. L. Food additives. *Nutrition Today 8(4)*: 20. 1973.

Hopkins, H. Color additive scoreboard. *FDA Consumer 14(2)*: 25. 1980.

Larkin, T. Herbs are often more toxic than magical. *FDA Consumer 17(8)*: 4. 1983.

McWilliams, M. and H. Paine. *Modern Food Preservation*. Plycon Press. Redondo Beach, Calif. 1977.

Ryno, R. R. and M. W. Leftwich. Exposure time of warm leftovers to temperatures suitable for microbial growth in home type refrigerator. *J. Food Protection 44(7)*: 513. 1981.

Sauer, F. Control of yeasts and molds with peservatives. *Food Tech. 31(2)*: 66. 1977.

Walker, H. W. Spoilage of foods by yeasts. *Food Tech. 31(2)*: 57. 1977.

Zottola, E. A. and J. D. Wolf. Recipe hazard analysis—RHAS—a systematic approach to analyzing potential hazards in a recipe for food preparation/preservation. *J. Food Protection 44(7)*: 560. 1981.

Study Questions

1. What types of food poisoning may result from poor handling of food during processing or in the home?
2. What are some precautions that can be taken to reduce the possibility of contracting a food-borne illness?

3. What foods are the probable source of the various types of food-borne illnesses?
4. What type of poisoning may result from eating improperly processed home-canned vegetables or meats? How may this hazard be controlled?
5. Why might an additive be introduced in the commercial preparation of a food?
6. What agency enforces the Food, Drug, and Cosmetic Act and the Food Additives Amendment?
7. Explain the use of five different additives commonly used.
8. Identify five sources of natural toxicants.

PART TWO

FOOD IN THE CONTEXT OF LIFE

Grant Wood, "Fall Plowing." Courtesy John Deere Art Collection.

CHAPTER 18

NUTRITION AND FOOD

NUTRITION, THE
ULTIMATE APPLICATION OF FOOD

Throughout this book, the nutritional merits of various foods and the implications that preparation techniques have on nutritive value have been discussed, for the ultimate purpose of food is to provide nourishment. These comments will be particularly meaningful when you know the reasons the body needs various nutrients.

Everybody needs energy to do work, even simply to maintain life itself; children also must have energy for their dynamic growth. This energy is provided by three groups of nutrients: carbohydrates, lipids, and proteins. Carbohydrates and proteins, gram per gram, provide less than half as much energy as is available from lipids (fats). Although it is true that all people need energy to live, one of the most challenging and frustrating facets of food for many people is eating an appropriate quantity to get the right amount of energy. Too many *calories* (also called kilocalories) provide more energy than the body uses, and the surplus is converted and stored as fat. Overweight or obesity will be the result if this pattern of overeating persists. On the other hand, eating too few calories will cause people to be too thin. The amount of calories eaten regularly, day after day, can be controlled appropriately in relation to energy needs through wise food choices and also through use of sound principles of food preparation.

The preoccupation of the general public with the subject of dieting and weight control often tends to overshadow the fact that other nutrients are essential for a wide range of specific chemical reactions and for some other key functions. For example, some minerals are necessary to form the structure of the body, while certain minerals and vitamins are essential to catalyze innumerable chemical reactions and to synthesize vital compounds.

Calories Unit of energy provided in a food. One calorie (also called kilocalorie) is the amount of heat energy required to raise 1 kilogram of water 1° Celsius.

Carbohydrates

Carbohydrates capable of providing energy to the body include different types of sugars and certain complex carbohydrates, notably dextrins and starch. Among the sugars, sucrose (the type of carbohydrate constituting granulated, powdered, and brown sugar) is perhaps the most familiar, but fructose, glucose, galactose, maltose, and lactose are other sugars occurring in foods. These sugars are comparatively simple carbohydrates, being categorized as monosaccharides or disaccharides, depending on the size of their molecules.

To utilize the disaccharides (sucrose, maltose, and lactose), these sugars are digested to monosaccharides (fructose, glucose, and galactose) and then absorbed.

The simplest of the sugars, the monosaccharides do not require digestion because they are able to pass directly through the wall of the small intestine and into the blood. Through a series of chemical changes in the body, referred to technically as *metabolism*, absorbed monosaccharides are broken down to provide energy to the body.

Metabolism Chemical reactions in the body; the release of energy from carbohydrates is but one example.

Sugars of various types are used in preparing desserts, candies, and other foods which are sources of carbohydrates for energy.

Carbohydrates considerably larger than the disaccharides are common in some foods and also are good sources of energy. These compounds, called polysaccharides because of their size, include starch and dextrins. Starch actually represents the substance in which plants store energy. Fortunately, the human body can digest the starch in potatoes and other foods until finally the monosaccharide, glucose, is produced and absorbed for use in the body. Dextrins are quite similar to starch, but they are somewhat smaller molecules.

Fiber Components of food not digested and absorbed; cellulose, pectic substances, and gums are plant carbohydrates contributing to the fiber content of the diet.

Not only are carbohydrates valued for their energy value, but certain polysaccharides are important as *fiber* or roughage in the diet. Cellulose, pectic substances, and several gums from plants are polysaccharides. However, these carbohydrates are not digested and absorbed in the small intestine, as is the case with the disaccharides and polysaccharides mentioned previously. Instead, these particular carbohydrates serve as irritants to the gastrointestinal tract and help to keep the food mass moving through the intestines, thus providing useful momentum for the elimination of waste materials from the body. Although cellulose and the other polysaccharides comprising fiber are not incorporated into the body to serve as sources of energy, they nevertheless are key dietary components for good health.

Lipids

Lipids are fatty substances serving as carriers of the fat-soluble vitamins (vitamins A, D, E, and K) as well as providing the essential fatty acid, linoleic acid, and energy. Not only do fats make foods taste good, but they also add to the feeling of satisfaction after a meal. Their structures are largely carbon and hydrogen, with only a small amount of oxygen. It is this combination that causes fats to be more concentrated sources of energy than are carbohydrates.

When fats are eaten, they are digested to their two component parts: fatty acids and glycerol. Most fats contain three fatty acids and one glycerol

Triglyceride Fat containing three fatty acids.

unit. These fats, called *triglycerides*, are found in foods from animals and in oils from plants, such as corn oil and safflower oil. The fatty acids and glycerol are absorbed through the intestinal wall and are recombined into fats in the body. Eventually, the lipids in the body will be utilized by freeing the fatty acids and then metabolizing them into short fragments capable of joining with a compound formed during carbohydrate metabolism. After additional reactions, energy will be released.

Proteins

Proteins are extremely important constituents of the body. Muscle tissue, connective tissue, the blood, antibodies, and many other substances in the body contain proteins, each of which is made to meet specific physical requirements. It is not possible to eat the specific protein you need for a particular function. Instead, the protein molecules in meats and many other foods are digested in the gastrointestinal tract until the individual components, the amino acids, are released in the small intestine and absorbed. Remarkably, the body can take these individual amino acids and synthesize the needed proteins.

There are more than 20 amino acids required to make the various proteins your body needs. Each of these amino acids has a slightly different structure, but nitrogen (in combination with hydrogen as an amino group), carbon, hydrogen, and oxygen (forming an acid) are found in all amino acids. To make proteins in the body, many individual amino acids must be com-

Fish can be prepared with other ingredients to provide exciting flavor accents; nutritionally, fish of all types are excellent sources of complete proteins and are rather low in calories.

bined in the appropriate sequence for a specific product. Some of the necessary amino acids can be produced in the body, which is the reason these are termed nonessential amino acids. Others must be available from the food that is eaten because the body is unable to make these *essential amino acids*. There are 9 essential amino acids, and these must be eaten in adequate amounts if a person is to be nourished adequately and maintain good health.

Essential Amino Acids Amino acids that must be provided in the diet to maintain life and promote growth; unable to be synthesized in the body.

Minerals

Food contains many other constituents besides the energy nutrients. Although present in much smaller quantities than the carbohydrates, lipids, and proteins, minerals are widespread throughout the food supply in sufficient quantities to meet physical needs if a wide variety of foods is eaten. Actually, there are many different *minerals*. Those found in the largest amounts—calcium, phosphorus, potassium, sulfur, sodium, chloride, and magnesium—are termed macronutrients. The micronutrient minerals include iron, zinc, manganese, selenium, copper, and iodine, as well as some other minerals found in minute quantities.

Minerals Natural elements in foods that remain as ash if a food is burned; many are essential nutrients.

The various minerals play different roles in the body. Some are essential to the structure of the bones and teeth, as well as being components of numerous compounds, such as hemoglobin in the blood and thyroxin, an important hormone. The balance between acids and bases in the body is regulated by some of the minerals acting as buffers to prevent shifts that would create too acidic or too basic a medium. In conjunction with protein, minerals help to maintain the appropriate balance of water in the various parts of the body. The ability of some minerals to ionize enables them to help in transmitting nerve impulses and contracting and relaxing muscles. Certain chemical reactions are able to occur in the body because specific minerals act as catalysts.

Each mineral has some unique functions in human nutrition. A brief overview of these functions and some food sources of many of the essential minerals are presented in Table 18.1. Because of the diverse functions and the wide range of foods providing significant sources of these minerals, you will need to eat a diet that includes animal and plant foods to be certain that your diet is adequate.

Vitamins

If ever a group of nutrients was viewed by the general public as being pure magic, surely *vitamins* would be the group for many people feel that swallowing a vitamin pill will solve all of their nutritional problems. Certainly vitamins are vital to life itself, but they represent only a portion of the nutrients people must eat in order to live.

Vitamins Organic compounds needed in very small amounts by the body to maintain life and promote growth and that must be included in the diet.

On the basis of their solubility, vitamins are classified as fat soluble and water soluble. There are only four fat-soluble vitamins: vitamins A, D, E, and K. The water-soluble vitamins include the B vitamins and vitamin C, also called ascorbic acid. This simple listing of the water-soluble vitamins becomes

Table 18.1 Overview of Functions and Sources of Minerals Needed by Humans

Mineral	Functions	Selected Food Sources
Calcium	Promotion of bone structure and maintenance, structure of teeth, blood clotting, muscle contraction	Milk and milk-containing products, including cheese; broccoli, greens
Chloride	Formation of hydrochloric acid in stomach, fluid balance, acid-base balance	Salt, meats, milk, cheese, eggs
Chromium	Promotion of glucose uptake in cells	Fruits, vegetables, whole-grain cereals
Cobalt	A component of vitamin B_{12}	Meats, organ meats
Copper	Catalyzing hemoglobin formation, form connective tissue, energy release	Meats, cereals, nuts, legumes, liver, shellfish
Fluoride	Strengthening bones and teeth	Fluoridated water
Iodine	Formation of thyroxin to regulate basal metabolism	Iodized salt, ocean fish
Iron	Formation of hemoglobin and cytochromes for transporting oxygen and releasing energy, respectively	Meats, organ meats, dried fruits, whole-grain and enriched cereals
Magnesium	Promotion of energy reactions (ATP formation), bone maintenance, conduct nerve impulses	Milk, green vegetables, nuts, breads and cereals
Manganese	Development of bone, amino acid metabolism	Cereals, legumes
Molybdenum	Oxidation reactions	Legumes, meats
Phosphorus	Promotion of bone and tooth formation, bone maintenance; component of DNA, RNA, ADP, ATP, TPP for metabolic reactions	Meats, poultry, fish, milk, cheese, legumes, nuts
Potassium	Maintenance of osmotic pressure and acid-base balance, transmit nerve impulses	Orange, dried fruits, bananas, meats, coffee, peanut butter
Sodium	Maintenance of osmotic pressure and acid-base balance, relax muscles	Salt, cured meats, milk, olives, chips, crackers
Sulfur	A component of thiamin, part of structural proteins in hair, nails, and skin	Meats, milk, cheese, eggs, legumes, nuts
Zinc	Promotion of protein metabolism, transfer of carbon dioxide	Whole-grain cereals, meats, eggs, legumes

ATP = adenosine triphosphate; DNA = deoxyribonucleic acid; RNA = ribonucleic acid; ADP = adenosine diphosphate; TPP = thiamin pyrophosphate.

more complicated as the B vitamins, also called the B complex, are enumerated: vitamin B_1, commonly called thiamin; vitamin B_2, usually called riboflavin; vitamin B_3, almost always referred to simply as niacin; pantothenic acid; folacin, also titled folic acid; vitamin B_6 or pyridoxine; vitamin B_{12} or cobalamin; and biotin.

Although vitamins are needed in only milligram or even microgram quantities daily, attention must be given to selecting foods containing these important substances and to preparing these foods carefully to retain the vitamin content. Unlike minerals, which tend to be held tightly within foods, vitamins may be leached out into the cooking medium or may undergo chemical changes during preparation, resulting in reduced nutritive value of the food as actually consumed. Throughout this book, comments are given regarding vitamin content of foods and ways of retaining optimal levels compatible with the preparation of high-quality food products.

The various vitamins perform a wide range of functions within the human body. Unless adequate amounts of the individual vitamins are provided in the diet, deficiency conditions will develop. The functions, food sources, and deficiency conditions for the various vitamins are presented in Table 18.2.

Table 18.2 Vitamins, Their Functions, Sources, and Deficiency Conditions

Vitamin	Functions	Selected Food Sources	Deficiency Condition
Fat Soluble			
A	Promotion of night vision, growth, health of eye and skin, resistance to bacterial infections	Liver, egg yolk, milk, sweet potatoes, carrots, greens	Night blindness, xerophthalmia, Bitot's spots, poor growth
D	An aid in absorbing calcium and phosphorus	Vitamin-D–fortified milk, eggs, cheese	Rickets, osteomalacia
E	Spare vitamins A and C (prevent oxidation)	Vegetable oils, greens	
K	Formation of prothrombin and proconvertin for blood clotting	Greens, liver, egg yolks	Hemorrhage
Water Soluble			
Thiamin	Release of energy (in TPP), form ribose for DNA and RNA synthesis	Meats, whole-grain and enriched cereals	Beriberi
Riboflavin	Release of energy (in FMN and FAD), convert tryptophan to niacin	Milk, green vegetables, fish, meat	Ariboflavinosis

Table 18.2 *(Continued)*

Vitamin	Functions	Selected Food Sources	Deficiency Condition
Niacin	Release of energy (as part of NAD and NADP), fatty acid synthesis	Meat, poultry, fish, peanut butter, cereals	Pellagra
Pantothenic acid	Part of coenzyme A (to metabolize fatty acids), form hemoglobin and steroids	Whole-grain cereals, organ meats	Fatigue, lack of antibodies
Folacin	Transfer single-carbon units, make amino acids and other compounds	Greens, mushrooms, vegetables, fruits	Macrocytic anemia
Vitamin B$_6$	Transaminate and deaminate amino acids, convert tryptophan to niacin	Meats, whole-grain cereals, lima beans, potatoes	
Vitamin B$_{12}$	Aid in maturing red blood cells, energy for central nervous system, convert folacin to active form	Animal foods	Pernicious anemia
Biotin	Release energy, deaminate amino acids	Egg yolks, milk, cereals, nuts	
Vitamin C	Form connective tissue, absorption of calcium, strengthen capillaries	Citrus fruits, tropical fruits, tomatoes, cabbage	Scurvy

TPP = thiamin pyrophosphate; DNA = deoxyribonucleic acid; RNA = ribonucleic acid; FMN = flavin mononucleotide; FAD = flavin adenine dinucleotide; NAD = nicotinamide dinucleotide; NADP = the phosphate form of NAD.

Food and Nutrition Board A group operating under the auspices of the National Academy of Sciences–National Research Council; members appointed to the group are nationally recognized researchers in nutrition.

RDA Recommended Dietary Allowances specified by the Food and Nutrition Board to provide standards for professionals to utilize in planning diets and projects for groups of people in normal good health.

Recommended Dietary Allowances

Complete understanding of nutrition and the body's use of nutrients has not yet been achieved, but much is known to help guide people in their quest for good health through wise food selection. To aid professionals in working with groups to plan effectively for good nutrition, the *Food and Nutrition Board* of the National Academy of Sciences–National Research Council has developed tables of recommended dietary intakes, often termed simply the *RDA* or the Recommended Dietary Allowances. Table 18.3 presents the RDA for various nutrients; Tables 18.4 and 18.5 provide the Food and Nutrition Board's

Table 18.3 Recommended Dietary Allowances Designed for Maintenance of Good Nutrition for Practically All Healthy People in the United States, 1980[1]

Age and Sex Group	Weight (kg)	Weight (lb)	Height (cm)	Height (in.)	Protein (gm)	Vitamin A (μg R.E.)[2]	Vitamin D (μg)[3]	Vitamin E (mg α T.E.)[4]	Vitamin C (mg)	Thiamin (mg)	Riboflavin (mg)	Niacin (mg NE)[5]	Vitamin B6 (mg)	Folacin (μg)[6]	Vitamin B12 (μg)	Calcium (mg)	Phosphorus (mg)	Magnesium (mg)	Iron (mg)	Zinc (mg)	Iodine (μg)
Infants																					
0.0–0.5 yr	6	13	60	24	kg×2.2	420	10	3	35	0.3	0.4	6	0.3	30	0.5[7]	360	240	50	10	3	40
0.5–1.0 yr	9	20	71	28	kg×2.0	400	10	4	35	0.5	0.6	8	0.6	45	1.5	540	360	70	15	5	50
Children																					
1–3 yr	13	29	90	35	23	400	10	5	45	0.7	0.8	9	0.9	100	2.0	800	800	150	15	10	70
4–6	20	44	112	44	30	500	10	6	45	0.9	1.0	11	1.3	200	2.5	800	800	200	10	10	90
7–10	28	62	132	52	34	700	10	7	45	1.2	1.4	16	1.6	300	3.0	800	800	250	10	10	120
Males																					
11–14 yr	45	99	157	62	45	1000	10	8	50	1.4	1.6	18	1.8	400	3.0	1200	1200	350	18	15	150
15–18 yr	66	145	176	69	56	1000	10	10	60	1.4	1.7	18	2.0	400	3.0	1200	1200	400	18	15	150
19–22 yr	70	154	177	70	56	1000	7.5	10	60	1.5	1.7	19	2.2	400	3.0	800	800	350	10	15	150
23–50 yr	70	154	178	70	56	1000	5	10	60	1.4	1.6	18	2.2	400	3.0	800	800	350	10	15	150
51+ yr	70	154	178	70	56	1000	5	10	60	1.2	1.4	16	2.2	400	3.0	800	800	350	10	15	150
Females																					
11–14 yr	46	101	157	62	46	800	10	8	50	1.1	1.3	15	1.8	400	3.0	1200	1200	300	18	15	150
15–18 yr	55	120	163	64	46	800	10	8	60	1.1	1.3	14	2.0	400	3.0	1200	1200	300	18	15	150
19–22 yr	55	120	163	64	44	800	7.5	8	60	1.1	1.3	14	2.0	400	3.0	800	800	300	18	15	150
23–50 yr	55	120	163	64	44	800	5	8	60	1.0	1.2	13	2.0	400	3.0	800	800	300	18	15	150
51+ yr	55	120	163	64	44	800	5	8	60	1.0	1.2	13	2.0	400	3.0	800	800	300	10	15	150
Pregnancy					+30	+200	+5	+2	+20	+0.4	+0.3	+2	+0.6	+400	+1.0	+400	+400	+150	*[8]	+5	+25
Lactation					+20	+400	+5	+3	+40	+0.5	+0.5	+5	+0.5	+100	+1.0	+400	+400	+150	*[8]	+10	+50

Source: Reproduced by permission of the Food and Nutrition Board, National Academy of Sciences–National Research Council. Rev. 1980.

[1] The allowances are intended to provide for individual variations among most normal persons as they live in the United States under usual environmental stresses. Diets should be based on a variety of common foods to provide other nutrients for which human requirements have been less well defined.

[2] Retinol equivalents: 1 retinol equivalent = 1 μg retinol or 6 μg β-carotene.

[3] As cholecalciferol: 10 μg cholecalciferol = 400 i.u. vitamin D.

[4] α tocopherol equivalents: 1 mg d-α-tocopherol = 1 α T.E.

[5] 1 N.E. (niacin equivalent) = 1 mg niacin or 60 mg dietary tryptophan.

[6] The folacin allowances refer to dietary sources as determined by *Lactobacillus casei* assay after treatment with enzymes ("conjugases") to make polyglutamyl forms of the vitamin available to the test organism.

[7] The RDA for vitamin B12 in infants is based on average concentration of the vitamin in human milk. The allowances after weaning are based on energy intake (as recommended by the American Academy of Pediatrics) and consideration of other factors, such as intestinal absorption.

[8] The increased requirement during pregnancy cannot be met by the iron content of habitual American diets or by the existing iron stores of many women; therefore, the use of 30 to 60 mg of supplemental iron is recommended. Iron needs during lactation are not substantially different from those of nonpregnant women, but continued supplementation of the mother for two to three months after parturition is advisable to replenish stores depleted by pregnancy.

Table 18.4 Recommended Energy Intake for People of All Ages, 1980 (mean heights and weights)

Age and Sex Group	Weight (kg)	Weight (lb)	Height (cm)	Height (in)	Energy Needs MJ	Energy Needs kcal	Energy Range in kcal
Infants							
0.0–0.5 yr	6	13	60	24	kg×0.48	kg×115	95– 145 kg
0.5–1.0 yr	9	20	71	28	kg×0.44	kg×105	80– 135 kg
Children							
1–3 yr	13	29	90	35	5.5	1300	900–1800
4–6 yr	20	44	112	44	7.1	1700	1300–2300
7–10 yr	28	62	132	53	10.1	2400	1650–3300
Males							
11–14 yr	45	99	157	62	11.3	2700	2000–3700
15–18 yr	66	145	176	69	11.8	2800	2100–3900
19–22 yr	70	154	177	70	12.2	2900	2500–3300
23–50 yr	70	154	178	70	11.3	2700	2300–3100
51–75 yr	70	154	178	70	10.1	2400	2000–2800
76+ yr	70	154	178	70	8.6	2050	1650–2450
Females							
11–14 yr	46	101	157	62	9.2	2200	1500–3000
15–18 yr	55	120	163	64	8.8	2100	1200–3000
19–22 yr	55	120	163	64	8.8	2100	1700–2500
23–50 yr	55	120	163	64	8.4	2000	1600–2400
51–75 yr	55	120	163	64	7.6	1800	1400–2200
76+ yr	55	120	163	64	6.7	1600	1200–2000
Pregnancy						+300	
Lactation						+500	

Source: Reproduced by permission of the Food and Nutrition Board, National Academy of Sciences–National Research Council. Heights and weights stated are median values. Rev. 1980.

recommendations for energy intake and estimates of safe and adequate intakes of additional selected vitamins and minerals, respectively.

The RDA values are reviewed by the Food and Nutrition Board at intervals of approximately five years, and adjustments are made in relation to the most recent research findings about the various nutrients. This information is very helpful to professionals and is of value if you are interested in analyzing the adequacy of your own diet.

ACHIEVING GOOD NUTRITION

The Basic Four

It is fine to have the guidance of the RDA values, but individuals need to have a convenient way of checking periodically to see whether or not their diets are

Table 18.5 Estimated Safe and Adequate Dietary Intakes of Additional Selected Vitamins and Minerals, 1980

Age Group	Vitamins			Trace Elements[2]						Electrolytes		
	Vitamin K (µg)	Biotin (µg)	Pantothenic Acid (mg)	Copper (mg)	Manganese (mg)	Fluoride (mg)	Chromium (mg)	Selenium (mg)	Molybdenum (mg)	Sodium (mg)	Potassium (mg)	Chloride (mg)
Infants												
0.0–0.5 yr	12	35	2	0.5–0.7	0.5–0.7	0.1–0.5	0.01–0.04	0.01–0.04	0.03–0.06	115– 350	350– 925	275– 700
0.5–1.0 yr	10– 20	50	3	0.7–1.0	0.7–1.0	0.2–1.0	0.02–0.06	0.02–0.06	0.01–0.08	250– 750	425–1275	400–1200
Children and Adolescents												
1–3 yr	15– 30	65	3	1.0–1.5	1.0–1.5	0.5–1.5	0.02–0.08	0.02–0.08	0.05–0.1	325– 975	550–1650	500–1500
4–6 yr	20– 40	85	3–4	1.5–2.0	1.5–2.0	1.0–2.5	0.03–0.12	0.03–0.12	0.06–0.15	450–1350	775–2325	700–2100
7–10 yr	30– 60	120	4–5	2.0–2.5	2.0–3.0	1.5–2.5	0.05–0.2	0.05–0.2	0.1 –0.3	600–1800	1000–3000	925–2775
11+ yr	50–100	100–200	4–7	2.0–3.0	2.5–5.0	1.5–2.5	0.05–0.2	0.05–0.2	0.15–0.5	900–2700	1525–4575	1400–4200
Adults	70–140	100–200	4–7	2.0–3.0	2.5–5.0	1.5–4.0	0.05–0.2	0.05–0.2	0.15–0.5	1100–3300	1875–5625	1700–5100

Source: Reproduced by permission of the Food and Nutrition Board, National Academy of Sciences–National Research Council. Rev. 1980.

[1]Because there is less information on which to base allowances, these figures are not given in the main table of the RDAs and are provided here in the form of ranges of recommended intakes.

[2]Since the toxic levels for many trace elements may be only several times usual intakes, the upper levels for the trace elements given in this table should not be habitually exceeded.

Basic Four Food plan composed of milk and dairy products, meat and meat alternatives, vegetables and fruits, and breads and cereals.

adequate for maintaining optimal health. A simple, yet rather effective, way of checking is to use the *Basic Four* system, a food plan based on four groups of foods: milk and dairy products, meats and meat alternatives, fruits and vegetables, and breads and cereals. In the Basic Four, the numbers and sizes of servings recommended as a minimum each day are presented (Table 18.6). Anyone can check easily to see whether or not all the categories are being met on a regular basis. Depending upon the findings, changes can be made to ensure that the recommendations are being followed.

Some people find fault with the Basic Four system because it does not define exactly the entire spectrum of food needed to meet the RDA. For example, fats and oils are assumed to be consumed when eating meats, bread, or other food in the Basic Four. Such omissions are deliberate, for it was assumed that simplicity of the plan was more important than total precision. Since the typical American eats more fat than is deemed desirable, the lack of a specific recommendation for fat in the Basic Four does not appear to be a serious shortcoming.

To overcome the objection that some foods simply do not fit into the Basic Four framework, some professionals have adopted the Daily Food Guide to which a fifth group, a group often termed ''Other,'' has been added. The

This meal of shrimp, fruit medley, and corn bread, when served with an ice-cold glass of nonfat milk, provides representatives of all four groups in the Basic Four, yet is quite low in calories.

Table 18.6 The Basic Four

Food Group	Number of Servings per Day	Serving Size
Milk and dairy	Children under 9: 2 to 3 Children 9–12: 3 to 4 Teens: 3 to 4 or more Adults: 2 or more Pregnant women: 3 to 4 Lactating women: 4 or more	1 cup (8 fluid ounces)[1]
Meat and meat alternatives	2 or more	3 ounces lean, cooked meat, poultry, or fish; or 2 eggs; or 1 cup cooked legumes; or ¼ cup peanut butter
Vegetables and fruits	4 or more, including 1 serving of citrus fruit daily (or other good source of vitamin C) and 1 serving dark green, leafy, or deep yellow vegetable every other day for vitamin A	½ cup or a piece of fruit
Breads and cereals	4 or more (whole grain or enriched)	1 slice of bread; or 1 ounce ready-to-eat cereal; or ½ to ¾ cup cooked cereal, corn meal, or pastas

Source: U.S. Department of Agriculture.
[1]Alternatives providing equivalent calcium values are: 1 cup milk = 1″ × 1″ × 2″ cheddar cheese = 1¼ cup cottage cheese = 1⅔ cup cream cheese = 1½ cup ice cream.

addition is a bit confusing because this group, which includes sugars, fats, and any other foods that do not fit into the other four groups, is a group for which recommended numbers of servings are not given. In fact, the recommendation is just the opposite of the statements for the other four groups; instead of recommending intake, the suggestion is that foods from the ''other'' group should be eaten only sparingly.

Buying Good Nutrition

The food you buy is the cornerstone of good nutrition, for many decisions are made in the grocery store. Ideally, planning of the week's menus to provide adequate amounts of all nutrients is done before going to the store, and a shopping list is prepared for these menus only.

Realistically, such preparations often are not done, and impulse buying may dominate food purchases. When this occurs, some nutrient-dense foods (milk, for example) may be forgotten, and high-calorie, low-nutrient snack items (soft drinks are but one popular example) may find their way into the shopping basket. Since the food that is carried home is the food that comprises much of the food eaten that week, these shopping decisions definitely shape the nutrient intake of the family.

Nutrient Density Ex-pression of the per-centage of the day's re-quirement of a nutrient provided by a serving of a food in comparison with the percentage of caloric need in that serving; high nutrient density is desirable, preferably in regard to three or more of the nutrients.

INQ Index of nutrient quality; profile of the nutrient content of a food in comparison with its calorie content.

Nutrient Density One way of thinking about food selection is to consider the *nutrient density* or the index of nutrient quality (often called simply *INQ*). This is a system by which food can be categorized as being a good use of calories or a poor use. Nutrient density is an expression of the amount of various nutri-ents a food provides in relation to the calories it contains. To illustrate, if a food offers half the total amount of calcium you need and only a tenth of the calories recommended for the day, that food is high in nutrient density, which is another way of saying that this food is a good choice nutritionally. In contrast, if a food choice offers a tenth of the day's need for calories and only a hundredth of the vitamin C needed (or of any other nutrient), this food is low in nutrient density and has a low index of nutrient quality (INQ). Foods with a high INQ are wise food choices and should be used frequently; those with a low INQ should be eaten infrequently and then only in small quanti-ties.

Nutrition Labeling Although numerous foods have been analyzed carefully to determine the normal level of various nutrients contained in 100 grams or in a standard serving of the item, most people do not have ready access to this information, particularly when shopping in the grocery store. As an aid the Food and Drug Administration (FDA) has developed a system for informing shoppers about the nutrient content of many canned and packaged foods. Canned and processed food items for which nutritional claims are being made are required to have nutrition labeling provided on the package. Regulations for nutrition labeling are very specific and must include information on:

1. Serving size for the calculations reported on the label.
2. Number of servings in the container.
3. Calories per serving.
4. Grams of protein per serving.
5. Grams of carbohydrate per serving.
6. Grams of fat per serving.
7. Percentage of the U.S. RDA for protein, vitamin A, vitamin C, thi-amin, riboflavin, niacin, calcium, and iron.
8. Optional listing of percentage of U.S. RDA values for vitamin D, vita-min E, vitamin B_6, folacin, vitamin B_{12}, phosphorus, iodide, magne-sium, zinc, copper, biotin, and pantothenic acid.
9. Optional listing for cholesterol and sodium content.
10. Optional listing of nutritive value when served with a common com-bination, such as milk with cold cereals.

Nutrition informa-tion on labels is pre-sented as an aid to consumers in help-ing them plan menus with ade-quate levels of vari-ous nutrients. The format is mandated by the Food and Drug Administra-tion (FDA).

There are limitations in the usefulness of nutrition labeling because many food items, such as fresh produce, are not labeled, which makes it impossible to add up the nutrient content being purchased. Another limitation is that the nutrients are expressed in percentages of the U.S. RDA, a value established as being appropriate in most instances for adult males. This means that the U.S. RDA values are higher than they need to be for many people in the population. In other words, children and most females do not need to consume 100 percent of the U.S. RDA to be well nourished. Despite these problems, nutrition labeling can be a big help in selecting foods for good nutrition.

Retaining Nutrients in Food

Nutrients, particularly vitamins, may be lost during food preparation. Fortunately, these losses can be kept to a minimum if certain precautions are observed.

Water Solubility Some nutrients, notably the water-soluble vitamins, may be dissolved into the surrounding cooking water during preparation. This is not a problem if all of the cooking liquid is to be consumed with the food, as would be the case in a soup, but it does represent a problem in such items as boiled vegetables.

Loss of nutrients by dissolving out of foods can be minimized by avoiding soaking peeled and/or cut vegetables or other foods in water. By using as little cooking water as is consistent with producing a palatable food, losses can be kept low. Another good practice is to keep cooking times as short as possible so that the time for leaching the water-soluble vitamins from foods will be brief.

Cut surfaces increase solubility losses. If foods can be pared and/or cut into the desired pieces after cooking, the vitamin content can be kept higher than would be the case if considerable cut surface area were exposed throughout the period of boiling.

Heating Intense heat may cause proteins to be utilized less well by the body than is the case when mild cooking temperatures are used. This is particularly true of excessively high temperatures used in some deep-fat frying or in some instances of baking. The length of time for heating is also of concern, not only for proteins in foods, but also for vitamins, particularly some of the B vitamins, such as thiamin. As much as is consistent with palatability, foods should be cooked at moderate temperatures for a short time.

Oxidation Certain nutrients, particularly some of the vitamins (vitamin C, vitamin A, thiamin, riboflavin, vitamin B_6, and folacin) and the polyunsaturated fatty acids are susceptible to loss of activity because of oxidation. Such reactions occur when cut surfaces are exposed to air. By paring and cutting foods close to the time they are to be cooked and served, oxidation losses can be reduced. The practice of dipping pieces of cut fruit in some acidic fruit juice is an effective means of preventing air from oxidizing the vitamin C or other vitamins in foods.

Light A few nutrients are sensitive to light and will lose their activity when exposed to light for a period of time. The most light-sensitive nutrient is riboflavin. This B vitmin, which is particularly abundant in milk, is reduced significantly in its activity if milk is allowed to sit in sunlight in clear glass containers, which explains the impetus for marketing milk in tinted glass or opaque plasticized containers. Although also light sensitive, vitamins E and K and also vitamin B$_6$ are definitely more stable to light than is riboflavin.

pH   The pH of the medium in which a food is placed, that is, whether acidic or alkaline, will have an effect on the nutritive value of the food. Most vitamins are quite stable in acids, but they are unstable in an alkaline medium, such as occurs if soda is added or if extremely hard water is used. Thiamin is particularly susceptible to destruction if the medium is even slightly alkaline.

SUMMARY

Food quality is a term that broadly defines all aspects of a food, including the original ingredients, the sanitary handling of the food, and its preparation and service. To obtain food of an acceptable quality, people may select from a variety of approaches to suit their life-styles. Some may elect to prepare foods from the basic ingredients because of the creative aspects of preparation or because of the desire to avoid food additives. Others may prefer to use convenience foods and do a minimum of preparation, while still others may eat away from home.

Regardless of the style of food selected, the ultimate goal is to eat the nutrients needed to achieve and maintain optimal health. These nutrients include the energy nutrients—carbohydrates, fats (lipids), and proteins (which are important for forming tissues and many other compounds in the body as well as providing energy). Minerals are needed to help form the body's structure and many compounds within the body. They also help to maintain the normal balance of acids and bases in the body and to attain water balance in the various body compartments. Even the transmission of nerve impulses requires the presence of minerals. The last category of nutrients is the vitamins, which include the fat-soluble vitamins (vitamins A, D, E, and K) and the water-soluble B vitamins (thiamin, riboflavin, niacin, pantothenic acid, folacin, vitamin B$_6$, vitamin B$_{12}$, and biotin) and vitamin C.

The amounts of the essential nutrients that are needed by people of various ages are specified in the RDA, the Recommended Dietary Allowances defined by the Food and Nutrition Board of the National Academy of Sciences–National Research Council. A good guide for selecting a diet that will afford the necessary amounts of these various nutrients is provided by the Basic Four. This guide includes milk and dairy products, meats and meat alternatives, fruits and vegetables, and breads and cereals. Some people use the Daily Food Guide, with its fifth group (called "Other") that includes fats and sweets and is to provide only limited additions to the diet.

Selecting foods with high nutrient density will ensure eating many nutrients in comparison with the calories provided. Some help in food selection is available by using nutrition labeling. This gives considerable information about the nutrients in many canned and packaged items, the information being given primarily in terms of percent of the U.S. RDA.

To retain the nutrients in foods that are purchased, careful preparation needs to be done to avoid extensive losses, particularly losses of vitamins. By keeping cooking times short and at moderate temperatures and avoiding excessive contact with water, oxygen, light, and alkali, nutrient losses can be minimized.

Selected References

Guthrie, H. *Introductory Nutrition.* C. V. Mosby. St. Louis. 5th ed. 1983.

McWilliams, M. *Fundamentals of Meal Management.* Plycon Press. Redondo Beach, Calif. 1978.

Peterkin, B. et al. Nutrition Labeling. *Ag. Information Bulletin* No. 382. Washington, D.C. 1975.

Stare, F. J. and M. McWilliams. *Living Nutrition.* John Wiley. New York. 4th ed. 1984.

Study Questions

1. Keep a record of all of the food you eat for three days. Compare your food intake with the recommendations for the Basic Four. Identify the groups where your intake was adequate and those where you did not meet the recommendation.
2. What suggestions can you make to yourself to improve your usual nutrient intake?
3. Go to the grocery store and read nutrition labeling on some canned products, some cereals, breads, and frozen foods. What information did you find to help you in making wise food choices?
4. What are four ways you can help to reduce nutrient losses when you are preparing fruits and vegetables?
5. Why is nutrition an important subject to consider when studying food preparation?

Van Rych, ''The Cook.'' Fine Arts Museum, Ghent. Scala/Art Resource.

CHAPTER 19

MENU PLANNING AND MEAL PREPARATION

PUTTING IT TOGETHER

The previous chapters have provided probing exploration of the basic types of foods typical on the American scene and of the nutrients these foods contain. To make this information useful on a daily basis, these individual components need to be linked together to provide attractive and tempting, yet nutritious, meals day in and day out throughout life.

Good meals begin with good planning. The underlying goal in planning any meal is to meet the body's needs for the various nutrients. Fortunately, there are many ways to meet these requirements, and this is where much of the challenge is found. With thoughtful planning, meals and eating can be highlights of the day's activities.

Planning for Good Nutrition

A convenient and generally satisfactory way of beginning menu planning is to plan breakfast, lunch, and dinner menus for a single day and then check these menus against the Basic Four to be certain that they include two or more servings of milk, two or more servings of meat and meat alternatives, four or more servings of fruits and vegetables (including a source of vitamin C and frequently vitamin A), and four or more portions of breads and cereals. If any of these servings is missing, the additional portions needed can be identified and added to the menus.

Breakfast for many people is the simplest meal of the day, yet it is a particularly important one from the perspective of nutrition. An outline of the breakfast menu appropriately includes a serving of fruit juice rich in vitamin C, a glass of milk, and a food from the bread and cereal group. If desired, some cheese, an egg, or other food from the meat and meat alternatives group can be included.

Lunch patterns vary considerably from person to person and family to family. This meal often is eaten away from home. For children, this meal needs to be hearty enough to meet their energy needs. Ideally, the noon meal should be the heartiest meal of the day for adults, too. However, lunch for many is a moderate meal. A suggested pattern includes an entree containing the equivalent of a 3-ounce serving of meat, two servings from the fruit and vegetable group, bread or another cereal product (pasta, for example), and a glass of milk.

The largest meal for many families is at night; dinner serves a social function, as well as a nutritional function for families. In fact, dinner may be the only meal eaten during the day in an organized manner with all family members present. Because of the sociability of dinner, this meal often is the largest and most elaborate meal of the day. Emphasis in planning this meal needs to be on providing a good variety, including a serving from the fruit and vegetable group and also from the bread and cereal group, yet only a limited quantity of fat. One of the easiest ways to reduce fat intake and promote good nutrition is to include a low-fat selection (poultry or fish) from the meat and meat alternatives group at least three times a week and to keep the serving sizes in this group modest (only about 3 ounces of cooked meat). Inclusion of another glass of milk at this meal is helpful to bone maintenance in adults and sets a good example for children in the family. In line with the recommendation to keep fat intake low, the use of nonfat (skim) milk at dinner and all other meals is recommended.

Sensory Aspects of Menu Planning

Color   Food has the potential for providing aesthetic pleasure in life, and color is a key characteristic in creating beautiful meals. When planning menus, the combination of colors in the tentative menu must be visualized. Fruits and vegetables are particularly valuable in adding color interest to a meal. They may be planned as a serving of a particular fruit or vegetable, as an ingredient in mixtures of foods, or even as a garnish to accent the appearance of a meal. To illustrate, red apples can be used in a salad with their skins left on to provide an important color highlight, or a twist of lemon or orange can be added just to garnish a meal needing a touch of excitement. Broiled salmon with a bright yellow twist of lemon, French cut green beans with toasted almonds, and a stuffed baked potato in its russet skin constitute a colorful and tempting dinner plate; contrast this to the monotonous color afforded by a plate of sliced breast of turkey, mashed potatoes, and creamed onions. This turkey menu could be enhanced considerably by changing the menu slightly to mashed sweet potatoes and adding some bright green peas to the cream sauce on the onions. Color is a cornerstone of good menu planning. These are but a few ideas. With an awareness of the importance of thinking about color, the imagination can be exercised fully to create plates of beauty at any meal.

Shape   With most menus, there are choices to be made regarding the shape of the pieces of food. Carrots provide an excellent illustration of the types of choices to be made, for they can be cooked and served whole (with only the skin and the stem and tip being removed), cut in thin slivers, in matchsticks, in thin or thick disks, grated, or even curled. When the menu simply says carrots, that is only the beginning of planning for beauty. Many other foods afford opportunities for creative planning in regard to shape.

Harmony of shape is helpful in creating a visual picture of beauty in food. If several foods are to be cut up for making a salad or a casserole, the foods often are most attractive when they are cut into pieces of similar, but preferably not extremely, small size. Recognizable pieces invite the diner to sample food mixtures. When considering the shapes in a meal, the shapes in the different recipes being considered for the meal need to be chosen in relation to the total picture. If one dish is going to have comparatively small pieces, the other foods will complement this dish best if they are moderate or large slices.

Even the contour of the surface of the foods on the plate contributes to the visual effect. For example, a stalk of broccoli adds height to the area of the plate where the flower portion of the vegetable rises. Chicken wings and drumsticks are other instances of the use of food to add interesting contours. However, variety is the important feature. Not all foods on the plate should contribute height, or they will also contribute monotony.

Texture The range of textural experiences available from foods adds considerable excitement to a meal. Again, contrast is the guide to success. Crisp crackers are a pleasing complement to a smooth cream soup. A steak with its firm chewiness gains interest when accompanied by sliced mushrooms, which contribute a smooth, slightly slippery texture. Texture is influenced by cookery techniques as well as by the natural qualities of the food. By cooking pasta just to the *al dente* stage and vegetables to the point where they retain just a suggestion of crispness, these foods retain good textural qualities to heighten palatability of meals.

Flavor The basic taste characteristics—salt, sour, sweet, and bitter—can be valuable in small amounts but may be overpowering and even monotonous in

This imaginative meal of crab enchiladas topped with green chiles and grated cheese and complemented with guacamole and a crisp mixed vegetable salad combines the key elements of flavor, color, shape, texture, temperature, and satiety value that add up to a very special dining experience.

large amounts. Heightened interest can be achieved in meals where additional flavoring agents are utilized. Foods themselves should carry the primary flavor message, with spices and other seasonings being added to provide a flourish to the various recipes. Menus will be pleasing when they present some delicate and some moderately strong flavors concurrently. This combination gives the palate a chance to rest occasionally, rather than constantly challenge the flavor receptors. However, a bland meal is monotonous. Variety is important to avoid the inevitable fatigue experienced when the same flavor keeps impacting the tongue and nasal passages. For example, a meal containing cauliflower and broccoli would be rather uninteresting, because the flavors of these two vegetables are quite similar. Familiarity with a broad array of spices is invaluable in creating flavor excitement in meals.

Temperature   Perhaps the best illustration of the importance of temperature contrasts in foods is provided by a Baked Alaska. Its warm meringue is a wonderful complement to the sharp coldness of the ice cream within. On a less dramatic note, the use of at least one cold food when the meal is basically a hot meal or one hot food when the meal is cold will add interest to the meal. A cold glass of milk is welcomed when hot soup is served; a hot roll is a very pleasing addition to a luncheon featuring a salad plate.

Some foods have a hot, burning taste, for example, Jalapeno peppers and many Indian curries, while some others are soothingly cool, for example, peppermint. People's enjoyment of this type of heat in foods varies greatly. Some variety in temperature adds interest to a meal, but this aspect of seasoning and food selection needs to be consistent with the preferences and gastrointestinal tolerances of the people who will eat the meal.

Satiety Value Ability to satisfy and provide feeling of fullness.

Satiety Value   The *satiety value*, or the feeling of satisfaction and fullness, is an important aspect of a meal. Although a meal may be beautiful to view and appealing to eat, it may fail to provide a feeling of satisfaction, or, conversely, it may be too filling. The inclusion of an adequate amount of protein and fat in a meal aid in providing the desired satiety value, but very rich menus can lead to discomfort following the meal.

Portion sizes are an important factor in determining the feeling of satiety following a meal. There are no rules to apply in planning portion sizes, for exact nutritional needs vary with the individual and are influenced by activity levels and basal metabolic requirements. The appropriateness of the weight of various family members is a good indication of whether or not appropriate serving sizes are the usual practice. If excess weight is evident, portion sizes need to be decreased; the reverse is true if family members are underweight.

Variety   Even menus planned to satisfy the various criteria just outlined can be dull and uninteresting if they are served too frequently. Variety is needed to spark interest in food and to add zest to mealtimes. Meal planning is more exciting and less routine if an attempt is made to include new foods and recipes as time and interest dictate. Considerable inspiration can come from browsing through cookbooks and reading articles on food in newspapers and magazines. Ideas may range from the very exotic and expensive to something as simple as using a different seasoning in a familiar food. Such explorations in the realm of food help to relieve the possible monotony of meal preparation each day, but they also aid in broadening the food tastes of family members.

Planning for Energy Management

Human Energy   Wonderful menus meeting the many palatability concerns can be developed, yet they may fail to hit the mark if the human energy factor is not considered. For example, the time and energy available for preparing a meal can make complex menus inappropriate, particularly during the week if nobody is at home during the day to do the preparation. Even on the weekend, difficult menus may prove too taxing. A warm welcome in a relaxed mealtime atmosphere is the appropriate background against which to enjoy fine food and friendship. The menu being prepared and served should be tailored to the cook(s) so that the dining experience will meet this description.

Appliances   With some thought, use of appliances can overcome some of the human energy and time constraints in preparation. For instance, a crock pot can be loaded and turned on before the cook leaves for work in the morning so that a meal is almost ready to be served the minute the front door is opened at night.

Judicious use of the freezer represents another approach to solving energy and time problems. Foods that freeze well can be prepared on the weekend and then frozen in serving portions, so that weeknight dinners are largely a matter of thawing and warming to serving temperature. In some instances, meals may even be placed in the oven and the time set to turn on the heat at an appropriate hour—though this practice must consider the potential for food spoilage if meat is held in the oven for several hours before being heated. Frozen meats and casseroles, however, do lend themselves to this type of meal preparation. Note that electric ovens are safer than gas for this use because the temperature is cooler than in a gas oven, which derives some heat from the pilot light. (Pilotless gas ovens are comparable to electric ovens in temperature.)

MANAGING COSTS

Planning

Food costs and menu planning go hand in hand in the management of meals in the home. For optimum efficiency in planning and shopping, meals should be planned for a week at a time so that effective use can be made of special purchases and unnecessary shopping trips can be avoided. The simple act of limiting trips to the grocery store to one each week is a big step toward controlling food costs, for this significantly limits the opportunities for impulse buying. Rare is the shopper who refuses to buy any item not on the shopping list.

Planning for the week also can effectively reduce food waste. When the week's menus are checked over, it is easy to see whether or not lefovers have been identified and worked into subsequent meals so that they will not spoil and have to be discarded. Any necessary modifications in the menus can be made before buying the food, either reducing quantities being purchased or changing menu items to utilize leftovers.

Some flexibility in menu items is recommended so that sensible use of specials can be planned at the grocery store. Usually grocery stores run week-end specials, and these sometimes can provide substantial savings without seriously altering menu plans. However, these changes are recommended only if the substitution is compatible with family food preferences and with the other foods being planned in the meal.

The Shopping List

A shopping list is a valuable tool in managing costs, for it is prepared in concert with the weekly menu plan. In addition, staple items, such as flour, sugar, salt, milk, and eggs, should be checked and added to the list, if needed. This list is most helpful if it is arranged in the same sequence as the floor plan of the grocery store, with the canned and nonrefrigerated items being first, followed by the refrigerated and frozen items, and last, the fresh produce. This arrangement makes it possible to do one efficient tour of the store and helps to keep optimum quality of perishable foods.

The quantities of the various food needed will vary considerably from family to family, depending on the number in the family, the age of family members, and the food consumption patterns of the various people being served. Fortunately, patterns do become known gradually to those doing the shopping, which simplifies this aspect of food purchasing and avoids shortages or waste. The U.S. Department of Agriculture has made a study of the amounts of foods that predictably might be utilized for good nutrition by people of various ages. This information for people on a moderate food budget is presented in Table 19.1.

Storage Considerations

When planning and shopping for food for a week, the storage facilities that are available in the home must be considered to avoid losses. There is a finite amount of frozen storage space in most homes, and frozen foods must either be prepared at the time of purchase or stored in a freezer. Marvelous buys on ice cream and various other frozen items cease to be bargains if they cannot be held satisfactorily. Fresh produce also requires special storage; in this instance, hydrator drawers are the preferred space for most items, particularly lettuce and other succulent items. Plastic bags that are closed tightly can serve as an alternative to hydrator drawers in the refrigerated storage of produce. Even winter squash, onions, and potatoes need to have space available so that they can be held at a cool room temperature.

Table 19.1 Moderate-Cost Food Plan—Amounts for One Week[1]

Family Member	Milk, Cheese, Ice Cream[2] (qt)	Meat, Poultry, Fish[3] (lb)	Eggs (no.)	Dry Beans and Peas, Nuts[4] (lb)	Dark Green, Deep Yellow Vegetables (lb)	Citrus Fruit, Tomatoes (lb)	Potatoes (lb)	Other Vegetables, Fruit (lb)	Cereal (lb)	Flour (lb)	Bread (lb)	Other Bakery Products (lb)	Fats, Oils (lb)	Sugar, Sweets (lb)	Accessories[5] (lb)
Children															
7 mo–1 yr	6.46	0.80	2.2	0.13	0.41	0.49	0.06	3.98	0.64[6]	0.02	0.06	0.05	0.05	0.19	0.08
1–2 yr	4.04	1.69	4.0	0.15	0.29	1.24	0.59	3.44	1.03[6]	0.26	0.81	0.33	0.12	0.28	0.79
3–5 yr	4.74	1.88	3.0	0.22	0.30	1.46	0.85	3.51	0.74	0.27	0.82	0.73	0.41	0.81	1.42
6–8 yr	5.79	2.60	3.3	0.34	0.37	1.94	1.17	4.39	0.84	0.39	1.14	1.11	0.56	1.03	1.97
9–11 yr	6.68	3.31	4.0	0.38	0.45	2.61	1.40	5.76	1.03	0.51	1.47	1.51	0.66	1.31	2.63
Males															
12–14 yr	7.02	3.77	4.0	0.48	0.48	2.44	1.52	4.66	0.94	0.56	1.69	1.54	0.85	1.34	3.65
15–19 yr	6.65	4.65	4.0	0.29	0.47	2.73	2.00	5.45	0.80	0.67	1.98	1.82	1.05	1.15	4.41
20–54 yr	3.38	5.73	4.0	0.29	0.59	2.92	1.94	5.93	0.76	0.65	1.97	1.65	0.95	0.96	2.95
55+	2.97	4.64	4.0	0.19	0.70	2.91	1.69	5.88	0.89	0.53	1.58	1.45	0.87	1.05	1.50
Females															
12–19 yr	6.22	3.32	4.0	0.24	0.53	2.62	1.21	5.38	0.68	0.56	1.34	1.22	0.56	0.97	3.36
20–54 yr	3.35	4.12	4.0	0.19	0.62	2.84	1.35	4.94	0.54	0.49	1.28	1.08	0.65	0.81	2.89
55+	3.35	3.21	4.0	0.14	0.72	3.09	1.17	5.50	0.81	0.52	1.20	0.98	0.45	0.73	1.39
Pregnant	5.44	4.57	4.0	0.25	0.91	3.52	1.60	6.13	0.73	0.83	1.77	1.28	0.46	0.85	3.50
Nursing	5.31	5.01	4.0	0.26	0.91	3.76	1.73	6.52	0.74	0.81	1.84	1.42	0.69	1.00	3.79

Source: Current costs are available in *Food and Home Notes,* issued by the Office of Communication of the U.S. Department of Agriculture. The *Family Economic Review* is published by the Consumer and Food Economics Institute, Agricultural Research Service of the U.S. Department of Agriculture and also carries this information on a quarterly basis.

[1]Amounts are for food as purchased or brought into the kitchen from garden or farm. Amounts allow for a discard of about one-sixth of the *edible* food as plate waste, spoilage, and so on. Amounts of foods are shown to two decimal places to allow for greater accuracy, especially in estimating rations for large groups of people and for long periods of time. For general use, amounts of food groups for a family may be rounded to the nearest tenth or quarter of a pound.

[2]Fluid milk and beverage made from dry or evaporated milk. Cheese and ice cream may replace some milk. Count as equivalent to a quart of fluid milk: natural or processed cheddar-type cheese, 6 oz.; cottage cheese, 2½ lb; ice cream, 1½ qt.

[3]Bacon and salt pork should not exceed ⅓ lb for each 5 lb of this group.

[4]Weight in terms of dry beans and peas, shelled nuts, and peanut butter. Count 1 lb of canned dry beans—pork and beans, kidney beans, and so on—as 0.33 lb.

[5]Includes coffee, tea, cocoa, punches, ades, soft drinks, leavenings, and seasonings. The use of iodized salt is recommended.

[6]Cereal fortified with iron is recommended.

For large families, adequate refrigerator space for storing milk and meat may be the limiting factor in shopping. Where available, home delivery of milk two or three times a week can be a solution, but when service often cannot be obtained, supplementary shopping in the middle of the week may be necessary to solve the milk supply problem. Another possible solution is to supplement the fluid milk with the use of some reconstituted dry milk solids.

Consumer Aids

Ingredient Labeling
Listing of ingredients, beginning with the one present in the largest amount by weight and continuing in descending order.

Grocery shopping can be very educational as well as time consuming. With the excellent *ingredient labeling* on many foods today, a considerable amount of information regarding nutrient content and ingredients is available. However, time may limit the advantage consumers take of labels. For items used frequently, a few minutes spent in comparing labels from different brands can serve as the basis of making informed decisions for many subsequent shopping trips. For persons who are allergic to some ingredients or who have other health reasons for needing to avoid certain items, ingredient labeling can be a vital source of information to aid in selecting appropriate foods. Ingredient labeling is of considerable merit when comparing the relative cost of various brands of the same item. Since ingredients must be listed in descend-

Considerable information regarding the ingredients and the nutritive value can be obtained by reading labels carefully. Smart shopping can save money and improve food quality.

ing order of their weight in foods, comparisons can be made between formulations. For example, a soup mixture listing chicken before noodles would be higher in chicken than would one listing the noodles before the chicken.

Open Dating Date stating clearly pull date or other freshness date.

Open dating of foods is another aid to consumers. Increasingly, the dates are accompanied by an explanation, such as "Best if used before Nov. 27." Dates without explanations can be confusing, for the date could mean the packing date, or it might indicate the pull date to remove the item from the grocery shelves, or it might even mean that the food should not be eaten after the date. Such vagueness is seen fairly infrequently today, although many foods still are marketed with no date on it at all.

Comparison Shopping

Comparisons of cost between competitive brands can save consumers a good bit of money. Since package sizes often are different, such comparative shopping can take a good bit of time unless a calculator is a part of the shopping gear. Many stores now are providing *unit pricing* information on the shelves to let consumers know the price of an ounce or other sensible unit of measure of various products. This saves consumers a great deal of time, for comparisons can be made quickly when the shelf information can be scanned. Even with unit pricing, consumers still need to stay alert when making selections. One of the clearest examples of the need for being careful is afforded by comparing the drained weight of canned peaches. Some packers will sell a good bit of water and a small amount of fruit, while others may have the can well filled with fruit and include only a small amount of juice. If the two products were the same price, the one with the abundance of fruit clearly would be the better buy. Numerous examples of this sort can be found throughout the market.

Unit Pricing Cost of a designated amount of an item to make price comparisons easy for consumers.

Often money can be saved by buying store brands rather than nationally advertised brands. An even greater saving usually is available with basic products by buying generics. Such products bear only a label indicating what they are. The simple, uncolored label identifies the contents. Frills definitely are not added to labels on generic products. The quality of these items may be every bit as good as a leading brand in some instances, while in others consumers may find a large difference. Experience is the best criterion for making such decisions. The one clear thing is that generics are less costly than nationally advertised products.

Universal Product Code Pattern of bars printed on packages to code inventory and cost information for translation by electronic scanning at the check stand.

Universal Product Code (UPC) is the name for the familiar bar coding seen on packaged food items in the market. This bar pattern was developed to aid markets in maintaining inventory information and to facilitate utilization of computers in the marketing process. An electronic scan of the UPC can be done at the check stand to generate the cash register tape for the consumer and to maintain necessary inventory and sales records for the store. By using scanners, errors at the check stand reportedly are reduced, and consumers receive a tally of their purchases with all of the items spelled out on the slip, complete with brand, product, and price all documented as a permanent receipt. One of the goals of the use of the UPC is to eliminate the cost of having items individually marked by human labor when they are being stocked onto the shelves, thus saving some labor costs that presumably are passed on to the consumer. Initially, consumer reaction to unmarked items was extremely negative, and grocers were forced to continue marking to halt consumer complaints. However, familiarity with the system in operation has developed consumer confidence to the point where many stores no longer are marking items.

TIME MANAGEMENT

A key to a successful meal is the timing of food preparation times so that everything is ready at the same time. Success in this area requires careful thought in advance. Actually, time management needs to be considered in the menu planning phase as well as in preparation so that the menu planned will be able to fit the time constraints of the person preparing the food. If dinner needs to be served soon after the cook returns from work, a simple meal with a brief cooking period fits the time demands. For inexperienced people, a meal with rather simple preparation requirements will help to guarantee success in preparation and timing.

When first learning to prepare meals, development of a detailed time plan will make the actual preparation proceed smoothly. Such a plan needs to anticipate all of the details that must be tended to in preparing and serving the meal, including time to set the table.

Development of a time plan is done most easily by starting at the serving time desired and then calculating the time needed for preparing each item in the menu. With this information, the time to begin preparing each item can be calculated. The actual cooking time for many recipes is stated on most recipes and will vary only slightly depending upon the equipment being used. However, the mixing time and the time needed for assembling or cutting and washing ingredients will vary greatly from one person to another. This is the main reason that individual time plans are important. With experience, relatively good estimates of preparation time can be made.

Such variables as interruptions by small children and telephone calls can throw off the best of plans. A time plan that considers probable interruptions will reduce frustration considerably. Educated guesses regarding the amount of time needed for these distractions during meal preparation can be made and incorporated into the plan.

Adequate time needs to be allowed for arranging a centerpiece and completing other details of table arrangement. For family meals, little time will be needed for setting the table, including doing the centerpiece. However, company meals may require the assembling of serving dishes that are stored in a remote cupboard and may even need washing before using. Silverware may need to be polished and washed before the table can be set. Special goblets or other glassware may also need washing and drying before being used at a special meal. These arrangements take a considerable amount of time. Even bringing extra chairs to the table for a company meal may be a time problem unless a detailed plan has been developed to include all aspects of setting the table. These special tasks often can be done the day before or at least earlier in the day of the special event.

Novices in meal preparation may find considerable comfort in developing a checklist of tasks needing to be included in the time plan. Details such as preparing ice water are important to the success of a meal, but are likely to be forgotten in a time plan unless a checklist is utilized. Even a listing of the serving dishes and the serving silver to be used can help to bring organization to a meal plan. With experience, some of these matters will become so natural that they may be done without the formality of writing them down. However, an appreciation of the need for time to do them must be maintained if meals are to be organized, rather than chaotic.

When possible, the time plan should be evaluated after the meal to see where the planning was good and where some modifications need to be made if the time plan is to be used again. When tasks that require less time or more time than was allocated can be identified, reality can be built into the next time plan. This evaluation process, whether done informally or by writing ideas on paper, is important to the development of time management skills. By modifying future time plans in relation to the time plan that has been tested, corrections in planning can be made, and the preparation of a meal in an organized and pleasing manner can be accomplished with increased ease.

MANAGING LEFTOVERS

Preplanning

Leftovers can be the result of deliberate planning or of miscalculation. If efficient use of time during the week is a goal, a pot roast may be prepared on the weekend, with the expectation that there will be enough meat left to make a vegetable beef soup and also a beef casserole during the week. Such planning allows purchase of large, but comparatively inexpensive cuts of meat or other foods. It also saves preparation time ultimately, because essentially no extra time is required to have the leftover meat ready to use in the other recipes.

If leftovers are being prepared deliberately, it is essential that the menu plans for the week provide for the utilization of the leftovers while they are of high quality and safe to eat. Leftovers that ultimately are thrown out do not represent an economy or a convenience. Frozen storage of leftovers can be a practical part of the plan for using certain leftovers.

When leftovers are not desirable, preplanning can be used to have no food left after a meal. Usually a fairly accurate calculation of the amount of food needed can be made so that extra food is not prepared. Occasionally, the diners will want more of a certain item than has been prepared, but this is only a minor problem, for many Americans tend to eat more food than they really need. However, to an energetic, athletic adolescent, too little food can be a real frustration and should be avoided. Experience quickly tells people how much food probably will be eaten by a family.

For people who are battling the bulges, it is generally not a kindness to cook more than might be needed. Urging a small bit of extra food on someone who already has had enough to eat can lead to weight difficulties. This approach—of limiting the food served—is contrary to the traditional practice of showing hospitality and friendliness by serving people as much as they possibly could hold. However, awareness about weight control and desire for good nutrition is spreading throughout the country, and quality is beginning to take precedence over quantity as a mark of hospitality.

Care of Leftovers

Many foods are at their height of quality when they are first prepared, and this quality can deteriorate fairly quickly if proper measures are not taken to control changes. Immediate care of leftovers after the meal has been finished can maintain quality. Protein-containing foods need to be refrigerated or frozen immediately, depending upon the food and the plans for its use. A protective covering of plastic wrap or aluminum foil will help to prevent the absorption of other flavors and loss of moisture from the food during refrigerator storage. Foods to be frozen need to be placed in containers with tightly fitting covers to avoid desiccation during frozen storage. Leftover vegetables and fruits also should be stored covered in the refrigerator even though they will not promote growth of microorganisms nearly as readily as will the protein-containing foods.

Breads and other baked goods do not require refrigeration, but they do need to be covered to protect them from drying out. For long-term storage, leftover breads and other baked products can be wrapped tightly and stored in the freezer.

To avoid growing microbiological wonders in the refrigerator or other storage areas, weekly tours of the stored food should be conducted. This should be done when the shopping list is being developed so that appropriate purchases will be made and edible items will not be duplicated. During this tour, food that will not be used should be discarded. Hydrator drawers and refrigerator shelves should be wiped clean in preparation for the arrival of the new food. If defrosting is needed, this also should be done before the shopping is done. This way the new food will be able to be placed immediately into the cold storage area safely.

SUMMARY

Meal management begins with planning of the meals for the full day and a review of these menus to be sure that all of the foods needed for good health are included in the menus. Check against the Basic Four to be sure that all of the recommended servings are being provided. Breakfast may be as simple as a serving of a food high in vitamin C, a glass of milk, and a bowl of cereal. Lunch should include a source of meat or a meat substitute, a couple of servings from the fruit and vegetable group, a slice of bread or other cereal product, and a glass of milk. Dinner can follow the same pattern as lunch. Ideally, dinner will be a meal of modest size unless a person is particularly active and needs more nutrients than the average individual.

To meet these guidelines, variety in menus is recommended. The sensory qualities of food to be considered include color, shape, texture, flavor, and temperature. Meals need to be planned to provide a feeling of satiety and should have enough variety from day to day to stimulate the appetite.

Menu planning should be done with the resources of human energy and appliances being utilized appropriately. Meals should not require such elaborate preparations that those fixing them are too exhausted to be a pleasant part of the social group at the table. Some menus can be planned to utilize time-saving appliances, such as a crock pot. Food safety also needs to be considered if items are to be held at room temperature a significant period of time.

Food costs can be controlled by shopping only once a week and by utilizing special buys that can be incorporated into family meals. A shopping list can be a real money saver when it is planned well and followed. Purchase of an appropriate amount of food so that safe storage can be done and the food will be eaten while still of high quality can be an important aspect of money management. Ingredient labeling, open dating, and unit pricing are important consumer aids in the marketplace. Comparison shopping and selection of generics or other products providing adequate quality at a reasonable price are other techniques for controlling food costs. Use of the Universal Product Code has been implemented in many markets to help control food costs.

Just by developing a careful time plan, the task of having all foods ready at the same time can be mastered. Such concerns as polishing silverware and arranging centerpieces also need to be considered when making the time plan. Evaluation of the plan is important after a meal so that improvements in subsequent time plans can be made. Experience is a great aid in gaining mastery of the timing of a meal.

Following a meal, proper care of leftovers is important as a means of controlling costs and quality. Planned leftovers can be a good way of saving time in meal preparation as long as the foods are properly stored and are used while still of high quality. Freezing leftovers can sometimes help in assuring high quality in leftovers. When leftovers are not a part of the plan, appropriate amounts of food should be cooked for a meal. The practice of cooking a bit more than probably will be needed is not only costly because of food waste but may also lead to overweight in a family if the extra food is pressed on people who have already had enough to eat.

Protein-containing foods need to be covered and either refrigerated or frozen just as soon as possible after a meal to avoid spoilage. Breads and other baked products need to be covered tightly to prevent them from drying out during storage. Frozen storage is appropriate if the items will not be used quite soon.

Removal of unused leftovers and careful cleaning of storage areas are important steps in maintaining control over food in the kitchen. This should be done in preparation for the next shopping expedition. This allows an inventory of existing food supplies to help in the development of an appropriate shopping list.

Selected References

Barer-Stein, T. *You Eat What You Are*. McClelland and Stewart. Toronto. 1979.

Hallberg, L. et al. Deleterious effects of prolonged warming of meals on ascorbic acid content and iron absorption. *Am. J. Clin. Nutr. 36:* 846. 1982.

Henderson, D. Using the store shelf as a food label. *FDA Consumer 16(6):* 22. 1982.

Kramer, M. and M. Spader. *Contemporary Meal Management*. John Wiley. New York. 1972.

Kinder, F. and N. R. Green. *Meal Management*. Macmillan. New York. 6th ed. 1984.

McWilliams, M. *Fundamentals of Meal Management*. Plycon Press. Redondo Beach, Calif. 1978.

Nickell, P. et al. *Management in Family Living*. John Wiley. New York. 5th ed. 1976.

Peet, L. J. et al. *Household Equipment*. John Wiley. New York. 7th ed. 1975.

Peterkin, B. et al. *Nutrition Labeling—Tools for Its Use*. U.S. Dept. Agriculture. Washington, D.C. 1978.

Peterkin, B. and C. Cromwell. Your Money's Worth in Food. *Home and Garden Bulletin No. 183*. U.S. Dept. Agriculture. Washington, D.C. 1977.

Stare, F. and M. McWilliams. *Living Nutrition*. John Wiley. New York. 4th ed. 1984.

Taylor, E. et al. Food retailers and open date labeling. *National Food Situation*. Economic Research Service. U.S. Dept. Agriculture. Washington, D.C. May, 1976.

Walker, M. A. and M. Hill. *Homemaker's Food and Nutrition Knowledge, Practices, and Opinions*. Home Economics Research Report No. 39. Agricultural Research Service. U.S. Dept. Agriculture. Washington, D.C. 1975.

Walker, K. E. and M. E. Woods. *Time Use: A Measure of Household Production of Family Goods and Services*. Am. Home Economics Assoc. Washington, D.C. 1976.

Waters, E. P. Checking the retail shelves. *FDA Consumer 9(5):* 4. 1975.

Study Questions

1. What factors need to be considered in planning appealing menus? Why do these aspects of food need to be coordinated in a menu?

2. Plan a lunch menu for an adolescent boy. How would you vary the menu if his mother were to eat the same meal? Would any changes be needed if his father were also to eat the meal? Explain your recommendations for the mother and for the father. What considerations did you use in planning the original menu for the boy?

3. Develop a time plan to prepare the lunch you planned in the previous question. Is the menu a workable one? If so, develop the shopping list for it. If changes appear to be needed, revise the menu and develop a shopping list for the revised menu.

4. Visit a supermarket and determine which foods have nutrition labels and which do not. Also examine ingredient labeling and open dating codes on packages. Do you think that consumers in the store you visited were using the consumer information provided for them? What did you learn from examining various products?

Norman Rockwell, "Freedom from Want." Reprinted from The Saturday Evening Post, © *1943*
The Curtis Publishing Company.

CHAPTER 20

MEAL SERVICE AND HOSPITALITY

A MATTER OF
AESTHETICS AND PRACTICALITY

A fully satisfying meal transcends the basic aspects of planning and preparation; the actual presentation of the food and the setting in which it is eaten are also important to total success. As noted earlier, food serves psychological and social functions—as well as meets nutritional needs—and the total experience at the table enhances one's ability to satisfy the total expectations for a meal. Whether a meal is intended as a family occasion, a social gathering, or a setting for doing business, the environment should be designed to suit the situation.

Table appointments set the tone for a meal. Sometimes informality may be the desired atmosphere; other times, a very formal occasion may be appropriate. By choosing linens, silverware, and other appointments for the table to fit the mood desired, the parameters for the meal are defined subtly. The method of service for the meal adds to this ambience desired for the group. Even the manners used at the table are a part of the total environment of the meal. These aspects of meal service are considered in this chapter.

No single definition of table setting, service, and hospitality is appropriate because the meals of different groups vary according to the occasion. The intent in this chapter is to heighten awareness of the importance of creating the desired environment for a meal and using available resources to achieve the desired effect.

TABLE APPOINTMENTS

Linens

The term "table linens" is used to designate table coverings and napkins, regardless of the type of fabric used. Choices range from tablecloths to place mats or even runners. There are no set rules to follow in selecting table linens for a meal, although the appearance and condition of the table itself may dictate the use of a tablecloth. If the surface finish of a table is unattractive, a tablecloth can mask this problem, whereas place mats can be the basis of a beautiful table setting if the table that shows under the mats is attractive. Similarly, a runner can be used effectively to provide the background for two people when the table surface that shows is pleasing to see.

The fabric in linens should be suited to the occasion. For an informal occasion, a coarsely woven or informal fabric helps to set the tone; for a more formal meal however, lace or damask is clearly appropriate. The color or pattern in a table linen should be complementary to the dishes and the food. Truly beautiful meals begin with creative selection of the linens. Often a contrasting napkin adds beauty to the setting. It is important that the linens do not compete with the food being served, for the whole purpose of table settings is to enhance the dining experience.

Tablecloths are always appropriate choices as table covers. Cloths should be large enough to extend beyond the table generously, usually about 8 to 10 inches on all sides. A textured fabric is a good choice for breakfast and lunch or even an informal dinner. Silence cloths under solid tablecloths help to protect the table surface and also help to keep the sound level down. When a cutwork or lace tablecloth is being used, a silence cloth is not used. Part of the beauty of these openwork tablecloths is to have the grain of the table surface show through the design of the cloth.

The popularity of tablecloths has been limited because they require more work in laundering than place mats do; fortunately, however, fabrics blended of easy-care fibers are used frequently for tablecloths so that a quick touching up with an iron is the most care required after the cloths are washed and dried. For people with limited time for doing laundry, selection of easy-care tablecloths can be an important time saver.

Place mats, a good choice for table settings when the dining table is attractive, are easy to care for and are available in many different colors, fabrics, and shapes to suit practically any occasion. The size of mats may vary slightly, but a convenient size for the individual place mat is about 22 inches long and 15 inches deep. The size of the table may dictate the use of slightly smaller mats. A circular table is easier to set if oval or round mats are used, rather than rectangular ones. Generally, the atmosphere for a meal is a bit less formal with mats than with a tablecloth, although delicate, lace-trimmed place mats can provide a very formal table setting.

When the dining table has a pretty surface, place mats can be used even for formal meals. For busy people, they save considerable time in laundering and yet they present a beautiful table setting. Note the arrangement of the silver and the placement of the napkin.

Tablecloths are pressed with a center crease extending the full length of the cloth. Although it often is necessary to fold cloths one or more times in addition to the original lengthwise fold, the other folds are not pressed in. Ideally, these other softer folds will be pressed out before the cloth is used if they do show after flat storage. The smaller size of place mats has dictated that mats be stored flat so that no creases can be found in them.

When place mats are used, a center runner is suggested as a basis for the centerpiece. If the table is too narrow to permit the use of a runner, this may need to be omitted. Some table should be showing if mats are being used, and mats should not overlap each other.

The napkins selected may match the mats or cloth selected, or they may contrast, if preferred. The size varies with the meal. Breakfast napkins usually are between 11 and 13 inches square, luncheon napkins are about 16 inches square, and dinner napkins range between 18 and 24 inches square. Regardless of size, napkins are folded in half, pressed, and then folded and pressed again. This results in a square one-fourth the size of the original napkin. Although cloth napkins are expected for special occasions, family meals often are served with paper napkins as a means of helping to reduce laundry duties.

Centerpieces

Artistry and imagination can be combined to develop centerpieces for various occasions. For a buffet, a large and dramatic centerpiece may suit the occasion, while somewhat smaller centerpieces are appropriate for the dining table where people will be seated. The purpose of a centerpiece is to add visual satisfaction and beauty to the occasion. The size needs to be adapted to suit the space requirements in the center of the table and also to provide eye contact between people seated around the table. A high centerpiece serves as a deterrent to conversation because people cannot see each other through or around the centerpiece. Consequently, centerpieces for most meals are fairly small and low. In no instance should the table appear crowded because of the centerpiece. There should be ample room for the centerpiece and any serving dishes being used at the meal.

Simple floral arrangements can be excellent centerpieces. A single flower with a touch of greenery floating in a simple bowl can be a lovely way of accenting the table appointments. Edible centerpieces featuring fruit arranged in a bowl or basket are attractive during the meal and can be functional as the dessert, if desired. Small sculptures or green plants are other possibilities. Candles often are used to heighten the sense of the occasion. If candles are used in the centerpiece, they should be lighted throughout the meal—regardless of the time of day.

Flatware

The common types of flatware are sterling silver, silver plate, and stainless steel. Each material has certain advantages and disadvantages that need to be considered when deciding what to buy. Sterling silver is surprisingly durable considering that silver is really a very soft metal. The shininess of new sterling silver gives way to a softer, more appealing appearance as numerous small scratches develop to impart a soft patina to the pieces. Two drawbacks can be cited in considering selecting sterling silver flatware. Sterling silver needs to be polished occasionally to remove the tarnish that develops on the surface, particularly if egg is in contact with the silver or if the silver is not dried thoroughly after being washed. Besides the time required for caring for sterling silver, silver prices are so high that consumers may want to spend their money elsewhere. However, the investment in sterling silver is one that will last a lifetime, with proper care.

Silver plate resembles sterling silver because silver is plated over a base metal and the silver coating on silver plate tarnishes just like it does on sterling silver. Plate has the disadvantage that eventually the silver will wear off in certain spots on the pieces, leaving the base metal showing through. This limits the useful life of silver plate. However, the reduced cost, in comparison with the price of sterling silver, provides a motivation to consider buying silver plate.

Stainless steel flatware has grown considerably in its acceptance for daily and even special use. There is a very large range of quality in stainless steel, from stamped pieces with sharp edges that jeopardize one's mouth when using it to very costly patterns almost rivaling silver in price. A real advantage of stainless steel is its ease of care. As the name implies, stainless steel is very resistant to damage of any sort. It does not require polishing, but it never develops the rich patina seen on sterling silver.

Many flatware designs are available to meet the preferences of various people. But the flatware design should probably be pleasing to its owners for a long time, for its cost dictates that it usually is intended for long-term use. Choices range from extremely simple to quite elaborate. Although this choice is a matter of individual preference, the flatware should be selected in relation to the dishes being selected so that the total effect will be consistent and pleasing. Once the choices of patterns are narrowed, it is wise to handle each of the different pieces of flatware in a place setting to be sure that the balance is pleasing. Note also the appearance of the various pieces, paying particular attention to the forks. The tines should be close enough together to permit food to be held easily while en route to the mouth. The tips of the tines should not feel sharp. These are details that can make quite a difference in the pleasure of eating with various flatware patterns.

Dishes

Just as was true in selecting flatware, the first decision in picking dishes is to determine the type of material desired, whether pottery or china. Even within these two major categories, there are choices of quality, with bone china being the most durable and also most costly of the alternatives. The breakable nature of dishes must be considered in making a decision about what to purchase. The initial purchase of bone china is very costly, yet the durability of this high-quality china can make this a choice that ultimately could prove to be less costly than purchasing and replacing sets of pottery over a period of

Choices of dishes and flatware need to be made carefully, for they usually are used for many years. The designs should complement each other.

years. Pottery is often much less expensive than bone china, but usually pottery is comparatively fragile.

Chipped and cracked dishes not only create an unattractive table setting, but they also present a possible health hazard because the defects serve as sites for the growth of some microorganisms that may be protected from destruction during dish washing. People who are particularly concerned about avoiding problems of breakage often select plastic dishes. Stoneware offers quite a durable and attractive alternative to the use of plastic. Unfortunately, stoneware often is quite costly. It also has the disadvantage of being quite bulky and heavy to lift. Nevertheless, the many attractive designs and the solid feeling of quality found in stoneware have combined to make this type of dishes quite popular, particularly for casual living.

Frequently, the patterns found in china are fairly formal, although there is a tendency recently to create some comparatively informal china patterns to add to the various product lines. On the other hand, pottery and plastic dish designs usually are quite informal. Clearly, a choice needs to be made regarding formality of design as well as formality and durability of material to be selected. If a set of dishes is to be used for all occasions in a home, a pattern that has a slight tendency toward formality without being stiff may prove to be a wise choice. An extremely informal design in dishes will prevent meals from being formal occasions. If a set of pottery and a set of china dishes will be chosen, the pottery dishes can be rather informal, while the china can be fairly formal. This arrangement makes it possible to set the table for any occasion.

Whether selecting a formal or informal design, the appearance of the food on the plate must be visualized. Very busy designs may distract the eye from the food, and the food really should be the focal point. Often a simple, stylized design may provide a pleasing background for food. The colors in the design also should enhance the food.

Once a tentative selection has been made, check out the design of the various pieces. Of particular importance is the cup. The handle should be easy for men and women to hold. An extremely dainty handle can present a real hazard to the fingers of many men. A cup that is fairly narrow and deep is more functional than is one that is shallow and wide because the beverages will stay hot for a comparatively long time in the deep cup. The large surface area of the broad, shallow cup causes very quick heat loss; furthermore, spills also occur rather easily in cups of this design.

Ease of care is another factor to consider when picking dishes. Dishes with a sculptured, raised design are difficult to wash clean if food has been allowed to dry on the plates a bit before washing. If a dishwasher is to be used frequently for washing dishes, the dish design should have the design under the glaze so that the pigments or platinum or gold trim will be protected. In other words, dishes should be dishwasherproof and able to withstand dishwasher temperatures. Metallic trim needs to be avoided if the dishes are possibly going to be used to heat foods in a microwave oven.

Glassware

Of the items needed to set an attractive table, glasses clearly are the least durable. The possibility of breakage definitely needs to be recognized when glassware is being selected. For optimal beauty in table settings, crystal stemware is important. The leaded crystal goblets add a regal quality to a table setting. Even though the lead in the crystal adds to the durability of this type of glassware, there still is a risk that stemware will be broken. For people wishing to set a formal table without investing such a large sum of money in glassware, considerably less expensive, yet nicely designed, stemware is a very satisfactory alternative.

Although stemware adds a touch of elegance to a table setting, there are many times when glasses can be used to excellent advantage. Glasses are distinctly more durable than stemware. In addition, they are less likely to be bumped and tipped over than are goblets with their tall stems. The formality of glasses and also the price vary considerably. The choice of pattern and also color should be made in relation to the dishes and flatware selected. Sometimes colored glasses can add a very pleasing color accent to a table, but many times clear glass is desirable.

Practical considerations should be combined with the aesthetic when glasses are being considered. Stability is one of the key considerations. In stemware, stability is a particular problem, but it deserves some consideration in glasses, too. A broad base and/or a stem weighted toward the lower portion can be crucial to stable stemware. Glasses with heavily weighted bottoms may be a good choice, particularly if children will be at the table, for the low center of gravity of these glasses greatly reduces the likelihood of tipping. Thick glass is particularly important when young children will be using them, for they resist chipping around the edge. There even are times when plastic glasses may be the best answer.

SETTING THE TABLE

For a specific meal, place mats or a tablecloth and napkins should be selected. If it is a formal occasion and a tablecloth is being used, a silence cloth is helpful in reducing the mechanical sounds of dishes and glasses on the table, but this cloth is not used with lace cloths or cutwork. The tablecloth should be arranged carefully, being sure that the cloth is straight on the table so that all the overhanging edges are even. Place mats should be parallel with the edge of the table and about half an inch from the edge.

The flatware comprising a setting is arranged for orderly use in keeping with the menu. All flatware placed on either side of the plate should have the handles extending to an inch from the edge of the table so that the ends of the handles present an orderly appearance. The fork(s) should usually be arranged to the left of the dinner plate. If a fork is to be used for dessert, that fork is placed immediately adjacent to the plate (or above the service plate). The dinner fork and the salad fork are placed to the left of the dessert fork, with the salad fork being on the extreme left. The arrangement to the right of the plate begins with the knife. The blade of the knife should be turned so that the cutting edge of the knife is facing the plate. A teaspoon is placed immediately to the right of the knife. If a soup spoon or cocktail fork is a part of the arrangement, it is positioned to the right of the teaspoon. The butter spreader is placed on the bread and butter plate at the upper edge parallel to the edge of the table. Sometimes the flatware for dessert is placed above the plate, parallel to the edge of the table. Customarily, a maximum of three pieces of flatware is placed on each side of the plate, preferably with the same number on each side to create a balanced appearance.

Certain options sometimes are followed when placing the flatware. Sometimes the soup spoon or cocktail fork simply is placed on the liner on which the course is served. Similarly, dessert flatware can be brought when the dessert is served.

Napkins usually are placed just to the left of the forks, with the lower edge positioned an inch from the edge and parallel to the table. Before placing the napkin, it is folded over without any attempt to crease it. The open corner of the folded napkin traditionally is placed so that it is in the lower right-hand corner, nearest the edge of the table and immediately adjacent to the flatware. This makes it convenient to pick up the napkin and partially unfold it for placing in the lap.

Glasses are arranged above the flatware, the water glass being positioned immediately above the knife and any other glasses being arranged in orderly fashion to the right of the water glass and slightly closer to the edge of the table. When both a salad plate and a bread and butter plate are being used, the bread and butter plate is placed directly above the fork, and the salad plate is arranged to the left of the bread and butter plate and somewhat closer to the edge of the table. If a bread and butter plate is not being used, the salad plate is positioned immediately above the fork.

MEAL SERVICE

American Service
Method of meal service in which all of the food is placed in serving dishes on the table and passed around.

Various ways of serving a meal can be used to suit the occasion. The least formal form of service is *American service,* a service in which the serving dishes are placed on the table and the dining plates are arranged at each cover. When everyone is seated, people begin to help themselves to the food placed closest to them. Then the serving dish is passed to the person to the right. It is important that all the serving dishes be passed in the same counterclockwise direction to avoid a traffic jam of platters and serving bowls. American service has the advantage of allowing each person to select the portion size desired. Usually the food can be kept fairly warm with American service if it is really hot when the serving dishes are filled and if the serving at the table proceeds efficiently. The disadvantage of American service is the cold food that can result if some people are slow in helping to get the food passed.

Family Service Service of a meal by the host, who serves all of the food onto plates stacked in front of him and then passes the served plates to the hostess and others at the table.

Family service is similar to American service. The difference is that the host serves each plate from the stack of plates placed in front of him. All the serving dishes are arranged conveniently around the host to facilitate rapid service of the food. The first plate served is passed by the diners along the left side of the table to the hostess. As each plate is served, it is passed along the left side of the table to serve each person, beginning with the person nearest the hostess and moving back in sequence to the person nearest the host. Then the second side of the table is served in the same fashion. The host is the last person served. The obvious disadvantage of this type of service is that the food often is rather cool by the time the last plate has been served. However, there is less interruption of conversation than occurs in the passing of the dishes of food in American service.

English Service Meal service in which a waiter or waitress carries the dinner plate, which the host has served, to the diner.

English service is a somewhat more formal style of service than family service, for a waiter or waitress is used. The arrangements for English service are the same as those for placing the plates and serving dishes in family service. The host again serves the food onto the top plate of the stack placed at his cover. However, when the plate is served, the waiter or waitress takes the plate and carries it to the person for whom it is intended, starting with the hostess. The sequence of service is the same as is followed in family service. The plates are served from the left side of the diner. Beverages are served from the right side. The obvious advantage of English service is that the plates do not have to be passed from one person to another. However, the difficulty of serving the food while it is still pleasingly warm remains a disadvantage. Of course, the limited presence of help for serving meals frequently rules out the possibility of using English service in the home.

Blue-Plate Service The service of dinner plates from the kitchen.

Blue-plate service is a convenient style of service that is suited well to today's life-styles. In this service, the plates are served in the kitchen and are carried to the table. If an appetizer course is being served, this will be eaten and cleared before the dinner plates are served from the kitchen. When no appetizer is served at the table, the plates of food can be in place on the table when the diners are seated. This form of service permits control of portion sizes, which is a distinct advantage when people are trying to restrict their food intake for weight control purposes. It also has the advantage of not using serving bowls and platters, thus reducing the tasks of the dishwasher.

Russian Service Very formal form of service in which the waiters or waitresses serve the plates at a sideboard and carry them individually to the diners at the table; the meal is served in several courses, with the table being cleared between each course.

By far the most formal type of service is *Russian service.* This requires trained waiters or waitresses and thus fails to meet the needs of most American households today. For Russian service, a sideboard or buffet is mandatory, for this is the place where the food will be served. Each course is brought in serving dishes to the sideboard where the waiter serves it and then brings it to one of the diners. By the time each person has been served in this fashion, the food generally is cold. However, Russian service has the advantage to the host and hostess that they can devote their full attention to their guests and to leading a stimulating conversation. When diners have all finished a course, the plates are removed in preparation for the next course. Russian service is slow, which means that the dinner often serves as the primary entertainment of the evening.

The goals in serving meals are to have all diners enjoy the meal and to have the hot foods served hot and the cold foods well chilled. The type of service used for the meal should be selected to help meet these goals. Temperature control can be aided by warming dinner plates in a warm oven or on the dry cycle in the dishwasher. The refrigerator is helpful in chilling salad plates appropriately.

TABLE ETIQUETTE

Consideration for others is the underlying theme for defining rules of etiquette. When the welfare of another is the basis on which an action is performed, this ordinarily will result in appropriate social interactions. There are certain guidelines to be followed at any meal occasion to enhance the pleasure of all at the table. Diners should be sure to chew with their lips closed and to talk only when they do not have food in their mouths. They should keep the flatware they are using on the plate except when transporting food to the mouth. Explanations of a point being made in the conversation can be understood simply by choosing words appropriately; punctuation with the wave of a knife or the reinforcement of a fork loaded with food is frowned upon.

Aside from these general guidelines, diners can be assured that they are fitting into the expected social pattern if they will follow the example set by the hostess. It is the responsibility of the hostess to be certain that the people at the table have their dining needs satisfied and that they are all a part of the social occasion the meal provides. The meal begins when the people have all been seated. The hostess places her napkin in her lap by first unfolding it so that the napkin remains folded in half. She then begins to eat with the appropriate piece of flatware. The others at the table follow this lead. The hostess should eat at a rate that results in her completing a course at the same time that the slowest diner finishes. This is a mark of hospitality, for it says that there is no need to hurry. The flatware used in eating the appetizer should be placed on the liner used for serving that course when a person finishes the course. When the main course is finished, the knife and fork should be arranged parallel to each other and from the right side of the plate, with both the knife and the fork resting in the center of the plate and the handles extending a bit beyond the right edge of the plate. This arrangement makes it easy to remove plates without having the silverware fall off.

When a course is finished, the table is prepared for the next course. Often the table is cleared only between the main course and dessert. When everyone has finished eating, clearing is begun by removing the salt and pepper, butter plate, and any other serving items no longer needed. When this has been done, the plates are removed. Plates should be carried to the kitchen without stacking them in the dining area. Although this means a few more trips, the reduced confusion is well worth the extra effort.

At this point, water glasses and other beverages may need to be refilled. Service of beverages ordinarily is done from the right side of the diner. Sometimes crowded dining areas make it necessary to deviate from the pattern of placing and clearing plates from the left and serving beverages from the right. Common sense and practicality need to be used when accessibility is a problem.

A bit of practice with these rather basic guidelines will make it easy to be comfortable at the dining table. The emphasis really needs to be on being a contributing and congenial person at the table. All people, whether a family member or a guest, should participate in the conversation and help to make the meal a pleasant experience for everyone. Sometimes it is helpful to identify some topics that would be interesting conversation items for the group at the table. This is a particular help when one is the host or hostess, but it also is a useful idea when one is a guest.

SPECIAL TYPES OF HOSPITALITY

Buffets

Buffet Service Arrangement of the dinner plates and the food on a serving table, with guests helping themselves to their food as they move along the table.

When a large group of people is to be served, *buffet service* is often used. There are two different procedures that may be used with buffet service. If sufficient tables can be arranged for everyone to be seated, individual places can be set at the tables, with the linens, flatware, and glasses already set before the guests arrive. In this arrangement, guests need only to fill their plates at the buffet table and then proceed to a place at one of the tables. This avoids the problem of needing to try to juggle too many items en route to the table. The alternative is to place the flatware and napkins at the far end of the buffet table for guests to pick up after they have selected their food. Guests then proceed to find a chair or other place to sit with their food. Small tables can be positioned around the room so that each person can reach one. Beverages can then be placed on these tables.

With buffet service, appetizers usually are served prior to the actual beginning of buffet service. The main course is served in appropriate serving dishes on the buffet table. The table for this type of service can be arranged in a dramatic style. A fairly large, high centerpiece can be used because people will not need to be able to see above it while seated. The size of the centerpiece is dictated primarily by the size of the table in relation to the amount of food being served. There should be enough room so that the centerpiece can be seen well, without the plates of food overlapping with it. Sometimes a runner is used as the linen for a buffet table, while a tablecloth may be more appropriate in some other situations. If a runner is to be used, the table surface needs to be pretty, for it will become part of the overall effect of the buffet table.

Buffet service can be arranged so that people pass along both sides of the table, or it may be set up for only one line of service. In the former case, the centerpiece needs to be placed in the center of the table and be arranged so that both sides are attractive. For one-sided service, the centerpiece can be placed at the back of the table, with only one side being visible. When a large group is being served, the service will be speeded significantly by having the same food arranged on both sides of the table. This makes it possible for half of the people to go through on each side, thus cutting serving time approximately in half.

Once the linen and centerpiece have been arranged, the arrangement of the rest of the table can be planned. The dinner plates need to be placed at the beginning of the line. The food then is arranged along the side of the table so that it can be served easily with one hand as people move along. Meats should be arranged on a platter in individual slices or servings. Sometimes it is practical to have someone carve a roast or a turkey as people pass by that part of the table. If a sauce or other accompaniment is intended to be eaten with a specific food, the accompaniment should be placed right beside the food it is to augment. This placement helps to clarify the intended use of accompaniments. Often all of the hot foods are placed at the beginning of the food line, and the salads and rolls are toward the end. Each item on the line should have appropriate serving silver placed with it so that the service is easy for individuals. If a large group of people is being served by buffet style, it will be necessary to replenish serving dishes of food occasionally during the service. Sometimes the serving dishes are refilled when the last person has gone through the line so that people can return for additional servings, if they wish.

Dessert in buffet service can be handled in any of several different ways. One is to clear the buffet table of all of the main course serving dishes and to arrange the dessert, either on a serving platter or in individual servings, on the table. This can be quite attractive because the centerpiece shows off particularly well when there is only the dessert course on the table with it. The other approach is to serve the dessert to the guests where they are seated. The choice between these two methods of service is often dictated by the amount of help available for service. Regardless of which method is used for serving the dessert, the dishes from the main course need to be cleared before the dessert is served. The beverages also need to be refilled when the dessert is served. Following completion of the dessert course, all of the glasses and dishes are cleared.

Teas and Coffees

Some social occasions are held in the middle of the morning or afternoon, making a complete meal inappropriate, but nevertheless suggesting the need for some refreshments. In the morning, such informal gatherings in a neighbor's home or even in a business setting often are called coffees. The usual beverage served is coffee, but any hot beverage may be offered. A hot bread provides an excellent accompaniment for the steaming hot beverage. On special occasions, fruit might be added to the menu. In serving the refreshments, arrange the cups and coffee service from a cart or table that has been prepared with a simple cloth and a touch of decoration, perhaps a rose in a simple rose bowl. The cups are placed on the left side of the coffee pot with the handles turned so that the hostess can reach them easily. If convenient, the first cup is placed on a small tray in front of the hostess so that she can pour the beverage easily into the cup. Then the filled cup is placed on a saucer and is passed to a guest. Guests then help themselves to the platter of food and a napkin. The entire arrangement is planned for ease of service and maximum comfortable social conversation.

In contrast to a morning coffee, afternoon tea may be a formal social event, complete with silver tea service and rather elaborate foods. If there are several people attending the tea, a buffet table may be the best way to serve. The table for a formal tea is set with beautiful linens, often an elaborate floral centerpiece, and either silver or other formal candelabra. The beverage, usually hot tea, is arranged at one end of the table. The tea service ordinarily includes a large silver platter on which the silver tea pot and the silver creamer and sugar bowl are placed. The cups are placed just to the left or slightly in back of the platter, and the stack of saucers or small plates is adjacent to the cups. If several cups are needed, the cups may be stacked two high to save

Tea served graciously can set the tone for a leisurely visit with friends.

space. If space is limited, additional cups will need to be brought from the kitchen as needed during the tea.

Although the food for some teas may be very simple, the menu frequently is quite elaborate. Fancy tea sandwiches may be prepared in pin wheels, stacked to make ribbon sandwiches, or perhaps cut into special shapes with sandwich or cooky cutters. Small cookies and cakes may be arranged on another platter. Tarts, candies, and nuts are other foods popular at a tea. On the buffet table, the sandwiches are the first item the guest selects, followed by the dessert items, and finally the candies and nuts. The last items are the silverware and napkins.

SUMMARY

Table appointments cover a wide range of styles to fit the tastes and needs of many different people. Tablecloths of easy-care fabrics provide a colorful background for virtually any occasion. Place mats are convenient to use and can be excellent for meal service ranging from very informal to rather formal providing the dining table used has a pleasing surface to enhance the appearance of the mats. Matching or contrasting napkins complete the linens needed.

Centerpieces can be varied to suit the formality or informality of the occasion. It is important that the centerpiece complement the other pieces being used on the table and that the arrangement be low enough that people can see all of the other diners seated at the table. Elaborate arrangements can be used to advantage on a formal tea table.

Choices among flatware are sterling silver, silver plate, and stainless steel. Either of the silver products will need occasional polishing to remove tarnish. Sterling is attractive, yet costly, flatware that can be used for many years; silver plate costs less than sterling, but the plating will wear off at certain key pressure points in a few years of wear.

The price and durability of dishes are key considerations when selecting dishes. Bone china is particularly durable, but it is costly to buy. Pottery is of limited sturdiness, which may result in chips. However, the comparatively low cost of pottery helps to make pottery a sensible choice for many people. The patterns on dishes are very important in selecting a set of dishes, for they influence the formality of the table setting. Glassware should be compatible with the designs of the flatware and dishes. Because of the risk of breakage, decisions on glassware are not necessarily choices that must be lived with 10 years later, which provides an opportunity for a bit of experimentation or variety.

Table settings should be done carefully, with the flatware being arranged so that the handles are an inch from the edge of the table. Careful attention to arranging the flatware neatly and according to well-defined standards is essential to presentation of a meal of high quality in the home.

The same meal may be served in a variety of styles, the simplest of which is American service. The serving dishes are passed around the table, with each person serving his or her own plate. Family service is done by the host serving each of the plates from the post at the end of the table. English service is very similar to family service. However, English service requires that a waiter or waitress carry the served plates from the host to the diner. Blue-plate service is done by serving the dinner plates in the kitchen and carrying them to the table where the places are set. Russian service requires that a couple of people serve the food and otherwise wait on the guests. This very formal service is inconsistent with the life-styles of many U.S. households today.

The host and hostess are involved very directly with the development of excellent table manners for all family members. It is the hostess who carries much of the brunt of this assignment. She is the one who signals the beginning of the meal by lifting her fork to take the first bite. It also is her responsibility to be sure that she is eating at approximately the same pace as the slowest eater.

Buffets are a good way to serve large groups. In fact, a double line can be set up on the two sides of the table to save time. Once the buffet line has been toured, guests may be seated at tables equipped with the table service needed for gracious dining. Another service style is to have guests seated away from a regular dining table, but with a small table within reach to hold the beverages conveniently. Teas and coffees are popular in the United States as a social gathering. Coffees usually are rather informal occasions at which coffee and perhaps a bread are served. Teas ordinarily are held in the afternoon and boast rather elaborate dainty foods and formal service.

Selected References

Defenbacher, D. S. *Knife, Fork, and Spoon.* Colwell Press. Minneapolis. 1951.

Eberlein, H. D. and R. W. Ramsdell. *Practical Book of Chinaware.* J. D. Lippincott. Philadelphia. 1948.

Hill, A. L. *Table Setting and Flower Arrangement.* Greystone Press. New York. 1957.

Hirsch, S. *Art of Table Setting and Flower Arrangement.* Crowell. New York. 1962.

Stennett-Wilson, R. *Modern Glass.* Van Nostrand Reinhold. New York. 1975.

Study Questions

1. What criteria are important in selecting linens for the table?
2. Why is china more expensive than pottery to purchase?
3. Why is bone china more durable than pottery?
4. What are the advantages and disadvantages of sterling silver, silver plate, and stainless steel flatware?
5. Sketch a place setting, being sure to show how the knife is oriented.
6. What are the basic elements of each of the following forms of service: family, American, English, Russian, blue-plate?

APPENDIX A

SOME FOOD ADDITIVES

Additive	Functions
Acacia gum	Stabilizer, thickener, surface finisher
Acetanisole	Flavoring agent (nutty flavors)
Acetic acid	Acidulant, antimicrobial agent (bacteria and yeast)
Acetophenone	Flavoring agent (fruity flavors)
Acetone peroxide	Flour bleaching and maturing agent, solvent, oxidizing agent
Adipic acid	pH control
Agar agar	Thickener
Alanine	Nutrient enrichment (amino acid)
Alcohol	Solvent
Alginates	Water binder, thickener
Allyl disulfide	Flavoring agent (garlic, onion)
Aluminum phosphate	Anticaking agent
Aluminum sodium sulfate	Buffer
Aluminum stearate	Defoamer
Aluminum sulfate	Firming agent
Ammonium alginate	Stabilizer, thickener, texturizer
Amylase	Enzyme (digests starch)
Amyl propionate	Flavoring agent (fruity)
Annatto	Food coloring (used in cheese)
Arabic, gum (Acacia gum)	Stabilizer, thickener, surface finisher
Arabinogalactan	Stabilizer, thickener, texturizer
Arginine	Nutrient enrichment (amino acid)
Ascorbic acid	Antioxidant (to prevent enzymatic browning in fruits, color retention, curing, nutrient enrichment)
Aspartic acid	Nutrient enrichment (amino acid)
Azodicarbonamide	Flour bleaching and maturing agent
Baking powder	Leavening agent
Baking soda	Texturizing agent, pH modifier, leavener with acid
Beeswax	Surface finisher
Bentonite	Protein absorber
Benzoic acid	Antimicrobial agent (yeast and bacteria)
Benzoyl acetate	Flavoring agent (fruity flavor)
Benzoyl isoeugenol	Flavoring agent (spicy)
Benzoyl peroxide	Flour bleaching and maturing agent, oxidizing agent

Additive	Functions
BHA (butylated hydroxyanisole)	Antioxidant
BHT (butylated hydroxytoluene)	Antioxidant
Bisulfite salts	Antioxidants
Black pepper	Flavoring agent
Butyl paraben	Preservative
Butyl stearate	Defoaming agent
Calcium alginate	Stabilizer, thickening, texturizer
Calcium bromate	Maturing agent, bleaching
Calcium carbonate	Acidity control, leavening
Calcium citrate	Buffer, chelating agent
Calcium chloride	Firming agent
Calcium disodium EDTA	Chelating agent
Calcium gluconate	Buffer, chelating agent
Calcium lactate	Preservative
Calcium lactobionate	Foaming agent
Calcium oxide	Acidity control
Calcium peroxide	Oxidizing agent
Calcium phosphate	Buffer, chelating agent, leavener
Calcium propionate	Preservative
Calcium pyrophosphate	Buffer
Calcium silicate	Anticaking agent
Calcium sorbate	Preservative
Calcium stearate	Anticaking agent
Calcium stearoyl-2-lactylate	Emulsifier
Calcium sulfate	Processing aid
Canthaxanthin	Color enhancer
Carbon dioxide	Effervescent
Carnauba wax	Surface finisher
Carob bean gum (acacia gum)	Stabilizer, thickener, texturizer
Carotenes	Coloring agents
Carrageenan	Thickener, stabilizer, emulsifier
Cellulose	Stabilizer, thickener, texturizer
Cholic acid	Emulsifier
Citric acid	Acidifying agent, synergist, chelating agent, preservative, antioxidant
Citrus Red No. 2	Color
Cobalt sulfate	Source of cobalt and sulfur in diet
Cochineal	Beverage color
Cornstarch	Anticaking, thickener
Corn syrup	Formulation aid, texturizing agent, sweetener
Cupric chloride	Copper source
Cyclamates	Nonnutritive sweetener (banned in U.S.)
Decanoic acid	Defoaming agent
Desoxycholic acid	Emulsifier
Dextrin	Stabilizer
Dextrose	Formulation aid, sweetener (glucose)

Additive	Functions
Dicalcium phosphate	Acidity control, leavening, anticaking
Diglycerides	Emulsifiers
Dimagnesium phosphate	Anticaking agent
Dimethylpolysiloxane	Defoamer
Dioctyl sodium sulfosuccinate	Emulsifier
Disodium EDTA	Chelating agent
Disodium guanylate	Flavor potentiator
Disodium inosinate	Flavor potentiator
Disodium phosphate	Emulsifier
EDTA (ethylenediaminete-tra-acetate)	Sequestrant used in salad dressings, antioxidant
Ethyl caproate	Artificial fruit flavors
Ethylene oxide	Antimicrobial agent
Ethyl pelargonate	Alcoholic beverage flavors
Ethyl phenylacetate	Honey flavor
Ethyl vanillin	Chocolate and vanilla flavors
Eugenol	Defoaming agent
Fatty acids	Emulsifiers
F.D.&C. Blue No. 1	Coloring agent
F.D.&C. Red No. 3	Red coloring agent used in baked goods
F.D.&C. Yellow No. 5	Yellow coloring agent
Ferrous gluconate	Nutrient enrichment, iron source
Ferrous sulfate	Nutrient enrichment, iron source
Fructose	Sweetener, monosaccharide
Fumaric acid	Acidity control
Furcelleran	Texturizer
Gelatin	Thickening agent
Gibberellic acid	Fermentation aid
Glucose oxidase	Oxygen scavenger
Glycerine	Solvent, texturizer, humectant
Glycerol mono- and diesters	Emulsifiers
Glycocholic acid	Emulsifier
Glycerol monostearate	Dough conditioner
Guar gum	Thickener
Gum guiac	Antioxidant
Heptylparaben	Preservative
Honey	Sweetener, texturizer
Hydrochloric acid	Acidifying agent
Hydrogen peroxide	Bleaching, antimicrobial agent, oxidizing agent
Hydrolyzed vegetable protein	Stabilizer, thickener
Invert sugar	Sweetener
Iodate, potassium	Nutrient enrichment, iodine source
Iron oxide	Color
Karaya gum	Stabilizer, thickener, texturizer
Lactylic acid esters of fatty acids	Surface active agents, emulsifiers
Larch gum	Stabilizer, thickener, texturizer

Additive	Functions
Lauric acid	Defoaming agent
Lecithin	Emulsifier (from corn and soybeans)
Lipase	Dairy flavor developer
Locust bean gum (carob bean)	Dough conditioner
Magnesium carbonate	Anticaking
Magnesium silicate	Anticaking
Magnesium stearate	Formulation aid, anticaking
Magnesium sulfate	Nutrient enrichment, magnesium source
Manganese citrate	Nutrient enrichment, manganese source
Mannitol	Formulation aid, sweetener, anticaking, stabilizer, thickener, texturizer
Methyl bromide	Kill undesirable organisms
Methyl cellulose	Bulking agent
Methyl glucoside	Clouding and crystallization inhibitor
Methylparaben	Preservative
Mineral oil	Defoaming agent
Modified food starch	Stabilizer, thickener, texturizer
Monocalcium phosphate	Leavening, dough conditioner
Monoglycerides	Emulsifiers
Monosodium glutamate (MSG)	Flavor enhancer
Mustard	Flavoring agent
Nickel sulfate	Nutrient enrichment, nickel source
Nicotinamide	Nutrient enrichment, niacin source
Nitrates	Antimicrobial action, effective against spores of *Cl. botulinum*
Nitrites	Antimicrobial action, effective against spores of *Cl. botulinum*
Oleic acid	Defoaming agent
Oxystearin	Clouding and crystallization inhibitor, defoaming agent
Palmitic acid	Defoaming agent
Papain	Proteolytic enzyme used in meat tenderizer
Pectin	Stabilizer, thickener, texturizer
Pectinase	Clarifying agent for beverages (enzyme)
Peroxidase	Enzyme used to destroy glucose in dried egg white
Petroleum waxes	Defoaming agent
Phosphates	Acidity control
Phosphoric acid	Chelating agent, sequestrant, acidity control
Phostoxin	Fumigant
Polysorbate 60, 65, and 80	Emulsifiers
Polyvinyl pyrrolidine	Surface finisher
Potassium acid citrate	Buffer
Potassium alginate	Stabilizer, thickener, texturizer
Potassium bromide	Bleach and maturing agent for flour, dough conditioner, fermentation aid
Potassium citrate	Chelating agent
Potassium gibberellate	Fermentation aid

Additive	Functions
Potassium iodide	Nutrient enrichment, source of iodine
Potassium phosphate	Chelating agent, emulsifier
Potassium polymetaphosphate	Emulsifier
Potassium propionate	Emulsifier
Potassium pyrophosphate	Emulsifier
Propylene glycol	Formulation aid, humectant, solvent
Propylene glycol monostearate	Humectant
Propylene oxide	Antimicrobial agent
Propyl gallate	Antioxidant
Propylparaben	Preservative
Red No. 40	Color
Rennin	Enzyme, used to clot milk
Resins	Insoluble materials used to remove ions from water, juices, and other liquids; forms are acrylate-acrylamide, sulfonated copolymers of styrene, sulfonated anthracite coal
Rice wax	Surface finishing
Saccharin	Nonnutritive sweetener
Saffron	Colorizer
Shellac wax	Surface finish
Silica aerogel	Anticaking agent
Silicon dioxide	Defoaming agent, anticaking
Sodium acetate	Acidity control
Sodium acid phosphate	Leavening
Sodium acid pyrophosphate	Buffer, chelating agent
Sodium alginate	Stabilizer, thickener, texturizer
Sodium aluminum citrate	Anticaking
Sodium aluminum phosphate	Leavening, emulsifier in cheese
Sodium aluminum silicate	Anticaking
Sodium aluminum sulfate	Leavening
Sodium benzoate	Preservative
Sodium bicarbonate	Texturizer, pH influence
Sodium calcium alginate	Texturizer, stabilizer, thickener
Sodium caseinate	Formulation aid
Sodium carbonate	Acidity control, leavening
Sodium carboxymethylcellulose	Bulking agent
Sodium chloride	Flavor enhancer
Sodium citrate	Acidity control
Sodium diacetate	Chelating agent
Sodium erythorbate	Curing agent, preservative
Sodium gluconate	Chelating agent
Sodium hexametaphosphate	Chelating agent
Sodium hydroxide	pH control

Additive	Functions
Sodium lauryl sulfate	Surface active agent
Sodium metaphosphate	Sequestrant, curing agent, emulsifier
Sodium nitrate	Curing agent, prevent formation of toxin from *Cl. botulinum* spores
Sodium nitrite	Curing agent, prevent formation of toxin from *Cl. botulinum* spores
Sodium potassium tartrate	Buffer, chelating agent
Sodium propionate	Preservative
Sodium silicoaluminate	Anticaking agent
Sodium sorbate	Preservative
Sodium stearyl fumarate	Maturing, bleaching, conditioning agent
Sodium tartrate	Chelating agent
Sodium tripolyphosphate	Curing agent, humectant, chelating agent
Sorbic acid	Mold and yeast inhibitor
Sorbitan monooleate	Emulsifier
Sorbitan monostearate	Emulsifier
Sorbitan tristearate	Emulsifier
Sorbitol	Chelating agent, humectant, sweetener
Starch	Thickener, moisture retention, bulking
Stearic acid	Defoaming agent
Sucrose	Flavoring agent, preservative
Sugar	Flavoring agent, preservative
Sulfites	General antimicrobial agent
Sulfur dioxide	Preservative
Sulfuric acid	Acidity control
Tagetes	Aztec marigold, color; in chicken feed only
Tannic acid	Complexes protein
Tartaric acid	Chelating agent, acidity control
Tertiary butyl hydroquinone (TBHQ)	Antioxidant
Thiamin hydrochloride	Nutrient enrichment, thiamin
Thiiodopropionic acid	Decomposes hydroperoxide
Thiosulfate	Reducing agent
Titanium dioxide	Color
α-Tocopherol	Reducing agent, nutrient enrichment, vitamin E
Tragacanth gum	Stabilizer, thickener, texturizer
Triacetin	Solvent
Tricalcium phosphate	Synergist, anticaking
Triethyl citrate	Solvent
Turmeric	Flavor, color
Ultramarine blue	Color, animal feed only
Xanthan gum	Body, bulking agent
Yeasts	Leavening agents
Yellow No. 5	Color
Yellow prussiate of soda	Anticaking

APPENDIX B

GLOSSARY

Acid Hydrolysis   Cleavage of a molecule by utilizing a molecule of water in the presence of an acid, which serves as a catalyst.

Acidophilus Milk   Milk containing a culture of *Lactobacillus acidophilus*, which metabolizes the lactose in milk.

Acrolein   Aldehyde formed when glycerol loses two molecules of water.

Additive   Substance added by intent or by accident into foods.

Aerobic   Needing oxygen for survival and reproduction.

Aflatoxin   Mycotoxin produced by the growth of *Aspergillus flavus* or *Aspergillus parasiticus*, molds sometimes growing on peanuts, corn, seeds, or nuts that are not stored in a sufficiently dry environment or are grown in mold-containing soil.

Aged Beef   Prime beef that has been held in very cold storage for 15 to 40 days to intensify flavor, darken the color, and tenderize the muscles.

All-Purpose Flour   Flour from hard or hard and soft wheat blended; protein content of about 10.5 percent and suitable for making most baked products.

American Service   Method of meal service in which all of the food is placed in serving dishes on the table and passed around.

Amino Acid   Subunit of protein; contains an amino ($-NH_2$) group and an organic acid group ($-C\overset{\displaystyle\|O}{\underset{\displaystyle OH}{}}$).

Amorphous Candies   Candies with such a high sugar content that they are too viscous to permit an organized crystal structure to develop; very hard to extremely chewy candies.

Amphoteric   Ability to act as an acid (carrying a + charge) or as a base (a − charge). Their carboxyl and amino groups permit proteins to do this.

Amylopectin   The rather insoluble, nongel-forming fraction of starch; contains both 1, 4- and 1,6-α-glucosidic linkages, resulting in a bulky, branching molecule.

Amylose   Linear starch fraction (1,4-α-glucosidic linkages) that is soluble and capable of forming gels.

Anadromous   Fish living part of their lives in fresh water and part in salt water.

Anaerobic   Capable of surviving in an oxygen-free environment.

Angel Cake   Foam cake consisting primarily of egg white foam, sugar, and cake flour, with no fat or baking powder.

Anthocyanins   Group of flavonoids providing the reddish to bluish hues of fruits and vegetables.

Anthoxanthins   Group of flavonoids providing the white or creamy colors in fruits and vegetables.

Astringent   Characteristic of drawing together or puckering; green tea is noted for making the mouth feel a bit puckered and almost dry, particularly if the leaves have steeped more than 5 minutes.

Atmospheric Pressure The pressure of the atmosphere pressing downward on the surface of a liquid; varies with changes in elevation.

Bacteria Microscopic plants, often single-celled and of varied shapes (filamentous, rod-like, round, or spiral), some of which are causes of food-borne illnesses.

Baking Soda Bicarbonate of soda, an alkaline ingredient ($NaHCO_3$).

Basic Four Food plan composed of milk and dairy products, meat and meat alternatives, vegetables and fruits, and breads and cereals.

Beading Droplets of moisture on a meringue due to overbaking.

Beating Very vigorous agitation of food mixtures using an electric mixer at high speed or a wooden spoon to trap air and/or to develop gluten.

Beta-amylase Enzyme prominent in the catalytic release of maltose and glucose from starch to provide food for yeast.

Biscuit Quick bread made by cutting in the solid shortening and using a ratio of flour to liquid of 3:1, which results in a dough that is able to be kneaded, rolled, and cut into the desired round disk for baking.

Black Tea Brisk, rather mild, deep amber–colored tea produced by an extended fermentation period during the processing of tea leaves.

Blanching Boiling or steaming for a brief period to inactivate enzymes prior to freezing.

Blastoderm Germ spot in the egg yolk.

Bloom White or light gray discoloration on chocolate where the chocolate has softened and moisture has collected during storage; tempering is helpful in avoiding the development of bloom.

Blue-Plate Service The service of dinner plates from the kitchen.

Boiling Active agitation of liquid and transition of some liquid to the vapor state; occurs when vapor pressure just exceeds atmospheric pressure.

Boiling Water Bath (water bath canning) Preservation by packing high-acid foods, including fruits and tomatoes, into canning jars, covering closed jars with water, and heat processing for the appropriate time.

Botulism Type of food poisoning caused by eating the toxin produced by *Cl. botulinum.*

Bound Water Water held so tightly by other substances that it cannot flow.

Braising Cooking meat slowly in a small amount of liquid in a covered pan until the meat is fork tender, usually a matter of 2 hours or more.

Bread A baked mixture containing a flour or meal (usually wheat) as its primary ingredient.

Broiling Cooking by direct heat, usually at a distance of about 3 inches; fat is allowed to drain away from the meat.

Bromelin Enzyme that digests protein; fresh or frozen pineapple contains active bromelin, but canning destroys the action.

Buffet Service Arrangement of the dinner plates and the food on a serving table, with guests helping themselves to their food as they move along the table.

Bulgur Parboiled, cracked wheat; chewy and nutlike.

Buttermilk Skim milk sometimes containing flecks of butter and a bacterial culture.

Caffeine Compound in coffee credited with contributing the stimulating effect of the beverage and a touch of bitterness.

Cake Flour Flour from soft wheat; contains about 7.5 percent protein.

Calories Unit of energy provided in a food. One calorie (also called kilocalorie) is the amount of heat energy required to raise a kilogram of water 1° Celsius.

Camellia sinensis Shrub in the *Theaceae* family, the leaves of which are plucked and used in making tea.

Candling   Grading procedure based on silhouetting eggs in the shell.

Carbohydrate   Organic compounds containing carbon, hydrogen, and oxygen, with the hydrogen and oxygen being in the ratio of water (H_2O); category includes sugars, starches, pectic substances, cellulose, gums, and other complex substances.

Carcinogenic   Capable of causing cancer.

Carotenoids   Carotenes and related compounds producing the orange pigments in fruits and vegetables.

Casein   Chief protein in milk and is precipitated in the manufacturing of cheese from milk.

Catechin   A prominent polyphenol in green tea.

Cellulose   Complex carbohydrate in cell walls of plant foods, particularly in the dermal cells.

Chalaza   A fibrous structure at the side of the yolk, aiding in centering the yolk within the egg.

Chiffon Cake   Foam cake containing oil and baking powder, as well as the ingredients used in other foam cakes combined together and folded into an egg white foam beaten until the peaks just stand up straight.

Chlorogenic Acid   Most abundant acid in coffee; contributes some of the sour and bitter quality to coffee flavor.

Chlorophyll   Green, magnesium-containing pigment in fruits and vegetables.

Chloroplasts   Plastids containing chlorophylls in the cytoplasm of parenchyma cells.

Chromoplasts   Plastids containing carotenoids (orange pigments) in parenchyma cells.

Cis   Configuration at the double bond of an unsaturated fatty acid resulting in a change in the direction of the chain of a fatty acid;

$$\begin{matrix} H & & H \\ & \diagdown \quad \diagup & \\ & C{=}C & \\ & \diagup \quad \diagdown & \\ R & & R \end{matrix}$$

Clostridium botulinum   Type of bacteria producing a toxin that is highly poisonous and frequently fatal to humans when consumed.

Clostridium perfringens   Anaerobic, spore-forming bacteria that multiply readily at room temperature; ingestion can result in perfringens poisoning.

Coagulation   The clumping together of partially denatured protein molecules to make a relatively insoluble protein mass.

Coarse Suspension   Dispersion of particles larger than colloidal size mixed in water or other liquid.

Coddling   Simmering of fruit in a sugar syrup.

Coldpack (club) Cheese   Mixture of natural cheeses with an added emulsifier, but without heating.

Collagen   White connective tissue in meats; fibrous structural protein encasing muscle proteins.

Colloidal Dispersion   System containing protein or other molecules or particles between 1 and 100 millimicrons in size dispersed in a continuous phase.

Conching   Processing step in making chocolate in which the melted chocolate is held in constant motion for between 36 and 72 hours at temperatures ranging from 110° to 210°F, a process helpful in avoiding bloom during storage.

Conduction   Transfer of heat from one molecule to the next.

Conserves   Preserves with nuts added.

Continuous Phase   Liquid surrounding the suspended droplets in an emulsion.

Convection   Transfer of heat throughout a system by movement of currents of heated air, water, or other liquid.

Conventional Method Method of preparing shortened cakes, in which the fat and sugar are creamed, the beaten eggs are added, and the sifted dry ingredients are added (in thirds) alternately with the liquid (in halves).

Conventional Sponge Method Method of mixing shortened cakes, differing from the conventional method by separating the eggs and using part of the sugar to make a meringue to fold in at the end of mixing.

Creaming Mixing fat and sugar together vigorously to create an air-in-fat foam.

Cream Puff Quick bread used as a container for dessert fillings or main course mixtures; characterized by a very large cavity resulting from an appropriate combination of butter, water, and egg, in conjunction with flour, and baked in a hot oven.

Cross-Linked Starches Starches treated with various phosphate compounds prior to gelatinization to reduce rupturing of the starch granules.

Crustaceans Shellfish covered by a horny protective layer; shrimp, lobsters, and crabs are familiar examples.

Cryophilic Thriving at temperatures well below room temperature; cold loving.

Crystalline Candies Candies with an organized crystal structure; easily bitten into or cut with a knife.

Curing Treating of meats with salt, sodium nitrate, and heat to achieve color and flavor changes and to promote shelf life and reduce spoilage.

Cutting In Process of cutting solid fats into small pieces with the use of a pastry blender or two table knives.

Cytoplasm Viscous layer just inside the cell wall of the parenchyma cell; contains plastids.

Dark-cutting Beef Darkly colored beef with a sticky and gummy character, the result of too little glycogen at slaughter, usually due to exhaustion or inadequate feeding at dispatch.

Delaney Clause Clause in the Food Additives Amendment mandating that additives shown to cause cancer at any level must be removed from the marketplace.

Denaturation A physical change in proteins, resulting in a change from native to denatured protein to decrease the solubility and alter the flow properties of food proteins.

Devil's Food Cake Shortened cake made with some excess of soda to achieve the desired deep mahogany color.

Dextrinization Chemical breakdown of starch to a more soluble carbohydrate as a result of intense, dry heat.

Dipole Molecule having both a positive and a negative charge.

Disaccharide Sugars occurring frequently in foods and more complex than monosaccharides, for instance, sucrose, maltose, and lactose.

Discontinuous (Disperse) Phase Droplets in an emulsion.

Double-acting Baking Powder Baking powder containing an acid salt that reacts at room temperature (phosphate salt) and one requiring heat for reaction (sulfate salt); common type of baking powder in the retail market.

Dressed Fish Fish from which the gills, fins, head, tail, and entrails have been removed.

Dripolator Coffee maker with a unit for the heated water, a section for the coffee grounds, and a pot to collect the coffee.

Drupes Fruit with a single seed surrounded by edible pulp; cherry is an example.

Dry Stage Point at which beaten egg white foam becomes brittle and loses the sheen normally seen on egg white foam; no longer useful in food preparation.

Durum Wheat A very hard, high-protein wheat grown primarily in North Dakota and particularly well suited to the production of pastas.

Dutch Process Chocolate Chocolate manufactured with the addition of alkali to produce a pH between 6.0 and 8.8, causing the chocolate to be dark in color, less acidic, and less susceptible to settling out than is true of chocolate made without adding alkali.

Edible Starch Films Films made from special starches containing about 80 percent amylose.

Elastin Extremely strong connective tissue; a yellow-colored protein in meat that is not tenderized by cooking.

Emulsifying Agent Substance forming a protective coating on the surface of droplets (the interface) in an emulsion.

Emulsion Colloidal dispersion of two immiscible liquids, with one type of liquid being dispersed as droplets in the other type of liquid.

English Service Meal service in which a waiter or waitress carries the dinner plate, which the host has served, to the diner.

Enriched Cereals Refined cereals to which thiamin, riboflavin, niacin, and iron have been added at specified levels.

Espresso Extremely strong and rather bitter Italian coffee resulting from brewing finely ground, dark-roasted coffee with steam.

Essential Amino Acid Amino acid that must be provided in the diet to maintain life and promote growth; unable to be synthesized in the body.

Evaporated Milk Canned milk product in which about half of the water content has been evaporated prior to canning; available in varying levels of fat, that is, ranging from nonfat to whole.

Family Service Service of a meal by the host, who serves all of the food onto plates stacked in front of him and then passes the served plates to the hostess and others at the table.

Fatty Acid Organic acid containing between 2 and 24 carbon atoms; combines with glycerol to form a fat.

FDA Food and Drug Administration; the federal agency regulating food additives.

Ferrous Sulfide Iron-sulfur compound formed on the surface of the yolk of hard-cooked eggs if eggs are of low quality or are held at high temperatures too long a time.

Fiber Components of food not digested and absorbed; cellulose, pectic substances, and gums are some carbohydrates contributing to the fiber content of the diet.

Filet Lengthwise piece of fish free of the backbone and associated bones.

Fish Cold-blooded aquatic animal, usually used as a term to designate those with fins, a backbone, skull, and gills.

Flavonoids Class of pigments contributing white and red to blue colors in fruits and vegetables; two main divisions are anthoxanthins and anthocyanins.

Flour Finely ground cereal grains; often used to imply wheat as the grain.

Foamy Stage Transparent, coarse, somewhat fluid foam; stage appropriate for adding the acid and starting to add the sugar to egg whites, but not suitable for use in food mixtures.

Folding Very gentle manipulation with a rubber spatula, narrow metal spatula, wire whisk, or whip to bring ingredients up from the bottom of the mixing bowl and to spread them over the upper surface to aid in blending them uniformly.

Food Additives Amendment of 1958 Amendment to the Food, Drug, and Cosmetic Act of 1938; regulates food additive usage.

Food and Nutrition Board A group operating under the auspices of the National Academy of Sciences–National Research Council; members appointed to the group are nationally recognized researchers in nutrition.

Freeze-dried Coffee   Soluble coffee product made by freezing brewed coffee and sublimating the aqueous portion to obtain dry solids.

Freeze-drying   Process of drying frozen foods.

Freezer Burn   Dessiccation or drying of part of the surface of frozen food where air contacts the surface.

Fruit Butter   Cooked fruit purée with spices.

Gel   A colloidal dispersion in which the solid is the continuous phase and the liquid is the disperse or discontinuous phase; a starch gel is an example.

Gelatinization   Physical change in starch when heated sufficiently in the presence of water; swelling of starch granules because of the entry of water.

Gelation   Formation of a colloidal dispersion in which the solid forms a continuous phase and liquid forms the discontinuous or disperse phase; a gelatinized starch system that does not flow.

Gliadin   Sticky fraction of gluten.

Gluten   Protein complex formed in batters and doughs when wheat flour is mixed with water (or other aqueous liquid).

Glutenin   Very large, elastic component of gluten.

Glycerol   Alcohol containing three carbon atoms and three hydroxyl (—OH) groups; common to the fats used in food preparation.

Glycogen   Polysaccharide in muscle, which breaks down to produce energy and lactic acid in the carcass following slaughter.

Gonyaulax catanella   One-celled organism in ''red tide'' that produces saxitoxin in infected shellfish.

GRAS List   List of over 680 additives considered to be safe and legal to use while testing of the numerous additives was being conducted.

Green Tea   Somewhat astringent tea that has not been fermented.

Grits   Coarsely chopped hominy.

Heat of Crystallization   Heat energy released when a viscous sugar solution crystallizes and forms a solid mass.

Heat of Solidification   Heat given off when water is transformed into ice; 80 kilocalories per gram of water.

Heat of Vaporization   Energy required to convert boiling water into steam; 540 kilocalories per gram of water.

Herb Tea   Beverage made by steeping herbs and other ingredients in water; chosen by some people because of absence of caffeine.

Hemicellulose   Complex carbohydrate contributing to the strength of cell walls and being particularly abundant in the walls of vascular and parenchyma cells.

High-Fructose Corn Syrup   Corn syrup in which isomerase has converted some of the sugar to fructose.

Hominy   Endosperm product made by soaking corn in lye.

Hydrogenation   Process of adding hydrogen to polyunsaturated fatty acids to change oils into solid fats.

Hydrolysis   Chemical reaction in which a molecule of water is used to split a compound into two molecules.

Hydrolytic Rancidity   Release of free fatty acids due to lipase action during storage of fats.

Hygroscopic   Water attracting.

Ingredient Labeling   Listing of ingredients, beginning with the one present in the largest amount by weight and continuing in descending order.

INQ   Index of nutrient quality; profile of the nutrient content of a food in comparison with its calorie content.

Instant Cereals Cereals that have been precooked to gelatinize the starch and then dehydrated to produce a product requiring only rehydration to serve.

Instant Coffee Soluble coffee solids remaining after the water vapor has been removed from brewed coffee; often made by spray drying.

Interfering Agent Butter, corn syrup, or other ingredient inhibiting crystal formation in candies.

Inversion Specific term for the hydrolysis of sucrose to glucose and fructose.

Invertase Enzyme catalyzing the inversion of sucrose to glucose and fructose.

Invert Sugar A mixture of equal amounts of glucose and fructose resulting from the hydrolysis of sucrose.

Isoelectric Point pH at which a protein molecule is essentially neutral, resulting in easy aggregation of protein molecules to form curds.

Isomerase Enzyme utilized to convert glucose to fructose in making high-fructose corn syrup.

Jam Pectin gel with pieces of fruit plus the juice.

Jelly Pectin gel made with fruit juice to yield a clear gel.

Kasha Buckwheat groats (hulled and fragmented particles).

Kneading Folding over of a ball of dough and pressing it with either the fingertips or the heels of both hands, depending upon the amount of gluten needing to be developed and the ratio of ingredients.

Leaf Lard Fat obtained from the abdominal cavity of hogs; the premium type of lard.

Lecithin Compound in egg yolk that is attracted to both oil and water, making it a very effective emulsifying agent.

Leucoplasts Plastids serving as the site for formation and storage of starch in cytoplasm in parenchyma cells.

Lipase Enzyme catalyzing the release of fatty acids from fats.

Lipids Compounds containing mostly carbon and hydrogen, plus a small proportion of oxygen, to provide concentrated sources of energy.

Low-Fat Milk Milk from which part of the fat has been skimmed, resulting in a product with fat usually at the level of 1 or 2 percent.

Lukewarm Approximately body temperature; about 100°F.

Lysozyme Protein involved in egg white foams; isoelectric point is pH 10.7.

Magnetron Tube Tube generating the microwaves in a microwave oven.

Maillard Reaction Browning reaction in food caused by reaction between protein and a sugar.

Marbling Deposition of fat within the muscles of meats.

Market Order Regulations for the marketing of specific food products under the guidance of a board, which is authorized by the U.S. Department of Agriculture.

Marmalade Citrus preserves.

Mellorine Frozen ice cream–like dessert in which the fat is not the original milk fat.

Metabolism Chemical reactions in the body; the release of energy from carbohydrates is but one example.

Microwave Oven Special type of oven that is able to heat food by sending waves of 915 or 2450 megahertz from a magnetron directly into foods, where water and/or fat molecules vibrate and heat foods.

Microwaves Form of electromagnetic energy; 915 and 2450 megahertz are the assigned frequencies for microwave ovens.

Milling Grinding and separating of the desired fractions of the cereal kernel to produce flour.

Minerals Natural elements in foods that remain as ash if a food is burned; many are essential nutrients.

Modified Conventional Method   Method of mixing a cake utilizing the conventional method, but separating the eggs and adding the whites as a foam folded in at the end of mixing.

Molds   Multiple-celled microorganisms capable of forming heads with spores that scatter and are viable even in moisture levels as low as 13 percent.

Mollusks   Shellfish protected by an outer shell; scallops, clams, and oysters are common examples.

Mono-, Di-, Triglycerides   Fat molecules containing, respectively, one, two, or three fatty acids esterified with glycerol.

Monosaccharide   The simplest of the sugars; common examples include glucose, fructose, and galactose.

Mother Liquor   Saturated sugar solution between the crystals in crystalline candies.

Muffin Method of Mixing   Method in which melted fat or oil is blended with other liquids, added all at once to the well-mixed dry ingredients, and stirred just enough to blend the ingredients.

Muffins   Quick bread with a cauliflowerlike, rounded surface resulting from careful mixing and baking of a batter with a 2:1 ratio of flour to liquid.

Muskmelon   One of two general subdivisions of melons; includes cantaloupe, honeydew, and other melons characterized by having a thick pulp surrounding a large central cavity full of small seeds.

Mycotoxin   Poisonous substance produced by the growth of some molds.

Myoglobin   Pigment in meat; compound similar to hemoglobin and capable of reacting with various substances to effect color changes in muscle.

Myosin   Key, elongated, and large protein molecule in muscle.

Natural Cheese   Concentrated curd of milk; ripening is optional.

Nonfat Milk   Milk resulting when almost all of the fat has been removed, leaving a maximum fat content of 0.5 percent, and usually the level is 0.1 percent or less.

Nonwaxy Potatoes   Potatoes with a low sugar content and high starch level; best suited for baking, mashing, and frying.

Nutrient Density   Expression of the percentage of the day's requirement of a nutrient provided by a serving of food in comparison with the percentage of caloric need in that serving; high nutrient density is desirable, preferably in regard to three or more of the nutrients.

Oolong Tea   Tea that has undergone limited fermentation, resulting in characteristics intermediate between green and black tea.

Open Dating   Date stating clearly pull date or other freshness date.

Orange Pekoe   Top grade of black tea.

Osmotic Pressure   The pressure exerted to move water in or out of cells to equalize the concentration of solute in the cell and in the surrounding medium.

Ovalbumin   Heat-sensitive, abundant protein in egg white.

Oven Spring   Sharp increase in volume in early phase of baking due to accelerated carbon dioxide production in a hot oven.

Overrun   The increase in volume of ice creams during freezing as a result of expansion as water turns into ice and the incorporation of air during freezing.

Ovomucin   Structural protein abundant in thick egg white.

Oxidative Rancidity   Uptake of oxygen (with loss of hydrogen at points of unsaturation in a fatty acid, causing undesirable flavor and aroma changes.

Pan Broiling   Cooking meat in a skillet, being careful to keep removing the fat as it drains from the meat.

Pan Frying   Cooking meat in a frying pan and allowing the fat to accumulate in the pan.

Parasite Organism living within another organism and deriving its sustenance from the host; worms, such as *Trichinella spiralis,* can cause weight loss and other health problems.

Parenchyma Cell Type of cell comprising most of the pulp of a vegetable or fruit.

Parevine Frozen imitation ice cream made without any dairy products.

Pasta Various dough pastes containing durum wheat and water and sometimes egg and shaped in a variety of flat and rounded or twisted shapes.

Pasteurization Heat treatment to kill disease-producing microorganisms in milk; usually heated to 161°F and held there for 15 seconds before cooling to less than 50°F.

Pectic Acid Pectic substance in overly ripe fruit; incapable of forming a gel.

Pectic Substances Complex carbohydrates acting as cementing substances between cells; sequence of change during ripening is protopectin to pectin to pectic acid.

Pectin Pectic substances in barely ripe fruit; capable of forming a gel.

Pectinic Acid A form of the pectic substance, pectin.

Peptide Bond Bond formed between the carboxyl of one amino acid and the amino group of a second amino acid with loss of water.

Percolator Coffee pot containing a basket for coffee grounds that is suspended on a hollow stem above the water in the pot.

Permanent Emulsion Viscous emulsion containing an emulsifying agent and that rarely separates into two layers.

Peroxide Value Content of peroxides in a fat; a measure of oxidative rancidity.

Petcock Small opening in the cover of a pressure saucepan to let steam escape and on which the pressure gauge is placed.

pH Hydrogen ion potential; values less than 7 are acidic, while those above 7 are alkaline.

Plasticity Ability of a fat to be spread easily into quite thin films.

Plastids Special structures within the cytoplasm of parenchymal cells.

Poaching Simmering a food in water or other liquid just below boiling until the food is tender.

Polymerization The joining together of free fatty acids to make long chains; occurs in heated oils.

Polyphenolase Enzyme active in converting polyphenols into theaflavins during fermentation of black tea leaves.

Polyphenols Compounds containing more than one six-membered phenolic ring; contribute astringency to tea.

Polysaccharide Complex carbohydrate made up of many units of monosaccharides joined together into single molecules.

Pome Fruit with a core containing five seeds and surrounded by thick, edible pulp; apples, pears, and quince are examples.

Popovers Quick bread made with a flour/liquid ratio of 1:1 and with egg and baked in deep cups in an oven heated to at least 425°F to generate steam for leavening.

Preserves Pectin gel with juice and fruit pieces larger than the pieces used in jam.

Pressure Canner Large, heavy kettle with tight-fitting lid capable of withstanding internal pressure of at least 20 pounds; used for canning low-acid foods.

Primal Cuts First cuts (wholesale cuts) to provide large sections, yet small enough to be handled by the butcher.

Process Cheese Blend of natural cheeses heated to at least 145°F, with the addition of an emulsifying agent and water; cheese that will not ripen.

Process Cheese Food Process cheese product with about 4 percent more water than in process cheese.

Process Cheese Spread Process cheese product with about 4 percent more water than in process cheese food, or about 8 percent more water than in process cheese.

Proofing Fermentation of a yeast-leavened batter or dough to produce the necessary carbon dioxide; usually controlled at a temperature between 85° and 95°F for about an hour to double the volume.

Proteolytic Enzyme Enzyme capable of catalyzing a break in a protein at a peptide linkage.

Protopectin Pectic substance in very green fruit; incapable of forming a gel.

Quick Bread Bread leavened with steam or carbon dioxide produced by a chemical reaction; a bread that does not require time for biological agents to generate carbon dioxide.

Quick-cooking Cereals Cereals treated with disodium phosphate to hasten softening during cooking.

Quick-rising Active Dry Yeast New strain of yeast capable of reducing rising time by half in yeast-leavened products.

Radiation Transfer of energy directly from the source to the food being heated.

RDA Recommended dietary allowances specified by the Food and Nutrition Board to provide standards for professionals to utilize in planning diets and projects for groups of people in normal good health.

Rearranged Lard Lard that has had special processing to remove the fatty acids from the glycerol and then to reunite them in a somewhat different configuration to achieve a product that tends to form beta prime ($_\beta{}'$) crystals.

Rennin Protein-digesting enzyme from calves' stomachs.

Retail Cuts Meat cuts available to consumers.

Retrogradation Formation of crystalline areas due to aggregation of amylose molecules in a starch gel; a physical process that can be reversed by heating.

Reversion Development of a fishy quality in polyunsaturated fats.

Rheology Flow properties.

Rigor Series of chemical changes occurring in the carcass following slaughter.

Roux Method Preparation of gravy by stirring starch into the measured drippings from fried or roasted meats.

Russian Service Very formal form of service in which the waiter or waitress serves the plates at a sideboard and carry them individually to the diners at the table; the meal is served in several courses, with the table being cleared between each course.

Saccharomyces cerevisiae Strain of yeast used to produce carbon dioxide in yeast-leavened products.

Saccharomyces exigus Yeast primarily responsible for the production of carbon dioxide in acidic, sourdough breads.

Salmonellae Bacteria capable of causing severe gastrointestinal upset when ingested in large quantities in food.

Salmonellosis Condition characterized by fever, nausea, abdominal cramps, and diarrhea resulting from ingestion of viable salmonellae.

Satiety Value Ability to satisfy and provide feeling of fullness.

Saturated Solution Homogeneous mixture that has as much solute in solution as is possible at that temperature.

Saxitoxin Poison secreted by *Gonyaulax catanella* within a shellfish host; capable of being concentrated enough to kill a person.

Scalding Temperature used to loosen fruit skins and perform other similar functions; about 150°F.

Scoring Cutting the fat and connective tissue at intervals of about an inch around the edge of a muscle to prevent curling of meat during broiling.

Self-rising Flour Flour containing a blend of hard and soft wheats, plus an acid salt, baking soda, and salt, making it necessary to eliminate these ingredients from recipes using self-rising flour.

Semipermanent Emulsion Emulsion that is quite viscous and separates into two layers very slowly.

Semolina Granular, milled durum wheat, with a maximum of 3 percent flour.

Shellfish Subcategory of fish; equipped with shell or horny outer covering.

Shellfish Poisoning Life-threatening poisoning from saxitoxin produced in shellfish feeding on *Gonyaulax catanella*; characterized by loss of strength and respiratory failure.

Shortened Cake Cake containing a solid fat (usually creamed with sugar), sugar, leavening agent, flour, and liquid.

Shortening Value Ability of a fat to interfere with gluten development and tenderize a baked product.

Simmering Range of temperatures between 180° and 211°F; bubbles form and rise, but rarely break the surface; more gentle heat treatment than boiling.

Single-Stage Method Method combining all of the ingredients except the egg and possibly part of the liquid, mixing, and then adding the egg and any remaining liquid with beating.

Sinigrin Compound in the cabbage family that ultimately is converted to hydrogen sulfide, causing an unpleasant flavor.

Skim Milk Milk resulting when almost all of the fat has been removed, leaving a maximum fat content of 0.5 percent, and usually the level is 0.1 percent or less.

Slurry Starch paste.

Smoke Point Temperature at which a fat smokes due to chemical breakdown to free fatty acids and acrolein.

Smoking Means of helping to promote shelf life of meat by hanging it in a smokehouse to dry out the surface and add flavor to the meat.

Soft Peak Stage Egg white foam beaten until the peaks just bend over, a point noted for ease of blending with other ingredients and for stability during mixing and baking.

Sol Colloidal dispersion in which the solid is the discontinuous phase or the disperse phase and the liquid is the continuous phase; a gelatinized starch paste is an example of a sol.

Sour Cream Viscous, acidic cream containing at least 18 percent fat; acidified by action of lactic acid bacteria on lactose.

Sponge Cake Foam cake comprised of an egg yolk foam and an egg white foam, plus a small amount of cake flour, water, lemon, and sugar, and usually baked in a tube pan.

Sponge Method Method of preparing a yeast dough, in which the salt and part of the flour are withheld until the batter has generated enough carbon dioxide to give a spongelike quality to the mixture; addition of the rest of the flour and the salt precedes the completion of the kneading and subsequent steps.

Stabilized Starches Starches resistant to retrogradation and syneresis because of formation of phosphate or acetyl esters of starch; often called modified starches.

Staphylococcal Poisoning Food poisoning due to ingestion of the enterotoxin produced by *Staphylococcus aureus*; violent disturbance of gastrointestinal tract for one to two days and occurring usually within 8 hours of eating the contaminated food.

Starch Granule Units of starch (usually consisting of about 20 percent amylose and 80 percent amylopectin) deposited in concentric layers within the leucoplasts in cells.

Steak Cross-sectional slice of a uniform thickness.

Stiff Peak Stage Point at which egg white peaks stand up straight, but the foam does not break apart; used in making hard meringues and chiffon cakes.

Stirring Gentle blending of ingredients when trapping of air and development of gluten are not necessary.

Straight Dough Method Method of making a yeast bread dough by combining all of the ingredients (scalded milk, sugar, salt, butter, and egg, with softened yeast added after mixture is sufficiently cool, and the flour) and kneaded prior to the proofing period.

Sublimation Change of state from ice directly to water vapor without passing through the liquid water state.

Sucrase Enzyme in yeast that catalyzes breakdown of sucrose to glucose and fructose to initiate the production of carbon dioxide in batters and doughs containing yeast.

Supersaturated Solution Solution in which more solute is dissolved than theoretically can be dissolved; created by boiling a true solution to a high temperature and then cooling very careful.

Surface Tension Tendency of a liquid to present the least possible surface area (to form a sphere rather than to spread into a film); low surface tension is essential to foam formation and stability.

Sweetened Condensed Milk Canned milk product made by evaporating about half of the water and adding a high percentage (44 percent) of sugar.

Syneresis Separation of liquid from a gel.

Tannins Previous term for polyphenols.

Temporary Emulsion Emulsion that separates very quickly into two layers.

Theaflavins Extremely astringent compounds in black tea that, in combination with caffeine, provide the brisk quality to black tea.

Theobromine Stimulant prominent in cocoa and chocolate.

Thermophilic Thriving at temperatures above room temperature; heat loving.

Thin-boiling Starch Starch that has undergone limited acid hydrolysis, resulting in a product that is fluid when the gelatinized mixture is hot, but forms quite a rigid gel when cooled.

Toxin Poisonous substance produced by metabolic reactions; *S. aureus* and *Cl. botulinum* are the bacteria most commonly responsible for food poisoning from toxins.

Trans Configuration at the double bond of an unsaturated fatty acid resulting in a continuation of the linear chain;
$$\underset{R}{\overset{H}{\diagdown}}C=C\underset{H}{\overset{R}{\diagup}}$$

Trichinosis Illness caused by the presence of viable *Trichinella spiralis*, a parasite sometimes found in pork and transmitted to humans if pork is heated inadequately.

Triglyceride Fat containing three fatty acids.

Triticale Grain produced by crossing rye and wheat; its flour has a protein mixture with some potential for making good baked products.

Turgor The tension in cells caused by water pressing against cell walls; a desirable characteristic in salad ingredients.

UHT Ultrahigh-temperature pasteurization of milk (280°F for 2 seconds) to make the milk sterile, permitting storage at room temperature when UHT-treated milk is aseptically packaged.

Unit Pricing Cost of a designated amount of an item to make price comparisons easy for consumers.

Universal Product Code   Pattern of bars printed on packages to code inventory and cost information for translation by electronic scanning at the check stand.

Vacuole   Largest region of the parenchyma cell; the portion encircled by the cytoplasm.

Vapor Pressure   Pressure within a liquid for individual molecules to escape from the liquid, varies with the temperature of the liquid and with dissolved substances.

Vegetable   Herbaceous plant containing an edible portion suitably served with the main course of a meal.

Vitamin   Organic compound needed in very small amounts by the body to maintain life and promote growth and that must be included in the diet.

Vitelline Membrane   Membrane surrounding the yolk of an egg.

Water-holding Capacity   Ability of muscles to hold water; an important contribution to juiciness of meats.

Waxy Potatoes   Potatoes with a high content of sugar and low amount of starch; best suited for boiling and other preparations where shape is important.

Waxy Starches   Starches from plants bred to produce a starch that is virtually all amylopectin and is free of amylose; valued for use in products where a gel is not desirable.

Weeping   Leakage or collection of fluid between the filling and meringue due to failure to denature the protein in the egg white.

Whey   Liquid removed from clotted milk in cheese manufacturing.

Whipping Cream   Cream capable of being whipped into a foam because of its fat content of at least 30 percent.

Whole Wheat Flour   Flour containing the bran and germ, as well as the endosperm.

Winterizing   Process of chilling an oil to 45°F and then filtering to remove any fat crystals.

Wok   Metallic bowl-shaped pan developed in the Orient for stir-frying.

Yeast   Single-celled fungus that reproduces by budding.

Yogurt   Milk-based food produced when milk is clotted by lactic acid—producing bacteria.

Yolk Index   Measure of egg quality out of the shell; height of the yolk divided by the diameter.

APPENDIX C

FOOD COMPOSITION

Source: Adams, C. A. and M. Richardson. Nutritive value of foods. *Home and Garden Bulletin* No. 72. Agricultural Research Service, U.S. Dept. Agriculture. Washington, D.C. 1981.

Appendix C: Nutritive Values of the Edible Part of Foods

(Dashes (—) denote lack of reliable data for a constituent believed to be present in measurable amount)

NUTRIENTS IN INDICATED QUANTITY

Item No. (A)	Foods, approximate measures, units, and weight (edible part unless footnotes indicate otherwise) (B)	Weight (Grams)	Water (C) Percent	Food energy (D) Calories	Protein (E) Grams	Fat (F) Grams	Fatty Acids — Saturated (total) (G) Grams	Fatty Acids — Unsaturated Oleic (H) Grams	Fatty Acids — Linoleic (I) Grams	Carbohydrate (I) Grams	Calcium (K) Milligrams	Phosphorus (L) Milligrams	Iron (M) Milligrams	Potassium (N) Milligrams	Vitamin A value (O) International units	Thiamin (P) Milligrams	Riboflavin (Q) Milligrams	Niacin (R) Milligrams	Ascorbic acid (S) Milligrams
	DAIRY PRODUCTS (CHEESE, CREAM, IMITATION CREAM, MILK; RELATED PRODUCTS)																		
	Butter. See Fats, oils; related products, items 103–108.																		
	Cheese:																		
	Natural:																		
1	Blue — 1 oz	28	42	100	6	8	5.3	1.9	0.2	1	150	110	0.1	73	200	0.01	0.11	0.3	0
2	Camembert (3 wedges per 4-oz container) — 1 wedge	38	52	115	8	9	5.8	2.2	.2	Trace	147	132	.1	71	350	.01	.19	.2	0
	Cheddar:																		
3	Cut pieces — 1 oz	28	37	115	7	9	6.1	2.1	.2	Trace	204	145	.2	28	300	.01	.11	Trace	0
4	— 1 cu in	17.2	37	70	4	6	3.7	1.3	.1	Trace	124	88	.1	17	180	Trace	.06	Trace	0
5	Shredded — 1 cup	113	37	455	28	37	24.2	8.5	.7	1	815	579	.8	111	1,200	.03	.42	.1	0
	Cottage (cottage cheese, 4% fat):																		
	Creamed (cottage cheese, 4% fat):																		
6	Large curd — 1 cup	225	79	235	28	10	6.4	2.4	.2	6	135	297	.3	190	370	.05	.37	.3	Trace
7	Small curd — 1 cup	210	79	220	26	9	6.0	2.2	.2	6	126	277	.3	177	340	.04	.34	.3	Trace
8	Low fat (2%) — 1 cup	226	79	205	31	4	2.8	1.0	.1	8	155	340	.4	217	160	.05	.42	.3	Trace
9	Low fat (1%) — 1 cup	226	82	165	28	2	1.5	.5	.1	6	138	302	.3	193	80	.05	.37	.3	Trace
10	Uncreamed (cottage cheese dry curd, less than 1/2% fat) — 1 cup	145	80	125	25	1	.4	.1	Trace	3	46	151	.3	47	40	.04	.21	.2	0
11	Cream — 1 oz	28	54	100	2	10	6.2	2.4	.2	1	23	30	.3	34	400	Trace	.06	Trace	0
	Mozzarella, made with—																		
12	Whole milk — 1 oz	28	48	90	6	7	4.4	1.7	.2	1	163	117	.1	21	260	Trace	.08	Trace	0
13	Part skim milk — 1 oz	28	49	80	8	5	3.1	1.2	.1	1	207	149	.1	27	180	.01	.10	Trace	0
	Parmesan, grated:																		
14	Cup, not pressed down — 1 cup	100	18	455	42	30	19.1	7.7	.3	4	1,376	807	1.0	107	700	.05	.39	.3	0
15	Tablespoon — 1 tbsp	5	18	25	2	2	1.0	.4	Trace	Trace	69	40	Trace	5	40	Trace	.02	.1	0
16	Ounce — 1 oz	28	18	130	12	9	5.4	2.2	.1	1	390	229	.2	30	200	.01	.11	.1	0
17	Provolone — 1 oz	28	41	100	7	8	4.8	1.7	.1	1	214	141	.1	39	230	.01	.09	Trace	0
	Ricotta, made with—																		
18	Whole milk — 1 cup	246	72	430	28	32	20.4	7.1	.7	7	509	389	.9	257	1,210	.03	.48	.3	0
19	Part skim milk — 1 cup	246	74	340	28	19	12.1	4.7	.5	13	669	449	1.1	308	1,060	.05	.46	.2	0
20	Romano — 1 oz	28	31	110	9	8	—	—	—	1	302	215	—	—	160	—	.11	Trace	0
21	Swiss — 1 oz	28	37	105	8	8	5.0	1.7	.2	1	272	171	Trace	31	240	.01	.10	Trace	0
	Pasteurized process cheese:																		
22	American — 1 oz	28	39	105	6	9	5.6	2.1	.2	Trace	174	211	.1	46	340	.01	.10	Trace	0
23	Swiss — 1 oz	28	42	95	7	7	4.5	1.7	.1	1	219	216	.2	61	230	Trace	.08	Trace	0
24	Pasteurized process cheese food, American — 1 oz	28	43	95	6	7	4.4	1.7	.1	2	163	130	.2	79	260	.01	.13	Trace	0
25	Pasteurized process cheese spread, American — 1 oz	28	48	82	5	6	3.8	1.5	.1	2	159	202	.1	69	220	.01	.12	Trace	0
	Cream, sweet:																		
26	Half-and-half (cream and milk) — 1 cup	242	81	315	7	28	17.3	7.0	.6	10	254	230	.2	314	260	.08	.36	.2	2
27	— 1 tbsp	15	81	20	Trace	2	1.1	.4	Trace	1	16	14	Trace	19	20	.01	.02	Trace	Trace
28	Light, coffee, or table — 1 cup	240	74	470	6	46	28.8	11.7	1.0	9	231	192	.1	292	1,730	.08	.36	.1	2
29	— 1 tbsp	15	74	30	Trace	3	1.8	.7	.1	1	14	18	Trace	18	110	Trace	.02	Trace	Trace

(A)	(B)		(C)	(D)	(E)	(F)	(G)	(H)	(I)	(J)	(K)	(L)	(M)	(N)	(O)	(P)	(Q)	(R)	(S)
	Whipping, unwhipped (volume about double when whipped):																		
30	Light	1 cup	239	64	700	5	74	46.2	18.3	1.5	7	166	146	0.1	231	2,690	0.06	0.30	0.1	1
31		1 tbsp	15	64	45	Trace	5	2.9	1.1	.1	Trace	10	9	Trace	15	170	Trace	.02	Trace	Trace
32	Heavy	1 cup	238	58	820	5	88	54.8	22.2	2.0	7	154	149	Trace	179	3,500	.05	.26	.1	1
33		1 tbsp	15	58	80	Trace	6	3.5	1.4	.1	Trace	10	9	Trace	11	220	Trace	.02	Trace	Trace
34	Whipped topping, (pressurized)	1 cup	60	61	155	1	13	8.3	3.4	.3	7	61	54	Trace	88	550	.02	.04	Trace	0
35		1 tbsp	3	61	10	Trace	1	.4	.2	Trace	Trace	3	3	Trace	4	30	Trace	Trace	Trace	0
36	Cream, sour	1 cup	230	71	495	7	48	30.0	12.1	1.1	10	268	195	.1	331	1,820	.08	.34	.1	2
37		1 tbsp	12	71	25	Trace	3	1.6	.6	.1	1	14	10	Trace	17	90	Trace	.02	Trace	Trace
	Cream products, imitation (made with vegetable fat):																		
	Sweet:																		
	Creamers:																		
38	Liquid (frozen)	1 cup	245	77	335	2	24	22.8	.3	Trace	28	23	157	.1	467	[1]220	0	0	0	0
39		1 tbsp	15	77	20	Trace	1	1.4	Trace	0	2	2	10	Trace	29	[1]10	0	0	0	0
40	Powdered	1 cup	94	2	515	5	33	30.6	.9	Trace	52	21	397	.1	763	[1]190	0	[1].16	0	0
41		1 tsp	2	2	10	Trace	1	.7	Trace	0	Trace	Trace	8	Trace	16	[1]Trace	0	[1]Trace	0	0
	Whipped topping:																		
42	Frozen	1 cup	75	50	240	1	19	16.3	1.0	.2	17	5	6	.1	14	[1]650	0	0	0	0
43		1 tbsp	4	50	15	Trace	1	.9	.1	Trace	1	Trace	Trace	Trace	1	[1]30	0	0	0	0
44	Powdered, made with whole milk.	1 cup	80	67	150	3	10	8.5	.6	.1	13	72	69	Trace	121	[1]290	.02	.09	Trace	1
45		1 tbsp	4	67	10	Trace	Trace	.4	Trace	Trace	1	4	3	Trace	6	[1]10	Trace	.02	Trace	Trace
46	Pressurized	1 cup	70	60	185	1	16	13.2	1.4	.2	11	Trace	13	Trace	13	[1]330	0	0	0	0
47		1 tbsp	4	60	10	Trace	1	.8	.1	Trace	1	Trace	1	Trace	1	[1]20	0	0	0	0
48	Sour dressing (imitation sour cream) made with nonfat dry milk.	1 cup	235	75	415	8	39	31.2	4.4	1.1	11	266	205	.1	380	[1]20	.09	.38	.2	2
49		1 tbsp	12	75	20	Trace	2	1.6	.2	.1	1	14	10	Trace	19	[1]Trace	.01	.02	Trace	Trace
	Ice cream. See Milk desserts, frozen (items 75-80).																		
	Ice milk. See Milk desserts, frozen (items 81-83).																		
	Milk:																		
	Fluid:																		
50	Whole (3.3% fat)	1 cup	244	88	150	8	8	5.1	2.1	.2	11	291	228	.1	370	[2]310	.09	.40	.2	2
	Lowfat (2%):																		
	No milk solids added																		
51		1 cup	244	89	120	8	5	2.9	1.2	.1	12	297	232	.1	377	500	.10	.40	.2	2
	Milk solids added:																		
52	Label claim less than 10 g of protein per cup.	1 cup	245	89	125	9	5	2.9	1.2	.1	12	313	245	.1	397	500	.10	.42	.2	2
53	Label claim 10 or more grams of protein per cup (protein fortified).	1 cup	246	88	135	10	5	3.0	1.2	.1	14	352	276	.1	447	500	.11	.48	.2	3
	Lowfat (1%):																		
	No milk solids added																		
54		1 cup	244	90	100	8	3	1.6	.7	.1	12	300	235	.1	381	500	.10	.41	.2	2
	Milk solids added:																		
55	Label claim less than 10 g of protein per cup.	1 cup	245	90	105	9	2	1.5	.6	.1	12	313	245	.1	397	500	.10	.42	.2	2
56	Label claim 10 or more grams of protein per cup (protein fortified).	1 cup	246	89	120	10	3	1.8	.7	.1	14	349	273	.1	444	500	.11	.47	.2	3
	Nonfat (skim):																		
	No milk solids added																		
57		1 cup	245	91	85	8	Trace	.3	.1	Trace	12	302	247	.1	406	500	.09	.34	.2	2

[1] Vitamin A value is largely from beta-carotene used for coloring. Riboflavin value for items 40-41 apply to products with added riboflavin.

[2] Applies to product without added vitamin A. With added vitamin A, value is 500 International Units (I.U.).

Appendix C: Nutritive Values of the Edible Part of Foods (*Continued*)

(Dashes (—) denote lack of reliable data for a constituent believed to be present in measurable amount)

NUTRIENTS IN INDICATED QUANTITY

Item No. (A)	Foods, approximate measures, units, and weight (edible part unless footnotes indicate otherwise) (B)	Grams	Water (C) Per cent	Food energy (D) Calories	Protein (E) Grams	Fat (F) Grams	Saturated (total) (G) Grams	Oleic (H) Grams	Linoleic (I) Grams	Carbohydrate (J) Grams	Calcium (K) Milligrams	Phosphorus (L) Milligrams	Iron (M) Milligrams	Potassium (N) Milligrams	Vitamin A value (O) International units	Thiamin (P) Milligrams	Riboflavin (Q) Milligrams	Niacin (R) Milligrams	Ascorbic acid (S) Milligrams
	DAIRY PRODUCTS (CHEESE, CREAM, IMITATION CREAM, MILK; RELATED PRODUCTS)—Con.																		
	Milk—Continued																		
	Fluid—Continued																		
	Nonfat (skim)—Continued																		
	Milk solids added:																		
58	Label claim less than 10 g of protein per cup. 1 cup	245	90	90	9	1	0.4	0.1	Trace	12	316	255	0.1	418	500	0.10	0.43	0.2	2
59	Label claim 10 or more grams of protein per cup (protein fortified). 1 cup	246	89	100	10	1	.4	.1	Trace	14	352	275	.1	446	500	.11	.48	.2	3
60	Buttermilk-------- 1 cup	245	90	100	8	2	1.3	.5	Trace	12	285	219	.1	371	[3]80	.08	.38	.1	2
	Canned:																		
	Evaporated, unsweetened:																		
61	Whole milk------- 1 cup	252	74	340	17	19	11.6	5.3	0.4	25	657	510	.5	764	[5]610	.12	.80	.5	5
62	Skim milk------- 1 cup	255	79	200	19	1	.3	.1	Trace	29	738	497	.7	845	[5]1,000	.11	.79	.4	3
63	Sweetened, condensed----- 1 cup	306	27	980	24	27	16.8	6.7	.7	166	868	775	.6	1,136	[5]1,000	.28	1.27	.6	8
	Dried:																		
64	Buttermilk------- 1 cup	120	3	465	41	7	4.3	1.7	.2	59	1,421	1,119	.4	1,910	[3]260	.47	1.90	1.1	7
	Nonfat instant:																		
65	Envelope, net wt., 3.2 oz[5]. 1 envelope	91	4	325	32	1	.4	.1	Trace	47	1,120	896	.3	1,552	[6]2,160	.38	1.59	.8	5
66	Cup[7]----------- 1 cup	68	4	245	24	Trace	.3	.1	Trace	35	837	670	.2	1,160	[6]1,610	.28	1.19	.6	4
	Milk beverages:																		
	Chocolate milk (commercial):																		
67	Regular---------- 1 cup	250	82	210	8	8	5.3	2.2	.2	26	280	251	.6	417	300	.09	.41	.3	2
68	Lowfat (2%)----- 1 cup	250	84	180	8	5	3.1	1.3	.1	26	284	254	.6	422	500	.10	.42	.3	2
69	Lowfat (1%)----- 1 cup	250	85	160	8	3	1.5	.7	.1	26	287	257	.6	426	500	.10	.40	.3	2
70	Eggnog (commercial)--- 1 cup	254	74	340	10	19	11.3	5.0	.6	34	330	278	.5	420	890	.09	.48	.3	4
	Malted milk, home-prepared with 1 cup of whole milk and 2 to 3 heaping tsp of malted milk powder (about 3/4 oz):																		
71	Chocolate-------- 1 cup of milk plus 3/4 oz of powder.	265	81	235	9	9	5.5	—	—	29	304	265	.5	500	330	.14	.43	.7	2
72	Natural---------- 1 cup of milk plus 3/4 oz of powder.	265	81	235	11	10	6.0	—	—	27	347	307	.3	529	380	.20	.54	1.3	2
	Shakes, thick:[8]																		
73	Chocolate, container, net wt., 10.6 oz. 1 container	300	72	355	9	8	5.0	2.0	.2	63	396	378	.9	672	260	.14	.67	.4	0
74	Vanilla, container, net wt., 11 oz. 1 container	313	74	350	12	9	5.9	2.4	.2	56	457	361	.3	572	360	.09	.61	.5	0
	Milk desserts, frozen:																		
	Ice cream:																		
	Regular (about 11% fat):																		
75	1/2 gal---------	1,064	61	2,155	38	115	71.3	28.8	2.6	254	1,406	1,075	1.0	2,052	4,340	.42	2.63	1.1	6
76	Hardened------- 1 cup	133	61	270	5	14	8.9	3.6	.3	32	176	134	.1	257	540	.05	.33	.1	1
77	3-fl oz container-	50	61	100	2	5	3.4	1.4	.1	12	66	51	Trace	96	200	.02	.12	.1	Trace
78	Soft serve (frozen custard). 1 cup	173	60	375	7	23	13.5	5.9	.6	38	236	199	.4	338	790	.08	.45	.2	1
79	Rich (about 16% fat), hardened. 1/2 gal	1,188	59	2,805	33	190	118.3	47.8	4.3	256	1,213	927	.8	1,771	7,200	.36	2.27	.9	5
80	1 cup	148	59	350	4	24	14.7	6.0	.5	32	151	115	.1	221	900	.04	.28	.1	1
	Ice milk:																		
81	1/2 gal---------	1,048	69	1,470	41	45	28.1	11.3	1.0	232	1,409	1,035	1.5	2,117	1,710	.61	2.78	.9	6
82	Hardened (about 4.3% fat)---- 1 cup	131	69	185	5	5	3.5	1.4	.1	29	176	129	.1	265	210	.08	.35	.1	1

(A)	(B)	(C)	(D)	(E)	(F)	(G)	(H)	(I)	(J)	(K)	(L)	(M)	(N)	(O)	(P)	(Q)	(R)	(S)
83	Soft serve (about 2.6% fat)—— 1 cup	175	70	225	8	5	2.9	1.2	0.1	38	274	202	0.3	412	180	0.12	0.54	0.2	1
84	Sherbet (about 2% fat)—— 1/2 gal	1,542	66	2,160	17	31	19.0	7.7	.7	469	827	594	2.5	1,585	1,480	.26	.71	1.0	31
85	1 cup	193	66	270	2	4	2.4	1.0	.1	59	103	74	.3	198	190	.03	.09	.1	4
	Milk desserts, other:																		
86	Custard, baked—— 1 cup	265	77	305	14	15	6.8	5.4	.7	29	297	310	1.1	387	930	.11	.50	.3	1
	Puddings: From home recipe: Starch base:																		
87	Chocolate—— 1 cup	260	66	385	8	12	7.6	3.3	.3	67	250	255	1.3	445	390	.05	.36	.3	1
88	Vanilla (blancmange)—— 1 cup	255	76	285	9	10	6.2	2.5	.2	41	298	232	Trace	352	410	.08	.41	.3	2
89	Tapioca cream—— 1 cup	165	72	220	8	8	4.1	2.5	.5	28	173	180	.7	223	480	.07	.30	.2	2
	From mix (chocolate) and milk:																		
90	Regular (cooked)—— 1 cup	260	70	320	9	8	4.3	2.6	.2	59	265	247	.8	354	340	.05	.39	.3	2
91	Instant—— 1 cup	260	69	325	8	7	3.6	2.2	.3	63	374	237	1.3	335	340	.08	.39	.3	2
	Yogurt: With added milk solids: Made with lowfat milk:																		
92	Fruit-flavored[9]—— 1 container, net wt., 8 oz	227	75	230	10	3	1.8	.6	.1	42	343	269	.2	439	[10]120	.08	.40	.2	1
93	Plain—— 1 container, net wt., 8 oz	227	85	145	12	4	2.3	.8	.1	16	415	326	.2	531	[10]150	.10	.49	.3	2
94	Made with nonfat milk—— 1 container, net wt., 8 oz	227	85	125	13	Trace	.3	.1	Trace	17	452	355	.2	579	[10]20	.11	.53	.3	2
	Without added milk solids:																		
95	Made with whole milk—— 1 container, net wt., 8 oz	227	88	140	8	7	4.8	1.7	.1	11	274	215	.1	351	280	.07	.32	.2	1
	EGGS																		
	Eggs, large (24 oz per dozen): Raw:																		
96	Whole, without shell—— 1 egg	50	75	80	6	6	1.7	2.0	.6	1	28	90	1.0	65	260	.04	.15	Trace	0
97	White—— 1 egg	33	88	15	3	Trace	0	0	0	Trace	4	4	Trace	45	0	Trace	.09	Trace	0
98	Yolk—— 1 egg	17	49	65	3	6	1.7	2.1	.6	Trace	26	86	.9	15	310	.04	.07	Trace	0
	Cooked:																		
99	Fried in butter—— 1 egg	46	72	85	5	6	2.4	2.2	.6	1	26	80	.9	58	290	.03	.13	Trace	0
100	Hard-cooked, shell removed—— 1 egg	50	75	80	6	6	1.7	2.0	.6	1	28	90	1.0	65	260	.04	.14	Trace	0
101	Poached—— 1 egg	50	74	80	6	6	1.7	2.0	.6	1	28	90	1.0	65	260	.04	.13	Trace	0
102	Scrambled (milk added) in butter. Also omelet.—— 1 egg	64	76	95	6	7	2.8	2.3	.6	1	47	97	.9	85	310	.04	.16	Trace	0
	FATS, OILS; RELATED PRODUCTS																		
	Butter: Regular (1 brick or 4 sticks per lb):																		
103	Stick (1/2 cup)—— 1 stick	113	16	815	1	92	57.3	23.1	2.1	Trace	27	26	.2	29	[11,13]3,470	.01	.04	Trace	0
104	Tablespoon (about 1/8 stick)—— 1 tbsp	14	16	100	Trace	12	7.2	2.9	.3	Trace	3	3	Trace	4	[11]430	Trace	Trace	Trace	
105	Pat (1 in square, 1/3 in high; 90 per lb)—— 1 pat	5	16	35	Trace	4	2.5	1.0	.1	Trace	1	1	Trace	1	[11]150	Trace	Trace	Trace	0
	Whipped (6 sticks or two 8-oz containers per lb):																		
106	Stick (1/2 cup)—— 1 stick	76	16	540	1	61	38.2	15.4	1.4	Trace	18	17	.1	20	[11,12]2,310	Trace	.03	Trace	0
107	Tablespoon (about 1/8 stick)—— 1 tbsp	9	16	65	Trace	8	4.7	1.9	.2	Trace	2	2	Trace	2	[11]290	Trace	Trace	Trace	0
108	Pat (1 1/4 in square, 1/3 in high; 120 per lb)—— 1 pat	4	16	25	Trace	3	1.9	.8	.1	Trace	1	1	Trace	1	[11]120	0	Trace	Trace	0

[3] Applies to product without vitamin A added.
[4] Applies to product with added vitamin A. Without added vitamin A, value is 20 International Units (I.U.).
[5] Yields 1 qt of fluid milk when reconstituted according to package directions.
[6] Applies to product with added vitamin A.
[7] Weight applies to product with label claim of 1 1/3 cups equal 3.2 oz.
[8] Applies to products made from thick shake mixes and that do not contain added ice cream. Products made from milk shake mixes are higher in fat and usually contain added ice cream.
[9] Content of fat, vitamin A, and carbohydrate varies. Consult the label when precise values are needed for special diets.
[10] Applies to product made with milk containing added vitamin A.
[11] Based on year-round average.

Appendix C: Nutritive Values of the Edible Part of Foods (Continued)

(Dashes (—) denote lack of reliable data for a constituent believed to be present in measurable amount)

Item No. (A)	Foods, approximate measures, units, and weight (edible part unless footnotes indicate otherwise) (B)	Grams	Water (C) Per cent	Food energy (D) Calories	Protein (E) Grams	Fat (F) Grams	Saturated (total) (G) Grams	Oleic (H) Grams	Linoleic (I) Grams	Carbohydrate (J) Grams	Calcium (K) Milligrams	Phosphorus (L) Milligrams	Iron (M) Milligrams	Potassium (N) Milligrams	Vitamin A value (O) International units	Thiamin (P) Milligrams	Riboflavin (Q) Milligrams	Niacin (R) Milligrams	Ascorbic acid (S) Milligrams
	FATS, OILS; RELATED PRODUCTS—Con.																		
109	Fats, cooking (vegetable shortenings). 1 cup	200	0	1,770	0	200	48.8	88.2	48.4	0	0	0	0	0	—	0	0	0	0
110	Lard— 1 tbsp	13	0	110	0	13	3.2	5.7	3.1	0	0	0	0	0	0	0	0	0	0
111	1 cup	205	0	1,850	0	205	81.0	83.8	20.5	0	0	0	0	0	0	0	0	0	0
112	1 tbsp	13	0	115	0	13	5.1	5.3	1.3	0	0	0	0	0	0	0	0	0	0
	Margarine (1 brick or 4 sticks per lb): Regular:																		
113	Stick (1/2 cup)— 1 stick	113	16	815	1	92	16.7	42.9	24.9	Trace	27	26	.2	29	[12]3,750	.01	.04	Trace	0
114	Tablespoon (about 1/8 stick)— 1 tbsp	14	16	100	Trace	12	2.1	3.1	3.1	Trace	3	3	Trace	4	[12]470	Trace	Trace	Trace	0
115	Pat (1 in square, 1/3 in high; 90 per lb). 1 pat	5	16	35	Trace	4	.7	1.9	1.1	Trace	1	1	Trace	1	[12]170	Trace	Trace	Trace	0
116	Soft, two 8-oz containers per lb. 1 container	227	16	1,635	1	184	32.5	71.5	65.4	Trace	53	52	.4	59	[12]7,500	.01	.08	.1	0
117	1 tbsp	14	16	100	Trace	12	2.0	4.5	4.1	Trace	3	3	Trace	4	[12]470	Trace	Trace	Trace	0
	Whipped (6 sticks per lb):																		
118	Stick (1/2 cup)— 1 stick	76	16	545	Trace	61	11.2	28.7	16.7	Trace	18	17	.1	20	[12]2,500	Trace	.03	Trace	0
119	Tablespoon (about 1/8 stick)— 1 tbsp	9	16	70	Trace	8	1.4	3.6	2.1	Trace	2	2	Trace	2	[12]310	Trace	Trace	Trace	0
	Oils, salad or cooking:																		
120	Corn— 1 cup	218	0	1,925	0	218	27.7	53.6	125.1	0	0	0	0	0	—	—	—	0	0
121	1 tbsp	14	0	120	0	14	1.7	3.3	7.8	0	0	0	0	0	—	—	—	0	0
122	Olive— 1 cup	216	0	1,910	0	216	30.7	154.4	17.7	0	0	0	0	0	—	—	—	0	0
123	1 tbsp	14	0	120	0	14	1.9	9.7	1.1	0	0	0	0	0	—	—	—	0	0
124	Peanut— 1 cup	216	0	1,910	0	216	37.4	98.5	67.0	0	0	0	0	0	—	—	—	0	0
125	1 tbsp	14	0	120	0	14	2.3	6.2	4.2	0	0	0	0	0	—	—	—	0	0
126	Safflower— 1 cup	218	0	1,925	0	218	20.5	25.9	159.8	0	0	0	0	0	—	—	—	0	0
127	1 tbsp	14	0	120	0	14	1.3	1.6	10.0	0	0	0	0	0	—	—	—	0	0
128	Soybean oil, hydrogenated (partially hardened). 1 cup	218	0	1,925	0	218	31.8	93.1	75.6	0	0	0	0	0	—	—	—	0	0
129	1 tbsp	14	0	120	0	14	2.0	5.8	4.7	0	0	0	0	0	—	—	—	0	0
130	Soybean-cottonseed oil blend, hydrogenated. 1 cup	218	0	1,925	0	218	38.2	63.0	99.6	0	0	0	0	0	—	—	—	0	0
131	1 tbsp	14	0	120	0	14	2.4	3.9	6.2	0	0	0	0	0	—	—	—	0	0
	Salad dressings: Commercial: Blue cheese:																		
132	Regular— 1 tbsp	15	32	75	1	8	1.6	1.7	3.8	1	12	11	Trace	6	30	Trace	.02	Trace	Trace
133	Low calorie (5 Cal per tsp)— 1 tbsp	16	84	10	Trace	1	.5	.3	Trace	1	10	8	Trace	5	30	Trace	.01	Trace	Trace
	French:																		
134	Regular— 1 tbsp	16	39	65	Trace	6	1.1	1.3	3.2	3	2	2	.1	13	—	—	—	—	—
135	Low calorie (5 Cal per tsp)— 1 tbsp	16	77	15	Trace	1	.1	.1	.4	3	2	2	.1	13	—	—	—	—	—
	Italian:																		
136	Regular— 1 tbsp	15	28	85	Trace	9	1.6	1.9	4.7	1	2	4	Trace	2	Trace	Trace	Trace	Trace	—
137	Low calorie (2 Cal per tsp)— 1 tbsp	15	90	10	Trace	1	.1	.1	.4	1	2	4	Trace	2	Trace	Trace	Trace	Trace	—
138	Mayonnaise— 1 tbsp	14	15	100	Trace	11	2.0	2.4	5.6	Trace	3	4	.1	5	40	Trace	.01	Trace	—
	Mayonnaise type:																		
139	Regular— 1 tbsp	15	41	65	Trace	6	1.1	1.4	3.2	2	2	4	Trace	1	30	Trace	Trace	Trace	—
140	Low calorie (8 Cal per tsp)— 1 tbsp	16	81	20	Trace	2	.4	.4	1.0	2	3	3	Trace	1	40	Trace	Trace	Trace	—
141	Tartar sauce, regular— 1 tbsp	14	34	75	Trace	8	1.5	1.8	4.1	1	3	4	.1	11	30	Trace	Trace	Trace	Trace
	Thousand Island:																		
142	Regular— 1 tbsp	16	32	80	Trace	8	1.4	1.7	4.0	2	2	3	.1	18	50	Trace	Trace	Trace	Trace
143	Low calorie (10 Cal per tsp)— 1 tbsp	15	68	25	Trace	2	.4	.4	1.0	2	2	3	.1	17	50	Trace	Trace	Trace	Trace
	From home recipe:																		
144	Cooked type[13]— 1 tbsp	16	68	25	1	2	.5	.6	.3	2	14	15	.1	19	80	.01	.03	Trace	Trace

FISH, SHELLFISH, MEAT, POULTRY; RELATED PRODUCTS

(A)	(B)		(C)	(D)	(E)	(F)	(G)	(H)	(I)	(J)	(K)	(L)	(M)	(N)	(O)	(P)	(Q)	(R)	(S)
145	Fish and shellfish: Bluefish, baked with butter or margarine.	3 oz---- 85	68	135	22	4	—	—	—	0	25	244	0.6	—	40	0.09	0.08	1.6	—
	Clams:																		
146	Raw, meat only	3 oz---- 85	82	65	11	1	—	—	—	2	59	138	5.2	154	90	.08	.15	1.1	8
147	Canned, solids and liquid	3 oz---- 85	86	45	7	1	—	—	—	2	47	116	3.5	119	—	.01	.09	.9	—
148	Crabmeat (white or king), canned, not pressed down.	1 cup--- 135	77	135	24	3	—	—	—	1	61	246	1.1	149	—	.11	.11	2.6	—
149	Fish sticks, breaded, cooked, frozen (stick, 4 by 1 by 1/2 in).	1 fish stick or 1 oz 28	66	50	5	3	—	—	—	2	3	47	.1	—	0	.01	.02	.5	—
150	Haddock, breaded, fried[14]	3 oz---- 85	66	140	17	5	1.4	2.2	1.2	5	34	210	1.0	296	—	.03	.06	2.7	2
151	Ocean perch, breaded, fried[14]	1 fillet 85	59	195	16	11	2.7	4.4	2.3	6	28	192	1.1	242	—	.10	.10	1.6	—
152	Oysters, raw, meat only (13-19 medium Selects).	1 cup--- 240	85	160	20	4	1.3	.2	.1	8	226	343	13.2	290	740	.34	.43	6.0	—
153	Salmon, pink, canned, solids and liquid.	3 oz---- 85	71	120	17	5	.9	.8	.1	0	[15]167	243	.7	307	60	.03	.16	6.8	—
154	Sardines, Atlantic, canned in oil, drained solids.	3 oz---- 85	62	175	20	9	3.0	2.5	.5	0	372	424	2.5	502	190	.02	.17	4.6	—
155	Scallops, frozen, breaded, fried, reheated.	6 scallops 90	60	175	16	8	—	—	—	9	—	—	—	—	—	—	—	—	—
156	Shad, baked with butter or margarine, bacon.	3 oz---- 85	64	170	20	10	—	—	—	0	20	266	.5	320	30	.11	.22	7.3	—
	Shrimp:																		
157	Canned meat	3 oz---- 85	70	100	21	1	.1	.1	Trace	1	98	224	2.6	104	50	.01	.03	1.5	—
158	French fried[16]	3 oz---- 85	57	190	17	9	2.3	3.7	2.0	9	61	162	1.7	195	—	.03	.07	2.3	—
159	Tuna, canned in oil, drained solids.	3 oz---- 85	61	170	24	7	1.7	1.7	.7	0	7	199	1.6	—	70	.04	.10	10.1	—
160	Tuna salad[17]	1 cup--- 205	70	350	30	22	4.3	6.3	6.7	7	41	291	2.7	—	590	.08	.23	10.3	2
161	Meat and meat products: Bacon, (20 slices per lb, raw), broiled or fried, crisp.	2 slices 15	8	85	4	8	2.5	3.7	.7	Trace	2	34	.5	35	0	.08	.05	.8	—
	Beef[18] cooked: Cuts braised, simmered or pot roasted:																		
162	Lean and fat (piece, 2 1/2 by 2 1/2 by 3/4 in).	3 oz---- 85	53	245	23	16	6.8	6.5	.4	0	10	114	2.9	184	30	.04	.18	3.6	—
163	Lean only from item 162	2.5 oz-- 72	62	140	22	5	2.1	1.8	.2	0	10	108	2.7	176	10	.04	.17	3.3	—
	Ground beef, broiled:																		
164	Lean with 10% fat	3 oz or patty 3 by 5/8 in 85	60	185	23	10	4.0	3.9	.3	0	10	196	3.0	261	20	.08	.20	5.1	—
165	Lean with 21% fat	2.9 oz or patty 3 by 5/8 in 82	54	235	20	17	7.0	6.7	.4	0	9	159	2.6	221	30	.07	.17	4.4	—
	Roast, oven cooked, no liquid added: Relatively fat, such as rib:																		
166	Lean and fat (2 pieces, 4 1/8 by 2 1/4 by 1/4 in).	3 oz---- 85	40	375	17	33	14.0	13.6	.8	0	8	158	2.2	189	70	.05	.13	3.1	—
	Relatively lean, such as heel of round:																		
167	Lean only from item 166	1.8 oz-- 51	57	125	14	7	3.0	2.5	.3	0	6	131	1.8	161	10	.04	.11	2.6	—
168	Lean and fat (2 pieces, 4 1/8 by 2 1/4 by 1/4 in).	3 oz---- 85	62	165	25	7	2.8	2.7	.2	0	11	208	3.2	279	10	.06	.19	4.5	—

[12] Based on average vitamin A content of fortified margarine. Federal specifications for fortified margarine require a minimum of 15,000 International Units (I.U.) of vitamin A per pound.
[13] Fatty acid values apply to product made with regular-type margarine.
[14] Dipped in egg, milk or water, and breadcrumbs; fried in vegetable shortening.
[15] If bones are discarded, value for calcium will be greatly reduced.
[16] Dipped in egg, breadcrumbs, and flour or batter.
[17] Prepared with tuna, celery, salad dressing (mayonnaise type), pickle, onion, and egg.
[18] Outer layer of fat on the cut was removed to within approximately 1/2 in of the lean. Deposits of fat within the cut were not removed.

Appendix C: Nutritive Values of the Edible Part of Foods (*Continued*)

(Dashes (—) denote lack of reliable data for a constituent believed to be present in measurable amount)

Item No. (A)	Foods, approximate measures, units, and weight (edible part unless footnotes indicate otherwise) (B)	Grams	Water (C) Per cent	Food energy (D) Calories	Protein (E) Grams	Fat (F) Grams	Fatty Acids Saturated (total) (G) Grams	Unsaturated Oleic (H) Grams	Unsaturated Linoleic (I) Grams	Carbohydrate (J) Grams	Calcium (K) Milligrams	Phosphorus (L) Milligrams	Iron (M) Milligrams	Potassium (N) Milligrams	Vitamin A value (O) International units	Thiamin (P) Milligrams	Riboflavin (Q) Milligrams	Niacin (R) Milligrams	Ascorbic acid (S) Milligrams
	FISH, SHELLFISH, MEAT, POULTRY; RELATED PRODUCTS-Con.																		
	Meat and meat products—Continued																		
	Beef,[1] cooked—Continued																		
	Roast, oven cooked, no liquid added—Continued																		
	Relatively lean such as heel of round—Continued																		
169	Lean only from item 168--- 2.8 oz	78	65	125	24	3	1.2	1.0	0.1	0	10	199	3.0	268	Trace	0.06	0.18	4.3	—
	Steak:																		
	Relatively fat—sirloin, broiled:																		
170	Lean and fat (piece, 2 1/2 by 2 1/2 by 3/4 in), broiled. 3 oz	85	44	330	20	27	11.3	11.1	.6	0	9	162	2.5	220	50	.05	.15	4.0	—
171	Lean only from item 170--- 2.0 oz	56	59	115	18	4	1.8	1.6	.2	0	7	146	2.2	202	10	.05	.14	3.6	—
	Relatively lean—round, braised:																		
172	Lean and fat (piece, 4 1/8 by 2 1/4 by 1/2 in). 3 oz	85	55	220	24	13	5.5	5.2	.4	0	10	213	3.0	272	20	.07	.19	4.8	—
173	Lean only from item 172--- 2.4 oz	68	61	130	21	4	1.7	1.5	.2	0	9	182	2.5	238	10	.05	.16	4.1	—
	Beef, canned:																		
174	Corned beef----- 3 oz	85	59	185	22	10	4.9	4.5	.2	0	17	90	3.7	—	—	.01	.20	2.9	—
175	Corned beef hash----- 1 cup	220	67	400	19	25	11.9	10.9	.5	24	29	147	4.4	440	—	.02	.20	4.6	—
176	Beef, dried, chipped----- 2 1/2-oz jar	71	48	145	24	4	2.1	2.1	.1	0	14	287	3.6	142	—	.05	.23	2.7	0
177	Beef and vegetable stew----- 1 cup	245	82	220	16	11	4.9	4.5	.2	15	29	184	2.9	613	2,400	.15	.17	4.7	17
178	Beef potpie (home recipe), baked[19] (piece, 1/3 of 9-in diam. pie). 1 piece	210	55	515	21	30	7.9	12.8	6.7	39	29	149	3.8	334	1,720	.30	.30	5.5	6
179	Chili con carne with beans, canned. 1 cup	255	72	340	19	16	7.5	6.8	.3	31	82	321	4.3	594	150	.08	.18	3.3	—
180	Chop suey with beef and pork (home recipe). 1 cup	250	75	300	26	17	8.5	6.2	.7	13	60	248	4.8	425	600	.28	.38	5.0	33
181	Heart, beef, lean, braised--- 3 oz	85	61	160	27	5	1.5	1.1	.6	1	5	154	5.0	197	20	.21	1.04	6.5	1
	Lamb, cooked:																		
	Chop, rib (cut 3 per lb with bone), broiled:																		
182	Lean and fat--- 3.1 oz	89	43	360	18	32	14.8	12.1	1.2	0	8	139	1.0	200	—	.11	.19	4.1	—
183	Lean only from item 182--- 2 oz	57	60	120	16	6	2.5	2.1	.2	0	6	121	1.1	174	—	.09	.15	3.4	—
	Leg, roasted:																		
184	Lean and fat (2 pieces, 4 1/8 by 2 1/4 by 1/4 in). 3 oz	85	54	235	22	16	7.3	6.0	.6	0	9	177	1.4	241	—	.13	.23	4.7	—
185	Lean only from item 184--- 2.5 oz	71	62	130	20	5	2.1	1.8	.2	0	9	169	1.4	227	—	.12	.21	4.4	—
	Shoulder, roasted:																		
186	Lean and fat (3 pieces, 2 1/2 by 2 1/2 by 1/4 in). 3 oz	85	50	285	18	23	10.8	8.8	.9	0	9	146	1.0	206	—	.11	.20	4.0	—
187	Lean only from item 186--- 2.3 oz	64	61	130	17	6	3.6	2.3	.2	0	8	140	1.0	193	—	.10	.18	3.7	—
188	Liver, beef, fried[20] (slice, 6 1/2 by 2 3/8 by 3/8 in). 3 oz	85	56	195	22	9	2.5	3.5	.9	5	9	405	7.5	323	[2]45,390	.22	3.56	14.0	23
	Pork, cured, cooked:																		
189	Ham, light cure, lean and fat, roasted (2 pieces, 4 1/8 by 2 1/4 by 1/4 in).[22] 3 oz	85	54	245	18	19	6.8	7.9	1.7	0	8	146	2.2	199	0	.40	.15	3.1	—
	Luncheon meat:																		
190	Boiled ham, slice (8 per 8-oz pkg.). 1 oz	28	59	65	5	5	1.7	2.0	.4	0	3	47	.8	—	0	.12	.04	.7	—
191	Canned, spiced or unspiced: Slice, approx. 3 by 2 by 1/2 in. 1 slice	60	55	175	9	15	5.4	6.7	1.0	1	5	65	1.3	133	0	.19	.13	1.8	—

NUTRIENTS IN INDICATED QUANTITY

(A)	(B)	(C)	(D)	(E)	(F)	(G)	(H)	(I)	(J)	(K)	(L)	(M)	(N)	(O)	(P)	(Q)	(R)	(S)	(T)
	Pork, fresh,[18] cooked:																		
	Chop, loin (cut 3 per lb with bone), broiled:																		
192	Lean and fat — 2.7 oz	78	42	305	19	25	8.9	10.4	2.2	0	9	209	2.7	216	0	0.75	0.22	4.5	—
193	Lean only from item 192 — 2 oz	56	53	150	17	9	3.1	3.6	.8	0	7	181	2.2	192	0	.63	.18	3.8	—
	Roast, oven cooked, no liquid added:																		
194	Lean and fat (piece, 2 1/2 by 2 1/2 by 3/4 in.). — 3 oz	85	46	310	21	24	8.7	10.2	2.2	0	9	218	2.7	233	0	.78	.22	4.8	—
195	Lean only from item 194 — 2.4 oz	68	55	175	20	10	3.5	4.1	.8	0	9	211	2.6	224	0	.73	.21	4.4	—
	Shoulder cut, simmered:																		
196	Lean and fat [3 pieces, 2 1/2 by 2 1/2 by 1/4 in.]. — 3 oz	85	46	320	20	26	9.3	10.9	2.3	0	9	118	2.6	158	0	.46	.21	4.1	—
197	Lean only from item 196 — 2.2 oz	63	60	135	18	6	2.2	2.6	.6	0	8	111	2.3	146	0	.42	.19	3.7	—
	Sausages (see also Luncheon meat (items 190–191)):																		
198	Bologna, slice (8 per 8-oz pkg.). — 1 slice	28	56	85	3	8	3.0	3.4	.5	Trace	2	36	.5	65	—	.05	.06	.7	—
199	Braunschweiger, slice (6 per 6-oz pkg.). — 1 slice	28	53	90	4	8	2.6	3.4	.8	1	3	69	1.7	—	1,850	.05	.41	2.3	—
200	Brown and serve (10–11 per 8-oz pkg.), browned. — 1 link	17	40	70	3	6	2.3	2.8	.7	Trace	—	—	—	—	—	—	—	—	—
201	Deviled ham, canned — 1 tbsp	13	51	45	2	4	1.5	1.8	.4	0	1	12	.3	—	0	.02	.01	.2	—
202	Frankfurter (8 per 1-lb pkg.), cooked (reheated). — 1 frankfurter	56	57	170	7	15	5.6	6.5	1.2	1	3	57	.8	—	—	.08	.11	1.4	—
203	Meat, potted (beef, chicken, turkey), canned. — 1 tbsp	13	61	30	2	2	—	—	—	0	—	—	—	35	0	Trace	.03	.2	—
204	Pork link (16 per 1-lb pkg.), cooked. — 1 link	13	35	60	2	6	2.1	2.4	.5	Trace	1	21	.3	—	—	.10	.04	.5	—
	Salami:																		
205	Dry type, slice (12 per 4-oz pkg.). — 1 slice	10	30	45	2	4	1.6	1.6	.1	Trace	1	28	.4	—	—	.04	.03	.5	—
206	Cooked type, slice (8 per 8-oz pkg.). — 1 slice	28	51	90	5	7	3.1	3.0	.2	1	3	57	.7	—	—	.07	.07	1.2	—
207	Vienna sausage (7 per 4-oz can). — 1 sausage	16	63	40	2	3	1.2	1.4	.2	Trace	1	24	.3	—	—	.01	.02	.4	—
	Veal, medium fat, cooked, bone removed:																		
208	Cutlet (4 1/8 by 2 1/4 by 1/2 in.), braised or broiled. — 3 oz	85	60	185	23	9	4.0	3.4	.4	0	9	196	2.7	258	—	.06	.21	4.6	—
209	Rib (2 pieces, 4 1/8 by 2 1/4 by 1/4 in.), roasted. — 3 oz	85	55	230	23	14	6.1	5.1	.6	0	10	211	2.9	259	—	.11	.26	6.6	—
	Poultry and poultry products:																		
	Chicken, cooked:																		
210	Breast, fried,[23] bones removed, 1/2 breast (3.3 oz with bones). — 2.8 oz	79	58	160	26	5	1.4	1.8	1.1	1	9	218	1.3	—	70	.04	.17	11.6	—
211	Drumstick, fried,[23] bones removed (2 oz with bones). — 1.3 oz	38	55	90	12	4	1.1	1.3	.9	Trace	6	89	.9	—	50	.03	.15	2.7	—
212	Half broiler, broiled; bones removed (10.4 oz with bones). — 6.2 oz	176	71	240	42	7	2.2	2.5	1.3	0	16	355	3.0	483	160	.09	.34	15.5	—
213	Chicken, canned, boneless — 3 oz	85	65	170	18	10	3.2	3.8	2.0	0	18	210	1.3	117	200	.03	.11	3.7	3
214	Chicken a la king, cooked (home recipe). — 1 cup	245	68	470	27	34	12.7	14.3	3.3	12	127	358	2.5	404	1,130	.10	.42	5.4	12
215	Chicken and noodles, cooked (home recipe). — 1 cup	240	71	365	22	18	5.9	7.1	3.5	26	26	247	2.2	149	430	.05	.17	4.3	Trace

[18] Outer layer of fat on the cut was removed to within approximately 1/2 in. of the lean. Deposits of fat within the cut were not removed.

[19] Crust made with vegetable shortening and enriched flour.

[20] Regular-type margarine used.

[21] Value varies widely.

[22] About one-fourth of the outer layer of fat on the cut was removed. Deposits of fat within the cut were not removed.

[23] Vegetable shortening used.

Appendix C: Nutritive Values of the Edible Part of Foods (Continued)

(Dashes (—) denote lack of reliable data for a constituent believed to be present in measurable amount)

Item No. (A)	Foods, approximate measures, units, and weight (edible part unless footnotes indicate otherwise) (B)		(Grams)	Water (C) Per cent	Food energy (D) Calories	Protein (E) Grams	Fat (F) Grams	Fatty Acids Saturated (total) (G) Grams	Unsaturated Oleic (H) Grams	Linoleic (I) Grams	Carbohydrate (J) Grams	Calcium (K) Milligrams	Phosphorus (L) Milligrams	Iron (M) Milligrams	Potassium (N) Milligrams	Vitamin A value (O) International units	Thiamin (P) Milligrams	Riboflavin (Q) Milligrams	Niacin (R) Milligrams	Ascorbic acid (S) Milligrams
	FISH, SHELLFISH, MEAT, POULTRY; RELATED PRODUCTS—Con.																			
	Poultry and poultry products—Continued																			
	Chicken chow mein:																			
216	Canned	1 cup	250	89	95	7	Trace	—	—	—	18	45	35	1.3	418	150	0.05	0.10	1.0	13
217	From home recipe	1 cup	250	78	255	31	10	2.4	3.4	3.1	10	58	293	2.5	473	280	.08	.23	4.3	10
218	Chicken potpie (home recipe), baked, 1/3 or 9-in diam. pie).	1 piece	232	57	545	23	31	11.3	10.9	5.6	42	70	232	3.0	343	3,090	.34	.31	5.5	5
	Turkey, roasted, flesh without skin:																			
219	Dark meat, piece, 2 1/2 by 1 5/8 by 1/4 in.	4 pieces	85	61	175	26	7	2.1	1.5	1.5	0	—	—	2.0	338	—	.03	.20	3.6	—
220	Light meat, piece, 4 by 2 by 1/4 in.	2 pieces	85	62	150	28	3	.9	.6	.7	0	—	—	1.0	349	—	.04	.12	9.4	—
	Light and dark meat:																			
221	Chopped or diced	1 cup	140	61	265	44	9	2.5	1.7	1.8	0	11	351	2.5	514	—	.07	.25	10.8	—
222	Pieces (1 slice white meat, 4 by 2 by 1/4 in with 2 slices dark meat, 2 1/2 by 1 5/8 by 1/4 in).	3 pieces	85	61	160	27	5	1.5	1.0	1.1	0	7	213	1.5	312	—	.04	.15	6.5	—
	FRUITS AND FRUIT PRODUCTS																			
	Apples, raw, unpeeled, without cores:																			
223	2 3/4-in diam. (about 3 per lb with cores).	1 apple	138	84	80	Trace	1	—	—	—	20	10	14	.4	152	120	.04	.03	.1	6
224	3 1/4-in diam. (about 2 per lb with cores).	1 apple	212	84	125	Trace	1	—	—	—	31	15	21	.6	233	190	.06	.04	.2	8
225	Applejuice, bottled or canned[24]	1 cup	248	88	120	Trace	Trace	—	—	—	30	15	22	1.5	250	—	.02	.05	.2	2[52]
	Applesauce, canned:																			
226	Sweetened	1 cup	255	76	230	1	Trace	—	—	—	61	10	13	1.3	166	100	.05	.03	.1	3[52]
227	Unsweetened	1 cup	244	89	100	Trace	Trace	—	—	—	26	10	12	1.2	190	100	.05	.02	.1	2[52]
	Apricots:																			
228	Raw, without pits (about 12 per lb with pits).	3 apricots	107	85	55	1	Trace	—	—	—	14	18	25	.5	301	2,890	.03	.04	.6	11
229	Canned in heavy sirup (halves and sirup).	1 cup	258	77	220	2	Trace	—	—	—	57	28	39	.8	604	4,490	.05	.05	1.0	10
	Dried:																			
230	Uncooked (28 large or 37 medium halves per cup).	1 cup	130	25	340	7	1	—	—	—	86	87	140	7.2	1,273	14,170	.01	.21	4.3	16
231	Cooked, unsweetened, fruit and liquid.	1 cup	250	76	215	4	1	—	—	—	54	55	88	4.5	795	7,500	.01	.13	2.5	8
232	Apricot nectar, canned	1 cup	251	85	145	1	Trace	—	—	—	37	23	30	.5	379	2,380	.03	.03	.5	2[36]
	Avocados, raw, whole, without skins and seeds:																			
233	California, mid- and late-winter (with skin and seed; 3 1/8-in diam.; wt., 10 oz).	1 avocado	216	74	370	5	37	5.5	22.0	3.7	13	22	91	1.3	1,303	630	.24	.43	3.5	30
234	Florida, late summer and fall (with skin and seed, 3 5/8-in diam.; wt., 1 lb).	1 avocado	304	78	390	4	33	6.7	15.7	5.3	27	30	128	1.8	1,836	880	.33	.61	4.9	43
235	Banana without peel (about 2.6 per lb with peel).	1 banana	119	76	100	1	Trace	—	—	—	26	10	31	.8	440	230	.06	.07	.8	12
236	Banana flakes	1 tbsp	6	3	20	Trace	Trace	—	—	—	5	2	6	.2	92	50	.01	.01	.2	Trace

(A)	(B)		(C)	(D)	(E)	(F)	(G)	(H)	(I)	(J)	(K)	(L)	(M)	(N)	(O)	(P)	(Q)	(R)	(S)
237	Blackberries, raw	1 cup 144	85	85	2	1	—	—	—	19	46	27	1.3	245	290	0.04	0.06	0.6	30
238	Blueberries, raw	1 cup 145	83	90	1	1	—	—	—	22	22	19	1.5	117	150	.04	.09	.7	20
	Cantaloup. See Muskmelons (item 271).																		
	Cherries:																		
239	Sour (tart), red, pitted, canned, water pack.	1 cup 244	88	105	2	Trace	—	—	—	26	37	32	.7	317	1,660	.07	.05	.5	12
240	Sweet, raw, without pits and stems.	10 cherries 68	80	45	1	Trace	—	—	—	12	15	13	.3	129	70	.03	.04	.3	7
241	Cranberry juice cocktail, bottled, sweetened.	1 cup 253	83	165	Trace	Trace	—	—	—	42	13	8	.8	25	Trace	.03	.03	.1	[27]81
242	Cranberry sauce, sweetened, canned, strained.	1 cup 277	62	405	Trace	1	—	—	—	104	17	11	.6	83	60	.03	.03	.1	6
	Dates:																		
243	Whole, without pits	10 dates 80	23	220	2	Trace	—	—	—	58	47	50	2.4	518	40	.07	.08	1.8	0
244	Chopped	1 cup 178	23	490	4	1	—	—	—	130	105	112	5.3	1,153	90	.16	.18	3.9	0
245	Fruit cocktail, canned, in heavy sirup.	1 cup 255	80	195	1	Trace	—	—	—	50	23	31	1.0	411	360	.05	.03	1.0	5
	Grapefruit: Raw, medium, 3 3/4-in diam. (about 1 lb 1 oz):																		
246	Pink or red[28]	1/2 grapefruit 241	89	50	1	Trace	—	—	—	13	20	20	.5	166	540	.05	.02	.2	44
247	White[28]	1/2 grapefruit 241	89	45	1	Trace	—	—	—	12	19	19	.5	159	10	.05	.02	.2	44
248	Canned, sections with sirup	1 cup 254	81	180	2	Trace	—	—	—	45	33	36	.8	343	30	.08	.05	.5	76
	Grapefruit juice:																		
249	Raw, pink, red, or white	1 cup 246	90	95	1	Trace	—	—	—	23	22	37	.5	399	(29)	.10	.05	.5	93
	Canned, white:																		
250	Unsweetened	1 cup 247	89	100	1	Trace	—	—	—	24	20	35	1.0	400	20	.07	.05	.5	84
251	Sweetened	1 cup 250	86	135	1	Trace	—	—	—	32	20	35	1.0	405	30	.08	.05	.5	78
	Frozen, concentrate, unsweetened:																		
252	Undiluted, 6-fl oz can	1 can 207	62	300	4	1	—	—	—	72	70	124	.8	1,250	60	.29	.12	1.4	286
253	Diluted with 3 parts water by volume.	1 cup 247	89	100	1	Trace	—	—	—	24	25	42	.2	420	20	.10	.04	.5	96
254	Dehydrated crystals, prepared with water (1 lb yields about 1 gal).	1 cup 247	90	100	1	Trace	—	—	—	24	22	40	.2	412	20	.10	.05	.5	91
	Grapes, European type (adherent skin), raw:																		
255	Thompson Seedless	10 grapes 50	81	35	Trace	Trace	—	—	—	9	6	10	.2	87	50	.03	.02	.2	2
256	Tokay and Emperor, seeded types	10 grapes[30] 60	81	40	Trace	Trace	—	—	—	10	7	11	.2	99	60	.03	.02	.2	2
	Grapejuice:																		
257	Canned or bottled	1 cup 253	83	165	1	Trace	—	—	—	42	28	30	.8	293	—	.10	.05	.5	Trace
	Frozen concentrate, sweetened:																		
258	Undiluted, 6-fl oz can	1 can 216	53	395	1	Trace	—	—	—	100	22	32	.9	255	40	.13	.22	1.5	[31]32
259	Diluted with 3 parts water by volume.	1 cup 250	86	135	1	Trace	—	—	—	33	8	10	.3	85	10	.05	.08	.5	[31]10
260	Grape drink, canned	1 cup 250	86	135	Trace	Trace	—	—	—	35	8	10	.3	88	—	[32].03	[32].03	.3	(32)
261	Lemon, raw, size 165, without peel and seeds (about 4 per lb with peels and seeds).	1 lemon 74	90	20	1	Trace	—	—	—	6	19	12	.4	102	10	.03	.01	.1	39
	Lemon juice:																		
262	Raw	1 cup 244	91	60	1	Trace	—	—	—	20	17	24	.5	344	50	.07	.02	.2	112
263	Canned, or bottled, unsweetened	1 cup 244	92	55	1	Trace	—	—	—	19	17	24	.5	344	50	.07	.02	.2	102
264	Frozen, single strength, unsweetened, 6-fl oz can.	1 can 183	92	40	1	Trace	—	—	—	13	13	16	.5	258	40	.05	.02	.2	81
	Lemonade concentrate, frozen:																		
265	Undiluted, 6-fl oz can	1 can 219	49	425	Trace	Trace	—	—	—	112	9	13	.4	153	40	.05	.06	.7	66
266	Diluted with 4 1/3 parts water by volume.	1 cup 248	89	105	Trace	Trace	—	—	—	28	2	3	.1	40	10	.01	.02	.2	17

[19] Crust made with vegetable shortening and enriched flour.
[24] Also applies to pasteurized apple cider.
[25] Applies to product without added ascorbic acid. For value of product with added ascorbic acid, refer to label.
[26] Based on product with label claim of 45% of U.S. RDA in 6 fl oz.
[27] Based on product with label claim of 100% of U.S. RDA in 6 fl oz.
[28] Weight includes peel and membranes between sections. Without these parts, the weight of the edible portion is 123 g for item 246 and 118 g for item 247.
[29] For white-fleshed varieties, value is about 20 International Units (I.U.) per cup; for red-fleshed varieties, 1,080 I.U.
[30] Weight includes seeds. Without seeds, weight of the edible portion is 57 g.
[31] Applies to product without added ascorbic acid. With added ascorbic acid, based on claim that 6 fl oz of reconstituted juice contain 45% or 50% of the U.S. RDA, value in milligrams is 108 or 120 for a 6-fl oz can (item 258), 36 or 40 for 1 cup of diluted juice (item 259).
[32] For products with added thiamin and riboflavin but without added ascorbic acid, values in milligrams would be 0.60 for thiamin, 0.80 for riboflavin, and trace for ascorbic acid. For products with only ascorbic acid added, value varies with the brand. Consult the label.

Appendix C: Nutritive Values of the Edible Part of Foods (*Continued*)

(Dashes (—) denote lack of reliable data for a constituent believed to be present in measurable amount)

Item No. (A)	Foods, approximate measures, units, and weight (edible part unless footnotes indicate otherwise) (B)		Grams	Water (C) Percent	Food energy (D) Calories	Protein (E) Grams	Fat (F) Grams	Fatty Acids Saturated (total) (G) Grams	Unsaturated Oleic (H) Grams	Linoleic Grams	Carbohydrate (I) Grams	Calcium (K) Milligrams	Phosphorus (L) Milligrams	Iron (M) Milligrams	Potassium (N) Milligrams	Vitamin A value (O) International units	Thiamin (P) Milligrams	Riboflavin (Q) Milligrams	Niacin (R) Milligrams	Ascorbic acid (S) Milligrams
	FRUITS AND FRUIT PRODUCTS—Con.																			
	Limeade concentrate, frozen:																			
267	Undiluted, 6-fl oz can	1 can	218	50	410	Trace	Trace	—	—	—	108	11	13	0.2	129	Trace	0.02	0.02	0.2	26
268	Diluted with 4 1/3 parts water by volume	1 cup	247	89	100	Trace	Trace	—	—	—	27	3	3	Trace	32	Trace	Trace	Trace	Trace	6
	Lime juice:																			
269	Raw	1 cup	246	90	65	1	Trace	—	—	—	22	22	27	.5	256	20	.05	.02	.2	79
270	Canned, unsweetened	1 cup	246	90	65	1	Trace	—	—	—	22	22	27	.5	256	20	.05	.02	.2	52
	Muskmelons, raw, with rind, without seed cavity:																			
271	Cantaloup, orange-fleshed (with rind and seed cavity, 5-in diam., 2 1/3 lb)	1/2 melon with rind[33]	477	91	80	2	Trace	—	—	—	20	38	44	1.1	682	9,240	.11	.08	1.6	90
272	Honeydew (with rind and seed cavity, 6 1/2-in diam., 5 1/4 lb)	1/10 melon with rind[33]	226	91	50	1	Trace	—	—	—	11	21	24	.6	374	60	.06	.04	.9	34
	Oranges, all commercial varieties, raw:																			
273	Whole, 2 5/8-in diam., without peel and seeds (about 2 1/2 per lb with peel and seeds)	1 orange	131	86	65	1	Trace	—	—	—	16	54	26	.5	263	260	.13	.05	.5	66
274	Sections without membranes	1 cup	180	86	90	2	Trace	—	—	—	22	74	36	.7	360	360	.18	.07	.7	90
	Orange juice:																			
275	Raw, all varieties	1 cup	248	88	110	2	Trace	—	—	—	26	27	42	.5	496	500	.22	.07	1.0	124
276	Canned, unsweetened	1 cup	249	87	120	2	Trace	—	—	—	28	25	45	1.0	496	500	.17	.05	.7	100
	Frozen concentrate:																			
277	Undiluted, 6-fl oz can	1 can	213	55	360	5	Trace	—	—	—	87	75	126	.9	1,500	1,620	.68	.11	2.8	360
278	Diluted with 3 parts water by volume	1 cup	249	87	120	2	Trace	—	—	—	29	25	42	.2	503	540	.23	.03	.9	120
279	Dehydrated crystals, prepared with water (1 lb yields about 1 gal)	1 cup	248	88	115	1	Trace	—	—	—	27	25	40	.5	518	500	.20	.07	1.0	109
	Orange and grapefruit juice: Frozen concentrate:																			
280	Undiluted, 6-fl oz can	1 can	210	59	330	4	1	—	—	—	78	61	99	.8	1,308	800	.48	.06	2.3	302
281	Diluted with 3 parts water by volume	1 cup	248	88	110	1	Trace	—	—	—	26	20	32	.2	439	270	.15	.02	.7	102
282	Papayas, raw, 1/2-in cubes	1 cup	140	89	55	1	Trace	—	—	—	14	28	22	.4	328	2,450	.06	.06	.4	78
	Peaches:																			
283	Raw: Whole, 2 1/2-in diam., peeled, pitted (about 4 per lb with peels and pits)	1 peach	100	89	40	1	Trace	—	—	—	10	9	19	.5	202	[3]1,330	.02	.05	1.0	7
284	Sliced	1 cup	170	89	65	1	Trace	—	—	—	16	15	32	.9	343	[3]2,260	.03	.09	1.7	12
	Canned, yellow-fleshed, solids and liquid (halves or slices):																			
285	Sirup pack	1 cup	256	79	200	1	Trace	—	—	—	51	10	31	.8	333	1,100	.03	.05	1.5	8
286	Water pack	1 cup	244	91	75	1	Trace	—	—	—	20	10	32	.7	334	1,100	.02	.07	1.5	7
	Dried:																			
287	Uncooked	1 cup	160	25	420	5	1	—	—	—	109	77	187	9.6	1,520	6,240	.02	.30	8.5	29
288	Cooked, unsweetened, halves and juice	1 cup	250	77	205	3	1	—	—	—	54	38	93	4.8	743	3,050	.01	.15	3.8	5

(A)	(B)		(C)	(D)	(E)	(F)	(G)	(H)	(I)	(J)	(K)	(L)	(M)	(N)	(O)	(P)	(Q)	(R)	(S)
	Frozen, sliced, sweetened:																		
289	10-oz container	1 container	284	77	250	1	Trace	---	---	---	64	11	37	1.4	352	1,850	0.03	0.11	2.0	[35]116
290	Cup	1 cup	250	77	220	1	Trace	---	---	---	57	10	33	1.3	310	1,630	.03	.10	1.8	[35]103
	Pears:																		
	Raw, with skin, cored:																		
291	Bartlett, 2 1/2-in diam. (about 2 1/2 per lb with cores and stems)	1 pear	164	83	100	1	1	---	---	---	25	13	18	.5	213	30	.03	.07	.2	7
292	Bosc, 2 1/2-in diam. (about 3 per lb with cores and stems)	1 pear	141	83	85	1	1	---	---	---	22	11	16	.4	83	30	.03	.06	.1	6
293	D'Anjou, 3-in diam. (about 2 per lb with cores and stems)	1 pear	200	83	120	1	1	---	---	---	31	16	22	.6	260	40	.04	.08	.2	8
294	Canned, solids and liquid, sirup pack, heavy (halves or slices)	1 cup	255	80	195	1	1	---	---	---	50	13	18	.5	214	10	.03	.05	.3	3
	Pineapple:																		
295	Raw, diced	1 cup	155	85	80	1	Trace	---	---	---	21	26	12	.8	226	110	.14	.05	.3	26
	Canned, heavy sirup pack, solids and liquid:																		
296	Crushed, chunks, tidbits	1 cup	255	80	190	1	Trace	---	---	---	49	28	13	.8	245	130	.20	.05	.5	18
	Slices and liquid:																		
297	Large	1 slice; 2 1/4 tbsp liquid	105	80	80	Trace	Trace	---	---	---	20	12	5	.3	101	50	.08	.02	.2	7
298	Medium	1 slice; 1 1/4 tbsp liquid	58	80	45	Trace	Trace	---	---	---	11	6	3	.2	56	30	.05	.01	.1	4
299	Pineapple juice, unsweetened, canned	1 cup	250	86	140	1	Trace	---	---	---	34	38	23	.8	373	130	.13	.05	.5	[2]80
	Plums:																		
	Raw, without pits:																		
300	Japanese and hybrid (2 1/8-in diam., about 6 1/2 per lb with pits)	1 plum	66	87	30	Trace	Trace	---	---	---	8	8	12	.3	112	160	.02	.02	.3	4
301	Prune-type (1 1/2-in diam., about 15 per lb with pits)	1 plum	28	79	20	Trace	Trace	---	---	---	6	3	5	.1	48	80	.01	.01	.1	1
	Canned, heavy sirup pack (Italian prunes), with pits and liquid:																		
302	Cup[36]	1 cup[36]	272	77	215	1	Trace	---	---	---	56	23	26	2.3	367	3,130	.05	.05	1.0	5
303	Portion	3 plums; 2 3/4 tbsp liquid[36]	140	77	110	1	Trace	---	---	---	29	12	13	1.2	189	1,610	.03	.03	.5	3
	Prunes, dried, "softenized," with pits:																		
304	Uncooked	4 extra large or 5 large prunes[36]	49	28	110	1	Trace	---	---	---	29	22	34	1.7	298	690	.04	.07	.7	1
305	Cooked, unsweetened, all sizes, fruit and liquid[36]	1 cup[36]	250	66	255	2	1	---	---	---	67	51	79	3.8	695	1,590	.07	.15	1.5	2
306	Prune juice, canned or bottled	1 cup	256	80	195	1	Trace	---	---	---	49	36	51	1.8	602	—	.03	.03	1.0	5
	Raisins, seedless:																		
307	Cup, not pressed down	1 cup	145	18	420	4	Trace	---	---	---	112	90	146	5.1	1,106	30	.16	.12	.7	1
308	Packet, 1/2 oz (1 1/2 tbsp)	1 packet	14	18	40	Trace	Trace	---	---	---	11	9	14	.5	107	Trace	.02	.01	.1	Trace
	Raspberries, red:																		
309	Raw, capped, whole	1 cup	123	84	70	1	1	---	---	---	17	27	27	1.1	207	160	.04	.11	1.1	31
310	Frozen, sweetened, 10-oz container	1 container	284	74	280	2	1	---	---	---	70	37	48	1.7	284	200	.06	.17	1.7	60
	Rhubarb, cooked, added sugar:																		
311	From raw	1 cup	270	63	380	1	Trace	---	---	---	97	211	41	1.6	548	220	.05	.14	.8	16
312	From frozen, sweetened	1 cup	270	63	385	1	1	---	---	---	98	211	32	1.9	475	190	.05	.11	.5	16

[2]Based on product with label claim of 100% of U.S. RDA in 6 fl oz.

[27]Weight includes rind. Without rind, the weight of the edible portion is 272 g for item 271 and 149 g for item 272.

[33]Represents yellow-fleshed varieties. For white-fleshed varieties, value is 50 International Units (I.U.) for 1 peach, 90 I.U. for 1 cup of slices.

[34]Value represents products with added ascorbic acid. Value in milligrams is 116 for a 10-oz container, 103 for 1 cup.

[35]Represents products with added ascorbic acid. For products without added ascorbic acid, value is 116 for a 10-oz container, 103 for 1 cup.

[36]Weight includes pits. After removal of the pits, the weight of the edible portion is 258 g for item 302, 133 g for item 303, 43 g for item 304, and 213 g for item 305.

Appendix C: Nutritive Values of the Edible Part of Foods (*Continued*)

(Dashes (—) denote lack of reliable data for a constituent believed to be present in measurable amount)

(A) Item No.	(B) Foods, approximate measures, units, and weight (edible part unless footnotes indicate otherwise)	Grams	(C) Water Per-cent	(D) Food energy Cal-ories	(E) Pro-tein Grams	(F) Fat Grams	(G) Saturated (total) Grams	(H) Unsaturated Oleic Grams	(I) Unsaturated Lino-leic Grams	(J) Carbo-hydrate Grams	(K) Calcium Milli-grams	(L) Phos-phorus Milli-grams	(M) Iron Milli-grams	(N) Potas-sium Milli-grams	(O) Vitamin A value Inter-national units	(P) Thiamin Milli-grams	(Q) Ribo-flavin Milli-grams	(R) Niacin Milli-grams	(S) Ascorbic acid Milli-grams
	FRUITS AND FRUIT PRODUCTS—Con.																		
	Strawberries:																		
313	Raw, whole berries, capped — 1 cup	149	90	55	1	1	—	—	—	13	31	31	1.5	244	90	0.04	0.10	0.9	88
	Frozen, sweetened:																		
314	Sliced, 10-oz container — 1 container	284	71	310	1	1	—	—	—	79	40	48	2.0	318	90	.06	.17	1.4	151
315	Whole, 1-lb container (about 1 3/4 cups) — 1 container	454	76	415	2	1	—	—	—	107	59	73	2.7	472	140	.09	.27	2.3	249
316	Tangerine, raw, 2 3/8-in diam., size 176, without peel (about 4 per lb with peels and seeds) — 1 tangerine	86	87	40	1	Trace	—	—	—	10	34	15	.3	108	360	.05	.02	.1	27
317	Tangerine juice, canned, sweetened — 1 cup	249	87	125	1	Trace	—	—	—	30	44	35	.5	440	1,040	.15	.05	.2	54
318	Watermelon, raw, 4 by 8 in wedge with rind and seeds [37] (1/16 of 32 2/3-lb melon, 10 by 16 in) — 1 wedge with rind and seeds [37]	926	93	110	2	1	—	—	—	27	30	43	2.1	426	2,510	.13	.13	.9	30
	GRAIN PRODUCTS																		
	Bagel, 3-in diam.:																		
319	Egg — 1 bagel	55	32	165	6	2	0.5	0.9	0.8	28	9	43	1.2	41	30	.14	.10	1.2	0
320	Water — 1 bagel	55	29	165	6	2	.2	.4	.6	30	8	41	1.2	42	0	.15	.11	1.4	0
321	Barley, pearled, light, uncooked — 1 cup	200	11	700	16	2	.3	.2	.8	158	32	378	4.0	320	0	.24	.10	6.2	0
	Biscuits, baking powder, 2-in diam. (enriched flour, vegetable shortening):																		
322	From home recipe — 1 biscuit	28	27	105	2	5	1.2	2.0	1.2	13	34	49	.4	33	Trace	.08	.08	.7	Trace
323	From mix — 1 biscuit	28	29	90	2	3	.6	1.1	.7	15	19	65	.6	32	Trace	.09	.08	.8	Trace
324	Breadcrumbs (enriched): [38] Dry, grated — 1 cup	100	7	390	13	5	1.0	1.6	1.4	73	122	141	3.6	152	Trace	.35	.35	4.8	Trace
	Breads: Soft. See white bread (items 349-350).																		
325	Boston brown bread, canned, slice, 3 1/4 by 1/2 in. [38] — 1 slice	45	45	95	2	1	.1	.2	.2	21	41	72	.9	131	[39]0	.06	.04	.7	0
	Cracked-wheat bread (3/4 enriched wheat flour, 1/4 cracked wheat): [38]																		
326	Loaf, 1 lb — 1 loaf	454	35	1,195	39	10	2.2	3.0	3.9	236	399	581	9.5	608	Trace	1.52	1.13	14.4	Trace
327	Slice (18 per loaf) — 1 slice	25	35	65	2	1	.1	.2	.2	13	22	32	.5	34	Trace	.08	.06	.8	Trace
	French or vienna bread, enriched: [38]																		
328	Loaf, 1 lb — 1 loaf	454	31	1,315	41	14	3.2	4.7	4.6	251	195	386	10.0	408	Trace	1.80	1.10	15.0	Trace
	Slice:																		
329	French (5 by 2 1/2 by 1 in) — 1 slice	35	31	100	3	1	.4	.4	.4	19	15	30	.8	32	Trace	.14	.08	1.2	Trace
330	Vienna (4 3/4 by 4 by 1/2 in) — 1 slice	25	31	75	2	1	.2	.3	.3	14	11	21	.6	23	Trace	.10	.06	.8	Trace
	Italian bread, enriched:																		
331	Loaf, 1 lb — 1 loaf	454	32	1,250	41	4	.6	.3	1.5	256	77	349	10.0	336	0	1.80	1.10	15.0	0
332	Slice, 4 1/2 by 3 1/4 by 3/4 in — 1 slice	30	32	85	3	Trace	Trace	Trace	.1	17	5	23	.7	22	0	.12	.07	1.0	0
	Raisin bread, enriched: [38]																		
333	Loaf, 1 lb — 1 loaf	454	35	1,190	30	13	3.0	4.7	3.9	243	322	395	10.0	1,057	Trace	1.70	1.07	10.7	Trace
334	Slice (18 per loaf) — 1 slice	25	35	65	2	1	.2	.3	.2	13	18	22	.6	58	Trace	.09	.06	.6	Trace

(A)	(B)	(C)	(D)	(E)	(F)	(G)	(H)	(I)	(J)	(K)	(L)	(M)	(N)	(O)	(P)	(Q)	(R)	(S)
	Rye Bread:																	
	American, light (2/3 enriched wheat flour, 1/3 rye flour):																	
335	Loaf, 1 lb	454	1,100	41	5	0.7	0.5	2.2	236	340	667	9.1	658	0	1.35	0.98	12.9	0
336	Slice (4 3/4 by 3 3/4 by 7/16 in)	36	60	2	Trace	Trace	Trace	.1	13	19	37	.5	36	0	.07	.05	.7	0
	Pumpernickel (2/3 rye flour, 1/3 enriched wheat flour):																	
337	Loaf, 1 lb	454	1,115	41	5	.7	.5	2.4	241	381	1,039	11.8	2,059	0	1.30	.93	8.5	0
338	Slice (5 by 4 by 3/8 in)	32	80	3	Trace	.1	Trace	.2	17	27	73	.8	145	0	.09	.07	.6	0
	White bread, enriched:[38]																	
	Soft-crumb type:																	
339	Loaf, 1 lb	454	1,225	39	15	3.4	5.3	4.6	229	381	440	11.3	476	Trace	1.80	1.10	15.0	Trace
340	Slice (18 per loaf)	25	70	2	1	.2	.3	.3	13	21	24	.6	26	Trace	.10	.06	.8	Trace
341	Slice, toasted	22	70	2	1	.2	.3	.3	13	21	24	.6	26	Trace	.08	.06	.8	Trace
342	Slice (22 per loaf)	20	55	2	1	.2	.2	.2	10	17	19	.5	21	Trace	.08	.05	.7	Trace
343	Slice, toasted	17	55	2	1	.2	.2	.2	10	17	19	.5	21	Trace	.06	.06	.6	Trace
344	Loaf, 1 1/2 lb	680	1,835	59	22	5.2	7.9	6.9	343	571	660	17.0	714	Trace	2.70	1.65	22.5	Trace
345	Slice (24 per loaf)	28	75	2	1	.2	.3	.3	14	24	27	.7	29	Trace	.11	.07	.9	Trace
346	Slice, toasted	24	75	2	1	.2	.3	.3	14	24	27	.7	29	Trace	.09	.07	.9	Trace
347	Slice (28 per loaf)	24	65	2	1	.2	.3	.3	12	20	23	.6	25	Trace	.09	.06	.8	Trace
348	Slice, toasted	21	65	2	1	.2	.3	.3	12	20	23	.6	25	Trace	.10	.06	.8	Trace
349	Cubes	30	80	3	1	.2	.3	.3	15	23	29	.7	32	Trace	.12	.07	1.0	Trace
350	Crumbs	45	120	4	1	.3	.5	.5	23	38	44	1.1	47	Trace	.18	.11	1.5	Trace
	Firm-crumb type:																	
351	Loaf, 1 lb	454	1,245	41	17	3.9	5.9	5.2	228	435	463	11.3	549	Trace	1.80	1.10	15.0	Trace
352	Slice (20 per loaf)	23	65	2	1	.2	.3	.3	12	22	23	.6	28	Trace	.09	.06	.8	Trace
353	Slice, toasted	20	65	2	1	.2	.3	.3	12	22	23	.6	28	Trace	.07	.06	.8	Trace
354	Loaf, 2 lb	907	2,495	82	34	7.7	11.8	10.4	455	871	925	22.7	1,097	Trace	3.60	2.20	30.0	Trace
355	Slice (34 per loaf)	27	75	2	1	.2	.3	.3	14	26	28	.7	33	Trace	.11	.11	.9	Trace
356	Slice, toasted	23	75	2	1	.3	.3	.3	14	26	28	.7	33	Trace	.09	.06	.9	Trace
	Whole-wheat bread:																	
	Soft-crumb type:[38]																	
357	Loaf, 1 lb	454	1,095	41	12	2.2	2.9	4.2	224	381	1,152	13.6	1,161	Trace	1.37	.45	12.7	Trace
358	Slice (16 per loaf)	28	65	3	1	.1	.2	.2	14	24	71	.8	72	Trace	.09	.03	.8	Trace
359	Slice, toasted	24	65	3	1	.1	.2	.2	14	24	71	.8	72	Trace	.07	.03	.8	Trace
	Firm-crumb type:[38]																	
360	Loaf, 1 lb	454	1,100	48	14	2.5	3.3	4.9	216	449	1,034	13.6	1,238	Trace	1.17	.54	12.7	Trace
361	Slice (18 per loaf)	25	60	3	1	.1	.2	.2	12	25	57	.8	68	Trace	.06	.03	.8	Trace
362	Slice, toasted	21	60	3	1	.1	.2	.3	12	25	57	.8	68	Trace	.05	.03	.7	Trace
	Breakfast cereals:																	
	Hot type, cooked:																	
	Corn (hominy) grits, degermed:																	
363	Enriched	245	125	3	Trace	Trace	Trace	.1	27	2	25	.7	27	[40]Trace	.10	.07	1.0	0
364	Unenriched	245	125	3	Trace	Trace	Trace	.1	27	2	25	.7	27	[40]Trace	.05	.02	.5	0
365	Farina, quick-cooking, enriched	245	105	3	Trace	Trace	Trace	.1	22	147	[41]113	(*[42])	25	0	.12	.07	1.0	0
366	Oatmeal or rolled oats	240	130	5	2	.4	.8	.9	23	22	137	1.4	146	0	.19	.05	.2	0
367	Wheat, rolled	240	180	5	1	—	—	—	41	19	182	1.7	202	0	.17	.07	2.2	0
368	Wheat, whole-meal	245	110	4	1	—	—	—	23	17	127	1.2	118	0	.15	.05	1.5	0
	Ready-to-eat:																	
369	Bran flakes (40% bran), added sugar, salt, iron, vitamins.	35	105	4	1	—	—	—	28	19	125	5.6	137	1,540	.46	.52	6.2	0
370	Bran flakes with raisins, added sugar, salt, iron, vitamins.	50	145	4	1	—	—	—	40	28	146	7.9	154	[42]32,200	(**)	(**)	(**)	0

[37] Weight includes rind and seeds. Without rind and seeds, weight of the edible portion is 426 g.

[38] Made with vegetable shortening.

[39] Applies to product made with white cornmeal. With yellow cornmeal, value is 30 International Units (I.U.).

[40] Applies to white varieties. For yellow varieties, value is 150 International Units (I.U.).

[41] Applies to products that do not contain di-sodium phosphate. If di-sodium phosphate is an ingredient, value is 162 mg.

[42] Value may range from less than 1 mg to about 8 mg depending on the brand. Consult the label.

[43] Applies to product with added nutrient. Without added nutrient, value is trace.

[44] Value varies with the brand. Consult the label.

Appendix C: Nutritive Values of the Edible Part of Foods (*Continued*)

(Dashes (—) denote lack of reliable data for a constituent believed to be present in measurable amount)

Item No. (A)	Foods, approximate measures, units, and weight (edible part unless footnotes indicate otherwise) (B)		(grams)	Water (C) Per-cent	Food energy (D) Calories	Protein (E) Grams	Fat (F) Grams	Fatty Acids Saturated (total) (G) Grams	Unsaturated Oleic (H) Grams	Linoleic (I) Grams	Carbohydrate (J) Grams	Calcium (K) Milligrams	Phosphorus (L) Milligrams	Iron (M) Milligrams	Potassium (N) Milligrams	Vitamin A value (O) International units	Thiamin (P) Milligrams	Riboflavin (Q) Milligrams	Niacin (R) Milligrams	Ascorbic acid (S) Milligrams
	GRAIN PRODUCTS—Con.																			
	Breakfast cereals—Continued																			
	Ready-to-eat—Continued																			
	Corn flakes:																			
371	Plain, added sugar, salt, iron, vitamins.	1 cup	25	4	95	2	Trace	—	—	—	21	(44)	9	(44)	30	(44)	(44)	(44)	(44)	[4]13
372	Sugar-coated, added salt, iron, vitamins.	1 cup	40	2	155	2	Trace	—	—	—	37	1	10	(44)	27	1,760	.53	.50	7.1	[4]21
373	Corn, oat flour, puffed, added sugar, salt, iron, vitamins.	1 cup	20	4	80	2	1	—	—	—	16	4	18	5.7	—	880	.26	.30	3.5	11
374	Corn, shredded, added sugar, salt, iron, thiamin, niacin.	1 cup	25	3	95	2	Trace	—	—	—	22	1	10	.6	—	0	.33	.05	4.4	13
375	Oats, puffed, added sugar, salt, minerals, vitamins.	1 cup	25	3	100	3	1	—	—	—	19	44	102	4.0	—	1,100	.33	.38	4.4	13
	Rice, puffed:																			
376	Plain, added iron, thiamin, niacin.	1 cup	15	4	60	1	Trace	—	—	—	13	3	14	.3	15	0	.07	.01	.7	0
377	Presweetened, added salt, iron, vitamins.	1 cup	28	3	115	1	0	—	—	—	26	3	14	(44)	43	[4]1,240	(44)	(44)	(44)	[4]15
378	Wheat flakes, added sugar, salt, iron, vitamins.	1 cup	30	4	105	3	Trace	—	—	—	24	12	83	4.8	81	1,320	.40	.45	5.3	16
	Wheat, puffed:																			
379	Plain, added iron, thiamin, niacin.	1 cup	15	3	55	2	Trace	—	—	—	12	4	48	.6	51	0	.08	.03	1.2	0
380	Presweetened, added salt, iron, vitamins.	1 cup	38	3	140	3	Trace	—	—	—	33	7	52	(44)	63	1,680	.50	.57	6.7	[4]20
381	Wheat, shredded, plain	1 oblong biscuit or 1/2 cup spoon-size biscuits.	25	7	90	2	1	—	—	—	20	11	97	.9	87	0	.06	.03	1.1	0
382	Wheat germ, without salt and sugar, toasted.	1 tbsp	6	4	25	2	1	—	—	—	3	3	70	.5	57	10	.11	.05	.3	1
383	Buckwheat flour, light, sifted	1 cup	98	12	340	6	1	.2	.4	.4	78	11	86	1.0	314	0	.08	.04	.4	0
384	Bulgur, canned, seasoned	1 cup	135	56	245	8	4	—	—	—	44	27	263	1.9	151	0	.08	.05	4.1	0
	Cake icings. See Sugars and Sweets (items 532–536).																			
	Cakes made from cake mixes with enriched flour:[46]																			
	Angelfood:																			
385	Whole cake (9 3/4-in diam. tube cake).	1 cake	635	34	1,645	36	1	—	—	—	377	603	756	2.5	381	0	.37	.95	3.6	0
386	Piece, 1/12 of cake	1 piece	53	34	135	3	Trace	—	—	—	32	50	63	.2	32	0	.03	.08	.3	0
	Coffeecake:																			
387	Whole cake (7 3/4 by 5 5/8 by 1 1/4 in).	1 cake	430	30	1,385	27	41	11.7	16.3	8.8	225	262	748	6.9	469	690	.82	.91	7.7	1
388	Piece, 1/6 of cake	1 piece	72	30	230	5	7	2.0	2.7	1.5	38	44	125	1.2	78	120	.14	.15	1.3	Trace
	Cupcakes, made with egg, milk, 2 1/2-in diam.:																			
389	Without icing	1 cupcake	25	26	90	1	3	.8	1.2	.7	14	40	59	.3	21	40	.05	.05	.4	Trace
390	With chocolate icing	1 cupcake	36	22	130	2	5	2.0	1.6	.6	21	47	71	.4	42	60	.05	.06	.4	Trace
	Devil's food with chocolate icing:																			
391	Whole, 2 layer cake (8- or 9-in diam.).	1 cake	1,107	24	3,755	49	136	50.0	44.9	17.0	645	653	1,162	16.6	1,439	1,660	1.06	1.65	10.1	1
392	Piece, 1/16 of cake	1 piece	69	24	235	3	8	3.1	2.8	1.1	40	41	72	1.0	90	100	.07	.10	.6	Trace
393	Cupcake, 2 1/2-in diam	1 cupcake	35	24	120	2	4	1.6	1.4	.5	20	21	37	.5	46	50	.03	.05	.3	Trace

(A)	(B)		(C)	(D)	(E)	(F)	(G)	(H)	(I)	(J)	(K)	(L)	(M)	(N)	(O)	(P)	(Q)	(R)	(S)
	Gingerbread:																		
394	Whole cake (8-in square)	1 cake	37	1,575	18	39	9.7	16.6	10.0	291	513	570	8.6	1,562	Trace	0.84	1.00	7.4	Trace
395	Piece, 1/9 of cake		37	175	2	4	1.1	1.8	1.1	32	57	63	.9	173	Trace	.09	.11	.8	Trace
	White, 2 layer with chocolate icing:																		
396	Whole cake (8- or 9-in diam.)	1 cake	21	4,000	44	122	48.2	46.4	20.0	716	1,129	2,041	11.4	1,322	680	1.50	1.77	12.5	2
397	Piece, 1/16 of cake		21	250	3	8	3.0	2.9	1.2	45	70	127	.7	82	40	.09	.11	.8	Trace
	Yellow, 2 layer with chocolate icing:																		
398	Whole cake (8- or 9-in diam.)	1 cake	26	3,735	45	125	47.8	47.8	20.3	638	1,008	2,017	12.2	1,208	1,550	1.24	1.67	10.6	2
399	Piece, 1/16 of cake		26	235	3	8	3.0	3.0	1.3	40	63	126	.8	75	100	.08	.10	.7	Trace
	Cakes made from home recipes using enriched flour:[47]																		
	Boston cream pie with custard filling:																		
400	Whole cake (8-in diam.)	1 cake	35	2,490	41	78	23.0	30.1	15.2	412	553	833	8.2	[48]734	1,730	1.04	1.27	9.6	2
401	Piece, 1/12 of cake		35	210	3	6	1.9	2.5	1.3	34	46	70	.7	[48]61	140	.09	.11	.8	Trace
	Fruitcake, dark:																		
402	Loaf, 1-lb (7 1/2 by 2 by 1 1/2 in).	1 loaf	18	1,720	22	69	14.4	33.5	14.8	271	327	513	11.8	2,250	540	.72	.73	4.9	2
403	Slice, 1/30 of loaf	1 slice	18	55	1	2	.5	1.1	.5	9	11	17	.4	74	20	.02	.02	.2	Trace
	Plain, sheet cake:																		
	Without icing:																		
404	Whole cake (9-in square)	1 cake	25	2,830	35	108	29.5	44.4	23.9	434	497	793	8.5	[48]614	1,320	1.21	1.40	10.2	2
405	Piece, 1/9 of cake		25	315	4	12	3.3	4.9	2.6	48	55	88	.9	[48]68	150	.13	.15	1.1	Trace
	With uncooked white icing:																		
406	Whole cake (9-in square)	1 cake	21	4,020	37	129	42.2	49.5	24.4	694	548	822	8.2	[48]669	2,190	1.22	1.47	10.2	2
407	Piece, 1/9 of cake		21	445	4	14	4.7	5.5	2.7	77	61	91	.8	[48]74	240	.14	.16	1.1	Trace
	Pound:[49]																		
408	Loaf, 8 1/2 by 3 1/2 by 3 1/4 in.	1 loaf	16	2,725	31	170	42.9	73.1	39.6	273	107	418	7.9	345	1,410	.90	.99	7.3	0
409	Slice, 1/17 of loaf	1 slice	16	160	2	10	2.5	4.3	2.3	16	6	24	.5	20	80	.05	.06	.4	0
	Spongecake:																		
410	Whole cake (9 3/4-in diam. tube cake).	1 cake	32	2,345	60	45	13.1	15.8	5.7	427	237	885	13.4	687	3,560	1.10	1.64	7.4	Trace
411	Piece, 1/12 of cake	1 piece	32	195	5	4	1.1	1.3	.5	36	20	74	1.1	57	300	.09	.14	.6	Trace
	Cookies made with enriched flour:[50][51]																		
	Brownies with nuts:																		
	Home-prepared, 1 3/4 by 1 3/4 by 7/8 in:																		
412	From home recipe	1 brownie	10	95	1	6	1.5	3.0	1.2	10	8	30	.4	38	40	.04	.03	.2	Trace
413	From commercial recipe[52]	1 brownie	11	85	1	4	.9	1.4	1.3	13	9	27	.4	34	20	.03	.02	.2	Trace
414	Frozen, with chocolate icing,[52] 1 1/2 by 1 3/4 by 7/8 in.	1 brownie	13	105	1	5	2.0	2.2	.7	15	10	31	.4	44	50	.03	.03	.2	Trace
	Chocolate chip:																		
415	Commercial, 2 1/4-in diam., 3/8 in thick.	4 cookies	3	200	2	9	2.8	2.9	2.2	29	16	48	1.0	56	50	.10	.17	.9	Trace
416	From home recipe, 2 1/3-in diam.	4 cookies	3	205	2	12	3.5	4.5	2.9	24	14	40	.8	47	40	.06	.06	.5	Trace
417	Fig bars, square (1 5/8 by 1 5/8 by 3/8 in) or rectangular (1 1/2 by 1 3/4 by 1/2 in).	4 cookies	14	200	2	3	.8	1.2	.7	42	44	34	1.0	111	60	.04	.14	.9	Trace
418	Gingersnaps, 2-in diam., 1/4 in thick.	4 cookies	3	90	2	2	.7	1.0	.6	22	20	13	.7	129	20	.08	.06	.7	0
419	Macaroons, 2 3/4-in diam., 1/4 in thick.	2 cookies	4	180	2	9	—	—	—	25	10	32	.3	176	0	.02	.06	.2	0
420	Oatmeal with raisins, 2 5/8-in diam., 1/4 in thick.	4 cookies	3	235	3	8	2.0	3.3	2.0	38	11	53	1.4	192	30	.15	.10	1.0	Trace

[45] Value varies with the brand. Consult the label.
[45] Applies to product with added nutrient. Without added nutrient, value is trace.
[46] Excepting angelfood cake, cakes were made from mixes containing vegetable shortening; icings, with butter.
[47] Excepting spongecake, vegetable shortening used for cake portion; butter, for icing. If butter or margarine used for cake portion, vitamin A values would be higher.
[48] Applies to product made with a sodium aluminum-sulfate type baking powder. With a low-sodium type baking powder containing potassium, value would be about twice the amount shown.
[49] Equal weights of flour, sugar, eggs, and vegetable shortening.
[50] Products are commercial unless otherwise specified.
[51] Made with enriched flour and vegetable shortening except for macaroons which do not contain flour or shortening.
[52] Icing made with butter.

Appendix C: Nutritive Values of the Edible Part of Foods (*Continued*)

(Dashes (—) denote lack of reliable data for a constituent believed to be present in measurable amount)

Item No. (A)	Foods, approximate measures, units, and weight (edible part unless footnotes indicate otherwise) (B)	Grams	Water (C) Per cent	Food energy (D) Calories	Pro-tein (E) Grams	Fat (F) Grams	Fatty Acids — Satu-rated (total) (G) Grams	Fatty Acids — Unsaturated Oleic (H) Grams	Fatty Acids — Unsaturated Lino-leic (I) Grams	Carbo-hydrate (J) Grams	Calcium (K) Milligrams	Phos-phorus (L) Milligrams	Iron (M) Milligrams	Potas-sium (N) Milligrams	Vitamin A value (O) International units	Thiamin (P) Milligrams	Ribo-flavin (Q) Milligrams	Niacin (R) Milligrams	Ascorbic acid (S) Milligrams
	GRAIN PRODUCTS—Con.																		
	Cookies made with enriched flour[50][51]—Continued																		
421	Plain, prepared from commercial chilled dough, 2 1/2-in diam., 1/4 in thick. 4 cookies	48	5	240	2	12	3.0	5.2	2.9	31	17	35	0.6	23	30	0.10	0.08	0.9	0
422	Sandwich type (chocolate or vanilla), 1 3/4-in diam., 3/8 in thick. 4 cookies	40	2	200	2	9	2.2	3.9	2.2	28	10	96	.7	15	0	.06	.10	.7	0
423	Vanilla wafers, 1 3/4-in diam., 1/4 in thick. 10 cookies	40	3	185	2	6	—	—	—	30	16	25	.6	29	50	.10	.09	.8	0
	Cornmeal:																		
424	Whole-ground, unbolted, dry form. 1 cup	122	12	435	11	5	.5	1.0	2.5	90	24	312	2.9	346	[53]620	.46	.13	2.4	0
425	Bolted (nearly whole-grain), dry form. 1 cup	122	12	440	11	4	.5	.9	2.1	91	21	272	2.2	303	[53]590	.37	.10	2.3	0
	Degermed, enriched:																		
426	Dry form 1 cup	138	12	500	11	2	.2	.4	.9	108	8	137	4.0	166	[53]610	.61	.36	4.8	0
427	Cooked 1 cup	240	88	120	3	Trace	Trace	.1	.2	26	2	34	1.0	38	[57]140	.14	.10	1.2	0
	Degermed, unenriched:																		
428	Dry form 1 cup	138	12	500	11	2	.2	.4	.9	108	8	137	1.5	166	[53]610	.19	.07	1.4	0
429	Cooked 1 cup	240	88	120	3	Trace	Trace	.1	.2	26	2	34	.5	38	[57]140	.05	.02	.2	0
	Crackers:[38]																		
430	Graham, plain, 2 1/2-in square 2 crackers	14	6	55	1	1	.3	.3	.3	10	6	21	.5	55	0	.02	.08	.5	0
431	Rye wafers, whole-grain, 1 7/8 by 3 1/2 in. 2 wafers	13	6	45	2	Trace	—	—	—	10	7	50	.5	78	0	.04	.03	.2	0
432	Saltines, made with enriched flour. 4 crackers or 1 packet	11	4	50	1	1	.3	.5	.4	8	2	10	.5	13	0	.05	.05	.4	0
	Danish pastry (enriched flour), plain without fruit or nuts:[54]																		
433	Packaged ring, 12 oz 1 ring	340	22	1,435	25	80	24.3	31.7	16.5	155	170	371	6.1	381	1,050	.97	1.01	8.6	Trace
434	Round piece, about 4 1/4-in diam. by 1 in. 1 pastry	65	22	275	5	15	4.7	6.1	3.2	30	33	71	1.2	73	200	.18	.19	1.7	Trace
435	Ounce 1 oz	28	22	120	2	7	2.0	2.7	1.4	13	14	31	.5	32	90	.08	.08	.7	Trace
	Doughnuts, made with enriched flour:[38]																		
436	Cake type, plain, 2 1/2-in diam., 1 in high. 1 doughnut	25	24	100	1	5	1.2	2.0	1.1	13	10	48	.4	23	20	.05	.05	.4	Trace
437	Yeast-leavened, glazed, 3 3/4-in diam., 1 1/4 in high. 1 doughnut	50	26	205	3	11	3.3	5.8	3.3	22	16	33	.6	34	25	.10	.10	.8	0
	Macaroni, enriched, cooked (cut lengths, elbows, shells):																		
	Firm stage (hot):																		
438	1 cup	130	64	190	7	1	—	—	—	39	14	85	1.4	103	0	.23	.13	1.8	0
	Tender stage:																		
439	Cold macaroni 1 cup	105	73	115	4	Trace	—	—	—	24	8	53	.9	64	0	.15	.08	1.2	0
440	Hot macaroni 1 cup	140	73	155	5	1	—	—	—	32	11	70	1.3	85	0	.20	.11	1.5	0
	Macaroni (enriched) and cheese:																		
441	Canned[55] 1 cup	240	80	230	9	10	4.2	3.1	1.4	26	199	182	1.0	139	260	.12	.24	1.0	Trace
442	From home recipe (served hot)[56] 1 cup	200	58	430	17	22	8.9	8.8	2.9	40	362	322	1.8	240	860	.20	.40	1.8	Trace
	Muffins made with enriched flour:[38]																		
	From home recipe:																		
443	Blueberry, 2 3/8-in diam., 1 1/2 in high. 1 muffin	40	39	110	3	4	1.1	1.4	.7	17	34	53	.6	46	90	.09	.10	.7	Trace
444	Bran 1 muffin	40	35	105	3	4	1.2	1.4	.8	17	57	162	1.5	172	90	.07	.10	1.7	Trace
445	Corn (enriched degermed cornmeal and flour), 2 3/8-in diam., 1 1/2 in high. 1 muffin	40	33	125	3	4	1.2	1.6	.9	19	42	68	.7	54	[57]120	.10	.10	.7	Trace

(A)	(B)		(C)	(D)	(E)	(F)	(G)	(H)	(I)	(J)	(K)	(L)	(M)	(N)	(O)	(P)	(Q)	(R)	(S)
446	Plain, 3-in diam., 1 1/2 in high. — 1 muffin	40	38	120	3	4	1.0	1.7	1.0	17	42	60	0.6	50	40	0.09	0.12	0.9	Trace
	From mix, egg, milk:																			
447	Corn, 2 3/8-in diam., 1 1/2 in high.[58] — 1 muffin	40	30	130	3	4	1.2	1.7	.9	20	96	152	.6	44	[57]100	.08	.09	.7	Trace
448	Noodles (egg noodles), enriched, cooked. — 1 cup	160	71	200	7	2	—	—	—	37	16	94	1.4	70	110	.22	.13	1.9	0
449	Noodles, chow mein, canned.[48] — 1 cup	45	1	220	6	11	—	—	—	26	—	—	—	—	—	—	—	—	—
450	Pancakes, (4-in diam.).[48] Buckwheat, made from mix (with buckwheat and enriched flours), egg and milk added. — 1 cake	27	58	55	2	2	.8	.9	.4	6	59	91	.4	66	60	.04	.05	.2	—
	Plain:																			
451	Made from home recipe using enriched flour. — 1 cake	27	50	60	2	2	.5	.8	.5	9	27	38	.4	33	30	.06	.07	.5	Trace
452	Made from mix with enriched flour, egg and milk added. — 1 cake	27	51	60	2	2	.7	.7	.3	9	58	70	.3	42	70	.04	.06	.2	Trace
	Pies, piecrust made with enriched flour, vegetable shortening (9-in diam.):																			
	Apple:																			
453	Whole — 1 pie	945	48	2,420	21	105	27.0	44.5	25.2	360	76	208	6.6	756	280	1.06	.79	9.3	9
454	Sector, 1/7 of pie — 1 sector	135	48	345	3	15	3.9	6.4	3.6	51	11	30	.9	108	40	.15	.11	1.3	2
	Banana cream:																			
455	Whole — 1 pie	910	54	2,010	41	85	26.7	33.2	16.2	279	601	746	7.3	1,847	2,280	.77	1.51	7.0	9
456	Sector, 1/7 of pie — 1 sector	130	54	285	6	12	3.8	4.7	2.3	40	86	107	1.0	264	330	.11	.22	1.0	1
	Blueberry:																			
457	Whole — 1 pie	945	51	2,285	23	102	24.8	43.7	25.1	330	104	217	9.5	614	280	1.03	.80	10.0	28
458	Sector, 1/7 of pie — 1 sector	135	51	325	3	15	3.5	6.2	3.6	47	15	31	1.4	88	40	.15	.11	1.4	4
	Cherry:																			
459	Whole — 1 pie	945	47	2,465	25	107	28.2	45.0	25.3	363	132	236	6.6	992	4,160	1.09	.84	9.8	Trace
460	Sector, 1/7 of pie — 1 sector	135	47	350	4	15	4.0	6.4	3.6	52	19	34	.9	142	590	.16	.12	1.4	Trace
	Custard:																			
461	Whole — 1 pie	910	58	1,985	56	101	33.9	38.5	17.5	213	874	1,028	8.2	1,247	2,090	.79	1.92	5.6	0
462	Sector, 1/7 of pie — 1 sector	130	58	285	8	14	4.8	5.5	2.5	30	125	147	1.2	178	300	.11	.27	.8	0
	Lemon meringue:																			
463	Whole — 1 pie	840	47	2,140	31	86	26.1	33.8	16.4	317	118	412	6.7	420	1,430	.61	.84	5.2	25
464	Sector, 1/7 of pie — 1 sector	120	47	305	4	12	3.7	4.8	2.3	45	17	59	1.0	60	200	.09	.12	.7	4
	Mince:																			
465	Whole — 1 pie	945	43	2,560	24	109	28.0	45.9	25.2	389	265	359	13.3	1,682	20	.96	.86	9.8	9
466	Sector, 1/7 of pie — 1 sector	135	43	365	3	16	4.0	6.6	3.6	56	38	51	1.9	240	Trace	.14	.12	1.4	1
	Peach:																			
467	Whole — 1 pie	945	48	2,410	24	101	24.8	43.7	25.1	361	95	274	8.5	1,408	6,900	1.04	.97	14.0	28
468	Sector, 1/7 of pie — 1 sector	135	48	345	3	14	3.5	6.2	3.6	52	14	39	1.2	201	990	.15	.14	2.0	4
	Pecan:																			
469	Whole — 1 pie	825	20	3,450	42	189	27.8	101.0	44.2	423	388	850	25.6	1,015	1,320	1.80	.95	6.9	Trace
470	Sector, 1/7 of pie — 1 sector	118	20	495	6	27	4.0	14.4	6.3	61	55	122	3.7	145	190	.26	.14	1.0	Trace
	Pumpkin:																			
471	Whole — 1 pie	910	59	1,920	36	102	37.4	37.5	16.6	223	464	628	7.3	1,456	22,480	.78	1.27	7.0	Trace
472	Sector, 1/7 of pie — 1 sector	130	59	275	5	15	5.4	5.4	2.4	32	66	90	1.0	208	3,210	.11	.18	1.0	Trace
473	Piecrust (home recipe) made with enriched flour and vegetable shortening, baked. — 1 pie shell, 9-in diam.	180	15	900	11	60	14.8	26.1	14.9	79	25	90	3.1	89	0	.47	.40	5.0	0
474	Piecrust mix with enriched flour and vegetable shortening, 10-oz pkg. prepared and baked. — Piecrust for 2-crust pie, 9-in diam.	320	19	1,485	20	93	22.7	39.7	23.4	141	131	272	6.1	179	0	1.07	.79	9.9	0

[48] Made with vegetable shortening.
[50] Products are commercial unless otherwise specified.
[51] Made with enriched flour and vegetable shortening except for macaroons which do not contain flour or shortening.
[53] Applies to yellow varieties; white varieties contain only a trace.
[54] Contains vegetable shortening and butter.
[55] Made with corn oil.
[56] Made with regular margarine.
[57] Applies to product made with yellow cornmeal.
[58] Made with enriched degermed cornmeal and enriched flour.

Appendix C: Nutritive Values of the Edible Part of Foods (Continued)

(Dashes (—) denote lack of reliable data for a constituent believed to be present in measurable amount)

(A) Item No.	(B) Foods, approximate measures, units, and weight (edible part unless footnotes indicate otherwise)		(C) Water	(D) Food energy	(E) Protein	(F) Fat	Fatty Acids			(J) Carbohydrate	(K) Calcium	(L) Phosphorus	(M) Iron	(N) Potassium	(O) Vitamin A value	(P) Thiamin	(Q) Riboflavin	(R) Niacin	(S) Ascorbic acid
							Saturated (total) (G)	Unsaturated Oleic (H)	Linoleic (I)										
		Grams	Percent	Calories	Grams	Grams	Grams	Grams	Grams	Grams	Milligrams	Milligrams	Milligrams	Milligrams	International units	Milligrams	Milligrams	Milligrams	Milligrams
475	Pizza (cheese) baked, 4 3/4-in sector; 1/8 of 12-in pie.[13] — 1 sector	60	45	145	6	4	1.7	1.5	0.6	22	86	89	1.1	67	230	0.16	0.18	1.6	4
	GRAIN PRODUCTS—Con.																		
	Popcorn, popped:																		
476	Plain, large kernel — 1 cup	6	4	25	1	Trace	Trace	.1	.2	5	1	17	.2	—	—	—	.01	.1	0
477	With oil (coconut) and salt added, large kernel. — 1 cup	9	3	40	1	2	1.5	.2	.2	5	1	19	.2	—	—	—	.01	.2	0
478	Sugar coated — 1 cup	35	4	135	2	1	.5	.2	.4	30	2	47	.5	—	—	—	.02	.4	0
	Pretzels, made with enriched flour:																		
479	Dutch, twisted, 2 3/4 by 2 5/8 in. — 1 pretzel	16	5	60	2	1	—	—	—	12	4	21	.2	21	0	.05	.04	.7	0
480	Thin, twisted, 3 1/4 by 2 1/4 by 1/4 in. — 10 pretzels	60	5	235	6	3	—	—	—	46	13	79	.9	78	0	.20	.15	2.5	0
481	Stick, 2 1/4 in long — 10 pretzels	3	5	10	Trace	Trace	—	—	—	2	1	4	Trace	4	0	.01	.01	.1	0
	Rice, white, enriched:																		
482	Instant, ready-to-serve, hot — 1 cup	165	73	180	4	Trace	Trace	Trace	Trace	40	5	31	1.3	—	0	.21	(⁵⁹)	1.7	0
	Long grain:																		
483	Raw — 1 cup	185	12	670	12	1	.2	.2	.2	149	44	174	5.4	170	0	.81	.06	6.5	0
484	Cooked, served hot — 1 cup	205	73	225	4	Trace	.1	.1	.1	50	21	57	1.8	57	0	.23	.02	2.1	0
	Parboiled:																		
485	Raw — 1 cup	185	10	685	14	1	.2	.1	.2	150	111	370	5.4	278	0	.81	.07	6.5	0
486	Cooked, served hot — 1 cup	175	73	185	4	Trace	.1	.1	.1	41	33	100	1.4	75	0	.19	.02	2.1	0
	Rolls, enriched:[38]																		
	Commercial:																		
487	Brown-and-serve (12 per 12-oz pkg.), browned. — 1 roll	26	27	85	2	2	.4	.7	.5	14	20	23	.5	25	Trace	.10	.06	.9	Trace
488	Cloverleaf or pan, 2 1/2-in diam., 2 in high. — 1 roll	28	31	85	2	2	.4	.6	.4	15	21	24	.5	27	Trace	.11	.07	.9	Trace
489	Frankfurter and hamburger (8 per 11 1/2-oz pkg.). — 1 roll	40	31	120	3	2	.5	.8	.6	21	30	34	.8	38	Trace	.16	.10	1.3	Trace
490	Hard, 3 3/4-in diam., 2 in high. — 1 roll	50	25	155	5	2	.4	.6	.5	30	24	46	1.2	49	Trace	.20	.12	1.7	Trace
491	Hoagie or submarine, 11 1/2 by 3 by 2 1/2 in. — 1 roll	135	31	390	12	4	.9	1.4	1.4	75	58	115	3.0	122	Trace	.54	.32	4.5	Trace
	From home recipe:																		
492	Cloverleaf, 2 1/2-in diam., 2 in high. — 1 roll	35	26	120	3	3	.8	1.1	.7	20	16	36	.7	41	30	.12	.12	1.2	Trace
	Spaghetti, enriched, cooked:																		
493	Firm stage, "al dente," served hot. — 1 cup	130	64	190	7	1	—	—	—	39	14	85	1.4	103	0	.23	.13	1.8	0
494	Tender stage, served hot — 1 cup	140	73	155	5	1	—	—	—	32	11	70	1.3	85	0	.20	.11	1.5	0
	Spaghetti (enriched) in tomato sauce with cheese:																		
495	From home recipe — 1 cup	250	77	260	9	9	2.0	5.4	.7	37	80	135	2.3	408	1,080	.25	.18	2.3	13
496	Canned — 1 cup	250	80	190	6	2	.5	.3	.4	39	40	88	2.8	303	930	.35	.28	4.5	10
	Spaghetti (enriched) with meat balls and tomato sauce:																		
497	From home recipe — 1 cup	248	70	330	19	12	3.3	6.3	.9	39	124	236	3.7	665	1,590	.25	.30	4.0	22
498	Canned — 1 cup	250	78	260	12	10	2.2	3.3	3.9	29	53	113	3.3	245	1,000	.15	.18	2.3	5
499	Toaster pastries — 1 pastry	50	12	200	3	6	—	—	—	36	[60]54	[60]67	1.9	[60]74	500	.16	.17	2.1	([60])
	Waffles, made with enriched flour, 7-in diam.:[38]																		
500	From home recipe — 1 waffle	75	41	210	7	7	2.3	2.8	1.4	28	85	130	1.3	109	250	.17	.23	1.4	Trace
501	From mix, egg and milk added — 1 waffle	75	42	205	7	8	2.8	2.9	1.2	27	179	257	1.0	146	170	.14	.22	.9	Trace

(A)	(B)		(C)	(D)	(E)	(F)	(G)	(H)	(I)	(J)	(K)	(L)	(M)	(N)	(O)	(P)	(Q)	(R)	(S)
	Wheat flours:																		
	All-purpose or family flour, enriched:																		
502	Sifted, spooned	1 cup	115	12	420	12	1	0.2	0.1	0.5	88	18	100	3.3	109	0	0.74	0.46	6.1	0
503	Unsifted, spooned	1 cup	125	12	455	13	1	.2	.1	.5	95	20	109	3.6	119	0	.80	.50	6.6	0
504	Cake or pastry flour, enriched, sifted, spooned.	1 cup	96	12	350	7	1	.1	.1	.3	76	16	70	2.8	91	0	.61	.38	5.1	0
505	Self-rising, enriched, unsifted, spooned.	1 cup	125	12	440	12	1	.2	.1	.5	93	331	583	3.6	—	0	.80	.50	6.6	0
506	Whole-wheat, from hard wheats, stirred.	1 cup	120	12	400	16	2	.4	.2	1.0	85	49	446	4.0	444	0	.66	.14	5.2	0
	LEGUMES (DRY), NUTS, SEEDS; RELATED PRODUCTS																			
	Almonds, shelled:																		
507	Chopped (about 130 almonds)	1 cup	130	5	775	24	70	5.6	47.7	12.8	25	304	655	6.1	1,005	0	.31	1.20	4.6	Trace
508	Slivered, not pressed down (about 115 almonds).	1 cup	115	5	690	21	62	5.0	42.2	11.3	22	269	580	5.4	889	0	.28	1.06	4.0	Trace
	Beans, dry:																		
	Common varieties as Great Northern, navy, and others:																		
	Cooked, drained:																		
509	Great Northern	1 cup	180	69	210	14	1	—	—	—	38	90	266	4.9	749	0	.25	.13	1.3	0
510	Pea (navy)	1 cup	190	69	225	15	1	—	—	—	40	95	281	5.1	790	0	.27	.13	1.3	0
	Canned, solids and liquid:																		
	White with—																		
511	Frankfurters (sliced)	1 cup	255	71	365	19	18	2.4	2.8	.6	32	94	303	4.8	668	330	.19	.15	3.3	Trace
512	Pork and tomato sauce	1 cup	255	71	310	16	7	2.4	2.8	.6	48	138	235	4.6	536	330	.20	.08	1.5	5
513	Pork and sweet sauce	1 cup	255	66	385	16	12	4.3	5.0	1.1	54	161	291	5.9	—	—	.15	.10	1.3	—
514	Red kidney	1 cup	255	76	230	15	1	—	—	—	42	74	278	4.6	673	10	.13	.10	1.5	—
515	Lima, cooked, drained	1 cup	190	64	260	16	1	—	—	—	49	55	293	5.9	1,163	—	.25	.11	1.3	—
516	Blackeye peas, dry, cooked (with residual cooking liquid).	1 cup	250	80	190	13	1	—	—	—	35	43	238	3.3	573	30	.40	.10	1.0	—
517	Brazil nuts, shelled (6-8 large kernels).	1 oz	28	5	185	4	19	4.8	6.2	7.1	3	53	196	1.0	203	Trace	.27	.03	.5	—
518	Cashew nuts, roasted in oil	1 cup	140	5	785	24	64	12.9	36.8	10.2	41	53	522	5.3	650	140	.60	.35	2.5	—
	Coconut meat, fresh:																		
519	Piece, about 2 by 2 by 1/2 in	1 piece	45	51	155	2	16	14.0	.9	.3	4	6	43	.8	115	0	.02	.01	.2	1
520	Shredded or grated, not pressed down.	1 cup	80	51	275	3	28	24.8	1.6	.5	8	10	76	1.4	205	0	.04	.02	.4	2
521	Filberts (hazelnuts), chopped (about 80 kernels).	1 cup	115	6	730	14	72	5.1	55.2	7.3	19	240	388	3.9	810	—	.53	—	1.0	Trace
522	Lentils, whole, cooked	1 cup	200	72	210	16	Trace	—	—	—	39	50	238	4.2	498	40	.14	.12	1.2	0
523	Peanuts, roasted in oil, salted (whole, halves, chopped).	1 cup	144	2	840	37	72	13.7	33.0	20.7	27	107	577	3.0	971	—	.46	.19	24.8	0
524	Peanut butter	1 tbsp	16	2	95	4	8	1.5	3.7	2.3	3	9	61	.3	100	—	.02	.02	2.4	0
525	Peas, split, dry, cooked	1 cup	200	70	230	16	1	—	—	—	42	22	178	3.4	592	80	.30	.18	1.8	—
526	Pecans, chopped or pieces (about 120 large halves).	1 cup	118	3	810	11	84	7.2	50.5	20.0	17	86	341	2.8	712	150	1.01	.15	1.1	2
527	Pumpkin and squash kernels, dry, hulled.	1 cup	140	4	775	41	65	11.8	23.5	27.5	21	71	1,602	15.7	1,386	100	.34	.27	3.4	—
528	Sunflower seeds, dry, hulled	1 cup	145	5	810	35	69	8.2	13.7	43.2	29	174	1,214	10.3	1,334	70	2.84	.33	7.8	—
	Walnuts:																		
	Black:																		
529	Chopped or broken kernels	1 cup	125	3	785	26	74	6.3	13.3	45.7	19	Trace	713	7.5	575	380	.28	.14	.9	—
530	Ground (finely)	1 cup	80	3	500	16	47	4.0	8.5	29.2	12	Trace	456	4.8	368	240	.18	.09	.6	—
531	Persian or English, chopped (about 60 halves).	1 cup	120	4	780	18	77	8.4	11.8	42.2	19	119	456	3.7	540	40	.40	.16	1.1	2

[19] Crust made with vegetable shortening and enriched flour.
[38] Made with vegetable shortening.
[59] Product may or may not be enriched with riboflavin. Consult the label.
[60] Value varies with the brand. Consult the label.

Appendix C: Nutritive Values of the Edible Part of Foods (Continued)

(Dashes (—) denote lack of reliable data for a constituent believed to be present in measurable amount)

(A) Item No.	(B) Foods, approximate measures, units, and weight (edible part unless footnotes indicate otherwise)	Grams	(C) Water Per‑cent	(D) Food energy Cal‑ories	(E) Pro‑tein Grams	(F) Fat Grams	(G) Saturated (total) Grams	(H) Unsaturated Oleic Grams	(I) Linoleic Grams	(J) Carbo‑hydrate Grams	(K) Calcium Milli‑grams	(L) Phos‑phorus Milli‑grams	(M) Iron Milli‑grams	(N) Potas‑sium Milli‑grams	(O) Vitamin A value Inter‑national units	(P) Thiamin Milli‑grams	(Q) Ribo‑flavin Milli‑grams	(R) Niacin Milli‑grams	(S) Ascorbic acid Milli‑grams
	SUGARS AND SWEETS																		
	Cake icings:																		
	Boiled, white:																		
532	Plain---- 1 cup----	94	18	295	1	0	0	0	0	75	2	2	Trace	17	0	Trace	0.03	Trace	0
533	With coconut---- 1 cup----	166	15	605	3	13	11.0	.9	Trace	124	10	50	0.8	277	0	0.02	.07	0.3	1
	Uncooked:																		
534	Chocolate made with milk and butter---- 1 cup----	275	14	1,035	9	38	23.4	11.7	1.0	185	165	305	3.3	536	580	.06	.28	.6	1
535	Creamy fudge from mix and water---- 1 cup----	245	15	830	7	16	5.1	6.7	3.1	183	96	218	2.7	238	Trace	.05	.20	.7	Trace
536	White---- 1 cup----	319	11	1,200	2	21	12.7	5.1	.5	260	48	38	Trace	57	860	Trace	.06	Trace	Trace
	Candy:																		
537	Caramels, plain or chocolate---- 1 oz----	28	8	115	1	3	1.6	1.1	.1	22	42	35	.4	54	Trace	.01	.05	.1	Trace
	Chocolate:																		
538	Milk, plain---- 1 oz----	28	1	145	2	9	5.5	3.0	.3	16	65	65	.3	109	80	.02	.10	.1	Trace
539	Semisweet, small pieces (60 per oz)---- 1 cup or 6‑oz pkg----	170	1	860	7	61	36.2	19.8	1.7	97	51	255	4.4	553	30	.02	.14	.9	0
540	Chocolate‑coated peanuts---- 1 oz----	28	1	160	5	12	4.0	4.7	2.1	11	33	84	.4	143	Trace	.10	.05	2.1	Trace
541	Fondant, uncoated (mints, candy corn, other)---- 1 oz----	28	8	105	Trace	Trace	—	—	—	25	4	2	.3	1	0	Trace	Trace	Trace	0
542	Fudge, chocolate, plain---- 1 oz----	28	8	115	1	3	1.3	1.4	.6	21	22	24	.3	42	Trace	.01	.03	.1	Trace
543	Gum drops---- 1 oz----	28	12	100	Trace	Trace	—	—	—	25	2	Trace	.1	1	0	0	Trace	0	0
544	Hard---- 1 oz----	28	1	110	0	Trace	—	—	—	28	6	2	.5	1	0	0	0	0	0
545	Marshmallows---- 1 oz----	28	17	90	1	Trace	—	—	—	23	5	2	.5	2	0	0	Trace	Trace	0
	Chocolate‑flavored beverage powders (about 4 heaping tsp per oz):																		
546	With nonfat dry milk---- 1 oz----	28	2	100	5	1	.5	.3	Trace	20	167	155	.5	227	10	.04	.21	.2	1
547	Without milk---- 1 oz----	28	1	100	5	1	.4	.2	Trace	25	9	48	.6	142	0	.01	.03	.1	Trace
548	Honey, strained or extracted---- 1 tbsp----	21	17	65	Trace	0	0	0	0	17	1	1	.1	11	0	Trace	.01	.1	Trace
549	Jams and preserves---- 1 tbsp----	20	29	55	Trace	Trace	—	—	—	14	4	2	.2	18	Trace	Trace	.01	Trace	Trace
550	---- 1 packet----	14	29	40	Trace	Trace	—	—	—	10	3	1	.1	12	Trace	Trace	Trace	Trace	1
551	Jellies---- 1 tbsp----	18	29	50	Trace	Trace	—	—	—	13	4	1	.3	14	Trace	Trace	.01	Trace	1
552	---- 1 packet----	14	29	40	Trace	Trace	—	—	—	10	3	1	.2	11	Trace	Trace	Trace	Trace	1
	Syrups:																		
	Chocolate‑flavored syrup or topping:																		
553	Thin type---- 1 fl oz or 2 tbsp----	38	32	90	1	1	.5	.3	Trace	24	6	35	.6	106	Trace	.01	.03	.2	0
554	Fudge type---- 1 fl oz or 2 tbsp----	38	25	125	2	5	3.1	1.6	.1	20	48	60	.5	107	60	.02	.08	.1	Trace
	Molasses, cane:																		
555	Light (first extraction)---- 1 tbsp----	20	24	50	—	—	—	—	—	13	33	9	.9	183	—	.01	.01	Trace	—
556	Blackstrap (third extraction)---- 1 tbsp----	20	24	45	—	—	—	—	—	11	137	17	3.2	585	—	.02	.04	.4	—
557	Sorghum---- 1 tbsp----	21	23	55	—	—	—	—	—	14	35	5	2.6	—	—	—	.02	Trace	—
558	Table blends, chiefly corn, light and dark---- 1 tbsp----	21	24	60	0	0	0	0	0	15	9	3	.8	1	0	0	0	0	0
	Sugars:																		
559	Brown, pressed down---- 1 cup----	220	2	820	0	0	0	0	0	212	187	42	7.5	757	0	.02	.07	.4	0
	White:																		
560	Granulated---- 1 cup----	200	1	770	0	0	0	0	0	199	0	0	.2	6	0	0	0	0	0
561	---- 1 tbsp----	12	1	45	0	0	0	0	0	12	0	0	Trace	Trace	0	0	0	0	0
562	---- 1 packet----	6	1	23	0	0	0	0	0	6	0	0	Trace	Trace	0	0	0	0	0
563	Powdered, sifted, spooned into cup---- 1 cup----	100	1	385	0	0	0	0	0	100	0	0	.1	3	0	0	0	0	0

VEGETABLE AND VEGETABLE PRODUCTS

(A)	(B)	(grams)	(C)	(D)	(E)	(F)	(G)	(H)	(I)	(J)	(K)	(L)	(M)	(N)	(O)	(P)	(Q)	(R)	(S)
	Asparagus, green:																		
	Cooked, drained:																		
	Cuts and tips, 1 1/2- to 2-in lengths:																		
564	From raw-------------- 1 cup--------	145	94	30	3	Trace	—	—	—	5	30	73	0.9	265	1,310	0.23	0.26	2.0	38
565	From frozen----------- 1 cup--------	180	93	40	6	Trace	—	—	—	6	40	115	2.2	396	1,530	.25	.23	1.8	41
	Spears, 1/2-in diam. at base:																		
566	From raw-------------- 4 spears-----	60	94	10	1	Trace	—	—	—	2	13	30	.4	110	540	.10	.11	.8	16
567	From frozen----------- 4 spears-----	60	92	15	2	Trace	—	—	—	2	13	40	.7	143	470	.10	.08	.7	16
568	Canned, spears, 1/2-in diam. at base. 4 spears-----	80	93	15	2	Trace	—	—	—	3	15	42	1.5	133	640	.05	.08	.6	12
	Beans:																		
	Lima, immature seeds, frozen, cooked, drained:																		
569	Thick-seeded types (Fordhooks) 1 cup--------	170	74	170	10	Trace	—	—	—	32	34	153	2.9	724	390	.12	.09	1.7	29
570	Thin-seeded types (baby limas) 1 cup--------	180	69	210	13	Trace	—	—	—	40	63	227	4.7	709	400	.16	.09	2.2	22
	Snap:																		
	Green:																		
	Cooked, drained:																		
571	From raw (cuts and French style). 1 cup--------	125	92	30	2	Trace	—	—	—	7	63	46	.8	189	680	.09	.11	.6	15
	From frozen:																		
572	Cuts----------------- 1 cup--------	135	92	35	2	Trace	—	—	—	8	54	43	.9	205	780	.09	.12	.5	7
573	French style--------- 1 cup--------	130	92	35	2	Trace	—	—	—	8	49	39	1.2	177	690	.08	.10	.4	9
574	Canned, drained solids (cuts). 1 cup--------	135	92	30	2	Trace	—	—	—	7	61	34	2.0	128	630	.04	.07	.4	5
	Yellow or wax:																		
	Cooked, drained:																		
575	From raw (cuts and French style). 1 cup--------	125	93	30	2	Trace	—	—	—	6	63	46	.8	189	290	.09	.11	.6	16
576	From frozen (cuts)--- 1 cup--------	135	92	35	2	Trace	—	—	—	8	47	42	.9	221	140	.09	.11	.5	8
577	Canned, drained solids (cuts). 1 cup--------	135	92	30	2	Trace	—	—	—	7	61	34	2.0	128	140	.04	.07	.4	7
	Beans, mature. See Beans, dry (items 509-515) and Blackeye peas, dry (item 516).																		
	Bean sprouts (mung):																		
578	Raw------------------ 1 cup--------	105	89	35	4	Trace	—	—	—	7	20	67	1.4	234	20	.14	.14	.8	20
579	Cooked, drained------ 1 cup--------	125	91	35	4	Trace	—	—	—	7	21	60	1.1	195	30	.11	.13	.9	8
	Beets:																		
	Cooked, drained, peeled:																		
580	Whole beets, 2-in diam. 2 beets------	100	91	30	1	Trace	—	—	—	7	14	23	.5	208	20	.03	.04	.3	6
581	Diced or sliced------ 1 cup--------	170	91	55	2	Trace	—	—	—	12	24	39	.9	354	30	.05	.07	.5	10
	Canned, drained solids:																		
582	Whole beets, small--- 1 cup--------	160	89	60	2	Trace	—	—	—	14	30	29	1.1	267	30	.02	.05	.2	5
583	Diced or sliced------ 1 cup--------	170	89	65	2	Trace	—	—	—	15	32	31	1.2	284	30	.02	.05	.2	5
584	Beet greens, leaves and stems, cooked, drained. 1 cup--------	145	94	25	2	Trace	—	—	—	5	144	36	2.8	481	7,400	.10	.22	.4	22
	Blackeye peas, immature seeds, cooked and drained:																		
585	From raw-------------- 1 cup--------	165	72	180	13	1	—	—	—	30	40	241	3.5	625	580	.50	.18	2.3	28
586	From frozen----------- 1 cup--------	170	66	220	15	1	—	—	—	40	43	286	4.8	573	290	.68	.19	2.4	15
	Broccoli, cooked, drained:																		
	From raw:																		
587	Stalk, medium size--- 1 stalk------	180	91	45	6	1	—	—	—	8	158	112	1.4	481	4,500	.16	.36	1.4	162
588	Stalks cut into 1/2-in pieces- 1 cup--------	155	91	40	5	Trace	—	—	—	7	136	96	1.2	414	3,880	.14	.31	1.2	140
	From frozen:																		
589	Stalk, 4 1/2 to 5 in long---- 1 stalk------	30	91	10	1	Trace	—	—	—	1	12	17	.2	66	570	.02	.03	.2	22
590	Chopped-------------- 1 cup--------	185	92	50	5	1	—	—	—	9	100	104	1.3	392	4,810	.11	.22	.9	105
	Brussels sprouts, cooked, drained:																		
591	From raw, 7-8 sprouts (1 1/4- to 1 1/2-in diam.). 1 cup--------	155	88	55	7	1	—	—	—	10	50	112	1.7	423	810	.12	.22	1.2	135
592	From frozen---------- 1 cup--------	155	89	50	5	Trace	—	—	—	10	33	95	1.2	457	880	.12	.16	.9	126

Appendix C: Nutritive Values of the Edible Part of Foods (*Continued*)

(Dashes (–) denote lack of reliable data for a constituent believed to be present in measurable amount)

Item No. (A)	Foods, approximate measures, units, and weight (edible part unless footnotes indicate otherwise) (B)	Grams	Water (C) Percent	Food energy (D) Calories	Protein (E) Grams	Fat (F) Grams	Fatty Acids Saturated (total) (G) Grams	Unsaturated Oleic (H) Grams	Linoleic (I) Grams	Carbohydrate (J) Grams	Calcium (K) Milligrams	Phosphorus (L) Milligrams	Iron (M) Milligrams	Potassium (N) Milligrams	Vitamin A value (O) International units	Thiamin (P) Milligrams	Riboflavin (Q) Milligrams	Niacin (R) Milligrams	Ascorbic acid (S) Milligrams
	VEGETABLE AND VEGETABLE PRODUCTS—Con.																		
	Cabbage:																		
	Common varieties:																		
	Raw:																		
593	Coarsely shredded or sliced-- 1 cup------	70	92	15	1	Trace	—	—	—	4	34	20	0.3	163	90	0.04	0.04	0.2	33
594	Finely shredded or chopped-- 1 cup------	90	92	20	1	Trace	—	—	—	5	44	26	.4	210	120	.05	.05	.3	42
595	Cooked, drained------ 1 cup------	145	94	30	2	Trace	—	—	—	6	64	29	.4	236	190	.06	.06	.4	48
596	Red, raw, coarsely shredded or sliced. 1 cup------	70	90	20	1	Trace	—	—	—	5	29	25	.6	188	30	.06	.04	.3	43
597	Savoy, raw, coarsely shredded or sliced. 1 cup------	70	92	15	2	Trace	—	—	—	3	47	38	.6	188	140	.04	.06	.2	39
598	Cabbage, celery (also called pe-tsai or wongbok), raw, 1-in pieces. 1 cup------	75	95	10	1	Trace	—	—	—	2	32	30	.5	190	110	.04	.03	.5	19
599	Cabbage, white mustard (also called bokchoy or pakchoy), cooked, drained. 1 cup------	170	95	25	2	Trace	—	—	—	4	252	56	1.0	364	5,270	.07	.14	1.2	26
	Carrots:																		
	Raw, without crowns and tips, scraped:																		
600	Whole, 7 1/2 by 1 1/8 in, or strips, 2 1/2 to 3 in long. 1 carrot or 18 strips---	72	88	30	1	Trace	—	—	—	7	27	26	.5	246	7,930	.04	.04	.4	6
601	Grated--------- 1 cup------	110	88	45	1	Trace	—	—	—	11	41	40	.8	375	12,100	.07	.06	.7	9
602	Cooked (crosswise cuts), drained 1 cup------	155	91	50	1	Trace	—	—	—	11	51	48	.9	344	16,280	.08	.08	.8	9
	Canned:																		
603	Sliced, drained solids------ 1 cup------	155	91	45	1	Trace	—	—	—	10	47	34	1.1	186	23,250	.03	.05	.6	3
604	Strained or junior (baby food) 1 oz (1 3/4 to 2 tbsp)---	28	92	10	Trace	Trace	—	—	—	2	7	6	.1	51	3,690	.01	.01	.1	1
	Cauliflower:																		
605	Raw, chopped--------- 1 cup------	115	91	31	3	Trace	—	—	—	6	29	64	1.3	339	70	.13	.12	.8	90
	Cooked, drained:																		
606	From raw (flower buds)------ 1 cup------	125	93	30	3	Trace	—	—	—	5	26	53	.9	258	80	.11	.10	.8	69
607	From frozen (flowerets)----- 1 cup------	180	94	30	3	Trace	—	—	—	6	31	68	.9	373	50	.07	.09	.7	74
	Celery, Pascal type, raw:																		
608	Stalk, large outer, 8 by 1 1/2 in, at root end. 1 stalk------	40	94	5	Trace	Trace	—	—	—	2	16	11	.1	136	110	.01	.01	.1	4
609	Pieces, diced--------- 1 cup------	120	94	20	1	Trace	—	—	—	5	47	34	.4	409	320	.04	.04	.4	11
	Collards, cooked, drained:																		
610	From raw (leaves without stems)- 1 cup------	190	90	65	7	1	—	—	—	10	357	99	1.5	498	14,820	.21	.38	2.3	144
611	From frozen (chopped)------ 1 cup------	170	90	50	5	1	—	—	—	10	299	87	1.7	401	11,560	.10	.24	1.0	56
	Corn, sweet:																		
	Cooked, drained:																		
612	From raw, ear 5 by 1 3/4 in--- 1 ear[61]----	140	74	70	2	1	—	—	—	16	2	69	.5	151	[6,2]310	.09	.08	1.1	7
	From frozen:																		
613	Ear, 5 in long------ 1 ear[61]----	229	73	120	4	1	—	—	—	27	4	121	1.0	291	[6,2]440	.18	.10	2.1	9
614	Kernels---------- 1 cup------	165	77	130	5	1	—	—	—	31	5	120	1.3	304	[6,2]580	.15	.10	2.5	8
	Canned:																		
615	Cream style---------- 1 cup------	256	76	210	5	2	—	—	—	51	8	143	1.5	248	[6,2]840	.08	.13	2.6	13
	Whole kernel:																		
616	Vacuum pack--------- 1 cup------	210	76	175	5	1	—	—	—	43	6	153	1.1	204	[6,2]740	.06	.13	2.3	11
617	Wet pack, drained solids---- 1 cup------	165	76	140	4	1	—	—	—	33	8	81	.8	160	[6,2]580	.05	.08	1.5	7
	Cowpeas. See Blackeye peas. (Items 585-586).																		
	Cucumber slices, 1/8 in thick (large, 2 1/8-in diam.; small, 1 3/4-in diam.):																		
618	With peel---------- 6 large or 8 small slices	28	95	5	Trace	Trace	—	—	—	1	7	8	.3	45	70	.01	.01	.1	3

(A)	(B)		(C)	(D)	(E)	(F)	(G)	(H)	(I)	(I)	(K)	(L)	(M)	(N)	(O)	(P)	(Q)	(R)	(S)
619	Without peel ---- 6 1/2 large or 9 small pieces.	28	96	5	Trace	Trace	—	—	—	1	1	5	0.1	45	Trace	0.01	0.01	0.1	3
620	Dandelion greens, cooked, drained --- 1 cup	105	90	35	2	1	—	—	—	7	147	44	1.9	244	12,290	.14	.17	1.9	19
621	Endive, curly (including escarole), raw, small pieces --- 1 cup	50	93	10	1	Trace	—	—	—	2	41	27	.9	147	1,650	.04	.07	.3	5
	Kale, cooked, drained:																		
622	From raw (leaves without stems and midribs) --- 1 cup	110	88	45	5	1	—	—	—	7	206	64	1.8	243	9,130	.11	.20	.9	102
623	From frozen (leaf style) --- 1 cup	130	91	40	4	1	—	—	—	7	157	62	1.3	251	10,660	.08	.20	.9	49
	Lettuce, raw:																		
	Butterhead, as Boston types:																		
624	Head, 5-in diam --- 1 head[63]	220	95	25	2	Trace	—	—	—	4	57	42	3.3	430	1,580	.10	.10	.5	13
625	Leaves --- 1 outer or 2 inner or 3 heart leaves.	15	95	Trace	Trace	Trace	—	—	—	Trace	5	4	.3	40	150	.01	.01	Trace	1
	Crisphead, as iceberg:																		
626	Head, 6-in diam --- 1 head[64]	567	96	70	5	1	—	—	—	16	108	118	2.7	943	1,780	.32	.32	1.6	32
627	Wedge, 1/4 of head --- 1 wedge	135	96	20	1	Trace	—	—	—	4	27	30	.7	236	450	.08	.08	.4	8
628	Pieces, chopped or shredded --- 1 cup	55	96	5	Trace	Trace	—	—	—	2	11	12	.3	96	180	.03	.03	.1	3
629	Looseleaf (bunching varieties including romaine or cos), chopped or shredded pieces. --- 1 cup	55	94	10	1	Trace	—	—	—	2	37	14	.8	145	1,050	.03	.04	.2	10
630	Mushrooms, raw, sliced or chopped --- 1 cup	70	90	20	2	Trace	—	—	—	3	4	81	.6	290	Trace	.07	.32	2.9	2
631	Mustard greens, cooked, drained --- 1 cup	140	93	30	3	1	—	—	—	6	193	45	2.5	308	8,120	.11	.20	.8	67
632	Okra pods, 3 by 5/8 in, cooked --- 10 pods	106	91	30	2	Trace	—	—	—	6	98	43	.5	184	520	.14	.19	1.0	21
	Onions:																		
	Mature:																		
	Raw:																		
633	Chopped --- 1 cup	170	89	65	3	Trace	—	—	—	15	46	61	.9	267	[65]Trace	.05	.07	.2	17
634	Sliced --- 1 cup	115	89	45	2	Trace	—	—	—	10	31	41	.6	181	[65]Trace	.03	.05	.1	12
635	Cooked (whole or sliced), drained. --- 1 cup	210	92	60	3	Trace	—	—	—	14	50	61	.8	231	[65]Trace	.06	.06	.2	15
636	Young green, bulb (3/8 in diam.) and white portion of top. --- 6 onions	30	88	15	Trace	Trace	—	—	—	3	12	12	.2	69	Trace	.02	.01	.2	8
637	Parsley, raw, chopped --- 1 tbsp	4	85	Trace	Trace	Trace	—	—	—	Trace	7	2	.2	25	300	Trace	.01	Trace	6
638	Parsnips, cooked (diced or 2-in lengths). --- 1 cup	155	82	100	2	1	—	—	—	23	70	96	.9	587	50	.11	.12	.2	16
	Peas, green:																		
	Canned:																		
639	Whole, drained solids --- 1 cup	170	77	150	8	1	—	—	—	29	44	129	3.2	163	1,170	.15	.10	1.4	14
640	Strained (baby food) --- 1 oz (1 3/4 to 2 tbsp)	28	86	15	1	Trace	—	—	—	3	3	18	.3	28	140	.02	.03	.3	3
641	Frozen, cooked, drained --- 1 cup	160	82	110	8	Trace	—	—	—	19	30	138	3.0	216	960	.43	.14	2.7	21
642	Peppers, hot, red, without seeds, dried (ground chili powder, added seasonings). --- 1 tsp	2	9	5	Trace	Trace	—	—	—	1	5	4	.3	20	1,300	Trace	.02	.2	Trace
	Peppers, sweet (about 5 per lb, whole), stem and seeds removed:																		
643	Raw --- 1 pod	74	93	15	1	Trace	—	—	—	4	7	16	.5	157	310	.06	.06	.5	94
644	Cooked, boiled, drained --- 1 pod	73	95	15	1	Trace	—	—	—	3	7	12	.4	109	310	.05	.05	.4	70
	Potatoes, cooked:																		
645	Baked, peeled after baking (about 2 per lb, raw). --- 1 potato	156	75	145	4	Trace	—	—	—	33	14	101	1.1	782	Trace	.15	.07	2.7	31
	Boiled (about 3 per lb, raw):																		
646	Peeled after boiling --- 1 potato	137	80	105	3	Trace	—	—	—	23	10	72	.8	556	Trace	.12	.05	2.0	22
647	Peeled before boiling --- 1 potato	135	83	90	3	Trace	—	—	—	20	8	57	.7	385	Trace	.12	.05	1.6	22
	French-fried, strip, 2 to 3 1/2 in long:																		
648	Prepared from raw --- 10 strips	50	45	135	2	7	1.7	1.2	3.3	18	8	56	.7	427	Trace	.07	.04	1.6	11
649	Frozen, oven heated --- 10 strips	50	53	110	2	4	1.1	.8	2.1	17	5	43	.9	326	Trace	.07	.01	1.3	11
650	Hashed brown, prepared from frozen. --- 1 cup	155	56	345	3	18	4.6	3.2	9.0	45	28	78	1.9	439	Trace	.11	.03	1.6	12
	Mashed, prepared from—																		
651	Milk added --- 1 cup	210	83	135	4	2	—	—	—	27	50	103	.8	548	40	.17	.11	2.1	21

[61] Weight includes cob. Without cob, weight is 77 g for item 612, 126 g for item 613.
[62] Based on yellow varieties. For white varieties, value is trace.
[63] Weight includes refuse of outer leaves. Without these parts, weight is 163 g.
[64] Weight includes core. Without core, weight is 539 g.
[65] Value based on white-fleshed varieties. For yellow-fleshed varieties, value in International Units (I.U.) is 70 for item 633, 50 for item 634, and 80 for item 635.

Appendix C: Nutritive Values of the Edible Part of Foods (*Continued*)

(Dashes (—) denote lack of reliable data for a constituent believed to be present in measurable amount)

Item No. (A)	Foods, approximate measures, units, and weight (edible part unless footnotes indicate otherwise) (B)	Grams	Water (C) Per-cent	Food energy (D) Cal-ories	Pro-tein (E) Grams	Fat (F) Grams	Satu-rated (total) (G) Grams	Oleic (H) Grams	Lino-leic (I) Grams	Carbo-hydrate (J) Grams	Calcium (K) Milli-grams	Phos-phorus (L) Milli-grams	Iron (M) Milli-grams	Potas-sium (N) Milli-grams	Vitamin A value (O) Inter-national units	Thiamin (P) Milli-grams	Ribo-flavin (Q) Milli-grams	Niacin (R) Milli-grams	Ascorbic acid (S) Milli-grams
	VEGETABLE AND VEGETABLE PRODUCTS—Con.																		
	Potatoes, cooked—Continued																		
	Mashed, prepared from—Continued																		
	Raw—Continued																		
652	Milk and butter added---- 1 cup	210	80	195	4	9	5.6	2.3	0.2	26	50	101	0.8	525	360	0.17	0.11	2.1	19
653	Dehydrated flakes (without milk), water, milk, butter, and salt added. 1 cup	210	79	195	4	7	3.6	2.1	.2	30	65	99	.6	601	270	.08	.08	1.9	11
654	Potato chips, 1 3/4 by 2 1/2 in oval cross section. 10 chips	20	2	115	1	8	2.1	1.4	4.0	10	8	28	.4	226	Trace	.04	.01	1.0	3
655	Potato salad, made with cooked salad dressing. 1 cup	250	76	250	7	7	2.0	2.7	1.3	41	80	160	1.5	798	350	.20	.18	2.8	28
656	Pumpkin, canned------ 1 cup	245	90	80	2	Trace	—	—	—	19	61	64	1.0	588	15,680	.07	.12	1.5	12
657	Radishes, raw (prepackaged) stem ends, rootlets cut off. 4 radishes	18	95	5	Trace	Trace	—	—	—	1	5	6	.2	58	Trace	.01	.01	.1	5
658	Sauerkraut, canned, solids and liquid. 1 cup	235	93	40	2	Trace	—	—	—	9	85	42	1.2	329	120	.07	.09	.5	33
	Southern peas. See Blackeye peas (items 585-586).																		
	Spinach:																		
659	Raw, chopped------ 1 cup	55	91	15	2	Trace	—	—	—	2	51	28	1.7	259	4,460	.06	.11	.3	28
	Cooked, drained:																		
660	From raw------ 1 cup	180	92	40	5	1	—	—	—	6	167	68	4.0	583	14,580	.13	.25	.9	50
	From frozen:																		
661	Chopped------ 1 cup	205	92	45	6	1	—	—	—	8	232	90	4.3	683	16,200	.14	.31	.8	39
662	Leaf------ 1 cup	190	92	45	6	1	—	—	—	7	200	84	4.8	688	15,390	.15	.27	1.0	53
663	Canned, drained solids---- 1 cup	205	91	50	6	1	—	—	—	7	242	53	5.3	513	16,400	.04	.25	.6	29
	Squash, cooked:																		
664	Summer (all varieties), diced, drained. 1 cup	210	96	30	2	Trace	—	—	—	7	53	53	.8	296	820	.11	.17	1.7	21
665	Winter (all varieties), baked, mashed. 1 cup	205	81	130	4	1	—	—	—	32	57	98	1.6	945	8,610	.10	.27	1.4	27
	Sweetpotatoes:																		
	Cooked (raw, 5 by 2 in; about 2 1/2 per lb):																		
666	Baked in skin, peeled------ 1 potato	114	64	160	2	1	—	—	—	37	46	66	1.0	342	9,230	.10	.08	.8	25
667	Boiled in skin, peeled------ 1 potato	151	71	170	3	1	—	—	—	40	48	71	1.1	367	11,940	.14	.09	.9	26
668	Candied, 2 1/2 by 2-in piece---- 1 piece	105	60	175	1	3	2.0	.8	.1	36	39	45	.9	200	6,620	.06	.04	.4	11
	Canned:																		
669	Solid pack (mashed)------ 1 cup	255	72	275	5	Trace	—	—	—	63	64	105	2.0	510	19,890	.13	.10	1.5	36
670	Vacuum pack, piece 2 3/4 by 1 in. 1 piece	40	72	45	1	Trace	—	—	—	10	10	16	.3	80	3,120	.02	.02	.2	6
	Tomatoes:																		
671	Raw, 2 3/5-in diam. (3 per 12 oz pkg). 1 tomato[66]	135	94	25	1	Trace	—	—	—	6	16	33	.6	300	1,110	.07	.05	.9	[67]28
672	Canned, solids and liquid---- 1 cup	241	94	50	2	Trace	—	—	—	10	[68]14	46	1.2	523	2,170	.12	.07	1.7	41
673	Tomato catsup------ 1 cup	273	69	290	5	1	—	—	—	69	60	137	2.2	991	3,820	.25	.19	4.4	41
674	Tomato catsup------ 1 tbsp	15	69	15	Trace	Trace	—	—	—	4	3	8	.1	54	210	.01	.01	.2	2
	Tomato juice, canned:																		
675	Cup------ 1 cup	243	94	45	2	Trace	—	—	—	10	17	44	2.2	552	1,940	.12	.07	1.9	39
676	Glass (6 fl oz)------ 1 glass	182	94	35	2	Trace	—	—	—	8	13	33	1.6	413	1,460	.09	.05	1.5	29
677	Turnips, cooked, diced------ 1 cup	155	94	35	1	Trace	—	—	—	8	54	37	.6	291	Trace	.06	.08	.5	34
	Turnip greens, cooked, drained:																		
678	From raw (leaves and stems)---- 1 cup	145	94	30	3	Trace	—	—	—	5	252	49	1.5	—	8,270	.15	.33	.7	68
679	From frozen (chopped)------ 1 cup	165	93	40	4	Trace	—	—	—	6	195	64	2.6	246	11,390	.08	.15	.7	31
680	Vegetables, mixed, frozen, cooked- 1 cup	182	83	115	6	1	—	—	—	24	46	115	2.4	348	9,010	.22	.13	2.0	15

MISCELLANEOUS ITEMS

(A)	(B)	Measure	(g)	(C)	(D)	(E)	(F)	(G)	(H)	(I)	(J)	(K)	(L)	(M)	(N)	(O)	(P)	(Q)	(R)	(S)
	Baking powders for home use:																			
	Sodium aluminum sulfate:																			
681	With monocalcium phosphate monohydrate	1 tsp	3.0	2	5	Trace	Trace	0	0	0	1	58	87	—	5	0	0	0	0	0
682	With monocalcium phosphate monohydrate, calcium sulfate.	1 tsp	2.9	1	5	Trace	Trace	0	0	0	1	183	45	—	—	0	0	0	0	0
683	Straight phosphate	1 tsp	3.8	2	5	Trace	Trace	0	0	0	1	239	359	—	6	0	0	0	0	0
684	Low sodium	1 tsp	4.3	2	5	Trace	Trace	0	0	0	2	207	314	—	471	0	0	0	0	0
685	Barbecue sauce	1 cup	250	81	230	4	17	2.2	4.3	10.0	20	53	50	2.0	435	900	.03	.03	.8	13
	Beverages, alcoholic:																			
686	Beer	12 fl oz	360	92	150	1	0	0	0	0	14	18	108	Trace	90	—	.01	.11	2.2	0
	Gin, rum, vodka, whisky:																			
687	80-proof	1 1/2-fl oz jigger	42	67	95	—	—	0	0	0	Trace	—	—	—	1	—	—	—	—	—
688	86-proof	1 1/2-fl oz jigger	42	64	105	—	—	0	0	0	Trace	—	—	—	1	—	—	—	—	—
689	90-proof	1 1/2-fl oz jigger	42	62	110	—	—	0	0	0	Trace	—	—	—	1	—	—	—	—	—
	Wines:																			
690	Dessert	3 1/2-fl oz glass	103	77	140	Trace	0	0	0	0	8	8	—	—	77	—	Trace	.02	.2	—
691	Table	3 1/2-fl oz glass	102	86	85	Trace	0	0	0	0	4	9	10	.4	94	—	Trace	.01	.1	—
	Beverages, carbonated, sweetened, nonalcoholic:																			
692	Carbonated water	12 fl oz	366	92	115	0	0	0	0	0	29	—	—	—	—	—	0	0	0	0
693	Cola type	12 fl oz	369	90	145	0	0	0	0	0	37	—	—	—	—	—	0	0	0	0
694	Fruit-flavored sodas and Tom Collins mixer.	12 fl oz	372	88	170	0	0	0	0	0	45	—	—	—	—	—	0	0	0	0
695	Ginger ale	12 fl oz	366	92	115	0	0	0	0	0	29	—	—	—	0	0	0	0	0	0
696	Root beer	12 fl oz	370	90	150	0	0	0	0	0	39	—	—	—	0	0	0	0	0	0
	Chili powder. See Peppers, hot, red (item 642).																			
	Chocolate:																			
697	Bitter or baking	1 oz	28	2	145	3	15	8.9	4.9	.4	8	22	109	1.9	235	20	.01	.07	.4	0
	Semisweet, see Candy, chocolate (item 539).																			
698	Gelatin, dry	1 7-g envelope	7	13	25	6	Trace	0	0	0	0	—	—	—	—	—	—	—	—	—
699	Gelatin dessert prepared with gelatin dessert powder and water.	1 cup	240	84	140	4	0	0	0	0	34	—	—	—	—	—	—	—	—	—
700	Mustard, prepared, yellow	1 tsp or individual serving pouch or cup	5	80	5	Trace	Trace	—	—	Trace	Trace	4	4	.1	7	—	—	—	—	—
	Olives, pickled, canned:																			
701	Green	4 medium or 3 extra large or 2 giant.[69]	16	78	15	Trace	2	.2	1.2	.1	Trace	8	2	.2	7	40	—	Trace	—	—
702	Ripe, Mission	3 small or 2 large[69]	10	73	15	Trace	2	.2	1.2	.1	Trace	9	1	.1	2	10	—	Trace	—	—
	Pickles, cucumber:																			
703	Dill, medium, whole, 3 3/4 in long, 1 1/4-in diam.	1 pickle	65	93	5	Trace	Trace	—	—	—	1	17	14	.7	130	70	Trace	.01	Trace	4
704	Fresh-pack, slices 1 1/2-in diam., 1/4 in thick.	2 slices	15	79	10	Trace	Trace	—	—	—	3	5	4	.3	—	20	Trace	Trace	Trace	1
705	Sweet, gherkin, small, whole, about 2 1/2 in long, 3/4-in diam.	1 pickle	15	61	20	Trace	Trace	—	—	—	5	2	2	.2	—	10	Trace	Trace	Trace	1
706	Relish, finely chopped, sweet	1 tbsp	15	63	20	Trace	Trace	—	—	—	5	3	2	.1	—	—	Trace	Trace	Trace	1
	Popcorn. See items 476-478.																			
707	Popsicle, 3-fl oz size.	1 popsicle	95	80	70	0	0	0	0	—	18	0	—	Trace	—	—	0	0	0	0

[66] Weight includes cores and stem ends. Without these parts, weight is 123 g.

[67] Based on year-round average. For tomatoes marketed from November through May, value is about 12 mg; from June through October, 32 mg.

[68] Applies to product without calcium salts added. Value for products with calcium salts added may be as much as 63 mg for whole tomatoes, 241 mg for cut forms.

[69] Weight includes pits. Without pits, weight is 13 g for item 701, 9 g for item 702.

Appendix C: Nutritive Values of the Edible Part of Foods (Continued)

(Dashes (—) denote lack of reliable data for a constituent believed to be present in measurable amount)

Item No. (A)	Foods, approximate measures, units, and weight (edible part unless footnotes indicate otherwise) (B)	(weight) Grams	Water Percent (C)	Food energy Calories (D)	Protein Grams (E)	Fat Grams (F)	Saturated (total) Grams (G)	Unsaturated Oleic Grams (H)	Unsaturated Linoleic Grams (I)	Carbohydrate Grams (J)	Calcium Milligrams (K)	Phosphorus Milligrams (L)	Iron Milligrams (M)	Potassium Milligrams (N)	Vitamin A value International units (O)	Thiamin Milligrams (P)	Riboflavin Milligrams (Q)	Niacin Milligrams (R)	Ascorbic acid Milligrams (S)
	MISCELLANEOUS ITEMS—Con.																		
	Soups:																		
	Canned, condensed:																		
	Prepared with equal volume of milk:																		
708	Cream of chicken---- 1 cup----	245	85	180	7	10	4.2	3.6	1.3	15	172	152	0.5	260	610	0.05	0.27	0.7	2
709	Cream of mushroom---- 1 cup----	245	83	215	7	14	5.4	2.9	4.6	16	191	169	.5	279	250	.05	.34	.7	1
710	Tomato---- 1 cup----	250	84	175	7	7	3.4	1.7	1.0	23	168	155	.8	418	1,200	.10	.25	1.3	15
	Prepared with equal volume of water:																		
711	Bean with pork---- 1 cup----	250	84	170	8	6	1.2	1.8	2.4	22	63	128	2.3	395	650	.13	.08	1.0	3
712	Beef broth, bouillon, consomme. 1 cup----	240	96	30	5	0	0		0	3	Trace	31	.5	130	Trace	Trace	.02	1.2	—
713	Beef noodle---- 1 cup----	240	93	65	4	3	.6	.7	.8	7	7	48	1.0	77	50	.05	.07	1.0	Trace
714	Clam chowder, Manhattan type (with tomatoes, without milk). 1 cup----	245	92	80	2	3	.5	.4	1.3	12	34	47	1.0	184	880	.02	.02	1.0	—
715	Cream of chicken---- 1 cup----	240	92	95	3	6	1.6	2.3	1.1	8	24	34	.5	79	410	.02	.05	.5	Trace
716	Cream of mushroom---- 1 cup----	240	90	135	2	10	2.6	1.7	4.5	10	41	50	.5	98	70	.02	.12	.7	Trace
717	Minestrone---- 1 cup----	245	90	105	5	3	.7	.9	1.3	14	37	59	1.0	314	2,350	.07	.05	1.0	—
718	Split pea---- 1 cup----	245	85	145	9	3	1.1	1.2	.4	21	29	149	1.5	270	440	.25	.15	1.5	1
719	Tomato---- 1 cup----	245	91	90	2	3	.5	.5	1.0	16	15	34	.7	230	1,000	.05	.05	1.2	12
720	Vegetable beef---- 1 cup----	245	92	80	5	2				10	12	49	.7	162	2,700	.05	.05	1.0	—
721	Vegetarian---- 1 cup----	245	92	80	2	2				13	20	39	1.0	172	2,940	.05	.05	1.0	—
	Dehydrated:																		
722	Bouillon cube, 1/2 in---- 1 cube----	4	4	5	1	Trace				Trace	—	—	—	4	—	—	—	—	—
	Mixes:																		
	Unprepared:																		
723	Onion---- 1 1/2-oz pkg----	43	3	150	6	5	1.1	2.3	1.0	23	42	49	.6	238	30	.05	.03	.3	6
	Prepared with water:																		
724	Chicken noodle---- 1 cup----	240	95	55	2	1				8	7	19	.2	19	50	.07	.05	.5	Trace
725	Onion---- 1 cup----	240	96	35	1	1				6	10	12	.2	58	Trace	Trace	Trace	Trace	2
726	Tomato vegetable with noodles. 1 cup----	240	93	65	1	1				12	7	19	.2	29	480	.05	.02	.5	5
727	Vinegar, cider---- 1 tbsp----	15	94	Trace	Trace	0	0	0	0	1	1	1	.1	15	—	—	—	—	—
728	White sauce, medium, with enriched flour. 1 cup----	250	73	405	10	31	19.3	7.8	.8	22	288	233	.5	348	1,150	.12	.43	.7	2
	Yeast:																		
729	Baker's, dry, active---- 1 pkg----	7	5	20	3	Trace				3	[70]17	90	1.1	140	Trace	.16	.38	2.6	Trace
730	Brewer's, dry---- 1 tbsp----	8	5	25	3	Trace				3	17	140	1.4	152	Trace	1.25	.34	3.0	Trace

[70]Value may vary from 6 to 60 mg.

PHOTO CREDIT LIST

CHAPTER 1 Page 5, Zoe Ann Holmes. Page 13, Taylor Scientific Consumer Instruments, Arden, North Carolina.

CHAPTER 2 Page 32, W. Atlee Burpee Company. Page 34, The Potato Board. Page 36, W. Atlee Burpee Company. Page 38, Plycon Press. Page 42, United Fresh Fruit and Vegetable Association. Page 43 & 44, Courtesy Andrea Mackey & the Oregon Agricultural Experiment Station. Page 58, H. J. Heinz Company. Page 62, Rice Council.

CHAPTER 3 Page 73 (left), California Strawberry Advisory Board, Courtesy Ketchum Public Relations; (right), Florida Department of Citrus. Page 75, Pacific Kitchen, Seattle, Washington. Page 76 (left), Oregon-Washington-California Pear Bureau, Pacific Bartlett Growers, Inc. Seckel Pear Alliance; (right), U.S. Department of Agriculture (USDA). Page 77, Oregon-Washington-California Pear Bureau, Pacific Bartlett Growers, Inc., Seckel Pear Alliance. Page 79, Calavo Growers. Page 84, Plycon Press. Page 90, Sun Diamond Growers, California. Page 92, Calavo Growers.

CHAPTER 4 Page 101, Mazola Corn Oil. Page 103, Hellmann's real mayonnaise. Page 106, United Fresh Fruit & Vegetable Association. Page 107, H. J. Heinz Co. Page 109, Western Growers. Page 113, General Foods. Page 117, American Spice Trade Association.

CHAPTER 5 Page 123, J. T. Colburn of Armour and Co. and Baker's Digest. Page 134, C. W. Hoerr.

CHAPTER 6 Page 147 (top), World Bank Photo by Randolph King; (margin), U.S. Department of Agriculture. Page 155, Karo Corn Syrup. Page 159, Carnation Company.

CHAPTER 7 Pages 168 & 169, North Central Regional Labs. Page 170, National Livestock and Meat Board. Page 173, from R. M. Sandstedt, *Cereal Science Today* 10:312, 1965. Reprinted by permission. Page 180, Borden Consumer Products. Page 193, Rice Council. Page 195, Canned Salmon Institute, Seattle.

CHAPTER 8 Page 206, American Dairy Association. Page 209, Reprinted with permission Dairy Council of California. Page 210, Courtesy of CP Division, St. Regis, Chicago, Illinois. Page 211, K. Bendo. Page 217, USDA. Page 231, American Dairy Association. Page 234, United Dairy Industry Association. Page 241, American Dairy Association.

CHAPTER 9 Page 248, Courtesy of S. B. Jones, USDA Eastern Regional Research Center, Philadelphia. Reprinted from Journal of Food Science 43:1182, 1978, Copyright © by the Institute of Food Technologists. Page 253, USDA Soil Conservation Service. Page 257, USDA. Page 259, National Livestock and Meat Board. Page 260, USDA. Page 266 and 267, National Livestock and Meat Board. Page 272, The Foley Company. Page 274, National Livestock and Meat Board. Page 275, Courtesy Chesebrough Pond's, Inc. Page 278 & 279, National Livestock and Meat Board. Page 281, Courtesy of the California Dried Fig Advisory Board. Page 285, National Turkey Federation. Page 288, Alaska Seafood Marketing Institute. Page 289 (top), USDA, (bottom) Alaska Seafood Marketing Institute. Page 290, National Marine Fisheries. Page 291, National Fisheries Institute. Page 292, W. Atlee Burpee Company.

CHAPTER 10 Page 302, USDA. Page 313, 315, 316, 317, American Egg Board. Page 319, Plycon Press. Page 320, General Mills. Page 322, J. Walter Thompson. Page 323, General Mills. Page 326, American Egg Board.

CHAPTER 11   Page 335, J. A. Dunn and J. R. White, Cereal Chemistry 16:96, 1939. Courtesy of Lever Brothers Company. Reprinted by permission. Page 337, American Egg Board. Page 338, Courtesy Fleishmann Laboratories.

CHAPTER 12   Page 349, Marketing Division Kansas State Board of Agriculture. Page 353 (left), Plycon Press; (right), General Mills. Page 362, Wheat Flour Institute.

CHAPTER 13   Page 372, Plycon Press. Page 373, Diamond Walnut Growers, Inc. Page 377, Plycon Press. Page 379, Courtesy Wheat Flour Institute. Page 382, Universal Foods. Page 383, Wheat Flour Institute.

CHAPTER 14   Page 391, from E. G. Halliday and I. T. Noble, *Hows and Whys of Cooking*, University of Chicago Press, 1946. Reprinted by permission of Isabel Noble. Page 393, California Plum Commodity Committee. Page 399, from Martha Jooste and Andrea Mackey, *Food Research* 17:192, 193. Copyright © 1952 by Institute of Food Technologies. Page 400, Plycon Press. Page 409, from D. Preonas, A. I. Nelson and M. P. Steinberg, "Continuous Production of Pie Dough," *Baker's Digest* 41(6): 34–40. Reprinted with permission from the December 1967 Issue of *Baker's Digest*, Chicago, Illinois. Page 410, Courtesy of Karo Corn Syrup.

CHAPTER 15   Page 410, National Coffee Association. Page 431, 433, Tea Council. Page 436, R. William Uhler. Page 437, Hershey Foods Corporation. Page 439, Calavo Growers.

CHAPTER 16   Page 445, USDA. Page 447, 448, USDA photo by Fred Faurot.

CHAPTER 17   Page 469, Armed Forces Institute of Pathology. Page 472, Carolina Biological Supply House. Page 475, American Spice Trade Association.

CHAPTER 18   Page 491, Emily Ferguson. Page 492, 500, National Marine Fisheries Service. Page 502, K. Bendo.

CHAPTER 19   Page 510, National Marine Fisheries Service. Page 515, K. Bendo.

CHAPTER 20   Page 525, Towle Silver. Page 528, Lenox China. Page 535, Tea Council.

INDEX